DECLINE OF THE U.S. PRESIDENCY

WILLIAM JEFFERSON CLINTON'S LEGACY
OF CORRUPTION

JOHN G. ANAGNOS

DECLINE OF THE U.S. PRESIDENCY

Songana Publishing Inc. Ocean View, DE

Copyright © 2018 by John G. Anagnos

Printed and bound in the United States of America. All rights reserved. No part of this book may be reproduced or transmitted in any form or by any means electronic or mechanical, including photocopy, recording, or any information storage and retrieval system now known or to be invented, without permission in writing from the publisher, except by a reviewer who wishes to quote brief passages in connection with a review written for inclusion in a magazine, newspaper, or broadcast. For information, please contact Songana Publishing Inc., 29L Atlantic Avenue, #314, Ocean View, DE 19970.

Although the author and publisher have made every effort to ensure the accuracy and completeness of information contained in this book, we assume no responsibility for errors, inaccuracies, omissions, or any inconsistency herein. Any slights of people, places, or organizations are unintentional.

First printing 2018

ISBN: 978-1-949345-02-5

LCCN: 2018956416

Visit us at www.songanapublishing.com

ATTENTION CORPORATIONS, Universities, Colleges, and Professional Organizations: Quantity discounts are available on bulk purchases of this book for educational, gift purposes, or premium use. For information, please contact Songana Publishing Inc. 29L Atlantic Ave., Ocean View, DE 19970, for information on discounts and terms.

*This book is dedicated to my parents
and to the late FF Demetrios G. Kalaris, John T. Tavlarides,
and Vasilios Penterides, and FF Nick Stavrakis, Steven P. Zorzos,
who taught me and guided me through this life
and have given me a solid foundation
to seek and learn the truth.*

CONTENTS

Acknowledgments   Vii
Introduction   ix

1. Bill Clinton (Family Origin) — 1
2. Bill Clinton (Early Years) — 6
3. Bill And Hillary At Yale — 18
4. Back In Arkansas — 23
5. The Governorship — 30
6. Mena Airport — 54
7. Election 1992 — 69
8. Inauguration Day — 83
9. 1993 Stumbles Part I — 86
10. Waco — 93
11. Ruby Ridge — 113
12. Travel Office Firings — 120
13. Foreign Policy Stumbles — 136
14. Health Care Reform — 158
15. 1993 Stumbles Part II — 166
16. Vince Foster — 170
17. The Troopers Talk — 200
18. Whitewater — 208
19. State Department File Search — 239
20. Vietnam — 245
21. Paula Jones Part I — 254
22. 1994 Stumbles — 272
23. Election 1994 — 284

24.	Ron Brown	292
25.	FBI Files	324
26.	1995 Through 2000 Stumbles	334
27.	Election 1996	341
28.	Oklahoma City Bombing	348
29.	Fund-Raising Scandals	363
30.	China	367
31.	Terrorism	403
32.	TWA Flight 800	425
33.	Paula Jones Part II	440
34.	Monica Lewinsky	451
35.	Impeachment	484
36.	Disbarment	516
37.	Pardons	519
38.	The Final Days Hillary's Book Deal/ White House Theft/Vandalism	533
39.	Bill Clinton (Legacy)	539
	Bibliography	548
	Endnotes	553
	Index	627

ACKNOWLEDGMENTS

There are many to thank for their part in this book. To begin with, I want to thank Mary Beth Reilly, who was the volunteer coordinator at the Bush-Quayle '92 campaign headquarters. I just happen to walk in to her office interested in volunteering and after a couple of minutes of small talk, Mark Nestlen, the deputy director for research walked into her office saying that he needed someone. Mary Beth recommended me to Mark, and I became, for the next three months, a full-time unpaid staff member. That's how it all got started.

I also want to thank Karen Kochenberg, then of Xulon Press, who took my phone call in 2003, in which I told her I was interested in writing a book on the Clinton presidency. For the next four years, I continued to research and write, but I was naively unaware about how much time and effort goes into composing a book. She was always there to help me and give me suggestions, and I will always be in debt to her graciousness and kindness.

I also want to thank the folks at SCORE DC for all of their teaching and instruction. This would include Arnie Westphal, Richard Rose, and my counselor, Hal Shelton.

Next, I want to thank the techs at Staples who have been with me for many years assisting me on my computer and laptop purchases, as well as the troubleshooting and the issues that came along. Kudos to Keith from Rockville and Kola from Germantown, Maryland. Kudos also goes to Scotty, Larry, Jeremy, and Garrett from Rehoboth Beach, Delaware, and Drew from Ocean City, Maryland.

I also want to thank Michael Klassen of Illumify Media Global who has been able to guide this book project from start to finish. Kudos also go to Geoff Stone who undertook the tenuous task of copyediting this book.

Finally, I want to thank my parents as well as my Sigma Phi Epsilon fraternity brothers from College Park, Maryland. Without all of your support, this book would not have been possible.

INTRODUCTION

January 26, 1998: "I want to say one thing to the American people. I want you to listen to me. I did not have sexual relations with that woman, Miss Lewinsky. I never told anybody to lie. Not a single time. Never. These allegations are false and I need to go back to work for the American people."[1]

January 15, 2001: "I had to come to terms with the fact that I made a terrible personal mistake, which I tried to correct in private and which then got dragged into public. That was dark for me."[2]

CHAPTER 1

BILL CLINTON (FAMILY ORIGIN)

We had two huge oak trees in my front yard, one of which had a lot of hedges around it. It was perfect for hiding. Right in front of my house was a thoroughfare, Park Avenue. We would wait for the cars to go by and try to hit the hubcaps with our acorns.

—Bill Clinton describing a game he played as a youngster[1]

William Jefferson Clinton, the forty-second president of the United States, was born William Jefferson Blythe IV on August 19, 1946, in Hope's Julia Chester Hospital in Hope, Arkansas. Bill's likely father, William Jefferson Blythe III, was born on February 27, 1918, in Sherman, Texas. His mother, Virginia Dell Cassidy, was born in Arkansas in 1923.[2]

In 1935, William Blythe III, who went by the initials W.J., was an up and coming traveling salesman who sold car-alignment equipment. That year, he married Adele Gash, the seventeen-year-old daughter of a saloon keeper. They lived in Sherman, Texas, but the marriage didn't last long, and they were divorced by the end of 1936. After the divorce, W.J. visited Adele several times while she was living in Sherman. On one of those trips, Adele became pregnant and in 1938, she gave birth to Henry Leon Blythe.[3]

On August 11, 1938, W.J. married twenty-year-old Maxine Hamilton in Ardmore, Oklahoma. They were divorced nine months later, and he was accused by the judge as "guilty of extreme cruelty and gross neglect of duty."[4]

In early 1940, W.J. met seventeen-year-old Wanetta Alexander at a Nevada, Missouri roadhouse. Later that year they met often at the

Netherlands Hotel in Kansas City where he sometimes stayed for weeks making his rounds in western Missouri and Kansas. By the end of 1940, Wanetta was pregnant, and W.J. had gone to northern California to see Adele and his first child. But after a few days, W.J. had run off with Adele's younger sister, Minnie Faye.[5]

On December 29, 1940, W.J. married Minnie Faye Gash in Durant, Oklahoma. Unfortunately, that marriage was soon over.[6]

Under pressure from the Alexander family, W.J.'s marriage to Minnie Faye was annulled in April 1941. On May 3, 1941, he was in the Jackson County courthouse in Kansas City, marrying Wanetta Alexander. Eight days later, on May 11, 1941, W.J. was on the road again while his new wife gave birth to a baby girl. They named her Sharron Lee Blythe.[7]

They lived for a short time in an apartment in Monroe, Louisiana. Wanetta remembered the place as "a dump." In six months, Wanetta left with their baby and headed back to Kansas City. She believed that W.J. was cheating on her.[8]

In July 1943, W.J. was out with another woman in Shreveport, Louisiana, when she suddenly had an acute attack of appendicitis. He took her to the emergency room of Tri-State Hospital for treatment. While his date was being treated, he noticed Virginia Dell Cassidy. Then, barely twenty, she was engaged at the time to her high school sweetheart, but was immediately taken with W.J. As he began to leave the hospital, he hesitated, and then turned around and walked up to the young nurse to ask her about the ring she was wearing. Without hesitation, she replied that it didn't mean a thing.[9]

Later that evening, W.J. took Virginia out for a soda and afterwards, he kissed her goodnight. Soon, he found an apartment to rent in Shreveport, Louisiana, and found a job selling automobiles. Virginia began pressuring him to get married. W.J. would never tell her about his current wife, Wanetta, his ex-wives, or his children.[10]

W.J. tried to resist marriage, but Virginia was not to be denied. It wasn't long before he wrote to Wanetta, saying he had "met a nurse down in Louisiana," and wanted out of their marriage. A Missouri court, on April 13, 1944, granted the divorce, and ordered the absent William J. Blythe III to pay forty-two dollars a month in child support. But, it was too late. On September 3, 1943, William Jefferson Blythe III committed bigamy by marrying Virginia Cassidy before a justice of the peace in Texarkana. Thus, the subsequent birth of William Jefferson Blythe IV, on August 19, 1946, was illegal under Arkansas law.[11]

Only five weeks after his marriage to Virginia, W.J. joined the army and was sent abroad. As a mechanic in an auto-maintenance battalion, he served first in North Africa, then in the liberation of Rome, and then the bloody Italian campaign north to the Arno River. After he went off to war, Virginia returned home to Hope, where, by several accounts, she resumed her prenuptial revelries. And here lies the discrepancy about who William Jefferson Blythe IV's actual father was.

According to his military records, W.J. arrived home from Italy on December 1, 1945 and was honorably discharged at Camp Shelby, Mississippi, on December 7, 1945. He then visited Sherman, Texas before he met up with Virginia in Shreveport, Louisiana. Given travel times in those days, that meant that they could not have seen each other until December 10, 1945. Bill was born on August 19, 1946. If you do the math, nine months before August 19, 1946, Tech 3 William J. Blythe was still in Italy. In response to inquiries, Virginia claimed that they had reunited in November 1945. That was not true. Then Virginia said that she had the baby early on doctor's orders. She claims a doctor insisted that labor be induced early because she had taken a fall. Yet, gossips in Hot Springs still whispered that Bill Clinton, born seven and a half months after Blythe's return from overseas, was actually the son of a car salesman Virginia had been dating in his absence.[12]

Author Gail Sheehy described in her book, *Hillary's Choice,* finding the one person still living who was present at the birth of the future president: the delivery room nurse, Wilma Booker. She asked Nurse Booker if Bill Clinton's birth could have been premature.[13]

"No, not at that weight," she replied unequivocally: "I remember he was a nice-size baby, between eight and nine pounds. [His mother noted he was 8.6 pounds.] Virginia got kinda big while she was pregnant."[14]

To summarize, according to R. Emmett Tyrrell, Jr., in his book, *Boy Clinton*, "It would seem that Bill Clinton, whether the son of Blythe or of an anonymous donor, is almost certainly America's first bastard to be elected president."[15]

Unfortunately, Bill would never see W.J. Three months before Bill was born, W.J. had secured a job with a Chicago, Illinois auto parts company. On May 17, 1946, on his way back to Hope, tragedy struck. On Missouri

Highway 60, halfway between Morehouse and Sikeston, his Buick sedan was found upside down on the shoulder. A full twenty-five yards from the car, William Jefferson Blythe III was found dead, belly down, drown in a ditch.[16]

Virginia Blythe and her parents, Edith and Eldridge Cassidy and little Billy lived together in Hope for less than a year before Virginia left for New Orleans, Louisiana, to resume her nursing studies and train at Charity Hospital as a nurse anesthetist. She left in the fall of 1947 when Billy was one, and he stayed with her parents, Eldridge and Edith Cassidy, for most of the next two years.[17]

Eldridge Cassidy owned a small grocery store in Hope, Arkansas. It was there, before she left for school in 1947, when Virginia met her second husband, Roger M. Clinton. She would continue to see him occasionally in New Orleans or during her trips home, which he usually paid for. Roger, who owned his own Buick dealership, was nicknamed "Dude," and loved to drink and gamble and have a good time. Virginia, though, was unaware that he was married and had two stepsons back in Hot Springs.[18]

Roger Clinton was soon leaving his wife, Ina Mae Murphy Clinton, of nearly fourteen years, and her family suspected that he was already involved with Virginia Blythe. In August 1948, Ina Mae filed for divorce, charging that Roger had abused her. To the dismay of her family, Virginia and Roger were married on June 19, 1950.[19]

In the autumn of 1951, Virginia enrolled Billy in Miss Marie's School for Little Folk, the nursery school and kindergarten run by Marie A. Purkins. In the school along with Billy was Thomas F. McLarty III, the son of one of the wealthiest men in town—another car dealer. Also, there was Vincent Foster, whose father was becoming extraordinarily successful in Arkansas real estate.[20]

In 1953, Roger Clinton lost his Buick franchise through mismanagement. His brother Raymond would come to the rescue, giving him a job as a parts manager in his own thriving Buick dealership in Hot Springs.[21] Roger and Virginia Clinton had a son Roger Cassidy Clinton born on July 25, 1956. But, things weren't always well.[22] At least twice during the late 1950s the police were called to their home and Roger landed in police custody. In April 1959, Virginia angrily filed for divorce. She later gave in to Roger's pleading after he promised to change.[23] Unfortunately, the changes never came and on April 9, 1962, Virginia told Roger she was divorcing him, and she fled with her boys and drove to the Motel Capri.[24]

The Garland County Chancery Court in Hot Springs granted the divorce on May 15, 1962, but it was messy. She had to obtain a restraining order to get her husband out of the old house on Park Avenue, although he continued to hang around outside, perched drunkenly on the stoop, begging her to let him come home.[25] Virginia got custody of her two children, a chandelier, and the 1960 Buick Le Sabre. Roger was ordered to sell the Park Avenue house, splitting the profits less expenses with Virginia, and to pay a minimum of fifty dollars a month child support for Roger. Billy received no child support.[26]

On June 12, 1962, nearly a month after her divorce, Virginia petitioned the Garland County Chancery Court on Billy's behalf to be able to adopt his former stepfather's name, so he would go from William Jefferson Blythe IV to William Jefferson Clinton. Since entering the first grade in the autumn 1952, he had been going by Billy Clinton and now it was official.[27]

Soon, Virginia began reconsidering remarrying Roger. Within two months, Virginia took Roger back and despite the objections of Billy, Virginia and Roger were remarried eighty-three days after their divorce on August 6, 1962. Roger would eventually deteriorate to a solitary, graying, silent drunkard. He died of cancer in November 1967.[28]

In December 1968, Virginia married Jeff Dwire, a hairdresser who had recently served nine months for investment fraud. He died in August 1974 from complications of diabetes. He left behind two daughters from a previous marriage. According to *Arkansas Gazette* journalist Meredith Oakley: "One was Diane Dwire Welch, whose life was fodder for the tabloids after the *National Enquirer* tracked her to Houston, Texas, and revealed her criminal record. Armed robbery and drug trafficking were among her offenses, and she eventually did time in the Mountain View Maximum Security Prison at Gatesville, Texas."[29]

CHAPTER 2

BILL CLINTON (EARLY YEARS)

They called him Tubby – even then he had weight problems. Also, he could not stop talking. Most college girls in those days inclined toward the tall silent type. Bill was tall, taller than I am, but he was a gasbag. The girls and I used to joke about Bill's loquacity. Did he ever shut down while attempting love? The girls doubted it and kept their distance.

—R. Emmett Tyrrell Jr.'s recollection of Bill Clinton as an undergraduate at Georgetown University.[1]

In high school, Bill was Beta Club president, junior class president, band major and Key Club president. In his senior year, alarmed by his titles and perks, the teachers stepped in and barred him from running for student body president. Bill responded by running for senior class secretary, which had always been a girl. He lost.[2]

Another highlight of Bill Clinton in high school was meeting his icon, President John F. Kennedy. Every year, the American Legion's division of National Americanism sponsored two high school juniors from each state, to travel to Washington as delegates to Boys Nation, an annual forum for civic training run by the American Legion. On July 24, 1963, Bill and the other ninety-nine delegates traveled from the University of Maryland College Park dormitories to the White House to see President Kennedy in the Rose Garden. After President Kennedy's speech praising the Boys Nation, he walked towards the group. Bill quickly got out in front and got his picture taken shaking President Kennedy's hand.[3]

Bill graduated fourth in his class of 323 students from Hot Springs High School in the spring of 1964 and entered Georgetown University's School of Foreign Service in the fall of 1964.[4]

In his first two years, Bill is elected freshman and sophomore class president. In the spring of 1966, he joined Alpha Phi Omega fraternity, which served as both a social club and service organization. Bill decided not to run for junior class president. Instead, he joined the campaign of Judge Frank Holt for the Democratic nomination of governor of Arkansas. Holt appeared to be the favorite to succeed Orville Faubus.[5]

This was his first full-time campaign. It was here that Bill met Paul Fray and his wife Mary Lee Saunders Fray, two people who would later play a pivotal role in Bill's 1974 congressional race. Judge Holt eventually lost in the Democratic primary runoff to segregationist Jim Johnson. In the general election, Winthrop Rockefeller won 54 percent of the general election vote and became the first Republican governor of Arkansas since Reconstruction. Afterwards, Bill Clinton got a part-time job paying $3,500 per year working in Washington for Arkansas Senator J. William Fulbright.[6]

From the autumn 1966 to the spring of 1968, Bill Clinton clerked on Capitol Hill on the Senate Foreign Relations Committee. By this time, Senator Fulbright had concluded that the Vietnam War was a tragic mistake and even publicly accused the Johnson administration of deceit.[7]

Clinton, who held a student deferment and was two years away from the threat of being drafted, viewed the ideological conflict between his boss and President Johnson with mixed feelings. Bill was for the war in the beginning. After researching the Gulf of Tonkin incidents of 1964, Clinton expressed disappointment that President Johnson had let "the Vietnam War and his own paranoid aggression consume him."[8]

During the summer of 1967, Bill was encouraged by a professor to broaden his scholarship and expand his horizons by applying for a Rhodes scholarship, an honor then awarded yearly to thirty-two American men who were sent off to Oxford University in England for further academic training. By the winter of 1967, armed with Senator Fulbright's crucial backing and recommendation, and competing in a region that comprised Texas as well as Arkansas, Clinton won his Rhodes scholarship.[9]

On February 16, 1968, President Johnson and the National Security Council (NSC) abolished draft deferments for graduate students except for those in various fields of medicine. Now, college seniors of 1968 stood exposed as the most vulnerable group in the draft.[10]

Senator Eugene McCarthy, campaigning the antiwar banner for president, almost defeated President Johnson in the New Hampshire primary. Four days later, Senator Robert Kennedy joined the Democratic presidential contest. Bill Clinton preferred Kennedy to McCarthy, arguing that timing is everything in politics and that Kennedy was smart to seize the moment. Unfortunately, Senator Robert Kennedy was assassinated on June 5, 1968.[11]

In June 1968, Bill Clinton graduated from Georgetown University. That summer, Bill went back to Arkansas to campaign for Senator William Fulbright. For the campaign, Bill served as Fulbright's driver.[12]

To understand how Bill was able to beat the draft, one will have to recognize that he must have had powerful connections in the Arkansas political establishment to devise such strategies. The source of those powerful connections was also the source of his comfortable life, namely Uncle Ray Clinton, owner of Buick dealerships.[13]

On March 20, 1968, Bill was reclassified 1-A and Raymond Clinton swung into action. "We started working as soon as [Raymond] got word that Billy was going to be drafted," said Henry Britt, the car dealer's longtime friend and personal attorney. It was a concerted effort "to get Bill what he wanted," Britt would say later, adding:

Of course Billy knew about it.

> . . . In late March 1968, Raymond called an old friend, Commander Trice Ellis, Jr., who was the officer in charge of the local naval reserve unit. The uncle asked the commander to create a billet, or enlistment slot, especially for Bill Clinton.
> Raymond then went to another old friend, William S. Armstrong, chairman of the Hot Springs draft board and asked him to "give the boy a chance to get into the navy." Britt himself would urge Armstrong to "put Bill Clinton's draft notice in a drawer someplace and leave it for a while." This is apparently what Armstrong did for several months."
> Then, at some point, Raymond and Henry Britt met Senator Fulbright at a dam dedication on the banks of the Arkansas River and got him to ensure that his office, too, would intercede with the

Hot Springs draft board. Soon, a Fulbright aide telephoned the Hot Springs office of the selective service to "give every consideration" to keeping young Bill Clinton out of the draft so that he could attend Oxford.

Meanwhile, Commander Ellis had in fact managed to arrange the extra naval reserve billet with the New Orleans headquarters and soon called his friend Raymond Clinton to ask, "What happened to that boy?" The car dealer replied cryptically, "Don't worry about it. He won't be coming down. It's all been taken care of."

Eventually, Bill Clinton would be scheduled to take his draft physical, though not until January 1969 at a U.S. base in England, nearly a year after it would have been set had he been treated like most inductees. The interval between his reclassification and his examination was "more than twice as long as anyone else" could expect, according to one account, "and more than five times longer than most area men of comparable eligibility" were granted. Of all those classified 1-A by his draft board in Arkansas during the turbulent, bloody year of 1968, Bill Clinton was the only one whose process was so extended.[14]

In October 1968, Clinton headed for England aboard the USS *United States*. The other thirty-one Oxford-bound Rhodes Scholars included Robert Reich and Strobe Talbott. As they sailed to England to flee the thoughts of the draft and Vietnam, the movie playing in the ship's cinema just happened to be John Wayne starring in *The Green Berets*."[15]

At Oxford, Clinton initially claimed to have enrolled for a degree in PPE—politics, philosophy and economics—an undergraduate program requiring a series of tutorials and examinations in the three broad subjects. Instead, he pursued what was called B. Litt. politics probational. The probational meant it was a tentative choice, the B. Litt denoted a research degree that required no tutorials or lectures, but a massive fifty-thousand-word dissertation at the end of two years.[16]

Thanks to the intercessions of his uncle, Raymond Clinton, and the office of Senator Fulbright, the Hot Springs draft board had consistently passed over Bill Clinton's file to facilitate his stay in Oxford. Coincidently, Senator Fulbright missed World War II himself (his mother was chairman of his draft board in one of those amazing Arkansas coincidences). But on January 13, 1969, eight months after his draft board first reclassified him 1-A, Clinton finally took his pre-induction armed forces physical examination at a U.S. air base near London. He passed it. Unless he could think of another way out, he was headed for boot camp.[17]

At the time, draft regulations allowed graduate students who received induction notices to finish the term they were in. There was some confusion on how it would be interpreted at Oxford, which worked on a three-term system.[18]

It was during this time that Clinton first experimented with drugs. Before attending a rock concert in London, Clinton was with a group at a London apartment and smoked marijuana. "Clinton did not know how to smoke and could not take the tobacco according to Martin Walker, a Balliol College journalist who was part of the group. His lasting image of Clinton is 'of the big southerner leaning his head out an open window gasping for fresh air.' "[19]

On April 7, 1969, Bill Clinton witnessed his first antiwar demonstration. While he was touring the National Gallery with a friend, Sharon Ann Evans, they noticed a demonstration in Trafalgar Square. They watched for about an hour from the steps of the gallery.[20]

Clinton started his final term at Oxford, but his studies deteriorated. He stopped attending tutorials, and though he continued reading a lot, he essentially stopped working toward his degree. In a letter back home, Clinton talked constantly about how much he was hurting and that he could not shake the feeling that he should return to America and fulfill his military obligation. But he hated the war and did not want to fight in it.[21]

It was also around this time in 1969 when, not well known at the time, a female student at Oxford raised the charge of rape against Bill Clinton. Her name was Eileen Wellstone. He claimed she was lying. Not long after her accusation was made, Clinton was asked to forgo his Rhodes scholarship by school authorities, his only apparent punishment. His Rhodes scholarship provided $2,760 annually for tuition, room, and board.[22]

On April 22, 1969, Bill Clinton received his second and final draft notice from Draft Board No. 26 in Hot Springs, Arkansas. It was the five-page SSS Form 252, the Order to Report for Induction, ordering him to return to America for military service. He called his mother and stepfather right away to tell them the news and to see what could be done. Fortunately, by the time the induction notice arrived, Clinton had begun the third school term, and according to draft regulations, he was allowed to finish out the term before reporting.[23]

Clinton's postponement would be until July 28, 1969. Clinton had been classified I-A (available for military service) for more than a year. The II-S student deferment he had obtained upon entering Georgetown, and which his draft board extended three times, had long since expired, and the United States government had stopped granting deferments to graduate students in late 1967.[24]

Clinton contacted his stepfather, Jeff Dwire, and gave him a list of officials to contact before he got back to Hot Springs, Arkansas. Clinton was trying to get into a National Guard or ROTC program. Clinton contacted John Spotila, a friend from Georgetown who was attending Yale Law School and asked him what it would take for him to get into that school and enroll in the graduate ROTC program there. He telephoned Paul Fray and asked him for help getting into the Air National Guard. Fray also arranged for Clinton to take an Air Force physical when he got back to the United States.[25]

According to friends at Oxford, Clinton returned to Hot Springs, Arkansas, on July 3, 1969, having made no living arrangements for the second year of study because he expected to be drafted. But he underestimated the efforts of a great many people busy lobbying on his behalf.[26]

Not long after arriving in Hot Springs, Clinton's first public display of temper occurred. He decided to go personally to the office of the draft board. "There he confronted its executive secretary, Opal Ellis, a twenty-year veteran of the selective service. Ellis remembered Clinton telling her he was too well educated to go. 'He was going to fix my wagon [and] pull every string he could think of.'"[27]

At this point, Clinton had no choice but to submit to the draft. His induction date was July 28, 1969. He took physicals for the Air Force and Navy officer programs. He failed both of them.[28]

On July 10, 1969, Clinton appealed to Cliff Jackson, a fellow Republican whom he had met at Oxford, and asked him to use his influence with the GOP administration in either Washington or Little Rock to "quash the July draft notice."[29] Eventually, Bill Clinton's only choice was the advanced ROTC program at the University of Arkansas which did not have quotas and was open to law students.[30]

Lee Williams who was a graduate of the University of Arkansas Law School, had several contacts there and worked the telephone from his Capitol Hill office, trying to arrange Clinton's enrollment. He contacted the commander of the army ROTC unit at the University of Arkansas, Colonel Eugene J. Holmes on July 16 to see if he could help Bill. On July 17, 1969, Bill Clinton made the 250-mile trip to Fayetteville to the home of Colonel Holmes. Holmes explained to Clinton that he would have to enroll at the University of Arkansas simply to be eligible for ROTC there. Clinton said he planned to "attend the law school."[31]

On July 20, 1969, Colonel Holmes enrolled Bill Clinton to a two-year summer only camp ROTC program at the University of Arkansas. Like others in Arkansas, Holmes was impressed by Bill's credentials and pleased by the bright student's interest in the ROTC program. He was proud to be "making it possible," he wrote later, "for a Rhodes Scholar to serve in the military as an officer." Clinton's July 28 induction was nullified, and his draft board granted Clinton a 1-D deferment as a reservist. On August 7, 1969, Clinton signed the formal letter of intent to join the University of Arkansas ROTC, but he did not legally file it until a few days later.[32]

Once Bill signed on for the ROTC program, he then became actively involved in the antiwar movement. According to David Mixner, a founder of what would later be called the Vietnam Moratorium Committee and who would later advise the 1992 Clinton presidential campaign on issues and policies pertaining to gay rights, said he and Clinton were two of about forty "young leaders" who attended a weekend retreat in the summer of 1969 at Martha's Vineyard "to explore ways that we could continue the important work started in the campaigns" of presidential hopefuls Robert Kennedy and Eugene McCarthy.[33]

There were three other co-founders of the Vietnam Moratorium Committee. One was Sam Brown, who was chief coordinator of the McCarthy campaign. The third was David Hawk who had worked for McCarthy in New Hampshire. The fourth co-founder was Marge Sklencar. Among the group's advisors was the Reverend Joseph P. Duffey, chairman of Americans for Democratic Action.[34]

The VMC's mission was to create a massive political movement to force the nation out of Vietnam. Most of its work had to do with undermining the American war effort in Southeast Asia by promoting nationwide work stoppages and through mass demonstrations. Clinton "volunteered his time and efforts" to organizing Vietnam Moratorium Committee-sponsored protests first in the United States and later in England.[35]

In mid-August 1969, Bill traveled to Washington and visited the Vietnam Moratorium Committee's headquarters on Vermont Avenue NW, where activists were planning a one-day nationwide protest against the war, scheduled for October 15, 1969. The first protest was aimed at college campuses and surrounding communities and it was a success. This persuaded the committee's founders to undertake an even larger show of force, and they officially signed on with the more radical New Mobilization Committee to End the War in Vietnam.[36]

In the fall of 1969, Bill Clinton was expected to enroll for the ROTC. He never showed up. Ed Howard, the drill sergeant, later recalled that there was great anger when word spread through the ROTC office that Clinton was not on campus.[37]

Bill Clinton was now back in Oxford in the fall of 1969, and through his work with the Vietnam Moratorium Committee, became a key contact and took credit for having helped organize the demonstrations held outside the American Embassy in London's Grosvenor Square in mid-October and near Grosvenor Square over the course of a weekend in mid-November 1969. According to fellow Rhodes scholar Tom Williamson, he and Clinton helped organize an "international student protest in London against the war in Vietnam" and served as unpaid marshal for the November 15 protest.[38]

That fall Clinton made a trip to Oslo, Norway, where he met Richard McSorley, a Jesuit professor at Georgetown and peace activist who was in Scandinavia to visit various antiwar groups. Clinton asked to accompany the priest on his rounds. They visited the Oslo Peace Institute where they talked with American conscientious objectors, Norwegian peace groups, and university students.[39]

On November 16, 1969, the day after Richard McSorley attended the moratorium demonstration of some five hundred Britons and Americans in front of the U.S. embassy in Grosvenor Square in London, Father McSorley encountered Clinton yet again. This time they met in another crowd of several hundred at an interdenominational church service for peace in England for which Bill Clinton was one of the organizers. Ten years later Clinton would tell the *Arkansas Gazette* that he had "only observed" protest marches in London and elsewhere.[40]

Bill Clinton's draft records show that he held the 1-D deferment from August 7 to October 30, 1969. Those two dates mark the days when the Garland County Draft Board met, considered Clinton's case, and reclassified him, first from 1-A to 1-D, then back from 1-D to 1-A. "Clinton gave up his deferment . . . [when] President Nixon, seeking to defuse the antiwar clamor on campuses, ordered the Selective Service System to change its policy for graduate students. From that day on, graduate students who received draft notices would be allowed to finish the entire school year rather than just the term they were in. Clinton was now safe until the following July 1970."[41]

On November 26, 1969, President Nixon signed H.R. 14001 enacting a draft lottery. It was to be held the following week on December 1. Fortunately for Bill Clinton, his birthdate of August 19 was the 311th day picked. Also, the yearly quota for 1970 would be about 350,000 men, which would be filled at least one hundred numbers short of Clinton's No. 311. Bill was basically free.[42]

On December 2, 1969, Bill Clinton jubilantly sent off an application to Yale Law School for the coming academic year. Now, Bill Clinton needed to cover his tracks. On December 3, 1969, Clinton wrote Colonel Holmes a letter explaining why he had decided not to enroll in the ROTC after all. He apologized for taking so long to write and explained how he had worked in a minor position on the Senate Foreign Relations Committee and strongly opposed the war. He went on to praise the actions of one of his roommates who was possibly indicted for resisting the draft and then wrote:

> I decided to accept the draft in spite of my beliefs for one reason: to maintain my political viability within the system. For years I have worked to prepare myself for a political life characterized by both practical political ability and concern for rapid social progress. It is a life I still feel compelled to try to lead.
>
> When the draft came, despite political convictions, I was having a hard time facing the prospect of fighting a war I had been fighting against, and that is why I contacted you. ROTC was the one way left in which I could possibly, but not positively, avoid both Vietnam and resistance. . . .
> After I signed the ROTC letter of intent I began to wonder whether the compromise I had made with myself was not more objectionable

than the draft would have been, because I had no interest in the ROTC program in itself and all I seemed to have done was to protect myself from physical harm. . . .

I am writing too in hope that my telling this one story will help you understand more clearly how so many fine people have come to find themselves still loving their country but loathing the military.

Merry Christmas

Sincerely,
Bill Clinton[43]

Colonel Holmes felt used. Joining the ROTC program had seemed so important to Clinton, who traveled to his home and engaged him in fervent conversation for two hours. The following day, the calls came in on Bill's behalf, calls from people too influential to be ignored. Holmes had secured that berth in good faith. Now, Colonel Holmes realized that it had all been a lie, a calculated, shoddy, fraudulent trick to avoid service to his country.[44]

Clinton did not understand the impact his letter would have on a career military man who had entered service in 1940, had volunteered for the Luzon campaign, and had been captured by the Japanese at Bataan and held prisoner for three and a half years. All he was doing was trying to tie up a loose end.[45] "The first effect of the letter, was dismay and outrage." Drill instructor Ed Howard said, "We all knew about it. Lieutenant Colonel Jones advised us about the letter. He was more upset than the average instructor." The letter "only intensified the anger the ROTC staff had felt toward Clinton since he had failed to enroll at the law school."[46]

Colonel Holmes angrily canceled Clinton's ROTC enrollment and sent no reply to Bill Clinton in England. Holmes would later reflect his reaction to a reporter during the 1992 presidential election. "Bill Clinton was able to manipulate things so that he didn't have to go in. Ethically, I think he should have stayed in the ROTC. He'd given his word and was backing out."[47]

Another effect of the letter was the creation of a Dissidents File on Bill Clinton at the ROTC headquarters in Fayetteville. Holmes placed the letter on the off chance that someday he would attempt once more to enter the ROTC program. A few days after sending his letter to Colonel Holmes, Clinton took off on a tour of Scandinavia, the Soviet Union, and Eastern

Europe. It is unclear how he managed this feat when, according to former girlfriends, he was always broke.

Interestingly, it was during this tenure that Bill Clinton's apparent ties to the intelligence community began. The Central Intelligence Agency had set up Operation Chaos, which recruited American student informants abroad to target and penetrate student antiwar movements, employing American students themselves as prime sources and de facto agents. It seems that Clinton's trip may have been paid for by the CIA. "According to at least two former agency station chiefs and two more deputies who received the instructions and directed such covert operations, the inducements for the young informers ranged from cash payments to help with local draft boards and even promised deferments to more general and sweeping proffers of future help and influence with careers."[48] All of these were things Clinton desired. "One former agency official would claim that the future president was a full-fledged 'asset,' and he was regularly 'debriefed,' and he informed on his friends in the peace movement in Britain."[49] After using Colonel Holmes and then this, it looked like Clinton was only interested in serving himself.

Now, going back to his trip, Bill stopped in Helsinki, Finland. There he visited a friend Richard Shullaw, a classmate from Georgetown. They spent several days touring the city. Bill's next stop found him at the Soviet border on December 31, 1969, with a visa that he obtained in London. Interestingly, the travel to the Soviet Union was not only costly back then, but had to be prepaid to Intourist, the government-owned and administered tourist board. The trip to Moscow alone in those days could have cost as much as five thousand dollars.[50]

In Moscow Clinton was booked for seven days at the prerevolutionary National Hotel overlooking Red Square. It was one of Moscow's more expensive hotels, and at the time was much favored by the Soviet elite. While there, he encountered a delegation of Americans who were negotiating with various Vietnamese, French, and Russian officials for an exchange of American prisoners of war in North Vietnam.[51]

"Bill stayed around with us while this was going on," recalled Charlie Daniels, a civilian member of the delegation who was there as a private citizen to obtain information about servicemen missing in action. "He was not important to us, he just hung around, always hungry and broke."[52]

On January 7, 1970, Clinton boarded the train for Prague, Czechoslovakia. Clinton stayed with Bedrich Kopold and Jirina Kopoldova, the parents of Jan Kopold, an acquaintance of Bill's from Oxford. He also met Marie Svermova, Jirina's mother and founder of the Czechoslovakian Party and a former member of the Party's central Committee from 1945-1951. Though the three were purged from the party in the 1950s, they still believed in a socialist motherland.[53]

On January 13, 1970, Bill left for Munich, West Germany and stayed with Rudi Loewe, a classmate from Georgetown, and his family. They toured the city and did a lot of partying. He finally arrived back in Oxford on January 19, 1970.[54]

Back at Oxford for his third term, Clinton tried to catch up on his studies, but his supervisor, Maurice Shock, maintained that he would not be ready for the June examinations to fulfill the B. Phil requirements and receive a degree from Oxford. Thus, he became the rare Rhodes Scholar to leave without a degree. By this time, though, Clinton had been accepted to Yale Law School.[55]

Back from Oxford, Clinton used his Rhodes contacts, notably Rick Stearns, to get a job for the summer of 1970 with Project Pursestrings, a Washington lobby backing the Hatfield-McGovern amendment to cut off appropriations for the Vietnam War. There he met Carl Wagner, a future Democratic political consultant and backer, and Anthony Podesta. It was also here that Clinton first met Harold Ickes and Susan Thomases.

On June 8, 1994, twenty-four years after he left Oxford, Bill Clinton would receive an Oxford degree, an honorary doctorate of civil law by diploma.

CHAPTER 3

BILL AND HILLARY AT YALE

The basic rationale for depriving people of their rights in a dependency relationship is that certain individuals are incapable of undeserving of the right to take care of themselves and consequently need social institutions specifically designed to safeguard their position. . . . Along with the family, past and present examples of such arrangements include marriage, slavery and the Indian reservation system.
—Hillary Rodham, *Harvard Educational Review,* 1973[1]

In the autumn of 1970, Bill Clinton arrived at Yale Law School. He was looking forward to going back to Arkansas to run for public office and eventually get to Washington as a congressman.[2]

Repeated often in the 1992 presidential race, the story of the first meeting of Hillary Rodham and Bill Clinton at the law school library became a kind of political celebrity folk tale. According to this tale, Hillary caught Bill staring at her across the room in the law library and marched over to introduce herself. The story had a nice feminist ring to it: a woman who took the initiative and forced the issue. The only trouble was, Hillary's story was a lie.[3]

Bill first became aware of Hillary through her work as coeditor of a Far-Left journal called *The Yale Review of Law and Social Action*. Even though she was hardly his type physically, he was interested in meeting her.[4]

Bill asked Jeff Rogers to introduce him to Hillary Rodham. Jeff and Kris Olson, Hillary's coeditor, lived together in a commune called Cozy Beach, which was affiliated with Ken Kesey's Oregon Hog Farm commune.

Bill and Hillary were invited to their commune for dinner and they hit it off right away.[5]

According to a classmate, "Hillary was soon a regular at Bill's group house in Milford, and the relationship took off. Hillary was clearly smitten. She seemed to hang on him. But Bill was not nearly as enamored. In fact, he continued to see other women, even after they moved into an apartment just off campus."[6]

In the fall of 1970, Tony Podesta, a political junkie who had worked with Bill at Project Pursestrings, got him involved in the U.S. Senate campaign in Connecticut for Joseph Duffy. He was a thirty-eight-year-old peace and civil rights activist and ethics professor at Hartford Seminary. He was also president of the liberal Americans for Democratic Action. He won the August 19 Democratic primary and was up against Republican Lowell Weicker. Bill was recruited to run the Third Congressional District based in New Haven. Lowell Weicker wins in the general election.[7]

Duffy may have lost, but Bill Clinton didn't. He acquired an encyclopedia of practical political knowledge and a network of friends who would jump to Clinton's congressional race in Arkansas in 1974 and later on to the national stage. Duffy's unsuccessful Senate campaign was invaluable in establishing the Clinton political network and philosophy.[8]

In September of 1971, Bill and Hillary moved into the ground floor of a house at 21 Edgewood Avenue. The apartment belonged to Greg Craig, a fellow student and friend from Yale Law School. Craig would go on to become one of President Clinton's lawyers during the Senate impeachment trial in 1999. It was also during this time that the seeds of Bill and Hillary's future began to take root.[9]

Early on in their relationship "Bill and Hillary struck a plan." Their strategy became the foundation of their relationship. "They agreed to work together to revolutionize the Democratic Party and ultimately make the White House their home. Once their 'twenty-year project' was realized, with Bill's victory in 1992, their plan became even more ambitious: eight years as president for him, then eight years for her."[10]

In the spring of 1972, Bill and Hillary teamed up for the Thomas Swan Barrister's Union Prize Trial. They prepared for the competitive trial, which began on April 29. Top-ranked lawyers competed against each other, two to a side plus two alternates. Bill and Hillary were the prosecution team. Michael Conway and Armistead Rood formed the defense team. They did not win, but they made a lasting impression on one of the judges, John Doar, who would soon play an important role in Hillary's future.[11]

In June 1972, Senator Fulbright recommended Bill Clinton for a position in the presidential campaign of South Dakota Senator George McGovern. Clinton was tapped to assist in Mr. McGovern's visit to Little Rock later that month. In July 1972, he attended the Democratic National Convention in Miami where McGovern was nominated.[12]

Afterward, for the rest of the summer, Bill Clinton went to Texas as a co-coordinator for McGovern's Texas campaign. Clinton was up in Austin at the McGovern headquarters, working under Gary Hart. There, he met Onie Elizabeth Wright, a native Texan known as Betsey. Hillary wangled herself an assignment in Texas, working in a pilot project to register Hispanic voters.[13]

No one would wind up being more important to Bill and Hillary than Betsey Wright. She was already neck-deep in politics when they met her in 1972. She had been working in campaigns at the county level at age fifteen, and by 1969, at age twenty-five, she had become the youngest president in the history of the Young Democrats of Texas. At thirty, she was already a mentor for many young women working on her campaigns.[14]

On November 7, 1972, Richard Nixon crushed George McGovern in Texas, winning 67 percent of the vote on his way to one of the most lopsided victories in American presidential history.[15]

As the end of her time in law school approached, Hillary voluntarily decided to take an eighth year of higher education, supplementing her legal studies with course work at the Yale Child Study Center. This allowed her to remain at Yale an extra year to be with Bill rather than graduate with her own class. After their graduation from law school in the spring of 1973, she went with Bill on her first trip abroad. They traveled to England and visited London, Oxford, and some of the places he had seen during his years as a Rhodes Scholar.[16]

In June 1973, Bill Clinton returned to Arkansas to take the bar exam. Hillary went along and took the exam with him. Supposedly, she was taking the test "just in case" she should find herself practicing in Arkansas. They both passed.[17]

Having passed the bar, Clinton planned to return to Arkansas and run for a congressional seat. Complicating matters was returning home with a girlfriend with whom he had been living out of wedlock for the past three years. Conservative voters in the state took it seriously the subject of "living in sin."[18]

Instead of moving to Arkansas, Hillary decided to accept a staff position at the Children's Defense Fund, an organization her mentor Marian Wright had recently founded. When Bill and Hillary parted after her brief stay in Arkansas, their situation seemed totally unsettled.[19]

On July 23 and 24, 1973, Hillary took the DC bar exam, according to records of the District of Columbia Bar Association. On November 3, 1973, the District of Columbia Bar Association notified her that she had failed the bar exam. Of 817 applicants, 551 of her peers had passed, most from law schools less prestigious than Yale. She kept this news hidden for the next thirty years.[20]

Bill flew to New England over the Thanksgiving holiday in 1973 to visit Hillary. They explored Boston together, and they talked about their future. They agreed that during the upcoming Christmas holidays Hillary would visit Arkansas again, so they could work toward a decision.[21]

A few days after Christmas, Hillary arrived in Fayetteville. As she was settling in to the house that Bill was renting, Bill received a phone call from John Doar, who had just been hired as chief counsel to the House Judiciary Committee's impeachment investigation of President Nixon. Doar had served the previous year as a judge during the Barristers' Union Prize Trial at Yale. Now Doar was saying that Bill was at the top of his list of recommendations for young lawyers to join the impeachment committee staff. Bill wanted to know if Clinton would take a year off from teaching law and come to Washington and suggest the names of other exceptional attorneys who might be available. Clinton excused himself from consideration: he was already gearing up to run for a US congressional seat in 1974. But, he recommended Hillary Rodham.[22]

Doar ran down Hillary's resume. When Hillary was offered the position, she accepted.

Doar's offer to Hillary represented a perfect solution to her and Bill's dilemma as a couple. If Nixon were investigated by the Judiciary Committee, then impeached by the House and tried by the Senate, the process would almost certainly take more than a year. If Bill won election to the House of Representatives in November 1974, he would begin the job in January 1975, about the same time the impeachment process was likely to end, and Hillary would not have to move to Arkansas.[23]

Hillary excitedly called Marian Edelman from Bill's house. Marian told her she could always return to the Children's Defense Fund, but that working on the impeachment inquiry was far more important.[24]

At the same time, second-guessing himself, Clinton asked David Pryor, the Democratic candidate for governor of Arkansas, whether he had made the right move regarding Hillary. He was worried if it was a political liability if his girlfriend took the job on the impeachment inquiry staff. It might be an asset, Pryor believed.[25]

CHAPTER 4

BACK IN ARKANSAS

I have no plans at this time to run for public office.
—Bill Clinton responding to a question from David Newbern,
August 1973[1]

On August 23, 1973, not long after Bill Clinton had been hired as an assistant professor at the University of Arkansas in Fayetteville, and had settled back in Arkansas, the campaigning began for Bill. He appeared at a watermelon party of the Washington County Democratic Central Committee. The party regulars were local figures of the sort that any aspiring politician would need to know, hard-core committed Democratic loyalists who performed the drudge work of organization and were the primary sources of inside political gossip.[2]

On February 25, 1974, Bill declared his candidacy for the Third Congressional District of Arkansas with press conferences in the state's four principal cities: Hot Springs, where he grew up; Little Rock; Fort Smith, with the biggest concentration of voters in the Third District; and Fayetteville, where he set up his campaign headquarters not far from the University of Arkansas campus.[3] He was running against John Paul Hammerschmidt, the first Arkansas Republican elected to Congress in one hundred years. Elected in 1966, Hammerschmidt who had amassed a fortune in the family lumber business, was one of the most popular politicians in Arkansas. He was a master at catering to his constituents' every need.[4]

Hillary soon became a significant player in the campaign. Almost daily, she began phoning advice from Washington to Bill and making her weight felt with his campaign managers. Hillary's political advice to the Arkansans, however, didn't necessarily rub well. Unfortunately for Hillary, she knew very little about Arkansas, its unique history and political environment. There were also several weekends when Hillary flew to Arkansas to be with Bill.[5]

That's when she realized that Bill had girlfriends in Little Rock and several towns in his campaign district, and, for several months, he had been seeing a young student volunteer (a.k.a. the College Girl) from the University of Arkansas who worked at campaign headquarters. His staff was aware of Bill's dalliances and they ignored them as long as they didn't interfere with the campaign.[6] That didn't sit well with Hillary. When she was back in Washington working on the impeachment inquiry, she brought in reinforcements. Two men in a fin-tailed Cadillac with Illinois license plates pulled into the parking lot of the Clinton for Congress headquarters on College Avenue in Fayetteville. "I'm Hugh Rodham, Hillary's dad." With him was Tony Rodham.[7]

"Well, how long are you going to be here to visit?" asked Ron Addington. "Hell, I don't know," Hugh said. "Hillary told me I ought to come down here and help out." Though Hugh did not explain what he meant by "help out," it soon became clear.[8] Then Hillary summoned her other brother, Hugh Jr., to Arkansas and "ordered *him* to give the College Girl the rush."[9]

According to Paul Fray: "Hughie stalked her every day, every way. She came to me and said, 'I want you to stop this son of a bitch bothering me.' Fray said, 'You're old enough to get rid of him yourself.' By the end of October [1974], she was gone."[10]

Hillary continued checking up on Bill, not just to learn the extent of his betrayals, but to assess the danger he posed to their joint political career. Hillary began her surveillance of Bill during this period by eavesdropping and checking his desk. She would search for scraps of paper with phone numbers on them and tear them up.[11]

According to liberal operative David Brock, "Bill was learning to master the politics of his home state, where the corrupt mixing of public and private interests was the coin of the realm. Public office was routinely used for private gain, and private interests routinely bought favors from public officials. Elections themselves were compromised: In the northwest Arkansas district where Clinton was running, paper ballots could be stuffed or dumped in the river for $250. Since many people didn't have checking accounts, contributions were made in cash and often disappeared. In the Fort Smith area of the district Clinton was running in, there were more than 10,000 black votes, all of them essentially for sale."[12]

Brock continued, "The power broker in the third congressional district was Don Tyson, who was well on his way to owning the biggest family chicken farm in the world. Clinton was introduced to Tyson by Billie Schneider, a woman who ran the Gas Lite, a local bar in town, as well as a roadside steakhouse on the way to Springdale where Tyson's headquarters was based. Tyson's support meant not only the assurance of personal contributions from him and his family but also contributions funneled through Tyson employees and use of the Tyson plane. Don's brother, Randall spent time at Clinton's Fayetteville headquarters and underwrote the campaign's phone bank. Bill appears to have amply returned these favors. In 1974, when Tyson failed to turn a profit and blamed U.S. sales of subsidized grain to the Soviet Union, which was driving up the price of chicken feed, Clinton campaigned against the US-Soviet grain deal."[13]

In June of 1974, Clinton won a runoff in the Democratic primary against Gene Rainwater, a state senator from Fort Smith with 69 percent of the vote. Clinton's opponent in the general election was John Paul Hammerschmidt. After winning his first election in 1966, he had built a solid reputation for constituent services, responding to inquiries and complaints from outside his district when no one else would. Clinton ran on a general election platform designed by Paul Fray to appeal to the varied constituents who comprised the vote in the third district—from chicken farmers to retired military people to college students. Clinton avoided mentioning his views on the military or his antiwar involvement during the Vietnam War. "The strategy was to wall off Fort Smith. He did not want to get into the posture of having to answer about his military record," said Paul Fray, to whom Clinton had confided his efforts to evade the draft in 1969.[14]

He also said little about his role in the 1972 McGovern presidential campaign. Behind the scenes, Bill Clinton was visibly agitated about how his evasion from the draft would be used by the Republicans. He was "red-faced scared," said an aide who heard him discussing it with another campaign volunteer, and the result would be the first of many efforts to suppress or obscure the record. Thus, Bill Clinton's first campaign had begun with a cover-up.[15]

"The campaign became a haven for drugs," according to *Washington Post* editor David Maraniss. One volunteer claimed people were smoking pot at a phone bank in a Fayetteville apartment. "Also, according to Clinton volunteer Neil McDonald, 'whenever eighteen-year old Roger Clinton, the candidate's younger brother, came up to Fayetteville, the scent of marijuana trailed him. It was no secret Roger was blowing smoke.' Neil continued, 'He and his buddies would be in the basement stenciling signs, and actually smoking joints.' "[16] The situation had gotten so bad that even Governor Dale Bumpers called the campaign to make sure Clinton himself wasn't using drugs along with his workers.[17]

The tension at Clinton headquarters in Little Rock came to a head on the night before election day. Paul Fray was contacted by a lawyer representing dairy interests, who had $15,000 ready for the campaign that could be used in Sebastian County, "to ensure that you are able to win the election." The Fort Smith area was heavily Republican, and this money would go to election boxes where votes could still be bought. Fray said later, "It was a question of me picking it up and delivering it. I knew there were places where we could spend a little money and it would turn out right."[18]

Clinton did not have much to say. Hillary rejected the proposal. "She nixed it," according to Fray. "She got adamant. She said to Bill, 'No! You don't want to be a party to this!' Fray said, 'Look, you want to win or you want to lose?' She said, 'Well, I don't want to win this way.' If we can't earn it, we can't go to Washington.' "[19]

The election was held on November 5, 1974. To Clinton's surprise, he even lost Garland County where he grew up. By midnight, Clinton was still leading by several thousand votes. By 3:00 a.m., it was all over: Clinton lost by six thousand votes or two percentage points. Bill, Hillary, and Paul Fray with his wife, Mary Lee, drove back to Fayetteville in their separate cars. Once they got there, all hell broke loose. Fray started swearing and throwing things out the window. "It was the goddamn money!" he said. Telephones and books sailed across the room. Paul Fray blamed Hillary. Hillary blamed Paul Fray, and Mary Lee blamed Bill.[20]

Then, the minute Paul walked into the back room at the Fayetteville headquarters, Hillary hit him between the eyes. She was angrier than Paul had seen her. "You fucking Jew bastard!" Hillary screamed.[21]

Hillary had cursed him out plenty of times before. But this was the first time she had used a racial slur, and it hit hard. It was not something he would ever forget. According to Fray: "I promise you it happened. It created a chasm I never really overcame," he said.[22]

In the summer of 1975, Hillary visited friends back East and began exploring her options. She told her friends that she was considering leaving Bill because of his womanizing. The truth was, Hillary was considering leaving Bill because she was worried that she had backed a loser. Hillary didn't care what Bill did with other women, as long as it did not hurt the Clintons' careers.[23]

Bill telephoned Hillary to tell her that he was going to run for attorney general. She was pleased, and when she returned to Arkansas, Hillary accepted his proposal of marriage. Thus was sealed the Faustian bargain that would shape the rest of her life: Hillary accepted Bill's womanizing as the price of political power.[24] The wedding occurred on October 11, 1975, in the front room of the house Clinton had just bought at 930 California Street in Fayetteville. Their new home, approximately one thousand square feet, cost $20,000.[25] A simple ceremony was performed by Vic Nixon, a Methodist minister in their new home, and attendance was limited to the immediate family.[26] Several blocks away, the reception was held at the backyard of the home of Morris Henry, a state Democratic chairman. The party appeared to be part wedding reception, part rally as it was understood that Bill Clinton was running again.[27]

Interestingly, Bill's infidelity didn't stop on their wedding day. In 1999, an old friend of the Clintons confided what she saw at their wedding reception to biographer Christopher Andersen. "One woman—a member of the Fayetteville contingent who would remain a friend of the Clintons for decades—pushed open the bathroom door and was 'totally floored' by what she saw: Bill 'passionately kissing a young woman. He was fondling her breasts. I was so shocked I just closed the door quickly and quietly.' "[28]

Dorothy Rodham discovered that the newlyweds had no plans for a honeymoon and found a package tour to Acapulco. Oddly, she booked the tickets for the whole Rodham family and excluded Virginia and Roger. The couple returned from Mexico and began planning the race for attorney general.[29]

On March 17, 1976, in a series of news conferences begun at Little Rock and repeated at Fort Smith, Texarkana, El Dorado, and Jonesboro,

Clinton announced his candidacy for attorney general. There were now three Democrats trying to win the primary. The Republican ticket lacked a candidate for attorney general that year.[30]

On May 27, 1976, Clinton avoided a runoff by amassing 55.6 percent of the vote. Without a general election of his own to worry about, Clinton signed up to work for the presidential campaign of Jimmy Carter. At the time, Clinton wrote a note to Betsey Wright in Washington claiming that he could not arouse much animosity toward Gerald Ford but felt freer to attack the Republicans "now that the biggest prick in Congress is on the ticket"—a reference, presumably, to Ford's running mate, Senator Bob Dole of Kansas.[31]

Clinton served as the Arkansas state chairman for Jimmy Carter as well as preparing for his new job and building more contacts for his political rise. Hillary left for Indianapolis, where she served as Carter's state field director through the November election.[32]

According to biographer Joyce Milton, "Bill and Hillary's early support for Carter over Ted Kennedy came as a surprise to some of their friends from Yale, but it was dictated by local politics. Jack Stephens, the younger of the powerful Stephens Brothers, had been Jimmy Carter's roommate at the Naval Academy, and there was little point in launching a career in Democratic politics without at least the tacit support of the Stephens's. Witt, the older and more influential brother, was the founder of Arkla, the Arkansas Louisiana Gas Company, and had been the financial angel behind Orval Faubus. Jack was president of Stephens, Inc., the largest bond firm outside Wall Street and a powerhouse in the Southeast."[33]

Preparing to move to Little Rock after the 1976 primary, Bill tried to help Hillary find a place in a major law firm. Clinton called Herbert Rule II partner of Rose, Nash, Williamson, Carroll, Clay & Giroir—the Rose Law Firm. The firm, which was founded in 1820—sixteen years before Arkansas became a state—had only nine partners, another of whom was his friend from childhood in Hope, Vince Foster. It was established as a standard bearer of the state's elite, and it represented the most powerful economic interests in the state: Tyson Foods, Stephens Inc., Wal-Mart, Worthen Bank, the *Arkansas Democrat-Gazette*, and the Hussman media empire in southwest Arkansas.[34] The firm saw her obvious value and offered the twenty-nine year old attorney a salary just under $25,000, far higher than the $6,000

Clinton himself would make as attorney general. Fortunately for Bill, his salary would soon be raised to $22,500 by the state legislature.[35]

In December 1976, Bill and Hillary found a house in the Hillcrest neighborhood of Little Rock, not far from downtown. It cost $34,000, and at 980 square feet, it was smaller than the house in Fayetteville.[36]

On January 11, 1977, Bill Clinton was sworn in as attorney general. Within days of taking over the attorney general's office, Clinton began exploring the limits of his influence with the Carter administration. Bill and Hillary would become somewhat regular dinner guests in the White House, and Bill traveled frequently to Washington for briefings and meetings with the president's staff and the Democratic National Committee.[37]

As attorney general, Clinton kept his staff working overtime, churning out pro-consumer lawsuits. Hardly a week went by without his office making news in some corner of the state, and from the day he took the oath of office he was laying the foundation of his campaign for governor. But campaigning wasn't the only thing that Clinton was up to.

"By the spring of 1977, he was involved in an affair with a reporter for KARK-TV named Gennifer Flowers. Hillary's husband couldn't be seen in public with another woman, but Flowers, in addition to her day job, was doing a cabaret act at the lounge in the Camelot Hotel, where Clinton occasionally showed up with friends. . . . According to Flowers, Clinton didn't talk much about his wife. When he did, he sometimes spoke admirably of her brains and professional accomplishments. At other times, he referred to her as 'Hilla the Hun.' Flowers allowed herself to imagine that his marriage was an experiment that hadn't worked out. In December 1977, she says, she discovered that she was pregnant. Clinton was about to announce his candidacy for governor, and when he heard the news, he gave Flowers $200 in cash to pay for an abortion."[38]

In late November 1977, eighty-two-year-old Senator John McClellan passed away. The death set off a scramble for the seat by two rivals, Governor Pryor and Congressman Jim Guy Tucker, and thus opened up the governorship to Bill Clinton. Clinton literally began to campaign at McClellan's funeral.[39]

CHAPTER 5

THE GOVERNORSHIP

From then on, they ran their campaigns themselves, going on their gut instincts, and they never again failed to hit back fast when the situation demanded it.

—Webb Hubbell
after Governor Clinton lost his reelection bid in 1980[1]

In the fall of 1977, Clinton's chief of staff, Steve Smith, placed a call to a thirty-year-old professional political consultant from the Upper West Side of Manhattan named Dick Morris who had been soliciting new clients around the country and had some novel ideas about how polls could be used to shape rhetorical arguments in campaigns. Morris flew down to Little Rock and met with Clinton at the attorney general's office. At the meeting, according to Morris, Clinton said that he had a difficult decision to make about whether to run for governor or senator. "I'd like to be governor; I feel there's a lot more I can do here," Clinton answered. "But the real action is in Washington," Clinton said.[2]

Morris agreed to do a poll for Clinton on the two races. The results showed that Clinton could win the governorship with no problem, and he "could possibly win" the senate race, but it wouldn't be easy. Clinton decided to run for governor.[3]

In March 1978, Clinton declared his candidacy for governor of Arkansas. At that point, he began running two campaigns at once. In public, he was the candidate for governor. But in private, he wanted Pryor to defeat Jim Guy Tucker, whom he viewed as his main competition as the rising star of State Democratic politics.[4] On May 30, 1978, Bill Clinton avoided a runoff by garnering 59.6 percent of the vote in the primary. David Pryor won in a runoff against Jim Guy Tucker and thus defeated the only real long-run threat to Bill Clinton.[5]

After winning the '78 primary, with Tyson's backing, Clinton was favored for the governorship over his GOP opponent, former legislator Lynn Lowe. Before the November election, Tyson secured a promise from Clinton to raise the legal limit on truck weight on state roads from about 73,000 to 80,000 pounds. Most other states used the higher limit, making it harder for Arkansas' producers to compete.[6]

On October 27, 1978, with Clinton ahead thirty points in the polls for the general election, his worst fears came true. Retired Air Force Lieutenant Colonel Billy Geren called a news conference in Little Rock and made the following statement: "The attorney general of Arkansas was a draft-dodger who had joined in protests against the United States government's involvement in the Vietnam War."[7]

Geren had written to members of the Arkansas Retired Officers Group, of which he was vice president, that Clinton was a "draft-dodger" who reneged on the commitment he had made to enter the advanced Reserve Officer Training Corps in exchange for a one-year deferment from the draft in 1969.[8]

Bill Clinton responded to the *Arkansas Gazette* claiming that the ROTC agreement was canceled "shortly after it was made." He said that he "never received the deferment" but had decided to "take advantage" of the ROTC option.[9]

"It was, of course, a brazen lie," wrote historian and journalist Roger Morris. Clinton believed he had "pressured Colonel Holmes in 1974 to remove the embarrassing letter from the files, and thus there could be no documentation for the charges." Geren had been on the air force ROTC staff at Fayetteville from 1972-76. He claimed to have seen the agreement between Clinton and the ROTC commander. Morris concludes: " 'It's obvious to me,' Clinton responded dismissively, 'that he [Geren] didn't know the facts and that he didn't want to follow them.' With the record still buried in a lone surviving copy of the letter outside Clinton's control, the issue died."[10]

The one person besides Geren who knew the facts wasn't talking. Contacted by a reporter at his home in Fayetteville, Eugene Holmes, by then retired, said he could not recall Clinton's case because there had been thousands of students since then. It was a response he would very much regret in later years.[11]

On November 7, 1978, Bill Clinton won an impressive 63.3 percent of the vote against the Republican candidate Lynn Lowe. At age thirty-two, the youngest attorney general in the nation was soon to become the nation's youngest governor and the second-youngest governor in state history.[12] Once elected governor, Clinton's goal was to serve three two-year terms, each one more progressive, more reform-minded than the last to position himself for a national campaign.[13]

On January 10, 1979, Bill Clinton took the oath of office to become the state's fortieth governor. On that day, a parade of Clintons' liberal friends from Georgetown, Yale Law School, Boys Nation, and assorted Berkeley and Harvard types stuck out as pointy-heads in the crowd. This was supposed to be a new progressive look for Arkansas, but it put an image out there that a lot of people didn't feel comfortable with. It was a poor, conservative state where a country song then popular in the South ridiculed such people as "long-haired hippie-type commie fags" who voted for McGovern.[14]

Some saw a certain infantile narcissism in Bill's behavior. It was captured by Arkansas cartoonist George Fisher. He began caricaturing the new governor as a baby in a buggy. Clinton expressed resentment at the caricature, snapping at Fisher in public, "Draw me ugly, but get me out of that baby buggy." That only encouraged the cartoonist. He graduated "Charming Billy" to a tricycle and put him into a little sailor's suit. Clinton was now thirty-three, and his nicknames were regressing from Wonder Boy or The Boy to the infantile Baby.[15]

As governor, Clinton declared the state highway system a disaster in need of $3.3 billion worth of improvements. The administration drafted a proposal that placed most of the burden on heavy trucks, but also raised car license fees, basing the rate of increase on the value of each car. The plan immediately encountered intense opposition from two powerful lobbies: the trucking industry and the poultry industry, a major user of trucks. Both were already upset at Clinton for backing away from a campaign promise to increase the weight allowed for trucks driving in Arkansas.[16]

When Tyson came in to complain about the new legislation, Clinton aide Rudy Moore left him to stew for a while. In an apparent effort to get back in Tyson's good graces, Clinton overruled the recommendations of his advisers and instead doubled fees for transferring vehicle titles and raised the cost of registration for cars and pickup trucks. Those who had older, heavier cars, had to pay the higher fees, setting off an anti-tax backlash.[17]

It didn't stop there. Clinton had been embarrassed by a story in the *Arkansas Gazette* which revealed that he and his wife were delinquent in personal property taxes owed in Washington County, the home of the University of Arkansas. Hillary's Fiat, which had been stolen and wrecked in 1978, had not been licensed or assessed for the years 1977 and 1978.[18]

Clinton insisted that this "oversight" was neither his fault nor his responsibility; one of his employees in the attorney general's office had been told to take care of licensing the car for the boss's wife, inadvertently revealing the couple's use of state employees for their personal business. Clinton subsequently paid the outstanding $77.82 in penalties and taxes for 1977 and 1978, and his employees in the governor's office made sure from then on that all personal bills were paid and all personal errands run in a timely manner.[19]

At the end of September 1979, Hillary announced her pregnancy, saying that the governor was "ecstatic" and that she did not know how soon she would return to Rose after the delivery. "Oh, it'll be Clinton," she said when asked by local reporters about the child's destined surname. Unfortunately, the circumstances that led to her pregnancy were very disturbing. The following is the sequence of events according to author Edward Klein in *The Truth about Hillary*:

> It was nearly one o'clock in the morning in June of 1979, and a group of boisterous vacationers were drinking and playing skittles, or nine pins, in the pub of the Horizons hotel in Bermuda. Among the collection of thirty-somethings was a couple from Arkansas—Hillary Rodham and her husband, Governor Bill Clinton.
> As the hours grew late, the wives retired to their rooms, leaving the husbands, who had met for the first time this night, to demolish what was left of a case of beer.
> After a few more beers, Bill Clinton—who normally was not a heavy drinker, and was clearly feeling no pain—made an announcement.
> "I'm going back to my cottage to rape my wife," he said.
> His new friends laughed at his drunken boast and bid him good night.

"The next morning, my phone rings at about eight-thirty, and it is Bill inviting me and my wife to breakfast," recalled one of the men from the night before, an investment banker from New York. "When we get there, the place looks like World War III. There are pillows and busted-up furniture all over the place. Obviously, Hillary got pissed off at Bill, and threw a few things across the room. I guess that's the price he paid for going back to his room and taking the initiative and demanding sex."

"The irony of it is, about two months later the phone rings in my office in Wall Street. It's Clinton, calling from the governor's mansion in Little Rock. I've heard he's been hitting up Wall Street a lot. Investment bankers are always targets for governors looking for a contribution or two."

"Anyway, we talk for a while, and then he says, 'By the way, Hillary hasn't been feeling well recently. She went to the doctor, and the doctor called a press conference, and lo and behold, I'm holding the *Arkansas Gazette* reading that my wife is pregnant.'

"That's the way he learns that Hillary is pregnant with Chelsea—in the newspaper.

"But the fact that his wife didn't tell him that she was pregnant before she told a reporter doesn't seem to faze him one bit, because he says, 'Do you know what night it happened?'

" 'No,' I say. 'When?'

" 'It was in Bermuda,' he says. 'And you were there!' "[20]

On February 27, 1980, Hillary gave birth, by caesarean section, to daughter Chelsea, whose name was derived from "Chelsea Morning," a Joni Mitchell song popularized by Judy Collins in the early 1970s.[21]

Roger Morris wrote in detail about the birth in his book *Partners in Power*:

Despite the public pregnancy and celebrated birth, a flow of tension and quarreling continued in the personal quarters of the mansion. From Clinton's first years as attorney general, Little Rock had been awash in gossip about his blatant womanizing, often unhidden from staff aides and escorts and seeming to accelerate after 1980 with the birth of his first child.

A young woman lawyer in Little Rock claimed that she was accosted by Clinton while he was attorney general and that when she recoiled he forced himself on her, biting and bruising her. Deeply affected by the assault, the woman decided to keep it all quiet for the sake of her own hard-won career and that of her husband. When the husband later saw Clinton at the 1980 Democratic Convention, he delivered a warning. "If you ever approach her," he told the governor, "I will kill you." Not even seeing fit to deny the incident, Bill Clinton sheepishly apologized and duly promised never to bother her again.[22]

Clinton then began appearing on the local bar scene, often with his brother Roger in tow. Dick Morris called him Saturday Night Bill as he made nightly rounds to visit his "constituents." Soon, people began noticing that Bill's nose was positively glowing. Little Rock began to whisper that the governor's brother was a cocaine abuser, and that maybe the governor was too.[23]

As reelection approached, Clinton had concerns on three fronts: crime, Cubans, and car tags. On crime, Clinton's liberalism was most evident in his refusal to schedule executions and his commutation of the life sentences of forty-four prisoners in his first term, many of them convicted murderers. One of them soon killed again, inciting a public uproar.[24]

Another major blunder was the issues of refugees from Communist Cuba. In the spring of 1980, more than 120,000 Cuban criminals, mental patients, and assorted "undesirables" were deported to the United States by Fidel Castro.[25]

The following events are detailed in *Arkansas Gazette* journalist Meredith Oakley's book *On the Make*:

> On May 7, 1980, the White House advised Governor Clinton that Fort Chafee, the federal installation near Fort Smith, Arkansas, which had proved its worth as an intermediary relocation camp for Vietnamese refugees in 1975, would be used as a temporary housing and processing site in resettling the Cuban refugees.
> Clinton, still eager to curry favor with the Carter White House, initially welcomed the unexpected influx of foreigners. . . .
> Alarm quickly turned to outrage when it became obvious that federal troops, under the command of General James E. Drummond, had

done nothing to restrain the refugees. They stood watching their weapons idle. Drummond's explanation, that federal law did not permit the use of military force against civilians, did nothing to mollify public opinion.

Voters went to the polls the next day determined to send Bill Clinton a message. Monroe Schwarzlose, a seventy-seven-year-old turkey farmer, received a stunning 31 percent of the vote. The message was not entirely lost on Clinton, who called the White House and asked for immediate intervention. Clinton then dispatched two hundred National Guardsmen to Fort Chaffee.[26]

There would be a second round of disturbances. On the morning of June 1, 1980, after staging a sit-in at the main gate, several hundred Cubans raced past the military guards and marched onto a nearby highway chanting "Libertad! Libertad!" They were met by the state police and retreated to the fort. But, later in the afternoon, the Cubans gathered at the main gate again, this time more than a thousand strong. They ran out of the gate and headed down state Highway 22, carrying sticks and bottles. The Cubans ran into the barricades manned by state troopers outside the town of Barling. A pitched battle broke out as officers brandishing nightsticks and rifle butts, beat the mob back from the town limits. When it was over, sixty-seven people were injured, including several officers.[27]

And then it got worse. Carter broke a promise to Clinton that no more prisoners would be sent to Fort Chaffee. On August 1, 1980, word came from the White House that about ten thousand Cuban refugees still being housed in Wisconsin, Pennsylvania, and Florida would be transferred to a single camp at Fort Chaffee. Travel aide Randy White was in the room at the Governor's Mansion when Clinton got the news. "You're fucking me!" White heard Clinton shout into the phone at a White House official. "How could you do this to me? I busted my ass for Carter. You guys are going to get me beat. I've done everything I could for you guys. This is ridiculous! Carter's too chickenshit to tell me directly!"[28]

There was nothing Clinton could do about the second round of refugees. Clinton had signed up as a floor whip at the Democratic National Convention and was chosen to be one of several speakers before Carter accepted the nomination on the final night of the convention.[29]

It was to be Clinton's first national television appearance, in prime time, although only one of three networks broadcast even a portion of his remarks. Clinton's eight-minute speech, the shortest of his career, impressed the twenty thousand or so delegates and onlookers crowded inside Madison Square Garden, but did little to boost his image back home.[30]

On September 27, 1980, the nickname Slick Willie, first appeared in an editorial by Paul Greenberg for the *Pine Bluff Commercial*. It was inspired by the two-faced attack Clinton made on his gubernatorial opponent, Frank White.[31] On the one hand, Bill was trying to place himself in the honored tradition of Arkansas' post-Faubus reform governors when he spoke at the party's state convention that year—even though he had embraced Orval Faubus himself, literally at the outset of his first term.[32] On the other hand, Governor Clinton welcomed the Cuban refugees at first, but by September of 1980, he was bad-mouthing Jimmy Carter for sending the Cubans to Fort Chafee. In the dishonorable Faubus tradition, he threatened to defy the U.S. Army if Washington sent any more our way. It was pretty slick.[33]

According to biographer Joyce Milton

> Clinton reacted to his woes by becoming strangely disengaged. He had installed a pinball game in the basement recreation room of the Governor's Mansion and spent hours hunched over the machine, his eyes glazed over. Arrested for speeding on his way to a campaign appearance, he joked perhaps he and Hillary should have called their daughter Hot-Rodham. In Little Rock, Clinton was a regular at popular nightspots like Busters. One longtime Clinton watcher would recall that during this period, Clinton became a "whirling dervish on the bar circuit. . . . That big red nose of his was unmistakable during the Christmas season. He was always with women, with an entourage, and you never knew whether this was his action or just staff members, but he was always with a pack. His wife was never there."
> Clinton was also subject to bad influences closer to home. His half-brother, Roger, had developed a heavy cocaine habit and was running with a rough crowd. As Roger recalls in his autobiography, he had fallen into the habit of using the guest house on the grounds of the Governor's Mansion as his private party shack. Rumors and allegations

abound that Clinton partied with his brother on occasion—perhaps when Hillary was out of town on business—and had developed a drug habit on his own. Also, cocaine use, which was the reason a lot of people became inordinately fond of the club scene in 1980, is one obvious explanation for Clinton's uncharacteristic lack of interest in getting elected."[34]

Bill's Republican opponent, Frank White, began a media offensive against Clinton on the car tags and the riots at Fort Chaffee. In one week, Clinton's lead dropped ten points. Clinton did not respond.[35] Hillary was conspicuously missing from the campaign. After being nominated by President Jimmy Carter in December 1977 to chair the Legal Services Corporation (LSC), she was spending much of her time flying back and forth from Little Rock to Washington, coordinating the election-year political efforts of the legal services movement.[36] In the end, it was too late. In the final weeks of the campaign, Hillary inserted herself in the campaign. She began scheduling Bill's activities on a daily basis. With eight days to go, she made the decision to bring Dick Morris back (whom they had fired). He had been replaced by another Democratic pollster, Peter Hart. She reached Morris's wife, Eileen McGann, in New York City. "We're losing, Frank White's gaining. He's hitting us with negatives. They're working. We need Dick."[37]

Morris was not in New York City. Instead, he was in Florida assisting Paul Hawkins, the Republican candidate. Hillary talked him into traveling to Little Rock for the remaining days of the campaign. When Morris took a poll, it showed Clinton under 50 percent. It was not a good sign. The Clinton campaign put up one last desperate negative ad against Frank White, hoping that it would make a difference.[38]

On November 4, 1980, which was election night, an early lead gave Clinton some hope. Unfortunately, by the next day, a popular DJ was announcing that Governor Bill Clinton and Hillary Rodham would soon be seen around town collecting cardboard boxes.[39]

Clinton had lost the election 52 percent to 48 percent. At 77 percent, the turnout was the highest in Arkansas in decades and Frank White won by 32,000 votes out of more than 800,000. Bill Clinton became the youngest defeated governor in American history and only the third Arkansas governor in the twentieth century to be denied a second two-year term. Though he began whining and feeling sorry for himself, he and Hillary were plotting a comeback.[40]

Clinton believed that the press had targeted him for defeat and went after them first. His first target was Bill Simmons, the Associated Press bureau chief in Little Rock. He called him and began screaming at him. Clinton's next target was the statehouse press corps. He gave most of them the silent treatment for several weeks. Finally, Clinton took his frustration out at Jimmy Carter, who was defeated by Ronald Reagan.[41]

According to R. Emmett Tyrrell Jr., founder of *American Spectator* "In the months ahead Clinton did some heavy drinking. In one lurid incident, at a small but popular Little Rock bar, the Afterthought, he engaged in an act of public indecency, oral sex with a female journalist. People in Little Rock also began spotting him standing around shopping malls and grocery stores, forlorn and dazed. At one point he stood by a checkout counter, alternately apologizing and seeking advice."[42]

Bill felt guilty that, by losing the election, Hillary would leave him, not because he had been unfaithful to her, but because he was a loser. Now their mutual arrangement of living in the White House could be unattainable.[43] According to investigative reporters Jeff Gerth and Don Van Natta Jr. "It was now Hillary's job to buck him up and try to reignite his political adrenaline. Hillary had "an uncanny knack for keeping me focused on the present and the future," Bill observed years later. As recalled by James McDougal, Hillary herself put it more bluntly: "Bill would not have amounted to anything if I hadn't kicked his ass." Bill would later be labeled the "Comeback Kid," but it was Hillary who carefully plotted and then orchestrated his political resurrection.[44]

The comeback began with three telephone calls. Hillary called Dick Morris again and said he had to return to Little Rock immediately to begin working on the next campaign. Morris was skeptical until Hillary convinced him that she was serious about using attack ads and attack campaigning. Ten days after the election, Hillary's second phone call was to Betsey Wright, who was working in Washington as executive director of the National Women's Educational Fund. She relinquished her job and moved to Arkansas to spearheaded Clinton's comeback.[45]

Without initially drawing a salary, Betsey moved into the guest house and began going through all the files that were stored in the basement recreation room. Wright began reorganizing the card files containing the names and addresses of ten thousand or so contacts Clinton had made since his college days. She also sent out brief notes, thanking the governor's loyal supporters and promising, "We'll have another day."[46]

Edward Klein, former editor-in-chief for *New York Magazine* described the following events in his book, *The Truth About Hillary*:

> Hillary's third phone call was to Ivan Duda, a well-known Little Rock private investigator.
> "She asked to see me," Duda told [Edward Klein], "and when we met, she said, 'I want you to do damage control over Bill's philandering.' I asked her, 'What do you mean?' And she said, 'Bill's going to be President of the United States.' I laughed at that, but she said, 'No, I'm serious.'
> "So," Duda continued, "I said, 'What do you want me for?' And she said, 'I want you to get rid of all these bitches he's seeing.' I said, 'Okay, I can do that.' And she said, 'I want you to give me the names and addresses and phone numbers, and we can get them under control.' "
> He claims to have reported to Hillary the names of about eight women he thought Bill was involved with, including one woman who worked at the Rose Law Firm. "That one really hurt and made her furious," Duda recalled.
> Hillary did not try to stop Bill from philandering; that would have been a fruitless exercise. All she asked of her husband was that he be more discriminating in his choice of women and not do anything to embarrass her in public. With Ivan Duda's reports in hand, Hillary was able to separate the "safe" women from the "trouble makers," and know who could be intimidated to keep their mouths shut.[47]

The wounded ex-governor entertained several job offers that would have taken him out of Arkansas. Instead, Clinton took a token job with the law firm of Wright, Lindsey and Jennings. This was arranged by Bruce Lindsey, the son of one of the firm's founders, and this would allow Clinton to regroup and mend his political fences. When asked by reporters about his duties at the law firm, Clinton said he was involved in some antitrust litigation. Clinton was to be paid $55,000 a year, a respectable Little Rock retainer at the time. Lindsey had called Clift Lane, former owner of Lane Processing, Inc., a major poultry company, to line up the retainer arrangement with the firm to help pay Clinton's salary. Hillary was receiving $49,290 as a junior partner at the Rose Law Firm. However, it was general knowledge that Clinton spent most of his time trying to revive his political career.[48]

The couple now purchased, for $112,000, a home on Midland Avenue in the capital's fashionable Pulaski Heights.[49] Dick Morris began visiting Little Rock a few days each month helping to plot Clinton's comeback. Morris believed that Clinton needed to seek redemption and apologize. According to Morris, "You have to recognize your sins, confess to them, and promise to sin no more. And in the act of contrition, you have to be humble. You can't be self-justified. You have to say, I am very sorry, ashamed, I know I did wrong and I'll never do it again." Morris ran the idea by Hillary and Betsey and they both liked it.[50]

Meanwhile, Clinton was looking for some financial deep pockets. Shortly after the election, he called former state senator George "Butch" Locke, asking him to set up a meeting with Dan Lasater, his partner in the bond brokerage house Collins, Locke and Lasater.[51]

The meeting took place in Lasater's apartment. Even though Clinton was, in Locke's words, "a crippled duck," he was pumped up about his prospects and talked for more than two hours about his vision of the state's future economic development. Clinton was bitter that the Stephen brothers had supported Frank White against him, and he was hoping that Lasater and Locke would want to back a candidate friendly to them.[52]

After the meeting Clinton set his sights on the religious community. He began appearing every Sunday at Little Rock's massive Immanuel Baptist Church, which he had never attended so regularly before. He was now seen prominently in the choir, just beyond the pulpit, as carefully arranged television cameras carried the service—and with it the former governor's grinning, nodding, hymn-singing presence—to thousands of viewers throughout the state.[53]

Hillary also got on the same program. She became a regular churchgoer, joining the First United Methodist Church in Little Rock. Hillary served on the board and provided free legal services.[54] "In another move that some of Bill's supporters viewed as hypocritical," David Brock reported. "Hillary began to assiduously court *Arkansas Democrat* editor John Robert Starr. Many observers believed that Starr's ranting against Clinton (for example 'Sweet

William' and 'Billion Dollar Bill') had cost him that election. Perceiving Starr's support as absolutely critical to the effort to remake Clinton's image, Hillary treated the columnist to a series of private lunches during which she laid out what Bill would do in a second term, and carefully gauged Starr's reaction. Knowing that Starr was married to a school-teacher, Hillary cannily broached the subject of a governor's initiative to reform Arkansas' schools in his second term."[55]

In early 1982, Hillary and Dick Morris scheduled two television spots to air just before Clinton was to begin his campaign. The ads were "intended to establish Bill in the new centrist mold to portray him as having embraced the core principles of the Republican opposition. The ad renounced the car-tag fees and other taxes imposed in his first term, and included a spot where Clinton pledged not to propose any new taxes in a second term. The second ad portrayed Clinton as tough on crime."[56]

On February 8, 1982, the thirty-second ads began airing in Little Brock.[57]

On February 27, 1982, Bill Clinton, with Hillary by his side holding Chelsea, now two years old, announced he was running for the governor again. He said he was "finished apologizing" and was now looking forward to a "good and hot" campaign.[58]

It became a three-way Democratic primary between Bill Clinton, Jim Guy Tucker, and Joe Purcell. The race soon became personal and bitter, especially between Bill Clinton and Jim Guy Tucker. They were both fighting for political survival.[59] When the Democratic primary votes were counted, Clinton received only 41.7 percent of the vote. This was the first time he was forced into a run-off against Purcell. Purcell was not a serious threat to Clinton and on June 8, 1982, in the run-off, Clinton received 53.6 percent of the vote.[60]

In the general election, Republican Frank White began ridiculing Clinton on his lack of real business experience. White claimed that Clinton had never "run anything in his life except an antiwar demonstration." Unfortunately, the editorial writers, who believed Clinton's previous denial of any antiwar activity, defended him against the attack.[61]

As the election approached, the Clinton campaign began organizing telephone blitzes literally every listed number and, more important, mobilized the African-American vote. "You and I know there's no such thing as a real Democrat for White," Clinton reportedly told black audiences.

"You and I both know that they ought to be called: 'White Democrats for White.' "[62]

In the November 1982 general election, Bill Clinton beat Frank White receiving roughly 54.7 percent of the vote. An analysis of election returns and voting patterns revealed that African-Americans had given Clinton the winning edge. In a race won by seventy-eight thousand votes, the ninety thousand African-American votes he took in Little Rock and the Delta were clearly the margin of victory.[63]

On January 11, 1983, Bill Clinton was inaugurated governor of Arkansas. Having learned his mistakes from his first term, he surrounded himself with a professional staff. Clinton also spent more time meeting with people and listening to their concerns. Bill Clinton and his inner circle had chosen education reform as the central issue of his governorship. Arkansas was ranked forty-ninth in the nation on education. Hillary took a leave of absence from the Rose Law Firm to spend the summer and early fall chairing the Education Standards Committee. Part of the package was competence for public school teachers.[64] The education reform package passed in November 1983 and Bill became known as the education governor. By the following year, Bill also became known as the governor whose brother was a substance abuser.[65]

According to *Arkansas Gazette's* Meredith Oakley:

Roger Clinton's first brush with notoriety as the governor's brother—not his first offense, but the first to draw statewide attention—came during Clinton's first year in office, when Roger was arrested for ignoring two traffic violations and an arrest warrant for failure to appear in court on one of the offenses. He called his big brother from the Little Rock jail, and in turn the governor called the chief of police and got him released without bond into the custody of their cousin, Sam Tatom, chairman of the state Crime Commission.
The governor defended his action, saying that it was prompted by Roger's obvious hysteria. Roger, he declared, had been 'terrorized' by his brief incarceration in a holding cell of the city jail, and his prompt release into a relative's custody was no more than police officials would do for anyone who had someone to vouch for him.
Virtually no one noticed when in March 1982, just before Bill Clinton officially launched his comeback campaign, Roger was arrested for

driving while intoxicated and possession of narcotics paraphernalia. After more than a year of dillydallying with the case, the sheriff's office and the prosecutor succumbed to political pressure and agreed to drop the charges.

The preferential treatment continued once Bill regained the governor's office. Generally, however, Roger's exploits—drinking, fighting, getting thrown out of bars for obnoxious behavior—were tamed enough for law enforcement officials to justify looking the other way."[66]

That would soon change.

In the spring of 1984, Rodney Myers approached Arkansas State Police narcotics investigator Robert Gibbs and Hot Springs detective Travis Bunn and told them that Roger Clinton was a cocaine dealer. They set up a sting operation in which they wired Myers with a hidden tape recorder and placed a video camera in his apartment to record Roger Clinton selling cocaine. Bunn recorded Roger Clinton saying:[67]

"I've got to get some for my brother, he's got a nose like a Hoover vacuum cleaner."[68]

The hidden surveillance cameras at Myer's apartment in Hot Springs caught Roger cutting a rock of cocaine for sale. "Boy, this is some good coke," says the undercover informant. "It's decent, it's decent," said Roger. He knew he was under suspicion but cockily assumed that he was untouchable. "I've got four or five guys in uniform who keep an eye on the guys who keep an eye on me," he explained.[69]

In early July 1984, Colonel Tommy Goodwin, head of the state police, went to Clinton's office to break the news. Goodwin explained that for several months, his brother had been the subject of an investigation into suspected drug trafficking in Arkansas and "would probably be arrested within a short period of time." This case was about to be presented to a federal grand jury, and Goodwin had no doubt that the evidence was solid. The United States attorney's office in Fort Smith was ready to make its announcement; Asa Hutchinson, the Republican appointee in charge of that office, was awaiting word that the governor had been notified.[70]

Bill Clinton would later turn his brother's scandal to advantage. He intimated that he had "signed off" on the police investigation of his brother, allowing the process of criminal justice to run its course without meddling.

His trouble-shooter, Betsey Wright, claimed that Clinton had written a note to the commander of the state police stating that there would be no interference from the governor's mansion and that he wanted the matter handled in a routine fashion.[71]

It was a lie. In reality, the Clinton machine had done everything it could to contain the case. Apparently, Detective Bunn felt he had enough evidence from the surveillance tapes to launch an investigation—in conjunction with federal authorities—of Governor Clinton himself. When he breached the question with the Arkansas State Police, they muscled in immediately and sabotaged his case.[72]

Roger Clinton was arrested before he could provide any more damaging revelations on surveillance tapes and was kept sequestered. In violation of usual police procedure, Bunn was denied access to the prisoner. He was told, tartly, that Roger "didn't know anything."[73] When Bunn complained to the head of the State Police Criminal Investigations Division, he discovered that the arrest of Roger Clinton had not been authorized by the proper officials. It was outside the normal chain of command. Nothing could be done. "The whole thing was damage control, orchestrated by the Governor's Mansion," said a state trooper close to the probe. "They had no right butting in on the Hot Springs police like that."[74]

Ambrose Evans-Pritchard summarizes the events: "The Governor was off the hook. But, it was too late to save Roger."[75] On August 2, 1984, a federal grand jury indicted Roger Cassidy Clinton, charging him with five counts of distributing cocaine and one count of conspiracy to distribute cocaine. Each count carried a maximum penalty of fifteen years in prison and a $25,000 fine.[76]

On August 14, 1984, Roger Clinton was arraigned in U.S. federal court. He pled not guilty to the six counts of drug dealing and conspiracy. He was released on a $5,000 bond. He was represented in the case by William R. Wilson, who nine years later, would be named to the federal bench by President Clinton, and by Steve Engstrom, who in December 1993 would assist Betsey Wright in drafting a statement in which a state trooper sought to retract statements he had made about a bribe the president allegedly offered him to quell controversy involving charges of Clinton's womanizing while governor.[77]

On November 9, 1984, three days after his brother's election to a third gubernatorial term, Roger arrived at the federal courthouse with his mother Virginia and her husband Dick Kelley. He changed his plea, which, it was learned, had been in the works from almost the moment of his arrest. Conveniently, Bill Clinton was out of town and did not attend the proceedings.[78]

Meanwhile, the news about Roger Clinton's drug activities continued throughout the legislative sessions. While Roger had been awaiting sentencing on federal drug charges, a federal grand jury returned additional indictments in the government's ongoing investigation of drug trafficking in Arkansas.[79] On January 28, 1985, Judge Oren Harris sentenced Roger Clinton to two years in a federal penitentiary on the conspiracy charge. A three-year sentence on the distribution charge was suspended. He was sent to the federal correctional institution in Fort Worth, Texas. As part of the plea deal, Roger agreed to testify in several other cocaine cases.[80]

One of the indictments resulted in the conviction of Sam Anderson, Jr. He was charged with two cocaine distribution counts and two conspiracy counts in connection with his dealings with Roger. Judge Harris sentenced Anderson to three years penitentiary and fined him $6,000.[81]

In October 1986, there was another indictment. Dan Lasater, an investment banker, received a six-month prison term for conspiring to deliver cocaine. Lasater would later be pardoned by Governor Clinton in November 1990, after winning reelection.[82]

According to Roger Morris:

> Clinton would run for reelection in 1984 with a nervous zeal. For a time, he put out rumors that he might run for the U.S. Senate against Pryor or take just one more term as governor before challenging Bumpers in 1986. But, the 1980 defeat had obviously altered timetables, and the extraordinary power of a third term and beyond in the statehouse still seemed to promise the ultimate price of the presidency.
>
> Clinton quietly raised more than $100,000 to push a state constitutional amendment on the 1984 ballot establishing a four-year term for governor beginning with the 1986 election, a provision that would allow him to run for the White House in 1988 and still hold on to the governorship and its base for yet another attempt at the presidency in 1992.

By the 1984 campaign, Clinton had assembled the most impressive list of corporate and individual donors ever recorded in Arkansas. The campaign also made sure that Arkansas's black community had their share of plentiful campaign funds which were duly dispensed as "walking-around-money." An aide who claimed to have guarded and carried the bags of money later told the *American Spectator* that it was variously handled in 1984 not only by Betsey Wright, but also by black aide Robert Nash and Delta boss Rodney Slater, and by Democratic National Committee agent Carroll Willis.

Those in the ranks who didn't get their cut were not above calling the governor directly to complain about inequities. 'That motherfucker hasn't spent that money! He hasn't spread it around,' the aide in charge of the bags remembered Clinton's yelling at Bobby Nash in a characteristic outburst. In 1984, Arkansas's black votes again went overwhelmingly for Clinton, some precincts by more than 90 percent.[83]

In the 1984 general election, Frank White decided to postpone a comeback for two years. Also, with Roger yet to change his plea and with no political damaging evidence in the case yet bruited, Clinton crushed his unfunded Republican opponent, Woody Freeman by a 63-37 margin.[84]

In the 1986 primary, Clinton faced former Governor Orval Faubus. Faubus's health and political influence were in rapid decline at the time, making him no match for the younger Clinton.[85]

In the 1986 governor's race, Bill Clinton faced Frank White in a bitter rematch. White claimed that the Clinton administration favored Lasater's company with state bond business only because Lasater was a political supporter who had contributed to Mr. Clinton's previous campaigns. White emphasized his statement by disclosing that the Rose Law Firm, whose partners included Hillary Rodham Clinton, had received a large portion of the legal business connected with state bonds while Clinton was governor.[86]

Clinton was able to survive the attacks and won reelection in November 1986 with 63.9 percent of the vote. By early 1987, one observer described Clinton's pace as "frantic." His schedule included a major speech in New Hampshire and visits to eighteen states. There were constant meetings and phone calls around the nation to raise money, which quickly yielded nearly $3 million in pledges, much of it from the wealthy individuals and large corporations he had long cultivated outside the state, including Wall Street financial houses, as well as the Arkansas interests. Clinton received some good news. Mario Cuomo decided that he would not be a candidate for the presidency. Then, Dale Bumpers, on March 13, 1987, also decided that he would not be a candidate for the presidency.[87]

On March 27, 1987, Clinton traveled to Los Angeles for an exclusive dinner with television producer Norman Lear and other major figures from the entertainment industry. Coincidently, among those dining with Clinton that evening was Don Henley, a member of the Eagles rock band. At the same time, in Miami, Florida, one of Henley's close friends, a young woman named Donna Rice, was boarding a yacht called the *Monkey Business* for a voyage that would change the course of American politics.[88]

On April 9, 1987, Gary Hart announced his candidacy for U.S. president. Four days later, Hart was the target of media speculation about his alleged womanizing. Acting on what it claimed was an anonymous tip, the *Miami Herald* followed a woman to Washington, staked out a townhouse where she was visiting Gary Hart, and on May 4, in a story that swept through the media nationwide, accused the front-runner of an illicit "relationship" with twenty-nine-year-old party girl Donna Rice of Miami.[89]

Hart aides then received a call from a *Washington Post* reporter who presented them with evidence of yet another illicit relationship and suggested that Hart drop out of the race or the story would run. Hart announced his withdrawal from the race the next day.[90]

The manner of the way Hart was removed must have shocked Bill Clinton. Suddenly, a candidate's private life and philandering seemed susceptible to scrutiny as never before. While Clinton had long been immune in Arkansas—almost cavalier in the openness of some of his extramarital affairs—the rules seemed to be changing just as he was reaching for his ultimate prize.[91]

Bill Clinton was clearly worried. In early summer of 1987, Clinton began asking friends and journalists, "Is there ever a time that your past is your past?" At a softball game one night, he tested the waters with journalist Max Brantley: "We've all done things that we'd be embarrassed about if they ever came out in public, but it's the nature of the game," he brooded, "that you never can be sure you don't have to answer for them." Brantley figured Clinton was talking about drugs, not sex.[92]

Before Clinton announced he was going to run, Betsey Wright decided to meet with him. As they sat in her living room, Betsey started listing the names of women Bill had allegedly had affairs with and the places where they were said to have occurred. Betsey, for many years, had been covering up for him. She was also convinced that some of the state troopers were soliciting women for him, and he for them.[93]

Betsey asked Clinton, "I want you to tell me the truth about everyone." She went over the list twice with Clinton and then again they went over the list, determining if any of the women might tell their stories to the press. After they had discussed each woman, Wright told Clinton he could not run for president.[94]

The list was a precursor of what would be called inside the 1992 campaign as the "doomsday list," a later and longer documented list of Clinton's substantial affairs or other sexual episodes, with each woman assessed and action recommended according to her potential for exposure or betrayal.[95]

On Wednesday, July 15, 1987, in the ballroom of the Excelsior Hotel, Bill Clinton held a luncheon with the national media and aides and backers from around the country to what many believed would be an announcement of candidacy. With his eyes watery and with Hillary at his side in obvious distress, Clinton said he had decided against a run because he wanted to spend more time with his daughter.[96]

On July 20, 1988, Bill Clinton gave the nominating speech at the Democratic National Convention in Atlanta, Georgia for Michael Dukakis, governor of Massachusetts. Clinton had been allotted twenty minutes for the speech. It did not go well. ABC cut away at the twenty-one-minute mark and began showing a film. On NBC, Tom Brokaw responded, "We have to be here too," and then gave up on the speech. CBS showed a red light flashing on the podium, a signal for Clinton to shut up. People could be heard shouting: "Get the hook! Get the hook!"[97]

After thirty-two minutes, when he uttered "in closing" the hall erupted in mocking applause. After the speech, Clinton threw a temper tantrum backstage, denouncing Dukakis as "that little Greek mother-fucker." The next day, he was crucified in the press on his performance. Frank Greer, a media consultant, said, "It was either the longest nominating speech or the shortest presidential campaign in history." Johnny Carson's writers delighted in the material Clinton had provided them for *The Tonight Show*.

Carson began his next monologue by saying, "in closing." Then he noted that the Surgeon General had just approved Governor Bill Clinton as an over-the-counter sleep aid; that Clinton's speech went over "about as big as the Velcro condom;" and that when it came to drama, Clinton was "right up there with PBS pledge breaks."[98]

Now Hillary was fighting for her husband and the future of their political partnership. She summoned Betsey Wright to Atlanta to manage the aftermath and telephoned Hollywood friends Harry Thomasson and Linda Bloodworth-Thomasson, who were sitcom producers. Within a few hours Clinton had an invitation to be on Carson's show, where his self-deprecating performance and saxophone solo seemed to redeem him.[99]

Clinton was also mocked by the Gridiron Club of Little Rock journalists and politicians. They put on a skit at a 1988 gathering that brought the house down. Members impersonated Gary Hart and Bill Clinton and sang a parody of a popular song, "To All the Girls We've Loved."[100] Michael Dukakis would go on to lose the presidential election to George H. W. Bush in November 1988. At this point, Bill Clinton was looking for advice on his next move. On December 23, 1988, Clinton met with John Poulard who had been the southern coordinator for Gary Hart's presidential campaign and with Clinton aide Randy White.

1. Should he run for governor in 1990, if he wanted to run for president two years later?
2. How much money did he need to raise in Arkansas?
3. Could he be the regional candidate?
4. What about another young southern moderate—Tennessee Senator Al Gore?[101]

Late in the summer of 1989, Betsey Wright told Clinton that she was burned out. She asked for and got a leave of absence. On November 17, 1989, Clinton's office announced her resignation. She was soon replaced by Gloria Cabe. Cabe was unhappy that Bill and Hillary still dealt with political operative Dick Morris whose other clients were Republicans.[102]

On March 1, 1990, Clinton officially entered the race for governor. He promised, yet again, to serve out his term, even as he began testing themes and discreetly raising funds for the 1992 presidential bid.[103]

In the Democrat primary, he faced Tom McRae, a former Bumpers aide who had presided over the Winthrop Rockefeller Foundation with mounting dismay at Clinton policies. Then, shortly before the filing period closed, Tucker changed his mind and filed instead for lieutenant governor. It appeared that Tucker and Clinton "came to an understanding" about the governorship. McRae posed little threat and took only 40 percent of the primary vote.[104]

Now Clinton had to decide whom to face in the general election. In the Republican primary, there was Tommy Robinson, the former Pulaski County sheriff and congressman who might or might not have any dirt on Clinton, but who Clinton knew would not hesitate to play hardball. Then there was Sheffield Nelson, who was not perceived to be a formidable opponent. The most logical choice was Nelson.[105]

According to Skip Rutherford, with assistance from the Clinton campaign, an unusually large number of Democrats crossed party lines and voted for Nelson in the May 1990 primary, which they could do because Arkansas was an open primary state that allowed registered voters to vote in the other party's primary. Robinson lost the nomination by a 58-42 margin.[106]

In the October 1990 debate, reporter-panelist Craig Cannon posed the question that everyone wanted asked: "Will you guarantee to us that if elected, there is absolutely, positively no way that you'll run for any other political office and that you'll serve out your term in full?"[107]

Clinton responded. "You bet! I told you when I announced for governor I intended to run, and that's what I'm going to do. I'm gonna serve four years. I made that decision when I decided to run. I'm being considered as a candidate for governor. That's the job I want. That's the job I'll do for the next four years."[108]

The Nelson campaign began attacking Clinton on the womanizing issue. Betsey Wright and Hillary responded by hiring, through the campaign, Webb Hubbell and Vince Foster from the Rose Law Firm to represent the women and obtain from the women their signed statements that they never had sex with Bill Clinton. Then, during the final days of the campaign, Nelson decided to play his ace. The campaign produced a commercial reminding voters how many times Bill Clinton had raised taxes during his tenure and overlaid with Clinton's own voice repeating the words "raise" and "spend," thus portraying Clinton as a big-tax liberal. The ad was devastating and Clinton fell twelve points in three days and was down to 44 percent.[109]

In response, Morris and Clinton wrote a response ad overnight and produced it early the next morning. To pay for the ads, Clinton took out a $50,000 personal loan and started running them on Sunday and Monday. They handed out thirty thousand dollars in hundred-dollar bills just days before the balloting, and the election day they handed out "palm cards" and voting booth strings in black precincts; bused voters in some areas from precinct to precinct, providing changes of shirts; and handed out free fried chicken at some polling places. Clinton won with 59 percent.[110]

After winning his fifth term as governor, Clinton began acting like a presidential candidate. Despite his promise to the voters that he would not run for president, Clinton spent much of the time traveling around the country, giving speeches, and conferring with Democratic strategists. According to Meredith Oakley of the *Arkansas Democrat* (she kept a log of Clinton's schedule) during one fifty-two-day period Clinton was in the state only fourteen days. On a trip to a Democratic Leadership Conference convention in Seattle, he was accompanied by an immense fourteen-person security detail.[111]

Hillary soon began to spread the word of Clinton's plans to his home supporters. In the spring of 1991, Skip Rutherford, an Arkla executive and close friend of Mack McLarty's, got the message during a softball game of the Molar Rollers, a softball team on which his daughter and Chelsea Clinton both played. While he sat with Hillary in the bleachers, she took advantage of a lull in the action to pass on her opinion that she thought Bill could win in a contest against Bush.[112]

On May 6, 1991, just six months after he took the pledge not to run for the White House, Bill Clinton emerged at a carefully staged Democratic Leadership Council convention in Cleveland, Ohio as the best of six possible Democratic presidential contenders against President George H. W. Bush. Clinton used the event to mark out what would be called the "Bubba tactic" in his campaign, pointedly excluding Jesse Jackson from giving a policy address at the gathering of the corporate-funded group that Jackson called the Southern White Boys Club.[113]

By the summer of 1991, Mickey Kantor, Hillary's old friend and a former Legal Services Corporation board member, began putting together the nucleus of a national campaign organization. This group would include only a few longtime Clinton enthusiasts, but a majority of professional operatives.[114]

CHAPTER 6

MENA AIRPORT

By 1986, there was an epidemic of cocaine, contaminating the political establishment [of Arkansas] from top to bottom. Parties were given at which cocaine would serve like hors d'oeuvres and sex was rampant" and that "Bill Clinton was in frequent attendance."

—Ambrose Evans-Pritchard[1]

On October 7, 1994, Sarah McClendon of the Washington press corps, asked President Clinton about nefarious activities that reportedly took place in the 1980s at the Mena airport in Southwest Arkansas. The question was about the rumors of the CIA covertly flying arms through Mena to Nicaragua's anti-Communist Contras. When they returned, much to the embarrassment of American intelligence officials, they supposedly brought vast quantities of drugs and cash into Arkansas. Clinton replied, "Well, let me answer that question." And then he said he knew nothing. Nobody told him anything. It was a federal matter not a state matter: "The state really had next to nothing to do with it. . . . We had nothing—zero—to do with it, and everybody who's ever looked into it knows that."[2]

Unfortunately for Bill, two days later, Ambrose Evans-Pritchard, Washington bureau chief for the *Sunday Telegraph* of London, wrote an article reporting that Arkansas was a "major point for the transshipment of drugs" coming into the United States from abroad in the 1980s. In the middle of the decade, he asserted, Arkansas "was perilously close to becoming a 'narco-republic'—a sort of mini-Columbia within the borders of the United States."[3]

Ambrose had spoken with a convicted drug pilot who flew cocaine into Arkansas from abroad. He quotes an associate of another drug smuggler, who claims that vast amounts of drugs were brought through Arkansas while the smuggler was performing some sort of function for the CIA. Then the CIA discovered that the smuggler was still a drug merchant, and according to the smuggler's associate, "the Dixie Mafia was blackmailing the CIA" and for a while, drug shipments became rampant. It also appears, through Mr. Evans-Pritchard's witness, that the Arkansas state troopers actually observed the smuggler fly drugs in the state.[4]

Now let us fill in the cracks concerning the Intermountain Regional Airport in Mena, Arkansas; Governor Bill Clinton; and the drug culture in Arkansas during the roaring 1980s.

When Bill Clinton stated that he knew nothing about Mena airport, there were some who knew Clinton was lying. John Bender, a mechanic, saw Clinton at Mena three times in the summer of 1985. There were no local dignitaries present and Clinton did not seem to be taking part in any official function. Bender said that Clinton arrived in a Beech aircraft and was still there when Bender left for the day. Clinton's stays lasted for hours.[5] Another is Arkansas state trooper Bobby Walker who said that "sometime in the mid-80s," he was at Mena with Clinton. When Walker saw a "huge dark green military plane" parked there, he was surprised at seeing a military plane at Mena. Clinton told him it was not military; it served another purpose. Then, there was Arkansas state trooper Larry Patterson. In a legally binding deposition, Patterson said that Clinton knew about Mena. He said he had overheard conversations about "large quantities of drugs being flown into Mena airport, large quantities of guns, and there was an ongoing operation training foreign people in the area." When asked, "Were any of these conversations in the presence of Governor Bill Clinton?" he replied: "Yes sir."[6]

And finally, there was Arkansas state trooper Larry Douglas Brown whose daybook records one visit, on May 21, 1984. Brown accompanied Clinton to Mena on several other occasions. Given the remoteness of Mena, it was curious that Governor Bill Clinton was showing up so frequently in the mid-1980s. The airport is small and handles little traffic. The town itself is sleepy and extremely rural, located in a remote area near the Oklahoma border. Its voter turnout is, perhaps, the lowest in the state. Maybe Mr. Brown's story can explain this.[7]

On April 1, 1984, Arkansas state trooper L.D. Brown, while reading the *New York Times*, saw an ad for employment at the CIA. "I was reading it when Bill walked in. . . . I showed him this ad and, you know, he read spy novels and things of that nature and he said, 'L.D. I've always told you you'd make a good spy. You need to fire off a letter to them.' . . . I sat down either that day or very soon thereafter and actually wrote a letter to this guy."[8]

As part of the application process, Brown had written an essay: "Marxist Influence in Central America." Three early drafts of the essay contain interpolations in Clinton's handwriting. Clinton also suggested that Brown study Russian, a suggestion Brown took seriously enough to begin making entries in his daybook in Cyrillic.[9]

As the process continued to move along, Clinton made a call to Langley. According to Brown, "He [Clinton] said he was going to make a phone call for me. . . . I don't know who he called within the Agency. . . . He told me he had made the call. Now, I didn't press it or pry, but I appreciated it."[10]

On August 30, 1984, four months after passing a CIA entrance examination, Brown went to the Hilton Hotel in Dallas for his first interview. A man called Dan Magruder was waiting for him. After watching the Iran-Contra hearings, Brown identified "Dan Magruder" as Donald Gregg, Vice President George H. W. Bush's national security advisor from 1982 to 1989. Gregg was a career veteran of the CIA. Gregg asked Brown if he would be interested in paramilitary or narcotics" work as well as security. Brown said he wanted to be considered for such assignments and, in the course of the interview, duly signed a secrecy agreement. Somebody, he was told, would be giving him a call.[11]

On September 5, 1984, Brown received formal notification of his nomination for employment from Ken Cargile, the Southwest personnel representative for the CIA. The letter to Brown said, "I am pleased to nominate you for employment with the Central Intelligence Agency." Scarcely a month later, the CIA call came to his unlisted number at home. As Brown testified, the caller "talked to me about everything I had been through in the meeting in Dallas, . . . made me aware that he knew everything there was to know." He asked Brown to meet him at Cajun's Wharf in Little Rock. His name, he said, was Barry Seal.[12]

Berriman Adler Seal was a legendary drug smuggler, known for having flown hundreds of drug smuggling flights from 1977 to 1983. In late 1981,

Seal had made direct contact with the Colombian cocaine cartels. Over the next three years, his fleet of aircraft would become the dominant smuggling conduit for the Medellin Cartel, which reportedly controlled 75 percent of all the cocaine exported from Colombia. The Colombians learned to respect him. They were losing loads of cocaine at a fearful rate as the Reagan administration cranked up its war on drugs in the Caribbean. Seal knew how to get through the defenses. He had never lost a single shipment for the cartel.[13]

Seal needed a sophisticated base of operations, far enough inland to evade the stringent patrolling of the Coast Guard along the coastal states. He chose Mena. According to Billy Bottoms, a pilot in the organization: "We had gotten so high-tech at that time. Rather than use barnyard mechanics, hiding in the back of hangars . . . [we needed] a professional shop. That whole airfield is one of the most professional aviation retrofit places in the country, and that's why we went up there."[14]

Seal took over Rich Mountain Aviation, an aviation outfit that repaired, retrofit, and fueled airplanes, and turned it into a command center with two hangars large enough to hide his aircraft. His fleet had secret fuel "bladders" installed in the floor of the aircraft to extend their flight range. Trap doors were fitted so that he could drop duffel bags of cocaine in mid-flight before landing empty.[15]

Barry Seal became an informer for the DEA after he was caught in Operation Screamer, conspiring to smuggle Quaaludes into Florida. Facing the likelihood of a long prison sentence, he made overtures to the Florida office of the DEA. When that failed, he went over their heads to Washington and was helped out by his lawyer, Richard Ben-Veniste.[16]

In April 1984, the DEA instructed its Miami office to "work him." Agent Ernest Jacobsen volunteered to take that assignment. He was known for his skill at cracking the hard nuts. "I knew if we could work a deal out, Barry Seal would be one of the best informants DEA ever had," he said. "I mean, every major trafficker in the world was talking to this guy." Seal was also taking to L.D. Brown.[17]

In the Spring of 1984, Seal became DEA informant number SGI-84-0028, working as an $800,000-a-year double agent in an elaborate sting operation against the Medellin cartel in Colombia and individuals in the Nicaraguan regime who had been dipping into the trade themselves. The bargain seemed plain: "Seal was flying weapons to central and south

America," an agent noted, recording what "was believed" within the DEA. "In return he is allowed to smuggle what he wants back into the United States."[18]

On September 5, 1984, Brown was notified of his nomination for employment. About a month later, Brown was asked to meet Seal at the Cajun Wharf in Little Rock. When Brown met Seal, he noticed that Seal clearly knew the details Brown had provided on his CIA application. Seal also spoke vaguely about working for the CIA: "He'd been flying for the agency, that's all I know." In conversations over the next few weeks, Seal referred casually to Clinton as "the guv" and "acted like he knew the governor," Brown recalled. He invited Brown to join him in an "operation" planned to begin at Mena's Intermountain Regional before sunrise on Tuesday, October 23, 1984.[19]

Brown met Seal at the Mena airport in the predawn darkness and was surprised to find them boarding not a small private craft but a C-123K military transport with twin engines. Seal had a tailgate at the end of its fuselage capable of loading such cargo as a small automobile. The plane was serviced and financed by Southern Air Transport, a well-known CIA front company. Seal ordered Brown matter-of-factly to leave behind all personal identification, including his billfold, keys, and jewelry. Seal was at the controls next to a co-pilot whose name Brown never learned. In the back of the aircraft sat two men, "beaners" or "kickers," the trooper called them. They were common laborers who looked like Central American Indians. Though he did not know it, Brown was aboard the *Fat Lady*, and his later account marked the flight as one of Mena's routine gun-and-drug runs.[20]

After the plane left the Mena airport, it made a refueling stop at Stennis Airfield in Gulfport, Mississippi, an airfield frequently used by the DEA. Everyone stayed on the plane during the refueling stop.[21]

Seal took off from the airfield, and while in flight, the plane dropped to what Brown called "an altitude a hell of a lot lower than what you'd think you'd fly." Brown believed that Seal was trying to evade radar. Soon, the airplane regained altitude, but then Seal descended the plane again and, according to Brown, "that's when these two crazy bastards get these pallets and roll them on casters." Parachutes opened from the cargo on the pallets. Later, Seal confirmed to Brown that the pallets carried M-16s for the Contras. Approximately thirty minutes later, Brown said, the C123K landed at a sleepy Central American airport, thought to be Tegucigalpa,

Honduras, but not confirmed. After landing, the plane was refueled. Seal and the kickers went to collect four duffel bags. Brown and the co-pilot remained on board. Afterward, they flew back to Mena.[22]

Seal did not say much when they returned to Mena. Brown was merely an observer on this mission. Seal gave Brown a manila envelope with $2,500 in cash and said he would be in touch. When Brown returned to the Governor's Mansion after his flight, Clinton greeted him, jovially asking, "Well, are you having any fun yet?"

"Yeah, but this is some scary stuff."

"Oh, you can handle it," Clinton said, patting Brown on the back. Obviously, he was aware of what Brown had done. Clinton, according to Brown, seemed very familiar with the CIA.[23]

With Clinton's encouragement, Brown again flew with Seal to Central America on what he still understood to be some kind of orientation mission for his CIA employment. This occurred on December 24, 1984. Seal picked up two duffel bags on the return through Honduras, and just as before, back at Mena, he offered Brown $2,500 in small bills. Yet this time, Seal also brought one of the duffels to Brown's Datsun 310 hatchback in the Intermountain Regional parking lot and proceeded to take out of it what Brown instantly recognized as a kilo of cocaine, a "waxene-wrapped package," as he called it, "a brick."[24]

Brown had had enough. He told Seal that he wanted no part of what was happening and proceeded to leave. Next, Brown approached Clinton and asked, "Do you know what they're bringing back on those planes?" Clinton froze. "They're bringing back coke," Brown told him. Clinton calmly responded to Brown telling him not to worry. Then Bill said, "That's Lasater's deal. That's Lasater's deal."[25]

Brown was upset. Clinton tried to calm him: "Settle down. That's no problem." But Brown turned away, hurried to his car, and drove off, leaving behind his once-promising CIA career.[26]

Brown immediately called the CIA to withdraw his application. "Just changed my mind," he recalled telling them. But he saw no recourse, no appeal to some higher level of government in a crime in which both the governor of the state and Washington were knowledgeable and thus complicit.[27]

According to R. Emmett Tyrrell Jr. in his book, *Boy Clinton*: "In January 1985, while Brown was on duty at the Governor's Mansion, he was paid a visit by a man he believed to be another contract employee of the CIA, Felix Rodriguez, alias Max Gomez. His familiarity with the place surprised Brown and he concluded that Rodriguez must have known Clinton and was in continuing contact with him. Eventually, Clinton made it clear to Brown that he knew Rodriguez."[28]

Tyrrell continues: "On the occasion of the first meeting with Brown, it seemed that Rodriguez's mission was to placate him. He wanted Brown to work with him on clandestine operations, but he wanted to reassure Brown that no more "monkeying around with Seal would be involved." At Rodriguez's mention of Seal, Brown explained, 'I have had some bad experiences.' Rodriguez responded, 'Don't worry about Barry. . . . We're going to take care of that.' He told Brown he would 'take care of things' with Clinton. Apparently he did. Clinton never talked to Brown about Mena or Lasater again."[29]

By the summer of 1985, Seal's usefulness to the government had expired, and a scapegoat for the illegal operation in Mena was imperative. That same year the CIA abandoned him, refusing even to acknowledge on camera to a federal judge his role in the Sandinista sting, much less his long and seamy clandestine service. In a tangled plea bargain on the old Quaalude charges, a bitterly defiant Seal, still holding onto his Mena secrets and still contemplating a profitable return to Arkansas, found himself on a court-ordered six months' sentence to a Salvation Army halfway house in Baton Rouge, even though the Medellin Cartel had put a $1 million contract on his head. He was a sitting duck.[30]

On February 19, 1986, two Colombian gunmen opened fire as Seal parked his car in front of the Salvation Army Center in Baton Rouge. The two were part of a six-man team of Colombians. Eventually, three were caught, and three got away.[31]

In May of 1986, Brown got a call from Rodriguez. "You hear about our man?" he asked. Brown had heard of Seal's murder in Baton Rouge. "Well, we know who was flying in the second seat." Brown suspected that Rodriguez was eliminating anyone who knew too much about Mena.[32]

Rodriguez assigned Brown the task of carrying out a political assassination. Seal had been gunned down three months earlier, and Brown suspected that Rodriguez was eliminating anyone who knew too much about Mena. Brown wanted to make sure that he was on the right side of the house-cleaning operation by the CIA, so he accepted the mission. Before he left, he consulted Bill Clinton. "I'm going to take care of that problem in Mexico," he told him. "Oh, that's good, L.D., that's good," replied the governor. Looking back on that exchange, Brown believes Clinton also knew the identity of Brown's quarry.[33]

The target was intended to be the co-pilot Brown had seen on Seal's C-123. Brown flew to Puerto Vallarta, Mexico on June 18, 1986. A disassembled FAL 7.62 mm rifle was waiting for him in a straw bag at the guard house of the port.[34]

Going by the alias Michael Johnson, a name he had used in undercover work in Arkansas, Brown, on the morning of June 21, 1986, was to arrive at the Hotel Playa Conchas Chinas. He was to identify himself as Johnson to the hotel clerk and give him fifty dollars. The clerk would then direct him to his target. All went well according to plan until the clerk pointed out Brown's intended victim. He looked across and saw an American in his mid-thirties, playing with his children by the fountain. He was horrified and walked out. It was the end of his adventure with the CIA.[35]

Brown had never seen the intended victim before. His name was Terry Reed, and he was another of the pilots who had worked for Air Contra.[36]

Reed would eventually provide evidence supporting Brown's claims. Unaware of Brown, Reed wrote a book in 1994, called *Compromised.* It described his misadventures with the CIA and with Arkansas officials while training the Contras. The book implicates Clinton in Mena and places Reed in Puerto Vallarta. Oblivious to the fate that was awaiting him at the Hotel Playa Conchas Chinas, Reed wrote that he was told to be at the hotel on June 21, 1986, to meet his new CIA handler. The man who ordered him there was Felix Rodriguez, known to Reed as Max Gomez. When Reed finally learned that there was an assassin waiting for him in the lobby of the hotel, it did not surprise him. Nor did it surprise him that the gunman would be an Arkansas State Trooper and a close aide of Governor Clinton.[37]

According to political journalist Ambrose Evans-Pritchard: "It was Terry Reed who was recruited to create a remote Arkansas air base to upgrade the skills of Contra pilots and teach them techniques for aerial resupply inside Nicaragua. Reed chose a spot called Nella in the Ouachita National Forest, twelve miles north of Mena. There were four flight instructors. It was not long before the State Police started getting reports of paramilitary activity. . . . If Terry Reed's role had been confined to flight training at Nella, he might not have become a liability to Governor Clinton. But Barry Seal needed his machine tool expertise to help with the clandestine production of weapons parts at a series of plants scattered around Arkansas. It was this side of the operation that drew Terry into the vortex of the conspiracy where he would witness meetings with the governor of Arkansas. Reed paints a colorful scene in his book *Compromised*."[38]

Oliver North, Felix Rodriguez, and Bill Clinton holed up together in an ammunition storage bunker at Camp Robinson while an envoy from the CIA reads the riot act. "We didn't plan on Arkansas becoming more difficult to deal with than most banana republics," says the man from the CIA, dripping with contempt. "Our deal with you was to launder our money. This has turned into a feeding frenzy by your 'good ole boy' sharks, and you've had a hand in it, too, Mr. Clinton. . . . Reed was flabbergasted by what he heard. Nobody had told him that the Governor himself was mixed up with the operation. As it happened, Clinton had gate-crashed the meeting. He had heard that the Enterprise was shutting down in Arkansas—where endemic corruption had become a security risk—and he had come demanding an assurance that the White House would take care of all the loose ends stemming from Mena. It was a foolhardy thing to do. He had now exposed himself to Reed."[39]

Evans-Pritchard summarizes: "Governor Clinton was eager to see Terry Reed move away from Arkansas. In April 1986, he chatted with Reed outside Juanita's restaurant in Little Rock and strongly encouraged him to take up a new venture being offered to him in Mexico. Terry agreed. Two months later, Trooper Brown was sent to Puerto Vallarta to carry out the assassination."[40]

Brown could still recall when he originally spoke to Clinton about the drugs coming into Arkansas and Clinton's reaction was, "That's Lasater's deal. That's Lasater's deal." So who is Lasater?

Dan Lasater is a multi-millionaire who made his money initially selling his stake in the Ponderosa steakhouse chain in Ohio and Indiana. He then became the most successful breeder and racer of thoroughbreds and moved into the bond business in 1980. Lasater was also a player in the cocaine trafficking network of the Dixie Mafia as early as the mid-1970s. Intelligence reports show that the DEA had opened a file on Lasater in 1983 and had assigned him a tracking number of 1411475. Lasater was tipped off at once. A source called him in 1983 to inform him that he was listed in the computer as the subject of a DEA probe.[41]

In partnership with a state legislator, George "Butch" Locke, Lasater's "bond daddy" brokerage made millions in profits by 1982 but was already infamous in local investment circles for its flow of cocaine as well as its shady financial practices.[42]

In 1982 Lasater's company received a professional censure from the National Association of Securities Dealers for excessive markups and unlicensed sales. His company was censured again in 1983 for buying and selling bonds for a savings and loan without authority of the thrift's board. Then in 1984, his company was censured for making more unauthorized trades and over a period of time for violating multiples securities rules and regulations. The state securities commissioner sanctioned the firm for "cheating customers" in 1982.[43]

By 1983 Lasater had personally given thousands of dollars to Clinton's gubernatorial campaigns. He also held fund-raisers for Clinton which amounted to tens of thousands of dollars including the critically important 1982 comeback.[44]

Clinton also attended Lasater's parties which presented his bodyguard, L.D. Brown, with problems. In addition to young girls, the parties also included plenty of cocaine. At one typical gathering, Brown tried to usher the governor out to avoid a scandal, though it was clear that Clinton knew about the rampant drugs.[45]

When Clinton needed a safe house for his delinquent half-brother Roger, it was Lasater who gave him a job as a "stable hand" in Ocala, Florida. And when Roger fell behind in payments to his Medellin contact—a stash of cocaine had been stolen from his convertible—it was Lasater who paid the debt, or perhaps a better word is ransom. The Colombians, apparently were hinting that there could be violent reprisals against the governor himself.[46]

In June 1983, Lasater hired as his chief assistant a longtime Clinton associate, Patsy Thomasson, who had begun as an aide to Congressman Wilbur Mills in the 1970s and later became a close friend of state legislator and Lasater partner George "Butch" Locke. A self-described "yellow-dog Democrat," Thomasson was a discreet, almost cryptic figure and was never to be charged in any of the crimes surrounding her employer.[47]

At Lasater's company, Patsy was viewed as a shrewd and important link to the Democratic Party by the firm's employees. "We'd all have to make contributions to the Clinton campaign funds, anywhere from $500 on up, scaled on earnings," said one bond salesman, describing the obligatory tithing system at the firm. "Patsy was the one who handled the money."[48]

By the mid-1980s, Lasater had its own ties to Madison Guaranty, what one accountant called "significant dealings." A decade later, the Whitewater special prosecutor reportedly was moved by the record of these dealings to investigate whether Lasater used the thrift to funnel money to the Clinton campaigns in 1984 and 1986.[49]

Dan Lasater's luck was about to run out with his criminal indictment on federal drug charges in the autumn of 1986. A federal-state narcotics task force had been formed in Arkansas in 1985 after reports of blatant cocaine trafficking and use, especially in the Little Rock bond business, became what one officer called "overwhelming." Lasater was soon implicated by a torrent of informants' reports and formal statements. But almost from the beginning, the investigation followed what agents remembered as "unusual procedures."[50]

Lasater was given "use immunity" in return for cooperation in other cases and was sentenced to only thirty months in prison, though he apparently never offered testimony in another major case. He served just six months in prison and four in a halfway house and would be pardoned by Clinton immediately after the 1990 gubernatorial election, claiming that the pardon was necessary to enable Lasater to regain his hunting license. The pardon was of dubious validity, because Lasater had been sentenced by a federal court, not a state court. But it sent a signal to the Arkansas authorities that Lasater should be allowed to resume his financial and brokering activities without hindrance.[51]

When a reporter asked the governor at the time of Lasater's indictment, "Have you ever used cocaine?" Clinton responded casually, "No. I'm not sure what it looked like if I saw it." Others disagreed.[52]

A teacher and social worker named Sally Perdue described her four-month affair with Clinton in late 1983. She said he would parade around her apartment in one of her black nightgowns playing his saxophone. He would smoke marijuana and use cocaine regularly, pulling joints out of a cigarette case and shaking cocaine out from a small bag onto a table in her living room. "He had all the equipment laid out, like a real pro," Perdue told a reporter.[53]

There was another woman named Sharlene Wilson. She had been a bartender at Le Bistro, a Little Rock nightclub where Roger used to play with his rock band Dealer's Choice. She would later become an undercover informant for the US Drug Enforcement Administration. Bill would come by from time to time with one or two of his state troopers.[54]

"Roger had all the pretty girls and drugs and the fast life, and Bill was pretty envious of this," she said. On one occasion, "Roger the Dodger" came back to the bar and said he needed two grams of cocaine right away. They carried out the deal near the ladies' room. Roger then borrowed her "tooter," her "one-hitter" as she called it and handed it to the governor... . "I watched Bill Clinton lean up against a brick wall," Sharlene recalled. "He must have had an adenoid problem because he casually stuck my tooter up his nose. He was so messed up that night, he slid down the wall into a garbage can and just sat there like a complete idiot." Afterwards, they all went back to the governor's mansion and continued to party into the early hours of the morning. According to Sharlene: "I thought it was the coolest thing in the world that we had a governor who got high." That was not the only time she snorted cocaine with Bill Clinton. Although, she claimed to have been present with him at a series of toga parties at the Coachman's Inn outside Little Rock between 1979 and 1981. "I was, you know, the hostess with the mostess, the lady with the snow," she said. "I'd serve drinks and lines of cocaine on a glass mirror."[55]

People shared sexual partners in what amounted to a Babylonian orgy. They were elite gatherings of ten to twenty people, mostly public officials, lawyers, and local notables, cavorting in a labyrinth of interconnected rooms with women that included teenage girls. Bill Clinton was there at least twice, she said, snorting cocaine "quite avidly" with Dan Harmon, a former Saline County prosecutor and future Seventh Judicial District prosecutor, an enforcer for the local smuggling enterprise. She gave a graphic description of the sexual activities that Bill Clinton preferred.[56]

She remembered seeing a distinctive mole at the base of his stomach. "It's darned me that he's managed to get elected through all this," she said.[57]

Sharlene had even done a stint for three or four months unloading bags of cocaine at the Mena Airport in the mid-1980s. The cocaine was flown in on two-engine Cessnas, sometimes as often as every day. "I'd pick up the pallets and make the run down to Texas. The drop-off was at the Cowboys Stadium. I was told that nobody would ever bother me, and I was never bothered. . . . If there was a problem, I was to call Dan Harmon. A lot of the cocaine that came into Mena was taken up to Springdale in northwest

Arkansas, she said, where it was stuffed into chickens for reshipment to the rest of the country.[58]

She also used to pick up cocaine deliveries on the railways tracks near the little town of Alexander, thirty miles south of Little Rock. "Every two weeks, for years, I'd go to the tracks, I'd pick up the package, and I'd deliver it to Dan Harmon, either straight to his office, or at my house. . . . Sometimes it was flown in by air, sometimes it would be kicked out of the train. A big bundle, two feet by one and a half feet, like a bale of hay, so heavy I'd have trouble lifting it. . . . Roger the Dodger picked it up a few times."[59]

In the summer of 1987, one of the drops disappeared. The next delivery was three to four pounds of cocaine and five pounds of weed. Sharlene was supposed to make the pick-up, but that night she had been high-balling, a mixture of cocaine and heroin and was totally strung-out. Instead, it was Dan Harmon who also brought some of his men to watch the delivery.[60]

A group of boys had intercepted the package at the drop sight. Most of them managed to get away, but Kevin Ives, seventeen, and Don Henry, sixteen, were captured. Harmon's men interrogated them as they were lying on the ground, face down, hands tied behind their backs. They were kicked and beaten, and finally executed. Then their bodies were placed across the railway tracks, so they would be mangled by the next train.[61]

Another witness to Clinton's drug use was Jane Parks, a middle-age Arkansan hired in the mid-1980s as a resident manager at a Little Rock apartment complex called Vantage Point. Vantage Point consisted of three buildings and Mrs. Parks office was in the middle building, apartment B107. The apartment had been subdivided by a partition. Mrs. Parks worked with her assistant on one side. On the other side was a temporary apartment referred to as Vantage Point's "corporate suite." In the summer of 1984, she was informed by the real estate agents that a nonpaying guest would be coming to stay for a while. She was told to take care of him, no questions asked. The guest turned out to be Governor Clinton's half-brother, Roger Clinton.[62]

Mrs. Parks said that she observed cocaine being brought into the apartment. At that time, Roger was nearing the disastrous culmination of a five-year cocaine addiction. "By mid-1984, Roger spent virtually every waking hour getting high or trying to get high," wrote Arkansas commentator Meredith Oakley, in her book *On the Make*. Dan Lasater was there at least once. In an interview with one of Tyrrell's colleagues, she stated, "Once when I opened the door, Bill Clinton was sitting on the couch. He was staring straight ahead, looking stoned." She mimicked the governor sitting with arms stiff, looking straight ahead, glassy-eyed. She saw "lines of cocaine on the table in front of him."[63]

Other times, Parks could clearly distinguish Bill's voice as he chatted with his brother about the quality of the marijuana joints they were smoking. She said she could hear them talking about the cocaine as they passed it back and forth." She could hear Roger saying what it was, where he got it from, what it was like. Then she could hear Governor Clinton boasting his approval: "This is really good shit."[64]

Two or three times a week, the governor was buoying his spirits with a snort of Kid Brother's Colombian rock. The aroma was coming through the vents. Parks was certain as if she had been in the suite herself. Sometimes the two brothers were alone. Sometimes, young women were invited to join, and the little party was consummated with raucous orgasms. The bed was pressed up against the partition wall, just a few feet from the desk of Mrs. Parks. On two occasions, she heard the governor copulating on the bed.[65]

Jerry Parks, Jane's husband, was then head of the Little Rock branch of Guardsmark, a security firm based in Memphis. He did private detective work on the side. When Jane mentioned to him what was going on at B107, he began his own discrete surveillance. He wrote down names, dates, license plate numbers, and snapped photos. By the end of Roger's stay, Parks had collected a thick dossier on the comings and goings of Governor Clinton.[66]

The word must have gone out because some of the material that was in the files was stolen from their house in July 1993. Then in September 1993, Jerry was shot dead in his car on an Arkansas road. The murder was described by police investigators as a "professional hit." After R. Emmett Tyrrell Jr. published Mrs. Parks interview in his syndicated column in October 1996. She was threatened. It was the third threat against her in recent weeks. This time a man telephoned her to say, "You will be dead before the election."[67]

There may be a reason why Bill Clinton never went public with his medical records. They might reveal a drug habit. They may also reveal a drug overdose. Rumor has it that Governor Clinton was admitted to the University of Arkansas Medical Center emergency room in 1980, just after his defeat for reelection. He was suffering from a cocaine overdose. At some point, Hillary arrived. Two nurses were later interviewed that had knowledge of the occurrence. Neither would state a categorical no when asked if she knew about Clinton's arrival at the emergency room. One of the nurses said, "I can't talk about that." The other nurse responded that if she were to discuss the matter, her life would be in danger.[68]

Throughout his time as governor, Clinton would continue to hear reports about Mena. Joining the security unit in 1987, trooper Larry Patterson would later testify about frequent conversations among state policemen "that there was [sic] large quantities of drugs being flown into the Mena airport, large quantities of money, large quantities of guns, that there was an ongoing operation training foreign people in that area. That it was a CIA operation."[69]

On September 11, 1991, barely a month before he declared his candidacy for president, during a press conference, Bill Clinton would make his only public statement as governor about the crimes of Mena.[70]

He was "pleased" the issue had been raised "again," Clinton said. "The state did all it could do to investigate the allegations about Mena airport's being used to run drugs and guns."[71]

CHAPTER 7

ELECTION 1992

I think voters always try to make judgments about a person's character and fitness to serve. The question is whether it's relevant and whether it's true. In this particular case, the charges are untrue and have been thoroughly investigated, are old news at home, and the person who made them has been discredited.

—Governor Clinton
responding to the womanizing allegations, January 17, 1992[1]

On October 3, 1991, Governor Bill Clinton, with his wife, Hillary Rodham Clinton, and their daughter, Chelsea, near him, announced that he was a candidate for president of the United States. His mom, Virginia, was there to hear him finally say those words. So were legislators, state workers, curious onlookers, staff members, and friends. Even Orval Faubus, the former governor of Arkansas and famous segregationist who opposed the integration of Little Rock high schools, was there in attendance, which numbered thirty-five hundred people.[2]

He gave a thirty-two-minute speech, in which he pledged himself to a presidency that would "restore the American dream." He talked about the middle class, on optimism in the future, and opportunity and responsibility. He promised his presidency would ensure universal access to higher education, universal health care, and universal literacy."[3] He also talked about being against "divisiveness." Here is what he said: "For 12 years, the Republicans have tried to divide us, race against race. . . . We know about race-baiting. They've used that old tool on us for decades now."[4] At the end of the speech, the loud-speakers were turned up and

Fleetwood Mac's song "Don't Stop Thinking About Tomorrow" began to be played.[5]

The campaign featured well-planned responses and, for the most part, a new staff that included James Carville, a Baton Rouge native who was credited with engineering one of the biggest congressional upset ever when Harris Wofford overcame a forty-point deficit to upset Republican Dick Thornburgh in a special election for a Pennsylvania Senate seat. Then there was George Stephanopoulos, a former Dukakis aide who had joined the staff of House majority leader Richard Gephardt after Dukakis's 1988 defeat. George came highly recommended by Midwestern Democrats. Then there was Paul Begala, who had worked alongside Carville in the Pennsylvania race. David Wilhelm was a former campaign aide to Senator Joe Biden and manager of Richard M. Daley's previous two mayoral races in Chicago. Rahm Emmanuel was another former Daley assistant. Finally, there was Dee Dee Myers, who handled the media in a 1991 mayoral race in San Francisco.[6]

The campaign also had an "extensive policy network." It featured individuals from the Democratic Leadership Council and the National Governors' Association, the "Rhodes gang" from his student days, influential lobbyists and Washington consultants, and finally Wall Street backers. You also had Mickey Kantor, the former chairman of the campaign and one from Hillary's own circle of confidants. They came from different precincts of the political or business establishment and Washington culture. But they all had a governing orthodoxy and mentality in common, along with the obligatory, sometimes fierce loyalty to their candidate.[7]

During the 1992 presidential campaign, Clinton strategists famously huddled in a so-called war room under Hillary's direction. It was Hillary who gave the war room its name.[8] The *Washington Post* described its activities:

> The war room was set up to gather as much intelligence as possible and quickly turn it to Clinton's advantage. Campaign advisers tried to anticipate what stories reporters were working on in hopes of shaping those stories before they were written. James Carville and others combed through daily news media reports like intelligence analysts, trying to ferret out information that would help them.[9]

While this was going on at Clinton's campaign headquarters in the old Arkansas Gazette building in Little Rock, there was a one-story building, a short walk across the back alley, where the campaign's real high-stakes action was taking place. According to investigative reporters Jeff Gerth and Don Van Natta Jr.:

> Inside that building, nicknamed "the bunker" by campaign aides, the most perilous assignment of Clinton's presidential quest fell to a handful of mostly anonymous workers, many of whom were women. They were known simply as "the Defense Team." It was an appropriate label for a group whose mission included defending Bill Clinton's twelve-year record as the governor of Arkansas, though that qualified as one of their easier tasks. The team was also expected to help defend Clinton from attacks against his personal behavior, including his alleged affairs with women and his careful avoidance of the military draft and the Vietnam War. The team was additionally charged with an equally delicate assignment: defending Hillary's professional record and her ethical conduct as a partner at the Rose Law Firm. The Defense team was to act like a hard-boiled PI—find the clues, gather the facts, be unafraid to throw a hard punch—with one distinction; they were to do all of this stealthily, invisibly, without anyone except a tiny group of Clinton insiders ever knowing what they were up to. Their secret work would be overseen by Hillary.[10]
>
> A previously undisclosed campaign memo, prepared on March 25, 1992, identified more than seventy-five "issues facing the defense team," ranging from Bill Clinton's "personal hits" to problems in state-related legal work done by Hillary. Her presence on the list was more than noticeable. Roughly two-thirds of the issues were matters relating to both Hilary and Bill or to Hillary alone. Many of the joint issues involved tax returns and financial disclosure reports. Eighteen of the issues solely involved Hillary's work at the Rose firm, some under the heading "Appearance of Influence through HRC."[11]
>
> There was much to defend and not enough time, or people, to do the defending. When David Ifshin, the campaign's counsel, went to the governor's mansion in the fall of 1991 to discuss the possibility of preempting the press by disclosing a number of potential liabilities, Bill's rejection of the idea stunned him. Ifshin remembered Bill telling

him, "I can't open my closet . . . . I'll get crushed by the skeletons." Thus the job at hand became not one of calculated exposure but of diligent burial.[12]

As Clinton started his presidential campaign, he faced three issues that could have sunk him in 1992. The first one was his affair with Gennifer Flowers, which would lead to the womanizing issue. The second was his use of marijuana. The third issue, which was huge, was avoiding the draft for Vietnam. Specifically, the media wanted to know how Clinton managed to escape Vietnam, despite being classified 1-A through much of 1968 and 1969? Clinton's answer: "I was just lucky, I guess." Amazingly, he seemed to be able to talk his way out of disaster by offering misleading accounts of events—only to be forced to change his story when subsequent revelations showed him to be lying. But each time, combined with attacks on his opponents, the strategy somehow worked.[13]

Clinton initially tried to separate himself from his Democratic rivals by emphasizing the importance of character and good old-fashioned values. Democrats "should not be afraid to defend the values they were raised with," Clinton insisted early on in his campaign. In the preseason of the campaign, Clinton aide George Stephanopoulos stated: "Specificity should be the character issue of 1992." After his candidate's personal character had been under fire for months amidst classic-Clinton part-denial/part-admission evasiveness, Stephanopoulos admitted those words were "really going to come back to haunt me." The campaign quickly turned from a "character counts" theme to "It's the economy, stupid."[14]

In New Hampshire, Bill Clinton began using the tag line "Vote for one, get two." Clinton believed that he and Hillary in the White House would become a bigger partnership than the partnership of Franklin Delano Roosevelt and his wife Eleanor.[15]

When polls showed that Americans overwhelmingly opposed the idea of a president sharing power with his wife, Clinton quickly dropped the "Vote for one, get two." Yet, Hillary's involvement in the election was very dominant. She was the brains and muscle behind the campaign.[16]

On February 6, 1992, twelve days before the New Hampshire primary, the *Wall Street Journal* brought up Clinton's draft history, and soon the press had a copy of Clinton's December 1969 letter to Colonel Holmes. Clinton's first reaction was that Bush campaign operatives had unearthed the letter from official files. Clinton angrily responded: "I want you to ask the President to call the Pentagon and find out who leaked this!" It would later be established that the letter came from the personal records of the National Guard commander Lieutenant Colonel Clinton D. Jones. The campaign began issuing a series of revisions of his draft history. Clinton would go on to swear to his staff that the *Journal* had it wrong when it claimed he had actually received an induction notice. Unfortunately for Mr. Clinton, AP reporter John King, on April 5, 1992, handed George Stephanopoulos a copy of the actual induction notice. When Stephanopoulos confronted Clinton with the evidence, he replied: "I forgot about it." Stephanopoulos was so depressed that he retreated to his bed and spent the morning hiding under the covers.[17]

The campaign then acknowledged that he recalled getting the notice but said it had been delayed in the mail and he had missed his induction date. Clinton insisted that he had "never intentionally misled anybody about this." The public seemed to accept his explanation.[18]

To do a preemptive strike on the womanizing issue, the Clintons decided to meet with a group of reporters at a Washington traditional function called the Sperling Breakfast, founded by Godfrey Sperling Jr. of the *Christian Science Monitor*. The event was held on September 16, 1991, at a Washington hotel. Hillary was there, and when asked by a reporter about Clinton's sex life, Bill said "Like nearly anybody who has been together for twenty years, our relationship has not been perfect or free of difficulties."[19]

When the issue of Gennifer Flowers came up, Clinton denied the accusations of adultery while not actually making a simple declaration that he had never had an affair with the former lounge singer. When the *Star* tabloid published a story about Larry Nichols, the former Arkansas state employee who was peddling a list of alleged Clinton ex-lovers that included Flower's name, Clinton called the story "bogus" and "trash." Later, when the *Star* published Flowers' tale of her affair with Clinton, he responded by saying, "The allegations in today's *Star* are not true. I have nothing to add to what I've said in the past."[20]

As the questions threatened his political survival in the New Hampshire primary, Hillary made the decision to confront the Gennifer Flowers scandal head-on, but she rejected a recommendation that Clinton appear on *Nightline*. Fortunately, Clinton enjoyed considerable support from others among the major media, including Don Hewitt of *60 Minutes*. With that knowledge, Hillary, Carville, and others saw an opportunity to seize control of the controversy. They offered *60 Minutes* an exclusive interview with the Clintons, and the producers quickly agreed to broadcast the interview in an unprecedented fifteen-minute "special-edition" of *60 Minutes* following the 1992 Super Bowl, on January 26, 1992.[21]

The Clintons appearance was carefully choreographed and meticulously planned to show Bill Clinton in the best possible light. It would be later disclosed that the interviewer, Steve Kroft, was given the precise wording of his questions about allegations of Clinton's infidelity and was ordered not to stray from the agreed-upon text.[22] Clinton acknowledged "causing pain" in their marriage. When reporter Steve Kroft said, "I'm assuming from your answer that you're categorically denying that you ever had an affair with Gennifer Flowers," Clinton responded, "I've said that before, and so has she." Obviously, that was a lie.[23]

The interview heated up when Kroft said: "I think most Americans would agree that it's very admirable that you've stayed together—that you've worked your problems out and come to some sort of understanding and arrangement." The word *arrangement* did not sit well with the Clintons, especially Hillary for obvious reasons. Speaking with a Southern drawl, she said: "You know, I'm not sitting here—some little woman standing by my man like Tammy Wynette. I'm sitting here because I love him, and I honor what we've been through together. And you know, if that's not enough for people, then heck, don't vote for him."[24]

The reference to the famous country-and-western singer quickly provoked a firestorm. For millions of stay-at-home women, whether they were Tammy Wynette fans or not, there was a hint of condescension in dismissing "some little woman standing by her man."[25]

Hillary would later tell reporters: "I suppose I could have stayed home, baked cookies, and had teas, but what I decided was to fulfill my profession." To many women, it was very offensive to be told that raising children and running a household while their husbands were in the workplace made them simpleton cookie-bakers.[26]

But Flowers—and the *Star*—had tapes. On the Monday afternoon following the Clintons' *60 Minutes* appearance, Gennifer held a press conference and played several minutes of audio tapes of phone conversations between her and Governor Clinton. On one tape, Clinton complained about the attention paid to his extramarital affairs compared to his Democratic opponent Bob Kerrey, a bachelor. Clinton said: "Since he's single, nobody cares who he's screwing." Kerry was offended. On another tape, Clinton talked about the impact the Flowers affair might have on his standing in the Democratic race. Clinton said: "I wonder if I'm just going to be blown out of the water with this. I don't see how they can [garbled] so far if they don't, if they don't have pictures." Then Clinton advised Flowers on what to do if approached by the press. Clinton said: "If they ever hit you with it, just say no and go on. There's nothing they can do. I expected them to look into it and come interview you. But if everybody is on the record denying it, no problem."[27]

It appeared that Clinton had finally been caught. Instead, Clinton's operatives launched an all-out effort to discredit the tapes. Since the transcripts came from supermarket tabloid the *Star*, they had to be suspect was their argument. Then they claimed that tapes were edited and taken out of context. They also proposed the narrative that the tapes might be fake.[28]

Hillary, for her part, decided to level the playing field by slipping into her interviews mentions of the unsubstantiated rumor that George H. W. Bush had had an affair with a former aide. "I don't understand why nothing's ever said about a George Bush girlfriend," Hillary said in a *Vanity Fair* interview. "I understand he has a Jennifer too," she said coyly.[29]

The day after the *Vanity Fair* story appeared, the *New York Post* published First Lady Barbara Bush's response. Mrs. Bush took Hillary to task for stooping so low. Now it was Bill Clinton who had to defend his wife for making a major gaffe. He told the reporters, "Well, you know, all of us make mistakes once in a while."[30]

Somehow, the strategy worked. Some news accounts began calling the recordings "alleged tapes," and other stories referred to Clinton's voice as "the male voice that Flowers says is Clinton's" or "the man," or "the voice." Flowers began to fade from the scene, even though Clinton would eventually concede that the voice on the tape was actually his. The reporters actually liked Clinton. That fact came out later when a Roper poll of 139 Washington journalists found that 89 percent voted for him.[31]

In March 1992, the Clinton campaign reached out to Betsey Wright to come back to Arkansas and join the campaign. At the time, she was a fellow at the John F. Kennedy School of Government at Harvard. When Betsey arrived in Little Rock, she established a special "box room" stocked with towers of the most sensitive files, including Bill's personal records and material from his years in public office inside the defense team bunker.[32] Soon, Wright, who was brash and loud, clashed repeatedly with campaign consultant James Carville. Carville was visibly upset when Wright told a reporter that her job involved quashing "bimbo eruptions."[33]

The darkest side of the Clinton sex scandals involved not Bill, but Hillary's attempts at damage control. She was able to silence most of her husband's accusers using tactics more appropriate to the mob than a presidential campaign. They were the private investigators.[34]

"I'm somebody you call in when the house is on fire, not when there's smoke in the kitchen," bragged San Francisco private detective Jack Palladino in a 1999 interview with *San Francisco Examiner*. "You ask me to deal with that fire, to save you, to do whatever has to be done."[35]

Palladino was told that there were nineteen women being chased by the tabloids, led by *National Enquirer* editor Dan Schwartz. Schwartz admitted that his newspaper was willing to pay six figures for stories about Bill Clinton's private life. Palladino was tapped to be the Clinton campaign's secret policeman. His duties were to get from the targeted women signed affidavits denying any sexual or romantic involvement with Hillary's husband.[36]

Palladino had some early successes. In April 1992, he killed off a story that was being pedaled by another private investigator. Then Palladino tracked down an Oklahoma City woman who claimed to have had an affair with Clinton in the 1980s. He was able to persuade her not to proceed with her story. On occasions when Palladino ran into resistance, he would visit former boyfriends and relatives and gather embarrassing material to convince the women to remain silent. He would eventually gather affidavits from six of the Jane Does that would later be subpoenaed by future independent counsel Ken Starr.[37]

For his services, Hillary and Wright arranged to pay Palladino $100,000. The money came from federally subsidized campaign funds and initially was disguised as legal fees. The payments were laundered by passing them through a Denver law firm (headed by Jim Lyons) and then on to Palladino's agency in California. After it was discovered in a *Washington Post* story by Michael Isikoff, the campaign began publicly disclosing their payments to Palladino. While Palladino was working his way through the names in Wright's "black book" on Clinton, Wright herself mounted what she called "a truth squad" to monitor the activities of reporters who were covering the campaign.[38]

For the election, the Clintons had planned the finances of the campaign with great precision and skill. The Worthen Bank line of credit from the Stephens Empire was set up in early January 1992, before any of the crises of the campaign were apparent. The $3.9 million was doled out in eleven installments, supposedly collateralized by federal matching funds. The first draw of $1 million occurred on March 4, 1992. And the money remained there when the draft controversy and the Flowers story broke and had a numbing impact on fund-raising. Unlike Gary Hart in 1987, the Clintons made sure that they would not be driven from the presidential race by financial blackmail. Fortunately, the early contributions made possible the federal matching funds, and thus the razor's edge collateralizing of the Worthen loan. Surprisingly, less than twenty-three thousand donors would make Bill Clinton president.[39]

World Wide Travel, a company from Little Rock, was carrying the campaign's huge travel costs. This allowed Clinton to emerge from his second-place finish in New Hampshire as a financial front-runner. This allowed the Clinton campaign to invest early and effectively in the Illinois and Michigan primaries. After those primaries, the media declared him a front-runner and likely nominee, and the money began to pour in again. The Worthen Bank money continued to finance the April 7 New York primary victory over Jerry Brown, a race fought in typical New York fashion with what participants on both sides would describe as "dirty politics." After New York, Clinton's opponents had no Worthen reserve, no comparable, long-cultivated bank of big contributors to keep them in the campaign. Basically, the race for the 1992 Democratic presidential nomination was over.[40]

By June 1992, Clinton may have had a lock on the Democratic nomination, but he was still a long shot to win. Perot was leading him in the polls and in second place. To win, Clinton knew he would have to play all his angles in the race game. The first obstacle was the same one Dukakis faced in 1988: Jesse Jackson. His advisors, Paul Begala and George Stephanopoulos, sold Clinton on a risky maneuver.[41]

At the end of an address to Jackson's Rainbow Coalition, Clinton "dissed" Jackson for providing a forum the previous night to Sister Souljah, an arguably racist black rapper. Although Clinton worried he had miscalculated, the media applauded his courage. And as for Jackson, although he felt "violated," he still presented Clinton with a memo outlining his credentials for the vice presidency.[42]

Clinton did not make the Sister Souljah gambit in a vacuum. Ten days earlier, he had appeared on the *Arsenio Hall Show*, playing the saxophone and talking to Hall for half an hour. According to DeWayne Wickam in his book, *Bill Clinton and Black America*, Clinton banked enormous good will with millions of African-Americans that night. The appearance, added Wickam, "helped cushion him" against any criticism for his comments before the Rainbow Coalition.[43]

By the time Clinton was approaching the July 1992 Democratic National Convention in New York, his oratory began to darken. Clinton was making the case that the most prosperous middle class in the world, was a casualty of a "decade-long recession." Despite the fact that there was only a mild recession in 1991, Clinton characterized the shallow recession as a "depression."[44]

Bill Clinton continued this theme when spoke at Georgetown University, on October 23, 1991. Clinton talked about "the people who have lost faith" in our country; "the people who have lost faith" in material improvement; "the quiet, troubled voices of forgotten middle-class Americans"; the lost souls "in your home towns and mine." And he railed against the "people who have power," who make "backroom deals," and worse, "the people who keep them there."[45]

By the July 1992 Democratic National Convention, polls showed Clinton a distant third and in trouble. His negatives were high and with all the beatings he had taken on the campaign trail, he was in the dumps. A *Washington Post*/ABC poll showed Bush with 42 percent, Perot with 30 percent, and Clinton with 20 percent.[46]

Amazingly, despite Betsey Wright overseeing the bimbo-eruptions and Hillary sending private investigators to chase Bill's ex-girlfriends to sign affidavits saying that they didn't have sex with him, it also happened to be the Year of the Woman. The Democratic National Convention devoted its entire Tuesday evening to a prime-time showcase for women candidates. The DNC also put out a special women-in-politics newsletter entitled *Getting It*—presumably no double standard intended.[47]

On the fourth day of the convention, Al Gore warmed up the crowd for Clinton by attacking the rich and the powerful. He attacked the sitting administration for "ignoring the suffering of those who are victims of AIDS, of crime, of poverty, of hatred and harassment." He accused them of having "nourished and appeased tyrannies." There was also this statement: "The task of saving the earth's environment must and will become the central organizing principle of the post-Cold War world."[48]

Then Bill Clinton came out to give his acceptance speech. He had been nominated the day before by Mario Cuomo. Clinton's speech was an unbelievable fifty-four minutes. Network television cameras caught children in the audience fast asleep and adults nodding off or repairing to the restrooms with unnatural frequency. Some of the highlights of the speech:

* I have news for the forces of greed and the defenders of the status quo: your time has come . . . and gone.
* Those who play by the rules and keep the faith have gotten the shaft. And those who cut corners and cut deals have been rewarded.
* Our country is falling behind . . . thirteenth in the world.
* The incumbent president . . . took the richest country in the world and brought it down.
* I end tonight where it all began for me: I still believe in a place called Hope.[49]

On July 16, 1992, the day after the Democratic National Convention ended, Ross Perot dropped a bombshell. Perot said that he decided to drop out of the race after he "uncovered" a plot by the Bush "dirty tricks" campaign to sabotage his daughter's wedding. Perot believed that the Democratic Party had been "revitalized" and gave his support to Clinton. Clinton, who was in third place, immediately jumped to 56 percent in the polls and in first place.[50]

Things continued to go well for Bill Clinton, until his past caught up to him again. On September 7, 1992, Colonel Eugene Holmes signed an affidavit labeled Memorandum for Record and released it on September 16. It recorded Holmes's memories of his dealings with Bill Clinton in 1969. In one passage he said: "Even more significant was his lack of veracity in purposefully defrauding the military by deceiving me, both in concealing his anti-military activities overseas and his counterfeit intentions for later military service. These actions cause me to question both his patriotism and his integrity." In another passage he said: "When I reflect on not only the willingness but eagerness that so many of them displayed in their earnest desire to defend and serve their country, it is untenable and incomprehensible to me that a man who was not merely unwilling to serve his country, but actually protested against its military, should ever be in the position of commander–in-chief of our armed forces."[51]

Once Holmes's affidavit became public, Clinton avoided making any comment on the matter. Since Holmes stated that he would make no further comments to any of the media, the questions were directed to his daughter, Linda Burnett. Ms. Burnett stated that Clinton's claim that he had advised Holmes in September or October of 1969 that he would not be participating in the ROTC program at the University of Arkansas was false. She said that according to her father, the December 3, 1969 letter was the first knowledge Holmes had of Clinton's true intentions.[52]

The next day, on September 17, 1992, Clinton was hounded with questions about Holmes's statement. He ignored them. Then, when he was on the tarmac in Denver, he literally turned his back on members of the national press travelling with him and walked over to a group of local reporters who, predictably, did not ask about the draft. Afterward, at a Denver hotel, Clinton was asked whether he could take a question from reporters. "No, no questions," he snapped.[53]

On September 18, the campaign finally acknowledged that in 1969, Clinton had "discussed options" to the draft with members of Fulbright's staff while he was seeking an ROTC slot at the University of Arkansas. But he stated that he had not sought assistance in avoiding military service. A few hours later, while campaigning in Albuquerque, New Mexico, Clinton made the following statement: "I think I should let the facts speak for themselves."[54]

In October 1992, candidate Bill Clinton said he could "not recall" many details of a trip he took to Moscow in 1969, six weeks after he helped organize a massive anti-war, anti-U.S. demonstration in London.[55]

The first presidential debate occurred on October 11, 1992 between President Bush, Bill Clinton and Ross Perot, who had reentered the race. President Bush never aggressively challenged Mr. Clinton. That largely set the tone for the first two debates. On the third debate, held on October 19, 1992, in East Lansing, Michigan, President Bush began attacking Bill Clinton on the flip-flops.[56]

During the Vice presidential debate, Ross Perot's running mate, Admiral James Stockdale, said that Bill Clinton and the others who staged protests against the Vietnam War, prolonged the conflict, increased the number of casualties and worsened conditions for American POWs. "Those comrades of mine that died—the extra 10, 15, 20 thousand—that blood is on your hands, you war protesters," Admiral Stockdale, a Navy fighter pilot held captive for seven and a half years said.

Admiral Stockdale, when he was shot down, was the senior Navy officer to fall into enemy hands. He acted as unofficial commanding officer of the Hoa Lo prison, nicknamed the Hanoi Hilton." It was the first time anyone in the Perot camp directly criticized Bill Clinton's antiwar activities.[57]

On October 24, 1992, Bill Clinton made the following statement: "Everybody knows that this [Bush] administration is the embodiment of unfairness. They do not believe that they have any obligation to the people who work hard and play by the rules."[58]

On October 28, 1992, more than nine thousand supporters had come to see Bill Clinton speak at the Freedom Hall in Louisville, Kentucky. They were shouting and cheering and waving Clinton-Gore signs. Yet, Clinton's speech gave a few listeners the impression that something was terribly wrong.[59]

Press reports finally began to report on the Arkansas governor's shrinking lead over President Bush in the polls. Bush appeared to be making headway with his constant attacks on Clinton's character, telling voters they could not trust a candidate who didn't always tell the truth in response to allegations about his personal life. As it had throughout the campaign, Clinton's rapid response team countered every accusation, and Clinton himself took up the attack. "Every time Bush talks about trust it makes chills run up and down my spine," he told the crowd. "The very idea that the word 'trust' could ever come out of Bush's mouth after what he has done to this country and the way he has trampled the truth is a travesty for the American political system."[60]

By the closing weekend of the 1992 campaign, a CNN survey showed President Bush had narrowed the gap to within 1 percentage point of Governor Clinton. Then the unthinkable happened.[61] On October 30, 1992, conveniently for candidate Clinton, and a mere *four days* before the election, a prosecutor working on Lawrence Walsh's Iran-Contra investigation issued an indictment of George Bush's defense secretary, Casper Weinberger, for withholding notes damaging to President Bush. It turned out that the indicting prosecutor, James Brosnahan, was a committed Clintonite and a $500 campaign contributor—whose law firm had contributed $20,000 to the Clinton campaign. Mysteriously, the press release tarring President Bush with Mr. Brosnahan's brush was dated October 29, 1992—a day before the indictment was filed and became public.[62]

The Clintons seemed so up to speed on the October surprise scandal that suspicion swirled as to whether they had received a heads-up on the pending Weinberger indictment. The same day of the indictment, Clinton himself went on the attack, referring to some of the evidence in the case that he just happened to have: "Weinberger's note clearly shows . . . Bush has not been telling the truth when he says he was out of the loop," he shouted to crowds along the campaign trail.[63]

Then the Clinton-Gore campaign issued a release headlined "New Iran-Contra Evidence Released by Prosecutor Shows Bush Flatly Lied About His Role in Arms-For-Hostages." That news release was dated October 29—again, the day before the indictment was disclosed, reported the *Washington Times* after Bush's election loss.[64] The next day Hillary Clinton joined in the attack. Speaking to an audience in Mankato, Minnesota, she criticized President Bush: "I think what we learned today is that President Bush was in the loop on trading arms for hostages," she said. "He denied it. He'll say anything to stay in office."[65]

The presidential election was held on November 3, 1992. Bill Clinton won with 43 percent of the vote (the lowest percentage of any president in the twentieth century). George H. W. Bush was second with 38 percent of the vote and Ross Perot was a distant third with 19 percent of the vote. Bill Clinton's 43 percent win was 3 percentage points less than Michael Dukakis, who lost badly in 1988 with 46 percent of the vote.[66]

CHAPTER 8

INAUGURATION DAY

The obligation of a President is more than the fulfillment of a set of Constitutional duties. The President must carry the mantle of hope and optimism in the battle against fear and despair.

—President Bill Clinton
proclaiming the National Day of Fellowship and Hope.[1]

On Inauguration Day, January 20, 1993, President-elect William Jefferson Clinton began his rituals at 6:30 a.m. with the daily presidential briefing on world affairs. Then a Bush aide explained the purpose of the Football—the small box conveying thermonuclear-attack codes. The electronic card to unlock the ciphers will pass to Clinton's side as he takes the oath of office at noon and will remain with him until the last moment of his presidency.[2]

Bill Clinton would soon start his presidency with a lot of goodwill with the public and with Congress. Clinton also understood that his relationship with Congress and his promise to end gridlock would be shared between the two and the public would judge them in two years if they were moving the country in the right direction.[3]

Unfortunately, Clinton stumbled early and often.

On Inauguration Day, some former presidents had expressed special feelings of emotion of what it meant to them. For Harry Truman, he felt as if all the stars and moon had fallen on him. In his memoirs, Ronald Reagan recalled walking into the White House with Nancy and after seeing his furniture from their home moved in becoming overwhelmed by the realization that the presidency was truly his to command.[4]

For Bill and Hillary, the tone and tenor turned out to be a public fight as reported by *Time* magazine. Standing on the steps of Blair House on Inauguration Day, Bill Clinton yelled at his wife. "Fucking bitch!" he screamed, causing Secret Service agents and well-wishers to cower. "Stupid motherfucker," was the reply from our First Lady Hillary Rodham Clinton.[5]

Tradition holds that the new president and first lady be received on inauguration morning at the White House by the outgoing president and first lady, and that the two presidents ride together to the Capitol. That morning, President-elect Clinton and Mrs. Clinton forced President George H. W. Bush and Mrs. Barbara Bush to wait twenty-seven minutes before they appeared for the traditional pre-inaugural coffee.[6]

When the Clintons arrived at the Blue Room, they were accompanied by Harry Thomason and Linda Bloodworth-Thomason (Hollywood producers of prime-time entertainment) and Ron Brown (Chairman of the Democratic National Committee). No president-elect had ever arrived late to take coffee with the outgoing president on Inaugural Day nor had any of Clinton's predecessors thought to bring any uninvited guests, let alone the Thomasons and Ron Brown. The Bushes were startled, and the White House staff was getting an early indication of the days ahead.[7]

After taking the oath of office, Bill and Hillary were taken to a holding room next to the library in the Capitol building. Minutes passed while everyone waited for Bill and Hillary to emerge to commence the inaugural festivities. A Capitol police officer was ordered to inform the Clintons that everyone was ready and waiting.[8]

The policeman knocked and opened the door of the holding room. He immediately shut the door and retreated. Several people among the Republican leadership reported hearing a loud fight next door. It was Hillary screaming "You fucking asshole!" at Bill in what was described as "uncontrolled and unbridled fury." Apparently, there was a matter of "office space" that had *not* been settled.[9]

The Capitol Hill police and the Secret Service quickly conferred about entering the room if it appeared the president's life might be threatened by the first lady. The question before them was, "How much physical abuse is too much physical abuse?"[10]

Bill Clinton's inauguration, which featured high tech and special effects, became the most expensive ceremony ever. According to Shep Gordon, manager of the singer Luther Vandross, who told a reporter for the

New York Times, "The inauguration has mobilized the whole entertainment community. We feel like we can be heard again after all these years."[11]

In his inaugural address, Bill pledged that the Clinton administration would be the most open and ethical in history, restoring honesty and candor to the political process.[12]

One final note: On May 17, 1993, the *Washington Times* reported that the Federal Protective Service and other law enforcement authorities estimate that at least $154,000 worth of radios, computers, televisions, VCRs, walkie-talkies, and pagers were taken by Clinton inauguration employees and volunteers. The goods were discovered during a mid-February 1993 inventory of the Presidential Inaugural Committee headquarters at the Federal Center Building, near the Navy Yard.[13]

Cash collected from the sales of tickets and memorabilia also was reported stolen, as were several cars, license plates, and an array of office-related equipment.[14]

CHAPTER 9

1993 STUMBLES PART I

If we can get our house in order, we can turn this country around.
—President Clinton, May 1993[1]

ATTORNEY GENERAL

The attorney general position was the one job that Hillary Rodham Clinton wanted, but couldn't as a matter of law. She settled for deciding who it would be. The person would have to be loyal and discreet, sufficiently liberal, and, of course, a woman.[2]

It was also decided that Webster Hubbell would direct the Justice Department from behind the scenes. The first prospective nominee for attorney general, DC Circuit Judge Patricia Wald—who had been a researcher with Hillary on the book *All Our Children* at Yale—could not accept Hubbell's role as a pre-condition.[3]

Then, on December 24, 1992, President-elect Clinton nominated Zoe Baird to be his attorney general. During the confirmation hearings, it was disclosed that Baird, an attorney for Aetna Life and Casualty, who made $507,000 in the previous year, and her husband, Yale Law School professor Paul Gewirtz, who made $100,000 in the previous year, failed to pay Social Security taxes for a Peruvian couple, who were in the United States illegally. They were employed as babysitters to help care for their eight-month baby.[4]

After meeting with transition lawyers, Baird and her husband voluntarily paid a little over $12,000 in back Social Security taxes and $1,000 in state taxes. The Immigration and Naturalization Service, which by coincidence the attorney general overseas, fined Baird and Gewirtz $950 each on the two counts of hiring an undocumented alien and $500 each on the failure to complete the required paperwork. Charles Cobb, the INS regional director in Boston, which has jurisdiction over Connecticut, where Baird and Gewirtz lived, determined the size of the fines. Baird and Gewirtz paid the civil penalty totaling $2,900.[5]

The Clinton administration was trying to stand behind the Baird nomination. Communications director George Stephanopoulos said, "Ms. Baird has taken responsibility for this matter and acknowledges that to have hired any employee before receiving the necessary authorization was a mistake. She deeply regrets the mistakes she made in the matter."[6]

Those in the media didn't see it that way. Jerry Knight of the *Washington Post* responded: "The claim that a lawyer good enough to be nominated for attorney general and her equally successful lawyer husband making $600,000 a year between them didn't know it was against the law to hire illegal immigrants and not pay taxes is simply not credible. Every working mom and diaper-changing dad knows how this game is played: You can save a hundred bucks a week in child care if you're willing to hire an illegal to work "off the books.""[7]

Knight continued: "But that means ignoring immigration laws, ignoring social security, ignoring unemployment compensation, ignoring the minimum wage, ignoring taxes and ignoring health and welfare of the person entrusted to care for your children. Should a person that ignorant be attorney general?"[8]

On January 22, 1993, Zoe Baird withdrew her name for the nomination in a post-midnight letter that was faxed to the White House at 12:42 a.m. Bill Clinton later acknowledged that he knew nothing about Zoe Baird's hiring of undocumented aliens before he nominated her to be attorney general. This was Clinton's first defeat.[9]

Bill thought that this would be the end of "Nannygate," as it began to be called, but that was just the beginning. His next nomination for attorney general was Judge Kimba Wood.[10]

On January 28 and 29, 1993, Judge Wood met with President Clinton and White House counsel Bernard Nussbaum, at the White House about the attorney general appointment. Wood was asked by Clinton if she had a "Zoe Baird problem." She responded, "I did not, and I do not." On February 4, 1993, the White House confirmed to two major newspapers that Wood was to be named to be the next attorney general.[11] Around the same time, the vetters discovered that Wood and her husband, political writer Michael Kramer, had employed an illegal alien as a babysitter, but before the law was passed that made such employment illegal. The next day, February 5, 1993, the White House ditched the nomination of Judge Wood.[12]

George Stephanopoulos was now angry that many newspapers and networks quickly portrayed Judge Wood as the likely nominee. He cornered three network correspondents, scolded them for touting the judge in their broadcasts, and told them the White House never said she was the top choice. Many reporters disputed that assertion. "You go too far, and we get penalized," Stephanopoulos said to the reporters.[13]

This left the fledgling Clinton administration in the humiliating situation of publicly ditching two female attorney general candidates. Not well known at the time was that Clinton was looking at Stephen Breyer. Unfortunately, he too, had failed to pay his cleaning lady's Social Security taxes.[14] Eventually, the position went to Janet Reno, a Dade County, Florida, prosecutor who made a name for herself by losing high-profile cases and for pressing dubious charges of child abuse. Yet Reno had all the right qualifications for Hillary Clinton. She was loyal. She was liberal, and she was warmly regarded by her friend Marian Wright Edelman. And, of course, she was a woman, though Camille Paglia, a noted feminist, would say what everyone thought that Reno was "the most masculine Clinton appointee."[15]

Above all, Reno had a great desire to get and keep the job, which made her pliable. One condition of Reno's appointment was to accept Webb Hubbell, who was made associate attorney general, the de facto attorney general. Another apparent condition was to fire all ninety-three US attorneys after she took office. This unprecedented move halted all of the inquiries in the assorted scandals that were percolating around in Arkansas.[16]

EXECUTIVE ORDERS

On January 22, 1993, in a televised Oval Office ceremony, with Hillary's full backing, Bill Clinton signed five executive orders lifting restrictions on abortion counseling and on federally sponsored research on medical use of fetal tissue, ending restrictions on the use of US funds for UN population programs that included abortion counseling, and restoring the right of US military hospitals overseas to perform abortions paid for with private funds, and ordering a review of the government ban on private importing of the French abortion pill, RU-486.[17]

Four days after the signing of the executive orders, the Vatican newspaper, *L'Osservatore Romano*, ran a dire editorial, stating grimly that the "renewal" that the man from Hope had promised during his campaign would now come "by way of death" and "by way of violence against innocent human being." The stage was set. As papal biographer George Weigel noted, it was the opening salvo in what would become "the most serious confrontation ever" between the US government and the Holy See.[18]

Unfortunately, the Clinton administration didn't realize until later that by making his first order of business the undoing of these orders, all of them on social issues, the president, who had run for office as a centrist, was governing from the left.[19]

CLINTON'S PHONY DRUG WAR

During the presidential campaign, candidate Bill Clinton proposed to make the drug czar a member of the cabinet. Clinton not only failed to name a candidate for the job, but instead his first action on drugs was to cut the drug office staff by more than 80 percent. In February 1993, the Office of National Drug Control Policy was cut from 146 employees to 25, less than half the size of the White House communications staff.[20]

In late April 1993, with no czar in place, the administration sent Alice Rivlin, the deputy director of the Office of Management and Budget, to the congressional budget hearing. When the hearing began, Ms. Rivlin confessed that she did not know a lot about the drug issue. By the time Ms. Rivlin left the hearing, President Clinton finally announced his choice to be the drug czar. It went to Lee Patrick Brown. Mr. Brown wouldn't start his job until July 1993. By that time, the House voted to cut $231 million from anti-drug programs. Unfortunately, the White House budget officials accepted the decision. Brown, by his own admission, learned about the whole thing when he read it in the *Washington Post*. "We have got to get back in the loop," he told the paper.[21]

GAYS IN THE MILITARY

In October 1991, fund-raiser Bill Clinton met with ANGLE, a group of twenty major gay and lesbian campaign donors he was connected with through his good friend David Mixner, a major gay leader and fund-raiser in California. Gays were a major force within the Democratic Party as organizers and fund-raisers. At the time Clinton met with this group, he was running third among gays, after Paul Tsongas and Jerry Brown. In the meeting, Clinton was asked if he would issue an executive order to end the ban on gays serving in the military. He said that he would do it as one of the first acts of his administration. There was no room for compromise on this, Clinton told the group.[22]

During the election of 1992, the homosexual lobby contributed $3.5 million to the Clinton-Gore campaign and turned out for him at the polls. Now with the election over, it was payback time. What was the payback? Lifting the fifty-year ban of gays serving in the military.[23]

The original policy had been developed out of necessity during World War II. Congress had reaffirmed the World War II era policies in 1982 when it declared that "homosexuality is incompatible with military service because it undermines discipline, good order, and morale.[24]

A few days after the election, following a Veterans Day event at the Arkansas statehouse, Andrea Mitchell of NBC asked Clinton whether he intended to fulfill his campaign pledge on gays in the military. Clinton said: "Yes, I want to." Veterans groups were outraged at Clinton's comments.[25]

Two days after Clinton's Veterans Day remarks, Gen. Colin Powell, who had openly expressed his opposition to lifting the ban, said that the Joint Chiefs of Staff and the senior commanders "continue to believe strongly that the presence of homosexuals within the armed forces would be prejudicial to good order and discipline." Powell continued to speak out against gays in the military with a speech to the midshipmen at Annapolis: "Homosexuality is not benign behavioral characteristic such as skin color. It goes to the core of the most fundamental aspect of human behavior."[26]

On January 23, 1993, Clinton announced that he was ordering Defense Secretary Les Aspin to stop enforcing the ban on recruiting homosexuals and to halt prosecutions of homosexuals and that he would be signing an executive order removing the ban.[27]

On January 24, 1993, President Clinton received a confidential memorandum from Defense Secretary Aspin, saying that a majority of Congress and top military leaders opposed an immediate attempt to lift the ban on homosexuals serving in the military. The next day President Clinton promised to issue an executive order ending the Pentagon's prohibition on homosexuals in the military. He never did and broke another campaign promise to a constituency. On February 3, 1993, the Pentagon issued orders to halt the dismissal of homosexuals serving in the military and to stop asking recruits about their sexual orientation.[28]

On March 12, 1993, President Clinton visited the aircraft carrier USS *Theodore Roosevelt*, as part of his effort to establish better relations with the military. Unfortunately, the visit didn't turn out too well. To Clinton's embarrassment, the press reports focused on complaints and wisecracks the sailors were making about Clinton's gays-in-the-military proposal. Also, the pictures of Clinton that appeared were not complimentary. According to an adviser, "The jacket they gave him on the *Roosevelt* was two sizes too small, and he looked like a sausage. We were paranoid. We thought it was deliberate."[29]

On April 25, 1993, an estimated 300,000 people marched in Washington for homosexual "civil rights." This was far short of the 1 million people that organizers hoped would come. President Clinton left town and did not attend the March. Some marchers were very unhappy with Clinton, showing pictures of him with a Pinoccio-style nose in front of the White House.[30]

Unfortunately, anger in the military continued to build. On May 27, 1993, a confidential Army report stated that eight out of ten homosexuals the Army court-martialed for sexual misconduct in the past four years, engaged in sexual assaults. Also, nearly half of the 102 assault cases involved child molestation, and most of the attacks occurred on base, the study said.[31]

On June 3, 1993, the Defense Readiness Council held a news conference to discuss the ban and statistics on sex crimes involving homosexuals in the military. Of more than 2,700 officers who responded to the survey, 91 percent supported the gay ban.[32]

Despite the military's objection, on July 19, 1993, President Clinton announced his new policy, "Don't ask, don't tell, don't pursue," in a speech at the National Defense University at Fort McNair, across the Potomac. Angry homosexual activists accused Clinton of betraying them by refusing to lift entirely the ban on homosexuals in the military. This would be one of many groups that Clinton used to get elected.[33]

CLINTON BREAKS HIS PROMISE FOR MIDDLE CLASS TAX CUT

During the 1992 presidential election, then candidate Bill Clinton pledged to the American people that if he were elected, he would give the

American middle class a tax cut. Once elected, his pledge didn't last long. On February 15, 1993, Clinton went on national television to assert that he had worked harder than he ever had before to avoid raising taxes on the middle class. Unfortunately, he was not successful.[34]

CHAPTER 10

WACO

I still maintain what I said from the beginning, that the offender there was David Koresh, and I do not think the United States government is responsible for the fact that a bunch of fanatics decided to kill themselves and I'm sorry that they killed their children.

—President Bill Clinton, April 23, 1993[1]

The Branch Davidians at Mount Carmel were an offshoot of the Seventh-Day Adventist Church (SDA). Of the seventy-two adults living there, all but seven had been members or in some way involved with the SDA Church.[2]

Vernon Howell, a.k.a. David Koresh, and his group of followers acquired possession of the Mount Carmel compound near Waco, Texas, in March of 1988. The first thing the group did was disassembled the methamphetamine lab and turn the equipment and manuals over to the sheriff. The Bureau of Alcohol, Tobacco, and Firearms (ATF) would later use the old drug lab to request for US military assistance in the raid. Authorities told Howell that in order to perfect title to the property his group would have to remain in continuous possession of it for five years. The five-year period was scheduled to end on March 22, 1993. The first government assault occurred on February 28, 1993. Reportedly, the Branch Davidians were very reluctant to surrender possession during the siege because of their fear of losing title to the property.[3]

On June 9, 1992, in the final year of the Bush administration, the ATF in Austin, Texas, opened an investigation of the Branch Davidians based on a phone call they had received a month before from the McLennan

County Sheriff's Department. The sheriff had been called by the United Parcel Service stating that they had delivered dummy grenades, explosive powder, and suspicious firearms to the Mount Carmel compound.[4]

On July 30, 1992, the ATF assigned agent Davy Aguilera to visit Koresh's gun dealer, Henry McMahon, and investigate whether David Koresh and his followers were violating the National Firearms Act by illegally converting semiautomatic firearms to fully automatic weapons. McMahon responded by calling Koresh directly. When Koresh heard the agent's concerns, he invited Aguilera to visit the Davidians' residence and carry out an inspection. Aguilera refused the invitation.[5]

The Davidians actually acquired all types of guns for both protection and investment purposes. They bought and sold the guns at gun shows throughout the state. They also sold vests made by the Branch Davidian women who spruced them up by sewing dummy hand grenades into them.[6] Despite any incriminating evidence, the ATF sought and obtained an arrest warrant for David Koresh and a search warrant for the Branch Davidian compound. Former US Attorney William W. Johnson helped draft the search warrant used by the ATF. The Treasury Department, in its internal report on Waco, somehow concluded that probable cause had been established for the arrest and search as of November 1992. Unfortunately, many of the allegations contained in the warrant applications were based on old information, involving activities that occurred between 1988 and 1992.[7]

The ATF believed that it had established probable cause for the arrest warrants by the end of 1992. This was disputed by former Branch Davidian Marc Breault, who stated ATF agent Davy Aguilera had told him, in December 1992, he could not do anything about Koresh because he lacked direct evidence. Likewise, ATF director Stephen Higgins, who would later testify before House subcommittees, confirmed that the ATF lacked probable cause as of December 1992.[8]

In early January 1993, then-Gov. Ann Richards (D-TX) authorized the use of Texas Air National Guard radar planes to fly over Mount Carmel as part of the ATF's surveillance, based on the drug allegations, and ATF secured assistance from the Army's Special Forces Command using the same information.[9]

At the same time, the ATF rented a house near the Branch Davidians' compound to use as an undercover surveillance post. Eight ATF agents were stationed in the building. The Davidians immediately became suspicious of their new neighbors. They were in their thirties, carried briefcases, and drove late-model cars. They claimed to be college students.[10]

When the surveillance cameras yielded no incriminating evidence, the ATF sent in Robert Rodriguez to work undercover. Eventually, Rodriguez was unable to obtain any evidence to support the warrant application. Despite this setback, the ATF pursued a warrant anyway.[11]

On February 19, 1993, nine days before the eventual raid, two undercover ATF agents, who were recognized as such by Koresh and the other Branch Davidians, invited Koresh to go shooting with them. Koresh, two other Branch Davidians, and the two ATF agents proceeded to have an enjoyable time shooting with two AR-15s, an ATF agent's .38 Super pistol, and two Sig-Sauer semiautomatic pistols. Koresh actually provided a majority of the ammunition. The undercover agents' report noted: "Mr. Koresh stated that he believed that every person had the right to own firearms and protect their homes."[12]

On February 25, 1993, the ATF obtained an arrest warrant for Koresh and a search warrant that covered, among other things, machine guns and destructive devices.[13]

The *Waco Tribune-Herald* began a series on David Koresh's "cult" on February 27, 1993, the day before the fateful raid. The story mobilized public opinion against the Mount Carmel residents.[14]

The question was, why would the ATF have decided on a high-risk military-style raid when they could have picked Koresh up on one of his regular jogs? Or, when he was out shopping, with his legal wife Rachel and their kids in local music stores and auto parts shop? Or when he was at one of the many gun shows he regularly attended?[15]

The answer may be that the Davidians weren't the only ones under the media spotlight. Its public image and morale had been devastated by an expose on the CBS show *60 Minutes*. The segment broadcast allegations by female ATF agents that had been sexually harassed on the job and that the agency intimidated and punished its victims and witnesses who had pressed sexual harassment claims.[16]

While the segment didn't air until January 12, 1993, it had been in production for some time. *60 Minutes* had first contacted ATF personnel around mid-November 1992, according to Bob Anderson, who produced the segment for CBS. It appears that the ATF's Koresh investigation changed radically in the weeks just after bureau officials would have learned that *60 Minutes* had planned to expose the sexual harassment.[17]

Furthermore, this story couldn't have aired at a worst time. Congressional budget hearings were scheduled for March 10, 1993. Unfortunately, we will never know for sure whether ATF superiors were considering the potential impact on congressional funding when they were planning the raid. But there are things we do know.[18]

ATF special agent Sharon Wheeler, a public information officer, was in charge of videotaping the agency's raid preparation and the raid itself, as well as handling the media that arrived. She had called editors at local ABC and NBC affiliates and told them, "we have something big going down." When she testified before Congress, Wheeler confessed, "You want to promote your agency in a good light, and ATF hired public information officers over the last two years to do that to show the agency in a good light." What the ATF got was their assault being repelled by the Branch Davidians and being shown live to the public.[19]

While the official name for the February 28 raid was Operation Trojan Horse, the agents themselves changed it to Showtime. It's hard to conceive that the agency wasn't hoping to score big points with its Hollywood-style assault.[20]

ATF Response Teams from three cities spent three days before the February 28 raid training at Fort Hood, near Killeen, Texas. The Posse Comitatus Act of 1878 prohibits any involvement of the US military with domestic law enforcement. In 1989, after then Defense Secretary Richard B. Cheney declared illegal drugs a threat to national security, Congress created an exception to this ban for cases involving narcotics. ATF officials were told the US military could not aid them unless there was a "drug nexus." A few days later, ATF officials deliberately deceived the US military officials claiming they suspected the Davidians had a methamphetamine lab in their basement. ATF agents were then trained in close-quarters combat. The ATF also called in military helicopters from the Texas Air National Guard to assist in their assault. The ATF requested that the military supply it with "100 gas masks, 500 sandbags, 90 sleeping bags, 15 night-vision goggles, a water tank truck, ten tents (including one for 'VIP sleeping'), along with electric generators and smoke generators 'to cover two square kilometers with concealment smoke.' " The drug charge vanished immediately after the raid; federal prosecutors never raised the issue at the Davidians' 1994 trial. A subsequent congressional investigation noted, "The only consistent mention of any drug activity by Branch Davidians in any of the ATF Waco documents is in requests for military assistance which required drug activity to justify military intervention and assistance."[21]

On Sunday morning, February 28, 1993, ATF agent Robert Rodriguez visited David Koresh about forty-five minutes before the raid to gauge his reaction to the *Waco Tribune-Herald* series about him entitled "The Sinful Messiah." Rodriguez had gained Koresh's trust during eight visits inside the Mount Carmel compound over several weeks.[22]

Informed that he had received a phone call, Koresh left the room for a moment, then returned, clearly shaken. A Davidian, who worked for the U.S. Postal Service, David Jones, told Koresh he had encountered reporters seeking directions to the compound to view the raid. Rodriguez, realizing that Koresh was aware of what was about to happen, hurriedly left the compound as soon as he could, unsure if the Branch Davidians would allow him to leave, and ran inside the undercover house. He informed James Cavanaugh, ATF's deputy tactical coordinator for the ATF operation that Koresh knew they were coming. Apparently unfazed by the news, Cavanaugh asked Rodriguez only whether he had seen any guns. When Rodriguez said he hadn't, Cavanaugh told him to report the news to Chuck Sarabyn, the tactical coordinator for Showtime.[23]

When Rodriguez phoned Sarabyn with the news, Sarabyn's response was not to cancel the raid, but to ask the same questions that Cavanaugh asked. Had he seen any guns? What were the Davidians wearing? And so forth. Sarabyn then met with Phillip Chojnacki, who headed the Houston ATF. Chojnacki asked Sarabyn whether he thought they should consider going forward. Sarabyn said yes, "If they hurried."[24]

Concerned about what might happen next, Rodriguez drove to the command center where the agents were supposed to gather but found they had already left for Mount Carmel. It was too late.[25] Despite having lost the element of surprise, seventy-six ATF agents in two cattle trailers, moved up to the front of the Branch Davidians' residence. They shouted "Showtime!" as they raced out for the attack. The ATF planned for one group of agents to storm the front door while a second group carried ladders and smashed in through second-story windows. A subsequent congressional investigation noted, "There was little else to the plan and, importantly, little or no discussion of what might go wrong." Also, three military helicopters were used to fly over the compound.[26]

When Koresh saw the cattle trailers pull up and ATF agents dressed in military-style uniforms race out, he opened the front door and asked, "Can't we talk about this? There's women and children in here." The ATF answered with a hail of bullets. Koresh was hit in two places, and his father-in-law, standing behind him, Perry Jones, was killed. After that, those on the inside ran to their rooms, got their guns and started shooting back."[27]

As the ATF agents assaulted the front of the building, the ATF agents in the Texas Air National Guard helicopters opened fire from above. One elderly Branch Davidian died when he was shot while lying in his bed on the upstairs floor; bullet holes in the ceiling of his room indicated that the shots entered from above. The Davidians reacted the way any normal family would. They placed emergency calls to the McLennan County Sheriff's 911 switchboard. In the first call, Wayne Martin, a top Koresh lieutenant and a Waco attorney who was well known and liked in the local legal community, pleaded with Sheriff's Lieutenant Larry Lynch:[28]

> **MARTIN:** "There's 75 men around our building and they're shooting at us at Mount Carmel!!"
> **LYNCH:** "Mount Carmel?"
> **MARTIN:** "Yeah. Tell them there are children and women in here and to call it off."
> **LYNCH:** "All right. All right. Hello? I hear gunfire. Oh, [expletive deleted]."
> **MARTIN:** Another chopper with more people and more guns going off. Here they come. Call it off."[29]
> Koresh himself placed a second 911 call:
> **KORESH:** "You see, you brought your bunch of guys out here and you killed some of my children. We told you we wanted to talk. No. How come you guys try to be ATF agents? How come you try to be so big all the time?"
> **LYNCH:** "Okay, David."
> **KORESH:** "Now, there's a bunch of us dead, and a bunch of you guys dead. Now—now, that's your fault."

LYNCH: "Okay, let's—let's try to resolve this now. Tell me this. Now, you have casualties. How many casualties? Do you want to try to work something out? ATF is pulling back, we're trying to—"
KORESH: "Why didn't you do that first?"[30]

In a third and final call, placed by Lynch, Martin repeatedly pleaded for a cease-fire, offers to arrange one, and claims at one point that the people inside had ceased their fire, but that incoming fire had continued unabated. "I have the right to defend myself," he said at one point." They started firing first."[31]

Sheriff Jack Hartwell, the chief law enforcement officer in the jurisdiction, had been largely left out of the loop by the ATF throughout the investigation and the raid. Might the outcome have been different if the ATF had brought his department into the investigation of the Branch Davidians?[32]

Another curious aspect of the raid is that the ATF had arranged for no telephone contact to be established with the Davidians in the event the raid didn't go as planned. Larry Lynch tried for thirty minutes to reach the ATF and only after thirty-eight minutes did he reach someone at the ATF command team. Yet, there was still no direct communication between the ATF and the Davidians. They had to communicate through Lynch.[33]

The shootout lasted for forty-five minutes. Four ATF agents were dead, sixteen were wounded, and six Davidians were dead. After a bitter gun battle, the Davidians agreed to a cease-fire and permitted the ATF agents to gather their dead and wounded and withdraw from the scene. The fact that the Davidians limited the carnage they inflicted was quickly swept aside in the coming weeks because it did not fit the fed's attempt to demonize the Davidians.[34]

Shortly after the raid and during the standoff, the government started to investigate itself. The ATF began its review almost immediately. No sooner had it started than it was ordered to back off by its parent, the Treasury Department. Treasury was yielding to a request from its sister, the Justice Department to curtail the internal investigation.[35]

According to American libertarian author and *USA Today* columnist James Bovard, "the government was worried about the embarrassing and damning evidence that was being uncovered. A confidential September 17, 1993, Treasury Department memo to Assistant Treasury Secretary Ron

Noble stated that on March 1 the Bureau of Alcohol, Tobacco, and Firearms initiated a shooting review and 'immediately determined that these stories [by the agents involved] did not add up.' Justice Department attorney Bill Johnston 'at this point advised [ATF supervisor Dan] Harnett to stop the ATF shooting review because ATF was creating exculpatory material that might undermine the government prosecution of the Davidians.' Thus, as early as thirty-six hours after the botched initial ATF raid on the Branch Davidian compound, the government began abandoning routine law enforcement procedure in order to avoid gathering evidence that might embarrass it. Yet, the government, under what is known as the Brady rule, is required to disclose evidence that might point to the defendant's innocence."[36]

On September 29, 1993, the two ATF supervisors, Phillip Chojnacki and Charles Sarabyn—who made the decision to proceed with the raid despite being aware that the element of surprise had been lost and who significantly altered the written plans for the assault after the disaster and then tried to conceal the changes from officials investigating the incident—were fired. It was one of the worst episodes in U.S. law enforcement history. Later, however, they were reinstated and awarded retroactive salary payments. Two other top ATF officials, Daniel M. Harnett and Edward D. Conroy told colleagues they were retiring.[37]

After the raid, the FBI became the lead agency for resolving the standoff. Special agent Jeff Jamar was named the on-site commander. By the afternoon, advance units of the FBI's Hostage Rescue Team (HRT) arrived, and telephone conversations were under way between Koresh, Steve Schneider, and Wayne Martin on one side and the ATF's Jim Cavanaugh and Waco Police Lt. Larry Lynch on the other. Koresh disclosed that he had been wounded in the hip and left wrist. Michael Schroeder, a Branch Davidian, was killed while he tried to return to the main building. Texas Rangers began an investigation but were barred by the FBI from continuing. At about 5:30 p.m., Jamar arrived at Waco and chose Byron Sage of the FBI as chief negotiator.[38]

In the following days of the siege, a group of Davidians came out of the compound. The adults were quickly arrested, slapped into handcuffs and leg irons, and paraded in front of the television cameras in bright orange prisoner suits. Then, after a few weeks of the siege, FBI spokesmen bitterly complained that none of the other Branch Davidians would come out and surrender. However, in at least seven instances, FBI agents threw flash-bang hand grenades—which emit a deafening explosion and blinding flash—at people who had left the compound, effectively driving them back into the building. The FBI agents at Waco requested permission from headquarters to shoot Branch Davidians who were leaving the building—regardless of whether they posed a direct threat to federal agents.[39]

Initially, the FBI intended to take all the time it needed to reach a peaceful solution. But, the FBI negotiators were baffled by the peculiar Davidian theology and were unwilling to engage outside religious experts to assist them with this highly unusual situation.[40]

Religious scholars Philip Arnold and James Tabor were pressing the FBI to allow them to assist in the negotiations. They were convinced that Koresh had to be approached from a theological perspective. Arnold had earned the respect of Koresh when he expounded on the seven seals and offered his assistance on a radio talk show during the siege. Though Koresh and his lieutenant, Steve Schneider, often asked to talk to Arnold, neither Arnold nor James Tabor was permitted to participate in the negotiations with Koresh.[41]

As the siege continued and government frustration swelled, the FBI launched psychological warfare and adopted numerous harassing tactics against the Davidians, including cutting off their electricity, shining blinding spotlights at night to prevent them from sleeping, harassing them with cacophonous music, and taunting them with derisive remarks. They ridiculed Steve Schneider, David Koresh's right-hand man, for letting Koresh "marry" his wife.[42]

None of the tactics worked. So the government upped the ante and began using tanks to destroy Davidian property outside the compound: cars, a mobile home, and even children's toys. They also used the tanks to flatten the Davidians' cemetery. The result of all this was to strengthen the resolve of the Davidians and diminish the chances of a peaceful resolution of the conflict. The chronology of the last days went like this:[43]

> On March 1, 1993, authorities negotiate but bring in a convoy of Bradley fighting vehicles, armored personnel carriers, helicopters and heavily armed officers on the road to the compound.
> On March 2, 1993, in a fifty-eight-minute taped message broadcast on several radio and TV stations, Koresh says: "I, David Koresh, agree upon the broadcasting of this tape to come out peacefully with

all the people immediately." A total of eighteen children and two adults were released.

On March 4, 1993, two more children were released, for a total of twenty children and two adults released. Twenty-four children and seventy-three adults remained in the compound.

On March 7, 1993, Koresh refused a compromise that would have ended the stalemate.

On March 16, 1993, Koresh's top lieutenants—Steve Schneider and Wayne Martin—met with government negotiators for the first time.

On March 19, 1993, Koresh asked for "a little more time."

On March 20, 1993, the FBI said negotiations had improved, and the standoff would end soon.

On March 28, 1993, the FBI said it feared sect members had signed suicide pacts.

On March 31, 1993, the FBI shut down all negotiations with the Branch Davidian sect.

On April 4, 1993, Koresh said he would end the standoff after Passover.

On April 9, 1993, Koresh said they had no plans to come out after Passover.[44]

The FBI squandered one final and genuine opportunity to end the siege when it chose to ignore Koresh's pledge to surrender when he completed work on his written exposition of the seven seals. On April 14, Koresh sent a letter to his lawyer, Dick DeGuerin. God, Koresh wrote, had told him that he would be "given over into the hands of man." Koresh said that after he finished his commentary of the seven seals, he would "stand before man to answer any and all questions regarding his actions." In the letter, Koresh even asked how he would maintain contact with DeGuerin once he was in prison. Steve Schneider offered to provide the FBI some of Koresh's work in progress to convince the government that he was sincere.[45]

Tragically, the FBI interpreted the letter as another stalling tactics. DeGuerin said that when he told the FBI that the Davidians would surrender upon Koresh's completion of the writing, agent Bob Ricks was contemptuous. A few days after the April 19 assault, FBI agent Jeff Jamar said the FBI discounted Koresh's surrender promise because they had "absolute certain intelligence" that it was a sham. This intelligence has never surfaced.[46]

On April 13, 1993, the FBI announced at a White House meeting that it had scrapped its Waco negotiating tactics and opted for a raid with tear gas and tanks. The records show that none of those in attendance, including White House Counsel Bernard Nussbaum, senior adviser Bruce Lindsey, White House Deputy Counsel Vincent Foster, and Associate Attorney General Webster Hubbell raised any objection.[47]

The next day, on April 18, 1993, Attorney General Janet Reno had a fifteen-minute telephone conversation with President Clinton, giving him a detailed presentation of the plan for ending the standoff. She also told the president that negotiators had given up hope of ending the siege by talking. The president signed off on the plan, and Ms. Reno gives the FBI the go-ahead.[48]

The plan was to spray gas into the compound gradually, over a forty-eight-hour period, and get the Branch Davidians to evacuate. While the stated objective was to save the children, the FBI had to know that there were no gas masks available to fit the children. There is no question that the children suffered horribly. Even worse, FBI tanks blocked the residents' access to the one place in the compound where they could safely seek refuge, an "underground bus"—a bus that had been buried to serve as a tornado shelter.[49]

As it turns out, there was never a realistic possibility that the assault would be gradual, as Reno had promised. Even the agent in charge, Jeff Jamar, admitted there was a 99 percent likelihood that the Davidians would respond to the gas with gunfire. As some have accurately observed, the plan for a gradual assault was doomed from the beginning. It was inevitable that the "gradual" assault would accelerate into a full-blown operation almost immediately after it began. In this case, "immediately" was no exaggeration. What follows is a chronology of the final hours of the standoff at the Branch Davidian compound outside Waco, Texas on April 19, 1993:[50]

- **At 5:56 a.m.** FBI chief negotiator Byron Sage phoned into Davidian's residence and announced: "We are in the process of putting tear gas into the building. This is not an assault. We will not enter the building."

- **At 6:02 a.m.** two modified M-60 tanks, equipped with thirty-foot booms and bulldozer blades to "insert" the CS gas with needlepoint precision, began punching holes in the compound walls. Two minutes later, the tanks were fired on.
- **At 6:30 a.m.** experienced FBI agents, such as then Deputy Assistant Director Danny Coulson, who had been running the Waco siege from a command center in the FBI's Washington headquarters, were kicked out of the center and replaced by Attorney General Janet Reno; Associate Attorney General Webster Hubbell; FBI Director William Sessions; and Session's deputy, Floyd Clarke.
- **At 6:55 a.m.** authorities call Hillcrest Baptist Medical Center in Waco to be on alert.
- **At 8:00 a.m.** an armored vehicle with a large battering arm rips into the second floor of the compound and minutes later another hole is punched into the back of the compound. Armored vehicles then withdraw.
- **At 9:20 a.m.** an armored vehicle returns to the compound and bashes another hole in the front wall, taking out the front door.
- **At 10:00 a.m.** two tanks drove up to the side of the Davidian's residence and began pumping the residence full of a combination of CS gas and methyl chloride. At the same time, other tanks and Bradley Fighting Vehicles maneuvered around the Davidians' home; grenade launchers on those vehicles fired almost four hundred ferret rounds of CS gas through the thin wooden walls and the windows of the building. Throughout the morning, FBI loudspeakers blared: "This is not an assault."
- **At 11:30 a.m.** armored vehicles continue battering the buildings.
- **At 12:15 p.m.** a couple of hours after the gas had flooded the buildings, fires began in different parts of the building and within minutes the compound and all but eight of its remaining inhabitants were incinerated. FBI transcripts reveal that when the fires were breaking out, FBI broadcasters on the scene uttered words over the loudspeakers such as, "David,

you have had your fifteen minutes of fame" and "Vernon is finished. He's no longer the Messiah." Also, the ATF removed the Davidian's flag, a Star of David, from the compound's flag pole. Over the smoldering heap of gassed and charred American citizens, they ran up the ATF flag in its place. This act alone did more to illustrate the government's warlike attitude toward its own citizens than any words could ever convey. Complete conquest had been achieved.

- **At 12:28 p.m.** a person with hands raised walked to an armored vehicle and appeared to surrender. A second person appeared to come out of the compound, dragging something—possibly another person—toward the armored vehicle. Fire had destroyed much of the compound.
- **At 12:38 p.m.**, after receiving a 911 call from a nearby resident, fire trucks began approaching the scene. But the FBI stopped the trucks far from the burning building, claiming that it was not safe to allow them to get any closer because the Davidians might shoot people dousing the fire that was killing them. The FBI's "fire plan" consisted of preventing fire trucks from coming close to the Davidians' home until all fires were out.
- **At 4:00 p.m**. federal authorities say eight survived and presumed a "massive loss of life" among the remaining cult members.[51]

Actually, eighty-six Branch Davidians were killed (sixty-two adults and twenty-four children). Seventeen of the dead children were under age ten. Eleven Branch Davidians escaped the blaze. What was not reported by the Justice Department was the Branch Davidians' ethnicity. More than half the dead were, in fact, racial minorities. Twenty-eight of them, aged six to sixty, were black. Also, the chemical used, called O-chlorobenzalmalononitrile (CS), was banned at the Chemical Weapons Convention in Paris in January 1993. Attorney General Janet Reno would later say that she was not told that the CS gas had been banned. [52]

"The chemical would have panicked the children. Their eyes would have involuntarily shut. Their skin would have been burning. They would have been gasping for air and coughing wildly," said Benjamin C. Garrett, executive director of the Chemical and Biological Arms Control Institute in Alexandria. He continued, "Eventually, they would have been overcome with vomiting in a final hell. It would not have been pretty."[53]

A few weeks later, the FBI razed the crime scene. A former arson investigator for the ATF, whose wife was still on the ATF payroll and whose business cards included the ATF insignia, came in and did an "independent investigation" that supposedly proved the Davidians started the fire. The investigation was later criticized as a whitewash with a preordained conclusion. Lawyers for the surviving Davidians complained that the destruction of the crime scene "prevented examination of the blast hole in the ceiling, the scraping and removal of the remains of the building including concrete foundation slabs, and dirt which contained thousands of expended bullet slugs from government firearms, evidence of lethal chemicals, accelerants and other dangerous elements used in the assault and other evidence."[54]

President Clinton distanced himself from the decision to use force. He actually hid from public view. On April 19, 1993, when he appeared in public, he was asked, when the federal agents were moving on the compound but before the fire began, if he had authorized such action. He said, "The attorney general . . . recommended that we proceed with today's action, given the risks of maintaining the previous policy indefinitely. I told the attorney general to do what she thought was right, and I stand by that decision."[55]

Later that evening, Attorney General Janet Reno went on *Nightline* and announced: "I made the decision. I'm accountable. The buck stops with me." Reno then asserted that the fiery end was all somebody else's fault: "I don't think anybody has ever dealt with a David Koresh, who would purposely set people afire in that number." *Nightline* host Ted Koppel asked Reno why the feds used "tanks to ram the compound down." Reno replied, "I think that what we were trying to do was to give everybody an opportunity to come out in the *most unobstructive way* possible, not with a frontal assault."[56]

The embarrassed and incompetent attorney general later stated that before the raid, her "fatigued agents" gave her reports that babies were being beaten and molested. After the raid, she pleaded it was the Clintons' concern with children that justified setting in motion a plan that got all of the children killed. Reno also let it be known that on that night she had been unable to reach the president—thus compounding the picture of a president hiding. The episode set off tensions between Reno and the White House.[57]

Early in the morning of April 20, 1993, White House spokesman George Stephanopoulos went on all three morning news shows to emphasize that the children had been abused—at least in the past—and that Mr. Koresh was the "murderer" responsible for the deaths. "Protecting the kids was the ultimate rationale for going in," Mr. Stephanopoulos said. He also stated: "Cult leader David Koresh was marrying children and sexually abusing children and children were being taught how to commit suicide, how to put guns in their mouths, how to clamp down on cyanide."[58]

Later in the morning, Clinton was enraged by the stories in the papers suggesting he had been lying low. "That's shit," he said to his aides—an expression he employed often. It was obvious that he would have to take questions on the matter at some point, so in a Rose Garden ceremony that day to present the Teacher of the Year award, Clinton expressed his sorrow over the loss of life, announced that he had instructed the Departments of Defense and Treasury to undertake an investigation of the siege, and reiterated his support for the attorney general.[59] He also declared: "There is nothing to hide here. This was probably the most well-covered operation of its kind in the history of the country." As he spoke, Reno raced to put the fix in on the Justice Department's Waco investigation. Reno chose Edward Dennis, a former assistant general in the Bush administration, to head the investigation. Dennis was an unusual choice to evaluate the Justice Department's behavior since his law firm had many clients with cases currently before the Department.[60]

The Justice Department's final report was widely derided as a whitewash. Edward Dennis announced at a Washington press conference that Reno or the FBI could had done nothing that would have changed the final assault. "I find no fault in the performance of law enforcement during the standoff and the tear gas assault," Dennis said. "Ultimately, the outcome was not within the power of law enforcement to effect. He [Branch Davidian leader Koresh] choreographed his own death and the deaths of most of his followers." Reno initially justified the final assault because of ongoing child abuse; the report found no evidence to support that charge. Reno announced, "I now understand that nobody in the [FBI] told me that it was ongoing. We were briefed, and I misunderstood." The Treasury Department wrote a separate report, which concluded that several ATF officials had lied and the agency had committed blunders. The report avoided or swept under the rug the most serious allegations of ATF wrongdoing.[61]

The eleven surviving Branch Davidians were tried for murder and various other charges in early 1994. A grand jury indictment accused them of conspiring "with malice aforethought" to kill ATF agents "on account of the performance of their duties." The trial was presided over by federal judge Walter Smith, a former personal injury lawyer and chairman of the McLennan County Republican Party.[62]

Judge Smith initially proclaimed that "the government is not on trial." Smith then limited defense attorneys in offering evidence that the Davidians acted in self-defense when the ATF attacked their home. Smith even prohibited the defense attorneys from introducing into evidence the official Treasury Department report on ATF actions at Waco. Since the credibility of ATF witnesses was crucial to the government's case, the Treasury Department's findings of false statements and incompetence by ATF officials could have been decisive. Smith also denied requests by the attorneys to acquire testimony from ATF Chief Stephen Higgins and from Attorney General Janet Reno. Finally, the judge refused to allow defense attorneys to call ATF agents who had been in the Blackhawk helicopters to determine whether shots had been fired from there. During the trial, the pictures of the four dead ATF agents were displayed, but the judge refused to let the jurors see pictures of the twenty dead children.[63]

On February 26, 1994, after six weeks on trial, the jury found all eleven Branch Davidian defendants not guilty of murder in the deaths of four ATF federal agents. Five of the eleven were found guilty of the lesser charge of voluntary manslaughter and two others of weapons violations. The verdicts represented a clear rebuke to federal prosecutors and to Janet Reno. Judge Smith "appeared visibly upset when the jury acquitted" the Davidian defendants. Bill Johnston, the lead federal attorney at Waco, shed tears in bitter disappointment at the verdict. The *New York Times* characterized the verdict as a "stunning defeat" for the federal government.[64] Then, two ATF agents, Phillip Chojnacki and Chuck Sarabyn, who had come under disciplinary action, were reinstated January 9, 1995, with full back pay and benefits and with all references to Waco removed from their personnel files.[65]

On April 24, 1995, Clinton appeared on *60 Minutes*, and was asked if he had "any second thoughts" about the raid at Waco. He exploded: "Before that raid was carried out, those people murdered a bunch of innocent law enforcement officials . . . and when that raid occurred it was the people who ran that cult compound who murdered their own children, not the federal officials. They made the decision to destroy all the children that were there." On July 20, 1995, Clinton charged that the Republicans were conducting a "war" on federal police by suggesting they are part of an "armed bureaucracy acting on private grudges and hidden agendas."[66]

In the summer of 1995, after capturing control of Congress in November 1994, the Republicans began holding hearings on Waco, much to the dismay of the White House and congressional Democrats. Treasury Secretary Robert Rubin fired the opening shot by sending an open letter to journalists suggesting that the hearings might become a "witch hunt" targeting federal law officers. Rep. Charles Schumer (D-N.Y.) said: "We know what that was all about. That was an attack on the ATF. This planned hearing is simply some red meat to some of those extreme right forces." White House Chief of Staff Leon Panetta denounced proposals for new hearings as "despicable."[67]

When the House hearings on Waco ended in August 1995, many Americans believed that the Justice Department, the FBI, and the Clinton administration had been caught repeatedly lying about what happened at Waco. Previously, in May of 1995, we had learned that Peter Smerick, the FBI's lead criminal analyst of the Waco case, disclosed how he was pressured by federal powers above to change his fifth and final memo which stressed "waiting Koresh out" rather than treating him and his followers as if the situation were a hostage crisis, which "if carried to excess could eventually be counterproductive and could result in loss of life." The Republicans, unfortunately, allowed the story to die.[68]

It would later appear that the government may have provided more assistance to the debacle than the FBI would have liked. According to the *Washington Times*:

- An ex-CIA employee told the *Dallas Morning News* in late August 1999 that ten Delta Force commandos participated in the tear-gassing and even drove armored vehicles lent to the FBI in the final day's action in Waco. Delta members bragged to him of their role when he subsequently served with them in Europe. James B. Francis, Jr., chairman of the Texas

Department of Public Safety, confirmed there is evidence that the Delta Force participated in the final assault against the Davidians.
- The "national security" excuse, repeatedly invoked for not turning over key files to congressional investigators, is wearing thin. According to the *Dallas Morning News*, "The military has estimated that at least 6,000 pages of its documents are classified, and CIA, FBI, Treasury, ATF [Alcohol, Tobacco and Firearms] and Justice Department officials have indicated that their agencies have a number of secret documents relating to the standoff." In September 1999, the Texas Department of Public Safety blocked the release of a report listing all the evidence it collected after the fire because the information contained military secrets. If there's so much to hide, was the military testing new weapons on American citizens during the standoff?
- In early October 1999, the FBI turned over thousands of key documents to congressional investigators—information previously withheld because it had supposedly been mislaid in boxes kept at Quantico, Virginia, home base of the FBI's Hostage Rescue Team.
- Infrared footage from an FBI plane circling 9,000 feet above the Davidians' home on the final day reveals that federal agents fired machine guns at or into the back of the building—either shortly before or just after the fire had broken out. According to former Pentagon infrared expert Edward Allard, the film showed gunfire directed at the Davidians. Additional newly released infrared footage made by an FBI plane, featured in 1999 movie, Waco: A New Revelation (made by Mike McNulty), shows two figures exiting from the back of the tank and then spraying the back of the Davidians' residence with automatic weapons fire. One FBI agent stated in an after-action report that he heard gunfire from the sniper post occupied by Lon Horiuchi, the same FBI agent who killed Vicki Weaver as she held her baby daughter in the cabin door of her Idaho home in 1992. The FBI may have attempted to keep the Davidians inside while its tanks crushed in

the walls and collapsed the roofs—long after the air inside was nearly unbreathable of a massive six-hour attack with CS gas.
- The FBI deceived Congress and a federal judge by withholding information that it had six closed-circuit television cameras monitoring the Davidians' home throughout the siege. The resulting films may contain information to resolve the major issues of Waco. Incredibly, the FBI claimed none of the cameras contained tape—the very same excuse made by the ATF, which had cameras both in the helicopters and on the ground when it launched its February 28, 1993, commando-style raid on the Davidians' home.[69]

It was now clear that a massive cover-up had occurred—in either the FBI or the Justice Department, or both. *Newsweek* reported that, according to a senior FBI official, "as many as 100 FBI agents and officials may have known about" the military-style explosive devices used by the FBI at Waco—despite Reno's and the FBI's endless denials that such devices were used.[70]

In September 1999, Janet Reno appointed former three-term Republican senator from Missouri, John C. Danforth, as special counsel to reopen the investigation on Waco to specifically, find out if the FBI fired their weapons during the final siege. Edward F. Allard, former director of the Defense Department's night vision laboratory at Fort Belvoir and a pioneer of infrared thermal imaging technology, concluded that heat sources observed on a tape taken by the FBI were forty-four distinct muzzle flashes from automatic-weapons fire being directed at the compound from behind an armored tank.[71]

Carlos Ghigliotti, owner of Infrared Technologies Corp. in Laurel, Maryland, disclosed in an interview with the *Washington Post* that a review of the tape showed "without a doubt" that the FBI had fired into the compound. Ghigliotti had been hired by the House Government Reform Committee to study the tape and testify when the hearing would be scheduled. He never made it to the hearing.[72] On April 28, 2000, Ghigliotti's badly decomposed body was found sitting at his desk in his office at Infrared Technologies Corp. Police said there was no evidence of forced entry into his office. He was forty-two.[73]

On July 22, 2000, Special counsel Danforth cleared the government of any wrongdoing in the April 19, 1993, raid. Mr. Danforth said that his ten-month-long investigation concluded that government agents did not start the Waco fire, did not shoot at the Davidians, did not improperly use the U.S. military, and did not engage in a conspiracy and cover-up. "There is no evidence of any wrongdoing on the part of Attorney General [Janet] Reno, the present and former director of the FBI, other high officials of the United States or members of the FBI hostage team who fired pyrotechnic tear gas on April 19, 1993."[74]

Unfortunately, in the end, the Justice Department was adamant that no federal agents or officials deserved even a slap on the wrist for carrying out a military-style assault on American civilians that ended with eighty-six dead.[75]

CHAPTER 11

RUBY RIDGE

*The real measure of our progress is whether responsibility
and respect for the law are on the rise.*

—President Bill Clinton, April 6, 1998[1]

Nothing illustrates the Clinton administration philosophy of civil rights better than the investigations and lawsuits involving Ruby Ridge. The shootings at Ruby Ridge, Idaho, occurred during the latter end of the George H. W. Bush administration. But most of the cover-up and almost all the whitewashing occurred on President Clinton's watch. Ruby Ridge became a symbol of federal agents being above the law and spurred millions of Americans to distrust Washington.[2]

The Weaver family moved from Iowa to Idaho in 1985 and then bought a plot of land. The Weaver family lived in a cabin located thirty miles south of the Canadian border in the Idaho panhandle in an area called Ruby Ridge. The case involved the entrapment of Randy Weaver on firearms charges by an informant for the Bureau of Alcohol, Tobacco and Firearms (ATF), "Gus Magisono," a.k.a. Kenneth Fadley. The entrapment included false ATF reports to federal prosecutors and dozens of intrusions by U.S. marshals on Weaver's land. The attack was triggered when Randy Weaver did not show up for a court appearance in 1991. It was discovered that, because of a clerical error, the wrong date appeared on the summons. Then began eighteen months of surveillance in preparation for Mr. Weaver's arrest. On August 21, 1992, three U.S. marshals dressed in full camouflage and ski masks ambushed Weaver's fourteen-year-old son, Sammy, and twenty-five-year-old family friend, Kevin Harris, firing submachine guns at them as they came down a road in the woods. Marshal Arthur Roderick started the clash by shooting the boy's dog Striker in the rear end, indicating that the dog was running away. The dog was killed by the second shot. Soon, a firefight began which resulted in the death of Marshal William Degan. As Sammy Weaver was leaving the scene and running back toward the cabin, Marshal Larry Cooper shot him in the back and killed him.[3]

That evening, Randy Weaver and Kevin Harris retrieved Sammy's body and wrapped it as best they could. They put the body in the birthing shed near the main cabin. A siege that was to last eleven days was under way.[4]

The next day, FBI snipers arrived on the scene and received their "rules of engagement."

1. If any adult male is observed with a weapon prior to [a surrender] announcement, deadly force can and should be employed if the shot can be taken without endangering any children.
2. If any adult in the compound is observed with a weapon after the surrender announcement is made and is not attempting to surrender, deadly force can and should be employed to neutralize the individual.
3. If compromised by any animal, that animal should be eliminated.
4. Any subjects other than Randall Weaver, Vicky Weaver, Kevin Harris presenting threats of death or grievous bodily harm, the FBI rules of deadly force are in effect. Deadly force can be utilized to prevent the death or grievous bodily injury to one's self or that of another.[5]

Within an hour of the snipers taking their positions, every adult in the cabin was either dead or severely wounded, despite the fact that they had not fired a shot at the FBI. It is worth noting that the FBI never called them out to surrender. FBI sniper Lon Horiuchi shot Randy Weaver in the back as he stood outside his cabin, and then fired a shot that went through the glass window and entered Vicki Weaver's temple, killing her instantly as she stood in the cabin doorway holding their ten-month-old baby, Elisheba. According to former Green Beret and FBI intermediary Bo Gritz, "an agency official told me that the FBI had 'targeted' Vicki Weaver during the standoff." But Mrs. Weaver herself had committed no crime. A second shot passed through Vicki Weaver and struck Kevin Harris. Afterward, the FBI proclaimed Ruby Ridge a great success.[6]

In April 1993, Randy Weaver and Kevin Harris went on trial for killing Marshal Degan and other charges. Federal prosecutors sought to prove that Weaver had conspired for nine years to have an armed confrontation with the government. Yet the conflict actually began when heavily armed federal agents trespassed on his land and opened fire. The government then tried to prove that Harris had shot first in the initial confrontation, but this claim was contradicted by other government witnesses. Finally, the federal prosecutors claimed that Marshal Degan had never fired a shot before he was hit. Ballistics evidence showed that he had fired seven rounds.[7]

Weaver's lawyer, Gerry Spence, did not call a single witness for Weaver's defense, relying instead on all the contradictions provided by the government's witnesses. On August 8, 1993, a jury acquitted Randy Weaver and Kevin Harris in the killing of Marshal Degan. Randy Weaver was convicted on lesser charges. Federal Judge Edward Lodge condemned the FBI: "The actions of the government, acting through the FBI, evidence a callous disregard for the rights of the defendants and the interests of justice and demonstrate a complete lack of respect for the order and direction of this court." Judge Lodge issued a lengthy list detailing the Justice Department's misconduct, fabrication of evidence, and refusals to obey court orders.[8]

After the debacle, the FBI and Justice Department launched separate investigations. In December 1994, the Justice Department completed their review of the siege, concluding that the FBI agents at the Weaver cabin violated bureau policies and constitutional guidelines. The report also concluded that numerous federal officials may have obstructed justice, perjured themselves, or otherwise broken the law. A task force of twenty-four Justice Department and FBI officials recommended that sniper Horiuchi face federal charges for the killing of Vicki Weaver. After that report was completed, the Justice Department's Office of Professional Responsibility (OPR) came in and urged that neither Horiuchi nor his boss, Richard Rogers, face charges. Assistant Attorney General for Civil Rights Deval Patrick, in an October 15, 1994, memo, disregarded the initial task force and ruled that the federal agents had not used excessive force in the killings of Sammy Weaver and Vicki Weaver. The Justice Department refused to release Patrick's memo.

However, a *New York Times* article noted that Patrick "said that when the sharpshooter fired the fatal shot, the agents had a reasonable belief that their lives were in danger. Agents had not intentionally used excessive force." The Justice Department refused to release any of the reports.[9]

A few weeks later, on January 6, 1995, FBI Director Louis Freeh announced the results of the FBI's internal investigation. Freeh declared that the Randy Weaver "crisis was one of the most dangerous and potentially violent situations to which FBI agents have ever been assigned." This was odd, considering that camouflaged FBI snipers had been hiding in the woods two hundred yards away when the Weavers were gunned down.[10]

Freeh did find twelve FBI officials guilty of "inadequate performance, improper judgment, neglect of duty and failure to exert proper managerial oversight." However, the heaviest penalty that Freeh imposed was fifteen days unpaid leave, and that on only four agents. Freeh had imposed heavier penalties on FBI agents who used their official cars to drive their children to school. Freeh gave especially lenient treatment to Larry Potts, an old friend and Freeh's pick as acting deputy FBI director. Potts was the senior FBI headquarters official in charge of the Idaho operation. Despite the finding of a Justice Department confidential report that the rules of engagement had violated the Constitution, Freeh recommended that Potts face only the penalty of a letter of censure—the same penalty that Freeh had imposed on himself when he lost an FBI cell phone. A month later in Senate testimony, Freeh would declare that "no misconduct" by FBI officials had occurred in the handling of the Weaver case.[11]

Freeh justified the FBI shooting of Randy Weaver by saying that sniper Lon Horiuchi "observed one of the suspects raise a weapon in the direction of a helicopter carrying other FBI personnel." But, other federal officials testified at the trial that no helicopters were flying in the vicinity of the Weaver's cabin when Horiuchi opened fire. Chuck Peterson, an Idaho lawyer who was part of Weaver's defense team, observed that "the federal judge threw out the [charge that Weaver aimed at] the helicopter because it was so incredibly weak—it was not supported by anything." Dean Miller was a reporter for the *Spokane Spokesman-Review* who had covered the original siege and subsequent federal trial.[12]

Freeh was also satisfied that Horiuchi's second shot was justified and that the killing of Vicki Weaver was an accident. An internal FBI report completed shortly after the confrontation justified the killing of Mrs.

Weaver by asserting that she had just put herself in harm's way. A Senate report later noted that the FBI "assault plan . . . was based on the premise that Vicki Weaver would kill her children." Freeh declared, "The question is whether someone running into a fortified position is going to shoot at you is as much a threat to you as somebody turning in an open space and pointing a gun at you. I don't distinguish between those."[13] Freeh's allegation that Weaver was "running into a fortified position" was a joke. As Gerry Spence, Weaver's lawyer observed, "The cabin was built with sticks and plywood so fragile a wolf could have blown it down."[14] And Weaver had never fired upon the FBI agents; he was shot in the back outside his cabin. According to Freeh: "if a government agent shoots and wounds a private citizen, the agent acquires an unlimited right to kill the target because otherwise the citizen might shoot back at the government agent."[15]

The press rallied around the Clinton administration. The *Washington Post*, in a January 9, 1995, editorial titled "Ruby Ridge and Waco," declared: "No criminal charges against law enforcement agents are contemplated, and none would be justified." Then you had a July 14, 1995, *New York Times* editorial describing Randy Weaver, his wife, their ten-month-old baby, thirteen-year-old son, sixteen-year-old daughter, and family friend, Kevin Harris, as "an armed separatist brigade."[16]

James Bovard, in his book, *Feeling Your Pain*, reports the following:

> In June 1995, the confidential 542-page Justice Department report on Ruby Ridge leaked out and was placed on the Internet by *Legal Times*. The revelations in the report made a mockery of Deval Patrick and Louis Freeh's earlier statements. The task force was especially appalled that the adults were gunned down before receiving any warning or demand to surrender: "There was no attempt by the FBI to give notice to the individuals in the cabin prior to the shots taken by Horiuchi . . . While the operational plan included a provision for a surrender demand, that demand was not made until after the shootings . . . The absence of such a [surrender demand] subjected the Government to charges that it was setting Weaver for attack."
> The report concluded that the FBI's rules of engagement at Ruby Ridge flagrantly violated the U.S. Constitution: "The Constitution allows no person to become fair game for deadly force without law enforcement evaluating the threat that person poses, even when, as

occurred here, the evaluation must be made in a split second." The report illustrated the rules of engagement as a license to kill: "The Constitution places the decision on whether to use deadly force on the individual guest; the Rules attempted to usurp this responsibility." The report concluded that the rules were a decisive factor in the wrongful killing of Vicki Weaver.[17]

On July 12, 1995, Michael Kahoe, the director of the FBI's Violent Crimes and Major Offenders Section, was suspended because he was suspected of shredding the FBI after-action report on Ruby Ridge. A month later, Deputy Director Larry Potts and four other high-ranking officials were also suspended from their positions because they were suspected of also having destroyed evidence, or for their role in issuing illegal rules of engagement.[18]

On August 15, 1995, the Justice Department agreed to pay the family of Randy Weaver $3.1 million to settle the deaths of Vicki Weaver and their son. The Weavers had filed civil claims against the government and a lawsuit against specific federal agents seeking $200 million in damages. With the settlement, the government admitted no wrong-doing or legal liability. According to the Justice Department, "the settlement reflects the loss to the Weaver children [three daughters] of their mother and brother. By entering into a settlement, the United States hopes to take a substantial step toward healing the wounds the incident inflicted."[19]

On September 6, 1995, Sen. Arlen Specter (R.-Pa.), chairman of the Senate Judiciary Subcommittee on Terrorism, Technology and Government Information began hearings focused on the Bureau of Alcohol, Tobacco and Firearms' efforts to target Mr. Weaver on a minor weapons charge at Ruby Ridge.[20]

During the hearings it came out that ATF agent Herb Byerly, the person who set up Weaver to violate firearms law, had lied about Weaver, telling the U.S. attorney that Weaver had previous convictions. Weaver had never been convicted of anything in his life. Asked about these slanders during his testimony, Byerly insisted they had been merely "typographical errors," which elicited roars of laughter from the hearing room.[21] Five FBI agents ended up taking the Fifth rather than telling the incriminating truth about their activities on Ruby Ridge case.[22]

The investigation that began in 1995 dragged into the summer of 1997. On August 15, 1997, on a Friday afternoon, when most reporters were not working, the Justice Department surprisingly announced that it would file no criminal charges against any high-ranking FBI agents in the Ruby Ridge case. It claimed there "was substantial evidence that FBI law enforcement efforts were undertaken by on-site supervisors with the belief that Randall Weaver and Kevin Harris posed a severe threat to law enforcement officers requiring the use of deadly force."[23]

Despite the whitewash of any FBI agents facing criminal charges from the Justice Department, on October 10, 1997, FBI Agent Michael Kahoe, who was on trial for his role in the Ruby Ridge incident, pleaded guilty to obstructing justice in the Ruby Ridge siege. U.S. District Judge Ricardo Urbina sentenced Kahoe to eighteen months in prison and gave him two years' probation after his release from federal prison. Kahoe had faced up to ten years in prison and a $250,000 fine.[24]

On September 22, 2000, the U.S. government paid $380,000 to Kevin Harris, who was wounded during the 1992 siege. It was the last remaining civil lawsuit and the U.S. government did not admit any liability.[25]

There is simply no question that the ATF, the FBI, the Justice Department, and Attorney General Reno bear some responsibility for the tragic outcome of Ruby Ridge. Since the buck stops at the top, ultimately President Clinton also bears some responsibility for the tragedy. In the end, the U.S. government did not consider killing innocent civilians a crime.[26]

CHAPTER 12

TRAVEL OFFICE FIRINGS

This man [Billy Dale] and his colleagues were screwed . . . for greedy purposes by people who just got to the White House, who thought they had total power and could put any of their friends they wanted into this lucrative travel office business.
—Senator Orrin G. Hatch (R-UT), September 12, 1996[1]

After the 1992 election, there was a plan to replace the White House travel office with a hand-picked travel agency, World Wide Travel, a Little Rock travel agency that had booked all the travel for the Clinton campaign.[2]

The travel operation got its start during Andrew Jackson's administration when aides helped reporters following the president book train tickets. By 1993, the small operation on the Old Executive Office Building's ground floor consisted of seven employees who handled about $7 million a year in travel arrangements for the White House press corps.[3]

Then came the long-standing political and business relationships in Arkansas. World Wide Travel was originally owned by the Worthen Bank, which was in turn controlled by the Stephens family. In 1979, Stephens, Inc. was forced to sell the agency when banks had to divest themselves of their travel services. Stephens arranged for it to be bought by its manager, Betta Carney. By 1993, World Wide was the twenty-fourth largest U.S. travel agency, with annual business of $158 million. Then you had David Watkins, who ran the Worthen-owned Advertising Associates, Inc., becoming a client of World Wide. Then you had Mack McLarty, the chief executive officer of the Stephens-owned Arkla Gas Company, who was a

World Wide client. And you had Wal-Mart, on whose board of directors Hillary Rodham Clinton sat, who was also a client.[4]

Carney made well over $1 million as the Clinton presidential campaign's travel agent, in a contract arranged on a non-competitive basis by Watkins, who by then was the deputy manager and chief financial officer of the campaign. Though the arrangement was not disclosed in either the White House Review or the GAO audit, according to a 1992 report in *Travel Weekly*, World Wide did the Clinton campaign a huge favor. It agreed to bill the campaign based on the amount of money it was taking in, rather than on the money it was spending. Thus, a major portion of the campaign's travel debts was thereby deferred until federal matching funds started pouring in.[5]

The agency also adopted an unusual billing policy for journalists. When members of the press flew on the candidate's chartered aircraft, the campaign billed them a pro-rated fare plus 10 percent. World Wide required journalists to charge their tickets in *advance* and made sure that those funds were wired back into the campaign's coffers within a few days. The campaign, which spent an estimated $100,000 a week chartering planes, also tried to force the Secret Service to pay immediately. The arrangement enabled the campaign to instantly pump money into advertising in crucial races like Michigan and Illinois, for example. The funds would have otherwise been only a ledger entry in accounts receivable for weeks. *Travel Weekly* quoted Watkins as saying that "were it not for World Wide Travel here, the Arkansas governor may never have been in contention for the highest office in the land."[6]

Thus, World Wide needed to be rewarded. According to an article in the *Washington Times*, by the time Clinton locked up the nomination, Carney was already secretly analyzing the White House travel office operation. Two weeks after the election, Steve Davison, director of customer services for World Wide, was quoted in a little-noticed *Arkansas Business* article as saying that "World Wide is studying the possibilities of opening an office in Washington, D.C., to handle travel plans for Clinton's staff when he becomes president." Shortly after the 1992 presidential campaign ended, World Wide was rewarded with the Democratic National Committee's travel business.[7]

Betta Carney and David Watkins enlisted twenty-five-year-old Catherine Cornelius, a fellow Arkansan who served as the liaison between the Clinton campaign and World Wide and whose great-grandmother was a sister of Clinton's great-grandfather. Catherine was told to come up with a rationale for gutting the current travel office and assuming the same role in the White House that she had played in the campaign. Though Watkins masterminded the Cornelius scheme from the get-go, future White House aide Patsy Thomasson allegedly told Cornelius to lie if she were ever asked whether Watkins had read her memos before Clinton took office.[8]

In December 1992, Catherine Cornelius and representatives from World Wide met in Little Rock with David Watkins, at that time a transition official, to discuss strategy for World Wide's takeover of the travel operation. On December 31, 1992, Cornelius sent Watkins a memo specifying that by privatizing the White House travel office, that would let Clinton fulfill his campaign promise to reduce White House personnel and make it easier to get discounted airfares. Also, there would be additional revenue generated through a rebate scheme in which 3.5 percent of the agency's ten-percent commission on tickets would be sent to the White House Travel Account. Cornelius estimated that on a travel budget of nearly $6 million a year, (it was actually $7 million a year), it would get a $210,000 rebate. Cornelius neglected to point out that the remaining 6.5 percent (or $390,000 a year) would go directly to World Wide. Cornelius proposed that the White House disregard regular procedures and select the private contractor itself.[9]

The day after Inauguration Day, January 21, 1993, phone calls began coming in to the White House Travel Office for the "new director," Catherine Cornelius. She had not, of course, been given the job.[10]

On January 26, 1993, six days after Mr. Clinton's inauguration, Cornelius wrote a memo proposing that she and Clarissa Cerda, who had supervised the campaign's early-billing operation, could perform the functions of the White House travel office in conjunction with World Wide. Watkins quickly named both Cornelius and Cerda to his White House staff as assistants, with the apparent intention of moving them to the travel office at the right time.[11]

On February 15, 1993, Cornelius sent another memo, co-authored by Clarisa Cerda, for staffing the White House that included an organization chart that consisted of her name and those of Clinton campaign aides. The chart listed World Wide Travel as handling the arrangements. The document was called "The White House Travel Office: Briefing Book and Proposal."[12]

Then, apparently tipped off by Carney and Cornelius, there was another group of close associates of the Clintons who began maneuvering for a piece of the White House business. Penny Sample, whose company, Air Advantage, had brokered charter planes to the campaign for World Wide, was eager to perform the same service for the White House press corps. Darnell Martens, Sample's boyfriend, was president of a small Cincinnati-based aviation consulting firm that had done billing and consulting for Air Advantage. Martens had chartered "Air Elvis," the airplane that transported Clinton and his aides during the presidential race.[13] Marten's firm was called Thomason, Richland & Martens (TRM). It was co-owned by Martens; Hollywood producer Harry Thomason, a longtime Arkansas friend of the Clintons; and Dan Richland, the agent of Thomason's wife Linda Bloodworth-Thomason.[14]

On January 29, 1993, Martens wrote a memo to Thomason suggesting the two needed "some form of official status to the White House for general aviation policy matters." One of the suggestions was review of all nonmilitary aircraft. Another idea was taking over the scheduling for the White House travel office. Martens also advised Thomason to change the name of the company to Harry Thomason and Associates, in order to "capitalize on 'Thomason' name recognition." Martens estimated the cost of the audit alone at half a million dollars.[15]

The Clintons were very loyal to the Thomasons—even more than to Betta Carney. The couple hosted countless Hollywood fund-raisers for Bill Clinton, and their production company donated $60,000 to the Democratic National Committee. In 1992, the Thomasons went to extraordinary lengths to make film editors, cameramen, make-up artists, and wardrobe people, as well as studio facilities and equipment from their TV shows, available for Clinton campaign videos, according to a report in the *Los Angeles Times*.[16]

In early February, Thomason began to make discreet inquiries about the travel office. He asked Dee Dee Myers if the White House charter business was open for competitive bidding, and Myers said she thought it was. Thomason suggested that Martens call Myers to follow up. Myers, perhaps naively, referred Martens to Billy Dale, the long-time travel office director who would soon become one of the Travelgate Seven. On February 17, 1993, Bill Clinton took a moment to review a note from Darnell Martens suggesting that TRM be awarded a government consulting contract to review government use of nonmilitary aircraft. "These guys are sharp," the president wrote to Mack McLarty on a note accompanying Marten's proposal. "Should discuss with Panetta, [Philip] Lader," the director and assistant director, respectively, of the Office of Management and Budget.[17]

On May 10, 1993, Thomason and Martens sent a three-page "confidential" memo to the White House, outlining their efforts to penetrate the White House travel business. They were interested in getting the lucrative White House press charter business. The charters were worth an average of $40,000 a day.[18]

Martens also wrote a memorandum for his files about the Dale telephone call. Martens referred to an interest in "earning" White House business for TRM and conveyed his frustration that Dale "refuses to discuss business opportunities with legitimate charter operators." But Martens's company was a charter *broker*, not a charter operator, and the White House already had a charter broker—the travel office itself. It was clearly the brokerage Dale was referring to when, according to the memo, he was adamant that there was "no chance" the White House would change its current operation.[19]

Martens made a case for replacing the current charter airline, UltrAir—formerly Airline of the Americas (AOA), which had been founded by ex-Pan Am executives using Pan Am's old planes after Pan Am's bankruptcy in 1991.[20] Dale politely declined, saying he had no need for "a middleman," since that is basically the function served by the travel office itself. Martens and Thomason did not take this rejection kindly. This was Bill Clinton's White House, after all.[21]

On May 10, 1993, Thomason arrived at the White House, at this time he had his own office in the East Wing and had a reminder on his calendar to "call Hillary." In preparation for the call, he began to collect information, checking in with Watkins about the travel office, and asking Martens to fax a copy of his memo seeking business for their own company. Thomason would later clarify that the memo was meant to say that they would act on behalf of charter companies they had worked with, firms that had complained the travel office had shut them out of competition for the business of transporting the White House press corps. Before leaving the White House that day, according to his calendar, Thomason called McLarty, Watkins, and Cornelius to set up a White House meeting for the following morning. He also wrote himself a note: "Call Susan Thomases at home after 9:30 p.m."[22]

The next morning Thomason received a message to call Craig Livingstone, who had worked in Thomases' advance operation during the 1992 campaign: "Come over while Susan is here." Harry Thomason and Susan Thomases met later that afternoon. Then Thomason, later in the day, met at the White House with Harold Ickes, another Hillary adviser, who was not yet a member of the staff.[23]

That same day, on May 11, 1993, White House Chief of Staff Mack McLarty met with Harry Thomason. McLarty would later tell the General Accounting Office that he "never met with" Harry Thomason before the travel office firings. Both of their calendars show Mr. Thomason and Mr. McLarty meeting on May 11, 1993.[24]

Also on May 11, a reporter from *Time* magazine called the White House Travel Office to inquire about Catherine Cornelius, who had begun to travel with the president. Unlike other travel office employees, she flew on Air Force One and rode in the presidential motorcade instead of on the press bus. Reporters who covered Clinton's trips could see for themselves that Cornelius appeared to be quite friendly with the president. Cornelius was in Chicago with Clinton when the *Time* reporter's inquiry was passed on to her. Her first reaction was to accuse the career travel office employees of gossiping about her relationship with the president.[25]

Jeff Eller, the director of media affairs at the White House, came to her defense. He told *Time* Cornelius was a distant cousin of the president. Though the revelation came as a shock to people who had worked with her in both the White House and the campaign, it was evidently intended to quash a rumor that Cornelius was having an affair with the president.[26]

On the morning of May 12, 1993, Thomason met with Bill Clinton in the Oval Office. Afterward, Cornelius met with Thomason at the White House and reported her observations. They met with Watkins and Martens. Martens brought up an allegation that a travel office employee had solicited a kickback from a charter airline. With no hard evidence of any wrongdoing by the current employees, Cornelius called Betta Carney and told her to prepare to send staffers to Washington to take over the travel operation. Cornelius believed the staff was about to be fired. Cornelius disclosed to the GAO that Watkins ordered her to make the call. That same day, Martens applied for a White House pass, according to the GAO. But Watkins, Cornelius, and Thomason did not have the ability to execute the purge and cover it up. Thus, on the same day, Thomason, who had already spoken to Bill Clinton earlier in the morning, arranged and met with Hillary Rodham Clinton to express his concerns. She told him to "stay ahead" of the problem.[27]

Later that day, Watkins brought in White House deputy counsel Vincent Foster to meet with Cornelius and Thomason on the alleged travel office problems.[28] Associate counsel William Kennedy then joined Foster in a second meeting with the trio. What came next was a reprise of Rose Law Firm days, where Foster had been the brains and Kennedy, the bad cop. Foster asked Kennedy to contact the FBI about initiating an investigation of the office. With this, Foster drew the FBI and the Justice Department into the plan to get rid of the travel office workers by setting up a criminal probe. Late that day, Kennedy contacted FBI agent Jim Bourke. Kennedy told Bourke that there was a problem in a White House office, that he was unsure how to proceed and that he sought guidance on handling the matter. Bourke indicated that he would determine appropriate agents with whom Kennedy could talk. The next morning, May 13, Kennedy called Bourke, who demanded to know "within 15 minutes" what the FBI was going to do. Otherwise, Kennedy warned, he would call in the IRS.[29]

That threat seemed to have resonated at the FBI. Two senior agents in the criminal division, Howard Apple and Pat Foran, went to the White House and met with Kennedy following what Apple described to the GAO as a "nebulous and cryptic" telephone call from Kennedy. Apple said he told Kennedy that if normal procedure were followed, the matter would be referred to the FBI's Washington Metropolitan Field Office or even the local police rather than involve FBI unit chiefs. But Kennedy was adamant. According to an FBI report prepared on June 1, 1993, for Attorney General Janet Reno, it stated Associate White House Counsel William Kennedy "insisted that an FBI Headquarters manager meet with him, noting that the matter to be discussed [the Travel Office] was both extremely sensitive and being directed at the 'highest level' at the White House." Kennedy did not recall making this statement but did recall indicating that his superiors—Foster and Watkins—were looking over his shoulder.[30]

Kennedy told the agents of "rumors" about lavish lifestyles among travel office personnel. Apple was clearly unimpressed, telling Kennedy he needed more information before deciding whether to investigate, according to the GAO. Apple and Foran then consulted with their boss, Daniel Coulson, a deputy assistant director of the FBI. Later in the day, Coulson sent a second team of senior agents, Richard Wade, the chief of the governmental fraud unit, and Tom Carl, a supervisor in that unit, to meet with Kennedy. Then came the key meetings.[31]

First, Wade, Carl, and Kennedy met with Foster. The FBI agents told the White House lawyers that there was insufficient grounds for an investigation. Cornelius, who had returned to her home to retrieve the travel office documents, was then summoned. She told the FBI that a small amount of checks made out to cash were not accounted for and hinted at unsubstantiated stories about kickbacks. Pressure from the White House and Cornelius's observations led to the decision to open a criminal investigation. The White House Review portrayed the decision to investigate as an independent judgement reached by the FBI: "Following this conversation [with Cornelius], [Wade and Carl] determined there were grounds for further investigation." On May 14, the day after this determination, Carl briefed three Justice Department lawyers: Joe Gangloff, Jerry McDowell, and Jack Keeny, a deputy assistant attorney general. "None raised an objection."[32]

Foster must have realized the horrible mistake of asking Kennedy to call the FBI on May 12. The rule was that any requests for information or assistance from any branch of the Justice Department, including the FBI, must be cleared through the Attorney General's office. Thus, on the next day, May 13, 1993, Vince Foster, consulting with Watkins and Patsy Thomasson, who worked under Watkins as an assistant to the president, came up with a strategy to conceal the activities of the White House staff contacting the FBI, while at the same time concealing the involvement of the Clintons and their friends, in the travel office firings.[33]

A quick financial audit of the travel office would be undertaken as the basis for the decision by the FBI and the Justice Department to open an investigation. This would serve as the basis for installing Clinton's friends in the travel office. The press would be told than an audit had turned up allegations of wrongdoing. Then a criminal probe would be ordered. Then the decision will be made to fire the travel office employees. In this case, the events happen in reverse.[34]

Why have an audit when the matter had already been elevated to the level of potential criminality? On May 13, 1993, then-FBI Director William Sessions sent a letter to then-Minority Leader Bob Dole responding to his question about what the FBI agents recommended to Kennedy as a course of action: "No course of action was recommended to Mr. Kennedy. He was advised that the FBI was only authorized to conduct criminal investigations." From this response, it appeared clear that Kennedy and Foster had asked the FBI to do an audit and that the FBI refused.[35]

What happened next? Normal procedure in such a case would have been for the FBI to seize everything that might be evidence and seal the office. But the agents didn't do that because there were no credible allegations. Instead, they agreed to Foster's request that they wait until the audit was done.[36]

Conveniently, an auditor with political ties to the administration, Larry Herman of the accounting firm KPMG Peat Marwick, was already in residence in Vice President Gore's office doing early work on the examination of government management that would come to be known as the National Performance Review. This would be the cover meant to justify the unjustified firings.[37]

On May 13, 1993, Foster met with Hillary Rodham Clinton on another matter, and she asked him about the travel office. He told her that Kennedy was looking into the matter. Later, Foster told her KPMG would conduct a review.[38] Then, on the same day, Hillary increased the pressure to take action on the Travel Office situation when she met with Mack McLarty. "Are you aware that there are potentially very serious problems in the Travel Office." He said he was. On May 13, 1993, Hillary Rodham Clinton met with Mack McLarty and asked what was being done about the "problems" in the travel office.[39]

Mack McLarty signed off on the Foster-Watkins-Thomason cover-up plan late Thursday, May 13, 1993. The next day, there were several additional contacts between Kennedy and the FBI once the decision was made.[40]

Throughout Friday, May 14, 1993, and during the weekend, Kennedy attempted to feed any preliminary findings he could get his hands on to the FBI in an effort to cover his tracks. These contacts were divulged in the Sessions letter. Unfortunately, the White House Review and the GAO audit omitted them entirely. Sessions revealed to Dole that twice on May 14, Kennedy called Wade, "providing additional information on the audit being conducted at the Travel Office and discrepancies being found by the auditors." The next day, on May 15, according to Sessions, FBI agents Tom Carl and David Bowie went to the White House "at the behest of Mr. Kennedy . . . to receive a further update about the preliminary findings of the 'performance review.' " Sessions also mentioned that the two agents met not only with Kennedy, but also with Patsy Thomasson and Larry Herman of KPMG.[41]

Considering Herman's ties to the administration, the audit could not be represented as independent. Consider this: two aides from Watkin's office, Deputy Brian Foucart and Jennifer O'Connor, a staff assistant, worked with Herman, checking back with Thomasson on their progress throughout the weekend. Thomasson then called Watkins. Watkins then called Foster. Then Foster told Watkins to call Hillary.[42]

Why call Hillary? It turns out that the sense of urgency in the White House on May 13, the day Kennedy gave the FBI fifteen minutes to jump, was at least partly due to Hillary's inquiries about the travel office to Mack McLarty and Vince Foster about what was being down about the "problems" in the travel office.[43]

How Hillary first became aware of the "problems" has been one of the enduring mysteries of Travelgate, a question glossed over entirely in the White House Review. Recall on May 12, Thomason and Martens had met with Watkins—and then Watkins told Cornelius to call World Wide with news of imminent firings. Though none of the press accounts picked up on it, the missing piece of the puzzle was disclosed by the GAO. Following the meeting with Watkins, Thomason "repeated his concerns" to Hillary, and then reported back to Watkins on the conversation. Through his lawyer, Thomason said he could not recall any conversation with Hillary.[44]

Yet, Thomason's interests were getting a lot of attention with what White House sources described as Hillary's obsession with clearing out "Republican holdovers" from the White House staff. On a May 14, 1993, memo, Watkins recounted that Mrs. Clinton told him to replace a team of travel office aides, who for decades had arranged press and staff trips, with a travel firm partly owned by Harry Thomason. "Harry says his people can run things better, save money, etc. And besides, we need those people out—we need our people in. We need the slots."[45]

Foster told Hillary late Thursday that the audit would start the next morning. But even that was not soon enough for Harry Thomason, Catherine Cornelius, or Jeff Eller, who met with Mack McLarty on Friday morning to urge him to fire the travel office employees by 5 p.m. that day. McLarty was probably unaware that Cornelius had already told World Wide to come to Washington.[46]

Foster objected to the immediate firings, because the audit had to happen first, and McLarty backed him up. "McLarty decided that no action would be taken until the completion of the Peat Marwick review," according to the Review. The action, of course, was already pre-determined by Hillary on May 12, 1993, after she spoke with Thomason.[47]

On Sunday evening, May 16, 1993, Mack McLarty brought the news to Bill and Hillary at a private dinner in the White House residence. McLarty's handwritten notes of that day reflected "HRC pressure." Later that night, Foster had a meeting with Clinton.[48]

On Monday, May 17, 1993, KPMG sent its report to Kennedy, questioning the travel office operations. This included petty cash procedures. The report was sent to Watkins who then sent a memo to McLarty reporting the results of a draft of the Peat Marwick review and informing him of the pending firings. Watkins carbon-copied only Hillary on this memo, placing the "cc" designation prominently across the top of the first page, yet another sign that Hillary was privy to the firings before they occurred, as well as to the plan to appoint Cornelius to head the re-organized office working hand in glove with World Wide Travel. Watkins needed Hillary's imprimatur to implement the plan. Copying the first lady in this bold way suggests the two had a quite close relationship, and Watkins was willing to call in some chips for Carney. That same day, Vince Foster, who started keeping a diary detailing the events of the travel office did the following: In the margin near another note dated May 17 regarding the imminent firings, Foster wrote "HRC problem" and circled it. On another page entitled "Coordination," he reminded himself to defend the firings as a management decision and "thereby defend HRC role whatever is, was in fact or might have been misperceived to be."[49]

On May 18, 1993, Hillary Rodham Clinton received a memo from David Watkins, saying that the White House Travel Office staff workers would be fired the next day.[50]

On Wednesday morning, May 19, 1993, Watkins gave White House press secretary Dee Dee Myers, written talking points on the travel office firings, which were to occur within the hour. In an apparent effort to bolster the White House position and make the allegations credible, Watkins included in the talking points the White House contacts with the FBI. When Foster saw the talking points, he was distressed and told Watkins to remove any mention of the FBI. However, Watkins could not locate Myers before she took a press call and disclosed the FBI contacts. The disclosure of these contacts violated longstanding FBI policy against confirming or denying the existence of an investigation. The policy was designed to protect the innocent. The disclosure also raised the question of whether the White House had used any political pressure to create a criminal probe.[51]

There was a second problem. Though there had been contacts between the White House and the FBI, the bureau had not started an investigation. Now in damage-control mode, the White House pressured the FBI into confirming that a probe was in fact under way. John Collingwood, the chief spokesman for the FBI, was summoned to a White House meeting by George Stephanopoulos and attended by Bernard Nussbaum, Foster, and Kennedy. Being a veteran of the Watergate inquiry, Nussbaum, of all people, should have been particularly concerned of the White House contacts with the FBI. Stephanopoulos pressured Collingwood to modify the bureau's public statement that would strengthen the case for firing the employees. The White House now had its statement confirming the "criminal investigation," despite the fact that the FBI statement was not meant for public release.[52]

On the morning of May 19, 1993, David Watkins, abruptly fired all seven of the travel office employees, telling them the White House was trying to reorganize and pare down the travel office. He told them they had two hours to pack their things and be out by noon. As they packed, the employees watched in horror as press secretary Dee Dee Myers revealed during the news conference that the FBI was actually investigating them. Then they were put in a seatless, windowless cargo van and driven from the White House to Pennsylvania Avenue. Then they were marched across Pennsylvania Avenue under Secret Service escort. The official White House line was that the travel office was being reorganized as part of Vice President Gore's initiative to reinvent government.[53]

When asked about this, Clinton said, "I had nothing to do with any decision except to save the taxpayers and the press money. That's all I know." Clinton added, "The FBI sounds like a huge deal to you, but when you're in Washington, you're the president, you can't call the local police or local prosecutor, that's who you call."[54]

The seven fired workers were Billy Dale, director of the travel office, who had been at the White House for thirty-two years; Gary Wright; John Dreylinger, who worked twenty-six years in the travel office, John

McSweeney, thirteen years; Barney Brasseaux, eleven years; Robert Van Eimeren, nine years; and Robert Maughan, nineteen years. Mr. McSweeney, who was in Ireland at the time of the firings, returned later to empty his desk and discovered his personal possessions had been thrown away.[55]

Then, Linda Bloodworth-Thomason decided, unwisely, to speak out and defend her husband. She appeared on *Good Morning America* and said that Harry would never have thought: "Ooh, I'm going to like take my six-figure salary a week and fly off to Washington and see if I can't get those seven little guys out of that Travel Office in the White House. It's sort of the equivalent of taking over a lemonade stand."[56]

At the time of the firings, Penny Sample of Air Advantage and Catherine Cornelius and World Wide began handling the travel office operations. In the first week of the new operation Sample, who was an unpaid volunteer, received a $1,400 commission for arranging a $31,000 Midwest Air news media charter flight to New Hampshire. It was the first flight she arranged. When asked about it, George Stephanopoulos said, "It was a mistake. She did not realize the funds were going to her firm." Sample returned the payment and soon left the White House to return to her business in Albuquerque, New Mexico.[57]

On Friday morning, May 21, 1993, Stephanopoulos released the Peat Marwick audit of the travel office, which found improper financial record keeping and funds that were missing. At 8:00 p.m., Stephanopoulos announced that World Wide Travel itself was dumped to quiet the growing criticism. By the following Monday, American Express Travel Offices was handling travel arrangements for press and White House officials until bids could be taken for a permanent service.[58]

On May 25, 1993, the president again faced reporters and was asked about the travel office firings: "I've told you all I know about it. All I knew was there was a plan to cut the size of the office, save tax dollars, save the press money." Just a day later, with word emerging that the whole affair was part of a scheme between the First Lady and presidential friend Harry Thomason to steer business to Clinton's friends, the president said: "The press complained to me repeatedly about being gouged by the White House travel office. I kept hearing it everywhere."[59]

Actually, Bill Clinton was told about the plan to fire the travel office workers by aide Bruce Lindsey on the night of May 17, 1993. This information was also deleted from the White House internal review and final report.[60]

Then you have the possible abuse by the IRS. On May 21, 1993, three IRS agents arrived unannounced at the offices of UltrAir (formerly Airline of the Americas), in Smyrna, Tennessee. The agents had been dispatched from the Nashville IRS District Office to investigate allegations of bribery and kickbacks in connection with the White House charters. They seized its financial records and launched an investigation that lasted two years. In the end, UltrAir was cleared. Curiously, the IRS does not usually investigate such crimes unless there are tax implications, and in the case of UltrAir there was no tax return to trigger an audit. UltrAir had just been formed in 1992 and had not even filed its first tax return because it had obtained an extension. Ultra was dubbed a "Republican airline" by Clinton allies seeking to take over the travel office, according to a confidential memo revealed in the White House report.[61]

On May 25, 1993, after a week of nonstop criticism, Mack McLarty decided to rescind the firings of the five travel office employees who had no responsibility for financial accounting and placed them on administrative leave at full pay. Having removed the World Wide employees, McLarty ordered a management review, undertaken by John Podesta, soon to be known around the White House as the "Secretary of Shit" for his role in cleaning up messes.[62]

Throughout the inquiry, McLarty, Foster, Watkins, and Thomason all downplayed Hillary's role in the Travelgate fiasco. Foster, in particular, pressured Watkins to protect Hillary by preventing disclosure that she had suggested cleaning house to get "our people" in the travel office.[63] To minimize the impact of the disclosures, the report was released late in the day on Friday, July 2, 1993. Advance copies of the report were not available. The White House permitted live coverage only of the opening statements of McLarty, Panetta, and other officials. Then the rather hostile question-and-answer session that followed was yanked off the air. Podesta's report criticized the decision of several White House employees to bring in the FBI as being made from "inexperience and just plain stupidity.". Vince Foster was spared and Hillary's role in the firings was minimized, but four people were reprimanded:[64]

- David Watkins, White House director of administration;
- William H. Kennedy III, White House Associate Counsel;
- Jeff Eller, White House Deputy Communications Director; and
- Catherine Cornelius.[65]

On August 4, 1993, the Justice Department dropped its probe into alleged wrongdoing by five of the White House travel office workers, forcing the White House to put them back to work. They were John Dreylinger, John McSweeney, Barney Brasseaux, Robert Van Eimeren, and Robert Maughan. The sixth individual, Gary Wright, retired. The Justice Department, though, continued to investigate Billy Dale. On October 26, 1995, Dale went to trial being accused of embezzlement. Judge Gladys Kessler, a Clinton appointee, was the presiding judge for the case. Her clerk, Adam Rosman, was a former intern in the White House Counsel's office from mid-July through August 1994. Coincidently, his direct superior was Clarissa Cerda.[66]

Billy Dale's life at that point was turned upside down. The FBI examined his finances, questioned his wife about her drinking habits, called numbers from his address book looking for a mistress, and forced his daughter to document where she got the money to pay for her wedding. To minimize his legal bills, Dale offered to plead to a misdemeanor. The Justice Department refused to deal, but word of Dale's proposal was leaked to President Clinton's personal lawyer, Robert Bennett, who mentioned it on national TV. Another revelation occurred in December 1993, when the White House counsel's office, then under the direction of Bernard Nussbaum, wrote the FBI requesting its entire file on Billy Dale. The FBI responded two weeks later with "11 letters and 11 memos."[67]

On November 16, 1995, a U.S. District Court jury acquitted Billy Dale of embezzling $68,000 from the White House travel office. It took the jury only two hours and twelve minutes to reach the verdict. Mr. Dale's father died without ever seeing his son exonerated. After the verdict, Billy Dale said, "It's been 30 long months is all I can say . . . I've been angry for 2 ½ years," he said as he wiped tears from his eyes. This was a major embarrassment for the White House which had pressed for the prosecution of Billy Dale.[68]

When President Clinton heard about the verdict he said, "I'm very sorry about what Mr. Dale had to go through, and I wish him well. I hope that he can get on with his life and put this behind him." Kind of reminiscent of "better put some ice on that." The *Washington Post* upbraided Clinton for that non-apology. It editorialized that Clinton misspoke when he expressed sorrow about what Billy Dale "had to go through." It would have been more accurate to say, "He was sorry for what Mr. Dale was 'put through' by the White House."[69]

CHAPTER 13

FOREIGN POLICY STUMBLES

The biggest mistake America ever made with Africa over the long run was neglect.
—President Clinton's remarks during an overseas trip
to Africa in March 1998

On October 14, 1993, Bill Clinton told reporters at the White House that his foreign policy was as good if not better than that of Presidents Reagan and Bush.[1]

"I've had people who were involved in the two previous administrations say that our national security decision-making process was at least as good as the two previous ones, perhaps better," said Clinton.[2]

In the book *Legacy* Rich Lowry wrote: "The formative experience of many Clinton foreign policy aides were in the anti-Vietnam War movement. They were veterans of the George McGovern presidential campaign in 1972, which had as its motto, 'Come Home, America,' and wanted the country to quit the struggle with the Soviets. Then, many of them went on to serve in the Carter administration, led by a president who had warned his fellow Americans against having 'an inordinate fear of Communism.' A defeatist, apologetic attitude toward American power was instinctual for much of the Clinton team." Let's look at five examples.[3]

HAITI

Haiti has been a geo-political disaster since the French first set foot on its ill-fated soil. The Haitian military had overthrown its elected president Jean-Bertrand Aristide on September 30, 1991. It was the latest in a long line of coups to plague Haiti since it emerged as the world's first black republic in 1804. Although President George H. W. Bush had pledged to restore Aristide to power, he and his advisors must have realized that there was not an easy and quick solution to the problems and decided to leave the mess for his successor.[4]

As irrelevant as Haiti might have seemed to Bush, it mattered to Clinton. There was a reason why. African-Americans, especially the Black Caucus, cared about Haiti. Bill Clinton cared about African-Americans. Eighty-two percent of African-Americans voted for him in the 1992 presidential election. Clinton could not have been elected without their support.[5]

During the 1992 presidential campaign, Clinton attacked Bush for sending the refugees back to Haiti and promised to return Aristide to power. At the Democratic convention, Democrats put Clinton's stand on repatriation into their platform: "Forcible return of anyone fleeing political repression is a betrayal of American values."[6]

Clinton calculated that his position would resonate with Kweisi Mfume, the Congressional Black Caucus chairman and his colleagues. Mfume would later admit he was "very concerned about that situation."[7]

To Mfume's disbelief, however, once in office, Clinton embraced Bush's policy of repatriating fleeing Haitians. Unfortunately, there were many Haitians who believed in Clinton's campaign promises. Some had gained the attention of authorities as they withdrew money from their banks and hurriedly hammered together oceangoing boats. Others actually put out to sea and were lost. Survivors were often returned and arrested by the Haitian government.[8]

On May 8, 1993, Clinton stopped the summary forced repatriation of the Haitian boat people. His new policy called for hearings aboard U.S. ships or in a third country. Unfortunately, nearly two months later, on July 6, as thousands of Haitians took to the sea, the Clinton administration announced a new policy that only those who apply for asylum from offices in Haiti, would be allowed into the United States. The boat people would be returned or taken to "safe havens."[9]

On July 3, 1993, Aristide and Haiti's military leader, Lt. Gen. Raoul Cédras, signed the Governors Island agreement, a U.N.-brokered deal that set out steps for the restoration of Haiti's democratically elected government by October 30 and the lifting of the international economic sanctions.[10] When those steps were not initiated, the Clinton administration, on

July 21, 1993, asked for U.N. approval for the invasion. Ten days later, on July 31, the U.N. Security Council voted 12-0, with two abstentions, to authorize the use of force against Haiti.[11]

On October 11, 1993, the USS *Harlan County*, an amphibious landing ship, was anchored eight hundred yards offshore of Port-au-Prince, Haiti. Its mission was to land two hundred American and Canadian troops, mostly military medics, engineers and civil affairs specialists.[12]

At the same time, a band of twenty-five to fifty men, some of them armed, appeared on the dock and protested the arrival of the troops to land. Guards at the dock refused to let Vicki Huddleston, Deputy Chief of Mission at the U.S. Embassy, enter the gate to the port. Then the mob became unruly and shoved the diplomats and reporters gathered for the scheduled docking. Once the thugs began punching and kicking their cars, they fled.[13]

As the ship waited offshore for two days, the question in Washington was whether the United States would look worse if the *Harlan County* hovered at sea, unable to land, or if there were pictures of it turning around and leaving. On Tuesday, October 12, the world was treated to a picture of the mighty United States sailing away from the clutch of rioters and withdrew to the U.S. military base at Guantanamo Bay, Cuba. It was a humiliating embarrassment for the United States. Lt. General Cédras set the tone for the resistance by laying flowers at the downtown statue of Jean-Jacques Dessalines, who destroyed an invading French force to win independence in 1804.[14]

As Clinton left the White House to speak at the University of North Carolina that evening, trying to look forceful in the face of his second humiliation in little over a week (the first one was Somalia), he said: "I want the Haitians to know that I am dead serious about seeing them honor the agreement they made."[15]

On October 30, 1993, Aristide remained in exile in the United States as the deadline for his return passed.[16]

The Congressional Black Caucus and other black leaders had had enough. On March 23, 1994, they went after President Clinton for abandoning his policy on Haiti and urged him to take stronger action to restore President Aristide to power. According to Rep. Maxine Waters (D-Calif), she had a message for the Clinton administration: "We have no faith in you. As a matter of fact, we're suspicious of you."[17]

Congress was divided on the issue. In May 1994, the House of Representatives voted 223-204 against a Haitian invasion. On July 31, 1994, the U.N. approved Resolution 940 to "use all necessary means" to oust Haitian military leader Cédras and his aides and restore President Aristide. Yet, a poll by ABC-News found that 73 percent of Americans wanted no part of Haiti.[18]

President Clinton had had enough. On September 15, 1994, Mr. Clinton held a televised speech on Haiti. He warned Haiti's military coup leaders to "leave now or we will force you from power."[19]

On September 17, 1994, former President Jimmy Carter, accompanied by retired General Colin Powell and Senator Sam Nunn, Georgia Democrat, arrived at Port-au-Prince airport to meet with Haiti's top three leaders to leave the island. They included Lt. Gen. Raoul Cédras, Brig. Gen. Philippe Biamby and Lt. Col. Michel François.[20]

By the next day, Mr. Carter telephoned Bill Clinton with the news that they had struck a deal and spelled out the terms. Despite Warren Christopher's objection, Clinton agreed to the last-ditch Carter peace deal. Originally, the negotiations with Lt. Gen. Cédras were strictly confined to when the military leader would relinquish power. Instead, once in Port-au-Prince, Mr. Carter freelanced, broadening discussions to include how Gen. Cédras' troops would greet a U.S. led peacekeeping force and when economic sanctions would end.[21]

According to a former State Department official, "The White House has got to be worried on how it looks when it has to turn to Jimmy Carter to solve a problem." It also demonstrated President Clinton's basic lack of confidence in his own foreign policy team.[22]

SOMALIA

In early December 1992, towards the end of the Bush administration, it had received a U.N. mandate to send American troops to Somalia to assist and secure the distribution of food aid for the starving people in the country. President-elect Clinton responded to the news: "I have felt for a long time that we should do more in Somalia. The thing I think is so heartening is that the United States is now taking the initiative .... I think it is high time. I'm encouraged, and I applaud the initiative of President Bush and his administration."[23]

On December 9, 1992, Operation Restore Hope began as U.S. military forces landed at Mogadishu with no resistance and secured the delivery of food and medical supplies essential for the survival of the civilian population. President Bush's goal was strictly a relief effort and at his insistence, they remained at all times under direct U.S. command.[24]

When Clinton took office, rather than winding down the mission, the mission wound up. In March 1993, the Clinton administration drafted and pushed through a resolution at the United Nations establishing a new, wide-ranging mandate. Somalia would be a test case for then-UN Ambassador Madeleine Albright's "assertive multilateralism." The warring factions would be disarmed, and the country would be made anew. The resolution called for the "reestablishment of national and regional institutions and civil administration in the entire country, [the] economic rehabilitation of Somalia, [and] conditions under which Somali civil society may have a role, at every level, in the process of political reconciliation." The Clinton administration was delusional.[25]

This wasn't just "mission creep," it was "nation-building." Albright believed that this action was a dawning of a new era. She claimed: "With this resolution we will embark on an unprecedented enterprise aimed at nothing less than the restoration of an entire country." Secretary of State Warren Christopher responded to the news in a cable to his ambassadors: "For the first time there will be a sturdy American role to help the U.N. rebuild a viable nation-state." Les Aspin was ecstatic: "We are staying there now to help those people rebuild their nation."[26]

On May 4, 1993, U.S. Marine Lt. Gen. Robert Johnston, handed over control of the relief mission to the U.N. "It's all yours," he told the new U.N. commander, a Turkish general, as he departed with most of his U.S. troops in tow. Operation Restore Hope ended. Clinton left forty-five hundred American men and women in Somalia to begin the United Nations Security Council operation UNOSOM II (United Nations Operation in Somalia), with enforcement powers and a mandate to disarm warring factions, in accordance with the Addis Ababa agreements of January 1993.[27]

On Wednesday May 5, 1993, the day after Johnston's troops left Somalia, President Clinton welcomed back a contingent of soldiers from Somalia. A little parade was arranged, in which the president marched with the servicemen, dressed in their camouflage uniforms, across the South Lawn. It wasn't clear where they were going, and it appeared awkward. Nevertheless, the scene was an attempt to show Clinton mixing comfortably with the military.²⁸ Clinton proclaimed: "General Johnston has just reported to me, 'Mission accomplished.'" Thus, the Bush mission to Somalia lasted five months, from December 1992 to May 1993.²⁹

Then the turning point began. The new mission antagonized the warlords, since it explicitly threatened the basis of their power. On June 5, 1993, twenty-five Pakistani soldiers contributing to the U.N. effort were attacked and killed by Mohammed Farah Aideed's militia. The Clinton administration had singled out Aideed as one of the chief barriers to peace in Somalia, and his attack on the Pakistani troops was the start of a situation that was sliding toward chaos. U.N. bases came under fire with mortars. U.S. helicopters suddenly came under attack by ground-fired missiles. Then the enemy snipers appeared, trying to pick off U.N. and American troops. The Clinton administration insisted that "engagement and enlargement" were to be achieved while the military presence itself was shrunk. This was obviously a recipe for disaster.³⁰

On June 17, 1993, Clinton held his first prime-time press conference. He began with an announcement that was designed to make headlines: "General Powell has reported to me this afternoon that this operation is over and that it was a success." He continued, "The United Nations, acting with the United States and other nations, has crippled the forces in Mogadishu of warlord Aideed." That was a lie.³¹

The next escalation of violence began on August 8, 1993, when a U.S. Army Humvee drove down a road in southern Mogadishu and hit a land mine. Four American military policemen were killed. They were among the first Americans murdered in Somalia. Clinton did nothing.³²

On August 22, 1993, another bomb exploded near a U.S. Army Humvee. In this attack, six Americans were wounded and their vehicle was destroyed. It was now obvious that Aideed's al Qaeda-trained men were serious about killing American troops. Within hours of the attack, the U.S. Army Rangers and America's elite Delta Force, combined as "Task Force Ranger," were ordered to deploy in Mogadishu.³³

Then the administration decided to pivot to a new approach: emphasizing a political settlement. Aideed, like every tyrant and killer around the globe in a confrontation against the United States, contacted Jimmy Carter, who urged Clinton to emphasize more diplomacy. Clinton approved the idea, and the State Department began to prepare for possible peace talks.³⁴ "The Pentagon's understanding of the policy," Clinton defense secretary Les Aspin would explain later, "was to move to more diplomatic efforts but snatch Aideed on the side, if you can." The policy, in other words, was half devoted to seeking a diplomatic accord with Aideed, and half devoted to attempting to capture or kill him.[35]

In the beginning of September 1993, Lieutenant General Thomas Montgomery, the military commander for Somalia, sent a request to Secretary Aspin for additional tanks. There was no response. At the same time, on orders from Khartoum, Sudan, the Islamic elite forces, under the banner of the Somali Islamic Union Party (SIUP), which were secretly in Somalia, were ready to engage the American forces. Although they had been preparing for combat even before the arrival of U.S. forces back in early December 1992, the SIUP forces had not intervened in the fighting until this point and had let Aideed conduct most of the fighting. On September 5, 1993, they joined the battle with Aideed's forces, and they ambushed the Nigerian contingent, which was part of the U.N. forces, killing seven soldiers.[36]

Then on September 10, 1993, the true escalation in the Islamist confrontation with U.S. forces started. The assault began with a series of diversionary attacks by the Islamist Habar Gidir tribal forces on Somalis that were considered friendly to the United Nations. The U.S.-U.N. forces intervened and fell into a trap. What appeared to be an intra-Somali clash suddenly turned into an organized ambush and attack on the U.N.-U.S. forces. The U.S. forces retaliated against the attack. The next day, September 11, 1993, U.S. forces attacked sites of Aideed's SNA forces. Aideed interpreted the attack as an intentional U.S. effort to affect the balance of power in Mogadishu.[37]

Two days later, on September 13, 1993, Cobra gunships began attacking Aideed's key sites, including a hospital that he used as his headquarters and a storage facility. Aideed's people claimed that civilians were killed in their attacks and they vowed revenge.[38]

The next day, September 14, 1993, Army Major General Thomas Montgomery "transmitted another call for help. He requested Bradley fighting vehicles, M-1 tanks, six artillery pieces and AC-130 gunships 'at the earliest feasible date.' 'I believe that U.S. forces are at risk without it,' "he said in his classified dispatch. General Joseph Hoar, commander of the U.S. Central Command that dispatched forces to Somalia, told General Montgomery, "There is no stomach in D.C. for new forces, but I think I can get something."[39]

Gen. Colin Powell, at the time chairman of the Joint Chiefs of Staff, was unable to get Aspin to approve the military's request. General Powell was "upset" when the matter was turned over to Frank Wisner, undersecretary of defense for policy, and other Pentagon civilians. "The policy shop was a mess with all those assistant secretaries overlapping each other," General Powell said. "Nothing happened."[40]

Mr. Wisner would later tell investigators that he misunderstood the purpose for the armor. He also said "there was no need to increase the violence nor increase the aggressiveness" of the U.S. special forces.[41]

Soon, there was another confrontation with Aideed. U.S. Rangers captured Osman Hassan Ali (Ato), Aideed's close friend and right-hand man. In response, Aideed ordered retaliatory attacks to deter future raids on his people. The Islamist terrorists and the SNA forces began ambushing American helicopters.[42]

On September 26, 1993, Somalis fired a rocket and shot down a U.S. UH-60 Black Hawk helicopter over Mogadishu. In the United States, the televised specter of the jubilant Somalian mob dragging the defiled bodies of American servicemen through the streets of Mogadishu, and the wreckage of the U.S. helicopter, brought home the extent of the debacle. For the Islamists and SNA forces, the clash served to ramp up further confrontations against the United States.[43]

By late September 1993, the Islamists considered the United States to be trapped in a Mogadishu quagmire, with some similarities to Vietnam. Aideed, growing more confident, instructed his troops to "be ready, in concert with our friends and allies, to get rid of the Western occupiers of our country [and] send American and Pakistani soldiers back home in coffins."[44]

On October 3, 1993, the improved capabilities of the Islamist-supported Somalis became evident. The U.N.-U.S. forces learned about the whereabouts of two of Aideed's senior foreign policy advisers, Osman Salah and Muhammad Hassan Awali, at the Olympic Hotel. About one hundred American troops with helicopter support was organized at the last minute and swiftly captured the two targets, as well as twenty-two other Aideed supporters on-site. What seemed a highly successful raid suddenly turned into a major confrontation. As the troops prepared for their departure by helicopter, they fell into a well-organized ambush by more than a thousand Islamist-supported Somalis. Two UH-60 helicopters were shot down, and a third crash landed at the Mogadishu airport. The American troops established a defensive perimeter around the crash site but were then surrounded and subjected to a sustained fire attack for about eleven hours until they were relieved by a U.S.-U.N. rescue force. In the firefight eighteen American troops were killed, seventy-eight wounded, and one helicopter pilot was captured. He would be released ten days later. At least seven hundred Somalis, both fighters and civilians, were injured in the fighting, and some three hundred of them were killed. It was the largest firefight the U.S. had been involved in since Vietnam. The next day, October 4, 1993, the bodies of dead American servicemen were dragged through the streets of Mogadishu. They also showed the frightened face of Chief Warrant Officer Michael Durant, a member of the Delta Force (this was not made known at the time), who was being held captive.[45]

The October 3 operation was the first major endeavor by Muhammad al-Zawahiri, the brother of Ayman al-Zawahiri, and his staff in the Mogadishu area. Additional Iranian senior advisers were on site, operating under the cover of journalists, with Aideed and his military commanders. There were also Iranians present, under the cover of journalists, which conducted interviews with Aideed on Radio Tehran and in Iranian magazines.[46]

On October 4, 1993, the day after the battle, Clinton was at the Fairmont Hotel, a landmark tower perched on San Francisco's Russian Hill. His trip to California was part of a multi-million-dollar campaign fund-raising tour. When he turned on the television, he saw what everyone in the United States had been seeing for hours. It was CNN footage of dead Americans being dragged through the streets of Mogadishu while a crowd of Somalis joyfully jumped up and down shouting "God is great."[47]

Clinton became upset that he believed the American people would hold him responsible for the eighteen deaths in Somalia. He was also angry with his foreign policy advisers whom he blamed for this humiliation. The White House went into damage control.[48]

At first, Clinton said the American soldiers had "lost their lives in a very successful mission against brutality and anarchy," and proclaimed, "you may be sure that we will do whatever's necessary . . . to complete our mission." That statement didn't sit well with the American people. Then, about a week later, even though his administration had authored the U.N. resolution advocating nation-building in Somalia, Clinton said: "It is not our job to rebuild Somalia's society." Then, in a CYA letter to Congress, the

White House began rewriting history: "The U.S. military mission is not now nor was it ever one of 'nation-building.' "[49]

The Black Hawk Down incident would shape the president's use of military action abroad in the future. Incur the least amount of risk and avoid actual combat. Four days after the Black Hawk Down failure, on October 7, 1993, Clinton announced the withdrawal of American combat troops and most logistical units. The U.S. role in Somalia would end by March 31, 1994.[50]

According to Lt. Col. Robert "Buzz" Patterson in his book, *Dereliction of Duty*: "In September 1994, we [U.S. troops] began our pullout from Mogadishu and the U.N. operation in Somalia. In less than four years, the world's most powerful military force had come from the historic successes in the Persian Gulf to being beaten by a ragtag group of thugs in Somalia, and all because of an administration that had no real, definable idea of what it was doing there and none of the military and foreign policy expertise requisite to complete a mission of this complexity. More significant, an Arab extremist whose name few Americans had ever heard—Osama bin Laden—had achieved a victory, and his international al-Qaeda terrorists, who were fighting alongside Aideed's thugs, were emboldened to strike again."[51]

KOSOVO

Kosovo was a province of Serbia that held a symbolic importance to the Serbs since the sixteen century. By the late 1980s, it had become 90 percent Albanian. In 1989, Serbian President Slobodan Milosevic revoked Kosovo's autonomous status and put it on a path to civil war.[52]

For the remaining 10 percent of the population, a reign of terrorist ethnic cleansing would soon begin, courtesy of the Kosovo Liberation Army (KLA), a militant Albanian group that the United States deemed "terrorist." The KLA began carrying out attacks in 1996-1997 on Serbian police and their families, a reign of terror against Slavic Orthodox churches and Orthodox Christians. Wells were poisoned and crops burned. The KLA also murdered Albanians allegedly collaborating with the Serbs. The KLA wanted an "ethnically pure" region and called for the expulsion of all Serbs. They also wanted to provoke the Serbs into a brutal response that would drag NATO into the war. The Serbs responded.[53]

By 1998, a full-scale civil war was ranging in Kosovo. The KLA controlled about 40 percent of the territory of the province. The KLA was reinforced by hundreds of Iranian fighters arriving via Albania. The key trainers and elite-unit fighters of the KLA included many veteran Afghans, Bosnians, Iranians, Algerians, Saudis, Egyptians, and even some Chechens who had fought in Afghanistan and Bosnia. That amounted to seven thousand mujahideen. Most of them were loyal to bin Laden and al-Zawahiri, and the financial and logistical system that allowed them to travel to Kosovo via Albania, was overseen by bin Laden.[54]

On September 23, 1998, the U.N. Security Council adopts Resolution 1199, demanding a cessation of hostilities in Kosovo and warning that "additional measures" to restore peace will be considered. Unfortunately, it did not stop the fighting. According to former Secretary of State Henry Kissinger, 80 percent of the cease-fire violations in the months before the NATO bombing campaign began were committed by the KLA.[55]

The U.S. and its NATO partners began a long series of negotiations to pressure the Serbian government to agree to a set of demands purportedly to end the ethnic violence in Kosovo. The deal, which was negotiated at Rambouillet, France, was the equivalent of unconditional surrender for the Yugoslavian government. When Milosevic refused, NATO bombed. On March 24, 1999, the day the bombing began, Clinton denounced Milosevic for rejecting "the balanced and fair peace accords that our allies and partners, including Russia, proposed [in February 1999], a peace agreement that Kosovo's ethnic Albanians courageously accepted." However, according to John Pilger, who reported for the British *New Statesman*, wrote: "Anyone scrutinizing the Rambouillet document is left in little doubt that the excuses given for the subsequent bombing were fabricated. The peace negotiations were stage-managed, and the Serbs were told: surrender and be occupied, or don't surrender and be destroyed.[56]

Mr. Clinton bombed for seventy-eight days. When the bombing started, then-White House Spokesman Joe Lockhart was asked if Mr. Clinton believed congressional support was "constitutionally necessary." Mr. Lockhart said, "Well, I don't think he believes it's constitutionally necessary because we don't believe that." Congress, in fact, declined to authorize it.[57]

This marked the first time that NATO forces had engaged in acts of war against a sovereign nation. It also violated the NATO treaty itself, which is purely defensive and calls on all NATO members to treat an attack on any other member as an attack on itself. Yugoslavia, the nation Clinton bombed, was neither a member of NATO, nor had it attacked a member of NATO.[58]

As the bombing continued, the *Los Angeles Times* detailed many of the "mistakes" made by U.S. and British war planes:

- April 5: An attack on a residential area in the mining town of Aleksinac kills 17 people.
- April 12: NATO missiles striking a railroad bridge near the Serbian town of Grdelica hit a passenger train, killing 17.
- April 14: 75 ethnic Albanian refugees die in an attack on a convoy near Djakovica.
- April 22: NATO bombed Serb television production facilities in downtown Belgrade killing 16 people.
- April 27: A missile strike in the Serbian town of Surdulica kills at least 20 civilians.
- May 1: A missile hits a bus crossing a bridge north of Pristina, killing 47.
- May 7: A cluster bomb attack damages a marketplace and the grounds of a hospital in Nis, killing at least 15.
- May 8: Fighter pilots using outdated maps attack the Chinese Embassy in Belgrade, killing 3 journalists and injuring 20 other people.
- May 13: 87 ethnic Albanian refugees are killed and more than 100 injured in a late-night NATO bombing of a Kosovo village, Korisa.
- May 20: At least three people are killed when NATO missiles hit a hospital in Belgrade.
- May 21: NATO bombs a Kosovo jail, killing at least 19 people and injuring scores.
- May 31: NATO missiles slam into a bridge crowded with market-goers and cars in central Serbia, killing at least nine people and wounding 28.[59]

When questions were being raised about the civilian casualties, NATO spokesmen responded by bragging even louder about how smart the bombs were that they were dropping. Imagine if Serbian terrorists had blown up hospitals, schools, bridges, neighborhoods in the United States, at the same rate that NATO hit the same targets in Serbia, the American people would have viewed the war differently. According to *Human Rights Watch*, at least five hundred civilians were killed by NATO bombing. The Serbian newspaper, the *Yugoslavia,* claimed that two thousand civilians were killed.[60]

On June 10, 1999, when it became clear that the Russians weren't going to stand by Milosevic, NATO and the Serbian government reached an agreement to end the conflict. Clinton could now claim victory, or was it a victory?[61]

Consistent with his tilt towards Islam everywhere in the world, Bill Clinton had gotten the United States in a war against Christian Serbians. The United States was now on the side of Albanian Muslims trying to set an Islamic State in Europe, in the Serbian province of Kosovo. The United States was now on the side of the Muslim KLA, which was supported by Muslim radicals in the Middle East, including Hamas and Osama Bin Laden, which were enemies of the United States.[62]

NORTH KOREA

For the entire half century since the Truman Administration, U.S. policy had stood firm against the self-appointed Communists Kim Il-Sung and his son, Kim Jong-Il. To the very last day of the Bush administration, North Korea received no U.S. aid, subsidies, or trade. Thus, Clinton's initiation of U.S. taxpayer subsidies for North Korea, and his plan to completely normalize relations with this bizarre and dangerous Communist country, was a radical break with longstanding American policy.[63]

North Korea, which freely signed the Nuclear Nonproliferation Treaty (NPT), was required to allow two kinds of inspections of its potential nuclear facilities: regular inspections of self-declared nuclear sites and challenge inspections of sites undeclared by the host country but suspected by the world of harboring nuclear bomb work.[64]

According to reporter Bill Gertz in his book *Betrayal*: "It was clear from the beginning of the Clinton administration that the North Koreans had no intention of limiting its nuclear program to producing electrical power. In February 1993, North Korean technicians at Yongbyon, north of the capital of Pyongyang, reprocessed spent fuel from a nuclear reactor to create plutonium out of the fuel rods used in the reactor. The North Koreans claimed they produced only one hundred grams of plutonium, but it became obvious to nuclear experts working for International Atomic

Energy Director Hans Blix that the North Koreans had at least the eight kilograms necessary for one nuclear warhead, and probably more."[65]

On November 7, 1993, Clinton made a major announcement: "North Korea cannot be allowed to develop a nuclear bomb." A few months later, the administration began back-tracking, and within a few months, administration officials were saying that Clinton had "misspoken." Secretary of Defense William Perry explained: "Our policy right along has been oriented to try to keep North Korea from getting a *significant* nuclear weapons capability." That statement suggested that North Korea would be allowed to keep any nukes it had already built.[66]

Then, the administration began to have harsh words for the International Atomic Energy Agency (IAEA). It stemmed from the fact that Hans Blix was much tougher and more demanding against North Korea than the U.S. government. One Clinton official denounced Blix as a "fanatic," while Clinton official Robert Gallucci condescendingly spoke of the IAEA as having "medieval or perhaps Talmudic" operations.[67]

By late 1993, when the IAEA demanded challenge inspections of two North Korean waste dumps for evidence of weapons-grade plutonium, North Korea refused. It then announced that it would not allow regular inspections either.[68]

In January 1994, the Clinton administration capitulated to the North Koreans by allowing only a one-time inspection of seven declared sites. In return, the U.S. canceled its "Team Spirit" exercises with South Korea. The results of the deal:

* NPT was dead.
* North Korea broke the deal and got a huge payoff from the United States, not for returning to it, but pretending to.
* North Korea's nuclear program proceeded unmolested.[69]

In the spring of 1994, Blix reported that inspectors at Yongbyon had spotted a second reprocessing facility in an advanced state of construction that had never been inspected. The North Koreans refused to let the inspectors into the second site. By June 1994, Blix was convinced the North Koreans had amassed enough plutonium to make nuclear weapons. "North Korea has more plutonium than it has reported," Blix said.[70]

On June 13, 1994, North Korean Foreign Minister Kim Yong Nam sent a diplomatic note to Secretary of State Warren Christopher, announcing that the International Atomic Energy Agency "has jeopardized the supreme interests of the DPRK, flagrantly encroached upon its sovereign rights and dignity, and created such a circumstance which makes it impossible for the DPRK to maintain normal relations with the IAEA any longer . . . I have been authorized to inform . . . the Government of the United States of America, the depository government, that the Government of the Democratic People's Republic of Korea has decided to withdraw from the International Atomic Energy Agency as of June 13, 1994."[71]

According to Bill Gertz President Clinton's response was "an attempt to appease the North Koreans with negotiations in Geneva, which began in the summer of 1994. The negotiations were nearly scuttled at the last minute by former President Jimmy Carter. Carter—in his role as a self-styled international peacemaker—launched his own private diplomatic mission to Pyongyang and began making promises for the U.S. government, such as claiming the United States would not seek sanctions against North Korea over the nuclear program. Asked if the president was willing to put off sanctions, as Carter had promised, an angry Clinton snapped at reporters, 'No, I gave my position yesterday.' The United States would not forgo sanctions until there was an acceptable agreement from the North Koreans."

"What is President Carter talking about?" he was then asked.

"None of us have talked directly with President Carter," Clinton said. "We don't know what he said."

"President Clinton," Gertz wrote, "had done nothing to stop the former president from conducting his own foreign policy without even consulting the White House. The incident revealed the president and his advisers to be amateurs. The president had been threatening to go to war with North Korea over the nuclear problem, posing great risks to the lives of thousands of soldiers and millions of civilians, and allowed former President Carter to meddle in important matters of state without authorization."[72]

In early October 1994, the *New York Times* reported: "After weeks of watching in silent frustration as the United States tries to negotiate a halt to North Korea's nuclear program, President Kim Young Sam of South Korea lashed out at the Clinton administration today in an interview for what he characterized as a lack of knowledge and an over eagerness to compromise. Mr. Kim directly attacked Washington's basic stance in the discussions with

North Korea as naïve and overly flexible. He said that the North Korean government was on the verge of an economic and political crisis that could sweep it from power, and that Washington should therefore stiffen its position in pressing Pyongyang to abandon its suspected nuclear weapons program."[73]

Instead, on October 21, 1994, the Clinton administration allowed itself to get intimidated into a deal. It was called the Agreed Framework, which was ideal for Pyongyang. Enclosed is what President Clinton gave up to the Stalinist regime:

- $263 million in food from 1996 to 1998
- $146 million in fuel oil from 1995 to 1998
- $198 million in food commitments for 1999
- $55 million in fuel commitments for 1999
- Two "safe" nuclear reactors to be built by 2005[74]

Also, according to the deal Clinton cut with the North Koreans, the United States was required to ship five hundred thousand metric tons of oil to North Korea each year until the promised reactors were completed, sometime between 2003 and 2005. That oil was valued at over $60 million.[75]

Unfortunately, North Korea's missile proliferation dramatically accelerated after this agreement was implemented. There were no known No-dong missile sales abroad until after the 1994 Agreed Framework. For example:

- It sold technology to Iran for the Shahab missile that now threatens U.S. forces across the Middle East.
- It sold technology to Pakistan for the Ghauri missile that in 1998 disrupted the fragile stability of South Asia.[76]

On February 17, 1996, while giving a speech in Rochester, New York, President Clinton said: "Our diplomacy backed with force persuaded North Korea to freeze its nuclear program." Unfortunately, that was a false statement.[77]

Five days earlier, on February 12, 1996, Communist Party official Hwang Jang-yop, the chief ideologist for the ruling Korean Worker's Party, defected by walking into the South Korean embassy in Beijing. It set off a major diplomatic confrontation in the Chinese capital that lasted for almost a month.[78] Hwang was a member of the ruling inner circle in North Korea. In his capacity, he had unprecedented access to what was occurring in North Korea, and he revealed that the North Koreans planned to turn South Korea into a "sea of flames."[79]

"Hwang had another startling revelation for the West that was not made public either by the South Koreans or by the Clinton administration," wrote Gertz. The revelation became known only when a secret U.S. intelligence report based on Hwang's testimony was disclosed by Bill Gertz on June 5, 1997. "In the April 1996 debriefings in South Korea, Hwang disclosed that North Korea already possessed nuclear weapons and had planned to conduct an underground nuclear test—the final step in nuclear weapons development. According to Hwang, the North Korean Foreign Ministry had argued against the provocative action in order to avoid arousing new suspicions about the secret nuclear weapons program, because a test of a nuclear device would end all speculation about the covert effort by Pyongyang. The intelligence tip, once exposed, prompted further investigations into the North Korean nuclear program, which helped uncover the secret underground facility at Kumchangni several months later."[80]

According to Gertz:

> Hwang also revealed new information about North Korea's huge chemical and biological weapons arsenal, describing the chemicals as 'high grade' deadly poisons, including nerve agents, blistering agents, and blood agents.
>
> On July 8, 1998, before the Senate Finance Committee, Albright testified that the nuclear accord has "frozen North Korea's dangerous nuclear weapons program." But that was not all. She had fed this line to Congress several times previously. As far back as February 12, 1997, Albright had said this to the House Appropriations Committee: "The Framework Agreement is one of the best things the administration has done because it stopped a nuclear weapons program in North Korea." Later, on February 10, 1998, she defended the request for $35 million to fund the agreement's implementation organization, stating that the funds were needed to "secure continued DPRK compliance with its non-proliferation obligations." And on March 4, 1998, she

told the House Foreign Operations Appropriations Committee that the agreement "has succeeded in freezing North Korea's dangerous nuclear program."

When, in August 1998, Albright was confronted by angry senators who questioned her about the new intelligence on Kumchangni, she said that she had not learned about the new evidence until July. Sitting in the room with her was Army Lieutenant General Patrick Hughes, director of the Defense Intelligence Agency in charge of the special access program to monitor North Korean nuclear weapons development. Hughes politely interrupted her. "Madame Secretary, that is incorrect," Hughes said. The Defense Intelligence Agency had reached its conclusions that North Korea was still building a new underground nuclear facility some eighteen months before and had provided the information to Albright's office. Albright was silent.[81]

The administration was eventually allowed to inspect the facility at Kumchangni in early 1999, but it came at a price. The North Koreans initially demanded $300 million in exchange for the inspection. Instead, it settled on receiving several hundred thousand tons of grain from the U.S. The administration denied that it had cut a deal with the North Koreans. That was a lie. A North Korean official would later explain: "There was sufficient debate on and agreement on the payment of the 'inspection fee.' The United States, though belatedly . . . decided to adopt politico-economic measures as demanded by the DPRK." The South Korean government confirmed the North Korean account. This illustrated that Pyongyang was more forthcoming in this instance than the Clinton administration.[82]

On December 8, 1998, after four years of Clinton-Gore-directed U.S. foreign aid, North Korean Defense Ministry officials publicly announced they were "ready to annihilate U.S. imperialists," and said they would "plunge the damned U.S. territory into a sea of flame."[83]

On February 25, 1999, testifying before the House International Relations Committee, Secretary of State Albright finally admitted: "We have suspicions that North Korea has engaged in construction activities that could constitute a violation of its commitment to freeze its nuclear-related facilities under the Agreed Framework."[84]

On March 11, 1999, the *Washington Times* reported publicly on a Department of Energy intelligence report widely available within the Clinton administration that, "North Korea is working on uranium enrichment techniques" for nuclear weapons, reporter Bill Gertz plainly stated.[85]

Alarmed by the potential consequences of the Clinton administration's willful blindness toward North Korea's work on nuclear weapons, Republican House Speaker Dennis Hastert commissioned a group of House leaders and committee chairman to evaluate U.S. policy toward North Korea. The Speaker's Advisory Group on North Korea, on which Rep. Chris Cox served, concluded in its November 1999 report that "North Korea's WMD [weapons of mass destruction] programs pose a major threat to the United States and its allies . . . . There is significant evidence that undeclared nuclear weapons development activity continues, including efforts to acquire uranium enrichment technologies and recent nuclear-related high explosives."[86]

On July 16, 1999, *Human Events* reported that two senior South Korean officials have claimed that the North Koreans are building a hardened missile launch site on the backside of a mountain only a few miles from the Chinese border. The launch site is reportedly configured to accept the Taepo Dong-1, which can reach Hawaii and Alaska, and the developing Taepo Dong-2, which could reach deep into the continental United States. The site is strategically positioned to make a U.S. or Southern Korean attack against it difficult.[87]

On September 17, 1999, in a joint press conference with Secretary of State Albright, former Defense Secretary William Perry announced the U.S. is ready to make even greater concessions to stave off the North Korean threat. "We must deal with the North Korean government as it is, not as we wish it would be," he began. Perry then announced that the U.S. would lift economic sanctions and allow U.S. companies to invest in North Korea, if it *promised* to temporarily suspend testing its latest long-range missile, which it's developing jointly with the Islamic Republic of Iran. "If, on the other hand, North Korea demonstrates, by its actions, that it's not willing to forego those dangerous programs," Perry continued, "then we have to pursue an alternate strategy. We have to take the actions necessary to protect our own security."[88]

For nearly a week, Perry and Albright waited anxiously for the North Koreans to respond publicly to the U.S. offer. Finally, on September 24, 1999, a North Korean Foreign Ministry spokesman announced that his government had agreed to halt missile testing, but only for as long as "meetings with the United States are taking place." Basically, North Korea reserved the right to resume tests if it felt slighted by the United States. Despite any tangible progress in the negotiations, the administration decided to lift the sanctions on North Korea without any specific agreement on a missile moratorium."[89]

In June 2000, the Japanese and Chinese were able to confirm reports of another underground uranium processing plant in Choma, about seventeen miles away from Kumchangni.[90]

Clinton's final gesture to North Korea was to send Albright to Pyongyang in October 2000 on a first-ever official U.S. visit. This gave Kim Jong Il his long-sought-after legitimacy. Nothing was actually accomplished, but Kim and Albright clinked wine glasses and exchanged starry eyes. As Albright told PBS's Jim Lehrer: "Basically, you know, we've had such weird stories about him, but it turns out that we had very good discussions. . . . And he seems pragmatic . . . not hostile."[91]

As the Clinton administration ended on January 20, 2001, U.S. citizens and soldiers were still undefended against a missile attack because of the policies of President Clinton. In the president's view, having an agreement limiting arms took precedence over building missile defense systems that could defend the growing threat of long-range missiles, especially from rogue states like North Korea and Iran. There were also other concerns coming from nuclear powers like Russia or China, which had exponentially advanced its offensive weapons capability while Clinton was president. The lack of missile defense system was a betrayal to the American people, especially if in the future, a rogue nation is successful launching a long-range missile armed with a nuclear, chemical, or biological weapon warhead which will be able to reach the United States.[92]

RWANDA

In Rwanda, there had been atrocities committed between the Government of the Republic of Rwanda (the Hutus, which comprised about 85 percent of the Rwandans) on one side and the Rwandese Patriotic Front (the Tutsis, which comprised 15 percent of the Rwandans) on the other side. One of the causes of the violence was that the minority Tutsis actually controlled Rwanda up until 1961 through their cooperation with the country's colonial masters. There was an initial ceasefire agreement signed at Arusha on July 12, 1992. Then there was the Protocols of Agreement on Power-Sharing signed at Arusha on January 9, 1993. Then, the Protocol of Agreement on the repatriation of Rwandese refugees and the Resettlement of Displaced Persons was signed at Arusha on June 9, 1993. A U.N. peacekeeping force was set up to enforce the agreements. The debate over the exact composition and mandate of the force, however, came just as the fighting in Somalia began to escalate.[93]

On October 5, 1993, two days after the Black Hawk Down incident, the U.N. Security Council voted on the composition of the peacekeeping force. Suddenly, saving Rwanda from a renewed escalation of fighting didn't seem important. The U.N. officials that were actually on the ground, understood the potential of horrible violence, and requested eight thousand troops. The western countries of the U.N. recommended three thousand troops. The Clinton administration wanted to send only one hundred troops. The U.N. settled on 2,548 troops, who would be stationed to the capital of Kigali.[94]

The whiff of mass murder had been in the air by January 1994. Unfortunately, the mass killings still might have been prevented. Maj. Gen. Roméo Dallaire, who would become the U.N. commander on the ground, arrived in Rwanda at the end of 1993. As luck would have it, Dallaire found a "top level" informant in the Rwandan militia. He told Dallaire where the militia's weapon caches were located, and of plans to use the weapons to exterminate the Tutsis. Dallaire immediately cabled Kofi Annan, then the chief of U.N. peacekeeping, requesting permission to place the informant and his family under protection and then evacuate them from Rwanda. Annan, unfortunately, made a horrible decision and disagreed. He told Dallaire he could neither seize the weapons, nor offer asylum to the informant. Instead he told Dallaire to share his information with Rwandan President Habyarimana, even though the informant had said the weapons were to be used in Habyarimana's own campaign to exterminate the Tutsis. In effect, the U.N. was now an accomplice to mass murder.[95]

On April 4, 1994, a plane carrying Rwandan president Juvenal Habyarimana, a Hutu, was shot down. His death was a trigger for Hutu extremists who wanted to scuttle the Arusha agreements and kill all the Tutsis. The Hutus almost immediately began their genocide.[96]

On April 7, 1994, ten U.N. Belgian soldiers were encircled by Hutus and ordered to give up their weapons. When they radioed their superiors for instructions, they were told to surrender their weapons. The Hutus then tortured and chopped them to pieces, eventually dumping a collection of body parts at the Kigali hospital. The savagery was calculated to horrify the U.N. It worked.[97]

Dalliare immediately requested reinforcements. He pleaded for another twenty-five hundred troops, which would bring his troop strength to about five thousand. He believed he could bring the killings to a halt with that force. No additional reinforcements arrived. By April 21, 1994, two weeks went by and one hundred thousand were murdered. Unfortunately, on the same day, the U.N. Security Council voted to reduce the U.N. force by 90 percent, leaving it with only 270 troops. Madeleine Albright, then the U.S. ambassador to the U.N., opposed leaving even that token force. With the death toll in Rwanda continuing to rise, the Security Council decided, in May 1994, to vote again. This time, Albright got the vote postponed for four days. Meanwhile, the death toll kept increasing.[98]

The following month, June 1994, without any imminent U.N. action, eight African nations announced that they would intervene in Rwanda if the Clinton administration would provide them with fifty armored personnel carriers. The White House responded that it would. Then, instead of turning the vehicles over to the Africans, the White House decided to rent them to the U.N. for $15 million. Then, the armored personnel carriers sat on a runway in Germany, while the U.N. negotiated for a $5 million reduction in the rental charge. Eventually the White House agreed to the reduction, but by then there was another problem. There were no planes available to transport the vehicles. The personnel carriers didn't arrive in Uganda until the end of June 1994, and not in Rwanda until August 1994. By then the Rwandese Patriotic Front (Tutsis) had conquered the country and the genocide was over.[99]

On July 12, 1994, the International Red Cross made the grim announcement that the genocide had taken one million lives.[100]

The Clinton administration did not offer stern words or impose sanctions nor authorized deployment of additional U.S. troops to the multinational U.N. force. The Clinton administration officials blamed the "Somalia Syndrome," and they did not want to send in more troops into more humanitarian missions after the disastrous retreat from Mogadishu, Somalia in late 1993.[101]

Later, President Clinton expressed deep regret. "I feel terrible," he said at one appearance, "because I think we could have sent 5,000 or 10,000 troops and saved a couple hundred thousand lives. I think we could have saved about half of them [400,000 lives]."[102]

CHAPTER 14

HEALTH CARE REFORM

We are basically taking the billions and billions of dollars we spend on financing health care and dropping it in a black hole as far as I'm concerned.
—First Lady Hillary Rodham Clinton,
February 1994[1]

During the presidential primary, the reason candidate Bill Clinton proposed a health care plan was that the issue was the centerpiece of Bob Kerrey's campaign in New Hampshire. Kerrey was proposing a Canadian style single-payer system to be paid for through taxes. Clinton responded with a jerry-built plan, made up of a variety of ideas that were thrown together to get him through New Hampshire. Clinton wasn't pleased with his proposal, and he avoided talking about health care through the rest of the nominating contest.[2]

In early January 1993, President-elect Clinton decided that Ira Magaziner, a businessman and friend of Bill's would run the health care effort. Magaziner had gotten to know Clinton at Oxford, where he organized protests against the Vietnam War. Magaziner wanted someone with authority to keep the project on track within the government. Clinton replied that Hillary would do that.[3]

As President Clinton prepared to govern, health care took on increasing importance for the American people. Polling would eventually show that health care was a major reason people had voted for him. If he was able to pull off scrapping and rebuilding the American health care system, Clinton would create a massive Democratic coalition.[4]

Going back to their days in Arkansas, the Clintons had come up with a simple strategy to advance their policy agenda. Whenever there was opposition to them, they would demonize the individuals or companies that opposed them. For the health care fight, the Clintons would attack the "greedy hospitals, greedy doctors and greedy insurance companies," as a campaign advisor put it.[5]

In February 1993, shortly after the election, the Clintons began publicly attacking pharmaceutical companies for allegedly charging exorbitant prices for their products and defrauding consumers. Magaziner actually told an insurance company lobbyist that by portraying pharmaceutical companies, doctors, and insurers as the "enemy," it would help sell the health care plan. During a speech at a Virginia clinic in the same month (February 1993), Bill Clinton said: "The pharmaceutical industry is spending $1 billion more each year on advertising and lobbying than it does on developing new or better drugs. Meanwhile, its profits are rising at four times the rate of the average *Fortune* 500 company. Compared to other countries, our prices are shocking."[6]

Wall Street began to have concerns about the new health care plan. Once it became public that price controls on medicines would be central to the administration's plan, the stock prices of pharmaceutical firms began to nosedive. According to a study from the Catalyst Institute, pharmaceutical stock prices plummeted over 27 percent, relative to the rest of the stock market between the period of January 1 and September 9, 1993. The negative rhetoric was criticized as irresponsible for draining half of the equity out of the pharmaceutical industry and driving down the value of biotech stocks. Another negative side effect was the decline of new capital sources for the biotech industry. This hurt research and thus, the development of new life-saving drugs.[7]

On June 23, 1993, opposition to President Clinton's health care reform began. A group of eight-four Democratic congressmen sponsored a bill to create a government-run health system, a so-called single-payer approach. But, when lawmakers went to the White House to lobby for a single-payer system, Hillary Rodham Clinton gave no encouragement the administration would shift gears. Later, White House press secretary Dee Dee Myers reinforced the administration position. While the Clinton plan is likely to give states flexibility, she said, "We have said repeatedly that we're not pursuing a single-payer plan."[8]

In mid-August 1993, Clinton was besieged by members of his administration who warned him that the deficit would be in danger of exploding if he continued to listen to Hillary on health care reform. The plan she was developing as too big and too costly. They advised that his presidency would be successful only if he would scale back the plan and agree on a more manageable and incremental approach. Frustrated, Clinton responded that he would reach a final decision after his vacation at Martha's Vineyard.[9]

After the Clintons returned from their vacation, Bill stood in front of the cameras and explained the relationship between health care, his economic plan, and deficit reduction. "Our competitiveness, our whole economy, the integrity of the way the government works, and ultimately, our living standards, depend upon our ability to achieve savings without harming the quality of health care." Then he took a blue plastic card, which was the size of a credit card, out of his pocket. He continued: "Every American would receive a health care security card that will guarantee a comprehensive package of benefits over the course of an entire lifetime, roughly comparable to the benefit package offered by most *Fortune* 500 companies."[10]

The Health Insurance Association of America (HIAA) is an insurance industry lobbying group that had filmed a series of ads featuring an ordinary middle-class couple named Harry and Louise. They spoke of their concerns about how the new health care reform would affect them. On September 22, 1993, the day President Clinton was to give a speech to a joint session of Congress, the group offered to cancel its ad campaign, provided the concerns of the insurance industry got a more respectable hearing from Mr. Magaziner and Mrs. Clinton. The White House did not bother to reply to the HIAA.[11]

As the ads hit the airwaves, Hillary became frustrated and dismissed as "non-sense" claims that health insurance premiums would rise under the new health care plan. In a speech attended by twenty-one hundred doctors from the American Academy of Pediatricians, Mrs. Clinton said: "They have the gall to run TV ads [claiming] there is a better way—the very industry that has brought us to the brink of bankruptcy because of the way they have financed health care." Interestingly, an employee of the Democratic National Committee actually called up the actress who played Louise in the ad and tried to talk her into denouncing them. When the actress declined, the DNC staffer threatened to see that she never worked in the industry again.[12]

The reply to the Harry and Louise ads was a media campaign that attacked the insurance companies but did little or nothing to answer the public's questions about what the reforms would mean to them, especially when every citizen would be subject to civil and criminal penalties under the enforcement provisions of the plan.[13]

Soon, Bill joined Hillary in lambasting the pharmaceutical industry for imaginary offenses. This had the immediate effect of causing those companies to lose billions of dollars in value and forcing them to lay off employees. Hillary displayed no particular concern that her health care proposal would cause people to lose jobs. She dismissed the concerns of a young, female independent insurance agent with the biting put-down: "I'm sure someone obviously as brilliant as you could find something else to do." That was not the voice of Marie Antoinette, it was closer to Robespierre.[14]

On September 29, 1993, Mrs. Clinton began three days of lobbying on Capitol Hill to redesign America's health care system. Most of the lawmakers treated her with kid gloves. The only outburst occurred when Rep. Dick Armey, (R-TX), who previously had sniffed at the concept of a "government-run health care system" and had once referred to Hillary's health care plan as "a Dr. Kevorkian prescription" for American jobs. vowed to make the ensuing debate "as exciting as possible." Mrs. Clinton responded, "I am sure you will do that, you and Dr. Kevorkian." Armey though, got in the last word. "The reports of your charm are overstated, and the reports of your wit are understated," he said.[15]

On September 30, 1993, Elizabeth McCaughy wrote about some of the things that troubled her:

> Under the Clinton plan, most Americans will not be able to hold onto their personal physician or buy the kind of insurance that 77 percent of Americans now choose. Such fee-for-service insurance allows them to pick a doctor, go to a specialist when they feel they need one, get a second opinion if they have doubts and select the hospital they think is best.
> The Clinton plan will make almost all Americans buy basic health coverage through the 'regional alliance' where they live. Regional

alliances are huge, government monopolies that will purchase basic health care for everyone in the area. Unless you now receive health care through Medicare, military or veterans benefits, or unless you or your spouse works for a large company, the law will require you to buy basic health coverage from the limited choice offered by your alliance. It will be illegal to buy it elsewhere.

Under the plan, the federal government will set ceilings on how much each regional alliance can spend on payments to insurers and HMOs annually. The goal is to limit private health care spending. Alliances can reject any health insurance option that would push spending through the ceiling. Fee-for-service insurance, which tends to be more costly than HMO coverage, will be the first to go.

Finally, McCaughey puts the Clinton plan in perspective: "The Clinton plan is coercive. It takes personal health choices away from patients and families, and it also imposes a system of financing health care based on regional alliances that will make racial tensions fester and produce mean-spirited political struggles and lawsuits to shirk the cost of medical care for the urban poor.[16]

Soon, some budget analysts on Capitol Hill had concerns that the proposal contains some fiscal time bombs. "Over the last quarter of a century, we have all been wrong" in predicting the true cost of entitlement programs, Sen. Daniel Patrick Moynihan (D-N.Y.) warned Hillary Rodham Clinton during a Senate hearing. He was talking about the past efforts to forecast programs such as Medicare, Medicaid, Social Security, veteran's payments, student loans and farm price supports. Those forecasts have proved dismal failures. For example, when Congress enacted Medicare legislation in 1965 to expand health care coverage to the elderly, government actuaries predicted annual costs of $9 billion by 1990. Instead, the program cost $106 billion that year. Medicaid, also enacted in 1965, was intended to be a limited program with an unusual budget of about $1 billion by 1992. Medicaid actual costs topped $76 billion, an increase many times the rate of inflation.[17]

On December 18, 1993, the full 1,342-page Health Security Act had become public. In addition to providing health security, it also was also going to provide a litany of fines and prison sentences for everyone involved in health care—Physicians, health alliance and health plan employees, lawyers, drug manufacturers, medical suppliers and even patients—if they didn't comply.[18]

The only hope for the plan, which was a longshot, was to build a groundswell of public support and force a bill through Congress before the opposition got organized. Even within the administration, the health care plan had almost no support. Prominent critics included Health and Human Services Secretary Donna Shala, Alice Rivlin of the Office of Management and Budget, and Treasury Secretary Lloyd Bentsen.[19]

The bad news continued. On February 3, 1994, the U.S. Chamber of Commerce refused to support Clinton's health care reform bill, specifically the part that required companies to pay for their workers' health insurance. Even President Clinton's Council of Economic Advisers concluded that job losses from the plan would be at least 600,000. Other estimates put the figure as high as 2.1 million jobs lost.[20]

In early June 1994, the HIAA brought back its "Harry and Louise" campaign for another month's run, this time targeting provisions in the Clinton plan that would impose backup controls on health care spending and require standard premiums for all those insured. Pro-reform groups fought back but were badly outspent. On June 10, 1994, Magaziner attempted to mobilize the White House for its final fight. He drafted a five-page confidential memo—titled simply Where Do We Go From Here?—for Bill Clinton and his top advisers. It was Magaziner's attempt to sound the "panic alarm."[21]

On July 19, 1994, Bill Clinton addressed the summer meeting of the National Governors' Association in Boston. He stunned reporters and White House aides by declaring that his bottom-line demand for universal coverage can be satisfied by a "phased-in deliberate effort" to expand the ranks of the insured from the current 85 percent to "somewhere in the ballpark of ninety-five percent upwards." As if that was not enough, Clinton also said he was "open to any solution" on how to pay for more coverage and that "there may be some other way for an employer mandate to do this." Chaos quickly spread as the White House scrambled to erase the impression that he had backed down.[22]

On the evening of July 21, 1994, with the President's health care plan in trouble, Democratic leaders traveled to the White House to inform Clinton that their bill could not pass and that the leaders would try to wrest some new health care plan from the Congress. Administration officials, with straight faces, called this a "relaunch" of the health care bill, the third or fourth, depending on how one counted.[23]

The next day, on July 22, 1994, trying to win back the kind of political support that brought them to the White House, the administration planned a bus trek across America to generate their own grassroots message to Congress for reform. A kickoff rally in Portland, Oregon, was marred by anti-Clinton protesters. When the first buses reached the highway, they found hitched to a tow truck a broken-down bus wreathed in red tape labeled "This is Clinton Health Care. It symbolized government bureaucracy.[24]

On July 24, 1994, in an interview with Newt Gingrich (R-GA), the *New York Times* reported that Gingrich had united the House Republicans against the passage of health reform and hoped "to use the issue as a springboard to win Republican control of the House." Gingrich went on to predict that Republicans would pick up thirty-four House seats in the November elections and that half a dozen disaffected Democrats will switch parties to give Republicans control. The story attracted little attention.[25]

On July 30, 1994, the bus caravan rolled into Independence, Missouri, and was met by President Clinton, Mrs. Clinton, Vice President Al Gore, and his wife, Tipper Gore. They came to energize the Health Security Express bus tour. Mr. Clinton used the symbolism of former President Truman's hometown, who also introduced a national health insurance plan in 1948. It was defeated in Congress.[26]

At the event Clinton was greeted by thousands of protestors shouting "no," "liar" and "go home." Many of the protestors came to Independence at the request of talk-show host Rush Limbaugh. Some of the signs at the protest read, "Rush rules"; "It's socialism, stupid"; and "What public health clinic will Chelsea go to?"[27]

The buses arrived in Washington, D.C., on August 3, 1994, and Clinton gave an emotional address in the White House Rose Garden. It was timed to coincide on the day Democratic Majority Leader George Mitchell introduced his health care "rescue" in the Senate and Democratic Majority Leader Gephardt introduced his bill in the House. Mitchell's compromise was much less bureaucratic and government-driven than the Clinton plan. It put off any requirement that employers provide employees health insurance until early in the next century. It made a major concession to small businesses by exempting any employer with twenty-five or fewer employees from providing coverage. And it aimed at guaranteeing insurance for 95 percent of Americans by the year 2000.[28]

On August 16, 1994, the final round of "Harry and Louise" commercials began airing nationally. At the same time, the final outpouring of faxes, phone calls, and letters mounted by the small-business lobby flooded Washington offices. Nine days later Democratic leaders of both congressional chambers gave up on health care and announced they were letting their members go home for their much-postponed vacation. Neither the Senate (where Democrats outnumbered Republicans 56 to 44) nor the House (with a Democratic majority of 257 to 176) came close to passing, or even voting on, any health bill.[29]

On September 19, 1994, Congress reconvened. Mitchell hoped to set aside four days for Senate debate on the new mainstream bill and then schedule a straight up-or-down vote. Republicans began mobilizing for a filibuster to keep the bill from reaching the floor. Supporters realized they didn't have enough votes to break the filibuster.[30]

On September 26, 1994, Mitchell announced that, "It is clear that health insurance reform cannot be enacted this year." It perished without even one test vote.[31]

On November 2, 1994, President Clinton replaced Hillary Rodham Clinton and Ira Magaziner as his coordinators for his health care reform. Domestic Policy Advisor Carol Rasco and Robert E. Rubin, the head of the National Economic Council, would now head the Clinton administration's second attempt at health care reform. Any decisions of the 1995 health care package was going to wait until after the midterm elections.[32]

CHAPTER 15

1993 STUMBLES PART II

I'll tell you what went wrong. What went wrong was I was not able to keep the public focus on the issues that we're working on after I gave the State of the Union address, even though that's what we kept doing.

—President Clinton, 1993[1]

GENERAL LOSES HIS JOB

On May 24, 1993, at a thirteen-dollar-a-plate, off-base Air Force awards banquet for Air Force maintenance workers stationed at Soesterberg Air Base, Netherlands, Maj. Gen. Harold N. Campbell described President Clinton to 250 attendees as a "gay-loving," "pot-smoking," "draft-dodging," and "womanizing" commander in chief. Afterwards, some members of the audience took offense at General Campbell's remarks and reported them to Air Force leaders. The Air Force then launched an investigation into General Campbell's remarks.[2]

General Campbell was a former fighter pilot who had served two combat tours in Vietnam and flew one hundred combat missions over North Vietnam. He won numerous medals and commendations, including a Silver Star for gallantry during his thirty-two years in the Air Force.[3]

Unfortunately, the general was saying what most Air Force personnel at the air base believed was the truth. Most of the military families at Soesterberg didn't support Mr. Clinton because they believed he was undermining the military by opening the ranks to openly homosexual enlistees, cutting back on Pentagon spending, and reducing U.S. military strength.[4]

The Air Force finished its investigation of General Campbell's remarks and concluded that General Campbell violated Article 88 of the Uniform Code of Military Justice by making unspecified disparaging remarks about the president. He was docked one month's pay and was forced to retire on July 1, 1993.[5]

Mr. Clinton when asked during a news conference about the incident said that he did not take personal offense at the remarks by General Campbell, but it was not the proper way for an officer to talk about the commander in chief.[6]

ANCHORWOMAN FORCED TO DO CLINTON'S MAKEUP

On May 26, 1993, President Clinton arrived in Concord, New Hampshire, for an interview with Nanette Hansen, an anchorwoman at ABC affiliate WMUR-TV. One of President Clinton's staff insisted that the anchorwoman prepare the president's makeup if she wanted the interview. Ms. Hansen, astonished about the request, went to her studio and returned with the required powders and creams. Ms. Hansen got her revenge by reporting the episode on the evening news. Now it was national news and an embarrassment to the Clinton White House.[7]

According to White House spokeswoman Dee Dee Myers, "We certainly didn't mean to embarrass anybody or make anybody uncomfortable. As you know we've apologized."[8]

CLINTON VISITS VIETNAM MEMORIAL WALL

On May 31, 1993, President Clinton visited the Vietnam Veterans Memorial Wall, a war that he evaded. Chairs had been set up for about seven hundred guests with special tickets. This group was made up of staff members, friends, and some veterans.[9] The Clinton White House ordered the Wall be encircled with an ugly snow fence to keep the two thousand veterans who came to protest about five hundred yards away. You could go inside through the airport-style security detectors, but not if you were carrying a protest sign. TV reporters began interviewing some of the veterans asking: "But don't you think your protest is contrary to the spirit of the Wall?" and "After all, this Wall is for *healing* the wounds of Vietnam."[10]

A veteran named Terry responded: "That's a myth. Why don't you go down and film the inscription on the Wall and show it on television tonight? That's why we're here, and why Clinton shouldn't be. This wall was built to honor everyone who served in Vietnam, which most emphatically does not include Mr. Clinton."[11]

The inscription reads:

> IN HONOR OF THE MEN AND WOMEN OF THE ARMED FORCES OF THE UNITED STATES WHO SERVED IN THE VIETNAM WAR .... OUR NATION HONORS THE COURAGE, SACRIFICE AND DEVOTION TO DUTY AND COUNTRY OF ITS VIETNAM VETERANS.[12]

As President Clinton began to speak, the shouting began. Some yelled "Coward," "Draft Dodger," "Liar," "Where was Bill?" and "Shut up." Others held signs which read, "Slick Willie," "The Artful Draft Dodger," "You Lied, You Dodged, Refused to Go." Others stood silently at attention and turned their backs on the president who they said turned his back on them.[13]

To many, it seemed that President Clinton used the sacred Memorial Day as a political event to heal his own conscience instead of honoring the dead. The president, unfortunately, hadn't learned that sometimes good taste consists of declining an invitation and letting time heal wounds.[14]

CLINTON MEDIA FLOP

On June 7, 1993, David Gergen joined the administration to help President Clinton move back to the political center and repair things for the White House. One of his first moves was to put Mr. Clinton in a prime-time appearance for the American people. With the kind of TV props that former President Reagan used so well, Clinton was to explain his economic package.[15]

Two of the three networks refused to delay their prime-time shows. The president came on looking like hell, and NBC switched to other programming just as Clinton began talking about his "remarkable progress." It was a disaster.[16]

CLINTONS MEET JOHN PAUL II

From August 12-15, 1993, the Pope John Paul II came to the United States for the fourth international World Youth Day, held in Denver, Colorado. It was his first trip during the presidency of Bill Clinton. On Thursday, August 12, the pope stepped off the plane at Denver's Stapleton

International Airport ready to speak to a throng of faithful. He was greeted by President Clinton, the First Lady, Hillary Rodham Clinton, and their daughter, Chelsea. The president offered welcoming remarks.[17]

According to his biographer, the pope departed from his prepared text after hearing what Clinton had to say and did so in a pointed way. He first thanked the president, Mrs. Clinton, and Chelsea for their "kind gesture in coming here personally to welcome me," and then expressed gratitude to the young people who were present. The pope said that this would be a World Youth Day for serious reflection on the themes of life: "The human life, which is God's marvelous gift to each one of us."[18]

The pope then got to the substance of what he felt was the critical message that America and its first family needed to hear. He said that America had been founded on the assertion of certain self-evident truths concerning the human person, including the inalienable right to life of every human being. Now, with the Cold War over, said the pope, all the "great causes" led by the United States "will have meaning only to the extent that you guarantee the right to life and protect the human person." He said that the "ultimate test" of America's greatness was the way that Americans treated "every human being, but especially the weakest and most defenseless ones. The best traditions of your land presume respect for those who cannot defend themselves." He then raised his voice: "If you want equal justice for all, and true freedom and lasting peace, then, America, defend life!" The speech left little doubt by anyone in the crowd that the words were aimed not just at the nation but at its president and first lady standing at the pontiff's side.[19]

CHAPTER 16

VINCE FOSTER

My deepest hope is that whatever drew Vince away from us this evening, his soul will receive the grace and salvation that his good life and good works earned. Hillary and I love his wife, Lisa, and their three children and we want to draw them close to our hearts and keep them in our prayers in this painful moment of grief. The family has lost a loving husband and father. America lost a gifted and loyal public servant. And Hillary and I lost a true and trusted friend.

—President Clinton after Vince Foster was found dead[1]

On July 20, 1993, White House Deputy Counsel Vincent W. Foster Jr. was found dead of an apparent self-inflicted gunshot wound at Fort Marcy Park, a small Civil War park overlooking the Potomac River. When the body was discovered, it was clothed in a tie, shirt-sleeves and suit pants. He was found beside an ornamental cannon.[2]

Foster was a presidential counselor, one who was rumored to have had a romantic attachment to the First Lady Hillary Rodham Clinton and had worked in the White House for six months without an FBI background check or a permanent pass. Supposedly, he had a gun in his car when he parked that morning inside the White House compound, although no weapon was detected by the gun-sniffing dogs who patrol the grounds.[3]

Events would soon surface surrounding Vince Foster's "apparent suicide" and the roles the people around him played before and after July 20, 1993, to insulate the Clintons. And that is where we will begin.

Foster had come to Washington a week before the inauguration. He was excited and filled with high hopes. In the months before his death, he had been working on two separate personal financial projects on behalf of the Clintons that were Little-Rock-related. One was helping out Denver attorney James Lyons, who was doing his best to reconstruct the records of the Whitewater Development Company. The second was working with Brantley Buck, the Rose firm attorney who was setting up Hillary's blind trust.[4]

Hillary further burdened Foster with much of the weight of health care reform. At the time, there was a lawsuit filed against the health care task force. If they lost in court, Hillary feared something akin to Humpty Dumpty's fate. She was not sure her health care initiative could ever be put back together again.[5]

Foster worried that the tax treatment of the Clintons' Whitewater real estate venture would trigger an IRS audit. Whitewater was a real venture that Bill and Hillary Clinton invested with Jim and Susan McDougal in 1978. A thorough overview of Whitewater is described in Chapter 18. Foster also feared that Hillary would be embarrassed by the public revelations of her stock holdings, which occurred when the Clintons released their disclosure forms in May 1993.[6]

"I think the beginning of Vince's downturn was when the health care task force was sued," said Webster Hubbell, whom Foster immediately enlisted to help him. Hubbell had always known Foster to be cool and methodical. Not now. Reporters were constantly calling him. "Fix it, Vince!" he said Hillary had hissed. It hurt him deeply.[7]

Soon, Foster, according to David Watkins, believed that he was being monitored by the White House. Foster had apparently told his wife not to talk on their home phone because he believed he was under surveillance. "I don't know who he thought was listening and watching," Watkins says, "but he was really nervous."[8] Vince confided in her that he thought he had made a mistake and wanted to resign. She talked him out of it.[9] On Sunday morning, July 11, 1993, Foster went to the home of James Hamilton and the two spoke for two hours about Mr. Foster's "need for legal representation in the upcoming investigation in the travel office matter." Mr. Hamilton was a Washington lawyer who had been deputy counsel to the Senate Watergate committee. He was also a friend of the Clintons who had done some scandal-containment work for the 1992 campaign. He took three pages of notes.[10]

The next day Vince Foster consulted his brother-in-law, Washington lobbyist and former Arkansas Congressman Beryl F. Anthony Jr., about hiring a lawyer. He was concerned about a congressional inquiry and was seeking outside legal counsel on the travel office affair.[11]

On July 14, 1993, Vince Foster met with Susan Thomases, who was in Washington on one of her midweek working visits. Foster discussed his fear that David Watkins would try to shift the blame for the travel office mess onto Hillary. Foster's main problem was that he was feeling overworked and overburdened, but despite the eighty-hour weeks he was putting in, he was not being very productive.[12]

On July 16, 1993, James McDougal left a message for Foster, regarding "tax returns of HRC, VWF and McDougal." The documents in Mr. Foster's office at the time of death included a file on Whitewater and his notes of conversations with Clintons' accountant, Yoly Redden, concerning the tax treatment of the sale of Whitewater. The notes identified the tax problem as a "can of worms you shouldn't open" and further warned: "Don't want to go back into that box. Was McDougal trying to circumvent bank loss—why HRC getting loan from other."[13]

On July 16, 1993, Vince telephoned his sister, Sheila Anthony, and told her that "he was battling depression for the first time in his life" but was reluctant to visit a psychiatrist because it might endanger his security clearance. He also wanted to be absolutely sure that everything revealed in therapy would be confidential and beyond the reach of subpoenas.[14] Sheila called Dr. Charles Hedaya in Chevy Chase and explained that her brother was handling top secret issues at the White House and "that his depression was directly related to highly sensitive and confidential matters."[15]

On the same day Vince had his blood pressure checked at the White House infirmary. It was 132/84, a normal reading for a man of his age. One of the issues was that he had stopped his regular routine of jogging three or four times a week. He was no longer burning off the adrenaline. But something else was eating at him.[16] On July 16, 1993, the Fosters were scheduled to have dinner with Webb and Susie Hubbell. But, the Fosters broke off the engagement and instead drove to Easton on the Chesapeake Bay. Hubbell, for some reason, followed them to the Eastern Shore and tracked them down at the Tidewater Inn. For the rest of the weekend, the Fosters were corralled by Hubbell and his friends Michael Cordozo and his wife, Harolyn, the daughter of wealthy Democratic contributor Nate Landow. They had an immense estate outside Easton.[17]

When asked about the weekend, Lisa told the Park Police that "it had not gone particularly well." The Arkansas Group, as the insiders called themselves at the White House, were somehow very interested in the outcome of that weekend, as if something were riding on it.[18]

The next day, Attorney General Janet Reno told FBI Director William Sessions that he would be fired by Monday unless he resigned. The meeting took place at the Justice Department. Sessions refused as a "matter of principle."[19] It was the same day Foster finally completed the blind trust for the Clintons' assets, nearly six months into Mr. Clinton's presidency.[20]

On Sunday, at around 9:30 p.m. eastern time, Foster telephoned Jerry Parks, a private investigator in Arkansas who ran the security operation for the 1992 Clinton-Gore campaign in Little Rock and was conducting his own research about Bill Clinton's shady activities (and was mentioned in chapter 6). Foster explained that Hillary had worked herself into a state about "the files," worried that there might be something in them that could cause real damage to Bill or herself. The conversation was brief and inconclusive. Jerry told Vince that there was indeed "plenty to hurt both of them. But, you can't give her those files; that was the agreement."[21]

The files in question, went back to the late 1980s when Foster trusted Parks enough to ask him to perform discreet surveillance on the governor. "Jerry asked him why he needed this stuff on Clinton. He said he needed it for Hillary," recalled Jerry's wife, Jane. It appeared that Hillary wanted to gauge exactly how vulnerable her husband would be to charges of philandering if he decided to launch a bid for the presidency.[22]

"Then," according to Jane, "he called a second time, and they spoke for thirty minutes or more." This time it was a heated exchange. Vince said that he had made up his mind. He was going to hand over the files and wanted to be sure he had the complete set. "You are not going to use those files!" said Jerry angrily. Foster tried to soothe him. He said he was going to meet Hillary at "the flat" and he was going to give her the files. "You can't do that," said Parks. "My name's all over this stuff. You can't give Hillary those files. You can't! Remember what she did, what you told me she did. She's capable of doing anything!"[23]

"We can trust Hil. Don't worry," said Foster.[24]

Jane did not know what Foster meant by "the flat." Some believe it to be the Randolph Towers (4001 N. Ninth St., Arlington, Virginia.) This building, coincidently, is located near Fort Marcy Park.[25] Strangely, on the afternoon of July 20, 1993, Hillary was flying from Los Angeles and landed in Little Rock instead of Washington. But that does not preclude the possibility that Foster *thought* he was going to a rendezvous with the first lady that same day at "the flat," but met his death instead.[26] The next day Parks was reportedly watching a news bulletin on the death of Vincent Foster when he turned from the television and muttered to his son, Gary, "I'm a dead man."[27] For the next two months, the beefy six-foot-three security executive was in a state of permanent fear. He would pack a pistol to fetch the mail. On the way to his offices at American Contract Services in Little Rock, he would double back or take strange routes to "dry-clean" the cars that he thought were following him. Once he muttered darkly that Bill Clinton's people were "cleaning house," and he was "next on the list."[28]

In late July 1993, after Vince Foster's death, the Parks family home was burgled in a sophisticated operation that involved cutting the telephone lines and disarming the electronic alarm system. The files Parks had on Clinton were stolen. Two months later, on September 26, 1993, Jerry Parks was assassinated. The murder remains unsolved.[29] As with so many other "Arkancides," the name given to the seemingly endless list of suspicious deaths suffered by Arkansas associates of the Clintons, the major media networks ignored the event.[30]

The next day after Jerry's assassination (September 27, 1993), the rambler-style home of the Parks family was swarming with federal agents. Jane remembers credentials from the FBI, the Secret Service, the IRS, and possibly the CIA. Nothing made any sense. The federal government had no jurisdiction over a homicide case, and to this day, the FBI denies that it ever set foot in her house, yet they confiscated files, records, and 130 tapes of telephone conversations without giving up a receipt. According to Jane Parks, "I've asked them to give it all back, but they told me there's nothing they can do about the case as long as Bill Clinton is in office."[31]

Interestingly, Linda Tripp, at the time an executive assistant in the counsel's office, would later testify about "the flurry of activity and the flurry of phone calls and the secrecy" when word came over the office fax machine that Jerry Parks had been shot to death in Little Rock. Tripp had no information to suggest why Park's murder should have been a cause for concern in the White House. She just noticed that it was.[32]

So back to Monday, July 19, 1993, Foster went off to see the White House Credit Union to sort out his overdraft problems. At the Rose Law

Firm, he was earning $295,000 a year as a litigation lawyer. In Washington, he was earning less than half that figure. Yet, there was something strange going on. Without telling his wife, Foster had made several large withdrawals of $3,500 each from the account.[33] That same day he called his sister and told her that he was "feeling good" and had decided not to see a psychiatrist.[34]

Vince then called his own doctor in Little Rock, Arkansas, Larry S. Watkins, who prescribed an anti-depressant known as Desyrel. This was something he had never before done for Mr. Foster. The Desyrel was delivered to his home later that day.[35] That afternoon, President Clinton called to tell FBI Director William Sessions that he had been fired. Clearly in a great hurry, Clinton called a second time, minutes later. Sessions was to leave the Hoover Building "effective immediately." It was the first time in American history that a president had summarily dismissed an FBI director. The putsch passed without protest. Mr. Sessions said that he "would not be a part of politicizing the FBI, from within or without." He would later state that his firing was the result of a power struggle that pitted the FBI director, seeking to maintain the FBI's political neutrality, against the Justice Department and the White House.[36]

The president appointed Deputy Director Floyd Clarke to take over the FBI until a successor could be found. It would later emerge that the White House had already been working quietly with Clarke for some time. This was convenient because when Foster was found dead, Clarke failed to assert FBI jurisdiction, leaving the Park Police in charge.[37]

The same afternoon the president fired Mr. Sessions, Marsha Scott, the White House Director of Correspondence, visited Foster. She had dropped in to find out how the weekend had gone.[38] Scott used to come over from the Old Executive Office Building quite often to visit Foster. But, their meeting the day before his death, was different. It was a closed-door session that lasted for over an hour, possibly as long as two hours.[39] Her last words to Foster: "If I talk to Bill before you do, what do you want me to tell him?" It would appear that she was an envoy from the president, sent to learn Foster's thoughts. In the handwritten notes of her FBI interview she admitted that she had been to see Clinton that afternoon.[40] Scott also spent the next night with Clinton after Foster's death. The Secret Service logged her into the living quarters of the White House at 00.50 on July 21, 1993, and she was not logged out again until the next morning.[41]

At 8:00 p.m., on July 19, 1993, President Clinton called to invite Foster to the White House to a private screening of the new Clint Eastwood movie, *In the Line of Fire*. Besides Bill Clinton, Webb Hubbell and Bruce Lindsey, the "inner core," were at the White House. Foster declined the invitation, saying he wanted to be with his family. He chatted with the president for ten to fifteen minutes about "organizational issues" and the two men agreed to meet Wednesday morning, July 21, 1993 at the White House. After supper he chatted with his youngest child, Brugh, about an idea they had for buying a boat.[42]

That evening, Foster took a fifty-milligram dose of Desyrel. Although the drug needs a week or two to take full effect,[43] the next morning his "mood seemed better than it had in a while," Lisa Foster told the Police. (Interestingly, ten months later, Lisa told a dramatically different version to the FBI, but by then she was being advised by White House "surrogate" James Hamilton.)[44] Foster drove his children to work, chatting happily enough. Vincent III commented afterward that "his dad was in such a happy mood when he dropped us off."[45]

Foster arrived at his White House office at 8:30 a.m. on July 20. He received two phone calls that morning. One was from lawyer James Lyons. Did Mr. Lyons tell Mr. Foster that a magistrate in Little Rock authorized a warrant for the search of David Hale's office? Lyons told investigators that he was calling to confirm a dinner appointment in Washington to discuss both personal and business matters, but that he never reached Foster that day. At 11:00 a.m., Foster spoke to a Rose firm colleague, who said he "gave no clue" to being suicidal.[46]

At noon, Foster asked Linda Tripp, executive assistant to Mr. Nussbaum, to go to the White House cafeteria to get him lunch. Ms. Tripp delivered Foster's lunch and added some M&Ms to the tray. Foster sat on the couch in his office and ate his lunch while reading the newspaper.[47] At about 1:00 p.m., Foster came out of his office, holding his suit coat. He told Ms. Tripp there were some M&Ms left on his tray if she wanted them. He said, "I'll be back," and then left. According to Tripp, Foster was not carrying a briefcase when he left the building.[48]

That same day, Foster's sister Sharon Bowman was coming up from Arkansas with her daughter Mary. Foster had also promised to take Lisa out for a "date" that evening. He was planning to take his niece to lunch at the White House as a special treat. When the Bowmans arrived that evening Foster was already dead. At about 5:00 p.m., she called his office at the White House to find out what his plans were but was told that he was "unavailable." She tried again later, but nobody knew where he had gone.[49] This is what we do know:

Between 4:15 and 4:30 p.m., Patrick Knowlton entered Fort Marcy Park, driving a Thrifty rental car. He saw two cars parked in the place where Foster's car would later show up—an old, beat-up brown Honda and a blue car parked in front of it. A Hispanic-looking man with close-cropped hair sat in the blue car, fixing Knowlton with a menacing look. When Knowlton left his car to relieve himself in the woods, the Hispanic-looking man got out of the car and continued staring at Knowlton over the roof of his car. His behavior suggested he was acting as a guard or lookout.[50]

Frightened, Knowlton quickly left the park, but mentally noted some of the contents of the Arkansas Honda, including a suit jacket and a brief case. "I remember thinking these people from Arkansas must be really stupid to leave a briefcase on the front seat," he said. The U.S. Park Police claim that no briefcase was found in the car. Foster's briefcase later turned up at the White House.[51]

Mr. Knowlton was the first known eyewitness to see Foster's car, which he described as an older model brown Honda with Arkansas plates. Interestingly, Foster owned a light gray Honda of recent vintage with Arkansas plates.[52]

Next, a confidential witness came forward and said that he pulled into Fort Marcy Park at around 5:45 p.m. driving his white utility van. The witness said he clearly remembered seeing Mr. Foster's car with its Arkansas plates. He said there was a man, possibly Hispanic, in a light blue Honda parked beside it. The witness said the man gave him a menacing look when he walked passed him toward the bushes.[53] He had to go to the bathroom badly. After he relieved himself, he spotted a body. It was lying in the dense foliage, concealed from view by a berm, more or less in the line of fire of an antique howitzer. He started to walk away, but then he noticed that the face was swollen, so he moved in close, stepping to where his foot was within feet of the man's head, and looked straight down into his face.[54]

"He looked as if he'd been dead for a long time, I mean hours," he said. There was no blood on his white shirt. There was nothing to explain why a man wearing a "$400 or $500 suit" and sparkling "dress shoes" would be lying dead in the shrub with a bottle of wine cooler at his elbow.[55]

The body was bloating in the heat. There were traces of blood around the nostrils and mouth, and flies were crawling over those areas of the body. The eyes were partially closed and already glazed and his "hands at [his] sides, palms open and angled upwards." At the bottom of a slope near the body, "the brush was 'trampled' as if someone had been walking back and forth at that spot." He observed both hands of the body and that neither held a gun. Again, there was no gun. If a shot had been fired, it would have been heard by the guards at the home of the Saudi Ambassador's residence across the road. It actually was eerily silent, so silent that he could hear people talking across Chain Bridge Road.[56] After observing the body for several moments, the man walked back to his van and drove to a nearby U.S. Park Service facility, where he told two uniformed employees in the parking lot about the body and where it could be found.[57] Francis Swan, a National Park Service maintenance worker went to a pay phone and made two calls. First, he placed a 911 telephone call to the Fairfax County Public Safety Communications Center saying he had been told about a dead body. He then made a call to the U.S. Park Police.[58]

Between 5:00 and 5:15 p.m., two other witnesses, Josie and Duncan, entered the parking lot. They said there was only one car parked in the lot—a brown Honda, which resembled Foster's car, and a white utility van.[59] Josie said that "a white male without a shirt was seated in the driver's seat" of the Honda. She said he had dark hair.[60] Duncan remembered the hood of the car was up and a white male was standing by the front the car. He was in his "mid to late 40s, approximately six feet in height, medium build, long blonde hair and beard, appearing unclean and unkept [sic]." Duncan said the blond male wandered off into the woods.[61] (Blond hairs were found on Foster's undershirt, his trousers, belt, socks, and shoes, but the FBI never tried to identify whose they were.[62]

At one point, remembered Josie, a dirty, light-colored, beaten-up sedan came into the parking lot. The driver was a big bruiser in his thirties with long shaggy hair. He drove past, looked at the couple, then did a U-turn, and went straight back out again onto George Washington Parkway.[63]

They stayed in the car until 5:45 p.m.—it seems they were having a romantic encounter—and then they exited the car and set off on foot to a secluded knoll inside the park to consummate their affection. They were at the south end when twenty-five minutes later the fire brigade came screeching into Fort Marcy Park, followed quickly by the U.S. Park

Police. They first learned of a problem, they said, when emergency workers stumbled upon them during a search for the body shortly after 6:00 p.m.[64]

At this point, four witnesses had seen an old brown mid-80s Honda parked in Fort Marcy Park, between 4:30 and 5:45 p.m. It was *not* Vince Foster's car. Foster's light gray 1989 Honda arrived later. There was only one problem: Foster was already dead by the time his car arrived. His body was discovered around 5:50 p.m.[65]

All four witnesses would later give consistent testimony. None contradicted the others. Their combined testimony showed that Foster's body arrived in the park *before* his car. Naturally, this created a problem for investigators intent on proving that Foster committed suicide in Fort Marcy Park.[66]

At 6:05 p.m., U.S. Park Police Kevin Fornshill responded when a "DB" alert came over the radio.[67] The paramedics from the Fairfax County Emergency Medical Services were arriving when Officer Fornshill reached the park. Fornshill and the rescue workers fanned out in different directions to search for the body. Fornshill was joined by Emergency Medical Technician Todd Hall and Paramedic Sgt. George Gonzalez from the McLean Fire Service, Company One. Sergeant Gonzalez instructed the two paramedics to go one way while he went off alone to a hidden grove in the top corner of the park.[68]

At 6:14 p.m., Fornshill found Foster's body and almost half an hour after the body had been discovered by the confidential witness. In an interview with prosecutors and FBI agents assigned to Mr. Fiske, Fornshill described Foster's body as lying "straight up with his head slightly tilted to the right." From his position at the top of a berm, he told investigators, he could not see a gun, but he said the foliage around the body blocked his view. He would later tell investigators that everything, including Foster's white shirt, was really "neat," with no blood on it.[69]

At 6:15 p.m., U.S. Park Police Detective John Rolla was contacted. In his notes he wrote: Dead Body. Ft. Marcy. Warm Sunny Day[70] As Todd Hall reached the grove, he saw men running away from the scene on a footpath just below the slope where Foster was found and toward the rear entrance. He pointed this out to Fornshill, but Fornshill did not respond. Later, the FBI suggested to him that he might have mistaken men for cars moving along Chain Bridge Road.[71] During grand jury proceedings, the Park Police claimed they were unaware of the second entrance. Prosecutors had evidence, however, that police were regularly stationed at the rear entrance during the Gulf War, since the entrance is directly across the street from the Saudi Arabian ambassador's residence.[72] It turns out several people entered during the night through the rear entrance and encountered Park Police. The police had not secured that entrance and the officers also violated standard police procedure by not recording the names of the individuals who came into the park on the night of July 20, 1993.[73]

By the time Todd Hall got to the body to check the carotid pulse a gun has appeared. The weapon was in Foster's right hand, with parts of it tucked under his right leg. No one could explain the fact that the confidential witness didn't see a gun and then, forty-five minutes later, there was a gun in Mr. Foster's hand—a gun, we would later learn, without any fingerprints on it. Normally, a discrepancy of this magnitude would set off alarm bells.[74]

After two minutes, Fornshill contacted Park Police communications and announced that "it appeared to be a suicide." But it was not obvious to the paramedics that this DB was a suicide, and the paramedics had far more experience with violent deaths than the Park Police.[75]

Sergeant Gonzalez also noticed Mr. Foster's body. He said it was lying neatly on a gentle incline with a .38-caliber revolver in one hand. "Usually a suicide by gunshot is a mess," Mr. Gonzalez said. But in this case, the paramedic recalled only a "thin trickle of blood" in the corner of Mr. Foster's mouth. He said Mr. Foster's body was laid out neatly," as if ready for a coffin.[76]

According to a pathologist, it is "extremely rare" to find the gun in the hand of a man who has shot himself in the mouth. "A reflex action of the arm usually propels the gun a fair distance from the body, up to twenty or thirty feet. Another pathologist, a retired coroner, said he has "never heard of the gun remaining in a suicide's hand after delivering such trauma to a man's head."[77]

Richard Arthur, another EMT at the scene and one who had attended to twenty-five or thirty gunshot deaths in his nine years as a rescue worker, believed it was a homicide. "I've just never seen a body lying so perfectly straight after a bullet in his head," he said.[78]

The Park Police ruling of suicide had the effect of crimping further inquiry. It was cited by the Justice Department as grounds for backing off its original pledge to conduct a vigorous investigation. It also kept the FBI at bay. Under the Assassinations Statute, the FBI would have been compelled by law to take over the case if there was any question that it might have been homicide.[79]

There are five homes within 570 feet of the spot where Foster's body was found. One of them belonged to then-Senator Bennett Johnston of Louisiana. The closest is three hundred feet away. Yet somehow nobody heard a shot.[80]

At 6:35 p.m., Investigator Cheryl Braun arrived from the Anacostia police station. After a quick briefing by the shift commander, she began going through Foster's Honda.[81] There was a map of the Washington metropolitan area on the floorboard with no annotations or ink marks. A blue silk tie with swans was lying on top of a suit jacket, which was neatly folded on the front passenger seat. In the inside pocket of the jacket was a brown leather wallet. It contained $292 in cash, Foster's Arkansas driver's license, an American Express gold car, an Exxon card, a Delta Frequent Flyer card, and a White House Federal Credit Union card. But there was no briefcase. This was odd because paramedic Sgt. George Gonzalez told investigators: "The Honda contained a necktie, suit coat, and a black briefcase/attaché case."[82] Emergency medical technician Todd Hall also told the grand jury and Fiske investigators that he also saw a briefcase in the car.[83]

Detective John Rolla showed up and ran the Honda's plates. Within two minutes a trace revealed that it belonged to Vincent Foster, Jr. Detective Rolla noticed the following:

- Foster had a Motorola pager on his belt with the letters WHCA (White House Communications Agency).
- His White House ID was sitting on the front passenger seat of the unlocked Honda.
- There was a White House parking sticker clearly visible on the windscreen of the car.[84]

Detective Rolla checked all the pants pockets for car keys or a possible suicide note. No keys were found.[85]

By 7:00 p.m., members of the Special Forces, an elite unit of the U.S. Park Police, closely associated with the White House security, arrived at Fort Marcy Park. One of the individuals present was Officer William Watson, who later claimed that he forgot to pass on the message that there was a White House official lying dead in the park.[86]

What was the Park Police SWAT team doing at Fort Marcy at 7:00 p.m. on July 20, 1993, attending to a routine suicide? Why was this information withheld from the American people until it was forced into the open by a *Pittsburgh Tribune-Review* reporter Chris Ruddy's Freedom of Information Act lawsuit?[87]

At 7:00 p.m., Bernie Nussbaum and Betsy Pond left the White House Counsel's suite, room 208. Before leaving, Pond switched on the alarm system, which happened to be located in a box inside Foster's office, and then called the Secret Service Control Center to notify them that the Counsel's suite was being vacated. If anybody entered that set of rooms later that evening, their movements would be picked up by a sensor in the ceiling.[88]

At 7:05 p.m., an intruder alarm went off in the White House counsel's office as Patsy Thomasson checked into the suite and Ms. Thomasson didn't have clearance. At 7:10 p.m., a Secret Service unit called the MIG GROUP was logged into the offices of administration. At 7:44 p.m., both Thomasson and the MIG GROUP were logged in a second time. So what is the MIG GROUP? It appears that the unit is the Maintenance and Installation Group. It is part of the Technical Security Division, which handles alarms, locks, safes, surveillance, bugs, and the like. Very high tech. Very capable. Foster had a locked file cabinet in his office. Nobody was allowed to touch this cabinet. His executive assistant Deborah Gorham remembers that he kept a file on the Branch Davidian siege at Waco in there, but she did not have a key and never got to look inside. The most sensitive material was kept in a safe in Bernie Nussbaum's office. If there was any unit in Washington that was capable of getting into Foster's safe, quickly and cleanly, the MIG GROUP could do it. They were in the West Wing, between 7:10 to 7:44 p.m., with Patsy Thomasson. Keep in mind at the time of entry, Ms. Thomasson did not have a White House security clearance and did not receive one until March 5, 1994, fourteen months into her tenure at the White House[89]

At 7:37 p.m. eastern time, First Lady Hillary Rodham Clinton, who was on her way from Los Angeles to Little Rock on a U.S. Air Force flight, called the White House signals office and was patched through to the apartment of her chief of staff. "Maggie, are you at home? She asked. "I'll call you when I land." The first lady did not want to discuss details until they had a secure landline. The aircraft touched down in Little Rock at 8:26 p.m. eastern time.[90]

At 8:10 p.m., Corey Ashford, a McClean EMT, had the unpleasant task of moving Foster's corpse from Fort Marcy Park to the Fairfax County Hospital morgue. His was the cleanup crew. It can be a horrible business dealing with a gunshot death. A .38 Special will take the back of your head off. Blood everywhere, brain matter. Funny thing, though. He didn't notice any blood.[91]

Ashford picked up the corpse from the shoulders, cradling the head against his stomach as he lifted it into the body bag. Still no blood. He didn't get a drop of blood on his white uniform, or on the disposable gloves he was wearing for the job. There was no blood on the ground underneath the body, either, that he could see. He coded Foster's body a homicide on his incident report.[92]

Roger Harrison didn't see any blood either, as he helped Corey slide Foster's shoulders into the body bag. No blood on the ground. No blood on the corpse. No blood on anybody who had touched it. The nineteen-year veteran of the Fairfax County Fire and Rescue Department did not file a hazardous materials report—which is mandatory if there is blood around.[93]

Interestingly, when they were recounting war stories back at Fire Station One, nobody saw an exit wound. Corey Ashford didn't see a wound.[94]

Richard Arthur didn't see one.[95]

Sgt. George Gonzalez didn't see one.[96]

The head was intact. None of the paramedics saw the "official" one-by-one-and-a-quarter-inch hole in the back of Foster's skull. They have forensic evidence on their side, too. No bone fragments were ever found behind the head.[97]

The body bag was then moved by ambulance to the Fairfax County Hospital morgue. The Park Police, still puzzled about the absence of keys (how did he get to Fort Marcy Park?), decided to go to Fairfax Hospital to recheck the body. When they got there, they saw White House Associate Counsel William Kennedy and White House aide Craig Livingstone. They had gone to the hospital's morgue to identify the body.[98]

When Detective Braun re-checked Foster's right front pants pocket, she found two sets of keys: one ring containing the car keys and the other containing four door and cabinet keys.[99] This begs a rather sinister question. Whoever had the keys, what were they doing with them in the first place?[100]

The night duty doctor at the morgue was Dr. Julian Orenstein. His job was to verify Vince Foster's death, nothing else. Reporter Ambrose Evans-

Pritchard decided to call Orenstein at his home in Falls Church to verify the existence of the "exit wound." What did this exit wound look like, he asked? "I never saw one directly," Dr. Orenstein said, clearly taken aback. "The hair was matted with drier blood, but I didn't get a clear look. I really didn't spend too much time looking back there; my suspicions weren't aroused."[101]

At 8:30 p.m., the Secret Service beeped White House adviser David Watkins, who with Detectives Braun and Rolla went to Mr. Foster's home in Georgetown to tell Lisa Foster about her husband's death.[102]

The Foster family was stunned when the Park Police first notified them of the death, "Mrs. Foster nor other relatives, or friends were able to provide any insight as to why Vince would take his life," wrote Detective Rolla in his report. "One of the last things I got from Mrs. Foster . . . I asked her, was he . . . did you see this coming, were there any signs of this, and of course everyone said, no, no, no. He was fine. This is out of the blue."[103]

The two officers were turned away after Lisa Foster and family members became too distraught to talk. Police investigators were not allowed to interview Lisa Foster until nine days later. Vulnerable and confused, Lisa Foster surrendered herself totally to the political agenda of James Hamilton, the attorney for the 1992 Clinton-Gore campaign. He was described as the Foster "family lawyer" but an internal White House memo describes him more accurately as a lawyer performing a "surrogate role" for the White House. The interview took place at the K Street law offices of Swidler & Berlin, under the auspices of Mr. Hamilton. "[Mrs. Foster] was presented with a photograph of the weapon found with Mr. Foster's body but was unable to identify it," stated the Park Police interview with Lisa Foster.[104] The gun was a 1913 Colt made up from parts of two separate weapons. It was too old to trace. Foster's fingerprints could not be found. Nor could the bullet. No matching ammunition was found in Foster's homes. According to U.S. Park Police Chief Robert E. Langston, Foster's widow had been unable to identify the gun that was found at Fort Marcy Park. There was a good deal of confusion about this. It was said that the vintage Colt was an heirloom from Vince's father. But Vince's nephew, Lee Bowman, who used to go hunting with his grandfather and knew guns well, did not recognize it. He told the FBI that he "didn't remember the black handle and the dark color of the metal. In the end, the gun was never positively identified by the family.[105]

Shortly after 9:00 p.m., White House Chief of Staff Mack McLarty was notified of Mr. Foster's death and he then telephoned Mrs. Clinton in Little Rock with the news.[106] The night of his death, Hillary launched one of the most shameful—and illegal—cover-ups of her entire career. She sent two of her most trusted aides, White House loyalists—Maggie Williams, her chief of staff, and Patsy Thomasson—into Foster's office to retrieve embarrassing and incriminating documents related to Whitewater and Hillary's other personal affairs. While Bernard Nussbaum barred investigators from entering Foster's office, Maggie Williams, Patsy Thomasson and Craig Livingstone, director of White House security, removed armloads of files and loose-leaf binders after the MIG Group had sacked the office.[107]

In addition, White House lawyer Jack Quinn even tried to rewrite the factual record, deleting words in the titles of memos, changing "HRC's Travel Office Chronology" to "Chronological Analysis of Travel Office Events." "HRC Role" became "Draft chart analysis and comparison of various Travel Office investigations." The removal of the first lady's initials from the White House memos, said Chairman William Clinger, brought "a scent of obstruction of justice . . . [to the] changing of documents in an attempt to rub out . . . the role of the First Lady."[108]

At around 10:00 p.m., Williams called her assistant, Evelyn Lieberman, at her home and told her the news. Lieberman jumped into her car, picked up Williams and drove to the White House. At 10:29 p.m., they arrived at the White House and then headed to the second floor of the West Wing.[109]

At 10:01 p.m., Mr. McLarty told President Clinton of the death as the president completed an appearance on *Larry King Live*. Or so we are told.[110]

Did Bill Clinton already know something before he appeared on the show? As the CNN makeup artist was putting the final touches to the President in the White House Map Room, shortly before the program's 9 p.m. air time, an unidentified male presumed to be an aide notified Clinton that a note had been found in Vince Foster's office.[111] The two left immediately from the White House for Mr. Foster's Georgetown home.[112]

At 10:34 p.m., David Watkins beeped Patsy Thomasson, who was now at the Sequoia Restaurant in Georgetown. She called in from a pay phone and then took a taxi back to the White House to look for a suicide note in Foster's office. By the time she left the White House Counsel's suite with Bernie Nussbaum and Maggie Williams in tow, her fresh fingerprints were all over Foster's desk, drawers, and filing cabinet.[113]

Ms. Thomasson would later testify to the Senate Whitewater Committee, on July 25, 1995, that she spent only ten minutes in Mr. Foster's office on the night of his death looking for a suicide note and, finding none, left with no papers.[114]

At 10:42 p.m., Bernard Nussbaum arrived at Foster's office to find Ms. Thomasson at Foster's desk and Margaret Williams sobbing on the sofa. They claimed that they went into the office to look for a suicide note. They instead secretly removed records of business deals involving the Clintons in an Arkansas real estate venture (Whitewater) from Foster's office. This information did not become public until reported by the *Washington Times* on December 21, 1993.[115]

At around 11:00 p.m., Secret Service agent Henry P. O'Neill, who worked nights in the West Wing escorting the cleaning crews who worked in high security areas, observed Evelyn Lieberman walk out of the Counsel's office. Then a few seconds later, Mr. Nussbaum walked out behind her and walked through the hallway toward the stairs past the elevator. Within a few more seconds, he saw Margaret Williams walk out of the suite and turn to the right, in the direction that Officer O'Neill was standing.[116]

"She was carrying what I would describe, in her arms and hands, as folders," he said. "She walked past me and she continued on down the hallway . . . and she started to enter her office. She had to brace the folders in her arms on a cabinet and then she entered the office and came out within a few more seconds and locked the door."[117]

Maggie Williams would later testify to the Senate Whitewater Committee, on July 28, 1995, that she did not take any papers from the office on the night of Vince Foster's death: "I took nothing from Vince's office," she said. "I did not look at, inspect, or remove any documents. . . . I disturbed nothing while I was there." She would eventually quit her job and move to Paris, France.[118]

Another Secret Service agent, Bruce Abbott, would later testify, that he saw Craig Livingstone carrying a brown "leather or vinyl briefcase, opening at the top, much in the fashion of a litigator's bag or lawyer's briefcase." The agent said he also saw Livingstone leaving the White House with an unknown person "carrying one or perhaps two boxes with what appeared to be, looked to me to be, loose-leaf binders." Livingstone denied that he took any documents from Foster's office.[119]

At 11:10 p.m., Cheryl Braun had a "brief conversation" with White House official David Watkins on securing the White House deputy counsel's office, and he agreed to do so. The records show that, at the time Ms. Braun made her request, Patsy Thomasson, Bernard Nussbaum, and Margaret Williams, had been in the Foster office about twenty minutes.[120]

After speaking with Hillary, Susan Thomases paged Margaret Williams while Ms. Williams was searching Mr. Foster's office, presumably to monitor the progress of the search. After the completion of her search, Ms. Williams returned home and called Mrs. Clinton at 12:56 a.m. on the morning of July 21. Upon the conclusion of her eleven-minute conversation with Mrs. Clinton, Ms. Williams called Ms. Thomases at 1:10 a.m. and spoke for fourteen minutes.[121]

Susan Thomases would later testify to the Senate Whitewater Committee in early August 1995 and deny that her seventeen phone calls to the White House in the forty-three hours after the death of Vince Foster were aimed at shielding documents in his office from investigators.[122]

"I know that I never, never received from anyone or gave to anyone any instructions about how the review of Vince Foster's office was to be conducted or how the files in Vince's office were to be handled," Ms. Thomases said.[123]

At 11:41 p.m., having found no note, Mr. Nussbaum, Ms. Thomasson and Ms. Williams leave the office.[124]

At 11:41 p.m., 10:41 p.m. Arkansas time, First Lady Hillary Rodham Clinton is believed to have called the White House and spoken for ten minutes to Mack McLarty. The number she dialed was later disconnected.[125] Interestingly, on December 8, 1995, First Lady Hillary Rodham Clinton filed an affidavit with the special Senate Whitewater committee and said she does not remember whom she talked with at the White House on the night of Foster's death during a call routed through the White House.[126]

Foster's office was open and unguarded for three hours the next morning (July 21)—from the time the first secretary arrived at 7:01 a.m. until 10:20 a.m., when a Secret Service agent was posted by the door, according to White House security logs. It was during this time that Mr. Nussbaum's personal secretary, Betsy Pond, also rummaged through Mr. Foster's office—ostensibly to straighten it up—thereby disturbing important evidence.[127]

On the morning of July 21, 1993, President Clinton, before hundreds of staff members, reflected on Vince Foster in a brief televised statement in the Rose Garden saying, in part: "What happened was a mystery about something inside of him. In times of difficulty he was normally the Rock of Gibraltar while other people were having trouble."[128]

On July 21, 1993, Park Police and FBI agents arrived at the White House to search Vince Foster's office for his work-related papers. Unfortunately, citing "national security" concerns, White House officials and Secret Service agents blocked the FBI and Park Police from searching Mr. Foster's office.[129] Around 5:00 p.m., Deputy Attorney General Philip B. Heymann had struck a deal with Mr. Nussbaum to allow his top deputies, Roger C. Adams and David Margolis, to review documents with the White House Counsel to determine their relevance to the Foster probe the next morning.[130]

The next morning, July 22, 1993, Margaret Williams was at the White House well before the search was to start and spoke with Nussbaum. Then, the following sequence occurred:

- 7:44-7:51 a.m.: (6:44 a.m. in Arkansas) Ms. Williams spoke with Hillary Rodham Clinton.
- 7:57-8:00 a.m.: Mrs. Clinton called her friend, confidant and fixer, Susan Thomases, in Washington.
- 8:01 a.m.: Ms. Thomases paged Mr. Nussbaum at the White House.[131]

Two hours later, when the search of Foster's office finally commenced, Nussbaum clashed over procedures with the two Justice Department lawyers, Roger Adams and David Margolis. Nussbaum suddenly went back on the deal. Nussbaum unilaterally cancelled his agreement with the Justice Department. It doesn't take a very suspicious mind to construct an interpretation of this string of calls that puts Mrs. Clinton in the driver's seat.[132]

Nussbaum insisted that he and he alone would look at the files. The FBI agents, who were joined by the Park Police investigators and the lawyers for the Foster family, were required to move to the other side of the room while Nussbaum hurriedly separated files having to do with Foster personally, the Clintons, and White House business into three piles.[133]

The investigators were also not allowed to see any of the materials that had been retrieved from his trash and were denied access to papers in a "burn bag" in the office, on the grounds that they were privileged. They were also not allowed to turn on his computers to check for information it might contain.[134]

At one point, an FBI special agent Scott Salter stood up to peer into the room. He was challenged immediately by Clifford Sloan, associated counsel for the president, and was accused of trying to sneak a look at documents being handled. Mr. Salter was later reprimanded. The document review lasted from 1:15 p.m. to 3:30 p.m.[135]

At 4:00 p.m., on July 22, 1993, Nussbaum and Williams conducted a second search of Foster's office for personal papers belonging to the Clintons. Nussbaum also directed his staff attorneys to monitor interviews of White House employees by Park Police investigating the death of Foster. "It is standard procedure to have lawyers sit in as people are being interviewed," he said. He "wanted to be fully aware of what's going on" and learn any facts he could about the death of his deputy.[136]

Then the following sequence occurred:

- At 5:13 p.m., Ms. Thomasses called Maggie Williams. They spoke until 5:22 p.m.
- At 5:23 p.m., Ms. Thomases called Bruce Lindsey, a presidential aide. They spoke until 5:26 p.m.
- At 7:12 p.m., Ms. Thomases called Mrs. Clinton's mother's residence in Arkansas. The call lasted until 7:13 p.m.[137]

On July 23, 1993, Vince Foster was buried at St. Andrew's Roman Catholic Cathedral in Little Rock, Arkansas. Bill and Hillary, as well as other staff members, attended the funeral services. But there seemed to be some kind of tension between Hillary and the Foster family concerning rumors about Hillary and Vince Foster having an affair.[138]

On July 26, 1993, six days after Foster's death, Associate White House Counsel Stephen Neuwirth, while packing Mr. Foster's belongings, picked up the briefcase and pieces of yellow legal paper that had been invisible before and suddenly materialized. The yellow paper was a note that had been torn into twenty-seven pieces—the twenty-eighth piece was missing.[139] The note in Foster's briefcase may well have been found several days before the counsel's office claim it had been discovered. Several people testified they had seen scraps of paper in Foster's briefcase some days before the note was "discovered" on July 26 by Nussbaum's aide Neuwirth. Deborah Gorham,

Foster's secretary, says that she told Nussbaum on the day after Foster's death that Foster had "placed shredded remnants of personal documents" in his briefcase. Michael Spafford, one of the lawyers for the Foster family who was present during the July 22 search of Foster's office, testified that he overheard Nussbaum and Clifford Sloan, talking about "scraps in the bottom of the briefcase."[140]

So who actually found the note? Documents now lodged with the National Archives refer to a handwritten note by White House aide Bill Burton dated July 26, 1993. "Far happier if discovered [by] someone other than Bernie," it says. Burton was describing a meeting shortly after the discovery of the note that was attended by Neuwirth, Nussbaum, Burton himself, and Hillary Rodham Clinton. Bill Burton and Steve Neuwirth witnessed Mrs. Clinton look at the reconstructed note. She then loudly questioned her own presence in the room and quickly left. Thus, it is natural to infer that the Neuwirth story was concocted. If so, Neuwirth perjured himself in congressional testimony, and Hillary Rodham Clinton was party to that deception.[141]

The FBI's Louis Hupp used state of the art equipment to check for fingerprints, but all he could find of any use was a single palm print. It did not belong to Foster. When asked in close-door testimony if it was Bernie Nussbaum's print, he was instructed not to answer by a lawyer for the Starr investigation (Mark Tuohey).[142]

On the evening of July 27, 1993, the note was turned over to the Justice Department, thirty hours after it was discovered, following meetings in the White House residence between Hillary Clinton, Susan Thomases, and Webster Hubbell. Congressional investigators believe that a leak from inside the White House to the press of the note's existence may have forced its release.[143]

As news of the search of Foster's office filtered out in early August 1993, the *New York Times* was the first to raise the specter of a special counsel investigation into the events surrounding Foster's death: "Ideally, an independent counsel wholly free from executive branch control needs to be appointed. First, there must be a thorough reinvestigation of the White House travel office and the attempt in the spring to shift its function to Clinton campaign supporters. . . . A special prosecutor-style inquiry is also needed into how the White House handled Mr. Foster's death."[144]

On August 10, 1993, the Justice Department concluded that Vince Foster committed suicide.[145]

On December 22, 1993, the White House refused to publicly release the records pertaining to the Clintons secretly taken from Foster's office. Myers says the records were given to the couple's personal attorney, David Kendall.[146]

On December 24, 1993, the Justice Department secretly issued a subpoena concerning the Vince Foster case. On January 5, 1994, it was announced that Clinton's lawyer had successfully negotiated with Justice Department officials to limit what would be turned over and to keep the records from being released publicly.[147]

In mid-February 1994, Deputy Attorney General Philip Heyman, who took exception to the White House's handling of the Foster investigation, was abruptly terminated. He was replaced with Jamie Gorelick, who had close ties to the embattled lawyers in the White House.[148] Around the same time the Republicans on the House Government Operations Committee launched a new investigation into the death of Vince Foster. The Republican probe was to determine "exactly what role the White House played and to what degree, if any, White House officials hindered or impeded the investigation."[149]

On March 7, 1994, Christopher Ruddy, whose exposés on the Vincent Foster case began running in the *New York Post* in January 1994, reported that Park Police had no "relationship photos" of the crime scene—that is, photos showing the relationship of Foster's body to its overall surroundings. Ruddy also said that other "crucial" crime scene photos were missing.[150]

Then, ABC *World News Tonight* aired a report, on March 11, 1994, claiming that they had seen a complete set of photographs showing Mr. Foster's body.[151] ABC even aired one close-up photo of the death scene showing his thumb in the trigger of the gun. It was a photograph that the public had not seen. The implication was clear. Though the segment never mentioned Ruddy by name, it strongly implied that this photo disproved his story. But did it?[152]

In fact, the Polaroid did not affect Ruddy's story one way or the other. Ruddy had never claimed that every crime scene photo was missing, only that certain *crucial* pictures were missing. And he was right. The close-up of Foster's hand was not a "relationship photo." Nor was it particularly crucial. It did not prove or disprove any part of Ruddy's theory. Moreover, it was just a Polaroid, which police shoot as back-ups until the real photos—shot on 35 mm film—are developed.[153]

ABC News claimed that it had seen a "complete set" of crime-scene photos. But had it really? One year after the broadcast, the government released documents showing that all 35-mm negatives taken at the Foster crime scene were "underexposed" and useless. There were no relationship shots and no videotape. Moreover, the most crucial and revealing Polaroids had gone missing. Only thirteen Polaroid close-ups remained in the police file—stunningly poor documentation for any homicide investigation. So how could ABC News have seen a "complete set" of crime scene photos?[154]

It turned out that Ruddy had been right all along. But his vindication came too late. ABC News had done its damage. It had destroyed Ruddy's credibility and killed the story. He was terminated by the *New York Post* in September 1994.[155]

On March 11, 1994, the *Washington Times* reported that Hillary Rodham Clinton ordered Rose Law Firm employees to shred documents during the 1992 presidential campaign when Whitewater became an issue. They admitted to shredding records belonging to Hillary and her three partners that she placed in the Clinton administration: Webster Hubbell, William Kennedy, and Vincent Foster. Also, two Rose Law Firm employees, Jeremy Hedges and Clayton Lindsey, said they shredded, on instructions from the firm, records from the files of Vincent Foster after the special prosecutor announced he was reopening the investigation of Mr. Foster's death.[156] Under U.S. law, a subpoena does not have to be in effect, or legal proceedings pending, in order for document shredding to be a federal crime. It is obstruction of justice to conceal, alter, or destroy evidence in anticipation of possible proceedings.[157]

On April 4, 1994, the Fiske investigation leaked to reporter Ellen Pollock of the *Wall Street Journal* that the investigation would conclude "suicide" even though no real investigation had taken place by that date, including FBI lab work and an independent autopsy review.[158] A month later an FBI report stated that after conducting a microscopic analysis of Foster's shoes, they found that they "did not contain coherent soil." How could that happen if Mr. Foster, who allegedly walked more than six hundred feet through the park to the spot where his body was found, not have any soil or even grass stains on his shoes?[159]

On June 12, 1994, Fiske came to the White House to question Bill and Hillary. Reluctantly, Kendall had acceded to the special counsel's insistence that they be examined under oath. Fiske's questioning of the Clintons at the White House was a courtesy—a respectful gesture to the office of the presidency. In lieu of a traditional appearance before a grand jury, he would take Bill's and Hillary's testimony and then have it read to the grand jurors who were considering evidence under his auspices.[160]

On June 30, 1994, Robert Fiske issued a fifty-eight-page report that Vince Foster committed suicide in Fort Marcy Park on July 20, 1993 and "there is no evidence to the contrary." He also said there was no evidence that Whitewater "or other personal legal matters of the president or Mrs. Clinton, were a factor in Foster's suicide." It should also be noted that Mr. Fiske refused to launch a grand jury investigation.[161]

Questions still remained unanswered:

- Where was Foster in the hours prior to his death?
- Why did no one see him alive or hear the fatal shot in the park?
- Why didn't Fiske investigate the hairs which the FBI found on Foster's clothes and underclothes. Where did they come from?
- Why didn't Fiske investigate how carpet fibers of various colors came to be all over his expensive clothing?
- Why was FBI Director William Sessions hurriedly fired the day before Foster's death, leaving no permanent head of the FBI for several weeks?
- Was the investigation, as Session has charged, "compromised from the beginning" by this action?
- Why were the U.S. Park Police given exclusive jurisdiction over the investigation of the death of such a high-ranking White House official?
- Why was an inexperienced officer, someone who had never conducted a homicide probe, permitted to serve as lead investigator?
- Why did the U.S. Park Police, within hours of Foster's death, give away critical pieces of evidence, like Foster's pager to the

Secret Service and the next day, his personal effects to the White House?
- How could the most elemental part of any homicide investigation, the key crime scene photos, have been "underexposed" in the U.S. Park Police labs?
- How could Fiske so easily accept the medical examiner's explanation that there were no X-rays of Foster's body because the machine was "inoperable," when both the autopsy report and the U.S. Park Police report clearly stated X-rays were taken?
- Why do blood tracks on Foster's face indicate his head assumed four distinct positions after his instantaneous death?
- How did blood run uphill, as one of the blood tracks on Foster's face shows, when his head was found in a normal, upright position on a steep slope?
- Why did neither the U.S. Park Police nor Fiske's investigators follow basic police practice by interviewing the many neighbors around Fort Marcy Park to see if they heard or saw anything unusual that fateful day?
- Why didn't anyone interview the person who spent the previous weekend with Mr. and Mrs. Foster?
- Why did Fiske's investigators, according to published reports, badger the confidential witness into changing his testimony about the crime scene to fit their own conclusions?
- Why is conflicting evidence, such as the claim by the same confidential witness to have seen wine cooler bottles near the body and in Foster's car, left out of the Fiske report?
- Why were observations by emergency workers noting additional wounds on Foster's head not recorded in their official reports?
- How did the FBI find traces of two drugs in Foster's blood when the original medical examiner's blood analysis found none?
- Why did Fiske accept the White House claim that a torn-up note, allegedly written by Foster, was found several days after his death in his briefcase, when the U.S. Park Police, in several published reports, said the briefcase was empty?

- How could Foster have torn a note into twenty-eight pieces without leaving any fingerprints?
- How did Foster's eyeglasses "bounce" nineteen feet from his body through dense foliage?
- Why was Foster's body not exhumed?
- Why was neither the fired bullet nor any bone fragments from Foster's head found at the site the police supposedly found the body?
- Why didn't Fiske's staff interview Charles Easley, the White House staffer in charge of safe combinations, including Foster's?
- Why was Craig Livingstone parked outside of Foster's house the morning after he died?[162]

On August 5, 1994, Appeals Court judges David Sentelle, John Butzner, and Joseph Snead rejected Reno's request to appoint Fiske as independent counsel. Instead, the three judges fired him and named former solicitor general and Appeals Court Judge Kenneth Starr as Independent Counsel.[163]

Soon, the White House spin machine went into overdrive. Clinton's spin doctors made a great show of courage, accusing Starr of being a "partisan" Republican with a vendetta. But, according to Christopher Ruddy, it was all an act.[164]

Privately, the Clintons celebrated Starr's appointment. So says Nolanda Hill, longtime lover and business associate of late Commerce Secretary Ron Brown. "[W]hen Starr was appointed, they were opening champagne bottles in the White House; they were celebrating," Hill told Ruddy. In fact, said Hill, Starr had been on Janet Reno's "short list" for special counsel before she appointed Robert Fiske to the post. "They would never have put him on the short list if they were worried about him," said Hill.[165]

Hill told Ruddy that Starr's entire investigative team had been infiltrated by Clinton operatives. Even the FBI agents assigned to Starr "were not working for Ken Starr in his Whitewater probe but for Reno and the White House, giving the Clinton administration de facto control over the Starr investigations," writes Ruddy.[166]

As Ruddy paints him, Starr was the sort of man who makes police states work. He may well have been the decent fellow as friends described, upright and diligent in his work. But Starr had a vice that outweighed all his virtues. He was a coward, so paralyzed with fear in the face of naked evil that he would look the other way and pretend not to see it. He was just the sort of man that Bill and Hillary needed.[167]

In October 1994, Ken Starr appointed Whitewater Associate Counsel Miguel Rodriguez to head up the Foster probe. Starr's mandate for a thorough investigation, though apparently conflicted with the desires of Mark Tuohey, Rodriguez's superior.[168] At one point, Tuohey took Rodriguez aside and told him that it would be ill-advised to challenge the essential findings of the Fiske Report. Nevertheless, Rodriguez soldiered on.[169]

The first thing Rodriguez noticed were little roadblocks left in his path. His requests for subpoenas were being held up. He was unable to call witnesses before the grand jury in a timely fashion. He was even having trouble obtaining Foster's credit card and travel records.[170]

Starr's staff did not choose new agents to work with Rodriguez on the case but kept the same agents to review their own work for Special Counsel Fiske. Notable was the lead FBI agent William Colombell. Colombell had been a senior agent working for Fiske in the Foster case. He along with Special Agent Larry Monroe testified in Senate hearings in the summer of 1994 and concluded Foster's death a suicide.[171] They also testified that their investigation found no major improprieties in the Park Police handling of the case. Monroe retired from the Bureau shortly after the Foster case was concluded by Fiske.[172]

One of Rodriguez's first requests to Colombell was that the FBI prepare a map of Fort Marcy Park, after he discovered, to his astonishment, that the Fiske investigation had drawn no survey map. Colombell refused, citing the fact the case had been concluded by Fiske and was not to be reopened.[173]

Rodriguez also noted that a rear entrance to the park had been misidentified in the Fiske report as for pedestrian access only when, in fact, vehicles are permitted to park there and regularly do so. An aerial photo of the park also showed a maintenance trail that led to the area where the body was claimed to have been discovered. That trail has since been allowed to overgrow.[174]

Rodriguez and Colombell remained at loggerheads for approximately three months, during which Rodriguez's requests for evidence and the questioning of witnesses were regularly denied. Eventually, Colombell was transferred from handling matters dealing with Foster's death.[175] Soon after that the campaign of leaks began. On January 5, 1995, Scripps Howard

News Service ran a story claiming that "sources familiar with the Starr inquiry," said that Kenneth Starr was ready to announce that Vincent Foster "committed suicide for reasons unrelated to the Whitewater controversy." Rodriguez was furious. He had just begun grand jury proceedings the day before. Who on earth would have leaked the news that the probe was finished?[176]

In February 1995, stories started appearing in the Washington press alleging that he had been badgering the Park Police officers at the grand jury. It was half-true. He had been reading them the perjury statutes in a deliberately pointed manner and with good reason. Their accounts were flatly contradicted by the Fairfax County paramedics, who had no obvious incentive to lie. One Park Police officer ultimately broke ranks under cross-examination and testified that the crime scene had been tampered with after he arrived.[177]

Then, in a disturbing twist, Rodriguez found that he could not trust the FBI investigators to do their job. The FBI lab had concluded that a set of crime scene photos were unusuable. But he knew this to be absurd, so he sent the film to a private laboratory, which had no trouble enhancing the photos. According to Ruddy, the photos revealed that the gun in Foster's hand was being moved around after the Park Police had arrived, with blades of glass protruding between different fingers in different photos.[178]

The *Tribune-Review* reported that a set of Polaroid photos had been deliberately blurred by the FBI. Rodriguez was able to obtain original copies, one of which was a photo of Foster's neck. It showed that Foster had a wound or bruise in the neck that had been dismissed as a blood "contact stain" in earlier reports and was not mentioned in the autopsy report. Evidently, somebody had taken a photo of the original and then touched it up to disguise the incriminating evidence. This second-generation copy had then been used to create an enhanced "blow up." It was blatant obstruction of justice. Indeed it was worse. Whoever had done this was now an accessory after the death of the Deputy White House Counsel, and they had made the mistake of failing to destroy the original.[179]

Wary of entrusting anything to the FBI crime labs, Rodriguez turned to the Smithsonian Institution to enhance the original. The work was done by the Smithsonian's subcontractor, Asman Custom Photo Service on Pennsylvania Avenue. A set of five "blowups" of the original were made. They revealed a dime-sized wound on the right side of Foster's neck (his left side) about half way between the chin and the ear. It was marked by a black "stippled" ring—a sort of dotted effect, like an engraving—that was suggestive of a .22 caliber gunshot fired at point blank range into the flesh.[180]

The photograph, which investigative journalist and author Ambrose Evans-Pritchard examined carefully, was one of the few surviving Polaroids taken at Fort Marcy Park that night. The rest disappeared, including most of the Polaroids taken by detective John Rolla.[181]

By the early spring of 1995, Rodriguez was starting to probe a hypothesis that the crime scene at Fort Marcy Park had been staged, that the gun had most likely been planted in Foster's hand, and that a crucial photograph of Foster's neck and head had been falsified. But, Rodriguez believed that the investigation was being sabotaged by prosecutors and FBI agents in his own office, He turned to Starr for support. Nothing was done to resolve the matter.[182]

The word was put out that Rodriguez was unstable. It was whispered that his conduct was becoming unprofessional. Drip, drip, drip. Rodriguez was being roasted slowly on the Beltway spit. It was how the Clinton administration dealt with people who refused to submit.[183]

Rodriguez then claimed that FBI agents bullied him, making threats against his "personal well-being," if he did not shut up. "The FBI told me back off, back down. I have been told to be careful where I tread," said Rodriguez.[184]

Rodriguez had had enough. He left Starr's Washington staff on March 29, 1995 and returned to his position as Assistant U.S. Attorney in Sacramento, California.[185] His sudden resignation could have exploded in scandal. But Big Media virtually ignored it. Indeed, Rodriguez claims that he tried to go public with his story, giving extensive interviews to reporters from *Time*, *Newsweek*, ABC's *Nightline*, the *Boston Globe*, the *Atlanta Journal-Constitution*, and the *New York Times*. Rodriguez says he spent six hours with the *New York Times* reporter alone. To all of them, Rodriguez told the same story: Starr's probe of Vincent Foster's death was a sham. Yet, none of the news organizations that interviewed Rodriguez aired or published his account. Several reporters admitted to Rodriguez that their editors had spiked the story.[186]

On July 15, 1997, Kenneth Starr issued a terse statement: "Based on investigation, analysis and review of the evidence by experts and experienced investigators and prosecutors, this Office concluded that Mr. Foster committed suicide by gunshot in Fort Marcy Park, VA, on July 20, 1993."[187]

On October 10, 1997, Ken Starr's three-year investigation of Foster's death concluded. In a 114-page report, he reaffirmed earlier findings of suicide.[188] "It is the Rosetta Stone to the Clinton administration," Richard Mellon Scaife—billionaire oil and banking heir, philanthropist, newspaper publisher, and funder of political causes told the late John F. Kennedy Jr. in an exclusive interview in the January 1999 issue of *George* magazine. "Once you solve that one mystery, you'll know everything that's going on."[189]

Pressed to explain further, Scaife responded: "Listen, [Clinton] can order people done away at his will. He's got the entire federal government behind him. . . . God, there must be 60 people . . . who have died mysteriously—including eight of Clinton's former body-guards. . . . There have been mysterious deaths.[190]

Whatever the circumstances of Vince Foster's death, he was clearly a man who knew many of the money secrets of both the campaign of 1992 and the Clinton presidency, just as he knew the secrets of the Rose Law Firm and of Hillary Rodham Clinton's business and financial dealings over the previous decade, dealings that would become the subject of numerous investigations and would cast an even greater shadow over the White House than his death would.[191]

CHAPTER 17

THE TROOPERS TALK

What does that whore think she's doing to me?
—Bill Clinton, January 1992[1]

Under Arkansas state law, the state troopers were responsible for safeguarding the first family of Arkansas, as well as the grounds of the gubernatorial mansion in downtown Little Rock. Yet, during the five terms that Clinton held office, the troopers functioned as chauffeurs, butlers, bodyguards, errand boys, and baggage handlers. They did everything for the Clintons from receiving and placing the telephone calls to changing bicycle tires and cleaning up after Socks the cat.[2]

The troopers said their "official" duties included facilitating Clinton's cheating on his wife. That meant, on the state payroll and using state time, vehicles and resources, they were instructed by Clinton on a regular basis to approach women and solicit their telephone numbers for the governor. The troopers also drove Clinton in state vehicles to rendezvous points and guarded him during sexual encounters. This included securing hotel rooms and other meeting places for sex, to lend Clinton their state cars so he could slip away and visit women unnoticed. Lastly, the troopers were used to deliver gifts from Clinton to various women and to help Clinton cover up his activities by keeping tabs on Hillary's whereabouts and lying to Hillary about her husband's whereabouts.[3]

By the end of the summer 1993, Bill Clinton had been tipped off that Arkansas state troopers who had previously worked on his security detail were now talking to journalists about what went on at the Governor's

Mansion. Two of the troopers, Danny Ferguson and Ronnie Anderson, were upset that the Clintons had passed them over for government jobs and didn't want to be identified. Two others, Roger Perry and Larry Anderson, would have remained silent, but Bill Clinton ignored their request for autographed pictures. When one of the troopers asked Clinton to sign some photographs for his family after the election, he said the president-elect snapped: "I don't have time for that shit."[4]

After the 1992 election, Clinton made Buddy Young, the former chief of Governor Clinton's security detail, the regional head of FEMA in Denton, Texas. When the troopers began talking to reporters, Young, at Clinton's request, warned them about the consequences. "I represent the president of the United States," Young told Roger Perry. "If you and whoever do that, your reputations will be destroyed, and you will be destroyed." Young called the wavering Danny Ferguson and Ronnie Anderson and delivered similar messages, while dangling the possibility of a White House job for Ferguson's wife. Governor Jim Guy Tucker reinforced the point with Trooper Perry: "Roger you will not survive this." Clinton called Danny Ferguson three times, offering him and Roger Perry federal jobs like Buddy Young's, which paid $92,300 a year. Ferguson recalled the president saying, "Dan, would you like to have a job? Would you like to come to D.C.? On the second call to Ferguson, Clinton asked what precisely Perry and Patterson were saying, Perry said. "If you tell me what stories Roger and Larry are telling, I can go in the back door and handle it and clean it up," Clinton allegedly said.[5]

The troopers believed the Clintons' relationship was a political partnership, more of a business relationship than a marriage. They described Bill as the public face, the more personable of the two. He was the good cop, the communicator, the conciliator, a man who loved to be liked and even talked with the troopers about his "star" qualities.[6]

Hillary, on the other hand, played the bad cop. She was gutsy and decisive. She was more obsessed than Bill with his political fortunes. According to trooper Patterson, one time when Bill had been quoted in the morning paper saying something that Hillary didn't like she "came into the mansion and Bill was standing at the top of the stairs and Hillary was standing at the bottom screaming at him." Patterson went into the kitchen, and the cook, Miss Emma, turned to him and said, "The devil's in that woman."[7]

The troopers themselves were, at times, objects of Hillary's wrath. Patterson recalled an incident that occurred in the early morning of Labor Day in 1991. Hillary came out of the mansion, got in her car, an Oldsmobile Cutlass, and drove off. About a minute after leaving the gate, she quickly turned around and came speeding back into the grounds. Obviously, the trooper thought something was wrong, so he rushed out to her. She screamed: " 'Where is the goddamn fucking flag?' It was early and we hadn't raised the flag yet. And she shrieked, 'I want the goddamn fucking flag up every fucking morning at fucking sunrise.' "[8]

According to Patterson, Bill Clinton had many long-term mistresses from 1987 to early 1993. To begin with, there was Gennifer Flowers. Then you had a staffer in Clinton's office; an Arkansas lawyer Clinton appointed to a judgeship; the wife of a prominent judge; a local reporter; an employee at Arkansas Power and Light, a state-regulated public utility; and a cosmetics sales clerk at a Little Rock department store. Clinton would visit one of these women, either early in the morning or the late evening. Sometimes, one of them would come to the residence to see him, at least two or three times a week.[9]

Again, according to Patterson, Clinton visited his regular Little Rock girlfriends in the early morning, during what were long jogs. "He would jog out of the mansion grounds very early most mornings and then we would go pick him up at a McDonald's at Seventh Street and Broadway." Patterson continued. "When we picked him up, half of the time he would be covered in sweat and the other half of the time, there wouldn't be a drop of sweat on him, even in the middle of July in Little Rock. Sometimes I'd ask him, 'How far did you run today governor?' And he would say, five miles. 'I'd tell him there must be something wrong with his sweat glands because he didn't have a drop of sweat on him.' He'd say, 'I can't fool you guys, can I?'"[10]

There were times when the troopers drove Clinton from the Governor's Mansion late in the evening to various women's homes and waited for hours for him to emerge. Patterson recalled that the first time he did this was in 1987, when he parked his car outside the home of a Clinton staffer. Patterson sat in his car from midnight until about 4:30 a.m., waiting for the governor. Finally, Clinton emerged, got in the car, and congratulated him on his stealthiness. "He told me it was our responsibility to cover his ass so he wouldn't get in trouble," Patterson said. Bill did get caught once in a while.[11]

Hillary is generally a heavy sleeper. One time, Hillary woke up in the middle of the night, turned on the bedroom light, and called down to the guard house looking for Bill. "The sorry damn son of a bitch!" she screamed when told the governor had gone out for a drive. Perry grabbed the cellular phone to inform Clinton, who was up at one of the women's homes, to get back to the residence fast. "He started saying, 'Oh god, god, god. What did you tell her?'" Perry recalled. When Clinton finally arrived, Hillary was waiting for him in the kitchen. Then, a wild screaming match began. When Perry entered the kitchen after the Clintons were gone, the room was a wreck, with a cabinet door kicked off its hinges.[12]

Clinton usually tried to conduct his liaisons in private. There were other occasions, however, when the troopers actually witnessed the acts. In the fall of either 1988 or 1989, as Patterson remembered it, he was driving Clinton to an annual reception for the Harrison County Chamber of Commerce in a hospitality suite at the Camelot Hotel in Little Rock. On the way, Clinton recommended a detour to Chelsea's school, Booker Elementary. When they arrived, Clinton told Patterson the sales clerk was sitting in her car, which was parked in the otherwise deserted front parking lot. "I parked across the entrance and stood outside the car looking around, about 120 feet from where they were parked in a lot that was pretty well lit. I could see Clinton get into the front seat and then the lady's head go into his lap. They stayed in the car for thirty or forty minutes," Patterson recalled.[13]

On another occasion, Patterson was on duty at the residence when, late in the evening, the same woman drove up in a yellow and black Datsun or Nissan pick-up truck and asked to see Clinton. "The governor came out of the residence and climbed into the front seat of the truck, which was parked in an area off the rear drive," Patterson recalled. This time, Patterson said, he got an even clearer view of the sex act by aiming a remote-camera with a swivel base mounted on a thirty-foot pole in the back yard of the house right into the truck. The image was projected onto a twenty-seven-inch video screen in the guard house. "He was sitting on the passenger side and she was behind the wheel. I pointed the thing directly into the windshield and watched on the screen as the governor received oral sex," Patterson said.[14]

Clinton also had a series of brief affairs and one-time encounters from 1987 to early 1993. He often met women at social functions in Little Rock or on the road. Sometimes he would even use troopers as intermediaries, sending them off with messages and outright propositions to women to retire to back rooms, hotel rooms, or offices with him.[15]

One of the troopers told the story of how Clinton had eyed a woman at a reception at the Excelsior Hotel in downtown Little Rock. According to the trooper, who told the story to Patterson and Perry as well, Clinton asked him to approach the woman, whom the trooper remembered as Paula (soon to be Paula Corbin Jones), to tell her how attractive the governor thought she was and take her to a room in the hotel where Clinton would be waiting to meet her. As the troopers explained it, the standard procedure in a case like this was for one of them to inform the hotel that the governor needed a room for a short time because he was expecting an important call from the White House.[16]

There were also times when Clinton would spend a lot of time speaking with an attractive woman at a public event. At one such event several troopers recalled hearing Hillary complain bitterly. "She would say, 'Come on Bill, put your dick up. You can't fuck here,'" as Patterson remembered the unforgettable phrasing.[17]

The troopers believed that Hillary tolerated this behavior much as eighteenth-century aristocrats maintained marriages of convenience to suit the social and material needs of both parties. As for Hillary, "it was common knowledge around the mansion that Hillary and Vince were having an affair," said Larry Patterson. Whenever Bill Clinton left town, no sooner would he be out of the mansion gates than Foster would appear, often staying in the residence with Hillary into the early hours of the morning. One of the off-the-record troopers drove Hillary and Foster to a mountain cabin in Heber Springs. It was maintained by the Rose Law firm as an out-of-town retreat for its lawyers. Evidently, the two spent significant amounts of time alone there. On several occasions, at the Heber Springs retreat, once stopped at a traffic light in Little Rock, the troopers said they observed Foster and Hillary embracing and open-mouth kissing.[18]

Many believed that Bill Clinton was aware of the affair, starting around the mid-1980s, and accepted it as part of the bargain in their marriage. "Bill knew, of course he knew," said a lawyer close to Foster who was familiar with them all. "But, what the hell is he supposed to say to anybody about being faithful?"[19]

On January 16, 1993, the Clinton family were scheduled to fly from Little Rock to Washington to prepare for Bill Clinton's coronation as the forty-second President of the United States. That morning, Bill awoke unusually early. He walked past his sleeping daughter's bedroom and sneaked down to the game room in the basement. It was five in the morning. He was expecting a special gift to be delivered.[20]

The governor had told his new Secret Service detail that a staffer would be arriving early. At 5:15 a.m., state trooper Danny Ferguson drove through the mansion gates. His instructions were to deliver his passenger at the basement door. Out of the official car stepped Marilyn Jo Jenkins, a tall, slender figure wrapped in a long coat, her face half hidden by a baseball cap. She quickly went inside.[21]

At about 6:00 a.m., Clinton emerged like a happy camper. He turned her over to Ferguson. The trooper, who had often taken presents from the governor to her, tucked her into his official car to drive her back to her place.[22]

Then, later on in the day, there was a scene at the Little Rock airport where Hillary noticed a state trooper escorting one of the women to the farewell ceremony and became very angry. "What the fuck do you think you're doing?" she asked Larry Patterson. "I know who that whore is. I know what she's doing here. Get her out of here." Once caught, Clinton simply shrugged and the trooper took the woman back to the city.[23]

The stories would eventually get out. On Friday, December 17, 1993, the *American Spectator* began to fax copies of the article, "Living with the Clintons," by David Brock around Washington. By Saturday, the White House knew that the *Los Angeles Times* and CNN were considering running articles on the troopers' stories. David Gergen, a White House counselor, was trying to discourage the stories, relaying rumors that the troopers had been paid for their story.[24] That afternoon, the Clintons gathered in the residence with the following advisers: Mack McLarty, David Gergen, George Stephanopoulos, Bruce Lindsey, as well as David Kendall, the Clinton's private attorney and another attorney from the firm. They were there to talk strategy about what was coming. Clinton had received a copy of the *American Spectator* story. He pressed his advisers for their opinions on how big the trooper story would be, where it would lead, and what they should do. No one knew whether the story would be picked up by the mainstream press.[25]

The next day, on Sunday, December 19, at six o'clock on CNN, Roger Perry and Larry Patterson, the two troopers who had gone on the record with the *American Spectator*, talked about Clinton's sexual activities and said that Clinton had offered another trooper, Danny Ferguson, a job in exchange for his silence. Soliciting anything of value in consideration for the promise of federal employment was a federal crime. The trooper was allegedly offered a job either as U.S. Marshall in Little Rock or as a regional director of the Federal Emergency Management Agency.[26]

On Sunday night, Bruce Lindsey issued a statement which was the first in a series of non-denial denials of the allegations about Clinton's sex life:

> The allegations are ridiculous. Similar allegations were made, investigated, and responded to during the campaign, and there is nothing here that would dignify a further response. . . . [The President] has had conversations about the fact that false stories were being spread about him.[27]

Bruce Lindsey and Dee Dee Myers dealt with the public response while the president stayed quiet. Myers announced that the press briefings for Monday and Tuesday, December 20 and 21, were canceled. Hillary had been scheduled to do interviews Tuesday on ABC, CBS, and NBC, to be broadcast during Christmas week. All three network news organizations canceled after Lisa Caputo informed them they could only inquire about the observance of Christmas at the White House: "about the crafts and the ornaments and the kind of entertainment the Clintons were having."[28]

On Tuesday, December 21, 1993, the *Los Angeles Times* published its story reporting that telephone logs revealed that Governor Clinton had called one of his mistresses fifty-nine times from 1989 to 1991. The woman insisted that he was helping her with a "personal" problem. One of his calls was made at 1:23 a.m. and lasted ninety-four minutes. It appears the "personal" problem persisted, for after the presidential election, Clinton met the woman in the basement of the Governor's Mansion, early in the morning, as a trooper stood lookout while Hillary slept soundly upstairs.[29]

On the same day, Hillary responded by calling the troopers' accounts "outrageous, terrible stories." Blaming the furor on the president's right-wing enemies, she said, "I find it not an accident that every time he is on the verge of fulfilling his commitment to the American people and they respond . . . out comes yet a new round of these outrageous, terrible stories that people plant for political and financial reasons."[30]

Mrs. Clinton would later call the troopers' story "trash for cash," and a "political vendetta." Author James Stewart reported in his book *Blood Sport* that Betsey Wright admitted to White House counselor David Gergen that, as far as she could tell, the troopers were telling the truth.[31]

The next day, Wednesday, December 22, 1993, the president himself addressed the issue. Echoing the first lady's earlier statements, he called the charges "outrageous." But he carefully avoided a specific denial of the facts of the case. Finally, a radio reporter asked, "So none of this ever happened?" It took Clinton nearly ten seconds to get a word out. "I have nothing else to say," he began. "We . . . we did, if, the, the, I, I, the stories are just as they have been said. They're outrageous and they're not so." When the tape was played on one of the network news broadcasts, the effect was very damaging.[32]

White House attorney Bruce Lindsey, doing his best damage control, accidently interrupted an on-the-air interview that ABC-TVs *World News Tonight* was doing with Trooper Patterson's former supervisor, Buddy Young. Mr. Lindsey, who had no idea Mr. Young was in the middle of a live interview with his speaker on, said after being told he was talking to ABC, "We may need you to do CNN, too, at some point."[33]

Finally, on April 11, 1994, Arkansas state trooper L.D. Brown, a fourteen-year veteran, came forward and stated that he solicited "over a hundred" sex partners for then-governor Bill Clinton. Not all were successful though. Mr. Brown worked with then-Governor Bill Clinton's security detail from late-1982 to mid-1985. On May 4, 1994, Mr. Brown was demoted from his position as an investigator with the white-collar crimes division to patrol duties in Pulaski County, which included Little Rock. The transfer order was signed by Col. Tommy Goodwin, who had been the state police director of several Arkansas governors, including Mr. Clinton.[34]

CHAPTER 18

WHITEWATER

As you know, in March 1992, the Clinton Campaign released a report by an independent accounting firm which establishes that the Clintons lost at least $68,900 on Whitewater Development Corporation. They received no gain of any kind from their investment. The Clintons were not involved in the management or operation of the company, nor did they keep its records. We see no need to supplement the March 1992 CPA report or to provide further documentation.

—Bruce Lindsey on Whitewater[1]

In the spring of 1978, Jim and Susan McDougal met Bill and Hillary Clinton one night at the Black-Eyed Pea restaurant in Little Rock where Jim offered them a profitable development on the banks of the White River in Marion County. The project would be called Whitewater. The Clintons were interested as Bill had nearly doubled his money in another investment with McDougal.[2]

On August 2, 1978, the McDougals and the Clintons bought the 230 acres along the White River from 101 River Development, Inc. It was a local partnership that was splitting up a larger parcel.[3] The financing of the deal was the best part. The land cost $202,611 and they could buy it no money down. Part of the money would come from a bank that was supporting Clinton's election for governor of Arkansas. The rest would come from another bank. It was agreed that Susan and Jim McDougal would manage the business and bear most of the risk and liability. They also personally guaranteed nearly $200,000 of the total loans, while Bill and Hillary would retain a 50 percent ownership. The Clintons could even deduct interest paid on the loans amounting to $10,000 in 1978 and $12,000 in 1979.[4]

It was a remarkable opportunity for a young couple who less than two years before were modestly paid law school instructors. In 1977, their combined taxable income in Little Rock had been only $41,000. Obviously, they never would have qualified for such financing or investment opportunities without conventional collateral or capital.[5]

On June 19, 1978, Bill Clinton and Jim McDougal signed for a $20,000 loan from Union National Bank. Though the $20,000 down payment was also borrowed, the Clintons and McDougals never told Citizen's Bank that they had no equity in the deal. Clinton himself lobbied Union National for the money, and former bank official Don Denton would later tell the Senate committee that his bosses told him to make the loan because Clinton was an "up and coming political . . . a rising star.[6]

Then you had the following financial transactions conducted on Whitewater:

* On August 2, 1978, the Clintons and McDougals signed for a $182,611 mortgage loan from Citizens Bank of Flippin.
* On June 18, 1979, Jim McDougal signed stock certificate to Hillary Rodham representing 150 shares of Whitewater stock.
* On June 19, 1979, Bill Clinton and Jim McDougal signed for a $20,000 loan renewal from Union National Bank.
* On September 17, 1979, Bill Clinton and Jim McDougal signed for a $20,000 loan renewal from Union National Bank.
* On September 30, 1979, the Clintons and McDougals signed a warranty deed associated with Whitewater property.
* On November 9, 1979, there was a meeting at the Governor's Mansion attended by Governor Clinton and Jim McDougal. They signed for a $182,611 mortgage loan received from Citizens Bank of Flippin.
* On December 17, 1979, Bill Clinton and Jim McDougal signed for a $20,000 loan renewal from Union National Bank.
* On August 5, 1980, Bill Clinton and Jim McDougal signed for a $182,611 mortgage loan renewal from Citizens Bank of Flippin.[7]

In 1980, McDougal bought the Bank of Kingston and changed its name to Madison Bank and Trust.[8] On December 16, 1980, Hillary

Clinton obtained a $30,000 loan from Jim McDougal's Bank of Kingston. The purpose of this loan was to place a pre-fab house on Whitewater's Lot 13, which was positioned near the entrance to the development in an attempt to spur lot sales. Consequently, the Clintons must have known as early as December 1980 that Whitewater was experiencing slow lot sales. The loan marked the beginning of the tangled web of deals, transfers, and co-mingling of individuals and corporations that later investigators found riddled with legal and ethical discrepancies.[9]

Enclosed is the tale of Lot 13:

- The mortgagor released Lot 13 to Whitewater Development, which transferred it to Hillary Rodham Clinton without payment of one penny.
- Hillary used the land as collateral to get the $30,000 loan. A check for that amount, without any notation, was deposited into the Whitewater account.
- A modular home was purchased and placed on Lot 13. Hillary was given the deed for the lot and the house.
- In a strange legal twist, Whitewater—not the owner, Hillary Rodham Clinton—regularly paid the principal and most of the interest payments on the $30,000 loan.
- On December 14, 1981, Hillary sold the lot and house to Hillman Logan for $27,900, and may have pocketed the down payment, which Jim McDougal had hinted at.
- Mr. Logan made several payments, then went bankrupt, after which he died. Hillary bought back the land and the house from the bankruptcy court for $8,000.
- Meanwhile, Governor Clinton borrowed $20,000 from another bank to pay off the balance of Hillary's loan.
- Hillary resold Lot 13 and the model house for $28,000. She paid off the loan, on which she had never made any principal payments. The Clintons kept the balance of the money and though they made a profit of $20,000, they reported a capital-gains tax of only $1,640.
- Bill and Hillary Clinton later sold the same lot for $18,666. An October 31, 1988, warranty deed transferring the 2.66-acre parcel to John and Marilyn Lauramoore was signed only

by the Clintons. The sale was recorded at the courthouse in Yellville on Nov. 28, 1988, three weeks after Mrs. Clinton sought power of attorney over the Whitewater project.[10]

Interestingly, Hillary Clinton claimed tax deductions in the first year, 1979, on Whitewater, even though the Whitewater Development Corporation was making the payments. She took the deduction anyway. She illegally took the deduction again in 1980.[11]

On August 5, 1981, the Clintons and the McDougals signed for a $129,241 mortgage loan renewal from Citizens Bank of Flippin. On March 1, 1982, Jim McDougal sent a letter to Bill Clinton stating, "I have paid from Whitewater Development Corporation the note you owed Citizens Bank of Jonesboro. You are correct in your belief that the sum of money borrowed was part of your investment in Whitewater." A handwritten note on the bottom of the letter read, "Response to Hillary," indicating that Mrs. Clinton apparently inquired about the matter and requested the above statement from Jim McDougal, possibly for tax purposes.[12]

By May 1982, Whitewater's books showed land sales of about $300,000. In some cases, buyers defaulted, allowing Whitewater Development Corp. to sell the lots again.[13]

On August 5, 1982, Theresa Pockrus of Madison Bank and Trust sent a letter to Hillary Rodham reminding her that her loan was past due. Six days later Hillary Rodham sent a letter to Theresa Pockrus stating, "I ask that you speak with either Mr. or Mrs. McDougal who have made all the arrangements for this loan."[14]

On November 1, 1982, the Clintons and McDougals signed for a $20,000 interest funding loan from Citizens Bank of Flippin. The purpose of the loan was to pay accrued interest due on the land mortgage because Whitewater was not generating sufficient income to service the bank debt. Consequently, the Clintons must have known at this point that the land venture could not pay its bills.[15]

On March 28, 1983, Mrs. Clinton sent a letter on the Governor's Mansion letterhead to "Dear Gaines" which reads, in part, "Here are my records. I've tried to list all categories of income and deductions on the enclosed typed pages . . . I do not as yet have the tax info from McDougal's accountant about White River. I will try to get it but may want you to contact him. After you've had a chance to review these, I'd be glad to meet with you." Obviously, Mrs. Clinton was actively involved in the handling of Whitewater's financial records.[16]

Governor Clinton began hopping around to different banks in the area to continue funding Whitewater. On September 30, 1983, Governor Clinton signed for a $20,800 loan from Security Bank of Paragould, the proceeds of which were remitted directly to Madison Bank and Trust and applied to Hillary Clinton's loan from 1980 to build a modular home at Whitewater. An undated payment of $5,796 completed repayment of the original loan.[17]

On June 26, 1984, after summoning Madison Guaranty's (McDougal's bank) directors to Dallas, and despite the warning signs, the Federal Home Loan Bank Board authorities decided not to close down the bank nor seriously disciplined Jim McDougal. Instead, McDougal received a "supervisory agreement," a relatively mild form of probation.[18]

On September 30, 1984, the Clintons signed for a $18,800 loan renewal from Security Bank of Paragould. Whitewater paid $4,811.19 on the loan for accrued interest and a $2,000 principle reduction. The Clintons improperly deducted the $2,811.19 interest payment paid by Whitewater on their personal tax returns.[19]

It appeared, throughout 1984, that the relationship between Jim McDougal and Governor Clinton grew even closer and even more lucrative for Mr. Clinton. A federal investigation later found evidence that at least $60,500 had been appropriated from Madison Guaranty to Governor Clinton's 1984 reelection campaign and the governor's official campaign committee would be named in Justice Department criminal investigative documents as an alleged coconspirator in the diversion of depositors' funds. Even then, the suspected appropriating appeared to be only a fraction of the money that campaign aides saw pouring into the 1984 race.[20]

In the later part of 1984, after his reelection, Clinton interrupted his morning jog to appear unannounced at McDougal's Quapaw office, looking for a favor. Bill Clinton began complaining about his personal income and expenses, that his statehouse salary and Hillary's law partnership were not enough. "I asked him how much he needed, and Clinton said, 'about $2,000 a month,'" McDougal later told the *New York Times*. In response McDougal promptly put Hillary on a $2,000-a-month retainer, with the unusual arrangement that it be paid to her personally rather than to or through the firm. Afterwards, the governor was there at the Quapaw office on his morning jog regularly each month to pick up the check, and on occasion Hillary herself came for the money.[21]

On November 26, 1984, the Clintons and McDougals signed for a $100,121 mortgage loan renewal from Citizens Bank of Flippin. The Clintons should have questioned how a $27,954 principal reduction was made in light of past chronic shortfalls and minimal lot activity since the last renewal. Related correspondence indicates that the loan renewal was not actually signed on this date.[22]

In mid-January 1985, Bill Clinton, at the urging of McDougal, replaced Lee Thalheimer, the outgoing State Securities Department director and McDougal critic, with Beverly Bassett, an attorney with a Little Rock firm that had done work for Madison. Beverly Bassett was the sister of Clinton's former student and aide Woody Bassett and would become the wife of Archie Schaffer, a Tyson executive and a nephew of Senator Bumpers.[23]

Then, within days, Clinton came back for his own favor. As McDougal remembered, the governor telephoned in late January 1985 and asked him to "knock out the deficit of the 1984 campaign, meaning the $50,000 Clinton had borrowed personally from Maurice Smith's Bank of Cherry Valley for a final barrage of ads."[24]

"Bill's in trouble, and we're going to have to get together and help him out," Madison employees remembered McDougal's telling them after Clinton's call. Some were "promised," by one account that they would be "reimbursed" for donations, though from what source was not disclosed.[25]

On March 26, 1985, Governor Clinton received a memorandum from his staff about attending Jim McDougal's fund-raiser on April 4, 1985, around 4:00 or 4:30. Governor Clinton responds with a handwritten note on the bottom of the memorandum stating, "really needs at least one hour."[26]

On April 3, 1985, Davis Fitzhugh, Madison's in-house counsel, called the Arkansas Securities Commission and floated the idea of the preferred stock deal to Charles Handley, Beverly Bassett's second in command. Unfortunately, on April 16, Fitzhugh reported the bad news that the S&L could only issue common stock, not preferred stock to Madison executive John Latham, who was serving on the securities commission board. McDougal was upset at the news and, on April 18, 1985, wrote to Latham and said: "I want this preferred stock matter cleared up immediately as I need to go to Washington to sell stock."[27]

The next day, Jim McDougal hosted a fund-raiser for Governor Clinton at Madison Guaranty to help him retire his personal $50,000 loan he used to finance his 1984 re-election campaign. About $35,000 is raised at that event. Federal auditors would later find that $12,000 in certified checks were drawn on Madison Guaranty, yet attributed to "phantom contributors" who made no donations. Provoked by the bogus checks, an examination of Madison books showed similarly suspicious movements of cash-inflated closing costs, commissions, and transfers, coinciding with the final, free-spending weeks of the Clintons' 1984 run.[28]

Interestingly, records would later show that not all of the fund-raiser donations went to pay off the Clintons' note. Authorities said a May 1986 campaign report shows that $8,000 of the $35,000 went to provide seed money for Mr. Clinton's 1986 reelection bid. The records also show that as much as $14,000 of the funds raised by Mr. McDougal went unreported on Mr. Clinton's campaign filings, including four checks investigators suspect were illegally diverted from Madison.[29]

In April 1985, two letters to Beverly Bassett from the Rose Law Firm, pointedly referred to Hillary Rodham Clinton as the senior lawyer on the matter and pressed for swift approval of the stock plan. Both letters showed clearly that Hillary and her Rose associates were aware that Madison had not met federally mandated requirements for cash reserves.[30]

That same month McDougal and Latham met with Hillary and retained the Rose Law Firm. Interestingly, a file marked "Madison Guaranty— Sale of Stock" had been opened at the Mitchell firm, McDougal's regular counsel, in early February 1985, but something caused McDougal abruptly to switch the project to Rose. On April 29, Hillary telephoned the state's banking regulator, Beverly Bassett and assured her that the preferred-stock proposal would meet state requirements. That conversation occurred a day before the proposal was formally submitted to the Securities Department for review. Was Hillary improperly using her influence with Bassett, an appointee of her husband's on McDougal's behalf?[31]

On April 30, the Rose Law Firm submitted a plan to the Arkansas Securities Department for Madison's recapitalization. The letter was signed "the Rose Law Firm," but the last sentence pointedly stated: "Should you require further information or assistance, please advise Hillary Rodham Clinton or Richard Massey of this firm." On May 14, 1985, in a return letter addressed to Hillary, Beverly Bassett ruled to approve McDougal's issue of the stock, despite continuing vocal opposition among her staff. But the stock was never issued, and the condition of Madison Guaranty grew more desperate. Overdrafts were building up and a new federal examination was scheduled in early 1986.[32]

In May, McDougal sold off the remaining twenty-four Whitewater lots to Chris Wade, the local real estate broker who had handled the sale of the land to McDougal. Wade put up no cash, but he agreed to pay $35,000 toward the Citizens Bank mortgage and gave McDougal a twin-engine Piper Seminole airplane, which was valued at about $30,000. None of the transactions were reported in the Clintons' 1985 tax returns.[33]

On November 8, 1985, Jim McDougal sent a letter to Charles Campbell, Security Bank of Paragould Vice President, and copied Bill. In it McDougal enclosed a $7,322.42 Whitewater check to be applied to Bill Clinton's loan. Whitewater paid $2,322.42 on the loan for accrued interest and a $5,000 principal reduction. It is not clear why Mr. McDougal would pay off a debt owed by Mr. Clinton that, according to the records, had nothing to do with Whitewater. On top of that, the Clintons improperly deducted the $2,322.42 interest payment paid by Whitewater on their personal tax returns.[34]

In the fall of 1985, McDougal began looking for a new source of revenue. This is where David Hale comes in. David Hale was a judge and banker. McDougal began inquiring about his lending company. One evening, Hale said, Jim Guy Tucker drove him to McDougal's office at his Castle Grande development. Once there, McDougal asked him how much he could help in cleaning things up for their "political family."[35]

David Hale and Arkansas State Trooper L.D. Brown both stated that during the first week of February 1986, Hale encountered Governor Clinton returning from his morning jog on the steps of the State Capitol, and that Governor Clinton pressured Hale to make a loan during that encounter, asking if he was going to "help him and Jim out."[36]

When Mr. Clinton brought it up, "David was kind of taken aback, a little bit shocked; he dropped his head. It was more than normal conversation. It was like this is the kind of thing you discuss behind closed doors," Trooper Brown said.[37]

David Hale confirmed the encounter and also confirmed that Jim McDougal asked him to meet Clinton after work at Castle Grande. McDougal had already asked him for a $150,000 loan for Madison, mentioning an upcoming federal examination. At the meeting "Jim said we'll put it in Susan's advertising company" Hale said. "When we talked about how to structure it, Clinton explained that his name could not show up anywhere. McDougal made the statement that that was all taken care of. What he meant, I don't know." If Bill Clinton and Jim McDougal had in fact been secret beneficiaries of the Small Business Investment Company (SBIC) loan to Susan, their use of her to conceal their involvement in the loan in all likelihood would have been indictable fraud. Clinton has said that he didn't remember such a meeting. But now we have phone logs that bear Hale out:

- February 3, 9:15 a.m., "Bill Clinton called Re David Hale."
- February 3, 9:23 a.m., "Bill Clinton called, 'Be in my office in hour,' "
- February 4, 1:40 p.m., "David Hale called."[38]

When Hale asked what type of security should be listed on the federal loan documents, Clinton said that he and the McDougals owned property in Marion County. Hale initially balked at the development as too remote and problematic to list as collateral. Despite that, the loan would go forward. After twenty minutes Hale left, agreeing to provide the federal money.[39]

Within days, McDougal called Hale about the loan for Clinton and out of the blue asked him to double the amount to $300,000. Hale agreed yet again to make the loan.[40]

On March 4, 1986, barely nine months after Hillary Rodham Clinton and the Rose Law Firm assured Beverly Bassett that Madison was free of its old problems and safe for new investors and depositors, the Federal Home Loan Bank Board auditors issued a seventy-eight-page confidential audit that exposed a far different reality for Madison. It was a catalog of "financial abuse, accounting discrepancies, missing records, high-risk land developments, poor asset quality, inadequate income and net worth, etc., which constituted a significant threat to the continued existence of the institution."[41]

On April 3, 1986, on the basis that the federal funds were going to a "disadvantaged" businesswoman (the McDougals had a net worth of over $2 million), David Hale made out a check for $300,000, payable to Susan H. McDougal, doing business as Master Marketing. Promptly deposited without endorsement, the check was stamped, "Guaranteed by Madison

Guaranty Savings and Loan Little Rock."[42]

On July 2, 1986, Arkansas Securities Commissioner Beverly Bassett sent a handwritten note to Governor Bill Clinton's top assistant, Sam Bratton, to tell him about a pending meeting in Dallas before federal regulators considering Madison. She said, in part, "Madison Guaranty is in pretty serious trouble. Because of Bill's relationship w/McDougal, we probably ought to talk about it." "Please note," Ms. Bassett continued, "that while all of the FHLBB restrictions in the letter are serious, #5 & #6 effectively put Madison out of business." This note tipped off a potential insider as to the progress of an investigation.[43]

Ms. Bassett also attached to her note to Mr. Bratton, a copy of the July Federal Home Loan Bank Board (FHLBB) report on Madison, listing six management concerns and suggesting that the thrift's owner, James McDougal, had operated the savings and loan in an "unsafe and unsound" manner.[44] On July 11, 1986, James and Susan McDougal were removed from the savings and loan association at a meeting of the Federal Home Loan Bank in Dallas attended by Bassett. Three days later, Mrs. Clinton sent Jim McDougal a letter returning Madison's $2,000 monthly retainer check for the month and another check for $4,622.53, the thrift's unused retainer credit, thus refusing to conduct any further business with Madison Guaranty.[45]

On July 14, 1986, Betsey Wright, an aide to Bill Clinton, sent the governor a separate note saying: "Whitewater stock (McDougal's company). Do you still have? (Pursuant to Jim's current problems). If so, I'm worried about it." Clinton, in a scribbled notation at the bottom of the Wright note responded: "No, don't have any more—B." This wasn't exactly true as records showed that the Clintons remained half-owners of the Whitewater venture until December 1992, after he was elected president.[46]

On November 14, 1986, Jim McDougal sent a letter to the Clintons about the status of Whitewater stating, "The company to date has experienced losses totaling approximately $90,000 . . . Susan and I have in large measure contributed to the company the funds necessary to cover these losses."[47]

In December 1987, Susan McDougal personally delivered Whitewater records to the Governor's Mansion at the request of Mrs. Clinton.[48]

On November 28, 1988, Hillary Rodham Clinton, on the letterhead of the Rose Law Firm, sought power of attorney from partners James B. McDougal and his wife, Susan H. McDougal, to "manage and conduct all matters related to Whitewater Development." Mrs. Clinton wanted: the power to endorse, sign, and execute "checks, notes, deeds, agreements, certificates, receipts or any other instruments in writing of all matters related to Whitewater Development Corp."[49]

In 1989, the Federal Deposit Insurance Corporation—the federal agency that insurers savings and loan deposits—hired the Rose Law Firm to represent the government in a lawsuit against Madison's accounting firm, Frost & Co. The suit, handled by Hubbell, contended that the accounting firm had failed to alert Madison's board to reckless lending and management practices that led to insolvency. The initial Resolution Trust Corporation suit in the Frost case sought to recover $10 million in damages on five counts. It was settled out of court in 1991 for $1 million, less than the insurance coverage Frost held. The Rose Law Firm was paid $369,776 by the government.[50]

What should have been apparent is that the Rose Law Firm (where she was a partner) was suing Frost & Co. (her former accountants). There is an ethics issue here, because Hillary should have been transparent to the U.S. government about her business ties to Frost & Co. To begin with, the firm had prepared her taxes. Secondly, Frost & Co. and TCBY Yogurt, on whose board Hillary served from May 1989 to May 1992, were partners in a company called Capital Avenue Development Co., which owned the $68 million TCBY Tower in downtown Little Rock. If Frost & Co. were bankrupted by the lawsuit, TCBY would suffer. Then you had the undisclosed political relationship between Bill Clinton and Frost & Co., who was a contributor to Clinton's campaigns. In August 1990, when the Rose Law Firm was seeking to settle the lawsuit for the U.S. government, Frost & Co. contributed $1,000 to Clinton's gubernatorial re-election campaign.[51]

In July 1989, James McDougal was indicted on fraud charges in connection with Madison. By this time, McDougal was nearly destitute and begging Clinton for help. McDougal had been living in a trailer on the Riley's property in Arkadelphia, surviving on $591 a month in Social Security disability. Unfortunately, Clinton gave his old friend no help and McDougal continued to face his ordeal without his longtime ally. At his trial in the summer of 1990 on eight counts of bank fraud and conspiracy, prosecutors concentrated on two tangled land sales by a Madison subsidiary. With McDougal's attorney invoking his frail mental state as part of the defense and contending mismanagement rather than conspiracy, McDougal was acquitted of all charges when the jury deadlocked.[52]

After the verdict, Bill Clinton remembered his old friend and called McDougal to congratulate him on his acquittal. Then, Clinton brought up a problem. Hillary, who had control of the Whitewater books, had spent about $3,000 on various expenses, and she wanted McDougal to reimburse her. This was very upsetting to McDougal. The Clintons were still 50 percent partners in the venture and had lost much less than he and Susan had.[53]

A few days later, Bill Clinton met with Sam Heuer, McDougal's court-appointed lawyer, and told him Hillary wanted to close the books on Whitewater. Heuer wrote a letter to Hillary laying out the steps that would have to be taken to dissolve the company. Hillary replied that she needed to gather more information on Whitewater's finances. Hillary never called Heuer back. It would appear that McDougal's acquittal made the matter seem less urgent.[54]

On October 3, 1991, when Bill Clinton announced his candidacy for president, he threw this line in about President George H. W. Bush: "When the rip-off artists looted our S&Ls, the president was silent." At the time, very few people saw the hypocrisy.[55]

On March 8, 1992, Jeff Gerth of the *New York Times* published his first Whitewater story on the eve of the critical New York primary. It detailed the history of the Whitewater land deal and alleged that the Clintons had put up little money and had taken improper tax deductions. It also alleged that Madison money had been used to subsidize the Whitewater project, which eventually went bust. It also alleged that Hillary Rodham Clinton had been retained by Madison, to help prevent it from being closed down by a state agency after it had been found insolvent. The *Times* reported that some of the Whitewater documents were missing.[56]

After the story ran, couriers from the Rose Law Firm were summoned to the Arkansas Governor's Mansion by Hillary Rodham Clinton and were given sealed, unmarked envelopes of records to be shredded at the firm's downtown office. The couriers made at least six other "mansion runs" during the campaign. The shredding continued through the Nov. 3, 1992, general election.[57]

On September 1, 1992, the Kansas City RTC (Resolution Trust Corp.) sent one letter to Steve Irons of the FBI White Collar Crimes unit in Little Rock and one letter to Charles Banks, then the U.S. attorney for eastern

Arkansas, also in Little Rock. According to a November 1993 report in the *Washington Post*, the referral listed dozens of questionable transactions. Apparently tracking federal thrift examination reports, the document reportedly mentioned business partnerships involving former Clinton aide Stephen Smith, James McDougal, and Jim Guy Tucker. It singled out bank checks that might have been involved in Clinton's 1984 campaign finances, including an April 4, 1985 fund-raiser held at Madison Guaranty to help retire a $50,000 personal debt incurred by Governor Clinton himself. The referral described check-kiting and revolving overdrafts.[58]

According to others in the U.S. attorney's office, Banks, realizing how politically hot it was, immediately sent the referral to main Justice in Washington, D.C. There, in the last stages of the 1992 presidential campaign, it languished for over a year.[59]

The criminal referral wasn't the only time bomb landing in Washington, D.C. David Hale had used a fraudulent maneuver to recapitalize his Capital-Management Services company in 1992, and auditors in the Small Business Administration began going through his books. Their curiosity was bound to cause heartburn in the Governor's Mansion.[60]

At the end of the 1992 presidential campaign, Webster Hubbell inherited the files on Whitewater and Madison Guaranty Savings and Loan gathered by Clinton aides. He kept them at his home and turned them over to David Kendall in November 1993, when he was associate attorney general. That was after it became publicly known that Justice was weighing a criminal investigation of Madison that would touch on the Clintons. The records were then subject to attorney-client protection.[61]

After the election, the Clintons considered Whitewater a liability, and they wanted to eliminate any association with the venture. On December 22, 1992, Jim McDougal and his attorney, Sam Heuer, met with Vince Foster as power of attorney for the Clintons, to handle the Clintons transfer of their Whitewater interest to Jim McDougal. The cost would be $1,000. After fourteen years, Jim McDougal became the sole owner of Whitewater Development.[62]

In January 1993, just before the inauguration, Clinton aide George Stephanopoulos contacted Mitchell Stanley, a high-ranking Small Business Association (SBA) official, praising the way SBICs had helped out in Arkansas, several SBA officials would later testify to the Senate Whitewater committee. He also asked pointed questions about the way assistant SBA administrator Wayne Foren was running the program. At the time, Hale's company was the only SBIC in the state. White House spokesman Mark Fabiani would later state that George Stephanopoulos denies making such a call.[63]

In March 1993, Albert Casey stepped down as head of the RTC. President Clinton appointed his friend, Roger Altman, as acting RTC chief. On March 23, 1993, at his first staff meeting, Altman asked about any high-profile issues of which he should be aware. Senior Vice President William Roelle quietly told him of an earlier criminal referral on Madison that had mentioned the Clintons. That evening, and again the next morning, Altman faxed a year-old newspaper clipping about Madison and Whitewater to White House counsel Bernard Nussbaum. Both men later testified that they "remembered nothing" about the fax or related discussion.[64]

On May 5, 1993, SBA administrator Erskine Bowles gave White House Chief of Staff Mack McLarty a "heads-up" that the SBA's investigation had centered on David Hale, who had publicly charged that Bill Clinton, while serving as governor, asked him to help Clinton's Whitewater business partner with a government-backed $300,000 loan. The Justice Department was also concerned in early 1994 that the White House had sought and obtained from SBA a confidential file on Hale's activities. (Bowles later testified, on November 28, 1995, that he could "not recall" some of the briefings his aides said they gave him on Hale, or the May 5, 1993, "heads-up" they said he reported giving to Mack McLarty.)[65]

In May 1993, Jean Lewis, from the Kansas City RTC, began inquiring to Steve Irons and to Charles Banks for a response to the referral. A secretary in the attorneys' office told Lewis her boss had said that, after the case went to Washington, "we'd probably never hear about it again." Lewis then called main Justice in Washington to get some answers. To begin with, the case wasn't in the computer, and second, it had been passed up directly to the attorney general. "Any time a referral comes in that would make the department look bad or has political implications," Lewis says she was told by a person bearing the title ethics program manager, "it goes to the attorney general."[66]

In June 1993, Lewis, after several more inquiries, learned that the referral had turned up in the fraud section of the criminal division, where the unidentified person assigned to it "didn't want to deal with it." This person turned out to be Donald Mackay, a career lawyer in the division who later served briefly as special prosecutor in the Madison case until the appointment of Robert Fiske. Main Justice in Washington sent it back to Little Rock.[67]

After eight of these conversations, the Kansas City office decided to go ahead itself. Lewis took another trip to the Little Rock warehouse and noticed that the Madison records were much tidier this time. In fact, a number of boxes, she said, were missing. Her team spent another three months on the case. This produced nine more criminal referrals.[68]

On July 20, 1993, the same day that Vince Foster was found dead in Fort Marcy Park, the U.S. District Court in Little Rock granted a warrant to FBI agent Steven Irons. The document demanded the following: Hale's papers on "Master Marketing, Susan of [sic] James McDougal," and on two Little Rock development companies, Castle Sewer and Water Corporation and Southloop Construction. The last two companies were spin-offs from a large real estate development in Little Rock financed by McDougal's Madison Guaranty. Their legal work was handled by Jim Guy Tucker, who was the governor of Arkansas. Their business dealings involved Little Rock civic leader Seth Ward, who happened to be the father-in-law of Webster Hubbell, deputy attorney general.[69]

On August 17, 1993, Randy Coleman, David Hale's attorney, told Associate White House Counsel that Mr. Hale was under investigation by the Federal Bureau of Investigation, that he expected to be indicted soon, and that the investigation could affect President Clinton.[70]

On September 7, 1993, Randy Coleman met Paula Casey, the new U.S. attorney in Little Rock, for a last-ditch meeting. By Ms. Casey's account, she gave him a flat no on immunity or reduction of charges. Hale had to stand trial on a felony count, she said. If after the conviction he were still willing to testify against others, she said, her Litigation Committee would consider filing a motion to reduce his sentence. Coleman was floored.[71]

On September 15, 1993, Coleman wrote a letter to Casey, asking her to step aside and bring in an independent prosecutorial staff. She was a former law-school student of Bill Clinton. Coleman stated: "I can certainly understand the reluctance of anyone locally to engage in these matters, political realities being what they are." Casey disregarded the suggestion in the letter.[72]

On September 17, 1993, Hale started giving long interviews to Jeff Gerth of the *New York Times*. When Gerth called Casey for comment, she went ballistic, to use Hale's words. Hale asserted that she passed the word to stop talking to the press. If not, her office was going to start "stacking" charges. Casey wrote a letter to Coleman, warning, "Your client faces potential criminal exposure on a number of items." On September 23, 1993, Hale was indicted on charges of defrauding the Small Business Administration. When his prosecution went on fast track and the Justice Department ignored his offers of information about Arkansas corruption, Hale decided that he was indeed the fall guy and resumed talking to the press.[73] Soon he noticed what looked like a regular surveillance. Some of his apparent tails were off-duty Little Rock policemen he recognized from his days on the municipal court. One day, an unmarked van followed him home and parked near his house. He refused to do long-distance telephone interviews, and some who came to Little Rock to meet him also felt they were being watched. But Hale continued to speak, and he refused to plead guilty.[74]

On September 27, 1993, RTC Senior Vice President William Roelle told Jean Hanson that criminal referrals in the Madison case name President and Hillary Clinton as possible witnesses and "further investigative work" could make them "more than just witnesses." Two days later, on September 29, 1993, Jean Hanson told White House counsel Bernard Nussbaum of an RTC criminal referral involving Madison Guaranty that mentioned Bill and Hillary Clinton. Nussbaum called White House assistant counsel Clifford Sloan and asked Hanson to repeat to him what she had said. Nussbaum asked Hanson to call Sloan if there were further developments.[75]

On September 30, 1993, a day after the Nussbaum briefing, RTC officials, under the direction of acting RTC Director Roger Altman, ordered Jean Lewis, who headed the Madison probe, to hold up her investigation for a legal review. Mrs. Lewis was told the RTC's professional liability section wanted to conduct a legal review of the Madison case. No other similar reviews had been ordered at the time. She later testified before the House Banking committee that the review gave Treasury the opportunity to "selectively disseminate sensitive criminal referral information."[76]

On October 4, 1993, Denver lawyer James Lyons contacted Bruce Lindsey with the news that there had been additional media inquiries about the RTC referrals. They included information about checks written on Madison Guaranty to Mr. Clinton's 1984 gubernatorial campaign and concerns that the checks were at issue in the nine RTC criminal referrals. That same day, Bruce Lindsey relayed the information to Bill Clinton during a trip.[77]

When Bill Clinton was asked by reporters on March 8, 1994 how he found out about the "criminal referral," he responded: "My clear—I don't even remember when or exactly how I learned it—but my clear impression was that the RTC had made a referral on this and that it—I understood the issue and I just absorbed it and did—I did nothing about it. I ordered no action to be taken. And I honestly don't remember what date it occurred on," Mr. Clinton said.[78]

On October 6, 1993, two weeks after the indictment, Governor Jim Guy Tucker made an unannounced visit to the Oval Office and met with Bill Clinton. Photographers were barred from the Clinton-Tucker meeting and afterward the governor declined to talk with reporters at driveway microphones set up for presidential visitors. Both men later denied discussing the referrals during the White House session. Mr. Tucker also met with Mack McLarty and Webster Hubbell.[79]

On October 7, 1993, Bruce Lindsey was advised by White House lawyer Clifford Sloan of additional information on referrals from Jean Hanson. The second Hanson briefing came after she was given a copy of a secret legal analysis by the RTC into the Madison probe. Glion Curtis, the RTC's general counsel, later claimed in a July 8, 1994, deposition that he showed the analysis to Mrs. Hanson and later made her a copy of it during a meeting with the general counsel and RTC Assistant General Counsel John Bowman.[80]

On October 27, 1993, U.S. Attorney Paula Casey in Little Rock, rejected the first RTC referral. It was that referral that contained specific "language," according to Mr. Roelle's account to Mrs. Hanson, that could have elevated the Clintons to something "more than just witnesses." Ms. Casey decided the referral contained "insufficient information to sustain many of the allegations." Five days later, on November 1, 1993, Paula Casey threw the other nine referrals out in a letter to the RTC, citing "insufficient information . . . to warrant the initiation of a criminal investigation."[81]

On November 1, 1993, President Clinton made a terse statement to reporters: "We did nothing improper, and I have nothing to say about it." Previously, White House spokeswoman Dee Dee Myers said Mr. Clinton "did not recall" any meetings with Mr. Hale and had "no recollection" about efforts by him to pressure the former judge for an SBA loan. That same day, the Clintons selected David Kendall of Williams & Connolly as their lawyer.[82]

Armed with details of the confidential RTC criminal referrals obtained from Treasury—as well as information on Mr. Hale's allegations from the SBA—there was an improper Whitewater defense meeting at David Kendall's law firm on November 3. David Kendall, William Kennedy, White House Counsel Bernard Nussbaum, and senior presidential adviser Bruce Lindsey were all present. The purpose was "to impart information to the Clinton's personal lawyers" and to arrange "a division of labor between personal and White House counsel for handling future Whitewater issues." Notes from Mr. Kennedy at the meeting say in part:

> Vacuum Rose law files. WWDC [Whitewater Development Corp.]
> Docs—subpoena
> Documents—never know go out
> Quietly.[83]

Kennedy's notes make a reference to payments to Hillary Rodham Clinton from a Whitewater bank account. During an apparent discussion of a $2,000 monthly retainer to her law firm by the thrift, the notation "$34,000—WWDC—Hillary" is written and then crossed out. Below that, Kennedy wrote "ANN check drawn on WWDC—payable to HRC."[84]

Certainly, the meeting produced immediate results. On November 9, 1993, Jean Lewis received an e-mail memo ordering her off the Madison investigation without warning or explanation. Coincidently, that same day, Paula Casey, U.S. attorney in Little Rock, recused herself and staff from the Madison investigation. She was replaced by Justice Department prosecutor Donald Mackay. Interestingly, after Ms. Casey recused herself, the referrals were reinstated and eventually resulted in the conviction of the McDougals and Jim Guy Tucker on twenty-four felony counts.[85]

On November 16, 1993, associate White House counsel Neil Eggleston, one of the seven lawyers at the meeting, obtained the confidential SBA case file on David Hale. In fact, he picked it up in person from SBA general counsel John Spotila, who had been appointed in mid-September 1993 on the recommendation of Hillary Clinton's office. The Justice Department was so horrified when it learned of this leak that Eggleston returned the file to the SBA two days later, on Sunday, November 18, 1993, but not before he photocopied at least one document. Mr. Eggleston's actions mark the third known time the White House had obtained confidential information from an ongoing investigation of Whitewater.[86]

On November 17, 1993, the *Washington Post* requested documents, including financial records, offering proof that the Clintons had lost what they claimed on Whitewater, plus records from the 1984 gubernatorial campaign and the fund-raiser in 1985. (All of these were related to items in the RTC criminal referral.) Mrs. Clinton, her defense lawyers, Nussbaum, and Lindsey were strongly opposed to turning over the material.[87]

On November 20, 1993, David Kendall and several other attorneys arrived in two station wagons at Webb Hubbell's home in Northwest D.C., to take possession of the files. They went into the vault at the Williams & Connolly offices that contained other Clinton material and were logged in as follows: "five larger Banker's boxes, ten smaller Miracle boxes, and a small metal two-drawer check file." A few weeks afterward, Hillary told Maggie Williams: "I didn't want anyone poking around twenty years of our lives in Arkansas." With the records safely in the vault, that would be extremely difficult.[88]

On December 10, 1993, Bernie Nussbaum, David Kendall, and Hillary Rodham Clinton persuaded the president to stonewall the *Washington Post*. All three were determined to follow a closed-hold strategy more appropriate for corporation litigation than presidential politics. Also, Hillary didn't want to create a fishing expedition for the *Post* for more inquiries.[89] On December 22, Hillary Rodham Clinton told reporters that there was no reason to release the records showing the couple's business dealings with Whitewater Development Corp. or Madison Guaranty Savings and Loan Association. "I am bewildered that a losing investment . . . is still a topic of inquiry," Mrs. Clinton said. "I think we've done what we should have done and don't feel the need to do any more than we've done."[90]

According to Rep. Jim Leach, Iowa Republican on the House Banking Committee, he believes the Clintons made money, not lost it, on Whitewater. He sums that up as follows:

- $8,000 in real-dollar tax gain from interest deductions on Whitewater.

- $20,000 in capital gains on the sale of Lot 13 and the model house.
- $500 capital gain in the $1,000 sale of their Whitewater share to Mr. McDougal, handled by Vince Foster.
- $35,000 (or more), the Clintons' share of infusions of capital that Madison Guaranty and its affiliated companies allegedly put into Washington, according to Resolution Trust Corp. investigators.
- $55,000, the Clintons' share of the $110,000 of Judge David Hale's illegal $300,000 loan to Susan McDougal that allegedly went into the Whitewater account.
- Payment of $9,200 by Whitewater to reduce the principal of Hillary's Bank of Kingston loan, and $12,133 payments by Whitewater on Bill Clinton's subsequent loan—a total of $21,333 he believes was income to the Clintons.[91]

Using these figures, we come up with a gross gain to the Clintons from Whitewater of $139,833. Deduct from that what the Clintons claim as $46,636 in loses, and there is still a net gain of $93,193. Whatever the exact amount, the Clintons apparently did not lose on Whitewater—except politically.[92]

On December 23, 1993, lead editorials in the *New York Times* and the *Washington Post*, called on the White House to turn over the Whitewater documents. Late in the day, President Clinton agreed to do so.[93]

That same day, David Kendall began secretly negotiating with Allen Carver, deputy chief of the Fraud Section at the Justice Department about issuing a subpoena. This maneuver would protect the documents from public and press scrutiny by immunizing them against FOIA requests. Through their negotiations, the subpoena was also broadened to include campaign documents and other records with no obvious connection to Whitewater.[94]

On January 1, 1994, President Clinton was so upset by the coverage of Whitewater that he asked comptroller of the currency, Eugene Ludwig, for advice on handling Whitewater-related legal difficulties. Mr. Ludwig, a friend of Mr. Clinton's since their days at Oxford and Yale, declined to offer any advice, saying it would be "impermissible" for him as an independent regulator to provide counsel. This prompted a flurry of concerned telephone calls from White House lawyers who did not think it advisable for the president to be discussing the matter with a banking regulator.[95]

Unfortunately, Senate investigators later learned that Ludwig secretly funneled copies of reporters' FOIA requests on Whitewater to White House senior advisor Bruce Lindsey.[96]

On January 2, 1994, Republicans Newt Gingrich and Bob Dole, then in the minority in Congress, called on Attorney General Janet Reno to appoint a special prosecutor. Reno denied the request.[97] A few days later, when the subpoena became public, Senator Bob Dole, Republican Minority Leader from Kansas responded: "It's almost unbelievable the White House would work with Justice in a matter of this kind. I don't know of any precedent for this," he complained. "It appears the White House is running the investigation and not the Justice Department."[98]

On the same day, Jean Lewis wrote a memo admitting that roadblocks had been erected to divert criminal referrals in the Whitewater-Madison affair and it was "beginning to sound like somebody, or multiple somebodies, are trying to carefully control the outcome of any investigation." She continued, "The beginnings of a cover-up may have already started months ago."[99]

On January 9, 1994, Sen. Daniel Patrick Moynihan of New York was the first Democrat to join Republicans in calling for a special prosecutor or independent counsel. Two days later, on January 11, a total of seven Democratic senators, including Russell Feingold of Wisconsin, Bill Bradley of New Jersey, Bob Kerry of Nebraska, and Charles Robb of Virginia, joined Moynihan in calling Janet Reno to name a special counsel to investigate Bill and Hillary Clintons' ties to Whitewater Development Corp. and Madison Guaranty S&L. When asked about this development, President Clinton, who was traveling overseas in Prague, told CBS News in Prague: "The most important thing to me and the most important thing to the American people is I'm completely relaxed about this because I didn't do anything wrong."[100]

On January 12, 1994, Senator Bob Dole held a news conference and quoted Mr. Clinton's 1992 campaign book, *Putting People First*, in which candidate-Clinton said, "Washington stood by while quick-buck artists brought down the savings and loan industry."[101]

Clinton had had enough. Later in the day, he directed Janet Reno to appoint a special counsel. Then he testily refused to answer reporters' questions about Whitewater. And it soon became apparent that the investigation had given him a new reason to remain silent. The presence of an independent counsel meant that Clinton could answer questions that he felt might be politically advantageous to him, and refuse to answer others, citing the confidentiality of the Whitewater investigation.[102]

On January 20, 1994, Janet Reno appointed Robert Fiske, special counsel to investigate President and Mrs. Clinton involvement in the Whitewater-Madison affair. Interestingly, after the appointment of Special Counsel Fiske, Washington RTC officials imposed censorship guidelines on Kansas City RTC employees. No discussion with Fiske could be made without going through Washington. There could be no meetings between Kansas City office and Fiske without accompaniment of Washington officials. No materials could be forwarded without going through Washington. All information concerning attorney-client privilege was to be redacted, with Washington RTC determining the scope.[103]

On February 1, 1994, Roger Altman had decided to recuse himself from the RTC investigation. The reaction from the White House was fierce. The Clintons didn't want Altman to recuse himself. His presence might protect them from what they saw as "partisan" actions on the part of the RTC staff. According to a senior official, the Clintons wanted Altman to "keep the lid on."[104]

The next day, Roger Altman called Maggie Williams to tell her that he had changed his mind and would not recuse himself. He then asked her to "get people together" at the White House so he could formally announce his decision. Mr. Altman went to the White House and met with Bernard Nussbaum, Ms. Williams, and Harold Ickes, the president's chief of staff. Mr. Altman gave them a "heads up" briefing on Madison.[105] On the same day, RTC attorney April Breslaw flew to Kansas City, her first and only visit to the RTC office, to gather documents on the civil investigation of Madison. At the end of the day, she met with Jean Lewis and told her that "head people" at RTC were concerned about her investigation and there were "certain answers" they would be happier about because it would "get them off the hook." Two of the "head people" Breslaw identified were then-Deputy Chief Executive Officer Jack Ryan and General Counsel Ellen Kulka.[106]

Ms. Lewis wrote in a memo documenting the meeting that she pointed out to Breslaw that the "business partners are intelligent individuals, the majority of them being attorneys, who must have concluded that McDougal was making the payments for their benefit. If you know your mortgages are being paid, but you aren't putting money into the venture, and you also know the venture isn't cash flowing, wouldn't you question the source of the funds being used for your benefit?"[107] In her memo, Ms. Lewis said Ms. Breslaw told her RTC officials in Washington, whom she described as "people at the top," would like to be able to say that "Whitewater did not cause a loss to Madison. . . . She asked how we could get to a clear-cut answer as to whether or not Whitewater caused a loss to Madison," Ms. Lewis wrote. "I stated that as far as I am concerned, there is a clear-cut loss. . . . I also stated that any attempt to extract Whitewater as one entity from the rest of the McDougal-controlled entities involved in the alleged check kite will distort the entire picture. I further pointed out I would produce the answers that were available, but I would not facilitate providing "the people at the top" with the politically correct answers just to get them off the hook."[108]

Ms. Lewis said the losses to Madison from the Whitewater account "would easily exceed $100,000," and the "end loss result from the entire scam," using twelve companies suspected of being involved, "would be hundreds of thousands of dollars in what were essentially unauthorized loans." The RTC investigator said she told Ms. Breslaw that both the U.S. Attorney's Office and the FBI field office in Little Rock believed the Madison case was "highly prosecutable."[109]

When the memo first came to light, Ms. Breslaw "categorically denied" the conversation and the comments attributed to her. It turns out Ms. Lewis recorded at least a portion of the Lewis-Breslaw meeting, and the tape was "completely consisted" with Mrs. Lewis' conversation.[110]

On February 11, 1994, the *Washington Times* reported that a fire had broken out on the fourteenth floor of the Worthen Tower, gutting some of the offices of an accounting firm that in 1986 audited Mr. McDougal's soon-to-be-bankrupted savings and loan. "Security personnel at the Worthen Tower waited for twenty-five minutes before calling" in their alarm.[111] Coincidently, the next day, President Clinton went to Hot Springs, Arkansas, for two days, supposedly to visit the husband of his late mother, and brought along Webster Hubbell to play golf. The conclusion in Washington, correct or not, was that the president went to Arkansas with his lawyer to check out documents that might bear on Whitewater.[112]

On February 25, 1994, George Stephanopoulos and Harold Ickes placed a conference call from Stephanopoulos' office to Roger Altman. They were furious about Altman's recusal—for weeks they had urged Altman not to do it—and were even more put out that they had learned of it only after Altman had divulged his decision to the *New York Times*. Then one of them asked, "What about Jay Stephens? Can anything be done about it, or are we stuck with this?" Altman reportedly cut off the conversation "quite quickly," telling his callers he "absolutely would not" be a party to sacking Stephens. Altman then reported the substance of the conversation to Josh Steiner, adding, "These guys are nuts."[113]

Stephanopoulos called Steiner and, according to others, Stephanopoulos began with the classic "this conversation never happened" line and proceeded to ask Steiner, "How can we get rid of Stephens?" After further contacts between Steiner and Stephanopoulos, the conclusion reportedly was that Stephens could not be removed easily, so the subject was finally dropped.[114]

Though Stephanopoulos was able to portray these two contacts as his sole role in the controversy to Senate investigators, largely unnoticed evidence was developed in the House that Stephanopoulos had been involved in the ouster of former RTC chief Albert Casey in March 1993, which put Altman in control of the agency. Shortly thereafter, the RTC reversed its position on extending the statute in the Madison case from favorable to opposed.[115]

Stephanopoulos later testified that in two telephone conversations on February 25, one with Altman and Ickes and one with Steiner, he was just inquiring about how Stephens was hired. He said he also "blew off steam," since he believed Stephens was out to get Clinton for removing him and all other U.S. attorneys in February 1993.[116]

So what was Stephanopoulos's real motive? An entry in Joshua Steiner's diary, which Steiner was not able to convincingly disavow, read: "George then suggested to me that we needed to find a way to get rid of him [Stephens]." Altman testified that Stephanopoulos suggested firing Stephens. And Hanson testified that Steiner told her that people at the White House wanted to get rid of Stephens.[117]

Stephanopoulos testified that he did not recall asking Steiner if the RTC could get rid of Stephens. Then, he was asked: "Did you ever tell, request, ask, or suggest that Mr. Steiner or Mr. Altman or anyone else for that matter find a way to fire or get rid of Mr. Stephens," Stephanopoulos then retreated to the nonresponsive assertion that he "never *directed* anyone to take any action to impede an investigation." He then used the verb "directed" six more times, even after GOP Sen. Orrin Hatch of Utah called attention to his ducking. Stephanopoulos used the phrase, "I don't recall" a total of thirty-one times in his Senate deposition.[118]

On March 1, 1994, Harold Ickes sent a confidential twenty-five-page memo to Hillary Rodham Clinton describing in lengthy detail the findings of separate investigations by the RTC and the Federal Deposit Insurance Corporation (FDIC) into allegations of conflict of interest by Little Rock's Rose Law Firm in the handling of a 1989 FDIC lawsuit. The memo also detailed information on the RTC's hiring of former U.S. Attorney Jay Stephens to look into the possibility of civil lawsuits in the Madison case. Mrs. Clinton would later deny being involved in monitoring the investigation.[119]

The memo also included a copy of a February 28, 1994, letter by White House Associate Counsel Neil Eggleston to Mr. Ickes outlining the FDIC and RTC investigations. The letter addresses White House concerns that conclusions by the FDIC and RTC were "inconsistent."[120]

In a March 3, 1994, news conference, Bill Clinton said that he was unaware of any of the discussions between Treasury and White House officials over Whitewater-Madison.[121] Nine days later, President Clinton was interviewed in the Oval Office. When one of the two Knight-Ridder reporters changed the subject from jobs to the Whitewater-Madison controversy fifteen minutes into the interview, Mr. Clinton's face reddened as he stood and made a scene for five minutes, denouncing both reporters along with press coverage in general and the Republican Party. He then had them ushered out without even the ritual handshake.[122]

The next day James McDougal appeared in an interview on ABC-TV's *This Week* and said he couldn't file his taxes for 1993 because the Clintons refuse to give him records in their possession. Mr. McDougal speculated that the Clintons were holding them back because of "possible embarrassment from some aspect of it."[123] The next day, March 14, Associate Attorney General Webster Hubbell resigned his position at the Justice Department. Later that evening, President Clinton, while attending a thousand-dollar-a-plate fund-raiser in Boston, lashed out at Republicans in a lectern-pounding denunciation near the end of a rambling, eighteen-minute speech. Mr.

Clinton said: "Why then are we confronted in this administration with an opposition party that just stands up and says, 'No, no, no, no, no, no, no, no, no?'" he said with a red face and clenched jaw as he pounded the podium with each syllable. Mr. Clinton also charged the GOP with the "politics of personal destruction."[124]

On March 22, 1994, David Hale pleaded guilty to fraudulently applying for federal money for his government-backed lending company in February 1986. (That's the same month Hale said Mr. Clinton first approached him about the McDougal loan.) With the plea agreement, Mr. Hale began cooperating with special counsel Robert Fiske.[125]

On June 29, 1994, Richard Iorio, the field director of RTC's Kansas City investigations office, and Lee Ausen, his department head, were summoned to Washington with their three Madison investigators for a review of their criminal referrals. Deputy General Counsel Andrew Tomback, who was recently recruited to the RTC, called the all-day meeting. Tomback wanted to get up to speed on the Madison case because it was the most political and sensitive one then facing the corporation. Iorio and his staff went point by point through all ten of their criminal referrals. But Tomback seemed especially interested in the additional "soft referral" on the alleged drug money laundering.[126]

The investigators told him their suspicions that Dan Lasater, the Little Rock bond dealer, convicted cocaine distributor, and family friend of Bill Clinton, may have used accounts at Madison and elsewhere to make his drug profits reappear as legitimate money. The Little Rock police department, they said, was providing material from its own investigation of Lasater. Tomback didn't seem interested in pursuing. He called the connection "tenuous" and argued against asking the independent counsel for a full-press series of witness interviews.[127]

On June 30, 1994, President Clinton signed the Independent Counsel Act back into law, allowing court-appointed special prosecutors to probe cases that might be a conflict of interest for a political Justice Department. It was originally passed in 1978, but it lapsed on December 15, 1992.[128]

On August 5, 1994, a three-judge panel of the U.S. Court of Appeals ousted Robert Fiske as special counsel. They appointed Kenneth W. Starr to investigate all crimes related to Madison Guaranty Savings & Loan, which lost $65 million in depositors' funds, and the Whitewater real estate development.[129]

On August 18, 1994, Jean Hanson resigned as Treasury Department General Counsel. She was the fourth Clinton administration official—following Mr. Altman, Bernard Nussbaum and Webster Hubbell—to be forced from office over the Whitewater matter. Other resignations included associate White House counsel William Kennedy, who resigned on November 18, and Treasury Secretary Lloyd Bentsen, who resigned in December. [130]

The convictions from Whitewater include:

* On March 21, 1995, Chris Wade, the real estate agent for the Clinton's Whitewater Development Corporation, pled guilty to bankruptcy fraud and to filing a false bank loan application to build a house on Lot 7 of the Whitewater property where a house was to be built for the Clintons.

* On April 14, 1995, Eugene Fitzhugh was sentenced to one year in prison for being a key player in a scheme to trick the Small Business Administration into giving David Hale's Capital Management Services Inc., $900,000 to lend. He was accused of misrepresenting the amount of private capital the company had.

* On May 2, 1995, Neil Ainley, president of the Bank of Perry County (June 1989-March 1994), pleaded guilty in U.S. District Court in Little Rock to two misdemeanor counts of "concealing" from the Internal Revenue Service and others "the withdrawals of large amounts of United States currency by the 1990 Clinton campaign"—on May 25, 1990, $30,000 and on November 2, 1990, $22,500. Federal law requires the reporting to the IRS of all cash transactions in excess of $10,000.

* On June 8, 1995, Stephen Smith pleaded guilty to defrauding the Small Business Administration to obtain a $65,000 loan, which was never repaid. Mr. Smith, who was president of the Bank of Kingston, also approved a questionable $30,000 loan to Hillary Rodham Clinton, in December 1980, to build a model home on Lot 13 at the Whitewater site.

* On June 16, 1995, Robert Palmer, a Little Rock real estate appraiser, was sentenced to three years' probation, including one year of home detention on his guilty plea of filing false loan appraisals for Madison Guaranty Savings and Loan Association. U.S. District Judge George

Howard in Little Rock also ordered Mr. Palmer to pay a $5,000 fine.[131]

On May 17, 1995, the Senate voted 96-3 to reopen Whitewater hearings. The Senate's special committee on Whitewater would be chaired by Alfonse D'Amato, New York Republican.[132]

On December 20, 1995, the Senate voted 51-45 to take President Clinton to court for refusing to turn over disputed Whitewater notes. The historic vote authorized Senate lawyers to begin legal action to sue the administration in federal court to enforce a committee subpoena for the release of notes taken by White House Associate Counsel William Kennedy during a November 5, 1993, meeting in the office of David Kendall, personal attorney for President Clinton and Hillary Rodham Clinton. The next day, facing a court showdown with the Senate, the White House agreed to surrender Mr. Kennedy's notes.[133]

On December 28, 1995, the Senate Whitewater Committee issued subpoenas for documents to sixteen people and institutions in Arkansas, continuing its attempt to sort out the connections between the Whitewater Development Corp.; the failed Madison Guaranty Savings and Loan; the suicide of old friend, law partner, and Whitewater legal adviser Vincent Foster; and the first couple themselves. The subpoenas had been issued to:

1. Gov. Jim Guy Tucker
2. James McDougal, former chairman of Madison Guaranty and part owner of Whitewater Development Corp.
3. Susan McDougal, also a part owner of Whitewater Development.
4. Christopher Wade, Whitewater Development real estate agent.
5. Loretta Lynch, staff member of the 1992 Clinton presidential campaign who was assigned to Whitewater issues.
6. Jack Palladino, a private investigator retained by the 1992 campaign.
7. First Bank of Arkansas, a lender to James McDougal.
8. Security Bank, which provided a loan to the Clintons for Whitewater.

9. Lawrence Kuca, a former director of Madison Financial Corp.
10. The Arkansas Public Service Commission.
11. The National Association of Security Dealers, a self-regulatory organization for stock trading.
12. Stephen Smith, a former business partner of James McDougal and Tucker.
13. Eugene Fitzhugh, a former associate of Hale in Capital Management.
14. E. Russell Webb, a former partner in Ozark Air Services Inc.
15. Robert Palmer, a former real estate appraiser for Madison Guaranty.
16. Charles Matthews, a former associate of Hale in Capital Management.[134]

On December 31, 1995, the Resolution Trust Corporation marked its last day of business. The next day, the FDIC took over statutory responsibility for the RTC.[135] A few days later, personal assistant Carolyn Huber "magically" discovered 116 pages of billing records covering Hillary Rodham Clinton's work as a Rose Law Firm lawyer for Madison Guaranty Savings and Loan after shelves had been built in her East Wing office. The billing records were found on a table in the White House residence's "book room," whose access is limited to President and Mrs. Clinton and "selected house guests." She called the Clintons' personal attorney, David Kendall. Conveniently, they appeared four days beyond the statute of limitations.[136]

The billing records show Hillary did nearly seven thousand dollars' worth of legal work—about sixty hours over fifteen months, including contacts with sixty-eight of the thrift's executives, other Rose lawyers and state regulators. An RTC billing recap also showed that at one point she was the lead attorney in the Madison matter. This contradicted Mrs. Clinton's sworn deposition before the resolution Trust Corp., said she did only minimal work for Madison Guaranty. During the 1992 presidential campaign, she said she did "little or no" work for Madison.[137]

The Rose Law firm billing records show Mrs. Clinton met with Arkansas officials about the Madison case on at least two occasions, contrary to earlier assertions that she did not represent clients before state regulatory agencies. The White House also confirmed Madison's monthly retainer. This contradicted a statement Mrs. Clinton made, through a presidential campaign spokesman in March 1992, denying getting a two-thousand-dollar-a-month retainer from Mr. McDougal for Madison's legal work. In statements, the campaign said she had not given Madison any legal advice on its dealings with state officials and that she did not "intervene or attempt to influence" the state concerning the Madison inquiry.[138]

On January 26, 1996, Hillary Rodham Clinton appeared before a twenty-three-member panel federal grand jury in Washington to answer questions under oath about the discovery of Rose Law Firm billing records in the White House living quarters. It marked the first time in U.S. history that the wife of a sitting president has been called to testify under subpoena before a sitting grand jury.[139]

On April 28, 1996, President Clinton testified on videotape for three hours and twenty-three minutes in defense of James and Susan McDougal and Governor Jim Guy Tucker. This marked Mr. Clinton's fourth appearance before Whitewater prosecutors. Mr. Clinton's testimony was taken in the Map Room at the White House, which was chosen because it had no distinguishing White House artifacts for the camera to capture. Some of his testimony, though, contradicted David Hale's:[140]

> **Mr. Heuer:** "Were you ever present at any time for any meeting between Jim McDougal and David Hale?"
> **President Clinton:** "Never, I never was present at any meeting."
> **Mr. Heuer:** "Were you ever present when there was any discussions of getting any kind of loan from David Hale or his S.B.I.C.?"
> **President Clinton:** "No."
> **Mr. Heuer:** "Did you ever ask David Hale to make Susan McDougal a loan?"
> **President Clinton:** "No, I didn't."[141]
> Furthermore, it would later contradict an April 21, 1997, CNN *Larry King Live*, appearance of Jim McDougal. Transcript is as follows:
> **King:** "Last time you were here . . . you absolved the President. What happened?"
> **McDougal:** "Well, we were involved in a great deal of lying then, on all sides."
> **King:** "You lied on this program?"

McDougal: "I lied to you, and for that I apologize. And I lied to the American people through your program by denying vehemently the story that David Hale was telling about a meeting with the President and Mr. Hale and I had concerning a loan made to Susan McDougal. . . ."
King: "You just saying he [the President] is lying about that meeting?"
McDougal: "Yeah."
King: "He was at the meeting, and saying he wasn't is lying?"
McDougal: "Right."[142]

The same day Clinton testified, the FBI announced that it found Hillary Rodham Clinton's fingerprints on copies of the Rose Law Firm billing records that disappeared in 1993 and then mysteriously reappeared on January 4, 1996, in the White House living quarters.[143]

On May 28, 1996, a federal grand jury found James and Susan McDougal and Governor Jim Guy Tucker guilty on twenty-four felony counts in the Whitewater fraud-and-conspiracy trial. After the verdict, Governor Tucker announced he would resign by July 15, 1996, making him the fourth governor in modern U.S. history to step down in the face of criminal charges. U.S. District Judge George Howard Jr. delayed James McDougal's sentencing until November 18, 1996, since he was cooperating with Ken Starr's inquiry. Susan McDougal was sentenced to two years in jail and three years' probation and was ordered to pay $300,000 in restitution for illegal loans. Governor Tucker, who was facing a maximum penalty of ten years in prison and $500,000 in fines, somehow managed to secure leniency for himself without any pretense of cooperating with Ken Starr. He received an astonishingly mild punishment of four years' probation and some $300,000 in fines and restitution.[144]

On March 8, 1998, James McDougal died as an inmate at the Federal Medical Center prison in Fort Worth, Texas.[145]

On September 21, 2000, after six years and fourteen convictions, the Whitewater inquiry came to a close. Madison Guaranty cost the taxpayers $74 million. Independent Counsel Robert Ray, who took over from Ken Starr, said: "This office determined that the evidence was insufficient to prove to a jury beyond a reasonable doubt that either President Clinton or Mrs. Clinton knowingly participated in any criminal conduct."[146]

CHAPTER 19

STATE DEPARTMENT FILE SEARCH

In the wake of Whitewater, in the wake of Travelgate, it is obvious the administration does not want another scandal. This is nothing but stonewalling.

—Mike Mitchell[1]

During the 1992 presidential campaign, Bush appointees at the State Department searched Bill Clinton's passport file looking for political ammunition concerning his trip to Moscow during the Vietnam War when Clinton was protesting the war while a student at Oxford University in England. As president-elect, Mr. Clinton applauded President Bush's firing of Elizabeth Tamposi, an assistant secretary of state implicated in the passport search. "I'm glad Miss Tamposi had to leave her job about six weeks early. I thought that was an appropriate thing to do," he told reporters at his transition headquarters in Little Rock, Ark. "I just want you to know that the State Department of this country is not going to be fooling with Bill Clinton's politics and if I catch anybody doing it, I will fire them the next day."[2]

It was only a few months into the Clinton administration that Miss Tamposi's confidential personnel folder at the State Department, with information from a secret FBI background investigation, was pulled by a White House liaison officer at State, who leaked a gossip item from it to the *Washington Post*. In the ensuing furor, the State Department discovered that about 160 other confidential personnel dossiers of Reagan-Bush officials at the State Department had been pulled from storage and searched by Clinton officials in an effort to find derogatory information in their personal or medical histories and law enforcement checks conducted by the FBI.[3]

The file searches had originally surfaced on September 1, 1993, when *Washington Post* reporter Al Kamen quoted State Department officials as describing information in the files of the Bush appointees. Sherman M. Funk, State Department Inspector General, conducted the investigation. Mr. Funk interviewed nearly sixty people, many under oath, and had conducted extensive searches of telephone and other records.[4]

On November 3, 1993, the Justice Department began a criminal investigation into searches by the Clinton White House's personnel office on Reagan-Bush appointees.[5] By mid-November 1993, Mr. Funk, after finding evidence of illegal searches and leaks of information from the files, delivered his report to the Justice Department's public integrity section. Divulging any information from a personnel file is a direct violation of the Privacy Act and a criminal offense.[6]

Mr. Funk identified Mark Schulhof, a GS-11 assistant in the State Department's office of Public Records, and Joseph Tarver, a GS-15 director of the White House liaison office at the State Department, as being "the sole [State] Department employees responsible for the unauthorized dissemination of privacy-protected information from these files outside of the Department." Both men worked on the Clinton-Gore campaign. Mr. Funk's probe found:

- State Department telephone records showing that Mr. Schulhof called the *Washington Post* reporter forty-five times between April 26, 1993 and September 1, 1993. This amounts to one phone call every two working days from the point at which Mr. Schulhof found out about the files to the publication of Mr. Kamen's article.
- One thirteen-minute call was made on the same day in July 1993 that Bush White House liaison files had been retrieved.
- Department employees other than Messrs. Tarver and Schulhof may have been responsible for acts of omission or commission in their official duties.
- One employee did not disclose what he knew about the leak and said another, apparently unwittingly, took actions which resulted in the destruction of relevant evidence.
- Evidence directly relating to the case was deliberately destroyed by another Clinton appointee, and other officials

were responsible for "acts of omission or commission" in this crime.[7]

Other high-ranking State Department officials, including Assistant Secretary of State Thomas Donilon and Richard Moose, undersecretary of state for management, also came under suspicion, but denied any knowledge or involvement in the incident.[8]

On February 1, 1994, despite Mr. Funk's findings that the Privacy Act had been violated, the Clinton Justice Department decided "not" to prosecute Joseph Tarver and Mark Schulhof. Coincidently, Mr. Funk's report was slated to be publicly released "the following day or two."[9]

Mr. Funk was surprised by the Justice Department refusal to prosecute in the case. Also upset were former Bush appointees who believed that their privacy was violated and some thought that the decision was an attempt at "stonewalling."[10]

"Why would we have expected anything different from the Clinton Justice Department?" asked Fran Wexner, a former Bush State Department official. "There are those of us who have come to believe the Clinton administration feels it is functioning under a separate set of laws."[11]

Attorney General Janet Reno ignored requests of Republican senators for a special prosecutor, as Democrats had requested in the case of Mr. Clinton's passport file and refused to launch a criminal probe.[12]

As pressure mounted for some action, Secretary of State Warren Christopher fired Joseph Tarver and Mark Schulhof.[13]

This left a lot of questions "conveniently" unanswered:

- How many files were pulled and examined? Mr. Tarver estimated that there were from 350 to 425 files. Mr. Kamen cited 160 in his article. State investigators took possession of 197. Mr. Schulhof and Mr. Tarver had access not only to political appointees' files but also to Ambassadorial files. How broad was their access?
- Who ordered the files to be pulled from storage?
- Were other agencies ordered to retrieve files of Bush appointees?
- What was their purpose?
- Why weren't Joseph Tarver and Mark Schulhof prosecuted under the Privacy Act by the Clinton Justice Department?[14]

Bill Clinton Taking the Oath of Office

The Official Photo President Bill Clinton

President Clinton and Vice President Al Gore witnessing the swearing in of the Cabinet

President Clinton Standing at Microphones, with Al Gore and Janet Reno

*First Lady Hillary Rodham Clinton
Speaking About Healthcare Reform at U.S. Capitol*

*President Bill Clinton, Newt Gingrich, Bob Dole,
and another man talking near table*

CHAPTER 20

VIETNAM

I've always been interested in and supportive of the military.... In some ways I wish I'd been a part of it. I wound up going through the lottery, and it was just a pure fluke that I wasn't called.

—Bill Clinton, December 1991[1]

In November 1992, after his election, President-elect Clinton appeared unalterably opposed to normalizing relations with Vietnam until Hanoi finally made good on longstanding pledges for full disclosure on Americans missing from the war. "I don't think we should normalize and then get accounting," he said. "I think we ought to know where our people are. That's putting the horse before the cart."[2]

Once in office, President Clinton sought to normalize relations with Vietnam. Unfortunately, he, as well as other politicians and some in the press, wanted the public to forget the MIA issue. But evidence continued to emerge that far more men were left behind than had been reported. There were other reports that some may have been alive as late as 1993.

> On January 23, 1973, U.S. Secretary of State Henry Kissinger and Le Duc Tho, a senior member of the Hanoi Politburo, signed the Paris Peace Accords ending the Vietnam War. "We have been told that no American prisoners are held in Cambodia," Kissinger told reporters the next day. "American prisoners held in North Vietnam and Laos will be returned to us in Hanoi."[3]

One week later, President Nixon sent a secret letter to Premier Pham Van Dong of North Vietnam, reflecting an unpublicized understanding reached by Kissinger and Le Duc Tho. Nixon told Pham that the United States would "contribute to postwar reconstruction in North Vietnam" in an amount that would "fall in the range of $3.25 billion of grant aid over five years." He also said that "other forms of aid . . . could fall in the range of 1 to 1.5 billion dollars."[4]

None of the aid was ever extended, and even the existence of the letter was not disclosed until years later. If the aid had been extended, however, Vietnam might have returned all its prisoners. The precedent was clear. The Vietminh guerillas of the 1950s had held back an unknown number of French soldiers after the fall of Dien Bien Phu. France quietly ransomed them back with government aid. Moreover, a 1969 study by the Rand Corporation had said that "a quid pro quo that the DRV [Democratic Republic of Vietnam] is likely to demand—and one that the United States may want to consider accepting—is the payment of reparations to North Vietnam in exchange for U.S. prisoners."[5]

But the concessions, or the aid programs, were not forthcoming. There was no possibility they were ever could be. Nixon would soon be undone by Watergate, and Congress wanted no more of the war. When it did release 591 POW's, in Operation Homecoming in March 1973, however, it was apparent that something was wrong. Hundreds of hospital beds had been set aside for the returnees. It had been assumed many would need medical attention. The 591 returnees, though, included no amputees or burn cases. There was no one maimed, disfigured, or blind. It is reasonable to believe that the most afflicted POWs either remained in Vietnam or were murdered.[6]

On March 29, 1973, President Nixon addressed the nation on television: "For the first time in twelve years, no American military forces are in Vietnam," he declared. "All of our American POWs are on their way home. . . . There are still some problem areas. The provisions of the agreement requiring an accounting for all missing in action . . . have not been compiled with. . . . We shall insist that North Vietnam comply with the agreement."[7]

Unfortunately, the Democratic-controlled Congress had walked away from the war. In May 1973, the Senate rejected a Republican amendment that would have allowed continued bombing if Nixon certified that North

Vietnam was not trying to account for all missing in action. Certainly, there already was evidence that men had been left behind:

- A March 1973 memo to the Joint Chiefs of Staff says, "There are approximately 350 U.S. military and civilian PW/MIAs in Laos." An earlier memo to Henry Kissinger says that some 215 of the 350 "were lost under circumstances that the enemy probably has information regarding their fate." No information was ever forthcoming, however, and only twelve prisoners returned from Laos.
- As shown by the enclosed Casualty Data Summary, a total of 1,303 American personnel remain officially unaccounted for after the completion of Operation Homecoming. . . . Of the 1,303 personnel, the debriefs of the returnees contain information that approximately 100 of them are probably dead (according to Defense Intelligence Agency memorandum to Deputy Secretary of Defense William Clements, May 22, 1973).
- The intelligence indicates that American prisoners of war have been held continuously after Operation Homecoming and remain[ed] in captivity in Vietnam and Laos as late as 1989 (according to Unpublished reports by Senate investigators, April 9, 1992).[8]

On April 12, 1993, the *New York Times* reported about a secret document found in Moscow. The document was purported to be a Russian translation of a speech by Gen. Tran Van Quang, deputy chief of staff of the Vietnamese People Army before the North Vietnamese Politburo. General Quang stated that 1,205 American military POWs were held in eleven North Vietnamese prisons in September 1972, while they were telling the United States that they held only 368.[9] According to him, each camp held about a hundred Americans and were divided by rank. Also, by 1972, Hanoi was the happy recipient of inside information on its captives, thanks to American informants within the so-called peace movement.[10] General Quang said they were deliberately deceiving us about the numbers, knowing we had no way of knowing exactly how many of our men they had captured.[11]

The document was discovered by Stephen J. Morris, a Harvard researcher in the tightly closed archives of the former Soviet Party in Moscow. Obviously, the communist masters in Hanoi, as anxious as they were for American trade, technology and tourism, were not about to part with their treasured diplomatic records from the war years. Yet, the communist regime was gone in Moscow and the question arose whether Boris Yeltsin and others were prepared to tell the truth about Vietnam as Nikita Khrushchev began to tell some of the truth about Stalin's murderous government.[12]

In Hanoi, Gen. John Vessey, the presidential emissary to Vietnam on POW-MIA affairs, said he had spoken to General Quang and that Quang denied he had made the report. "I have no reason to disbelieve him," Vessey said, although he had no reason to believe him either, which was one excellent reason to think Quang was lying. Quang could hardly admit that North Vietnam had held more prisoners than it had ever acknowledged.[13]

In the appalling history of POW-MIA policy, though, nothing is more scandalous than the issue of live sightings. From 1975 to 1989, the Defense Intelligence Agency received more than fifteen thousand live-sighting reports about American prisoners in Southeast Asia. Approximately 1,650 of the reports were first-hand. A first-hand sighting is when a source says he has actually seen an American held in captivity, or under conditions that cannot be easily explained. The remainder of the reports were hearsay, or when a source says he has been told by someone else about an American, or many Americans, held in captivity. The live-sighting reports came from many sources—refugees, defectors, diplomats, and travelers—with the preponderance from refugees. Many of the reports, even the ones that are hearsay, were quite specific, with physical details, exact locations, and an abundance of certifiable facts. No live-sighting reporting, however, were ever accepted as proof by the Defense Intelligence Agency that an MIA was still alive, or ever had been alive, in Southeast Asia.[14]

The Defense Intelligence Agency's (DIA) abysmal record led the six staff members on the Senate Select Committee on POW/MIA Affairs who were charged with investigating intelligence reports, to re-examine, in 1992, the 1,650 first-hand live-sighting reports. After discounting several factors, that left the investigators with 929 first-hand live sightings, all involving two or more men allegedly seen in conditions indicating they were prisoners.[15]

The investigators plotted the 929 sightings on a map of Southeast Asia, using pins to mark each one. Cambodia drew no pins. Laos and some areas of Vietnam drew only a few. Other areas of Vietnam, however, drew pins in clumps or clusters. In every place where there was a cluster, there was also a Vietnamese prison. The investigators, who, for technical reasons, were using live-sighting reports that extended only through 1989, drew an obvious conclusion: "that American prisoners of war have been held continuously after Operation Homecoming and remain[ed] in captivity in Vietnam and Laos as late as 1989."[16]

The conclusion, however, was not welcomed by the DIA, or even by most members of the Senate committee. On the morning the investigators were scheduled to present their report to the senators, one senator's aide let the Pentagon know what the investigators intended to say. A team from DIA immediately showed up to rebut their presentation. The investigators protested; their briefing was supposed to be closed to outsiders. In a remarkable display of bad judgement, however, the senators voted 7 to 2, to allow DIA to attend the briefing.[17]

By all accounts, what followed was contentious. The investigators and the team from DIA shouted at each other. Several senators shouted too. Committee Chairman and Massachusetts Democrat Senator John F. Kerry told one of the investigators that if the report ever leaked, "you'll wish you'd never been born." When the briefing was over, Frances Zwenig, the committee's staff director, ordered that all copies of the investigators' report be destroyed. She also said she wanted their computer files purged.[18]

In its 1,123-page final report on the hearings, the committee reached an evasive conclusion: "We acknowledge that there is no proof that U.S. POWs survived, but neither is their proof that all of those who did not return had died. There is evidence, moreover, that indicates the possibility of survival, at least for a small number, after Operation Homecoming."[19]

On May 26, 1993, Senator Kerry distributed declassified U.S. documents in a preemptive strike against the "hysteria" that he felt the *New York Times* created with its April 12 story, according to the *Washington Post*. The newly released documents showed that Dr. Dang Tan, a North Vietnamese army doctor who defected to the South in 1969, knew a lot about North Vietnamese policy toward U.S. POWs. He had even treated some of them. He said the number of prisoners being held was greatly understated and explained the reasons why. American POWs were regarded as valuable assets that could be exploited in various ways. He warned then that North Vietnam would be looking for excuses not to return all our POWs in the event an exchange was agreed upon.[20]

He said that "by not revealing the names or the number of American POWs, North Vietnam would hold the upper hand in any future negotiations." He said they did not wish to be held accountable at some future date for any POWs might not be alive then.[21]

Dr. Tan told his story to the press in May 1971. In the text of his remarks, approved in advance by the American Embassy and the CIA station chief in Saigon, he said there were more than eight hundred American POWs held by North Vietnam in 1967, but at the time of the press conference, they claimed to hold only 367. He said it was possible that some would never be released "as they [were] too valuable as sources of information and for the technical skills they possess[ed]."[22]

Dr. Tan confirmed what another defector, Le Dinh. Le Dinh, who defected in 1978, claimed when he put the number of POWs who remained in Vietnam at more than seven hundred, around the same number indicated by the Quang report.[23]

According to Senator Kerry, though, "analysts concluded at the time that the defector's story could not be true." Actually, the analysts placed considerable confidence in Dr. Tan, and what he told his interrogators at the time of his defection fit very well with what General Quang included in his report three years later.[24]

Soon, with the help of cooperative reporters, they immediately embarked on an effort to discredit the Quang report, seizing on disinformation supplied by Hanoi. They also received help from U.S. government officials who would have to acknowledge that all they had been saying for twenty years was false if they admitted the Quang report was true. This is why the Clinton Defense Department didn't come up with an official position on the Quang report even though the CIA certified it to be authentic.[25]

On September 8, 1993, Defense Secretary Les Aspin disclosed that the Pentagon was analyzing a second Soviet intelligence document concerning POWs in North Vietnam. Labeled Top Secret, it was a translation by the Soviet GRU military intelligence service of a report in Vietnamese by Khoang Anya, secretary of the North Vietnamese Communist Party Central Committee in December 1972, which stated that "The total number of captured fliers in the DRV [Democratic Republic of Vietnam] consists of

735 people." And it declared that they had "published the names of 368 fliers."[26]

The document also said that the North Vietnamese government would agree to release "these 368 people" if the United States agreed to withdraw its forces from South Vietnam. "When the Americans finish withdrawing their forces, we will give the rest back to them."[27]

Yet, the Clinton administration did not denounce the North Vietnamese record on the POWs. Could it be that the liberal Democratic leadership was not interested in discovering what the Communists were up to in Vietnam, a war they long ago denounced as illegal or immoral from the American point of view.[28]

Could you imagine Bill Clinton—who studiously avoided military service, who was surrounded by critics of the war and the sons and daughters of the anti-war '60s—making a serious effort to persuade Moscow, not to mention Hanoi, to open their archives to war? No. The only thing that President Bill Clinton, Senator John Kerry, and others were interested in was lifting the trade embargo on Vietnam.[29]

There was another reason, Clinton wanted to lift the trade embargo on Vietnam. As it happens, the Lippo Group, who was led by Mochtar Riady, was a Clinton fund-raiser who had a huge financial interest there; (including the fact that Vietnam Airlines is housed in Hanoi's Lippo Center). So it stood to benefit enormously for trade between Vietnam and the United States.[30]

On September 13, 1993, President Clinton announced that he would ease the trade embargo, which was imposed in 1975 and renewed every September since. He also permitted U.S. firms to bid on development projects in Vietnam. Mr. Clinton based his decision on the Vietnamese government's cooperation in accounting for Americans missing since the Vietnam War.[31]

On December 14, 1993, *Reuters* reported from Hanoi, Vietnam, that U.S. Assistant Secretary of State Winston Lord said that there are no U.S. prisoners of war (POWs) being held in Vietnam. "There has never been evidence uncovered of someone being held alive," he told a news conference after talks with Vietnamese officials.[32]

On December 23, 1993, Vietnam handed a major offshore oil exploration deal to a consortium, including U.S. oil giant Mobil Corp. The deal covers exploration of the Thanh Long, or Blue Dragon, offshore area. The deal marked the return to Vietnam for Mobil, which was a major corporate presence in the former South Vietnam before the communist victory of 1975.[33]

Vietnam had been pressing hard for a full restoration of diplomatic relations and an end to the embargo, which was a major hurdle in their efforts to develop the country's economy. Yet, POW-MIA groups were angry about the loosening of trade restrictions on Vietnam.[34]

"Our idea of cooperation is entirely different" from the president's, Dolores Alfond of the National Alliance of Families said. She said Vietnam withheld information on prisoners of war and those listed as missing in action. "Family members are totally against lifting the trade embargo since the Vietnamese have really not cooperated," she said.[35] On January 27, 1994, the Senate voted 62-38 to urge the Clinton administration to lift the trade embargo against Vietnam. The resolution was proposed by Senator John Kerry and supported by the Clinton White House. The vote angered veterans groups, most of which were strongly against relaxing restrictions on Vietnam without a full accounting of Americans missing from the war. "We were somewhat stunned that they didn't listen to the veterans and families" who thought Vietnam had not been forthcoming on the POW-MIA issue, said Phil Budahn, spokesman for the American Legion.[36]

On February 3, 1994, President Clinton ended the thirty-year trade embargo on Communist Vietnam, overriding objections from veterans and abandoning his own pledge to hold out for the "fullest possible accounting" of missing Americans before easing the policy. A total of 2,238 persons were listed as missing in action or prisoners of war throughout the Indochina theatre, including 1,647 in Vietnam.[37] On January 28, 1995, the United States and Vietnam signed agreements settling old property claims and establishing liaison offices in each other's capitals.[38]

On April 14, 1995, after a taped session with CNN, White House correspondent Wolf Blitzer asked President Clinton if he felt vindicated by former Defense Secretary Robert McNamara's new book, which called U.S. involvement in the Vietnam War a stupid and costly mistake, thus vindicating his draft dodging and anti-war organizing in the late 1960s. "Yes I do. I know that sounds self-serving, but I do," said Mr. Clinton.[39]

On July 11, 1995, President Clinton announced formal diplomatic relations with communist Vietnam. On August 5, 1995, the United States and Vietnam formally established diplomatic relations. Secretary of State

Warren Christopher and Vietnamese Foreign Minister Nguyen Manh Cam signed and exchanged the historic letters in Hanoi's Government Guest House. In Washington, the new Embassy of Vietnam, located at 2251 R St., NW, raised its red and yellow flag.[40]

Claims that better overall relations with the Vietnamese communists have led to better results in accounting for MIAs are disproven by the actual record. During the Reagan administration when U.S. officials adhered to strict negotiating principles: 169 MIA's from Vietnam were accounted for, an average of 21 per year. During the Bush administration, 96 MIAs were accounted for, averaging 24 per year. However, during the first 2 ½ years of the Clinton administration, 30 MIAs had been accounted for, a drop to only 12 per year. By the year 2000, the remains of 1,500 U.S. servicemen are still unaccounted for from the Vietnam War.[41]

On August 6, 1995, at 10:08 a.m., the Stars and Stripes was raised at the American Embassy in Vietnam for the first time since the fall of Saigon, on May 7, 1995.[42]

CHAPTER 21

PAULA JONES PART I

*How do you put up with mosquitos in summertime in Arkansas?
You just swat them and go on, it's part of living.*

—President Clinton on congressional Republicans
who supported the Paula Jones investigation[1]

On February 11, 1994, Paula Corbin Jones, using the Conservative Political Action Conference as a backdrop, accused President Bill Clinton of sexually harassing her when he was governor of Arkansas and she was a state employee, saying that he caused her "humiliation" and lasting emotional distress. So who is Paula Corbin Jones and what events led to this accusation?[2]

On March 11, 1991, Paula Corbin, who was not married at the time, began working at the Industrial Development Commission as a $10,270-a-year documents clerk. The job required regular visits to the governor's office in the capitol. A couple days later, the Arkansas Quality Management Governor's Conference was being held at the Excelsior Hotel in Little Rock, Arkansas. Paula Corbin, then twenty-four-years-old, and Pam Blackard were handing out name tags and literature at a booth for the Arkansas Industrial Development Commission. Governor Clinton arrived at the hotel for a meet and greet accompanied by Arkansas state trooper Danny Ferguson, a member of his security detail. Trooper Ferguson, whom Ms. Corbin had chatted with earlier, approached the booth and told her, "the governor said you make his knees knock."[3]

Ms. Corbin said that Trooper Ferguson returned a short time later, at about 2:30 p.m., and handed her a piece of paper with a four-digit room number on it. "The governor would like to meet you in his room and talk to you . . . in a few minutes," Ferguson said. He also assured Ms. Corbin by saying, "it's okay, we do this all the time for the Governor."[4]

In an interview, Blackard said she had seen Clinton staring at Corbin, watched the trooper ask Jones to meet Clinton, and talked with her about whether to go. "I did say to her . . . 'Find out what he wants and come right back. . . . If you're that curious, go ahead,'" Blackard recalled saying.[5] Ms. Corbin went to the room partially because she felt honored to meet the governor and with some hope of getting a better job, Blackard said. Clinton met her at the door. Once she was ushered into the room by Trooper Ferguson, he stood watch outside in the hallway.[6]

Once in the room, Mr. Clinton made small talk and referred to Ms. Corbin's boss, David Harrington, a Clinton appointee, as "my good friend."[7] After asking her about her job, she said, Clinton took her hand. She said she pulled it away and tried to distract him by chatting about Clinton's wife. But, she said, he persisted, kissing her neck and putting his hand on her thigh.[8]

Corbin objected, asking Clinton: "What's going on?" He told her he had noticed her downstairs and liked the curves of her body and the way her black hair flowed down her back. "I will never forget the look on his face," she said. "His face was just red, beet red."[9] Later when Corbin was asked why she didn't leave the room, she said: "I guess I didn't know what to do. This is the governor, this is not just anyone. I feel intimidated . . . by anybody that's higher than me. I feel I've got to do everything possible not to make them upset at me. I've always been like that."[10]

Corbin walked to the far end of a sofa and sat down, averting her eyes. The next thing she knew, Clinton had dropped his trousers and underwear and was sitting next to her on the couch. Then he asked her to "kiss it" (perform oral sex).[11]

Ms. Corbin jumped up. "No, I don't do that. I'm not that type of person. I need to be going back downstairs," she said as she tried to bolt the room. Mr. Clinton continued to fondle himself while saying, "Well, I don't want to make you do anything you don't want to do. Mr. Clinton then pulled up his pants and told Ms. Corbin that if she got in trouble with her boss for leaving the booth, he could fix it. "You are smart," he said. "Let's keep this between ourselves."[12]

When Paula returned to the booth, Ms. Blackard noticed that she was "walking fast" and "visibly shaken and upset" and asked what had happened. Paula told her about Governor Clinton's unwanted advances and implored her to tell no one. "We were both kind of scared," Ms. Blackard recalled. "We weren't thinking straight. I thought I could lose my job. She thought she could lose her job." Later that day, another friend, Debra Ballentine, said Paula showed up unexpectedly at her office and told her the story. Ms. Corbin trembled and "was breathing really hard," said Ms. Ballentine.[13] "I could tell just by looking at her that something was wrong. . . . She said, 'Debbie, he pulled his pants down to his knees and he asked me to [perform a sex act] right then.' He also told her," Ballentine confirmed, "he knew she was a smart girl and her boss—what's his name? Dave Harrington?—'is a good friend of mine.'"[14]

After her initial encounter, Paula had several more contacts with Ferguson and Clinton before she left her state job in February 1993. One time she ran into Ferguson, who told her Clinton had been asking about her, wanted her home phone number, and was interested in seeing her. Jones, who was living with Stephen Jones, the man she would marry, said she refused.[15]

Another time, Governor Clinton called out her name under the rotunda of the Arkansas capitol. He was accompanied by another bodyguard, Larry Patterson. After Clinton spotted her, he called out her name and walked over. Then, Jones (who was married at that point) said in an interview, "he squeezed me up close to him," her side to his. She said he turned with a smile to Mr. Patterson, his arm still around her shoulder, and said to Patterson: "Don't we make a beautiful couple? Beauty and the beast."[16]

"Well, you don't look like the Beast," Jones recalled responding. And with that, she said, Clinton bid goodbye, saying, "It was nice to see you, Paula." Trooper Patterson said in an interview that he recalled the encounter as Jones does.[17]

When the article about the Arkansas troopers came out in the *American Spectator* on December 20, 1993, Jones felt humiliated by the magazine's description of her encounter with Governor Clinton and believed that some of her friends and family would conclude that she was the "Paula" described in the article. She said she wanted to "clear [her] name."[18]

A short time after the article came out, then Mrs. Jones and Ms. Ballentine recalled that they ran into Trooper Ferguson, on January 8, 1994, at the Golden Corral Steakhouse in the Little Rock area. Jones said she asked Mr. Ferguson if he had been the magazine's source. Ferguson became apologetic, according to both Mrs. Jones and Ms. Ballentine.[19]

Asked why she did not complain during the 1992 presidential campaign, when his conduct with women was at issue, Jones said she did not accuse Mr. Clinton then because she still worked for the state and was convinced no one would believe her.[20] Her attorney, Daniel Traylor, expounded: "What do you do? Call the police? The police escorted her up there. Tell her boss? The governor has just said her boss is a close friend?"[21] Besides Mrs. Jones, Mr. Traylor also presented affidavits by Pam Blackard and Debra Ballentine, who were with Ms. Jones at the hotel the day she said Governor Clinton harassed her.[22]

White House spokeswoman Dee Dee Myers responded that "It is not true."[23]

On February 11, 1994, White House Communications Director Mark Gearan responded: "It is not true. He does 'not recall' meeting her. He was never alone in a hotel with her."

When George Stephanopoulos went to the Oval Office to get his response, Clinton said he didn't remember her. "What does she look like?" he asked. He even joked about the trooper angle: "I may be a fat old man now, but in my younger days I never needed any help getting women."[24]

"Only after Mr. Clinton and his staff denied that these events had ever happened, and called me 'pathetic,' and in effect a liar, did I decide to seek legal relief," Jones said. She then threatened to file a civil suit against the sitting president alleging sexual harassment and defamation.[25]

Daniel Traylor tried to mediate the matter with the White House in a way that would have secured his client an apology along with an acknowledgment of the incident by Mr. Clinton. After White House officials declined, he said, Mrs. Jones decided to seek the apology publicly.[26] On March 24, 1994, *Washington Post* reporter Michael Isikoff was suspended for insubordination for two weeks after a shouting match with National Editor Fred Barbash. Mr. Isikoff and two other reporters had spent six weeks working on the story, and he heatedly criticized his editors for burying their findings about sexual harassment charges leveled at Mr. Clinton by Paula Corbin Jones.[27]

A couple weeks later, Reed Irvine of *Accuracy in Media* payed $13,860 for a quarter-page ad in the *Washington Post* headlined: "WHO IS PAULA JONES AND WHY IS THE POST SUPPRESSING HER CHARGE OF SEXUAL HARASSMENT?" It appeared on page A19.[28]

Robert Kaiser, Managing Editor of the *Washington Post*, explained the failure to report Mrs. Jones charges this way: "We have an obligation to the *Post*'s readers to do our best to establish the truth and not simply to print damaging accusations the moment they are made." The *Washington Post* waited until May 4, 1994, nearly three months after Paula Jones' accusations, to begin seriously reporting one of the biggest stories of the year. It was triggered by President Clinton's hiring of Robert S. Bennett, a lawyer from the Washington law firm of Skadden, Arps, Slate, Meagher & Flom, to defend himself against Jones's charges.[29]

Before signing on—at $475 an hour—Bennett met with Hillary, then with Bill, who told him, "I swear to God, it didn't happen." The president also told Bennett, according to those familiar with the circumstances of his hiring, not to discuss the Jones case specifically with his wife. Bennett had already heard from others that Hillary did not want to settle the case; after all, if nothing had happened with this woman, why should Bill settle? She wanted the matter to disappear.[30]

Daniel Traylor—himself a Democrat whose father once served as a Democratic member of the Arkansas Legislature—looked right, left, and center for legal help: from the conservative Landmark Legal Foundation to the flamboyant Idaho defense lawyer Gerry Spence to the feminist NOW Legal Defense Fund. But it was not until the final week for the May 8 statute-of-limitations deadline that Northern Virginia–based attorneys Gilbert K. Davis and Joseph Cammarata volunteered their services.[31]

There was another group of volunteers that would soon begin secretly assisting Jones' defense team. Called the "elves," they were an informal group of conservative attorneys led by Philadelphia lawyer Jerome Marcus. Others included George T. Conway III from New York and Richard Porter from Chicago. Conway also brought into the group, from Washington, D.C, Laura Ingraham and Ann Coulter. Cammarata and Davis treated the group with absolute trust, faxing internal documents to them and often including them in strategic discussions as negotiations with the president's legal team proceeded.[32]

In May 1994, polygraph examiner James Wilt affirmed Paula Jones passed a lie detector test where she described Mr. Clinton's so-called genital defect. Mr. Wilt worked as a polygraph examiner for the Fairfax County Police Department from 1962 to 1975. He had conducted more than ten thousand examinations and served a Virginia legislature committee that drafted that state's polygraph laws.[33]

Mrs. Jones spoke truthfully in answering no to the following questions:

- Did you lie when you stated Governor Clinton placed his hand on your thigh?
- Did you lie when you stated Governor William Clinton exposed his penis to you?
- Did you lie when you stated Governor Clinton asked you to kiss his penis?[34]

On Thursday morning, May 5, 1994, Jones' attorney Gilbert K. Davis informed Clinton's attorney Robert S. Bennett that they would be filing Jones's case against Clinton by three o'clock that afternoon. "I've talked to the president about this for hours and hours," Bennett said, "and this just didn't happen. You have no case." The two men sparred inconclusively for a few minutes and then Bennett raised the stakes. "Did you know there are naked photos of your client?" Davis said he didn't know about any naked photos, but he would be interested to see them if they existed. Bennett said he had not seen them yet. Then it was Davis's turn to spring a surprise.[35]

"My client says your guy has a unique mark on his penis, and she can identify it." What followed was a considerable silence.[36]

The two attorneys came up with statements that each party would say publicly. Mrs. Jones accepted everything in the statement except Mr. Clinton's vague language about meeting her. Mr. Cammarata came up with a follow-up statement and Mrs. Jones wanted a six-month extension to file her compliant. Paula wanted the extension with the no-comment agreement, her attorney said, because the White House was leaking "false information" to the press during negotiations.[37]

According to Mr. Cammarata, "Mr. Bennett responded that Mr. Clinton wanted the case over on May 6 and that [an extension] was a 'deal breaker.'" In the end, the negotiations between the two sides failed and the next day, May 6, Jones' lawyers filed a sexual misconduct lawsuit in District Court in Arkansas against President Clinton and Trooper Danny Ferguson.[38]

The four complaints were as follows:

Complaint #1: Charges that Mrs. Jones was discriminated against because of her gender by Mr. Clinton by "sexually harassing and assaulting her on May 8, 1991," depriving Mrs. Jones "of her right to equal protection of the law."

Complaint #2: Charges there was a conspiracy between Mr. Clinton and Trooper Ferguson to lure Mrs. Jones to Clinton's room and "entice her on to have a sexual liaison with him." It says the actions violated her equal protection under the law.

Complaint #3: Sub-headed "Intentional Infliction of emotional distress," charges that Clinton's acts "caused Jones severe emotional distress."

Complaint #4: Charges the president and Trooper Ferguson with defamation of character. It says Mr. Clinton's defamation occurred after her February news conference when Mr. Clinton and his "agents" called Mrs. Jones a liar and labeled her charges "pathetic." Trooper Ferguson is charged with defamation for comments made in the January 1994 issue of the [American Spectator] magazine in which he said "Paula" had a consensual sexual encounter with Mr. Clinton.[39]

The complaint also contained an extremely significant statement that said: "There were distinguishing characteristics in President Clinton's genital area that were obvious to Mrs. Jones."[40]

The suit sought $175,000 on each of four complaints, ($75,000 in compensatory damages and $100,000 in punitive damages) per complaint. Mrs. Jones said she did not intend to profit personally from the proceeds of the lawsuit and that she would contribute all proceeds beyond legal fees to an Arkansas charity.[41]

Mr. Bennett called the lawsuit "tabloid trash with a legal caption of it." He continued, "We absolutely deny, without any question, that this incident occurred. This president did not engage in any inappropriate or sexual conduct with this woman. The president has 'no recollection' of ever meeting this woman . . . He does not deny that it is possible that he met her, but he absolutely denies the allegations, the thrust and the core of this complaint." And there was James Carville, Clinton's 1992 campaign manager who famously said: "Drag a hundred-dollar bill through a trailer park and you never know what you'll find."[42]

Obviously, there were plenty of people in Arkansas who were offended by the label "white trash." It was amazing how an administration filled with people who prided themselves on their sensitivity to racial and gender stereotypes could have come up with the strategy of attacking Paula Corbin Jones as trailer trash.[43]

President Clinton, pausing at an Oval Office meeting with Malaysian Prime Minister Mohammed Mahathir, was asked about the lawsuit. He responded, "I'm not going to dignify this with a comment,". Asked directly if Mrs. Jones' charges were false, the president referred to Mr. Bennett's earlier news conference. "I think Mr. Bennett did a fine job. I don't have anything to add to what he said. Bob Bennett spoke to me, and I'm going back to work."[44]

The truth was, the last thing Bennett, or Clinton, wanted was to challenge Paula Jones' story on the merits in a courtroom. In May 1994, only one date mattered to the president, and that was two and a half years away. He wanted all depositions and inquiries into his sex life to be put off until after the 1996 election.[45]

On May 9, 1994, the case was assigned to U.S. District Judge Susan Webber Wright. Judge Wright first met Mr. Clinton in 1974 when she took his course in admiralty law at the University of Arkansas law school and ended up challenging him over her grade. When Mr. Clinton later launched his first run for Congress, she campaigned for his opponent, Rep. John Paul Hammerschmidt.[46]

On August 10, 1994, President Clinton became the first U.S. president to request a broad constitutional claim seeking presidential immunity, except in extraordinary cases, lawsuits arising from private acts by a sitting president must be dismissed, with the option of being refiled after the president leaves office. Previously, there had been only one other lawsuit against a sitting president for his alleged actions before taking office. In 1960, Democratic National Convention delegates sued candidate John F. Kennedy, shortly before he was elected president, for injuries they suffered in a car rented by the Kennedy campaign. Kennedy did not invoke presidential immunity and settled the matter for $17,750 in 1963.[47]

On January 9, 1996, a three-judge panel of the Eighth Circuit Court of Appeals in St. Louis ruled 2-1 overturning a lower court's ruling that Mr. Clinton was immune from going to trial while in office. The two judges declared that Mrs. Jones was "constitutionally entitled to access to the courts and to equal protection of the laws."[48] Robert Bennett responded by seeking a review of the decision by the full Eighth Circuit Court of Appeals and, if necessary, by the Supreme Court. The months required to file legal papers in those courts meant that there would be little chance the matter would be decided before the November 1996 president election.[49]

On February 9, 1996, the *Washington Times* reported that Bill Clinton bought a $1 million insurance policy against personal claims in 1991, three months before Paula Jones' claim that she was sexually harassed by him. Pacific Indemnity, a subsidiary of Chubb Group Insurance, had turned over $900,000 to help Mr. Clinton fight Paula Corbin Jones' lawsuit and the president has access to another $1 million personal liability insurance policy that he bought in 1994 from State Farm.[50]

On May 8, 1996, the Eighth Circuit Court of Appeals denied President Clinton's second plea to delay Paula Jones' sexual misconduct lawsuit until he leaves office. The next stop would be the Supreme Court.[51] On May 15, 1996, Robert Bennett filed a petition to the Supreme Court to delay Jones' sexual misconduct lawsuit until after President Clinton had left office. Mr. Clinton asserted in legal papers that as commander in chief, he is in the military and a sexual harassment lawsuit against him must be postponed until his active duty is completed. In his papers, Mr. Bennett sought to defer the lawsuit against Mr. Clinton under the Soldiers' and Sailors' Relief Act of 1940, which grants automatic delays in lawsuits against military personnel until their active duty is over. Interestingly, it was Mr. Clinton who maneuvered to avoid military service in 1969, during the Vietnam War.[52] Several veterans' groups protested and demanded that the president withdraw his argument. Eventually he did, thirteen days later.[53]

On June 24, 1996, President Clinton won a Supreme Court reprieve that he would not have to face politically embarrassing testimony about sexual misconduct charges until after the November elections on January 13, 1997. Mrs. Jones responded by calling the president a "coward" for ducking a showdown on charges the president called baseless.[54]

On January 13, 1997, the Supreme Court began listening to oral arguments in the Paula Jones sexual misconduct lawsuit. Robert Bennett and Solicitor General Walter Dellinger continued to carve out a new constitutional rule that would spare President Clinton a trial for at least four years. Mr. Bennett contended that Mr. Clinton's schedule would be threatened even by allowing Mrs. Jones to begin gathering testimony and evidence from other witnesses.[55]

Outside of the Supreme Court, five men wearing Clinton masks and brown trench coats with trouser legs rolled up to suggest nudity underneath the coats mocked the president by yelling: "Where's the flasher? He's guilty." They opened their coats to expose signs that said, "Friend of the court briefs."

On May 27, 1997, the Supreme Court, in a unanimous 9-0 decision, refused to stall Paula Corbin Jones' sexual misconduct lawsuit against President Clinton. This was a major blow to Mr. Clinton who then had to immediately face Mrs. Jones' charges that he sexually harassed her in a Little Rock hotel room and defamed her from the White House when she complained.[56] Coincidently, feminist groups that had embraced Anita Hill reacted with a coolness bordering on hostility to the Supreme Court's refusal to stall Jones' sexual misconduct lawsuit against President Clinton. Patricia Ireland, president of the National Organization for Women, would not support Paula Jones.[57]

You also had people like Susan Estrich, legal scholar and feminist pioneer of date-rape and sexual harassment theory, on ABC's *Nightline*, denying that what Bill Clinton may have done to Paula Jones constitutes sexual harassment. So, we were now being led to believe that when a powerful man brings a young woman into his hotel room, reminds her he is her boss' boss, and drops his pants and requests oral sex, that's *not* sexual harassment.[58] For all of the feminists and militant feminists that were supporting Mr. Clinton because of women's issues, I wonder what Exhibit A would be during the eventual trial of Paula Corbin Jones vs. President Bill Clinton?[59]

On July 31, 1997, the *Washington Times* reported that the attorneys for Paula Jones had subpoenaed former White House employee Kathleen Willey for a sworn deposition concerning accusations that she also was a victim of sexual advances by President Clinton. The subpoena sought all documents Mrs. Willey had concerning Mr. Clinton, including diaries, journals, notes, and correspondence from "when William Jefferson Clinton began his first term as governor of Arkansas, through the present." It also sought all her government employment records.[60]

On August 5, 1997, Robert Bennett and his partner, Mitch Ettinger, invited Davis and Cammarata to a secret late-night negotiating session to see if they could settle the case. When Davis and Cammarata indicated a willingness to accept a six-figure settlement, Bennett began to pay attention.[61]

Bennett had tested out various settlement possibilities on some of his contacts in the news media. The consensus seemed to be that the lawyer could portray any payment of less than $1 million as a legitimate effort to dispose of a distraction to the president. Initially, Jones's lawyers had asked for $1.4 million in 1996.[62]

On September 9, 1997, after Paula Jones refused the $700,000 settlement offer, her attorneys Gilbert Davis and Joseph Cammarata were granted a motion to withdraw from the case by U.S. District Judge Susan Weber Wright. Judge Wright set a jury trial for May 27, 1998.[63] On September 13, 1997, Paula Jones, along with her husband Stephen, were targeted for an income tax audit by the Internal Revenue Service. It was the first time either had ever been audited. They were selected for an audit for their 1995 return, and they were asked questions about their 1994 and 1996 returns as well.[64]

According to Susan Carpenter-McMillan, who became Mrs. Jones key adviser and a frequent spokeswoman after being named chairman of the Paula Jones Legal Fund in July 1997, an audit seemed particularly suspicious because Mr. Jones earned $37,000 a year and Mrs. Jones, was a housewife and mother and not employed at the time.[65]

Two days later, on September 15, the White House denied using the Internal Revenue Service to attack Paula Corbin Jones as punishment for her sexual misconduct suit against the president: "We may do dumb things from time to time, but we are not certifiably insane," White House Press Secretary Michael McCurry said in denying the allegation.[66]

On September 16, 1997, William N. McMillan III, who became interim legal adviser to Paula Corbin Jones, met with Robert Bennett. They agreed for the time being, to keep their conversations confidential. The agreement came just as Mr. McMillan's wife, Susan Carpenter-McMillan, contacted reporters to insinuate that one of Mr. Bennett's law partners, Fred Goldberg, a member of Skadden, Arps, Slate, Meagher & Flom, spurred the audit. Mr. Goldberg served as IRS commissioner from 1989 to 1992.[67]

On September 26, 1997, President Clinton's attorneys filed a motion asking Judge Wright to order Paula Jones to immediately fax her affidavit describing the "distinguishing characteristic" in his groin that she says would prove he exposed himself to her. Three days letter, on September 29, 1997, at 5:55 p.m., Paula answered these demands with a two-page fax sent from her home. Some of the highlights:[68]

- I briefly observed the erect penis of William Jefferson Clinton in a hotel suite of the Excelsior Hotel on May 8, 1991. That is the only time I have seen his genital area, and I have never had it described to me by anyone, nor have I read anything on the subject.
- Mr. Clinton's penis was circumcised and seemed to me to be rather short and thin. I would describe its appearance as seeming to be five or five and one-half inches, or less, in length, and having a circumference of the approximate size of a quarter, or perhaps very slightly larger.
- The shaft of the penis was bent or "crooked" from Mr. Clinton's right to left, or from an observer's left to right if the observer is facing Mr. Clinton.[69]

On October 1, 1997, Robert E. Rader Jr., senior partner of Rader, Campbell, Fisher & Pyke with five other attorneys from the Dallas, Texas law firm, became Paula Jones' new legal team. Their expenses were to be paid by the Rutherford Institute.[70] The Dallas lawyers broadened the suit to include the charge that Clinton rewarded women who had sex with him. This opened the way to rummaging more widely, if not in Clinton's bedroom, at least in his hotel rooms and hideaway offices. Given Clinton's vulnerabilities, it made obvious sense for him to settle.[71]

The same day Jones got a new legal team, a group called the Campaign for Victims of Sexual Harassment held a press conference to announce "a special hot line for individuals who have been the victims of sexual harassment from President Clinton." The number, 888-HARASSU was being promoted through a number of billboards in Little Rock and a $250,000 nationwide radio and television advertising campaign.[72]

On October 12, 1997, the *Washington Times* reported that Cindy Hays, who was the director of the Paula Jones Legal Fund, complained about being "terrorized" by repeated Watergate-style raids on its phones, computers and files. "I have been terrorized in Washington, D.C. by someone or a group of individuals who have broken into my offices, breached my security systems, broken into and wiretapped my telephones and computer modem lines, stolen files from my offices, and probably taken information from my computer hard drives and copied all of the documents in my office," Hays told reporters. The intrusions were first detected on January 17, 1997, four days after Supreme Court arguments in the case, and they surged after May 27, 1997, when the court ordered Mr. Clinton to submit to trial.[73]

President Clinton emphatically denied all of the allegations made against him in Paula Jones' sexual-harassment lawsuit and claimed he never sexually harassed Mrs. Jones or any other woman. Yet, Bob Bennett was worried about Clinton lying in his deposition. He was particularly worried about Clinton lying about Marilyn Jo Jenkins, an executive with the Arkansas Power and Light Company. It turns out that Trooper Danny Ferguson had brought her to the basement of the Arkansas Governor's Mansion four times for forty-five minute visits after the November 1992 election, usually before 6:00 a.m. Bennett urged Clinton not to lie about his relationship with her, telling him if he committed perjury, "You are dead. You are dead!" Clinton was noncommittal. "I hear you," he said.[74]

On January 16, 1998, Attorney General Janet Reno and judges expanded independent counsel Kenneth Starr's mandate to investigate possible perjury and obstruction of justice relative to Clinton's testimony in the Paula Jones trial.[75] There were rumors everywhere about an intern and tapes. But nothing was in print yet. Michael Isikoff, despite the distractions, kept a lunch appointment with Lanny Davis, a White House lawyer who served as a spokesman on scandal issues. During the course of the lunch, Davis found Isikoff distracted and preoccupied. In the course of a conversation, Davis happened to say, "These womanizing stories are old hat and still haven't gone anywhere."[76]

"They're more real than you think," the reporter replied cryptically.[77]

By Friday afternoon, the circle of knowledge about Starr's sting was expanding. Frustrated that *Newsweek* hadn't yet committed to running a story in the next issue, Lucianne Goldberg decided to tip a reporter at the *New York Post* to call Isikoff and ask him about the big scoop he had in the works. By this time, the likelihood of a settlement was non-existent. Yet, Clinton was so confident, that he boasted to Bennett, "If Paula Jones wants a trial, go and give her one."[78]

On January 17, 1998, Bill Clinton became the first president in U.S. history to testify as a defendant in a criminal proceeding. The deposition, which was taken at Robert Bennett's office, were Mr. Clinton, Mrs. Jones, and U.S. District Judge Susan Webber Wright of Little Rock. In addition to Mr. Bennett, attorneys for Mrs. Jones and Trooper Danny Ferguson, who was a co-defendant, were there.[79] After being sworn in, the president was handed a legal document by the Jones' lawyers with a court-approved definition of "sexual relations." The definition was extremely specific. It listed the following: "contact with the genitalia, anus, groin, breast, inner thigh, or buttocks of any person with an intent to arouse or gratify the sexual desire of any person."[80]

Though the deposition was intended to deal with the alleged incident at the Excelsior Hotel in May 1991 between then-governor Clinton and Paula Jones, Jones' lawyer, James Fisher, began with a series of questions about a woman named Kathleen Willey and an encounter she claimed to have had with the president just a few short steps from the Oval Office. Then, not long into the deposition, the Jones' lawyers gave Clinton what his friends call his "Oh, shit," moment:[81]

> **Fisher:** "Now, do you know a woman named Monica Lewinsky?"
> **Clinton:** "I do."[82]

Fisher began with a series of questions about Lewinsky's employment history—her internship, her service in the White House, then her move to the Pentagon. After a short break, though, Fisher started to put his knowledge, courtesy of Linda Tripp.[83]

> **Fisher:** "Mr. President, before the break we were talking about Monica Lewinsky. At any time were you and Monica Lewinsky together alone in the Oval Office?"
> **Clinton:** "I don't recall, but as I said, when she worked at the legislative affairs office, they always had somebody there on weekends.

> I typically worked some on the weekends. Sometimes they'd bring me things on the weekends. She—It seems to me that she brought things to me once or twice on the weekends. In that case, whatever time she would be in there, drop it off, exchange a few words and go, she was there."

This, of course, was the cover story Clinton and Lewinsky had constructed to explain her visits to him on the weekends. It was why Lewinsky always carried a folder when she visited Clinton for their assignations.

> **Fisher:** "So, I understand your testimony is that it was possible, then, that you were alone with her, but you have no specific recollection of that ever happening?"
> **Clinton:** "Yes, that's correct. It's possible that she, in, while she was working there, brought something to me and that at the time she brought it to me, and she was the only person there. That's possible." [The president's answers were unequivocal lies.]
> **Fisher:** "Did it ever happen that you and she went down the hallway from the Oval Office to the private kitchen?"[84]

At that point, as if in an instant, Clinton's demeanor changed. To answer this question, and all of the remaining queries about Lewinsky, the president assumed the posture in which he would spend much of the following year—one of abject self-pity, coupled with sustained dishonesty.[85]

> **Clinton:** "Now, to go back to your question, my recollection is that, at some point during the government shutdown, when Ms. Lewinsky was still an intern but working the chief of staff's office because all the employees had to go home, that she was back there with a pizza that she brought to me and to others. I do not believe she was there alone, however. I don't think she was. And my recollection is that on a couple of occasions, after that she was there but my secretary, Betty Currie, was there with her. She and Betty are friends. That's my, that's my recollection. And I have no other recollection of that."
> **Fisher:** "At any time were you and Monica Lewinsky alone in the hallway between the Oval Office and this kitchen area?"

Clinton: "I don't believe so, unless we were walking back to the dining room with the pizza. I just, I don't remember. I don't believe we were alone in the hallway, no."
Fisher: "At any time have you and Monica Lewinsky ever been alone together in any room in the White House?"
Clinton: "I think I testified to that earlier. I think that there is a, it is—I have no specific recollection, but it seems to me that she was on duty on a couple of occasions working for the legislative affairs office and brought me some things to sign, something on the weekend. That's—I have a general memory of that. . . . "[86]

Then, a real surprise to his lawyers, if not to Clinton, Fisher asked about any letters that were sent by Lewinsky to Currie for Clinton. Clinton hedged, said it was possible. The questions grew more specific.[87]

Fisher: "Did she tell you she had been served with a subpoena in this case?"
Clinton: "No, I don't know if she had been."
Fisher: "Did you ever talk with Monica Lewinsky about the possibility that she might be asked to testify in this case?"
Clinton: "Bruce Lindsey, I think Bruce Lindsey told me that she was, I think maybe that the first person told me she was. I want to be as accurate as I can."[88]

Much to Clinton's surprise, Fisher then began asking about the gifts.

Fisher: "Have you ever given any gifts to Monica Lewinsky?"
Clinton: "I don't recall. Do you know what they were?"
Fisher: "A hat pin?"
Clinton: "I don't, I don't remember. But I certainly, I could have."
Fisher: "A book about Walt Whitman?"
Clinton: "I give—let me just say I give people a lot of gifts, and when people are around I give a lot of things I have at the White House away, so I could have given her a gift, but I don't remember a specific gift."
Fisher: "Do you remember giving her an item that had been purchased from the Black Dog store at Martha's Vineyard?"

Clinton: "I bought a lot of things for a lot of people, and I gave Betty a couple of the pieces, and she gave I think something to Monica and something to some of the other girls who worked in the office. I remember that because Betty mentioned it to me."[89]

At that point, Clintons' lawyers were dumbstruck. Bennett was getting nervous. Ettinger was also fidgeting a great deal. What was going on? Fisher obviously had a wealth of detail about contacts between Clinton and Lewinsky. The lawyers were hearing a great many of these things for the first time from their client, who was obviously laboring. There had to be a source who was feeding this stuff to the Jones lawyers. Finally, Fisher came to the heart of his examination.[90]

Fisher: "Did you have an extramarital sexual affair with Monica Lewinsky?"
Clinton: "No."
Fisher: "If she told someone that she had a sexual affair with you beginning in November of 1995, would that be a lie?"
Clinton: "It's certainly not the truth. It would not be the truth."
Fisher: "I think I used the term 'sexual affair' and, so the record is completely clear, have you ever had sexual relations with Monica Lewinsky as that term is defined in Deposition Exhibit 1, as modified by the Court?"
Clinton: "I have never had sexual relations with Monica Lewinsky. I've never had an affair with her."

At the end of the Lewinsky phase of questions, Clinton had a question of his own to Fisher:

Clinton: "Mr. Fisher, is there something, let me just—you asked that with such conviction and I answered with such conviction, is there something you want to ask me about this? I don't, I don't even know what you're talking about, I don't think."
Fisher: "Sir, I think this will come to light shortly, and you'll understand."[91]

Then, the questioning turned to Paula Jones.

Fisher: "Now, seated to my right, two chairs down, is Ms. Paula Jones. Do you recall ever having met her before today?"
Clinton: "No." I've said that many times. I don't."[92]

At the end of the deposition, Bennett held up a copy of Lewinsky's affidavit denying that she had had sex with the president. Clinton maintained that her affidavit was "absolutely true." Not only was Lewinsky's statement false, but Bennett wouldn't have helped lock his clients into this categorical denial unless he thought Clinton was denying sex entirely, which, for the most part, he was.[93]

What Clinton and his defense team didn't realize was that Linda Tripp had met the night before with a lawyer for Jones to fully brief him about Monica Lewinsky's purported affair with the president. The two-hour session in Tripp's Columbia home armed the Jones legal team with enough information to ask Clinton precise questions the next day about Lewinsky and his ties to her. By cooperating with Jones' lawyers even as she provided independent counsel Kenneth Starr with information about Lewinsky's alleged affair, Tripp proved the crucial link in a crisis that had imperiled his presidency.[94]

After the six-hour deposition, Paula Jones with her husband, Stephen Jones, together with their attorneys, Patricia Carpenter-McMillan, an adviser, and Chris Vlasto, a producer for ABC News had dinner together at a table in the window of the Old Ebbit Grill, a block from the White House. Later, this group celebrated with champagne. They had a lot to celebrate.[95]

That night, Bill and Hillary canceled plans to have dinner with Erskine and Crandall Bowles. When asked what they did that weekend, Hillary said they had spent much of the weekend "cleaning out closets." They had a lot to worry about.[96]

CHAPTER 22

1994 STUMBLES

His concern [Johnny Chung] about his safety was understandable, given that there had been three attempts on his life which required FBI protection . . . and given his knowledge of what happened to people such as Ron Brown, who as secretary of commerce, was deeply involved in arranging – and selling seats on – Clinton administration trade missions to China.

—Bob Abernethy[1]

CLINTON CHEATS ON CROSSWORD PUZZLE

In early 1994, President Clinton ordered a presidential aide to call the *New York Times* crossword puzzle cheat line and then brief him on the answers, enabling him to whip through the puzzle in front of amazed and unsuspecting White House guests. After news of the cheating broke, Mike Antonucci, editor of the California-based newsletter, *The Right Mind*, challenged Mr. Clinton to a one-on-one crossword puzzle duel—"I wanted to give him a chance to clear his name," Mr. Antonucci told us.[2]

Mr. Clinton ducked the challenge. "The president does appreciate your offer and is sorry he will be unable to accept," wrote Ricki L. Seidman, Mr. Clinton's director of scheduling and advance. "Unfortunately, the tremendous demands on the president as he works to move our country forward do not give him the opportunity to accept as many invitations as he would like."[3] Ms. Seidman, who composed and signed the letter, was reportedly the assistant in charge of calling the *New York Times* cheat line.[4]

A PECULIAR PATTERN OF SUICIDES AND VIOLENCE

In the summer of 1994, the *Economist* listed eight unpleasant incidents concerning a "peculiar pattern of suicides and violence" surrounding "people connected to the Clintons," a.k.a. "Clinton body count." That list would eventually grow to "over sixty." Here is the list:

1. **Susan Coleman—February 15, 1977**—She was pregnant at the time of her death and rumored to have had an affair with Clinton while he was still Arkansas attorney general. Clinton had been Coleman's law professor at the University of Arkansas in Fayetteville. Though Coleman died of a gunshot wound to the back of her head, her death was ruled a suicide.
2. **Barry Seal—February 19, 1986**—Drug running pilot out of Mena, Arkansas. Was assassinated by two Colombian gunmen when they opened fire with a Mac-10 machine gun as Seal parked his car in front of the Salvation Army Center in Baton Rouge, Louisiana.
3. **Florence Martin**—An accountant and sub-contractor for the CIA, was related to the Barry Seal Mena Airport drug smuggling case. He died of three gunshot wounds.
4, 5. **Kevin Ives and Don Henry—August 22, 1987**—Known as "The boys on the track" case. Reports say the boys may have stumbled upon the Mena Arkansas airport drug operation. A controversial case, the initial report of death said, due to falling asleep on railroad tracks. Later reports claim the boys had been slain before being placed on the tracks. Kevin Ives was 17 and Don Henry was 16. Many others linked to the case died before their testimony could come before a grand jury. They include the next seven persons.
6. **Keith Coney—July 1988**—Died when his motorcycle slammed into the back of a truck.
7. **Keith McMaskle—November 1988**—Died when he was stabbed 113 times.
8. **Gregory Collins—January 1989**—Died from a gunshot wound.
9. **Jeff Rhodes—April 1989**—He was shot, mutilated and found burned in a trash dump.
10. **James Milan**—Found decapitated. However, the coroner ruled his death was due to "natural causes."

11. **Richard Winters—July 1989**—A suspect in the Ives/Henry deaths. He was killed in a set-up robbery.

12. **Jordan Kettleson—June 1990**—Was found shot to death in the front seat of his pickup truck.

13. **C. Victor Raiser II and Montgomery Raiser—July 30, 1992**—The finance co-chairman of Bill Clinton's presidential campaign was killed along with his son, Montgomery, and three other passengers in a plane crash. Another passenger and the pilot were injured.

14. **Paula Grober—December 9, 1992**—Clinton's speech interpreter for the deaf from 1978 until her death. She died in a one-car accident.

15. **Jim Wilhite—December 21, 1992**—Vice chairman of ARKLA was killed in a one-man skiing accident. He reportedly "suffered severe head injuries when he skied into a tree on Snowmass Mountain in Aspen, Colorado, while on a family vacation." He was 54.

16. **Paul Tulley—September 1992**—Democratic National Committee Political Director was found dead in a hotel room in Little Rock. Described by Clinton as a "dear friend and trusted advisor."

17. **James Wilson—May 1993**—Found dead from an apparent hanging suicide. He was reported to have ties to Whitewater.

18. **Danny Casolaro**—Investigative reporter who was investigating Mena Airport and Arkansas Development Finance Authority. He slit his wrists, apparently, in the middle of his investigation.

19. **Paul Wilcher—June 22, 1993**—Attorney investigating corruption at Mena Airport with Casolaro and the 1980 "October Surprise" was found dead on a toilet in his Washington, D.C. apartment. Had delivered a report to Janet Reno three weeks before his death.

20. **Vince Foster—July 20, 1993**—Deputy White House Counsel and Hillary's friend and law partner who had connections to the Travelgate and Whitewater scandals was found dead in Fort Marcy Park with a fatal gunshot wound to his mouth and ruled a suicide. (See chapter 16.)

21. **Jon Parnell Walker—August 15, 1993**—Fell to his death from the top of the Lincoln Towers building in Arlington, Virginia. On July 10, 1994, Connecticut's *The Day* reported, "In March 1992,

Walker, and investigator for the Resolution Trust Corporation (RTC), had contacted the Kansas City RTC regional office for information concerning possible ties between Whitewater Development, Madison Guaranty Savings & Loan and the Clintons."

22. **Dr. Stanley Heard—September 10, 1993**—Was from Hot Springs, Arkansas, and had treated Bill Clinton's mother, stepfather, and brother. He was killed, along with his attorney, Steve Dickson, of Topeka, Kansas, in a plane crash fifty miles west of Washington.

23. **Jerry Luther Parks—September 26, 1993**—Head of security for Bill Clinton's headquarters in Little Rock, Arkansas, during the 1992 presidential campaign and gubernatorial years. Gunned down in his car at a deserted intersection outside Little Rock. Park's son said his father was building a dossier on Clinton. He allegedly threatened to reveal this information. After he died, the files were mysteriously removed from his house.

24. **Ed Willey—November 29, 1993**—Was found lying dead of a gunshot wound to his mouth in the woods near his car, parked on a hunting path in rural King and Queen County, Virginia.

25. **Gandy Baugh—January 8, 1994**—Had been an attorney for Clinton pal and drug convict Dan Lasater, who reportedly killed himself by jumping out a window of a tall building.

26. **James Bunch—February 11, 1994**—A Texas employee in Austin who ran a prostitution ring from his office, reportedly died from a suicide involving a gun. Bunch was said to have owned a "little black book" of influential people, including at least one "state legislator," from Texas and Arkansas who visited prostitutes. He was 46.

27. **Hershell Friday—March 1, 1994**—Attorney and Clinton fundraiser who died when his plane exploded.

28. **Kathy Ferguson—May 10, 1994**—Ex-wife of Arkansas Trooper Danny Ferguson, was found dead in her living room with a gunshot to her head. It was ruled a suicide even though there were several packed suitcases, as if she were going somewhere. Danny Ferguson was a co-defendant along with Bill Clinton in the Paula Jones lawsuit. Kathy Ferguson was a possible corroborating witness for Paula Jones.

29. **Bill Shelton—June 12, 1994**—Arkansas State Trooper and fiancée of Kathy Ferguson who questioned whether Ferguson had

actually committed suicide. Shelton was found dead of a gunshot wound also ruled a suicide at the grave site of his fiancée.

30. **Stanley Huggins—June 23, 1994**—Reportedly had been investigating the Madison Guaranty Savings and Loan collapse. Reports indicate he died of viral pneumonia before his 300 pages of findings could be released.

31. **Charles Meissner—April 3, 1996**—The Assistant Secretary of Commerce who had issued John Huang a security clearance. He and Ron Brown were killed in a plane crash.

32. **Ron Brown—April 3, 1996**—The U.S. Secretary of Commerce who was killed in a plane crash after Hillary Clinton dispatched him on a dubious mission to a war-torn corner of the world. "To protect his son Michael from prison, Ron Brown threatened to expose the White House's yet unrevealed Asian fund-raising scheme, in which Brown had played a major role," wrote WND contributor and investigative writer Jack Cashill. A pathologist close to the investigation reported that there was a hole in the top of Brown's skull resembling a gunshot wound.

33. **Barbara Wise—November 29, 1996**—Was a fourteen-year Commerce Department staff member who worked with Ron Brown and John Huang, who worked at the Worthen Bank in Little Rock, where he met then-Gov. Bill Clinton. Huang, who was born in China, was also a former executive of the Lippo Group in Indonesia. Wise's body was found partially nude and bruised in her office. Her death was attributed to natural causes, as Wise had reportedly received several blood transfusions for a liver ailment. She was 48.

34. **John Hillyer—November 29, 1996**—NBC cameraman John Hillyer had been working on an investigation of a drug-smuggling operation in Mena, Arkansas, while Clinton was governor. He also helped with a thirty-minute video called "Circle of Power" and "The Clinton Chronicles." Died of a heart attack.

35. **Mary Caitrin Mahoney—July 6, 1997**—Was a former White House intern up until 1995. She then became a night manager of a Starbucks and became friends with White House intern Monica Lewinsky, who frequented the café. Mahoney was shot five times, once in the back of the head that was described as a robbery, though nothing was taken. She had the key to the safe in her hand which

held $10,000 and wasn't touched. Despite the Starbucks' location in a densely populated neighborhood, no one reported hearing gunfire, sparking speculation that the gunman used a silencer. The murder happened just after she was about to go public with her story of sexual harassment in the White House.

36. **Ron Miller—October 12, 1997**—A principal in GAGE Corp., an Arkansas utility, who began cooperating with the FBI in their investigation of Dynamic Energy Resources started by Nora and Gene Lum. Miller turned over to the FBI on August 5, 1997, 165 tape-recordings of conversations he had with the Lums and their associates. He also helped investigators with the Government Reform and Oversight Committee on Aug. 12. On September 2, the committee subpoenaed documents from Miller concerning Ron Brown, the Lums and Dynamic Energy Resources. Three days later, the committee deposed former White House Chief of Staff Mack McLarty, who was a former chairman of ARKLA. He denied knowing the Lums, and questions about ARKLA and its convicted lobbyist were largely diverted by his attorneys. Seven days later, PBS *Frontline* broadcast interviews with Miller and former Commissioner Bob Anthony. The congressional committee was set to begin formal proceedings October 8. But, on October 3, Miller was admitted to the hospital with an unknown illness. He died nine days later. The cause is still unknown. He was 58.

37. **Eric Butera—December 4, 1997**—Was an informant who had information about the murder of Mary Mahoney. He was told to help police with an undercover drug buy, during which he was beaten to death.

38. **James McDougal—March 8, 1998**—A former business partner of the Clintons and the "brains behind the Whitewater Development Corp.," reportedly died of cardiac arrest in solitary confinement in federal prison. He had been cooperating with Independent Counsel Kenneth Starr in the Whitewater investigation. He was 58.

39. **Johnny Lawhorn Jr.—March 29, 1998**—A mechanic, reportedly discovered a large check from Madison Guaranty Savings and Loan made out to Bill Clinton. The check was said to have been found in a car at his repair shop. He was later killed in a car accident.

40. **Lt. Gen. David J. McCloud—July 26, 1998**—Served as Clinton's director for the Joint Chiefs of Staff Force Structure, Resources and Assessment Directorate, or J-8, from May 1996 to December 1997. He later became commander of Alaskan Command and Eleventh Air Force. McCloud was killed while he piloted his personal YAK-54, a Russian-built, single-engine acrobatic aircraft. The cause of the crash was reportedly unknown. Several blogs had printed unsubstantiated claims that McCloud had been part of a group of twenty-four flag officers that sought to arrest Clinton for treason under the Uniform Code of Military Justice while Clinton was president.

41. **Daniel Dutko—July 27, 1999**—Died from head injuries in a mountain biking accident in Aspen. Dutko served as vice chairman of finance for the DNC in 1996, when thousands of dollars were reportedly funneled from a Chinese military officer to Clinton's 1996 re-election campaign. He was 54.

42. **Charles Wilbourne Miller—November 17, 1999**—Was vice president and board member for Alltel, the company that created the White House's "Big Brother" computer system. An Arkansas medical examiner concluded "suicide" after Miller was found dead of a gunshot wound to the head in a shallow pit about three hundred yards from his ranch near Little Rock. He was 63.

43. **Carlos Ghigliotti—April 28, 2000**—A key figure in the Waco congressional investigation, was found mysteriously dead in his home outside Washington, D.C. His badly decomposed body was found sitting at his desk in his office. Police said there was no evidence of forced entry into his office. He was a respected expert in the field of thermal imaging, had been retained by the House Government Reform Committee to analyze surveillance film footage taken by means of Forward-Looking Infrared, or FLIR, during the siege and final inferno of Mt. Carmel, the Branch Davidian complex near Waco, Texas. He was 42.

44. **Charles Ruff—November 20, 2000**—An influential lawyer in Washington, D.C., who defended Clinton during the Monica Lewinsky scandal and impeachment trial, reportedly died after an accident at his Washington home. One report said he was found unconscious outside his shower. Other reports indicated he had a heart attack. He was 61.

45. **Gareth Williams—August 16, 2010**—A transatlantic MI6 spy, whose dead body was found naked, padlocked and stuffed in a thirty-two-by-nineteen-inch duffel bag that was sitting in his London bathtub. He had illegally hacked secret data on Bill Clinton, according to the UK *Sun*. The news site noted, "[H]is death is still one of Britain's most mysterious unsolved cases." Scotland Yard had announced the death as a suicide, saying he locked himself in the bag. But his DNA wasn't found on the lock. There were no palm prints on the edge of his bathtub.

46. **John Ashe—June 22, 2016**—Former United Nations General Assembly President was found dead in his New York home, and the cause of death was reported as a heart attack. But the local Dobbs Ferry police said "his throat had been crushed, presumably by a barbell he dropped while pumping iron." Ashe was scheduled to testify in just days with Chinese businessman and co-defendant Ng Lap Seng, who was accused of smuggling $4.5 million into the U.S. and lying that it was to buy casino chips and more.

47. **Seth Rich—July 10, 2016**—DNC staffer who was shot in the back and murdered near his neighborhood in Washington, D.C. In one interview, WikiLeaks founder Julian Assange appeared to suggest that Rich was the source of the WikiLeaks-exposed DNC emails. He was 27.

48. **Joe Montano—July 25, 2016**—Served as chairman of the Democratic National Committee before Debbie Wasserman Schultz and was an aide to Hillary's running-mate, Tim Kaine. He reportedly died of a heart attack after the WikiLeaks DNC email dump. He was 47.

49. **Victor Thorn—August 1, 2016**—Authored four books on the Clintons: *Hillary (and Bill): The Sex Volume, Hillary (and Bill): The Drugs Volume,* "*Hillary (and Bill): The Murder Volume,* and *Crowning Clinton: Why Hillary Shouldn't Be in the White House.* Thorn reportedly committed suicide with a gun on his fifty-fourth birthday on a mountaintop in Pennsylvania. *Inquistr* reported that Thorn made several appearances on *The Russell Scott Show* and told the host, "Russell, if I'm ever found dead, it was murder. I would never kill myself."

50. **Shawn Lucas—August 2, 2016**—An attorney who on July 3, helped serve the DNC with a lawsuit claiming then-DNC Chairwoman Debbie Wasserman Schultz "rigged the primary for Hillary Clinton." Less than one month after he helped serve the lawsuit, Lucas' girlfriend found him dead in his bathroom. Cause of death was still pending as of this writing. He was 38.[5]

The following Clinton bodyguards are dead:
51. Major William S. Barley Jr.
52. Captain Scott J. Reynolds
53. Sgt. Brian Hanley
54. Sgt. Tim Sabel
55. Major General William Robertson
56. Col. William Densberger
57. Col. Robert Kelly
58. Spec. Gary Rhodes
59. Steve Willis
60. Robert Williams
61. Conway LeBleu
62. Todd McKeehan[6]

BILL SPELLS R-E-L-I-E-F WITH THE MEDIA

On March 21, 1994, reporters accompanying President Clinton to a printing plant in Keene, New Hampshire, asked him for reaction to Rep. Lee Hamilton's call for congressional hearings to look into Whitewater. "I don't know," the president replied. "What did he say?" One of the reporters quoted Mr. Hamilton's remarks. "That's a discussion he ought to have with the special counsel," the president said testily. He turned away and, according to the press pool report written by the two reporters assigned to accompany the president, "emitted what the pool believed to be a flatulent sound and then turned back toward the pool and said, 'We've cooperated.'"[7]

STEPHANOPOULOS' SWEATHEART LOAN?

In May 1994, George Stephanopoulos bought an $835,000 D.C. building. The ground floor was occupied by the Eye Gotcha optical shop and the upper two floors comprise of an apartment. Mr. Stephanopoulos received a three-year adjustable-rate mortgage at a 6.375 percent rate (locked in until June 1, 1997). It was interesting that he qualified for a residential loan on a mixed-use property. A commercial loan would have been two points higher. Many began asking: How could someone who pulls down $125,000 a year, with a net worth between $30,000 and $100,000, be able to afford such pricey real estate?[8]

According to a NationsBank underwriting memo, it reveals that one of the three restrictions applying for residential lenders doing a loan on mixed-use properties is that "the borrower must be the owner of the business entity." The optical shop on the ground floor was owned not by Stephanopoulos, but by Robert McAlare.[9]

Stephanopoulos obtained a twenty-five-year mortgage on the $835,000 property with 80 percent ($668,000) being lent to him by NationsBank, which was five times his annual salary. A second trust was taken out with the previous owners, John and Miriam Fisher Reno for $83,500 at 8.5 percent with a balloon making the entire balance due on June 1, 2001. Until then, his payment was an additional $642 per month. A general calculation that banks use to determine how much they will lend you generally stands at 2.5 times income to loan amount. That would mean he should have received an estimated maximum of $312,500, or less than half of what he got.[10]

NationsBank's "Program Summary" details exactly what kind of loan Stephanopoulos received and the exceptions that were made. Nations designates loans between $650,001 and $1 million as an "AS3 Super Jumbo Loan Amount." Its "Conventional Program Matrix" specifics that cumulative loan-to-value ratios on Super Jumbo products are "70/90." The "90" means that both the first and second trusts together can make up no more than 90 percent of the total selling price. In other words, 10 percent must be put down, as was done in this case. Stephanopoulos did put down 10 percent, although approximately $60,000—or 72 percent— of that 10 percent was a gift from his father. When asked exactly how much he put down, Stephanopoulos responded, "That's none of your business. I put down my money." But the "70" means that the "first mortgage"—the actual NationsBank mortgage—can account for only 70 percent of the total selling price. Instead, the bank lent him $668,000 or 80 percent, $83,500 above its own stated limits.[11]

There were two other issues:

1. Super Jumbo guidelines also list various restrictions that apply. One of them required loans to be on "single-family

detached properties only." Unfortunately, the early 1900's row building with shared walls, did not qualify as "single-family detached."
2. The qualifying-debt ratio was violated. The Super Jumbo product lists a qualifying ratio of "28/36." One source with knowledge of Stephanopoulos's financing claims that he qualified for a "39/47" ratio, about 11 points over the maximum allowance.[12]

Credit must also be given to Stephanopoulos's real estate agent, George Furioso. He not only shopped around and found the property but then consulted Hugh McColl. Mr. McColl was not only the owner of NationsBank, but a friend and consultant to President Clinton, who called him, "the most enlightened banker in America." McColl dined at the White House, attended ball games with the president, and had put his seal of approval on everything from NAFTA to Clinton's economic plan. He was a high-profile participant at Clinton's Little Rock summit.[13]

McColl was one of the biggest proponents of interstate branching, which would allow banks to acquire institutions across state borders. Under current law, bank holding companies must maintain separate banks in every state. If such laws were lifted, behemoth banking entities would have a much easier time cornering combined commercial markets such as Virginia, Maryland, and the District of Columbia, where NationsBanc already controlled, at the time, a 22 percent market share.[14]

By coincidence, there just happened to be an interstate branching bill on Capitol Hill at the time. It had just cleared the House and, pending Senate approval, was soon to pass under Clinton's pen. When asked about this, Stephanopoulos said of the bill, "I never worked on it—didn't know anything about it." McColl, on the other hand, stood to save millions through the bill's enactment. The *American Banker* reported, "If NationsBank could cut its annual costs as much as $5,000 a branch, that would be a savings of $10 million."[15]

BOXERS OR BRIEFS?

In April 1994, President Clinton appeared on MTV and fielded questions from an audience of teenagers. Toward the end, a seventeen-year-old girl asked, "The world is dying to know—is it boxers or briefs?"[16]

"Usually briefs," the forty-second president of the United States, heir of the tradition of Washington, Jefferson, and Lincoln said. "I can't believe she did that," he said shaking his head.[17]

Joking about the underwear question after the broadcast, President Clinton told MTV President Judy McGrath that "I should have said, 'I'm too old to answer that question.'"[18]

PRESIDENT CLINTON ATTACKS TALK RADIO

In June 1994, President Clinton telephoned a radio call-in show from Air Force One and delivered a twenty-three-minute denunciation of the "violent personal attacks" he was suffering from conservative critics such as Rush Limbaugh, G. Gordon Liddy, and Michael Reagan. "I don't suppose there's any public figure that's ever been subject to any more violent personal attacks," Mr. Clinton complained, "than I have, at least in modern history."[19]

CLINTON REBUKED BY POPE JOHN PAUL II OVER ABORTION

On June 2, 1994, President Clinton held a forty-five-minute meeting with Pope John Paul II in the Vatican where he got an earful from the supreme pontiff of a billion Roman Catholics, about U.S. intent, at the U.N. Cairo conference in September 1993, to use U.S. leverage to impose abortion as a means of population control on the Third World.[20]

After the meeting, Clinton decided to tell reporters that he and the Pope had made "some progress" in reconciling their differences on abortion. Almost immediately, the Vatican spokesman, Joaquin Navarro, denied the statement and rubbed in some salt: "If he says there was a narrowing of differences, it's clear it can only be in one sense, that being that the American president had come closer to the Pope's total opposition to abortion."[21]

CHAPTER 23

ELECTION 1994

I must say, their term limits proposals are looking better to me every day!
—President Clinton, postelection speech 1994[1]

The Democrats had the most to lose in the November 1994 midterm election. To begin with, they had twenty-one of thirty-four Senate seats that were up. Five of eight open Senate seats (where incumbents were not seeking re-election) were held by Democrats. In the House, 257 of 435 were up. Among the forty-three members who were calling it quits, twenty-five were Democrats and eighteen were Republicans. The Democrats also had to defend thirty-one to thirty-six governorships.[2]

Republican officials predicted that voters would disapprove of Bill Clinton as a big-government liberal and would reject Democratic candidates. Also, Republican candidates also began to use talk radio to get their message out to voters. For example, the *Rush Limbaugh Show* broadcast five days a week on 600 radio stations with a potential audience of 20 million listeners. His TV show was carried on 225 local stations with a potential audience of 4.5 million.[3]

Republican candidates began buying local spots which aired during Mr. Limbaugh's syndicated radio show or during his TV show over a series of weeks. In a typical ad, the candidate talked about an issue: crime, welfare, taxes, education, or health care. Then the candidate invited listeners to share their views. Next came the campaign's toll-free number and address. Then, the campaign hoped that they would send a check, pound in a yard sign, or call a neighbor. With Mr. Limbaugh, for only ten thousand dollars you got a big bang for your buck.[4]

On May 3, 1994, President Clinton said he was looking forward to the mid-term election as a chance for Democrats to counter what he called the "venom" of Rush Limbaugh and the "right-wing extremist media." He continued:

> "I welcome the election. When the American people find out the truth, they're going to support people who didn't say no all the time. I think Democrats will do very, very well. Because they'll all have their own record to run on. So, I'm looking forward to it."[5]

On May 25, 1994, Republicans won two upset special House elections in the congressional districts of Kentucky and Oklahoma, states which Democrats comprised the majority of registered voters. The victories were referendums on Mr. Clinton in which voters sent Washington a message on his policies and character in the wake of the Whitewater-Madison investigation and new charges of womanizing.[6]

In the summer of 1994, White House pollster, Stanley Greenberg, assembled a focus group and gave the people assembled a list of phrases. Greenberg then asked them to pick the ones that best described President Clinton. "Over his head" was the most-stated phrase. The second most popular was "indecisive," followed by "immature."[7]

On August 18, 1994, Reuters reported on a *USA Today*-CNN-Gallup poll which put Mr. Clinton's approval rating at 39 percent and his disapproval rating at 52 percent. It was the first time this poll had recorded the majority of Americans disapproving of the job Mr. Clinton was doing.[8] The numbers had turned so negative for Mr. Clinton that his pollster, Stanley Greenberg, cautioned Democrats seeking re-election not to link themselves too closely to the president. In a memorandum sent to party leaders, he also urged Democrats to even avoid a close identification with Mr. Clinton on health care reform and the economy.[9]

Soon, a growing number of Democratic candidates for Congress and other high-profile offices across the nation were starting to keep their distance from President Clinton and his policies. Just two years before (1992), many of those Democrats either campaigned actively for Clinton or embraced him as the best hope to broaden the party's base of support.[10]

For example, freshman representative Don Johnson (D-GA), was widely quoted as saying he did not want either Clinton or Vice President Gore to campaign in his district unless "they are coming down to endorse my opponent."

On September 27, 1994, 152 Republican congressmen together with 185 congressional challengers, came together on the steps of the Capitol to sign the "Contract with America." The Contract bound those Republicans, if they were given the majority in the House of Representatives, to bring to a vote within the first one hundred days, the following ten proposals:

1. Term limits: Votes on two different constitutional amendments, one limiting House membership to six years, another making the limit twelve years.

2. Taxes: Include deductions for educational expenses, first-time home purchase and medical expenses; add tax incentives for child adoption.

3. Economic Growth: Exclude 50 percent of capital gains from taxation, and index capital gains to inflation; cut estate taxes; allow businesses to deduct the cost of new capital investment.

4. Regulation: Compensate property owners for regulatory damages and limit the total cost of all regulation.

5. Budget: Revise the balanced-budget amendment, requiring that any tax increase require a three-fifths vote. The idea is that this would create pressure for spending reduction.

6. Senior Citizens: Increase to $30,000 the Social Security limit on what can be earned without penalty; a dependent-care tax credit.

7. Courts: Reform product liability law, to prohibit outlandish jury awards; add a "loser pays" rule, to discourage frivolous suits; change expert witness rules, to exclude "junk science."

8. Defense: Prohibit placing U.S. forces under U.N. command; revive strategic defensive initiative, to defend the country against ballistic missiles.

9. Welfare: Return most decisions to the states, limit federal spending, require work, and forbid payments to teenage mothers not living with parent(s.

10. Crime: Remove federal impediments to the death penalty, tighten federal habeas-corpus rules, strengthen ability of states to treat juvenile offenders more severely, and target repeat offenders.[11]

The "Contract with America" was very Reaganesque. Even though the document didn't specifically mention former President Reagan's name, its theme of tax reduction, congressional and welfare reform, and a decentralized federal government were pure Reagan.[12]

On October 5, 1994, Ross Perot appeared on CNN's *Larry King Live* and proclaimed, "Give the Republicans a majority in the House and the Senate." Mr. Perot continued, "Stop the rush to big government, which is what the Democrats have given us." He was trying to reach out to an estimated 25 million "Perot-minded" voters to the GOP for the November midterm election. The Perot endorsement further depressed the Clinton White House which was already hammered by the growing number of Democratic candidates for the Senate and House who were avoiding President Clinton's personal help, and by its failure to make progress in winning over the Perot legions. The announcement moved GOP consultant Frank Luntz, who was the 1992 Perot campaign pollster, to project that "Republicans will win a majority in the House, something I wasn't willing to do before." The Republicans needed to gain forty seats for a majority in the House.[13] If the Republicans won a majority in the House, House Minority Whip Newt Gingrich, Georgia Republican, would become House Speaker. Mr. Gingrich would be the first Republican to hold that office since Rep. Joseph W. Martin Jr. of Massachusetts, who ruled the House in the Eighty-third Congress from 1953 to 1954.[14]

On October 11, 1994, President Clinton, in a speech at the Ford automotive plant in Dearborn, Michigan, began asking the audience of Michigan voters to reject going "back to the 1980s and trickle-down economics." Mr. Clinton did not mention former President Reagan by name, but his target was what Democrats used to call "Reaganomics," the combination of tax cuts and defense increases that Democrats blamed for running up the national debt from $1 trillion to $4 trillion. When asked about the Democratic strategy to go after former President Reagan, Democratic pollster Celinda Lake said, "No question, Reagan is very popular; he's the most popular living American among young voters." Still, Lake said, as long as Democrats are careful in their ads to "refer to the stale policies of the '80s," rather than Reagan personally, the tactic can work.[15]

What was President Reagan's message: "Stop putting faith in the false god of bureaucracy. Trust the genius of the American people again. Return to the principles of the Founders . . . limited government, free enterprise and respect for family, community, and faith."[16] President Reagan's message was straightforward: government is the problem, not the solution. To correct the problem, Mr. Reagan offered four commonsense proposals: tax cuts, sound monetary policy to reduce inflation, spending restraint, and deregulation. The result: ninety-three consecutive months of growth, 19 million more jobs, surging exports, and declining inflation and interest rates.[17]

What was the Democrats' alternative to the "Contract with America?" Clintonomics. It was the largest tax increase in the history of America, including tax increases on gasoline, Social Security, and small businesses. It was a government takeover of the health care system. It was broken promises, such as the tax relief for middle income Americans that was never produced. It was an administration that was aggressively fighting both the balanced budget amendment and term limits.[18]

Democratic candidates began approaching President Clinton the way Confederate hospital fund-raisers handled town madam Belle Watling in *Gone with the Wind*. They would take his cash, but only if he hides his face. On October 13, 1994, Rep. Bob Carr, a Democratic candidate for one of Michigan's U.S. Senate seats, became one such politician to sneak Mr. Clinton into a nighttime fund-raiser closed to the public.[19]

Facing questions that the president's October campaign schedule included few events pairing the president with Democratic candidates, White House spokeswoman Dee Dee Myers reeled off a handful of big-name lawmakers that Mr. Clinton had campaigned for or plans to campaign for: "You guys are going to have to end up eating your words, and I'm going to enjoy it," Ms. Myers told reporters.[20]

On October 21, 1994, a memo titled "Big Choices," was leaked to GOP strategist William Kristol. The eleven-page document, which was written on October 3 by Budget Director Alice Rivlin, outlined six politically difficult alternatives for keeping the deficit down while providing enough money for desired domestic programs over the next two years.[21]

Mrs. Rivlin's suggestions included a reduction in the Social Security cost-of-living allowance, entitlement caps for wealthier Americans, limiting mortgage interest deductions, and a variety of tax increases. Mrs. Rivlin drafted the memo to help President Clinton plot political and economic strategy for the next couple of years. The leaked memo embarrassed the Democrats. The President's party had been thrashing Republicans with accusations that the GOP's "Contract with America" would cut popular entitlement programs. The news that the Clinton administration had been secretly pondering similar options took the sting out of the Democrats' lash.[22]

On October 23, 1994, Democratic House Speaker Thomas Foley ducked President Clinton's campaign stop in Seattle, Washington, handing the president another embarrassing reminder of his drag on Democratic campaigns. Mr. Foley's absence, especially, was another measure of how Democratic candidates from coast to coast were distancing themselves from Mr. Clinton. In Washington state, the president's performance was regularly given negative marks in polls.[23]

That same day, the *Washington Times* reported that President Clinton was leaving the country for a six-nation, four-day trip through the Middle East with the hope of lifting his low approval ratings as a way to limit his party's losses on November 8. The president's strategists concluded that his low approval ratings were hurting many Democratic candidates who were closely tied to his agenda.[24]

On October 26, 1994, when Air Force One arrived at Amman, Syria's airport, President Clinton failed for more than fifteen minutes to appear in the doorway to meet his hosts, King Hussein and Queen Noor, who cooled their heals on the tarmac. As the delay continued, U.S. ambassador to Jordan, Wesley W. Egan, made two trips to the jet, apparently to find out what was wrong. Then National Security Council aide Martin Indyk walked up the stairs before the first family appeared in the doorway. Mr. Clinton had taken a nap during the flight.[25]

Dick Morris reported in his book *Behind the Oval Office* that on Monday, October 31, 1994, right after his return from the Middle East, the president called Mr. Morris to ask what he should do in the remaining week to capitalize on his new, broader public-approval ratings. Clinton got a bump by overseeing the signing of a peace treaty between Israel and Jordan. How could he translate these ratings into congressional and senatorial victories? In which states should he campaign? "Go back to the Middle East," Morris said somewhat facetiously. "Don't campaign for anyone; it will lower your approval ratings, and you will drag everyone down to defeat." As predicted, with Clinton back in the States his approval ratings skidded again. After a heady week for Democrats at the end of October, when their polls showed improvement as they rode the president's successes in Haiti and the Middle East, they lost their momentum in the first week of November. As the president dropped, so did his candidates.[26]

On November 4, 1994, four days before the midterm elections, Morris delivered the bad news to Bill by telephone. "You're going to lose the Senate and the House."

"Not the House, no way," he answered.

"*And the House*, Morris repeated. "And by significant margins."

"No way, no way. Not the House," he replied. "Not the House. You're wrong. You really think so? You're wrong."[27]

On November 7, 1994, on the eve of the midterm election, the breakout of parties was as follows:[28]

Senate	House	Governors
56 Democrats	256 Democrats	29 Democrats
44 Republicans	178 Republicans	20 Republicans
	1 Independent	1 Other

In the state legislature, the farm league of American politics, the breakout was as follows:[29]

Democratic Control	Republican Control	Split
25	8	16

On the evening of Election Day, November 8, 1994, the Republican Party rode a wave of anger across the nation as it seized control of the Senate for the first time since 1986 and the House of Representatives for the first time since 1954. Much of the anger appeared to have been directed at President Clinton as one of the most painful midterm defeats for a first-term president. The Republicans picked up fifty-four seats and won control in the House. Republicans won eight seats previously held by Democrats and also won control in the Senate. The Republicans also picked up eleven governorships, giving them a majority of the statehouses for the first time in decades, and in seven out of the eight largest states. They also won control of seventeen state legislative bodies previously held by the Democrats.[30]

"The 1994 defeat devastated Clinton," remembers Dick Morris. "He grieved for each member of Congress who lost his or her seat while loyally backing him. He would talk about them as he might have talked of family members who had passed away."[31]

On the morning of November 9, 1994, Hillary stayed out of sight. An exhausted, dejected and puzzled President Clinton held a news conference in the White House's East Room and vowed to join Republican congressional leaders in lowering taxes and shrinking government. "We're in the middle of a revolution here in the way organizations work in America and the world, and the government is still behind the 8-ball," Mr. Clinton said. "And we're going to have to keep pushing until people believe they have a government that works for them." Mr. Clinton continued, "With the Democrats in control of both the White House and the Congress, we were held accountable yesterday, and I accept my share of the responsibility in the result of the elections."[32]

That same day, the news got worse for the shell-shocked Democrats. Senator Richard C. Shelby of Alabama, a lifelong Democrat, switched parties to become the fifty-third Republican in the Senate. The new breakout of the parties was as follows:[33]

Senate	House	Governors
53 Republicans	230 Republicans	30 Republicans
47 Democrats	204 Democrats	19 Democrats
	1 Independent	1 Independent

The new breakout for the state legislatures, was as follows:[34]

Democratic control	Republican control	Split:
18	19	12

That stunning defeat knocked Bill Clinton back to his senses, and with the help of Dick Morris, he started to govern from the center, rather than from the left. From all appearances, Hillary went into hibernation. Bill Clinton's aides put out the word that Hillary no longer exercised significant influence over anything in the White House.[35]

CHAPTER 24

RON BROWN

I just want to say to my friend one last time: Thank you. If it weren't for you, I wouldn't be here.

—President Clinton at Ron Brown's funeral[1]

In 1991, Ron Brown, who was chairman of the Democratic National Committee, had a goal to get a Democrat elected president. It didn't seem possible in the beginning, though. When the Gulf War ended in early 1991, President George H. W. Bush's approval rating was an astonishing 91 percent, the highest ever recorded. It had even reached more than 55 percent among African Americans. To have any chance of victory, Brown had to find a new source of votes and, even more importantly, a new source of revenue. He knew one good place to look. It was the Asian Pacific American community.[2]

Brown had turned to this community before, back in 1988 when he had launched his own improbable bid for the DNC chair. In seeking their support, Brown had vowed to include Asian Americans in the DNC and to pay attention to their needs. It was one vow he chose to honor.[3]

In December 1991, Ron Brown with his then twenty-six-year-old son Michael, attended a luncheon at Matteo's Restaurant in Hawaii and first met the Lums. Gene Lum, Chinese by origin, was an attorney working for the Honolulu city council at the time as an advisor on land-use policies. Nora Lum, a Japanese American, began her career selling clothes in a tourist shop on Waikiki before moving into real estate. The Lums attracted Brown's attention by promising to make a large contribution to the DNC. That same month, Nora sent $10,000 to the DNC. On the same day, two businesses connected to the Lums sent an additional $11,000 to the DNC.[4]

Several months later, at the 1992 Democratic National Convention in New York, Ron Brown asked the Lums to move to California "to help promote the Democratic party to Asian-Americans there," according to a statement given by the Lums to the House Government Reform and Oversight Committee. Once the Lums moved to California, they founded the Asian Pacific Advisory Council, or APAC, and began organizing fund-raising events. From California APAC became something of a West Coast arm of the Democratic National Committee. The Lums would later release a statement claiming they used their own money to run the office and pay APAC's salaries. Their first fund-raiser was a dinner in Los Angeles honoring John Huang. Yet, according to the *Washington Post*, invitations were mailed from DNC headquarters in Washington, D.C. and were signed by candidate Bill Clinton. And the Lums weren't just giving through APAC. Again, from their statement, they acknowledged picking up the tab for other party events. "DNC officials," the statement reads, "solicited these payments and were aware of the transactions."[5]

Despite its short tenure, APAC raised somewhere between $250,000 and $1,000,000 for the Democrats in 1992. Not surprisingly, the Lums became welcome visitors at the White House. They sat at Ron Brown's table at a Clinton inaugural dinner in January 1993. They attended a state dinner for the president of South Korea. And they attended several events related to Asian-Americans.[6]

In late 1993, the Lums moved from California to Oklahoma. Despite the fact that they had no experience in the oil and gas business, they bought Gage Corporation, a small oil and gas company in Tulsa. They soon renamed it Dynamic Energy Resources. Though they did not appear to have the money to pull off a multi-million-dollar transaction, they did have a partner. His name was Stuart Price, a Clinton campaign official in Oklahoma. In a 1995 lawsuit that concerned some of Dynamic's business dealings, Price testified that he was invited into the deal by a friend at the Democratic National Committee but declined to elaborate.[7]

Although it was not clear where the Lums got the money to buy the company, it *is* clear that they made a killing by purchasing Gage and then turning around and selling some of its gas contracts for far more than they had spent buying the company. With this new windfall, they decided to hire a new high-level executive, Michael Brown. Mr. Brown, then twenty-nine, was the commerce secretary's son and like the Lums, had no experience in the oil-and-gas business. Brown was working as a lobbyist in the Washington office of the Miami firm of Greenberg, Traurig, Hoffman, Lipoff, Rosen & Quentel. The "Rosen" refers to Marvin Rosen, former finance chairman of the DNC.[8]

Brown was generously compensated by the Lums. First, they placed him on the board of directors, giving him five percent of the company's stock. It was worth $500,000 at the time. Then they gave him $7,500 a month in "consulting fees." After that, they gave him about $800 a month for expenses. Finally, they bought Brown a membership at the exclusive Robert Trent Jones Golf Club outside Washington that cost another $60,000.[9]

Now, I would like to introduce a businessman named Ly Tranh Binh. The story that follows comes largely from his recollection. In November 1992, Brown flew to Florida on a private jet. At a local restaurant he met with Lillian Madsen, Brown's girlfriend, and her brother-in-law, Marc Ashton, who was president of Gourmet Fresh Foods in Pompano Beach, Florida, and Nguyen Van Hao, a former deputy prime minister of Vietnam, president of Vietnam Development Corp. (VDC), an associate of Binh. Not yet nominated to anything but fully expecting to be, Brown listened to Hao's plans for stimulating investment in Vietnam once the trade embargo was lifted. Brown told him he wanted to be "the exclusive lobbyist" for Vietnam."[10]

After the meeting, Brown headed off to a DNC executive session in the Bahamas. Somewhere along the way, he hatched an idea and called Washington business executive and lover Nolanda Hill to get her take on it: "How about if he intervened on behalf of the Vietnamese for cash."[11] Hill was not happy. "I can't believe you're really talking about this," she responded, "especially on a cell phone." She suspected Brown was being set up and told him so. And that was the last she heard of it, at least for a while.[12] After the meeting, Nguyen Van Hao and Ly Tranh Binh traveled to Vietnam to meet with high-ranking Vietnamese officials to discuss the VDC proposal. Mr. Binh said that Mr. Hao was well connected in Hanoi and considered Vietnamese Prime Minister Vo Van Kiet a "personal friend." The visit, Mr. Binh said, included a session with Mr. Kiet, during which the two met privately for a half hour, and "when the session ended, Mr. Hao said the deal was done."[13]

Hao and Binh returned to the United States with a letter from the prime minister to Brown, urging Brown to continue discussions with the pair. The Vietnamese government denied any such meeting ever took place or that a letter was ever written, but on all verifiable points Binh would prove reliable, including his description of Hao's past history in Vietnam.[14]

On December 12, 1992, President-elect Clinton selected Ron Brown to be commerce secretary.[15] As soon as Binh learned that Ron Brown had been nominated as commerce secretary he knew they "had conflict-of-interest problems," adding that he relayed that concern to Mr. Hao but was told to be quiet.[16]

Once Brown accepted his cabinet position, he had to do two things. The first one was to open up his finances for inspection in order to win Senate approval. Then, he would have to learn to live on $145,000 once he was approved for the position.[17]

Hao must have sensed Brown's need. Without Binh, Hao sought a second meeting with Brown. Despite the discouragement from Hill and despite his recent nomination, Brown was willing to hear him out. His need for money was no longer merely speculative. He was about to lose his $750,000 a year Patton Boggs income, and he was also about to acquire new expenses.[18]

Brown's relationship with his Haitian mistress, Lillian Madsen, came at a price. As Hill observed, Brown had been paying the rent at Madsen's apartment "forever" and writing it off as his "insurance office." No sooner had Brown been nominated to the cabinet than he upped his investment. He bought Ms. Madsen a new townhouse on Westover Place, NW Washington, D.C., not far from his own residence. This deal struck close to home in more ways than the obvious. Brown had enlisted his son Michael to co-sign on the mortgage from PaineWebber.[19]

On December 15, 1992, Ron Brown met Nguyen Van Hao, Marc Ashton, and Ms. Madsen, at her home. It was in this meeting, according to Mr. Binh, that Ron Brown asked for an exclusive contract, subject to the approval of the Vietnamese government, and $700,000 cash to be deposited for him through Singapore in an offshore bank. The bank account was to be controlled by Marc Ashton, a former financial adviser to "Baby Doc" Duvalier of Haiti and brother-in-law of Lillian Madsen, Ron Brown's mistress. Mr. Binh elaborated:[20]

"My guts turned upside down," said Binh. He told Hao that with Brown now in government, he had serious doubts about their course of action. Hao tried to persuade him to see the deal through.[21] In a sworn affidavit, prepared in the spring of 1993, Binh was altogether specific in his account of what transpired. "Mr. Hao, after his trip to visit Mr. Brown, told me that the price was demanded by Mr. Brown for his lobby effort to be carried out by Patton Boggs and Blow but with close supervision and office coordination with Mr. Brown's contacts." In addition, Brown provided further detail about the $700,000 in cash to be deposited in an offshore bank account." Binh elaborated: "The price was personally delivered to Hanoi by Mr. Hao on his second trip to Vietnam and upon his return, he told me that everything was 'in order.' He told me that money was underway to be transferred to a Singapore bank account at Banque Indosuez. This account was opened by Mr. Le Quang Uyen, a partner of our group and a current vice president of Banque Indosuez Bangladesh branch."[22]

On December 26, 1992, according to Ly Tranh Binh, Ron Brown's contract was approved after a meeting between VDC executives and governmental officials in Hanoi. This occurred about two weeks after Mr. Brown had been nominated to head the Commerce Department.[23]

By the time of the third meeting in February 1993, the Senate had already confirmed Brown, with surprising ease, as secretary. This time Brown met Hao and Ashton at a Washington restaurant. Brown later took Hao alone to the Commerce Department for a brief tour, a fact later verified by Brown's own staff.[24]

According to Binh, Brown reached a tentative agreement with Hao to include oil royalties or concessions and interests of at least 30 percent in other business ventures in Vietnam as well as the cash. In exchange, Brown would work to adopt an eight-point agenda for U.S. assistance to Vietnam. This would start the lifting of the trade embargo and the establishment of most-favored-nation trading status for Vietnam, and it would include proposals for financial aid and industrial development.[25]

It was about that time the unthinkable happened. It was not that Brown had solicited a bribe from a country that was likely still holding American POWs. It appeared that the two Vietnamese partners, Hao and Binh, had a "falling-out."[26] Binh was sufficiently upset that he began telling his story to the media and federal officials. In the beginning, the media did not take him seriously, but the FBI did. In late February 1993, with Brown confirmed less than a month as secretary of commerce, the Miami office of the FBI launched a probe.[27] They interviewed Ly Tranh Binh on several occasions and gave him at least two polygraph examinations, one of which was videotaped. He passed the polygraphs. Mr. Binh was assigned a case agent, Steven Gurley, and given an FBI beeper, which he produced during a Washington interview.[28]

For six months, there was no news of the investigation mentioned in the media. It was not because of a lack of trying on Binh's part. The *New York Times* described his discussions with a lack of credibility: "For seven months, the small-time businessman has been spinning a wild tale of international intrigue." It should be noted that the *Times* offered up this bit of condescension *after* major parts of the "wild tale" had already been confirmed.[29]

On August 13, 1993, the Associated Press reported of an upcoming August 23 issue of *U.S. News & World Report* claiming that the FBI had been investigating Ron Brown since February 1993 on allegations made by Ly Tranh Binh, a Vietnamese businessman living in Florida, and that Mr. Brown accepted $700,000 in exchange for helping lift the U.S. trade embargo against Vietnam. *U.S. News* also said Mr. Brown had known about the investigation "for some time and has refused to discuss it." Mr. Brown denied the statement. In an impromptu news conference beside Air Force One at Alameda Naval Air Station in California, Mr. Brown said he had "no idea" whether the FBI was investigating the matter. "They have never contacted me," he told reporters accompanying President Clinton. "You have to ask the FBI. I assume . . . that when someone makes an absurd charge like this, that someone would look into it. I welcome that." Mr. Brown also called the *U.S. News Report*, "an absolutely ridiculous report. It has no validity to it."[30]

After the initial incident, things subsided. Both the solicitor of the bribe and the would-be recipient denied they had ever met, and this sucked the air out of the reporting, at least in the short term. Through his spokesman, Jim Desler, Brown was emphatic in his denials. Desler had told the *Washington Times* as early as May that Brown "never had any contact with any of the people named, not Mr. Hao or Mr. Binh, and never had any business dealings with the company."[31]

On September 26, 1993, things started to heat up when the *Miami Herald* reported that despite all the denials, Ron Brown and Hao had met three times, just as Binh had been alleging. Reid Weingarten, Mr. Brown's newly hired defense lawyer, responded, "No sane reporter or investigator believes there was any conspiracy between Mr. Brown and any Vietnamese. It's astonishing that this allegation still has legs."[32]

In late September 1993, right after it became known that Brown had deceived the public about his three meetings with Nguyen Van Hao, Brown met with Clinton at a White House ceremony where Clinton announced a new effort to boost U.S. exports. Clinton later defended Brown. "He's told me that he hadn't done anything wrong," Clinton told reporters. "He's done just about everything right as commerce secretary. I think he's done a great job, and I have no reason not to believe him."[33]

The investigation was thrown back to a federal grand jury in Janet Reno's Dade County, now under the watchful eyes of the Justice Department's Public Integrity Section. Stephen Dresch believed that then-Deputy Attorney General Webster Hubbell undermined the investigation, just as he had the Hawaii investigation into the Lums. The prosecutor never even called Ron Brown to testify.[34]

On February 2, 1994, after a yearlong investigation, the Justice Department cleared Ron Brown of all charges. According to a letter signed by Joseph E. Gangloff, acting chief of the Justice Department's Public Integrity Section criminal division, "We have completed a thorough investigation and have concluded that the evidence does not substantiate the allegation." Afterwards, Ron Brown responded that he was "very pleased" by the news. He had no further comment.[35]

Brown had been predicting for several months he would be exonerated. He had reason to be confident. For one, as he would tell Nolanda Hill shortly before his death, he had gotten an inside tip about the investigation from the Justice Department almost as soon as Binh went to the FBI. Agents on the case would tell *ABC News* that they always suspected that. That would explain why Brown never accepted the money.[36]

On February 10, 1994, a week after the Justice Department cleared Brown of his Vietnam charges, he led a delegation to Russia on the first of many large-scale trade missions. That same day, William Clinger, a Republican congressman from Pennsylvania, who was the ranking member of the House Committee on Government Operations, sent a letter of inquiry to Ron Brown, who ignored the letter. At the time, the Republicans had not controlled the House for forty years, and no one expected them to do so for another forty.[37]

The one person who stood out on the list for the Russian trip was Roger Tamraz. President Clinton had authorized him to travel with Ron Brown. So who was Roger Tamraz?

Roger Tamraz was a Lebanese oil financier who had donated $300,000 to the DNC between 1995 and 1996, and in return, received invitations to several White House functions, including a dinner at which he had asked the president for help on a Central-Asian pipeline deal. At the time of the Russian trip, the image of Mr. Tamraz was on an Interpol fugitive bulletin board. The Lebanese court had charged Tamraz with embezzling $200 million from his collapsed Beirut bank.[38]

Once in Russia, the administration officials arranged a series of meetings between Tamraz and Russian energy officials from the GAZPROM bureau. A month later, according to a now declassified telegram, Commerce Department representatives in Russia were ordered to arrange meetings between Tamraz and the Russian first deputy minister of fuels and energy.[39]

Clinton also began promoting the interests of his old friends from Arkansas. Notably, he was eager to reward the Entergy Corporation for its longtime political support and, perhaps, because it would benefit his "other love," Marilyn Jo Jenkins. She was now an Entergy executive and had made several trips to the White House in the first two years of the Clinton administration.[40]

On the next trip, in June 1994, the Commerce Department chose twenty-four American executives to be part of a trade mission to China. Fifteen of the group were heavy contributors to the DNC, among them Entergy's Jerry Maulden. The trip, led by Ron Brown, would net $6 billion in new business contracts. Entergy came home with the biggest chunk of that share. It was a $1.3 billion deal to manage and expand a power plant in northern China.[41]

Soon, Larry Klayman, general counsel of *Judicial Watch*, began to suspect that the Commerce Secretary was using his much-publicized "trade missions" as a means to repay big donors to the Democratic Party. And shake them down for more money. It turned out Klayman was on to something. In September 1994, *Judicial Watch* filed a Freedom of Information Act (FOIA) request with the department. Their intention was to review documents detailing Brown's foreign trade missions, and how businessmen who accompanied Brown on these missions were chosen. The Commerce Department ignored the *Judicial Watch* request.[42]

In the early morning of November 8, 1994, Nolanda Hill voted in Dallas, Texas, and immediately thereafter, flew to Washington. Soon after she arrived, Ron Brown invited her to come over to watch the returns. Hill did not have a good feeling. Brown was feeling about the same, less about the outcome of the election than his own role in it. The White House had been consulting him for nothing other than the distribution of "preacher money." His last official act, in fact, had been to deliver a large pile of it to Jesse Jackson.[43]

Brown hated this assignment. He was the man who had engineered the Democratic comeback in 1992—"I couldn't have done it without you," Clinton would later eulogize him. Now, two years after the election, he was reduced to the role of a bagman.[44]

Hill and Brown began sweating as the returns came in. It seemed like one state after another was throwing out the Democrats. It was a bloodbath. "You better fasten your seat belt," Hill told Brown. "We have had it." For the two of them, the threat was imminent and personal. Republicans, the same ones that Brown had been ignoring for the last two years, were going to be in control of Congress. According to Hill, "I knew that Ron's goose was cooked."[45]

Just a week after the disastrous 1994 midterm elections, Ron Brown, the soon-to-be-indicted Webster Hubbell, Bruce Lindsey, and the Clintons headed to the one place in the world that would be able to support a Clinton comeback. It was the Riady family home base of Indonesia. What is not well known is that it was the Riadys who bailed Clinton out as governor when he mismanaged Arkansas's Teacher's Retirement Fund. They also rescued him twice on the 1992 campaign trail. They had seemingly bought off Webster Hubbell before he had to seek a deal with Whitewater prosecutors. In the spirit of guanxi, they had shown their friendship.[46]

Ron Brown began feeling the pressure. The Clintons had "heavily stressed" the trip's importance. They not only had to impress the Riadys on their own turf, but they also had to start squeezing the CEOs accompanying them in a more systematic way. Hill believes it was about this time that the $100,000 donation morphed from a discreet expectation into the price of admission. Hill would later tell Brown, "They are going to use you and use you and use you until you are such damaged goods they can't use you anymore."[47]

Joining them all at the Asian Pacific Economic Conference in Jakarta were quite a number of shadowy individuals including: Hawaiian fundraisers Gene and Nora Lum, Little Rock restauranteur Charlie Trie, and Thai citizen Pauline Kanchanalak. Trie and Kanchanalak would later be charged by the Justice Department's campaign finance task force with funneling hundreds of thousands of dollars in foreign contributions to the DNC.[48]

On August 26, 1994, John Bryson, CEO of Mission Energy, wrote a "Dear Ron" letter to Brown. In one part of the letter, Bryson asked Brown to "indicate your support for ADB (Asian Development Bank) funding" for a massive new coal-fired electric plant for Indonesia called the Paiton project.[49] Lippo Group, an Indonesian-based conglomerate owned by the ethnic Chinese Mochtar Riady and his sons James and Stephen, had a stake in the deal. It turns out that Mission Energy was part of a larger consortium known as Edison International, and Edison was a Lippo partner. It doesn't stop there. Suharto in-law Hashim had secured an exclusive, no-bid, no-cut contract to supply clean coal to the Paiton power plant. Hashim's financial backer in his Indonesian coal mining business was none other than Mochtar Riady. The Lippo Group controlled one of the only two commercially viable low-sulfur coal mines in the world. Fortunately, one was located near the Paiton plant in Indonesia. The other source of clean coal was located in the United States (Utah). It gets worse. Mission CEO John Bryson had made donations to the Clinton-Gore campaign and also to President Clinton's legal defense fund. Thus, the Mission Energy people were able to travel to Indonesia with Brown and the Clintons.[50]

What happened next should have raised a series of troubling questions. On September 18, 1996, CNN reported the following headline: "Clinton Declares Utah Canyons a National Monument. CNN's Wolf Blitzer reported that Clinton "unilaterally" declared a new 1.7 million-acre national monument in southern Utah.[51] "We're saying, very simply, our parents and grandparents saved the Grand Canyon for us," Clinton told the crowd. "Today, we will save the Grand Escalante Canyons and the Kaiparowitz Plateaus of Utah for our children."[52]

The question was, why would Clinton make such a move just two months before the election. Obviously, it would play well to environmentalists, but Clinton had their votes already, and there were many safer gestures he could have made. Wolf Blitzer, to his credit, did raise the issue of the coal, specifically $1 trillion worth of clean, low-sulfur coal that would never be mined. Blitzer, however, did not know the deeper significance of the coal. Clinton obviously did. In this case, you don't need to be a conspiracy theorist to connect the dots between Utah and Indonesia.[53]

On January 19, 1995, after receiving no response from Ron Brown for three months on the (FOIA) request, Larry Klayman filed a ten-page complaint in U.S. District Court in Washington, D.C. The organization wanted to know if Ron Brown selected business executives to travel with him and promoted the interests of certain U.S. companies based on their financial contributions to the Democratic Party. The complaint stated:

> It has been reported that Secretary Brown had, in effect, sold access to and participation in these trips, as well as his personal promotion efforts with foreign governments and business interests, to those American companies and corporate officials who agreed to contribute large sums of money to the Democratic Party.[54]

On January 25, 1995, it was reported that Nolanda Hill paid $190,000 of Ron Brown's personal debt in 1994, including legal bills, lines of credit and vacation home mortgages. Corridor Broadcasting Corp. also took out an $875,000 promissory note payable to First International Communications. This conflicted with Mr. Brown's statements that he sold his share between $250,000 and $500,000.[55]

On February 7, 1995, it was reported that Mr. Brown's federal financial disclosure statement failed to reveal that a small firm called Kellee Communications, in which he owned stock, got most of its income from a joint venture with AT&T to operate pay telephones at Los Angeles International Airport. AT&T had financial interests pending before the Commerce Department. Its executives had accompanied Mr. Brown on trade missions, one of which resulted in a $4 billion contract for the communications giant.[56]

On February 15, 1995, the Justice Department announced that it would conduct a preliminary criminal investigation into the financial relationship between Brown and Nolanda Hill. The department said the probe was to determine if an independent special prosecutor should be named to review Brown's personal financial dealings.[57]

On April 9, 1995, the *Los Angeles Times* reported that Ron Brown had reaped generous tax breaks from investing in an apartment complex that defaulted on a $6 million loan and was declared partly "unfit for human habitation." The investment drew little notice because on two financial disclosure reports, Mr. Brown said the 150-unit complex called Belle Haven Apartments was located in the upscale Washington suburb of Potomac. In fact, it was low-income housing located in the poorer community of Landover, Maryland. It turns out that Mr. Brown invested $71,000 in Belle Haven in 1983 and enjoyed about $175,000 in tax write-offs in the years that followed, Stephen Moses, who was involved in putting together the original partnership, told the *Los Angeles Times*.[58]

The complex was lent $6.1 million by the Maryland Housing Fund in 1981 for renovations, but the state filed for foreclosure in February 1995 when payments on the renovation loan were about $500,000 in arrears.[59]

Things weren't getting any better for Ron Brown or Nolanda Hill. On May 17, 1995, Attorney General Janet Reno asked for an independent counsel to investigate Ron Brown. Reno also called for "the investigation of possible violations of federal criminal law by Nolanda Hill or her companies." Reno said an independent counsel is needed to determine whether Mr. Brown violated the law by accepting more than $400,000 from a former business partner and whether he filed misleading or false disclosure forms. This should have made Brown and Hill nervous.[60]

On May 17, 1995, President Clinton issued a statement supporting Ron Brown: "Secretary Brown's success as secretary of commerce is unparalleled. I know him to be a dedicated public servant . . . . I am confident at the conclusion of the process, the independent counsel will find no wrongdoing by Secretary Brown."[61]

In October 1995, Nolanda Hill and her seventy-nine-year-old mom had rented a Ryder truck in Dallas, Texas. They loaded it up with important documents and departed to her attorney's office in Kentucky. As they were passing through Memphis, a crew of agents from the DEA stopped them. They ordered Hill and her mother from the truck and spread-eagled Hill against it.[62]

The DEA agents detained the pair for five rainy hours in a parking lot while they searched the truck. She thought, "I know what this is all about." The First International case could not have generated this kind of heat. The independent counsel had to be on to something bigger, something hotter, and that something had to be Oklahoma. Hill was correct. Apparently, Gene and Nora Lum, in their heedless pursuit of wealth and power, had covered their tracks no better than a first-time bank robber. FBI agents had followed their paper trail from Washington back to Hawaii and on to California.[63]

The agents were particularly curious as to what happened to that APAC money raised in their Torrance, California, warehouse for the 1992 presidential campaign. Alas, the Lums had no records. As they told authorities, a car just happened to crash into the corner of their house where they kept their paperwork, destroying it all.[64]

From California, the FBI tracked the Lums to Oklahoma. There was a lawsuit filed in April 1995 by a Dynamic Energy shareholder named Linda Price. The suit accused the Lums of looting the business of $3 million. The Lums eased the FBI's work through their sheer recklessness. Truth be told, they knew little about a business other than how to loot it. And, it was Ron Brown who helped the Lums launch Dynamic Energy and become instant millionaires in the process.[65]

The independent counsel obviously had no trouble discovering the quid pro quo. Unfortunately for Ron Brown, the quid passed through his son, Michael.[66]

Price's lawsuit made another awkward revelation to Michael Brown. He "provided no services or value to the corporation in exchange for said transfers." When Linda's husband, Stuart Price, was deposed, he explained why Michael was hired: "He absolutely is there for them to gain influence with the Department of Commerce, and that's it, and [the Lums] think he's a buffoon, and their discussions with me is that because they want influence, and that's why he is getting paid, and that's why they gave him five percent of the stock for free."[67]

Linda Price claimed that Ron Brown's attorneys had met with Nora Lum and Michael Brown in March 1995 "to discuss personal, legal, and public relations issues regarding his father." It did not take FBI agents long to realize that they had struck gold. Ron Brown had "accepted things of value."[68]

In November 1995, Hill saw Brown about three or four times, but according to Hill, he was in denial. In late November, discreetly and without any public notice, Janet Reno requested the independent counsel add Michael Brown to the case. By 1996, after Michael had been officially but quietly targeted, Ron Brown turned serious.[69]

Sometime early in 1996, an extremely anxious Ron Brown removed from his ostrich skin portfolio a packet of documents about an inch thick and showed them to Nolanda Hill. Each letter was addressed to a trade mission participant, and each, according to Hill's testimony, "specifically referenced a substantial financial contribution to the Democratic National Committee." It was the "smoking gun," the elusive documents *Judicial Watch* had been seeking for more than a year under court order.[70]

In early February 1996, the White House dispatched Ron Brown to New York to personally receive a contribution from CEO Bernard Schwartz of defense contractor Loral. Obviously, Schwartz could have mailed it in. But by sending a cabinet member to him, the White House signaled both its respect for Schwartz and its recognition of his intent, namely to secure waiver approval for Loral's satellite launches. The two checks totaled $1.2 million and were never logged in to the DNC.[71]

On February 15, 1996, the *Washington Times* reported that the independent counsel, which was headed by Daniel Pearson, and his investigators, were zeroing in on loans and other debts, including taxes, that Michael Brown may have paid with money from Dynamic Energy.[72] This resulted in Ron Brown arranging a private meeting with Bill Clinton in the White House family quarters, where such meetings were held. As Nolanda Hill tells it, the meeting at the family quarters did not go well. Brown told the president to call off the dogs, to shut down the independent counsel, to do whatever had to be done because he was not about to let his son go to jail.[73]

The president kept his peace and let Brown talk. After Brown had finished, the president told Brown he doubted that he could do anything for him. The case was out of his hands. Brown disagreed. Without the IRS and the FBI, the independent counsel could not function, he reminded the president. If Reno wanted to starve the investigation, she could do just that and say no more. Obviously, there would be a public relations problem, but Reno loved her job so much she would do just about anything to keep it. This was her weakness, and both Clinton and Brown knew it.[74]

When Brown did not get the response he wanted from Clinton, he resorted to his ultimate bargaining chip. If he had to, he told Clinton, he was prepared to reveal the president's treasonous dealings with China, almost none of which had yet to make the news. It was on this subject—the president's ultimate Achilles' heel—that Hill had been focusing Brown.

Before Clinton had a chance to assess the threat, Brown unthinkingly upped the ante. He told the president he had "lost control" of Hill. Clinton said nothing directly, but he surely must have read this remark for the implicit warning that it was. So ended what may well have been the most critical and uncomfortable meeting of the Clinton presidency. The details of this meeting the president would not have shared with Leon Panetta or Vernon Jordan or even Dick Morris. The one person he would have told was Hillary. They would not have failed to recognize that if Brown went public on China, Clinton would certainly lose the election, probably the nomination, and quite possibly his freedom. The potential for disaster was that real and that imminent.[75]

Think about it. Ron Brown knew Bernie Schwartz. He knew Wang Jun. He knew the Riadys and the Lums and John Huang. He knew about the Chinese navy's attempt to secure a beachhead in Long Beach. He even knew about Mack McLarty and the Oklahoma deal. He knew what money was involved and where it went, and he transported a whole lot of it, much of which was never recorded. Ron Brown, in fact, knew way too much at a time when the media knew almost nothing. If there was any one man in America whose knowledge could sink Bill Clinton, it was Brown.[76]

On March 14, 1996, under court order, Brown submitted a sworn statement *Judicial Watch* would later claim to be "patently false and misleading." Brown swore he had played no role "in determining the scope of the Department of Commerce's search for and/or preparation of response to the Freedom of Information Act requests which made the basis this suit." Brown was committing perjury.[77]

Unlike Ken Starr, Daniel Pearson turned out to be a bulldog. On March 19, 1996, the independent counsel's office ratcheted up the pressure and zeroed in quickly on Brown's connections to Chinagate. Brown had worked with the Chinese to arrange illegal transfers of sensitive technology from U.S. corporations to the Chinese military. Also, Pearson obtained subpoenas for more than twenty individuals and organizations. He wanted to see the records of the DNC, the Lum's infamous Asian Pacific Advisory Council and their even more potentially explosive Oklahoma entity: Dynamic Energy Resources. If they were unaware before, the Clintons had to know now just where Pearson was heading, and they could not have been happy.[78]

Soon after the twenty subpoenas were issued, with return dates of April 2, 1996, Brown was informed that he would be participating in another trade-mission trip, this time to the Balkans. This news could not have sat well with either Brown or Hill.[79]

For some reason, everything about the trip seemed wrong. At first, Brown was told the State Department had asked for the trip, but this made no sense since the State Department typically wanted as little to do with Commerce as possible. The military could not have sought it either. Less than six months after the signing of the Dayton accords, the Balkan countryside remained unsettled and dangerous. Security would not come cheaply or easily. Brown could not call the trip off on his own. It was the White House that was organizing it. Brown still had one last White House meeting scheduled before he departed. Under pressure from Hill, he found a minute alone with the president and asked him to send someone else to the Balkans. The president refused his request.[80]

At home, Brown's pace quickened. Although his wife, Alma, was bedridden with the flu, Brown insisted she accompany him to the bank to refinance the mortgage at a lower rate. The day before he was to leave, he ignored Alma's objections and all but lifted her out of bed to get the mortgage signed. As Tracey Brown observes of her mother, "She couldn't understand his intensity."[81]

The night before he left for the Balkans, Brown visited his mother, then hospitalized for schizophrenia, in New York City. Afterwards, he returned to her apartment. He had not been there in years. Sitting alone in the dark, Brown called Hill and for three tearful hours walked her through the ruins of his life. According to Hill, "I was his old comfort. I was home to him."[82]

The day Brown left for Europe, he spent some time with "Sonny Junior," as Brown called his son. They played golf together, ironically enough at the Robert Trent Jones Golf Club, the club whose membership the Lums had purchased. Brown appeared to be in good spirits. After golf, his chauffeur arrived at the Brown residence to take him to the airport. Brown kissed his still ailing Alma goodbye, and he was gone.[83]

On March 31, 1996, Brown arrived in France and headed up to Lille, for a G-7 conference on employment. After the two-day conference, Brown returned to Paris where he stayed with Pamela Harriman, then the ambassador to France.[84]

On April 2, 1996, Brown boarded a military plane at the Villacoublay airport in France and headed to the Croatian capital of Zagreb. There he landed around midnight. Croatian ambassador Peter Galbraith and Brown aide, Morris Reid, met him at the airport, as did Croatian Prime Minister Zlatko Matesa. Brown was originally scheduled to meet Croatian strongman and President Franco Tudjman the next day in Zagreb. But Matesa informed him the meeting site had been changed to Dubrovnik, allegedly to help promote the walled city's potential as a tourist site. This added leg could not have pleased Brown. He left the hotel at 5:30 the next morning for a trip to Tuzla in Bosnia.[85]

What follows is a straightforward, multi-sourced account of that last flight and response:

* At 2:10 p.m. Croatia time on April 3, 1996, Captain Amir Sehic landed a twin-engine corporate jet at Cilipi Airport about ten nautical miles south of Dubrovnik on the Adriatic coast. For the record, a nautical mile equals 1.15 statute miles. (All future references will be to nautical miles.)
* Sehic's jet carried Croatian Prime Minister Zlatko Matesa and American ambassador Peter Galbraith. After Galbraith disembarked, he heard another plan descending and thought it might be Brown's. It wasn't. It was a Swiss Air charter carrying Enron executives, one of five planes to land routinely on the airport's sole runway in the hour before Brown's plane was scheduled.
* About fifteen minutes earlier, at 1:55 p.m., Ron Brown's CT-43A, the military version of a Boeing 737, call sign IFO-21, left Tuzla in Bosnia, 130 miles to the northeast. At this stage, the plane was five minutes ahead of schedule.
* A few minutes after take-off, IFO-21 contacted Air Force weather service and asked for Dubrovnik weather at the planned arrival time. The weather report was 500 feet broken, 2,000 feet overcast, five miles visibility and rain. Technically, this was below the legal minimum for landing, but the pilots proceeded apace. The weather had been highly variable all day. It would likely change again.
* At 2:34 p.m., the plane, now at 21,000 feet, crossed over the sophisticated VOR transmitter at Spit and banked southeast out over the Adriatic towards Dubrovnik's Cilipi Airport one hundred miles

away. The Zageb Center, which was controlling the plane, cleared it to descend first to 14,000 feet and then 10,000. At the later point, Zagreb transferred control to the Dubrovnik tower at Cilipi.

* Captain Sehic sat in the cockpit of his Challenger facing north to keep an eye out for Brown's plane. He watched as the rain ceased and the sky brightened. At 2:48 p.m., he called the incoming plane from his cockpit and told the pilots several other planes had successfully landed and the weather was, in his words, "on the minima," meaning above the minimum standards needed to land. If they needed to execute a missed approach, however, he recommended a route over the Adriatic to the right. "It is easy approach [sic]," he would tell USAF investigators. "I was not concerned." Now at about 5,000 feet and some sixteen miles away, U.S. Air Force Captains Ashley J. Davis, and Tim Shafer, thanked Sehic for his words of welcome.

* At 2:53 p.m., the control tower told another flight the weather was "500 broken and 2,000 overcast." This was below minimum. Davis and Shafer likely heard this, but they themselves did not ask for the current weather from the tower. If they had, it would have been on tape and they could have been reprimanded for starting an illegal approach. The only way they could get in trouble is if they crashed and they certainly did not expect to do that. They were well aware there was a mountain just 1.8 miles to the left of runway 12 and that mountain was shrouded in clouds.

* Because of the weather, the crew was required to fly an instrument approach into Cilipi. The only ground instrument the pilots could follow into this relatively primitive airport was a non-directional radio beacon (NDB) on Kolocep Island. This was not of great concern to Davis. As an evaluator pilot—that is, one who is skilled enough to evaluate other pilots—he did not lack confidence. He himself had recently tested "proficient" on this kind of approach, as the USAF report acknowledged. "The mishap pilot and copilot were described as the two best pilots in the flight."

* At 2:54 p.m., the plane passed over the radio beacon, seemingly on course, if a little too fast. The crew called the tower—"We're inside the locator, inbound"—and was then cleared for a landing. The published approach charts required the pilot to fly a 199-degree course from this beacon on Kolocep Island, the "final approach fix."

* To the pilots, all seemed in order. This was a routine landing. They descended through the clouds at an appropriate approach speed to an altitude of 2,200 feet smoothly and consistently, guiding themselves by the one beacon behind them. The tower took the pilots at their word. It had nothing else on which to rely. It had no radar.
* Lenadra Gluhan, an off-duty air traffic controller, knew something was wrong the moment she heard the plane pass behind her house. She lived just north of the airport. She could hear clearly because the light rain had ceased altogether, and she had just thrown open her rear windows. As Gluhan knew, the plane should have been in front.
* Only in the final seconds did Pilots Davis and Shafer realize they were off course. But they could not have begun to comprehend how far and how fatally. Before the plane's Ground Proximity Warning Systems could activate, just three minutes after last contact with the control tower, St. John's Peak rose up right in front of them.
* Davis would have instinctively yanked back on the control wheel and firewalled the throttles, but it was too late for either. At 2:57 p.m., the plane's inertia carried the hundred-thousand-pound craft at 150 knots into the jagged hillside, clipping its right wing and engine and cracking off the tail before any of the passengers even had a chance to pray for deliverance. The fuselage then skidded violently across the rocky slope, breaking up as it slid, disgorging its passengers randomly, and finally crunching to a fiery halt with the crew, likely dead or unconscious, trapped inside.
* At 3:01 p.m., the tower tried to contact the pilots but without success. At 3:10 p.m., the tower announced to Morris Reid, Galbraith, and the others that it had lost contact with Brown's plane. Ten minutes later, Prime Minister Matesa lamented that all contact with the plane had been lost. Galbraith returned to Matesa's plane and called the State Department in Washington. He reached Undersecretary Peter Tarnoff and expressed his concerns. Galbraith then turned his attention to organizing a multinational rescue operation. It would not be until 4:30 p.m. Croatia time that word reached the president in the Oval Office (9:30 a.m. local time).
* Search and rescue operations proceeded. Lacking helicopters in the Dubrovnik area, Croatian authorities called on NATO for help. Two French helicopters took off from nearby Ploce at about 4:50

p.m.—nearly two hours after the crash—and began searching. The first coordinates given to the French placed the crash site in the water between Kolocep Island and Dubrovnik. For the next hour, the French pilots continued to fly over and around the old city of Dubrovnik. "We didn't know anything about the location of the crash," conceded Lt. Col. Jean Francois Dupleix.

* At 6:45 p.m., two American helicopters arrived. They had crossed the Adriatic looking for a T-34, a single engine, training plane. They were not only looking for the wrong plane, but they were also looking in the wrong places. They had not been informed about the direction of approach for Brown's plane. After only a few minutes on site near Dubrovnik, however, they "pretty much knew it was on land." They saw no indication of the plane in the water, and the plane's crash position indicator was emitting a telltale signal. The weather, however, prevented an inland search. They landed at Cilipi airport, and had to sit there for the next frustrating few hours.

* At 6:45 p.m. Croatian time, almost four hours after the disappearance of the plane, a local villager named Ivo Djurkovic called the police to tell them that earlier in the afternoon he had heard a plane fly overhead, followed by a loud "grating sound" and then an explosion. He assumed it was a grenade. But, when the fog finally lifted off a nearby mountain called Sveti Ivan, or in English, St. John's Peak, one of the highest mountains in the area at 2,400 feet, there, to his horror, he saw the shattered wreckage of Ron Brown's plane.

* A message was relayed to Cavtat police chief Vitomir Bajac, and at 7:20 p.m. he called in the first official visual confirmation of the wreckage. He reached the site on foot about fifteen minutes later. About fifteen minutes after that (7:50 p.m.), police instructor Damir Raguz arrived with a group of about thirty other police. By this time, the rains were torrential and visibility non-existent. Some mystery surrounds how many survivors the rescue workers found or at exactly what time they found them.

* At 9:30 p.m., Raguz spotted Tech Sergeant Shelly Kelly, thirty-six of Zanesville, Ohio, who made an "ah" sound. She was bleeding from her mouth and nose and from her leg. At 9:35 p.m., he first alerted the outside world that there was at least one seriously injured survivor. With the bad weather, she was put on a stretcher found inside the

plane and carried down the hill. At the bottom of the mountain, they transferred Kelly to a waiting ambulance. An accompanying Croatian physician pronounced her dead on the way to the hospital. * More might have been known about what transpired at the scene were it not for an odd exchange of information at 9:40 p.m. Croatia time. Five minutes after Kelly was found, according to Commerce Department documents, Deputy Secretary of State Strobe Talbott was reported to have made a "strong request" that "HRT TV team in Dubrovnik not film the crash site." HRT is the acronym for Hrvatska Radiotelevizija, or Croatian Radio Television. Croatian officials readily complied.[86]

While the search continued on the hillside for survivors, the President and Hillary Rodham Clinton left the Brown residence and headed over to the Commerce Department to deliver a "eulogy" for Ron Brown and the other victims, at least one of whom was still very much alive. Besides Brown, there were eleven other Commerce Department employees on that doomed plane. The president dedicated only one paragraph to them, and mentioned none by name, not even Assistant Secretary of Commerce Charles Meissner. One labors to find a rationale for the Clintons' haste in this matter. They could not have known who was alive and who was dead. As we shall see, "haste" will shape much of the ensuing investigation.[87]

Less than an hour after the news reached Washington, two of Brown's secretaries ransacked his office, shredding an untold number of his personal papers and removing other files. Another man took documents and placed them in a safe at the Small Business Administration.[88]

In Dallas, after having received the news of Ron Brown from her brother-in-law, Louis Blaylock, shock and sorrow settled in which then yielded to thoughts of survival. Nolanda Hill called Brown's people at the Commerce Department. At Commerce, Brown kept a locked drawer filled with sensitive documents he had never turned over. "Don't let anyone in that drawer," Hill told them. She then called Michael Brown on his cell phone and expressed her concerns. Despite the shock at the loss of his father, Michael still had the presence of mind to tell her, "Any kind of documents that need to be shredded are being shredded as we speak." He was already one step ahead of her.[89]

The first American rescuers from the Special Tactical Squad would not reach the peak until 2:30 a.m. Croatia time. At 4:00 a.m. American military personnel set up a communications post at the base of the mountain. Toward morning, amidst the debris and carnage, Ron Brown's body was found. It was 9:00 a.m. in Croatia, 2:00 a.m. in Washington. Michael Brown took the call.[90]

Seven hours later, at 9:00 a.m. Washington time, President Clinton called Alma Brown. He told her Brigadier General Michael Canavan, special operations commander on site, had identified her husband.[91]

On April 4, 1996, a day after the crash, President Clinton made the connection between that sad day and a comparably sad one twenty-eight years earlier when Martin Luther King was slain in Memphis. Like King, claimed the president, Brown died "answering a very important challenge of his time." Clinton did not elaborate that this "important challenge" was getting him reelected by whatever means necessary.[92]

With Ron Brown's death, it also brought the independent counsel investigation to an end, and the case against Michael Brown was transferred to the Justice Department. And so the story would have ended. You had Ron Brown buried at Arlington National Cemetery with more pomp than any government official since RFK, a nation in mourning for its fallen hero, and a president bereft. But, Ron Brown's body had one more story to tell. From April 3, 1996, after Ron Brown's jet slammed into a mountainside in Croatia, there had been rumors that the secretary of commerce might have been murdered. His legal troubles soon became the basis for much speculation. Imagine if Mr. Brown had copped a plea deal in which he testified against the Clintons, it would have been curtains for Bill and Hillary. The talk was largely confined to black radio. That would soon change.[93]

On Easter Sunday, April 7, 1996, Chief Petty Officer Kathleen Janoski, a forensic photographer in the Office of the Armed Forces Medical Examiner (OAFME) at the Armed Forces Institute of Pathology (AFIP), and her colleagues went to work at Dover Air Force Base's huge mortuary, a building about the size of an airplane hangar, on the thirty-three bodies. Fully aware of the controversy around White House counselor Vince Foster's ill-handled death (see chapter 16), she took responsibility for photographing Ron Brown's body. She had scarcely begun when she saw something that took her breath away. "Look at the hole in Brown's head," she exclaimed. "It looks like a bullet hole."[94]

U.S. Army Lt. Col. David Hause, an experienced deputy medical examiner, left his examining table to take a look. "Sure enough," he remembers saying. "It looks like a gunshot wound to me, too." He would later add that the wound "looked like a punched-out .45-caliber entrance hole."[95]

Col. William Gormley consulted with the other pathologists, including Navy Cmdr. Edward Kilbane, and they all agreed it looked like "an entrance gunshot wound." Yet, despite the consensus, Colonel Gormley, the highest-ranking AFIP officer then at Dover, did not do the obvious. He did not call in the FBI. He did not ask the Brown family to permit an autopsy. Nor did he take the opportunity to look for an exit wound or test for gunshot residue.[96]

These oversights perplexed Janoski at the time, but she was hardly in a position to challenge a colonel. Meanwhile she continued to take photos, more than two hundred in all, ignoring the pressure to hurry up and "get the bodies out." That pressure, as contract investigator Bob Veasey disclosed, came directly from the White House.[97]

On April 8, 1996, Lt. Col. Steve Cogswell, a doctor and deputy medical examiner, arrived at St. John's Peak in Croatia. As was standard, the AFIP had sent one of its pathologists to the scene to help his colleagues back at Dover establish the cause and manner of each victim's death.[98]

Cogswell had no sooner descended on the scene than Col. Gormley called with a request. He wanted Cogswell to look for an object that might have punched a ".45 [inch] inwardly beveling, perfectly circular hole in the top of [Brown's] head." These were Gormley's words as Cogswell noted them at the time. The previous day's exam had apparently alarmed Gormley.[99]

There was much about this crash that seemed suspicious to Cogswell. For starters, the Air Force chose to skip the safety board phase of the investigation. With twelve years of experience at crash scenes, Cogswell could not understand why. This was the first time in his experience that there was no safety board.[100]

The same day, Monday, April 8, 1996, the press reported that the man responsible for the Cilipi Airport's navigation system, maintenance chief Niko Jerkuic, shot himself in the chest an hour after the bodies of Brown and the other Americans had been flown out of the airport on Saturday. Jerkuic had not been working on Wednesday, the day the plane crashed. The Croatian interior minister was quick to deny that his suicide had "any connections with the tragic crash of the U.S. aircraft." Unfortunately, he died before the U.S. team got a chance to question him" about the navigation aids.[101]

In Washington, the grieving for Brown continued, much of it painfully sincere, some of it less so. After a memorial service for Brown at St. John's Chapel near the White House, a TV cameraman captured the quintessential Clinton moment. As Clinton and the Reverend Tony Campolo were walking back to the White House, they were discussing, as Campolo recalls, the typically joyous black funerals they had attended in the past, and the conversation turned mirthful.[102]

As Clinton leaned back to laugh, he suddenly locked on to the camera and reflexively downshifted to a funeral gear, dropping his head in seeming sadness and wiping an imagined tear from his eye. Campolo, unaware of the camera, kept on talking and laughing. If it had been a Republican president, the media would have hung that transitional moment around his neck.[103]

Interestingly, the day of the funeral service, a friend in a position to know had told Nolanda Hill "for [her] own safety" that Brown had been found forty yards from the plane. "It looked," he said, "Like he was trying to get away." Neither he nor Hill could have known about the hole in Ron Brown's head.[104]

In June 1996, Air Force investigators concluded that pilot error and instrument failure had caused the crash. But Christopher Ruddy sensed a cover-up.[105]

Following the Vince Foster pattern, Washington officials immediately announced that the plane crash was an accident, before any investigation had gotten underway. Next, as mentioned earlier, the Air Force announced that it would circumvent standard procedure by not convening a safety board to investigate the crash. By canceling the safety board, it sent a message through the ranks that the brass did not want to hear from any potential whistleblowers. The official lies soon began.[106]

The first lie was the weather. The White House and the mainstream media claimed that Ron Brown's plane went down in a violent storm. It was not true. Hillary Rodham Clinton, who participated in a syndicated column at the time, wrote that the plane crashed "in a violent rainstorm." *Time* magazine called it, "the worst storm in a decade," and *Newsweek*, "the worst storm in 10 years." It was all lies.[107]

Christopher Ruddy learned from the Air Force's twenty-two-volume crash report that, "[T]he weather conditions broadcast by the control tower were basically good: winds were at 14 mph, with only a light to moderate rain.... The only possible hindrance to landing was scattered cloud cover at 500 feet and solid cloud cover at 2,000 feet."[108] Cloudy conditions are normal for Dubrovnik airport, which rests between the Adriatic Sea and a mountain range. Therefore, planes commonly follow Dubrovnik airport's ground beacons to find the runway. "In the minutes before Brown's plane crashed, five other planes landed at Dubrovnik without difficulty, and none experienced problems with the beacons," wrote Christopher Ruddy in the November 24, 1997, *Pittsburgh Tribune-Review*.[109] For some reason, however, Brown's plane failed to follow the beacon. It flew ten degrees to the left of the proper course, straight into a mountainside. The Air Force concluded that it must have been following the wrong beacon. But what sort of ground beacon would have led the plane into a mountainside?[110]

The Air Force report noted that a portable backup beacon had been stolen before the crash and never returned. Ruddy continued, "Conspiracy buffs have suggested Brown's plane may have been a victim of 'spoofing'— aviation slang for what happens when a spurious navigation beacon is used a trick a pilot to change course."[111]

The Friday morning after Thanksgiving 1996, the Associated Press broke a minor news story. It scarcely registered in the consciousness of most Americans, but in the hearts of a least a few, the story must have struck something close to terror:

> WASHINGTON (AP)—Police were investigating the death of a woman whose body was found today in an office at the Commerce Department. Anne Luzzatto, press secretary for Commerce Secretary Mickey Kantor, said the woman's body was found this morning by a Commerce Department employee, who notified security personnel in the building. 'It is my understanding that someone found the body in an office on the fourth floor,' Luzzato said. She said that District of Columbia police were conducting an investigation but she had no details on a cause of death. Her name was Barbara Wise.[112]

The Clintons heard the news that morning at Camp David. No doubt, Mickey Kantor, the new Commerce secretary, called them soon after the body was discovered. His spokesman would not have talked to the Associated Press without Kantor's approval, and Kantor would not have given it without the president's. Unlike Brown, the Clintons trusted Kantor. As U.S. trade representative, he had pulled insider rank on Brown often enough that Brown grew to despise him.[113]

A coworker had found Barbara Wise's bruised and half-naked body on the fourth floor in Commerce's International Trade Administration office at 7:45 a.m. Wise had worked in this office for fourteen years. This was the same office in which John Huang, soon to become a household name, had also worked.[114]

Wise was reportedly "very close to Ron Brown," according to *Insight* magazine editor Paul Roderiquez, who tracked this case closely. Apparently, she had been "under enormous pressures," emanating in part "from within the Department of Commerce not to cooperate with ongoing investigations on Capitol Hill." Nolanda Hill confirms Wise used to regularly brief Brown.[115]

At 5:21 p.m., that same Friday after Thanksgiving, the AP put on the wire the following story: "The name of the forty-eight-year-old woman was being withheld pending notification of relatives," the article stated before adding, "District of Columbia police spokesman J.C. Stamps said that an autopsy was being performed." In short, less than ten hours after a professional woman's body has been discovered, and before her relatives had been contacted, the DC medical examiners had it opened up on the table. This happens rarely if at all in the real world. It certainly did not happen to Ron Brown. One senses pressure from above.[116]

There was one good reason for the pressure. A finding of "natural causes" could put a quick lid on an extremely explosive story, to wit, a semi-naked woman, reportedly close to Ron Brown, found dead in John Huang's old office in the midst of a swelling fund-raising scandal and this just months after Brown's unlikely death.[117]

At 1:30 a.m. Saturday morning, the dead woman was identified as Barbara Alice Wise, forty-eight, of Gambrills, Maryland. The DC police claimed, "She died of natural causes." They also acknowledged, however, the autopsy was "unable to determine the cause of death."[118]

An article just 116 words long, wrapped up with the DC police saying Wise "probably died from natural causes," but they could not be certain until the medical examiner's office completed a toxicology test. Otherwise, despite the bruises, there was "no evidence of foul play."[119]

On August 28, 1997, Michael Brown pled guilty to one misdemeanor charge of illegally giving $4,000 to Ted Kennedy's 1994 Senate campaign. Specifically, Brown had given $2,000 to his secretary and $1,000 apiece to two co-workers, which they in turn gave to Kennedy's people.[120]

The Justice Department could have pursued felony charges against Brown, but prosecutor Raymond Hulser chose instead to charge Brown with a misdemeanor. "This case does not involve a large amount of contributions," Hulser said in explaining his decision. "We were looking to do what's right as to his conduct and the amount of money involved." The misdemeanor charge, Hulser added, was "a very fair and appropriate resolution" of the case. Sentencing was set for November 21, 1997.[121]

Brown's guilty plea wasn't exactly front-page news. It was just a misdemeanor. But there was a much larger story in the plea agreement, one that most reporters either missed or decided not to emphasize. In making the plea deal, the Justice Department agreed to close the book on an extensive investigation into several large and questionable payments made to Michael Brown by Gene and Nora Lum.[122]

On November 21, 1997, Michael Brown learned what the penalty would be for his misdemeanor—three years' probation and a $5,000 fine. He also had to perform 150 hours of community service and pay an additional $7,818 for the costs of his probation.[123]

Michael Brown and his new golf buddy, Bill Clinton, likely thought they had put the whole affair to bed that day. Just three days later, however, they would learn how wrong they were. As it turned out, Nolanda Hill was not the only one to go public in 1997. Lt. Col. Steve Cogswell decided to do so as well.[124]

On December 3, 1997, the *Pittsburgh Tribune-Review* ran an interview with Lt. Col. Steve Cogswell, the first of four military whistleblowers who would sacrifice their careers by going public, accusing the AFIP of a cover-up: "Brown had a .45-inch inwardly beveling circular hole in the top of his head, which is . . . the description of a 45-caliber gunshot wound," Cogswell told Christopher Ruddy. In his interview, Cogswell repeatedly described the injury as "an apparent gunshot wound." He said, "[W]hen you got something that appears to be a homicide, that should bring everything to a screeching halt."[125]

That same day Janoski was home on leave in Pittsburgh. She got the sense something was up when a tech sergeant called from the AFIP office wanting the combination to her safe. Two days later, on December 5, 1997, the AFIP imposed what was essentially a gag order on Cogswell. He was forced to refer all press inquiries on the Brown case to AFIP's public affairs. More intimidating still, military police escorted him to his house and seized all of his case materials on the Brown crash.[126]

On that same day, on December 5, 1997, F. Whitten Peters, acting secretary of the Air Force, sent an angry, apologetic letter to the families of the crash victims. "The alleged 'bullet fragments' mentioned in the *Tribune-Review* reports were actually caused by a defect in the reusable x-ray film cassettes," Peters wrote. "Medical examiners took multiple x-rays using multiple cassettes and confirmed this finding." He went on to claim that Brown had died of "multiple blunt-force injuries" suffered in the crash. Gag orders were imposed on all military personnel with knowledge of the Brown case.[127]

Lt. Col. David Hause ignored the heat and went public on December 9, 1997, in support of Cogswell. Unlike Cogswell, Hause had been present for the examination. Hause, who had won a purple heart in Vietnam as a combat infantryman, had been involved in autopsy procedures for twenty-five years. He was not one to be taken lightly. Two days later (December 11), a third pathologist, Air Force Maj. Thomas Parsons, also came forward. Although not present at the examination, he agreed the hole was suspicious and unusual" and worthy of an autopsy. Like Hause, he firmly denied he had ever signed off on a report backing Gormley's findings and just as firmly argued for an autopsy.[128]

On the same day, amazingly, the AFIP admitted that all the multiple new X-rays were all missing, as were the original ones. "Wecht's law," famed coroner Cyril Wecht called the phenomenon. The more controversial a case, the more likely evidence is to turn up missing. In real life Wecht described as "very, very rare" the times key X-rays actually disappeared.[129]

Then, the *Pittsburgh Tribune-Review* had brought Wecht in to review the case. The Pittsburgh coroner, a prominent local Democrat, could not be easily dismissed as a trafficker in Republican conspiracy commerce. He noted the "perfectly circular" nature of the wound, its "inwardly beveling path," the "tiny pieces of dull silver-colored" material around the edge of the wound, the "lead snowstorm" shown the photo of the X-ray, and came to an amazing conclusion:

> "There was more than enough evidence of a possible homicide to call the FBI so that [the autopsy could have been conducted] and a gunshot could have ruled out. The military had a duty to notify the family, and if the family didn't allow an autopsy, go to another authority and have it conducted."[130]

Tracey Brown would later concede that she learned about the hole only from the media and then more than a year and a half after the crash. "Had my family known about the suspicious wound at the time," says Tracey, "we would have requested an autopsy." Now the story had jumped from the conservative media stream to the black-oriented one.[131]

On December 11, 1997, the *Chicago Independent Bulletin* ran a story headlined "Pastor Demands Investigation into Late Ron Brown's Death." Two days later, the influential *Baltimore Afro-American* ran a lengthy front-page story, "Brown Head Suspected Bullet Wound." If the White House could ignore the conservative media, it could not ignore the black media.[132]

It looked bad for the Clintons. Black Entertainment Television (BET) devoted a one-hour show to the controversy on December 11, featuring an interview with Christopher Ruddy. Now, millions of African-Americans wanted to know what happened to Ron Brown.[133]

To head off the unrest, Colonel Gormley appeared on *BET Tonight* hosted by Tavis Smiley. Unfortunately for the White House, Gormley unwittingly admitted to Smiley that he had chosen not to pursue an autopsy based "on discussions at the highest level from Commerce, at the Joint [Chiefs of Staff], and the [Department of Defense], the White House." In other words, Gormley was sufficiently concerned about the wound to consult with his superiors at the time of the examination. This inquiry reached the White House. According to the relevant law that covers executive assassination, 18 U.S.C. S 351, the president should have referred the case to the FBI. At the very least, he should have informed the Brown family. That he did neither suggests he had good reason not to.[134]

The pressure from the black community was now starting to grow. On December 17, 1997, the *Washington Times* reported that the chairman of the Congressional Black Caucus and several other black figures asked President Clinton, Attorney General Janet Reno and General Henry H. Shelton, chairman of the Joint Chiefs of Staff, to evaluate published claims of two military pathologists "that a wound to the secretary's head may have been caused by a gunshot."[135]

On Christmas Eve, protestors showed up at the AFIP headquarters at Walter Reed Army Medical Center in Washington. Leading the charge was veteran activist and former comedian Dick Gregory. He staged a protest and prayer vigil that culminated in the TV-friendly gesture of wrapping yellow crime scene tape around the area. He was promptly arrested and went on a hunger strike in jail.[136]

The mainstream media largely ignored Gregory, just as they had Mfume. But there was one black leader neither the media nor the White House could ignore. That was Jesse Jackson, and he came forward on January 5, 1998. Jackson still had the perceived moral force to shake up Washington, and now he was exerting that force to call for an investigation.[137]

With Jackson on board, reporters finally raised the Brown question at a press conference on that same day. They obviously struck a nerve. "The Pentagon, I think, has very thoroughly and in very gruesome detail, and no doubt in ways painful to the Brown family, addressed the issue. And it's time to knock this stuff off," snapped press secretary Mike McCurry. "I'm not going to talk about this further or take any further questions on the subject."[138]

Despite the uproar in the black community, the Justice Department announced, on January 8, 1998 that it would not open a probe to Ron Brown's death.[139]

Despite the Justice Department ruling, momentum was still building in the black community for an investigation. On January 17, 1997, the *Washington Afro-American* ran a lengthy front-page story from the January 13, 1998, edition of the *Pittsburgh Tribune-Review* story by Christopher Ruddy, focusing on Chief Petty Officer Janoski claims that missing evidence of a possible homicide had been purposely destroyed.[140]

That same day, Nolanda Hill finally signed her affidavit for *Judicial Watch*. Only she had the knowledge that could move Larry Klayman's trade mission investigation to the next level. Hill had not made it easy for him. It wasn't that she feared Klayman. Instead, she feared the Clintons for her personal safety and her family's well-being, which she believed would be in jeopardy if she cooperated.[141]

On January 21, 1998, the Monica Lewinsky story inundated the land and left every other news story gasping for breath.[142]

Jesse Jackson had a choice to make. He could either pick away at the administration on a story that had just lost its legs, or he could come to the besieged president's aid. Nothing if not clever, Jesse Jackson chose to embrace the president once more. In an unintentionally comic sage, Jackson emerged as the president's spiritual advisor, with the aid of his comely assistant Karin Stanford, and comforted the repentant president in the midst of his moral crisis.[143]

Interestingly, it would be Jesse Jackson's comely assistant who would later be photographed with Jackson in the Oval Office when she was four months pregnant with Jackson's "love child." A $40,000 moving fee courtesy of Rainbow/PUSH and a $10,000 a month retainer would help keep the young Jackson child out of the news for more than a year.[144]

On March 13, 1998, ten days before her scheduled evidentiary hearing before Judge Royce Lamberth, the Clinton Justice Department indicted Hill, as well as her business partner, Ken White, on fraud and tax evasion charges. Larry Klayman was stunned. In a motion to the court, he wrote, "The timing of these events is neither accidental nor coincidental. Ms. Hill's indictment was likely an effort to retaliate against her and deter her from giving any further damaging testimony at the March 23, 1998 hearing."[145]

On March 23, 1998, Nolanda Hill reported to Washington's Federal District Court for the hearing *Judicial Watch v. Department of Commerce*. So anxious was she about testifying in public that when Judge Lamberth called her to the bench, she had to rush to his own restroom to throw up. Hill had spotted certain White House operatives in the packed courtroom, and she knew there would be hell to pay for telling the truth. She made the following statements:[146]

> * First Lady Hillary Rodham Clinton decided to use administration trade missions to raise political donations.
> * White House orchestrated a department cover-up of documents linking Commerce trade missions to political donations to the 1996 Clinton-Gore campaign and the Democratic National Committee.
> * A few weeks before his death (on April 3, 1996), Ron Brown showed

Ms. Hill "an-inch-thick" set of Commerce Department documents linking trade missions in which business executives were being asked to pay a minimum of $50,000 for seats on foreign trade missions.

* Ron Brown told her that he was under orders from the White House to withhold documentary evidence "prior to the 1996 election" that seats on administration-organized trade missions were bought with political donations. Ms. Brown's instructions came "through former Chief of Staff Leon Panetta and Cabinet Secretary John Podesta . . . to devise a way to comply with the court's orders" in the lawsuit.

* Melissa Moss, Commerce's business liaison and former DNC fundraiser when Ron Brown was DNC chairman, was responsible for writing the letters seeking donations.

* Mr. Brown first resisted pressure to use the trade missions for Democratic political donations, but Mrs. Clinton and White House officials overrode his objections after the Republican sweep of Congress in 1994.[147]

On June 15, 1999, Hill accepted her sentence. She reported to a halfway house in Seagoville, Texas.[148]

Hill could take some small comfort knowing that in September 1997 Gene and Nora Lum had been sentenced to ten months in custody, half in a community confinement center, the other half in home detention. The pair had pled guilty only to arranging about $95,000 in illegal contributions and those just in 1994 and 1995 for congressional campaigns—the mere tip of their illicit iceberg.[149]

Curiously, the Justice Department prosecutor alluded to the "abortive FBI investigation of public corruption" in Hawaii as well as "the support from Ronald H. Brown" in setting up the Lums' California operation, but there was no further pursuit of either. Nor, of course, were there any charges related to their Oklahoma gas company and their relationship with the Browns. Almost unbelievably, Michael Brown would emerge from the mess as the DNC's national finance vice chair.[150]

CHAPTER 25

FBI FILES

Once the initial rush [of appointments] subsides, we will begin to request copies of files from the FBI on carryovers. This will be our first glance at the background information of employees.

—Craig Livingstone,
1993 memo about collecting secret FBI files on Reagan and Bush aides[1]

On May 30, 1996, White House Counsel Jack Quinn was facing a contempt of Congress vote for not releasing the Travelgate documents requested by Bill Clinger, chairman of the House Government Reform and Oversight Committee. Mr. Quinn changed his mind about going to jail, and the administration turned over the documents. On June 5, 1996 Clinger released one thousand of the three thousand documents Congress requested. One of the documents was an explosive letter between the White House and the FBI.[2]

The next day, news broke that the FBI had illegally delivered to the White House more than three hundred (the number would grow to over nine hundred) confidential background-check files the FBI had compiled on Bush and Reagan administration appointees. The White House roundup of files was the project of White House personnel chief and former bar bouncer Craig Livingstone. The FBI files had almost bottomless blackmail potential. They included everything FBI agents heard or discovered while trying to determine the people's fitness to work for the president: biographical data, interviews, transcripts, bank records, and plenty of gossip. Disclosing the information in the FBI files is a federal crime carrying a penalty of a year in prison for each violation.[3]

The White House Office of Legal Counsel was the official entity that could approach the FBI about such matters. But, Clinton aides say nobody in the counsel's office can remember sending in the forms. Does this sound familiar? Also, coincidentally not a single person who worked for President Clinton was on the list. Does anybody seriously believe that those files would lie around unread for more than two years?[4]

This resurrected talk in Washington of an "enemies list" and political spying. With that single page, a new scandal, Filegate, was born.[5]

Charles Colson, President Nixon's special counsel, got a one-to-three-year prison sentence for "taking one FBI file and giving it to a reporter. [Special Prosecutor] Leon Jaworski said he'd been looking for a way to stop this practice, which he called an abuse of power." It was because of this incident that Congress passed the Privacy Act, which requires a legitimate public purpose for anyone seeking FBI files.[6]

Initially, the administration officials blamed what they called a clerical error involving a dated list of names submitted for background security checks by a low-level White House employee. Actually, this statement was not accurate: There were two people involved, and they weren't your ordinary low-level employees.[7]

The first person was Craig Livingstone, who was hired as director of White House security. His qualifications were as follows:

* Admitted using drugs.
* Fired from a previous job for making up stories about his education.
* Former bar bouncer in Pittsburgh.
* Former bartender in Georgetown (J. Paul's and Annie's).[8]

But more importantly, he was a Democrat Party operative whose previous duties included the following:

* Advance man and travel aide for presidential candidate Gary Hart in 1984 and 1988.
* Advance man and travel aide for vice presidential candidate Geraldine Ferraro in 1984.

* Planned Sen. Al Gore's presidential campaign announcement in 1988.
* Director of operations at the Democratic National Convention in Atlanta in 1988.
* Worked for the Democratic National Committee in 1992.
* Advance man and travel aide for vice presidential candidate Al Gore in 1992.
* Senior consultant to Counter-Event Operations, Clinton-Gore 1992, where he said he successfully deployed several of the infamous Pinocchio and Chicken George media events.
* Helped stage the celebration in Little Rock on election night.
* Director of security for the Clinton-Gore inaugural celebration in January 1993.[9]

Craig Livingstone's Washington career, unfortunately, did not start off on the right foot. Federal employees were trying to locate more than $150,000 worth of equipment lost or stolen from the inauguration, equipment Mr. Livingstone was in charge of. Then Associate Counsel William Kennedy asked FBI Special Agent Gary Aldrich, who was one of two agents stationed at the White House, how the FBI would feel about having Mr. Livingstone as director of White House security if "there were character issues in his background." When Mr. Aldrich expressed reservations, Mr. Kennedy responded: "I guess I see your point, but it doesn't matter. Hillary wants him." And Livingstone was hired.[10]

The second person was Anthony Marceca. He was a civilian investigator for the Army, who was detailed to Mr. Livingstone's office in mid-August 1993 and worked there until February 11, 1994. Mr. Marceca and Mr. Livingstone had worked together on the presidential primary campaigns of Gary Hart, Albert Gore Jr. and again on the Clinton inaugural committee. Also, according to Secret Service agents who control White House access Anthony Marceca visited Craig Livingstone's office on almost a daily basis from March 1 to July 31, 1993.[11]

After the clerical alibi was given, it began to take a pounding in some precincts.

"This didn't happen by mistake," said Roger Pilon, director of the Cato Institute's Center for Constitutional Studies. "There are just too many files and too much paper for that to have been the case. Mr. Pilon described the matter as part of a pattern of Clinton abuses, citing the FBI-led investigations and subsequent firings of seven White House travel office employees. "This administration has shown no reluctance to abuse the levers, including the government's investigative agencies," Mr. Pilon said.[12]

"I think once again the media are giving Clinton a pass," said radio talk-show host G. Gordon Liddy. "If there were a Republican president, they'd be tearing out throats. They'd be saying: 'Come on! What do you think, we're stupid?'" Mr. Liddy said. "But on this one, it's Clinton who had the files, but he didn't read them. He smoked the grass, but he didn't inhale."[13]

On June 9, 1996, President Clinton commented on the controversy for the first time, saying the White House had made a "completely honest" mistake: "It appears to have been a completely honest bureaucratic snafu when we were trying to straighten out who should get security clearances to come to the White House," Mr. Clinton said.

On June 12, 1996, President Clinton publicly apologized during a White House news conference with Italian Prime Minister Romano Prodi and European Commission President Jacques Santer. Mr. Clinton described the files request as "just an innocent bureaucratic snafu" and said the matter was being investigated by the White House counsel's office and the FBI. "And I'm sorry that it occurred, and I believe that we will correct it. I think the FBI will correct it on their end as well, so nothing like this will happen again, he said. The president said he first learned of the files from a newspaper story. "I knew nothing about it beforehand," he said.[14] Mr. Clinton also said he "would never tolerate or condone any kind of enemies list," and steps will be taken to make sure the White House's acquisition of confidential FBI reports on Republicans can never happen again.[15]

The FBI immediately tried to cover its hindside. On June 14, 1996, FBI Director Louis J. Freeh, a longtime friend of former White House Counsel Bernard Nussbaum, accused the White House of "egregious violations of privacy" in seeking secret background files and ordering sweeping new measures to protect the bureau's sensitive background information. "Unfortunately, the FBI and I were victimized. I promise the American people that it will not happen again on my watch," Freeh said.[16]

Four days later, however, Freeh amended his statement, claiming that his department was the victim of its own "lack of vigilance," not any impropriety by the White House. Afterward, Freeh appointed FBI General

Counsel Howard Shapiro to investigate. Shapiro promptly reported that no one at the FBI or the White House had violated federal law. Shapiro's investigation was discredited after congressional probers discovered that he had not even bothered to talk to any White House officials about what was done with the illegally acquired files.[17]

The question quickly arose as to who had hired Livingstone, and no one at the White House would take credit for his selection. FBI agent Dennis Sculimbrene submitted to a congressional committee his notes from a 1993 interview in which he was told by White House Counsel Bernard Nussbaum that Hillary Clinton had insisted on Livingstone's hiring—despite Livingstone's scant professional background. When FBI General Counsel Shapiro learned of Sculimbrene's notes, he dispatched two FBI agents (Duncan Wainwright and Jennifer Esposito) to pay a surprise visit to Sculimbrene's home in Haymarket, Virginia. Republican congressmen charged that the purpose of the visit was to intimidate Sculimbrene to change his report. Shapiro also alerted White House Special Counsel Jane C. Sherburne about the file notes. She, in turn, called Hillary Clinton and seven other top White House officials and the attorneys who represented Nussbaum and Livingstone. This happened one day before the FBI was provided the incriminating information demanded by congressional investigators. This kindly gesture caused an explosion on Capitol Hill. Shapiro quickly publicly admitted that he made a "horrible blunder," and Freeh issued a press release proclaiming his "full confidence" in Shapiro and declaring that "none of Howard's actions were done in bad faith or for partisan purpose."[18]

On June 18, 1996, Attorney General Janet Reno ordered the FBI to investigate the Clinton administration's unjustified search of secret background files of former Reagan and Bush aides. Some Republican leaders were skeptical that Miss Reno and Mr. Freeh—both Clinton appointees—had the credibility to conduct the investigation.[19] So on June 21, independent counsel Kenneth Starr, at Reno's initiation, was tasked to investigate Anthony Marceca and the "Filegate" scandal.[20] Five days later Craig Livingstone announced his resignation at the House Government Reform and Oversight Committee. "I bear the responsibility for the mistake that occurred," Livingstone said. Rep. Tom Lantos (D-CA) chastised Livingstone: "You should have done this sooner. With an infinitely more distinguished public record than yours, Adm. [Jeremy Michael] Boorda committed suicide when he may have committed a minor mistake."[21] At the same hearing, Bernard Nussbaum told the congressional panel that he never discussed hiring Mr. Livingstone with Mrs. Clinton. "I do not know who brought Mr. Livingstone into the White House," Mr. Nussbaum said.[22]

Just a few days later, on July 1, 1996, senior presidential adviser George Stephanopoulos said it wasn't Hillary who hired Craig Livingstone to vacuum raw FBI files to put together dossiers on their Republican enemies. "It was Vince Foster."[23]

Mrs. Clinton, who was traveling in Romania and Eastern Europe for the Fourth of July holiday, supported Mr. Stephanopoulos in his blaming of Vince Foster. Mrs. Clinton claimed she had no idea who hired Craig Livingstone: "I know I didn't," she told reporters.[24]

On July 7, 1996, Rep. Susan Molinari, New York Republican, was interviewed on *Fox News Sunday*, and pointed to a *New York Post* article that said "former Republican people, who were career employees" at the Department of Housing and Urban Development, the Agriculture Department, and the Interior Department were targeted for political reasons early in the Clinton administration. "Their files were [rifled] through, and a lot of these people lost their jobs shortly thereafter," Ms. Molinari said. She continued: "Obviously, somebody very high up has something to do with this. This has gone on too long . . . and this didn't just stop at the White House; it went through every agency. Craig Livingstone clearly can't be responsible for [all] that."[25]

Career employees are supposed to be protected from political changes. But the *New York Post* said it had documents that showed "Clinton appointees clearly believed it was their due to root out those whose political sympathies were suspect." For example, the *New York Post* said the American Federation of Government Employees sent HUD Secretary Henry G. Cisneros a list of thirteen career personnel it wanted out of the agency. The union accused some of those named of being "either Republican, racist, unethical, anti-union," or a "reputed personal friend" of George H. W. Bush.[26]

On July 11, 1996, the *Washington Times* reported that the number of FBI files improperly searched by the White House had exceeded nine hundred.[27] Less than a week later, on July 17, 1996, Secret Service agents John Libonati and Jeffrey Undercoffer testified before the Clinger committee that the Secret Service had given Marceca a more up-to-date list. This contradicted earlier White House explanations that a Secret Service misstep led to nine hundred FBI files ending up in the White House. Two days later, in retaliation for their testimony, the Inspector General's Office opened a criminal investigation of the two agents.[28] It was a shocking attempt to intimidate witnesses who could provide damaging testimony and was another example of Bill Clinton's penchant for using his public office to further his personal agenda and to protect himself from the consequences of his actions.[29]

On July 18, 1996, Anthony B. Marceca invoked his Fifth Amendment privilege against self-incrimination in the face of dozens of questions from members of the Senate Judiciary Committee. Also, as required by the subpoena, Mr. Marceca showed up with a thick briefcase full of documents bearing on the dispute. But he said he would turn them over only if the committee gave him a limited grant of immunity so that the act of producing the records could not be used against him.[30] It appears that the obvious explanation for Marceca's actions was that the Clinton White House wanted the Republicans' files around as a form of insurance. Coincidently, there had been several instances when critics of the Clinton administration have suspected that negative stories about them in the press were based on information gleaned from their FBI background files.[31]

On August 2, 1996, Dennis Sculimbrene, the twenty-four-year veteran FBI special agent who blew the whistle on illicit drug use by Craig Livingstone and other top Clinton White House officials, retired, citing political retaliation as the reason. Mr. Sculimbrene stated, "Unjustified changes in my professional assignments and assaults on my career over the past year have been difficult and more than any agent should have to endure."[32]

Mr. Sculimbrene said FBI background checks he conducted on many incoming Clinton appointees revealed they were "using illegal drugs repetitively, lying to law-enforcement officers, lying about school records [and] being fired." He said he found cases where even "older" incoming Clinton appointees "used illegal drugs . . . as recently as the Inauguration . . . and I'm not talking about junior staffers, either."[33]

On September 12, 1996, the first five of more than nine hundred former White House staffers came forward in a class-action suit, filed by *Judicial Watch*, which sought more than $90 million in damages for the Clinton administration's improper procurement of their secret FBI background files. Named as defendants in the suit were the White House, the FBI, First Lady Hillary Rodham Clinton, former White House Counsel Bernard Nussbaum, former White House personnel security director Craig Livingstone, and Anthony Marceca.[34]

Mari Anderson, an executive assistant who worked in Livingstone's White House office from February to September 1993, went into hiding after the Filegate story broke in June 1996—eluding U.S. marshals and a Judiciary Committee subpoena. Part of her job involved keeping a log of the people who checked out confidential FBI background files from the White House Personnel Security Office. The only two people who would review the files without having to log them out in Anderson's book—and then create a paper trail—were Marceca and Livingstone himself. Anderson's logbook, also subpoenaed by the committee, had a six-month gap. Suspiciously, there were no entries listed from March 29, 1994 to September 2, 1994.[35]

When the committee questioned Livingstone about this gap, he said, "I believe it [the log] wasn't kept." But, Anderson contradicted that claim in her October 1996 deposition. "I recall that background investigations were checked out and that we did log them [during that six-month period]," she said, adding that she definitely recalled making entries in April or May and in June. Livingstone never instructed her to stop keeping the log, Anderson testified. "I have no idea why [there is a six-month gap]," she said. "My version would be that there are pages that are not there." Anderson agreed with the committee that "some portion of the log" is missing. Thus, the missing log entries from March to September 1994 made it nearly impossible to determine whether those files were checked out, or by whom.[36]

On October 25, 1996, a special three-judge panel of the U.S. Court of Appeals for the District of Columbia, expanded Whitewater independent counsel Kenneth Starr's jurisdiction to investigate whether former White House counsel Bernard Nussbaum committed perjury when he testified before a House committee on June 26, 1996. Nussbaum said he had never discussed Craig Livingstone with First Lady Hillary Rodham Clinton, adding that "I do not know who brought Mr. Livingstone into the White House." But a month later, congressional investigators found a report from an FBI agent who said Nussbaum had "advised that he has known the appointee Craig Livingstone . . . [who] had come highly recommended to him by Hillary Clinton, who has known his mother."[37]

On January 14, 1998, Independent Counsel Kenneth Starr went to the White House to ask a series of questions to Hillary Rodham Clinton.

According to several published accounts, the First Lady told Starr she didn't know anything about the retrieval of hundreds of FBI files on Republicans from previous administrations. And she said she didn't know who hired Craig Livingstone.[38]

On December 15, 1999, Sheryl Hall, a former White House computer specialist, filed legal papers that the Clinton administration was trying to "stall" the Filegate lawsuit until after President Clinton left office with First Lady Hillary Rodham Clinton. Mrs. Hall said Michele Peterson of the White House Counsel's Office told her in late May or early June 1999 that their "strategy for the Filegate lawsuit was to stall because [they] had just a couple of more years to go."[39]

On January 7, 2000, Deborah Perroy, a former White House employee from 1988 to 1993, and a member of the National Security Council support staff, said in a sworn statement that she witnessed Robert Manzanares, director of NSC administration, and his assistant, Marcia Dimel, of looking through top-secret personnel files in 1993 in an office on the third floor of the Old Executive Office Building. In an affidavit taken by *Judicial Watch*, Ms. Perroy resigned after the incident and that White House officials threatened to "come after me with false charges and allegations in order to smear my good name. . . . I then informed the Clinton White House that I would sue them if they did something so egregious and that I would go public with information about, what I believed to be improper activities I witnessed while working at the White House," she said in the affidavit. Coincidently, Ms. Perroy's FBI file was requested by the White House Office of Personnel and Security in March 1994, six months after she had left her post and no longer required access or a security clearance.[40]

According to Ms. Perroy, "Based on my experience working for the Clinton administration, I believe my FBI file was obtained and repeatedly sought in part because of fear I would divulge information about improper activities I witnessed at the Clinton White House and so, if I did go public . . . confidential information about me from my FBI file could be used against me."[41]

On March 16, 2000, independent counsel Robert W. Ray, who took over for Ken Starr, filed a report with a three-judge panel that there was "no substantial and credible evidence to show that any senior White House official, or First Lady Hillary Rodham Clinton, was involved in seeking confidential FBI background reports of former White House staff from the administrations of President Reagan and Bush."[42]

The investigation also concluded, according to a statement issued by Mr. Ray, that prosecutors found no evidence showing that then-White House Counsel Bernard Nussbaum lied to Congress about the administration's hiring of the demonstrably unqualified Craig Livingstone. Finally, Mr. Ray said the investigation found no evidence showing that Mrs. Clinton was involved in Mr. Livingstone's hiring.[43]

The report also said that Anthony Marceca, a civilian Army investigator detailed to the White House Office of Personnel Security, sought the confidential FBI background reports in the wrong belief that the people still employed at the White House and needed access.[44]

Mr. Ray's office concluded that while some of Mr. Marceca's testimony to the House Government Reform Committee was false and that Mr. Marceca acknowledged "that he had knowingly testified falsely" to a grand jury and twice to the House committee in 1996 shortly after the controversy erupted, the independent counsel decided against prosecuting him. The report also said the evidence was insufficient to prove beyond a reasonable doubt that Mr. Marceca knowingly made false statements in requesting the reports.[45]

CHAPTER 26

1995 THROUGH 2000 STUMBLES

The official bywords of the [Clinton] administration's culture were confusion, inefficiency, mayhem, and dysfunction. But at the same time, the political machine was impressive, even if crisis-oriented in nature; it was committed to the president, and the energy level was high.

—Lt. Col. Robert "Buzz" Patterson,
on the Clinton culture[1]

BILL CLINTON'S RELEVANCY

On April 18, 1995, President Clinton, during a press conference, insisted that he remains "relevant." He alluded to the Constitution.[2]

V-E DAY

On May 7, 1995, President Clinton chose to celebrate the fiftieth anniversary of V-E Day in Moscow, Berlin's ally in invading Poland and starting World War II instead of the V-E celebrations in London. The gesture did not go unnoticed.[3]

"If the snub of the allies had been made by President Truman or President Kennedy or President Reagan," one prominent Brit remarked slyly, "our feelings would have been terribly hurt. But President Clinton's presence would have spoiled the party."[4]

DEE DEE MYERS COMPLETES ALCOHOL-EDUCATION PROGRAM

In late August or early September 1995, Dee Dee Myers concluded a special twelve-hour, alcohol-education program to avert a one-year sentence and $1,000 fine for driving while intoxicated down the wrong way of a one-way street.[5]

GEORGE STEPHANOPOULOS IS ARRESTED

On September 7, 1995, Washington, D.C. police arrested George Stephanopoulos for leaving the scene of an accident, driving with an expired license, and having expired plates on his car. It appeared that while he was pulling his little red Honda out of a parking space, he crunched the fender of someone else's car. Stephanopoulos paid no fine.[6]

POPE VETOES WHITE HOUSE VISIT

In the December 1995 issue, the *American Spectator* reported that Vatican officials politely but firmly rebuffed what they interpreted as "unseemly" overtures by the Clinton White House for a papal visit to 1600 Pennsylvania Avenue during John Paul II's trip to the U.S. A Vatican source says that the Pope was put off by Clinton's warm regard for Boris Yeltsin and what he viewed as the Clintons' shabby treatment of Mother Teresa during her visit to Washington in 1993.[7]

PARTIAL-BIRTH ABORTION

On April 10, 1996, President Clinton issued his first veto of the partial-birth abortion ban. That didn't sit well with one clergyman.[8]

On December 24, 1996, President Clinton was attending a Christmas Eve service at the National Cathedral. Reverend Rob Schenck, a leading pro-life activist, was approaching the Communion rail along with a small group of clergy. As Schenck walked past a seated Mr. Clinton, he whispered, "Mr. President, God will hold you to account for the babies." In response, an incensed Clinton ordered the Secret Service apprehend Schenck and search and interrogate him, which they did. To this day, he remains on a "flag list," meaning that various security details frequently deny him access to Washington events to which he is invited.[9]

"CLINTON IS AN UNUSUALLY GOOD LIAR"

In the January 1996 issue of *Esquire* magazine, Martha Sherrill wrote a profile of Sen. Bob Kerrey of Nebraska. In the middle of the story Kerrey was quoted as saying, "Clinton's an unusually good liar. Unusually good.

Do you realize that?" Interestingly, no Washington reporter noticed enough to write a story until the *Washington Times* mentioned it one month later.[10]

NASCAR

In 1996, President Clinton, running for re-election, appeared at the Darlington Raceway for the Southern 500. Entering the garage area where the teams housed their race cars, Bill Clinton toured the grounds seeking the drivers. To a man, the stars of the circuit hid out in their motor homes, refusing to be seen with President Clinton. Finally, the NASCAR officials, fearing reaction from a surly press corps, pleaded with driver Mark Martin, an Arkansas native, to perfunctorily greet Clinton. Understanding he was not welcome, Clinton left the track in a huff.[11]

MARRIOTT HOTEL

In 1996, Gary Aldrich, in his book, *Unlimited Access*, spoke of occurrences when Bill Clinton could not be found. Normally, the Secret Service should know where the president is at all times, but it was no longer the case since the First Lady had kicked them out of the Residence. Also, Hillary didn't know where the president was, because the Clintons slept in separate bedrooms.[12]

It appeared that the president was a frequent late-night visitor to the Marriott Hotel in downtown Washington, D.C. It has an underground parking garage with an elevator that allows guests to go to their rooms without passing through the lobby. The president did not have a room in his name, and the guest who rented the room was known only to the management, but was suspected to be a female celebrity.[13]

This is how it worked. Without Secret Service protection, Clinton would leave the White House around midnight alone through the West Executive Lobby. To the uniformed guard at the desk it would appear the president was walking to the Old Executive Office Building, which is across the parking lot from the West Wing. Once out of sight of the guard, the president immediately veered left and into a White House sedan, usually driven by Bruce Lindsey. The president would lie down on the back seat, covering himself with a blanket kept there for that purpose. Lindsey drove to the Marriott where he would park near the elevator and wait in the car until the president returned, often hours later. The car usually arrived after midnight and returned sometimes as late as 4:00 a.m.[14]

CLINTON LOSES HIS NUCLEAR CODES

The process the president has to go through to launch the U.S.'s nuclear weapons isn't as simple as pressing a button. The number of redundancies in the nuclear-launch process is staggering. All steps are "dependent on one vital element without which there can be no launch. That element, the president's authorization codes, is supposed to remain in close proximity to the president at all times, carried by one of five military aides, representing each branch of the military. The codes are on a card called the biscuit carried within the football, a briefcase that is officially known as the "president's emergency satchel."[15]

The first known disappearance of the nuclear codes occurred on January 21, 1998. Major Robert "Buzz" Patterson was the person on President Clinton's schedule. At seven in the morning, he was going to give the president his annual nuclear update briefing and his new set of nuclear "go codes."[16]

Kris motioned Patterson into the Oval Office. Clinton was seated behind his desk. He looked tired and beaten, blanched and swollen. He looked up at Patterson from behind his reading glasses.[17]

"Sir, if you'd like, we can just change out the codes now and I'll come back for the briefing later," said Patterson.[18]

"That'd be fine, Buzz. Thank you," said Clinton.[19]

Patterson handed Clinton the new card—the biscuit—with the new codes, which would be effective immediately. Clinton looked back down at his desk and the morning newspapers piled in front of him, which were littered with news of the Lewinsky scandal. Patterson was waiting for Clinton to respond in kind. Clinton didn't offer Patterson the old set of codes.[20]

A few days later, when one of the other military aides and Patterson returned to brief the president on changes to the launch codes of the football, they were in for a surprise. The military-aide briefed the president on the important changes. Patterson's expectation was that the president would finally return his old set to them. Instead, President Clinton looked up sheepishly and confessed, "I don't have mine on me. I'll track it down, guys, and get it back to you."[21]

They were dumbfounded—*the president lost his nuclear codes*. He is required to have the codes on him at all times. President Clinton normally kept the world's most sensitive document rubber-banded to his credit cards in his pants pocket.[22]

There had been one other time that he had misplaced the codes, but they were able to quickly track them down through his valets. He'd left them in the White House residence while he was leaving for a round of golf. This time, though, the codes were apparently lost.[23]

There was a long pause, and then the president merely went back to work on the pile of papers in front of him. As they left, they couldn't help wondering how long the codes had been missing. They immediately alerted the Joint Staff in the Pentagon. "What do you mean? How could this happen? You've got to find it ASAP!" They were incredulous. For days, they turned over everything in the White House. They talked to the ushers and valets and asked them to search the president's clothes and furniture in the residence. They asked the senior staff, specifically John Podesta and Bruce Lindsey, for help. The president finally threw up his hands and said casually, I just can't find it . . . don't know where it is." As far as he was concerned, that was the end of the story; Podesta and Lindsey's overriding concern was that the story might leak to the press. Only the military seemed remotely worried about the national security implications of the nuclear launch codes being lost. And they never were found.[24]

The second known incident of Clinton losing the nuclear codes comes from Gen. Hugh Shelton, who was chairman of the Joint Chiefs of Staff from October 1997 to September 2001. Around 2000, according to Shelton, a member of the department within the Pentagon that is responsible for all pieces of the nuclear process was dispatched to the White House to physically look at the codes and ensure they were correct—a procedure required to happen every thirty days. The set of codes was to be replaced entirely every four months. That official was told by a presidential aide that President Bill Clinton had the codes but was in an important meeting and could not be disturbed. The aide assured the official that Clinton took the codes seriously and had them close by. The official was dismayed, but he accepted the excuse and left.[25]

When the next inspection took place the following month, that official was on vacation, according to Shelton, and another official was dispatched to the White House. The new official was met with the same excuse—the president is very busy but takes the codes very seriously and has them on hand.[26]

"This comedy of errors went on, without President Clinton's knowledge I'm sure, until it was finally time to collect the current set and replace them with the new edition," Shelton wrote. "At this point we learned that the aide had no idea where the old ones were, because they had been missing for months," he added. "The President never did have them, but he assumed, I'm sure, that the aide had them like he was supposed to."[27]

Shelton and then-Secretary of Defense William Cohen were alarmed. The problem of missing codes had been resolved by changing the codes, but they quickly acted to change the process itself, mandating that the Defense Department official visiting the White House physically see the codes before leaving.[28]

Shelton and Cohen feared the saga would reach the press and become an embarrassing story. But word of the missing codes never made it out, and Shelton's recounting of it in his 2010 book was, to his knowledge, the first time it had been shared publicly.[29]

CLINTON'S *ESQUIRE* INTERVIEW

In late October 2000, President Clinton became involved in another controversy. Mr. Clinton, who was interviewed by *Esquire* magazine, appeared on the cover of its December issue. The picture caused quite a stir. It showed Mr. Clinton, with a mischievous smile on his face, seated with his legs spread apart and his hands, which appear large, on his knees. Also, a long blue tie is angled towards his crotch. Could this picture be construed as "Monica's view of the president?" This said everything about Bill Clinton and what he thought of the office and what he thought of the people who honored him with it twice. In your face, America.[30]

For the photographer to capture the essence of Bill Clinton for the cover photo, he would have had to shoot from below, focusing at the approximate level of the presidential belt. The angle alone tells much about Mr. Clinton. His hand and knees splayed wide apart as in the good old days of the government shutdown, thongs, and *Leaves of Grass*.[31]

In the interview, Mr. Clinton demanded an apology from Republicans who impeached him. Clinton calculated that the interview and cover photo would be published after the election when it would do no harm to Al Gore's presidential campaign. He miscalculated.[32]

The *Esquire* magazine was distributed on Saturday, October 28, 2000, ten days before the election. This infuriated both the Clinton and the Gore camp because it reminded voters of Clinton scandals in the final days of the vice president's struggling campaign.[33]

"I was promised faithfully that that interview would be . . . released after the election," Mr. Clinton snapped with obvious irritation in the Rose Garden. "And I believed it."[34]

The magazine's editor-in-chief, David Granger, strongly disputed the president's assertion. Mr. Granger said *Esquire* "had no formal agreement with the White House regarding the interview or the article accompanying it, other than that the president would be the cover subject of the magazine's December issue."[35]

CHAPTER 27

ELECTION 1996

We all look forward with great pleasure to four years of wonderful, inspiring speeches, full of wit, poetry, music, love and affection – plus more [expletive deleted] nonsense. He has not a creative bone in his body. Therefore, he's a bore, and will always be a bore.
—David Brinkley commenting on President Clinton's victory speech delivered from the state house in Little Rock, Arkansas, on November 5, 1996[1]

On May 10, 1994, the *Washington Times* reported that with troubles concerning Whitewater, sexual misconduct and sinking polls, President Clinton began taking steps to inoculate himself against a possible Democratic challenge in 1996. His strategists began building a state-by-state campaign team that could hit the ground running in 1996. The degree to which the Clinton White House was engaged in early preparations for 1996 presidential election was unprecedented. Don Sweitzer, Democratic National Committee (DNC) political director, said the long-term purpose of his early organizing efforts is to engage in "basic training for campaign workers in preparation for '96." The party was deploying "serious resources now to work with people we have an eye on to be in our organization in 1996."[2]

Presidents Johnson and Carter both faced challenges from people in their party who opposed their policies. Johnson decided not to seek re-election in 1968 as a result of a challenge from Sen. Eugene McCarthy, and Carter was so weakened by a challenge from Sen. Edward M. Kennedy that he lost his bid for re-election.[3]

On August 4, 1994, the DNC announced that Chicago was selected for the national convention in August 1996. For Chicago, the event marked the end of more than a quarter century of rejection after the 1968 Democratic National Convention, which was marred by violent clashes between police and anti-Vietnam War protestors.[4]

In December 1994, Dick Morris sat down with the president and Hillary for a secret meeting in the White House Treaty Room. Hillary had been the "principal link" between her husband and Morris, a political strategist who relished his role as the president's secret indispensable man. He even had a code name, "Charlie." No one else inside the Clinton inner circle knew he was there.[5]

Before Morris even had a chance to sit down in the Treaty Room, he looked Bill in the eye and said, "So, you want me to do basically for you what I did in 1980 or '82?"[6]

"I want you to come back and do the things for me that you did back in Arkansas," Clinton said. "I need new ideas and a new strategy. I'm not getting what I need here, and I want you to come in. I've lost confidence in my current team."[7]

A short time later, Morris met privately with Bill in the Oval Office. Morris was armed with an alarming set of polling data that had gauged the president's popularity. About one-third of those polled believed Clinton was immoral, and another third saw him as weak. Morris was convinced that Bill had the power to change the weak perception, but it would take some bold action. Then Morris broached a subject that almost no one dared bring up with Bill: Hillary. "The more she seems strong," Dick Morris told Bill, "the more you will inevitably be seen as weak."[8]

Bill blanched at the remark once made by Nixon before quickly changing the subject. But Morris returned to it a moment later. "Look," he said, "you and I know the reality of your marriage. Your strengths feed on each other. But people don't get it. They think either she's wearing the pants or you're wearing the pants."[9]

On May 17, 1995, Dick Morris met with George Stephanopoulos and Harold Ickes about the upcoming presidential campaign and described a Theory of the Race. It said that Clinton would win in 1996 if he "neutralized" the Republicans and "triangulated" the Democrats. Morris then broke it down to a relatively simple proposition: Steal the popular-sounding parts of the Republican platform, sign them into law, and you'll win. The fact that it would contradict Clinton's past positions and professed beliefs was barely relevant. Dick made obligatory references to avoiding "flip-flops," but his cardinal rule was to end up on the right side of a "60 percent" issue. If six out of ten Americans said they were for something, the president had to be for it too.[10]

Another idea that Morris had, after the devastating Democratic losses in the 1994 mid-term elections, was an unprecedented campaign of issue ads starting in mid-1995 that portrayed the Gingrich Congress as extreme and positioned Clinton in the political center. These ads cost millions and required massive fund-raising. Morris demanded weekly access to President Clinton.[11]

These strategy meetings began on March 2, 1995. Besides Clinton, they included Vice President Al Gore, Harold Ickes, Erskine Bowles, and other top figures from the White House, the Clinton-Gore campaign and the Democratic National Committee. In the beginning, Morris and Ickes argued about funding. Ickes didn't want to use up the $30 million limit on Clinton-Gore primary money imposed by the federal matching funds. Morris suggested the committee turn down the matching funds and go for unlimited spending. Clinton vetoed that idea. Around July, a plan B emerged, to pay for the ads through the unlimited "soft money" donated to political committees for party-building.[12]

On September 7, 1995, Morris and Clinton met in the Treaty Room for a strategy meeting. Morris believed that the entire fate of the Clinton presidency hinged on the key decision to run the ads.[13] Clinton presented the idea to DNC National Chairman Don Fowler at a Sunday night meeting. Others in attendance were Hillary Rodham Clinton, Al Gore, Chief of Staff Leon Panetta, and Harold Ickes. The first phase of the plan was to raise $10 million for the ads. It was a "go" decision. Clinton and Gore were committed, but without money, the Morris plan was going nowhere.[14]

Three days later, Clinton and Bruce Lindsey met in the Oval Office with James Riady, John Huang, and Lippo partner Joe Giroir. They decided that Huang would move from Commerce to become a major fund-raiser for the DNC, with the title of vice financial chairman. Who else would Clinton and Gore turn to besides the people who had bailed them out so many times before?[15]

The DNC was not enthused by this turn of events. Fowler and finance chair Marvin Rosen knew too much about Huang's reckless fund-raising history, and they resisted. Finally, on November 8, 1995, the president took Rosen aside at the DNC fund-raiser and laid down the law. John Huang was to be hired and there was an agreement on a ten-million-dollar budget for the balance of 1995. Between the September meetings and the November ultimatum, Huang made sixteen visits to the White House, visiting not only with the president and vice president, but also with Mrs. Clinton.[16]

Clinton complained bitterly at having to raise this much money. "You don't know, you don't have any remote idea," he said to Dick Morris, "how hard I have to work, how hard Hillary has to work, how hard Al has to work to raise this much money."[17]

From the beginning of the ad offensive, the Democrats worried that the Republicans would retaliate. But incredibly, the Republicans didn't go on the air. Each week, Morris and company monitored the TV stations. Once in a while, they would try to get press attention by running an ad on cable or by purchasing ad time in the Washington, D.C., media area and pretending that it was part of a national advertising buy. But they didn't go national.[18]

By the end of 1995, the Clinton and DNC ads had run unopposed by any Republican paid media for most of six months. The effect was devastating. In swing states like Michigan and Wisconsin, where ads had run, Clinton's lead over Dole was actually larger than in core Democratic states, like Rhode Island and New York.[19]

On January 14, 1996, the White House finished assembling a high-powered team of consultants to plot President Clinton's re-election campaign. Although they possessed different ideological pedigrees, they all shared reputations for ruthlessness. Dick Morris headed the team. Control of polling went to the New York firm of Penn & Shoen and Democratic consultant Robert Squier was hired to manage Mr. Clinton's television campaign. Penn & Schoen replaced Stanley Greenberg, and Mr. Squier replaced Paul Begala. James Carville, who co-managed the 1992 campaign, accepted a lesser role with Clinton-Gore '96. Key White House players, who were responsible for setting the campaign's overall tone and direction, included Deputy Chief of Staff Harold Ickes, White House political director Douglas Sosnik and senior policy adviser George Stephanopoulos. Evelyn Lieberman was elevated to deputy chief of staff alongside Mr. Ickes and Stanley Greenberg's role was reduced to polling analysis. Dick Morris's re-election strategy was to re-invent Bill Clinton politically as a more centrist president, but also effectively blurring the political distinctions between his campaign and that of his Republican rival.[20]

On January 17, 1996, the *Washington Times* reported that Republican pollster Frank Luntz predicted that "Bill Clinton will be re-elected. He is prepared to say anything and do anything to win. He's got the toughest, most negative team of consultants ever assembled. And he's a master debater. Going into the final weekend, he will have the lead."[21]

By the end of February, with Morris's ads still running full tilt, Clinton was polling 53 percent against Dole in a two-way race and at 50 percent in a three-way race with Perot. By contrast, in December 1994, Morris's polling showed Clinton at 33 percent of the vote in a two-way contest against Dole.[22]

On March 12, 1996, Senator Bob Dole wrapped up the Republican nomination. Three days later, he announced his resignation from the Senate as Majority Leader. Mr. Dole plainly stated, "Nowhere to go but the White House or home."[23]

On June 8, 1996, during his Saturday radio broadcast, Clinton mused about the recent spate of suspicious fires at southern black churches. "In our country during the '50s and '60s, black churches were burned to intimidate civil rights workers. I have vivid and painful memories of black churches being burned in my own state when I was a child." That was a lie. After his radio address, the *Arkansas Democrat-Gazette* quickly reported, there were no church burnings in Arkansas during Mr. Clinton's childhood—or, indeed, at any other time historians are aware of. There were, in fact, several arsons in Little Rock in the late 1950s, recalled Curtis Sykes, chairman of the state's Black History Advisory Committee. But they were set for insurance money—and the perpetrator turned out to be a black man. And there were a few bombings in 1959, apparently a delayed reaction to the 1957 integration of Central High School. All of the victims were white people who'd helped the desegregation effort, and no churches were involved. Apparently, Mr. Clinton was enhancing his re-election prospects by turning out his black supporters.[24]

On August 10, 1996, Bob Dole selected Jack Kemp as his vice-presidential running mate, and on the first two nights of the Republican convention, ABC, NBC and CBS averaged only twenty-five minutes apiece of podium coverage during their one-hour programs. When former president Gerald Ford spoke on opening night, none of the networks reported the speech. George H. W. Bush appeared on CBS and NBC, but hardly at all on ABC. It cleverly cut to him only when he introduced Barbara Bush as "a woman who unquestionably upheld the honor of the White House." No doubt Barbara wanted everyone to contrast her behavior with a certain First Lady who was knee deep in commodities trading, travel office firings, lost and then found billing records, and so on.[25]

On August 28, 1996, during the Democratic National Convention, Bill Clinton learned of a scandal involving his campaign strategist Dick Morris. The *Star*, a supermarket tabloid, had an upcoming September 10 issue showing Mr. Morris involved with a two-hundred-dollar-an-hour call girl named Sherry Rowlands. The *New York Post* showcased the issue on August 29, which coincided with Mr. Clinton's acceptance speech. Coincidently, on newsstands that week was *Time* magazine with Dick Morris on the cover telling how he was responsible for Clinton's comeback and how he had done it.[26]

The *Star* coverage though, was far worse. Not only had Morris been photographed with the prostitute in the $440-a-night suite at the Jefferson Hotel, which was five blocks from the White House, but, he had allowed Rowlands to listen in on his phone calls with the president. She was quoted extensively in the piece talking about her numerous meetings with Morris, who had bragged to her about writing the vice president's and First Lady's convention speeches.[27]

On August 29, 1996, Dick Morris submitted his resignation to President Clinton. The scandal not only overshadowed President Clinton's acceptance speech, but also affected the president's post-convention Midwest bus tour, which was scheduled to begin on August 31, 1996 from Cape Girardeau, Missouri, coincidently, the boyhood home of radio talk-show host Rush Limbaugh.[28]

Although Bill Clinton won reelection with 49 percent of the vote (Bob Dole received 41 percent and Ross Perot 8 percent), the election of 1996 was an enormous victory for conservatism. For the first time in sixty-eight years, a Republican House was re-elected—228 House seats— and the Republican Senate majority expanded by two seats to fifty-five.[29]

In 1996, although the Democrats still had a majority in state legislatures (2,880-2,536 legislatures and 990-930 state senators), Republicans held onto their 32-17 gubernatorial advantage. In 1992, only two states had a Republican governor and Republican-controlled state legislatures, versus seventeen for the Democrats. In 1997, Republicans had complete control of twelve states, the Democrats only six (and all of them are from smaller states: Georgia, Hawaii, Missouri, Kentucky, Vermont and Maryland).[30]

CHAPTER 28

OKLAHOMA CITY BOMBING

It broke a spell in the country as people began searching for our common ground again.

—President Clinton on owing his political revival to the Oklahoma bombing[1]

The searing destruction of the Alfred P. Murrah Federal Building on April 19, 1995, was the most traumatic event in the United States since the assassination of President Kennedy. One hundred and seventy-one-people were killed, including three unborn babies, and hundreds were injured.[2]

Clinton seized the moment. On April 24, 1995, he denounced the "loud and angry voices" that inflamed the public debate and called on the American people to speak out against "the purveyors of hatred and division." Addressing the bombing of the federal building in Oklahoma City, Clinton said the nation's airwaves are too often used "to keep some people as paranoid as possible and the rest of us all torn up and upset with each other. They spread hate, they leave the impression that, by their very words, that violence is acceptable. . . . It is time we all stood up and spoke against that kind of reckless speech and behavior," he said.[3]

The Republicans were dumbstruck. A few dared to reply that it was the deployment of tanks by a militarized FBI against women and children in Waco that had set off the deadly spiral. But, most were too intimidated, or horrified, to articulate a defense.[4]

Below is a list of events that occurred *before* the attack, written by Jayna Davis in her well-researched book, *The Third Terrorist*:

* On February 27, 1995, the Congressional Task Force on Terrorism, headed by Yossef Bodansky, forecasted an imminent international terrorism offensive, sponsored by an "Iran-sponsored Islamic attack" to be launched inside the United States. The strike date would likely occur sometime after the "start of the Iranian New Year on March 21." Washington, D.C., topped the hit list. The primary targets were Congress and the White House, a foreshadowing of the infernal events of 9/11.
* The warning was disseminated to the FBI and other federal intelligence agencies. After increased security stymied the terrorists' original strategy to hit the nation's capital, the focus shifted away from Washington, D.C., taking direct aim at the American Midwest. On March 3, 1995, Director Bodansky authored an updated warning that predicted the terrorists now planned to strike at "the heart of the U.S."
* Throughout the intelligence gathering phase, information crossed the wire that, if true, would pose a new and daunting challenge in preempting the cadre of predators. The Task Force learned that Middle Eastern terrorists had recruited two "lily whites" to carry out the bombing of an American federal building. Both Timothy McVeigh, a decorated Gulf War veteran, and Terry Nichols, a former soldier and Kansas farmer, fit the "lily white" criteria.
* Bodansky had unearthed the dead bang connection between the Middle East, the strike on the heart of America, and a Hamas terrorist training camp that reportedly took place in Chicago in preparation for the Oklahoma blast. "There are at least two young Arabs from Oklahoma City who were trained in 1993 in making car bombs of the type used in April 1995.
* Another revelation outlined by Bodansky centered on an Iran-sponsored strategy to specifically target government buildings and related objectives on American soil. The plan was disclosed in November 1994, at a summit in Larnaca, Cyprus, in which participants studied firsthand the status of specific terrorist networks (in the U.S.) and the "ability of local Muslim communities to withstand the aftermath of major strikes."
* Finally, Bodansky confirmed that bin Laden's No. 2 man, the notorious Dr. Ayman Al-Zawahiri, served as the Al-Qaeda field

commander who directed the Iraqi ex-military assets in the heartland attack. Intelligence data, which Bodansky had scrupulously authenticated, revealed that the Egyptian physician personally traveled to Oklahoma City in the spring of 1995.

* A few weeks before the attack on April 19, 1995, Zawahiri came to town in order to activate and prep members of the dormant terrorist cell. He instructed the local infrastructure how to neutralize public backlash against the Muslim community in the wake of the forthcoming attack. The shrewdly devised media campaign would undoubtedly exploit the prevailing political correctness of the day.

* Zawahiri's next order of business during his 1995 U.S. visit was to meet with two Islamic demolitions experts. The Oklahoma-based Arab operatives who were tasked with the job had previously attended a Hamas explosives training camp to hone their skills in constructing huge truck bombs from garden store materials. After bestowing his blessing upon the two Oklahoma bomb makers, Zawahiri returned to the Middle East.

* It was also during this time when a popular Islamist conference convened in Tulsa, Oklahoma, from April 14 through April 16, 1995. The convention attracted thousands of Muslim youth, which offered legal and legitimate activities. Yet, Bodansky pointed out that the conference organizers maintained a close relationship with the terrorist-sponsoring nation of Sudan and a grab bag of militant groups such as "Hamas, both FIS and GIA in Algeria, various Jihadist organizations in Egypt, and even Shi'ite Hezbollah"—all spiders in bin Laden's venomous web of influence. Now the plan went operational.[5]

Below are events that occurred *just before* the attack:

* On April 18, 1995, Ken Banks, who worked at an Oklahoma City gas station, noticed a large Ryder truck pull up to the diesel pumps. The driver, who looked Middle Eastern, entered the shop and paid one hundred twenty dollars cash for one hundred gallons of diesel fuel, despite the fact that the newer model Ryders took unleaded fuel. Days later, Ken picked out Hussain Al-Hussaini's photograph from a stack of surveillance pictures.

* The evening of April 18, two men entered the Cactus Motel and ordered a room for the night. The pair would be later identified as Timothy McVeigh and Hussain Al-Hussaini's fellow Iraqi army defector" known as Mohammed. They paid cash and stayed in Room 105.
* David Elmore, the Cactus maintenance man, would later testify that shortly before 8:00 a.m., he noticed Timothy McVeigh climb into the driver's seat of the Ryder truck. The Middle Eastern male named Mohammed stepped into the cab.
* Randy Christian, the owner of the Cactus Motel, arrived at the office and as he gazed outside, he noticed the Ryder truck. He watched McVeigh climb inside the truck cab behind the wheel. He saw Mohammed walk in front of the Ryder to the east side of the office where he jumped into a brown SUV. Simultaneously, a third person emerged on the scene. The Middle Easterner rounded the east corner of the office and leaped into the passenger side of the Ryder truck. Randy watched as the brown sport utility vehicle, which bore a strong resemblance to the Chevrolet Blazer and a yellow Mercury Marquis tail the Ryder truck as the convoy merged onto the interstate bound for downtown Oklahoma City.
* Shortly before 9:00 a.m., on April 19, 1995, thirty-four-year-old Manuel Acosta, a day laborer, arrived into the downtown area looking for work. As he approached a construction site manager, trying to score a job assignment, he noticed a Middle Eastern man waving a hand signal to a foreign looking male who was standing on the north side of Fifth Street. Both individuals were dark-complexioned with black hair. One of the men wore blue jogging pants, a black shirt, and black jacket. Manuel stood close enough to discern strands of gray hair in the beard of the second Middle Easterner.
* Fractions of a second later, both men spirited and jumped inside a brown Chevy pickup. Darkly tinted windows obstructed his view of the driver as the pickup peeled away from the curb. Five minutes later, a concussive wave of fire erupted beneath the shadow of the towering federal building.[6]
* At 9:02 a.m., on April 19, 1995, the Ryder truck packed with nearly five thousand pounds of explosives exploded. The front of the nine-story building had been torn off. Dozens of cars were

incinerated, and more than three hundred nearby buildings were damaged or destroyed. The explosion left one-hundred seventy-one dead, including three unborn babies and more than five hundred wounded.[7]

Below are a series of events *after* the explosion:

* Suddenly, a brown sport utility vehicle, which Randy believed was the same SUV that trailed the Ryder moving van that morning, screeched off the highway service road and stopped near a draining ditch at the back side of the Cactus. Randy watched as two men jumped out and headed to the west side of the vehicle and momentarily disappeared from sight. Shortly thereafter, the brown SUV backed up, zipped through the Cactus recreational vehicle park, and sped back to the freeway at approximately 9:30 a.m.

* Timothy McVeigh was driving north up Interstate 35 when Oklahoma Highway Patrol trooper Charlie Hanger noticed his 1977 Mercury Marquis had no license plate and signaled him to pull over. It was 10:17 a.m. as McVeigh stepped out of the driver's seat to meet the approaching officer. "I just bought the car and don't have a tag yet," he nervously explained as he reached into his pocket to retrieve his driver's license. The motion exposed a bulge under his blue jean coat. It was a .45 caliber Glock pistol. "Get your hands up and turn around," the patrolman directed as he thrust his weapon to the back of McVeigh's head. He felt the handcuffs clamp around his wrists.

* Manuel, through a translator named Claudia Rossavik, gave his story to an FBI agent who was on the scene. His account marked the first solid lead in a manhunt for those responsible. Enterprising reporters wasted no time tuning in to police scanner traffic to monitor the all-points-bulletin that flooded law enforcement channels. The bulletin would be repeatedly broadcast the morning of April 19.

* At 2:28 p.m., the Oklahoma Highway Patrol issued an all-points bulletin for a brown Chevrolet Blazer. The official Teletype identified several Middle Eastern occupants who were considered possible bombing suspects. The Blazer bore a license tag which was originally

issued to a Chevrolet Cavalier that a New York man of Pakistani descent rented from the National Car Rental Systems from Dallas/Fort Worth International Airport. Possible tag of PTF-54F.

* Afterwards, a second APB was sent out by the FBI: "Be on the lookout for a late model, almost new, Chevrolet full-size pick-up, will be brown in color with tinted windows and smoke-colored bug deflector on the front of pick-up." Acosta and several downtown witnesses who had seen the suspects speculated that the men riding in the cab of the speeding brown pick-up were of Arab descent. One male was reported to be in his mid-twenties. The second was described as thirty-five to thirty-eight-years-old. The truck's darkly tinted windows obscured the identity of a possible third terrorist, the driver.

* "Middle Eastern male, twenty-five to twenty-eight years of age, six feet tall, athletic build, dark hair and a beard, dark hair and a beard, break," the dispatcher for the Oklahoma County Sheriff's repeated throughout the morning. When an officer in the field questioned the authenticity of the information, the dispatcher responded firmly, "Authorization FBI."

* At 4:30 p.m., the FBI mysteriously withdrew the APB and issued a directive to local law enforcement agencies to immediately terminate its broadcast. A veteran officer with the Oklahoma County Sheriff's department demanded to know why the Teletype had been abruptly cancelled. "Just pull it!" the federal agent barked through the phone line. The conversation ended.

* By 5:30 p.m., nightfall, the APB for foreign terrorists dominated the evening news. "Police were told by one witness that he saw at least two men in blue jumpsuits running from a minivan outside the courthouse just before the blast. The witness told investigators the two men fled in a brown pickup," asserted NBC news correspondent Jim Cummins.

* ABC's *World News Tonight* opened the 6:30 p.m. April 19, 1995, evening broadcast exploring the probable involvement of terrorist factions. "Sources say the FBI has been watching dozens of suspicious Islamic groups throughout the American Southwest and several right in Oklahoma City," national security correspondent John McWethy reported.

* Vincent Cannistraro, the former chief of operations for the CIA's counterterrorism division, corroborated the legitimacy of McWethy's intelligence sources. "This is something professional. It really implies that the person who constructed the explosive device had experience, was trained in the use of explosives, [and] knew what they were doing." Cannistrano postulated in the ABC broadcast. Cannistraro based his information on the following events:

* A few hours after the bombing, Cannistraro received a phone call from Jeddah, Saudi Arabia. "The Saudi official told Cannistraro that he [the source] had information that there was a 'squad' of people currently in the United States, very possibly Iraqis, who have been tasked with carrying out terrorist attacks against the United States. The Saudi claimed that he had seen a list of 'targets,' and that the first on the list was the federal building in Oklahoma City, Oklahoma. The second target was identified as the INS office in Houston, Texas, and the third target was the FBI office in Los Angeles, California." The Saudi citizen's trustworthiness was never in question given the fact that Cannistraro had known this individual for "fifteen to twenty years." Cannistraro notified the FBI's Washington Metropolitan Field office and his call was sent directly to FBI Agent Kevin Foust. Yet, after the phone conversation, FBI Agent Foust noted that Cannistraro "could not comment on the reliability of the information, nor could he corroborate it." If true, Iraq might have controlled and orchestrated the Oklahoma attack, a provocation tantamount to an act of war. Federal prosecutors, not wanting to go down this road, stated that Cannistraro might have embellished the Saudi message or simply "made it up out of thin air."

* At 11:30 p.m., FBI agents, armed with a sealed warrant, raided a Northern Dallas apartment home where two Middle Eastern men were taken into custody for questioning. Meanwhile, authorities apprehended a third Arab male at an Oklahoma City motel. According to CNN, federal agents serving on the newly dubbed "Bombing Task Force" subjected all three men to intense interrogation. The Immigration and Naturalization Service (INS) then arrested the men for immigration violations.

* In the predawn hours of April 20, 1995, authorities eventually tracked down the blue Cavalier parked outside an Oklahoma City

motel where one of the Arab men had rented a room. Meanwhile, the Blazer was found at a Dallas residence that was thoroughly searched for evidence of bomb making materials. Unnamed federal officials told the *Dallas Morning News* that investigators seized several duffle bags from the North Dallas apartment and "sent them to a federal laboratory near Washington after a bomb-sniffing dog indicated the bags may have been exposed to chemicals used in explosives."

* In a succession of nationally televised press conferences, reporters asked the Justice Dept. and FBI officials about the all-points-bulletins for the brown Chevrolet pickup, blue Chevy Cavalier or Blazer, and Middle Eastern suspects. But that line of questioning would be instantly shut down with the clichéd "no comment." Then, the new on-site commander, FBI Special Agent Weldon Kennedy, deflected the questions. "Some people were detained last night who were riding in a Chevy Cavalier. Are they considered suspects?" a reporter shouted from behind the cameras' purview. "I cannot confirm that we have questioned any suspects, no," Kennedy answered.

* Meanwhile, at a news conference in Washington, D.C., Kennedy's boss, Attorney General Janet Reno, faced the same type questioning. "General Reno, there are broadcast reports of two men arrested in Dallas and one in Oklahoma. Are those reports incorrect?" the reporter asked.

* "I could not confirm that. I have no knowledge of that," Ms. Reno responded with a bit of observable annoyance. Undaunted, the journalist pressed further. "Reports concerning a New York City cab driver and his brother and another man named Mohammed . . . " "Neither [FBI] Director Freeh or I have information to that effect," Ms. Reno affirmed as she signaled another journalist to ask a question. Reno's stonewalling would not last long. By 2:14 p.m. on the afternoon of April 20, 1993, there was a report that British immigration officials had prohibited a Jordanian national arriving from the United States from entering the country.

* Now, the spin machine was spiraling out of control. In Washington, Justice Department spokesman Carl Stern portrayed the man being returned from London as a "possible witness who was refused admittance to Britain." When the London Associated Press inquired

if the detainee was considered a suspect, Stern replied, "You never know what's down the road." A background:

* At 9:30 a.m., on April 19, 1995, a nervous Middle Eastern passenger aroused the interest of vigilant employees posted at the American Airlines ticket counter. By the time of the FBI was notified, the man's flight had already lifted off from Oklahoma City's Will Rogers World Airport. His final destination was Amman, Jordan. During a scheduled stopover at Chicago O'Hare International Airport, federal agents placed the traveler, Jordanian national Abraham Ahmad, under temporary arrest. After a cursory interview, the thirty-one-year-old naturalized American citizen was released, allowing him to resume his international flight.

* Upon arriving at London's Heathrow Airport, British authorities seized him for further questioning. Meanwhile, Ahmad's luggage was rerouted to Rome, where Italian officials rifled through the commuter's overstuffed bags, yielding a provocative inventory of materials. Ahmad had stockpiled multiple car radios, shielded and unshielded wire, a small tool kit, solder, and caulking. These items which authorities theorized could be used to assemble a crude, "homemade" bomb. The vise of suspicion tightened with the discovery of blue jogging suits matching the description of the clothing worn by the Middle Eastern men profiled in the FBI's bulletin.

* At 12:07 p.m., on April 19, 1995, former Oklahoma congressman Dave McCurdy said the following in a CNN interview: "If you look at the nature of the destruction, this looks very similar to the destruction of the Israeli Embassy in Argentina and even the U.S. Embassy in Beirut." During his fourteen-year career as U.S. representative, Mr. McCurdy previously chaired the House Intelligence Committee, which allowed him access to national security threats.

* "My first reaction when I heard of the explosion was that there could be a very real connection to some of the Islamic fundamentalist groups that have, actually, been operating out of Oklahoma City. They've had recent meetings, even a convention, where terrorists from the Middle East who were connected directly to Hamas and Hezbollah participate," he passionately preached, touching off a media backlash. The local press scourged Mr. McCurdy for demagoguery, prompting

him to defend his remarks in an opinion column published by the Oklahoma *Gazette*.[8]

Evidence quickly led to Timothy McVeigh. A vehicle identification number led to a Ryder rental facility in Junction City, Kansas. On April 20, 1995, the FBI released a sketch of the man who rented the truck. The owner of the Dreamland Motel in Junction City, Kansas recognized him as a guest registered as Timothy McVeigh.[9]

A search of police records showed that McVeigh was in the Noble County jail in Perry, Oklahoma. As mentioned earlier, a state trooper had stopped him shortly after the bombing because his car was missing a license plate. He then arrested McVeigh for carrying a concealed firearm, and McVeigh was still in custody when the FBI called.[10]

The following sequence events come again from Jayna Davis, in her book, *The Third Terrorist*:

> * Driving home from the local lumber yard, forty-year-old military surplus salesman Terry Nichols flipped on the car radio. "James and Terry Nichols," two brothers from Michigan known to be associated with prime suspect Timothy McVeigh, were wanted for questioning in connection with the April 19 attack, the radio announcer reported.
> * The pair met in 1988 during basic training at Fort Benning, Georgia. Both were assigned to the First Infantry Division stationed at Fort Riley, Kansas. A year later, Nichols acquired a hardship discharge to raise his six-year-old son, Joshua, following his divorce from his first wife, Lana Padilla.
> * Nichols drove directly to the Herington Police Department, walked through the doors at 3:15 p.m., surrendered to the FBI, and agreed to unrestricted questioning. In an effort to appear cooperative, Nichols signed consent forms granting the search of his home and vehicle, without the benefit of legal counsel. However, he stopped short of submitting to a polygraph examination, claiming lie detector findings are unreliable. Teams of federal technicians swarmed the Herington residence. The most significant discoveries were the following:
>   1. Plastic barrels consistent with the fifty-five-gallon drums demolition experts theorized contained the truck bomb's deadly mixture.

2. Fertilizer prills strewn across the property.
3. A fuel meter.
4. Hand-drawn getaway map of downtown Oklahoma City.
5. Sales receipt bearing McVeigh's fingerprint. The pink slip documented the purchase of one ton of ammonium nitrate fertilizer from the Mid Kansas Co-op in McPherson. He went by the name "Mike Havens," a known alias of Terry Nichols.
6. Using phony identification, the bombers rented storage lockers throughout Kansas, Arizona, and Nevada to hide their loot until the time came to blend the lethal concoction of fertilizer and diesel fuel.
7. Five Primadet non-electric blasting caps with sixty-foot cords stashed under a stack of boxes.
8. A cordless drill which was linked to a padlock drilled open during a burglary of explosives from a Marion, Kansas rock quarry.
9. A telephone calling card issued under the alias "Daryl Bridges."

* It seems that McVeigh purchased the Daryl Bridges phone debit card in 1993 from *Spotlight* magazine. By using money orders to purchase more long-distance minutes on the same card, they figured they had covered their tracks. But, once the card fell into the hands of the authorities, FBI computer technicians were able to reconstruct the quest to purchase bomb components, successfully resurrecting a list of calls to manufacturers of barrels, demolitions, chemicals, racing fuel, motels, and the Junction City Ryder rental shop.

* A raised yellow flag emblazoned with the warning, "Don't Tread on Me," greeted FBI agents as they approached Michael Fortier's trailer in the arid Arizona desert. From the outset, the twenty-six-year-old hardware store clerk and former McVeigh Army pal portrayed himself as a shocked and stunned observer. McVeigh had served as the best man at his wedding and began a campaign to assist his anti-government friend.

* By May 1995, officials threatened to charge Fortier with conspiracy. If convicted at trial, he could have faced a possible death penalty. After months of playing hardball, Fortier broke down and discussed

his prior knowledge. He cut a plea that eventually led to a reduced twelve-year prison term in exchange for testifying against McVeigh and Nichols. The deal also secured immunity for his wife Lori.

* On the afternoon of April 21, 1995, law enforcement officials paraded Timothy McVeigh past a throng of cameras stationed on the lawn of the Noble County courthouse in Perry, Oklahoma. On August 21, 1995, a federal grand jury sealed the case. Timothy McVeigh and Terry Nichols, aided by Michael Fortier, conspired to murder innocents, apparently motivated by a desire to avenge the deaths of the Branch Davidians during the April 19, 1993, fiery standoff with the ATF and FBI at Waco, Texas.[11]

Rumors also began to circulate of people seeing bomb squads in downtown Oklahoma in the early hours of the morning before the blast. It was said that the ATF did not come to work that morning at the Murrah Building. The families noticed that none of the ATF agents were on the casualty list.[12]

On May 23, 1995, the day the ruined Murrah Building was brought down with demolition charges, Edye Smith, a mother who lost two children to the blast, erupted in a live interview on CNN: "Where the hell was the ATF, I want to know?" she thundered. "All fifteen or seventeen of their employees survived, and they were on the ninth floor. They were the target of this explosion and where were they? Did they have a warning sign? Did they think it might be a bad day to go into the office? They had the option not to go to work that day, and my kids didn't. They didn't get that option. Nobody else in the building got that option. And we're just asking questions. We're not making accusations. We just want to know. And they're telling us: 'Keep your mouth shut, don't talk about it.' "[13]

In August 1995, Timothy McVeigh and Terry Nichols were each charged with eleven federal crimes:

* Conspiring to use a weapon of mass destruction to kill people and destroy federal property;
* Using a weapon of mass destruction that caused death and injury;
* The malicious destruction of federal property by explosives; and
* Eight counts of first-degree murder of federal law enforcement officers.[14]

A federal jury found McVeigh guilty of all counts on June 2, 1997. A different jury found Nichols guilty of conspiracy and eight counts of manslaughter on December 23, 1997. He was sentenced to life in prison. Michael Fortier testified against McVeigh and was sentenced to twelve years in prison for failing to report the planned attack and for lying to the FBI.[15]

Though most people were convinced that McVeigh was guilty, and his own lawyer admitted as much during the sentencing hearings, the trial did not bring out the full story. Indeed, it was skillfully managed to ensure that collateral revelations were kept to a minimum.[16]

The prosecution withheld material from the defense that was exculpatory or impeached the credibility of government witnesses. It delayed a year in handing over FD-302 witness statements that were critical to the defense. It stonewalled, obstructed, and dragged its feet at every turn. It also told a series of demonstrable lies.[17]

On top of that, the FBI had been patting itself on the back for "solving" the Oklahoma bombing. Unfortunately, the report of the Justice Department's Inspector General lists the Oklahoma bombing case as one of the worst examples of de facto evidence tampering by the crime labs. To begin with, the FBI had no scientific basis for concluding that the Murrah Building was blown up by an ammonium nitrate fertilizer bomb. The FBI did not know in 1995, and does not know to this day, what actually caused the explosion.[18]

The Justice Department report concluded that the explosives unit simply guessed that the bomb was made of four thousand pounds of ammonium nitrate after "recovery of receipts showing that defendant Nichols purchased four thousand pounds of ammonium nitrate."[19] The labs guessed that the explosive charge was placed in fifty-gallon white plastic barrels, without conducting the requisite tests, after the discovery of fifty-gallon plastic containers at the house of Terry Nichols. They said that the detonator appeared to be a Primadet Delay system, but no trace of this was found at the crime scene. Primadet was, however, found at the house of Terry Nichols. You get the picture.[20]

Judge Richard Matsch had a responsibility to prevent the executive branch from conducting a politicized trial that obscured the facts. Yet, he seemed to go with the flow, acceding to the prosecution's request that the Inspector General's report be barred as evidence. It was never made clear to the jury that the FBI did not know what kind of bomb really caused the blast, nor that the FBI had forfeited its magisterial authority.[21]

Until the date of his execution, on June 11, 2001, McVeigh steadfastly maintained he acted alone, with minimal participation from Terry Nichols. Yet, even in death, the lingering suspicion of McVeigh's treasonous collusion with enemy soldiers persists.[22]

On September 15, 2001, just four days after the World Trade Center attack, Cactus owner Randy Christian came forward and said the following to investigative reporter Jayna Davis: "Jayna, I've toiled with coming forward with this, but I can't shake the image of their faces. I'm positive three of the 9/11 hijackers visited my motel a month before the attacks."[23]

It appears that the ringleader, Mohammed Atta, his sidekick Marwan Al-Shehhi, and surviving would-be hijacker Zacarias Moussaoui, entered the Cactus Motel lobby in early August 2001. The trio inquired about renting a room with a kitchenette, but the owner cordially explained there were no vacancies.[24]

Acting as the group's decision maker, Atta came across the room, standing an arm's length from the owner. "We're going to be attending flight school in Norman and would really like to stay at your motel because we have heard such good things about it," Atta said as he broke into a broad smile. He recited a series of compliments about the "outstanding" reputation of Randy's motel. In hindsight, the men appointed to die in a few short weeks, intended to deliver yet another humiliating slap in the face to American law enforcement by signing their names to the register at the very motel that served as the staging grounds for their Middle Eastern predecessors, as if to say, "Ignore us at your own peril."[25]

In February 2006, the Associated Press reported that two federal agencies appeared to have had advanced warning of an attack, specific enough to suggest Oklahoma City as the likely target, and April 19 as the probable date. Tragically, the information was apparently not passed along to other federal authorities.[26]

Agents from the Bureau of Alcohol, Tobacco and Firearms had an informant from the Oklahoma-based white supremacist group Elohim City, who told them before the bombing that individuals were "preparing for war against the U.S. government." Wayne Snell, who was from Elohim City, was scheduled for execution on April 19, 1995. As the date approached, Snell began making threats to FBI agents and prison officials about a bombing to avenge his death, FBI agents were so concerned about the possibility that a month before the blast, they questioned an associate of Snell, who had, with him, made a bomb plot against the same building.[27]

In December 2006, the House International Relations Committee issued a report criticizing the FBI's investigation of the 1995 bombing of the federal building in Oklahoma City. The FBI failed to pursue credible information that Timothy McVeigh and Terry Nichols had help, the committee said. The FBI shouldn't have abandoned its search for John Doe No. 2, the committee said, Jayna Davis, then a reporter for a television station in Oklahoma City, said she found at least 20 witnesses who identified Hussain al-Hussaini, a former Iraqi soldier, as the man they saw with Timothy McVeigh.[28]

In the end, any advanced information of a suspected bombing plot was not passed along to other federal agencies, in a failure of intelligence and communications reminiscent of those before the September 11, 2001 attacks. Yet, did any information get passed along to President Clinton through the Presidential Daily Brief (PDF) that he received each day? Thus, the question before us is, did Bill Clinton know beforehand about the Oklahoma City bombing and then use the tragedy to his advantage after the beating he and his party took in the '94 midterm elections?[29]

CHAPTER 29

FUND-RAISING SCANDALS

I see the White House is like a subway. You have to put in coins to open gates.
—Democratic fundraiser Johnny Chung[1]

On October 13, 1996, Vice President Al Gore appeared on NBC's *Meet the Press* and said the following, at the beginning of the campaign finance scandal: "I have worked closely with Bill Clinton for four years. . . . I've watched him demonstrate character, courage, moral leadership in making the right call, day after day. . . . You talk about ethics, he has imposed the toughest ethics code in the history of the White House."[2]

On March 10, 1997, President Clinton declared: "I don't believe you can find any evidence of the fact that I have changed government policy solely because of a contribution."[3]

Really!? Let us explore these statements.

On January 20, 1993, Bill Clinton was inaugurated as our forty-second president. That afternoon, the new team of presidential advisers gathered in the White House's Roosevelt Room, just across the hall from the Oval Office. The door opened, and Bill Clinton, *the commander in chief of the most powerful nation on the face of the earth,* entered smiling, and took his place at the head of the massive table. He began his first address to his staffers with a lecture on the value of the presidential ethics and personal integrity. "We just have to be dominated by high standards and clear vision and we ought to have a good time doing it," the new president told them.[4]

President Clinton's Executive Order Number 1, "Ethics Commitments by Executive Branch Appointees," required the new Clinton-Gore appointees to make three pledges: (1) no lobbying for five years after they left the government, (2) no activity on behalf of *a foreign government*, and (3) no representation of *a foreign government* or *foreign corporation* for five years after being engaged in a trade negotiation.[5]

The word *foreign* appeared twenty-one times in the executive order, making it clear that the president was demanding loyalty to the United States interests. To be absolutely clear, he told his new appointees, "The ethics rules that we have put forward will guarantee that the members of this administration will be looking out for the American people and not for ourselves."[6]

Yet how many of those present that day knew that they were there only because a foreign banker, later identified as a Communist Chinese agent, had rescued the Clinton-Gore team not once but twice in 1992? Could any of them have predicted that within five-and-a-half years the Clinton-Gore administration would be the subject of worldwide ridicule and a wave of congressional investigations for having maintained itself in power with a flood of foreign money? Who would have guessed that, in return for money, Bill Clinton and Al Gore would literally sit down to supper with a procession of agents for the Communist Chinese army, Chinese intelligence, the Macau criminal syndicate, and Cambodia's biggest drug trafficker? Who would have guessed that Clinton and Gore would use the power of the White House itself to lobby for a foreign power?[7]

It started on December 27, 1994, when President Clinton met with his campaign fund-raiser, Terry McAuliffe for plotting his re-election strategy. Mr. McAuliffe told Mr. Clinton at that meeting that raising whatever sums he needed for his campaign would be "no problem" and that he would do it "faster than it's ever been done before."[8]

According to a passage in *The Choice*, Bob Woodward's book on the 1996 campaign, Mr. Clinton responded by saying, "Is there anything I need to do?"[9]

There was, Mr. McAuliffe told him. "I need to get people to see you," adding that he needed to run key campaign organizers and big money donors through the Oval Office, allowing them to spend some time with the president. Mr. Clinton gave him the go-ahead, as he did his other top people in his re-election campaign at the Democratic National Committee.[10]

As a result, according to David Limbaugh in his book, *Absolute Power*: "The White House went to any lengths, including compromising the security interests of the United States, to obtain the money necessary to win in 1996 and to hold on to power. In the process, the president, vice president, the first lady, and so on down the line, sold access to themselves and to the institutions of the presidency and the White House. Wealthy donors, many of whom had business before the federal government or wanted favors from the administration, were rewarded with access in direct proportion to the size of their contributions. Fund-raisers who raised $100,000 and individual donors who gave $50,000 became managing trustees of the Democratic Party, entitling them to special privileges. Among those perks were opportunities to rub elbows with the first and second families, special seating at Democratic National Committee functions, access to White House coffees, and trips on Air Force One and Air Force Two. Other special privileges included sleepovers in the Lincoln Bedroom, seats in the President's Box at the Kennedy Center, use of the White House pool and tennis courts, tickets to DNC events, participation in trade missions, membership in party committees, and participation in other high-level White House meetings."[11]

President Clinton, the most proficient campaigner who always kept his eye on the prize, became absolutely obsessed and preoccupied with raising money. According to the Senate Governmental Affairs Committee report, Clinton spent "enormous amounts of time during the 1996 election cycle raising money. In the ten months prior to the 1996 election, President Clinton attended more than 230 fundraising events, which raised $119 million. The president maintained such a pace for over a year before the election, often attending fund-raisers five and six days each week."[12]

Then you had foreign nationals providing favors to the Clinton Administration. Edward Timperlake and William C. Triplett II in their book, *Year of the Rat*, laid out the Clinton-Gore record of campaign financial abuses. Enclosed is a partial list:

* Chinese agents ensured victory for the Clinton-Gore team in the 1992 general election with a massive cascade of illegally laundered foreign funds into key states.
* More than one hundred potential witnesses of illegal foreign campaign contributions to the Clinton-Gore team either fled the country, took the Fifth Amendment, or refused to be interviewed by investigative bodies.

* Chinese agents helped secure the 1992 Democratic presidential nomination for Clinton with a multimillion-dollar loan from an Arkansas bank under their influence.
* Chinese agents became the number one donors to Clinton and Gore in 1992.
* The Clinton Justice Department allowed the statute of limitations to run out so that illegal donations from Chinese agents could escape prosecution.
* Leading donors to the DNC were business associates of a major Tiananmen massacre war criminal that even the Chinese had jailed.
* Chinese agents helped fund Dick Morris's brilliant stealth advertising campaign against the Republicans in 1995-1996.
* A Macau criminal syndicate figure who exploited women for prostitution laundered more than $1,000,000 in illegal donations to the DNC; he met Clinton on a number of occasions, including on visits to the White House.
* A Chinese PLA spy laundered illegal campaign funds through an individual who met Clinton twice at fund-raisers.[13]

In the end, Clinton and Gore got away with it. They got themselves elected in 1992 and reelected in 1996 on foreign money, much of it coming from sources that were hostile to the United States. Despite the Congressional committees investigating the campaign finance abuses, they could not bring to account a single perpetrator.[14]

CHAPTER 30

CHINA

Chinese President Jiang Zemin emphatically denied to me personally that their government had tried to do anything to influence the outcome of this election.

—President Clinton
on Chinese influence in American political races in 1996

When Bill Clinton took office in 1993, China presented little threat to the United States. Its strategic missiles had technical problems, and its theater missiles were unreliable. It had no command-and-control systems, no modern air-defense systems, and no effective military communications system. It had no antisatellite weapons that could blind our early-warning systems, and it had no imaging or electronic eavesdropping satellites of its own. China, in fact, was ill-equipped to fight a modern war, or to threaten anyone other than its closest neighbors.[1]

Thanks to Bill Clinton, only six years later, China was able to hit any city in the USA, using state-of-the-art, solid-fueled missiles with dead-accurate, computerized guidance systems and multiple warheads. They likely have suitcase nukes as well. These enable China to strike by proxy—equipping nuclear-armed terrorists to do their dirty work, while the Chinese play innocent. Some intelligence sources claim that China maintains secret stockpiles of chemical, biological, and nuclear weapons on U.S. soil, for just such contingencies. A background:[2]

In 1992, candidate Clinton accused President George H. W. Bush of ignoring China's human rights abuses and neglecting to take action against its government. "Instead of leading an international effort to pressure the

Chinese government to reform, the Bush administration has coddled the dictators and pleaded for progress, but refused to impose penalties for intransigence."[3]

On January 20, 1993, when President Clinton took office, only the United States and Japan possessed any so-called supercomputers, the distribution of which was tightly controlled. The United States and Japan even had a bilateral agreement under which they would review any supercomputer exports before they took place. Supercomputers were not supposed to fall into the wrong hands. Eventually, that would change.[4]

In March 1993, Clinton issued a formal executive order, warning the Chinese leaders that he was giving them only one year to improve their record on human rights. If after a year there was no "overall significant progress" in several areas (including the treatment of political prisoners and the families of dissidents), the executive order said, China would be removed from the list of trading partners with Most Favored Nation status.[5]

Clinton was bluffing. I am sure he would have liked to see China improve its record on human rights, but it is doubtful that he ever felt it to be a serious concern. The executive order, though forcefully stated, was an empty threat. The same month in which Clinton issued the order he received a letter from Mochtay Riady. Marked "Personal & Confidential," the letter urged Clinton not to withdraw China's Most Favored Nation status. According to Riady: "The best way of achieving political reform in China is through capitalist interaction."[6]

To understand how China became a favorite trading partner, we need to look at former Carter administration official William Perry. He returned to government as deputy secretary of defense in 1993, giving the Chinese Communist government its first big break in gaining access to U.S. technology previously denied for export by the previous Reagan and Bush administrations. Perry personally overruled the objections of the National Security Agency (NSA) and the Joint Chiefs of Staff in approving the export of a buried fiber-optics Asynchronous Transfer Mode (ATM) telecommunications network to Hua Mei (Galaxy New Technology), and China Milky Way, front companies owned and controlled by COSTIND.[7]

"The Hua Mei deal was where it all began," said a former U.S. intelligence officer who spoke to the *American Spectator* on condition of anonymity for himself and his company. "When one of our clients asked us to check Hua Mei out and we discovered COSTIND was behind it, we told them there was no way they would ever get U.S. government or CoCom [Coordinating Committee on Export Controls] approval to export. The technology was extremely sensitive, and the Chinese end-user was a known government collection agency. COSTIND has always been on the watch list."[8]

Despite this initial reaction, the former intelligence officer met with Chinese officials in Hong Kong in October 1993 to learn more. "When I brought up the problem of export approvals, they just laughed," he recalls. "They boasted of their relationship to Perry and to John Lewis," a colleague of Perry's from Stanford who became the point man for the project once Perry joined the Clinton administration. In the end, thanks to William Perry, the Chinese were able to get U.S. export approval.[9]

Unknown to most people at the time was a plan devised by a future crop of Clinton administration appointees to lift export controls on a wide range of strategic technologies for China. The plan was first laid out in a 1992 National Academy of Sciences study authored by William Perry, Ashton Carter, and Mitchell Wallerstein, who all went on to top Pentagon jobs under Clinton. Calling export controls a "wasting asset," they argued that for U.S. high-tech firms to maintain a technological edge over their foreign competitors they needed to be allowed to export even-more sophisticated equipment, so they could plow those profits into developing new technologies.[10]

Once William Perry went to work putting the plan into action within the bureaucracy, Ron Brown, as secretary of commerce, was responsible with selling the decontrols to corporate America and Congress as part of an administration-wide "Trade Promotion" package, aimed at creating jobs and "growing" U.S. exports.[11]

As a globalist, Clinton promoted "multi-polarity," the doctrine that no country (including the United States) should be allowed to gain decisive advantage over others. To this end, Clinton appointed antinuclear activist Hazel O'Leary to head the Department of Energy. O'Leary set to work "leveling the playing field," as she put it, by giving away our nuclear secrets. She declassified eleven million pages of data on U.S. nuclear weapons and loosened up security at weapons labs.[12]

Kenneth Timmerman began investigating Chinese high-tech espionage activities in the United States in 1993 and discovered early on just how sensitive a subject this can be. As a congressional staffer working for California

Democrat Tom Lantos, Mr. Timmerman requested licensing records of U.S. high-tech exports to China from the Department of Commerce. When Commerce finally delivered the several-thousand-page print-out to the Rayburn House Office building in late March 1993, Timmerman was prevented for three weeks from even looking at it, despite the fact that the information was not classified. Leading the charge to prevent access was Rep. Sam Gejdenson (D-Conn.), and his top staffer John Scheibel, who went on to become a Washington, D.C. lobbyist for a computer export lobbying group. They did not want the story to leak out of just how much dual-use technology U.S. companies had been allowed to sell to the Chinese military, for fear that would impede the U.S.-China high-tech pipeline.[13]

Interestingly, after leaving the Hill in late 1993, Mr. Timmerman joined *Time* magazine. After a three-month investigation into Chinese procurement activities in the United States, he discovered that in 1993, an entity named CATIC, the procurement arm of the Chinese military aviation ministry, acquired the McDonnel-Douglas aerospace plant in Columbus, Ohio, took it apart, and shipped it home. Some 90 to 95 percent of the plant was defense related. It possessed sophisticated machine tools that were needed in the production of missiles and military aircraft, including the B-1 bomber. A Pentagon report later found that, at least 275 semitrailers were used to haul the plant's equipment from Columbus to the West Coast, where it was shipped to China. According to the *New York Times*, military experts affirmed that "the machines would enable the Chinese military to improve significantly the performance abilities—speed, range and maneuverability—of their aircraft. And if diverted, they could do the same for missiles and bombers."[14]

The CATIC deal was part of an unreported Chinese effort to buy cutting-edge U.S. defense manufacturing gear at auctions, as more and more defense plants closed in response to the Pentagon's defense build-down. Mr. Timmerman's story was pulled by *Time* the week O.J. Simpson burst onto the front pages, but not because of O.J. The Commerce Department had written a letter to *Time*'s editor's (which Mr. Timmerman subsequently obtained), calling his reporting "one-sided" and "unfair," all of this before his story was even printed! *Time* fired Mr. Timmerman within hours.[15]

Six months later, in March 1995, the *American Spectator* published Timmerman's article, "China Shops," and had since published nearly a dozen of his feature-length investigations of China's creeping infiltration of U.S. society. When he exposed the efforts of Defense Secretary William Perry to help the Chinese buy highly sensitive U.S. telecommunications gear over the objections of the National Security Agency, in his article "Peking Pentagon" in April 1996, Perry threatened to sue the *American Spectator* for defamation. Instead, he called prominent conservatives to his office in an attempt to organize a counter-attack against Mr. Timmerman. Meanwhile, Mr. Timmerman learned, photocopies of his article were being passed around gleefully behind Perry's back.[16]

On April 28, 1993, President Clinton waived the Tiananmen sanctions to allow Motorola to sign a contract with China's Great Wall Industries Corp. (CGWIC), to launch up to twelve satellites in China for its Iridium global wireless communications network. As part of the deal, the Chinese got help from U.S. companies in designing a "smart dispenser" that enabled them for the first time to launch multiple satellites from a single rocket. According to a December 1996 report from the Air Force National Air Intelligence Center, first revealed by *Washington Times* reporter Bill Gertz, the Iridium smart dispenser "could be developed into a credible PBV [post-boost vehicle] with a few relatively minor changes." Post-boost vehicles are used to deliver multiple nuclear warheads to separate orbits, so they can strike different targets independently. Multiple warhead technology was a key priority for the Commission of Science Technology and Industry for National Defense (COSTIND) collectors and was a capability the Chinese had previously lacked.[17]

In late May 1993, President Clinton betrayed the Chinese dissidents and their supporters by renewing China's most favored nation status. At the time, Clinton seemed willing to confront China's role in their proliferation. He claimed the United States was examining reports that China had shipped M-11 ballistic missiles to Pakistan in violation of the Missile Technology Control Regime. He vowed if he could prove China had transferred M-11 missiles or related equipment, he would "not hesitate to act."[18]

As it turned out, China did sell M-11 ballistic missile technology to Pakistan, and the administration was forced to respond. It did so in August 1993 when it sanctioned the very companies that launched satellites for Armstrong, Schwartz, and the others. The screams of outrage from Armstrong and the rest of the satellite maker CEOs caused the administration to back down immediately. The Clinton-Gore administration must have made some kind of pledge because, going forward, the administration would never again sanction the Chinese for missile proliferation, even when devastating news reports surfaced:[19]

- In June 1995 *Defense News* reported the existence of a top secret CIA study entitled, "China-Iran Missile Technology Cooperation: A Timeline Approach."
- On June 22, 1995, Italy's *La Stampa* quoted a Top Secret NATO assessment asserting than Iran would have 2,000-mile ballistic missiles thanks to a Chinese "command and control system disguised as space technology."
- On July 23, 1996, the *Washington Times* reported on Chinese shipments of missile guidance systems to Syria.
- On August 25, 1996, the *Washington Post* revealed that Chinese companies were building an entire turnkey ballistic missile plant in Pakistan.
- On February 1, 1997, the *International Defense Review* revealed that Chinese missile technicians were working at a defense complex outside Tehran, Iran.
- On June 16, 1998, the *Washington Times* reported that PLA companies were transferring missile technology to Libya. At a hearing that day a senator challenged Secretary of State Madeleine Albright, and she did not dispute the *Time's* account.[20]

In September-October 1993, according to the June 25, 1998, *Washington Post*, Michael Armstrong, CEO of Hughes Electronics, wrote two "blunt" letters to President Clinton in early fall of 1993, reminding him of "his support" and saying that the sanctions were damaging his company. Then he delivered a warning: "This will be public and political shortly. Thank you." Within weeks, he met with Clinton and eventually, he would receive most of what he wanted. And together with Loral Space and Communications, Hughes would have contributed $2.5 million to the Democratic Party from 1991—June 1998.[21]

On September 29, 1993, President Clinton announced a massive lifting of controls on supercomputers. Gary Milhollin, director of the University of Wisconsin Project on Nuclear Arms Control, immediately denounced Clinton's decision, accusing the administration of a payoff to California-based supporters and predicting that the Chinese would inevitably divert their American supercomputers to military uses. He was right. A U.S. supercomputer exported to a Chinese "civilian" project turned up in the hands of the PLA.[22]

On September 30, 1993, Secretary of Commerce Ron Brown, issued a report, "Toward a National Export Strategy," which first made the argument, often repeated until the Loral-Hughes satellite scandals erupted in 1998, that each additional $1 billion in U.S. exports creates twenty thousand jobs in the U.S. Brown's report urged the administration and Congress to facilitate exports to ten "Big Emerging Markets." It just happened that the largest of those markets, was Communist China. It was interested in purchasing precisely the type of technology that had long been subject to export restrictions because of its military and strategic applications.[23]

Regulations governing export controls are required under the Export Administration Act (EAA), first passed in 1979 to ensure that U.S. high-tech goods could not enhance the defense industries in Soviet bloc countries and Communist China. In 1993 and 1994, the Clinton administration tried to rewrite the EAA to eliminate most of the controls, but Congress objected. Then, they simply made an end run around the law, and dismantled the controls through executive branch regulations. The administration's efforts reduced the large licensing lists, and as a result, Defense Department officials began to complain that there were no more records of what had been shipped to the Chinese military and thus no way to gauge the damage to U.S. national security.[24]

On November 18, 1993, President Clinton decided to permit the sale to China of an $8-milllion supercomputer capable of performing 958 million per second. He also lifted the ban on selling components for China's nuclear power plants. On November 19, 1993, Chinese President Jiang Zemin meets informally with President Clinton at a conference for Asian-Pacific Economic Cooperation (APEC) leaders. Afterward, Clinton says, "I think anybody should be reluctant to isolate a country as big as China with the potential China has for good."[25]

On January 6, 1994, after intense lobbying by the U.S. aerospace industry, Mr. Clinton labels three satellites as "civilian," enabling them to circumvent the sanctions he had imposed only five months earlier. To permit the satellites to be launched from Chinese rockets, Mr. Clinton also issues the requisite presidential waivers, a procedure instituted by Mr. Bush after the 1989 Tiananmen massacre.[26]

In February 1994, Assistant Secretary of State Shattuck met secretly with Wei Jingsheng, the highest-ranking party member to have become a dissident and one of the founders of the "Democracy Wall" movement, the Chinese went public with *their* fury. They dared to break off what the *Human Rights Watch* called "an almost non-existent 'human rights dialogue.'"[27] Just ten days after Shattuck's meeting with Wei Jingsheng, Secretary of State Warren Christopher was sent to China to repair the damage. The Chinese never gave him a chance. To set the tone for Christopher's trip, authorities arrested Wei Jingsheng a week before his arrival. They were just warming up.[28]

When Mr. Christopher arrived in Beijing, he was notified that the Chinese would honor his presence, neither with a banquet nor an official welcoming at the airport. After Christopher deplaned, Tiananmen hardliner Li Peng verbally assaulted him. His insults were shrewd and studied. In a biting turn of phrase, he accused Christopher and Clinton of "losing China," a charge that in a slightly different context had haunted the Democratic Party since the days of Harry Truman.[29]

On March 30, 1994, the United States lifts export restrictions on telecommunications and computer technology imposed by the Coordinating Committee for Multilateral Export Controls. China and the former Soviet bloc are the primary beneficiaries.[30] On May 26, 1994, President Clinton shocked those who believed that he cared about human rights in China, by "de-linking" it from renewal of China's most favored nation status. Although Clinton admitted China had not made much progress on the issues outlined in his 1993 executive order, he suggested that, by following a new voluntary set of principles, American businesses could somehow turn things around. Now, almost no one was taking Clinton seriously. On June 2, 1994, President Clinton signed the executive order extending MFN to China for another year.[31] That same month, Loral CEO Bernard Schwartz sent the DNC a $100,000 soft-money contribution, eight times the size of his first soft-money donation in 1993. The next month, on July 13, 1994, President Clinton issued presidential waivers under P.L. 101-246 to allow U.S. satellites to be launched from Chinese rockets.[32]

Bernard Schwartz then became close to Commerce Secretary Ron Brown and received (purchased?) a highly coveted slot on a controversial

August 27 to September 3, 1994 trade mission to China. With Mr. Brown's help, Mr. Schwartz used his Chinese contacts to obtain satellite-transmission rights for a mobile telephone network in China, a deal worth billions. In a September 20, 1994 memo to the president, White House Deputy Chief of Staff Harold Ickes, who was directing the Democratic Party's fundraising from his West Wing office, suggested a presidential follow-up to Mr. Schwartz's lucrative China trip: "In order to raise an additional $3,000,000 to permit the [DNC] to produce and air generic tv/radio spots as soon as Congress adjourns," Mr. Ickes advised the president to call Mr. Schwartz and invite him and others to a White House breakfast "to impress them with the need to raise $3,000,000 within the next two weeks."[33]

So who is Bernard Schwartz?

An accountant by background, Schwartz took over the small, struggling Loral Corporation in 1972 when its stock was valued at thirty-six cents a share. He then produced ninety-six consecutive quarters of improved earnings before selling it to Lockheed Martin in 1996 for fifty-one dollars a share.[34]

In 1994, nearing seventy, the ever-ambitious Schwartz was about to shift his area of interest from the defense industry to telecommunications, specifically a cellular satellite network. Not coincidently, he was about to get interested in politics. In the 1992 election cycle. Schwartz had donated only $12,500 to help elect Clinton. After Clinton and Gore were elected, they had something Schwartz wanted. In the summer of 1994, he wrote a check to the Democrats for $100,000. Two months later, he was on Ron Brown's trade delegation to China. Brown arranged meetings between Schwartz and Chinese officials. In the 1993-1994 cycle, Schwartz contributed a total of $112,000 to the Democrats. Schwartz denied to newspapers any connection between the $100,000 and the Brown trade trip to China.[35]

Then, according to reporters Edward Timperlake and William C. Triplett: "In the 1995-1996 cycle, three things came together: (1) Clinton desperately needed money for Dick Morris's TV advertising blitz, (2) Schwartz needed antitrust approval from the Clinton administration's Justice Department for his spinoff of some parts of Loral to aerospace giant Lockheed, and (3) Schwartz desperately needed Clinton support (and later, cover) for his China satellite program. He wanted granting-authority for the export licenses he needed transferred to the user-friendly Commerce Department. He also wanted regular waivers of the Tiananmen sanctions on satellites, and, to avoid the proliferation sanctions, he had to persuade the Clinton administration to ignore Chinese missile sales to Iran."[36]

Timperlake and Triplett continued:

> Everyone got what they wanted. Bernie wrote a lot of checks. His personal contributions rose to an amazing $586,000 in the Clinton-Gore reelection cycle of 1995-1996. As of May 1998 Schwartz had contributed $421,000 to the Democrats' 1997-1998 campaign cycle. That made him the number one contributor to the Democrats in both the 1995-1996 and 1997-1998 campaign cycles. Between 1992 and May 1998, he had given the Democratic Party $1,131,000. His family, his companies, and his executives have given another $881,565 to Democratic candidates. Finally, he had contributed $217,000 to the Democratic Leadership Conference, a Clinton-associated think tank. Grand total: More than $2.2 million to the Clinton-Gore ticket, Democratic candidates, and Democratic causes.[37]
>
> Bernie got his antitrust exemption for Loral. On March 12, 1996, Clinton overturned an October 1995 decision by Secretary of State Warren Christopher and transferred authority for satellite export licenses to the Commerce Department. Tiananmen waivers became routine for Clinton. And, America's first line of defense against missile proliferation was dismantled. Loral would have gotten off the hook with the February 1998 Clinton waiver if somebody hadn't tipped off Jeff Gerth of the *New York Times*.[38]

In return for his largesse, Bernard Schwartz was allowed to sell out this country and walk away a free man. Ron Brown would help—but only to a point.[39]

On October 4, 1994, U.S. Secretary of State Warren Christopher and Chinese Foreign Minister Qian Qichen signed an agreement ending the ban on the export to China of U.S. high-technology, including satellite-launch equipment and computer technology. Three days later China conducted an underground nuclear test.[40]

On October 14, 1994, President Clinton proclaimed, "There is nothing more important to our security and to the world's stability than preventing the spread of nuclear weapons and ballistic missiles." The next day, President Clinton lifted sanctions he had imposed on China for selling missile technology to Pakistan, a major victory for the aerospace industry.[41]

On November 1, 1994, President Clinton issued a waiver on sanctions on China for missile-technology exports.[42]

On January 26, 1995, a Chinese Long March rocket carrying an Apstar-2 satellite manufactured by Hughes Space and Communications, exploded above its launch pad.[43]

On April 25, 1995, Larry Booth and Robby Henson, two key Los Alamos scientists doing the hard analytic work on China, sent (DOE) intelligence chief Notra Trulock a Top Secret memo outlining their conclusions about the purpose of the Chinese tests. Though the memo was classified, one report noted, "These tests led to suspicions in the U.S. Intelligence Community that the PRC had stolen advanced U.S. thermonuclear warhead "information". The two scientists believed that these tests were for the "purpose of developing smaller, lighter warheads for the PRC's new nuclear forces."[44]

There was a similarity between the W-88 and a recently tested Chinese warhead. It was then that the United States realized the theft had occurred. Detection came when experts analyzed data from recent Chinese underground nuclear tests and saw remarkable similarities to the W-88 U.S. warhead. Later in 1995, secret Chinese government documents confirmed that there had been a security breach at Los Alamos Laboratory.[45]

On May 26, 1995, in a White House announcement, President Clinton said, "I have decided that the United States should renew Most Favored Nation trading status toward China . . . . I am moving, therefore, to delink human rights from the annual extension of Most Favored Nation trading status for China.[46]

On September 1995, President Clinton personally "met with Long Beach officials to push their plan forward" to allow Chinese-government-owned COSCO to be given control of the mothballed Long Beach Naval Station, which was going to be deeded to the city.[47]

On October 6, 1995, President Clinton loosened restrictions on the sale of high-performance computers. China was allowed to import computers of less than 7 billion theoretical operations per second for civilian purposes. The Chinese could request greater capacity with special permission from the Commerce Department. The computers offered China's missile program increased simulation capability in assessing nuclear blast damage and kill zones.[48]

On October 9, 1995, after pressure from producers of communications satellites prompting a review of existing restrictions, Secretary of State Warren Christopher issued an order keeping commercial satellites on the munitions list, an inventory of strategic military and intelligence technology, reaffirming the jurisdiction of the State Department in the matter. According to the May 17, 1998, *New York Times* piece, Christopher wrote in a classified memorandum that lifting the export limitation would "raise suspicions that we are trying to evade China sanctions." The Commerce Department appealed Christopher's decision to the President.[49]

In late 1995 and early 1996, Trulock briefed the FBI on possible theft of W-88 plans from Los Alamos. FBI began investigating the three U.S. nuclear weapons labs.[50] Shortly thereafter, on February 15, 1996, a Chinese Long March rocket carrying a $200 million satellite for Loral Space & Communications blew up after liftoff, destroying the satellite.[51] February represented a moment of keen impasse between warring factions within the Clinton administration. With his generous support, Loral CEO Bernard Schwartz was hoping to overcome his obstacles.[52]

The obstacles in this case was the Pentagon and intelligence community. Much to Schwartz's frustration, they were standing firm on the question of commercial satellites. Given the vital technology contained therein, much of it secret, they had convinced Secretary of State Warren Christopher in October 1995 to keep satellites on the so-called munitions list, an inventory of the nation's most sensitive military and intelligence-gathering equipment.[53]

Almost immediately, Deputy National Security Advisor Sandy Berger had begun plotting to undermine Christopher. In November 1995, Berger sent a memo to Christopher's deputy and longtime Clinton buddy, Strobe Talbott. Berger claimed that Ron Brown, who "was far more sympathetic to the satellites makers," would appeal Christopher's ruling to Clinton. Clearly, Berger was setting up a paper trail that led directly to the hapless Ron Brown. He then added, as if Talbott needed to be told, "I, too, have real questions about the wisdom" of Christopher's decision.[54]

So who is Sandy Berger? Samuel R. "Sandy" Berger was President Clinton's national security adviser and a true friend of Bill's (and Hillary's). He met Bill and Hillary when all three were political operatives on the

McGovern campaign of 1972. In the years leading to Clinton's first inauguration in January 1993, Berger was a Washington-based lawyer-lobbyist. In an interview with *Washington Post* columnist Nat Hentoff, Representative Nancy Pelosi (D-CA) pointed out, "Sandy Berger was the point person at the Hogan and Hartson law firm for the trade office of the Chinese government." Despite the fact that he had no real foreign policy experience, Berger became the number two man at the NSA.[55]

Under those circumstances, authors Edward Timperlake and William Triplett believed that Berger should have recused himself from anything having to do with the PRC, especially trade. Instead, Berger seemed to be around whenever Clinton administration decisions were made that, in their opinion, favored PRC trade ties over American national security interests.[56]

On February 2, 1996, Poly Technologies, a company controlled by the People's Liberation Army, was issued a permit to ship more than 100,000 semiautomatic weapons and millions of rounds of ammunition into the United States. The chairman of the government-controlled conglomerate that runs Poly Technologies is Wang Jun. A background:[57]

According to a Rand Corporation report forced from the U.S. Department of Commerce by a federal lawsuit, one of Poly Technologies' profit centers was the "importation and distribution of semi-automatic rifles for the U.S. domestic market." Between 1987 and 1993, the company and its affiliates sold more than $200 million worth of these guns in the United States. When Clinton signed into law the banning of certain semi-automatic weapons in 1994, Poly Technologies only profited. They exploited export loopholes to circumvent the ban and ultimately resorted to old-fashioned smuggling.[58]

Four days later, on February 6, 1996, Wang Jun met with Secretary of Commerce Ron Brown at the Commerce Department and later attended a White House "coffee" with President Clinton. It was an only-in-America kind of moment. Wang Jun, China's top military-industrial arms dealer, who had cut arms deals with Chinese allies in places like Libya, Iran, Serbia, Iraq, and Afghanistan, now found himself at a cordial private coffee with the president of the United States. Wang Jun also had a multibillion-dollar stake in getting access to American satellites.[59]

Clinton pal and Chinese Triad mafia member, Yah Lin (Charlie) Trie had greased the Wang Jun meeting with a fifty-thousand-dollar payment.

Evidence suggested that Trie laundered the money through a Wall Street player named Ernest Green. Under oath, Green would later attribute the multi-thousand-dollar traveler's checks he received from Charlie Trie to "a gentlemen's bet on a basketball game."[60]

Charlie Trie was also a DNC fund-raiser who raised $640,000 for the President's Legal Defense Fund. Soon, all of it was returned when the source could not be verified. Trie fled to China rather than face questioning but later returned under indictment.[61]

The same day as the "coffee," President Clinton issued a waiver to lift sanctions and permit four satellites, including a Loral product, to be launched on Chinese rockets despite the January reports that China continued to export nuclear technology to Pakistan.[62] On February 14, 1996, about a week or so after Wang Jun's Washington visit, a Chinese Long March 3B rocket carrying a $200 million Loral-built Intelsat 708 satellite crashed just after liftoff onto a local village with an incredible explosion. According to an Israeli engineer who witnessed the disaster, "thousands of corpses were loaded in dozens of trucks and buried in mass graves." A COSTIND spokeswoman denied the Israeli's charge: "These are lies." They claimed that only about sixty people were killed or injured. But an American aerospace official, who was interviewed at the time by Edward Timperlake and William Triplett, confirmed the Israeli's account. This was the third Long March failure in the previous three years involving U.S.-built satellite payloads.[63]

The Pentagon welcomed the news. With the collapse of the Soviets, the People's Republic had emerged as America's most serious potential enemy, and its leaders weren't afraid to say so. Just a few months earlier, a Chinese military officer had warned American ambassador Charles Freeman, "If you hit us now, we can hit back. So you will not make those threats [about Taiwan]." The officer then offered this salient point: "In the end you care more about Los Angeles than you do about Taipei."[64]

American technical advice was making Chinese missile-rattling more than an empty threat. Unfortunately, with the Clintons' drive to raise money, they were prepared to broker that advice. In March 1996, Berger was able to send satellite control to Brown at Commerce and cost the Pentagon its veto power.[65]

According to the *New York Times*, which reviewed thousands of pages of unclassified documents, the deal was closed in a series of telephone calls involving Berger, Talbott, Brown, and John White, the deputy defense secretary. It appeared, according to the *Times*' review, that there was "no indication that Mr. Christopher was personally involved in the president's decision." On March 12, 1996, the president signed off on a "decision memorandum" that reversed Christopher's decision and awarded authority over satellite-export licensing to Commerce. Said an attached memo, "Industry should like the fact that they will deal with the more 'user friendly' Commerce system."[66]

Loral Space Systems, the builder of the satellite that crashed into the village, had a problem. So did the Chinese launchers, which had such a poor reputation for reliability that they were uninsurable. Without insurance, Loral and the other U.S. firms could not use Chinese rockets to launch their satellites. Something had to be done to make the Chinese rockets more reliable if the satellite makers were going to save a dollar or two on launch fees. Of course, since the Long March launch vehicle was nearly identical to a Chinese intercontinental ballistic missile, if you made one more reliable, then the other one is equally reliable. This is precisely the kind of technology transfer that some parts of the U.S. government didn't want.[67]

Indifferent to the fate of Taiwan and feeling confident about his relationship with the president, Schwartz sent a Loral-led review team to China to assess the failure of the Long March 3B rocket. For two months, scientists from Loral and Hughes studied the mishap to discover what corrections were needed in the Chinese missile system. They found an electrical problem in the flight guidance system caused a malfunction. They also identified other problems with the new Long March booster. Without informing the U.S. government, the team delivered to the Great Wall Industry, part of the Chinese government consortium known as China Aerospace Corporation, "200 pages of data, analysis evaluation and reports" that included discussion of "sensitive aspects of the rocket's guidance and control systems, which is an area of weakness in China's missile programs." The data must have been welcome news to the Chinese missile makers. It not only helped the Chinese company improve its commercial space launchers, but also helped make China's nuclear-tipped missiles more reliable as ICBMs.[68]

The State Department learned of this potentially illegal transfer of military technology and referred it to the Pentagon for a formal "damage assessment" investigation. This type of investigation is done after an act of espionage is discovered. After a year-long probe, the Pentagon concluded that "United States national security has been harmed."[69]

So serious was the offense that in 1998, the Criminal Division of the Justice Department launched an investigation. Amazingly, while the investigation was in process, Berger, who was the national security adviser in 1998, sent a memo to the president urging him to "waive the legislative restriction on the export to China of the communications satellites and related equipment for the Space Systems/Loral (SS/L) Chinasat 8 project."[70]

The waiver was suggested to derail the prosecution. Berger admitted as much: "Justice believes that a jury would not convict once it learned that the president had found SS/L's Chinasat 8 project to be in the national interest." But Berger was not about to let that stop him: "We will take the firm position that this waiver does not exonerate or in any way prejudice SS/L with respect to its prior unauthorized transfers to China." Berger was being dishonest, and he knew it. A waiver would make prosecution all but impossible.[71]

The president could issue a waiver, however, only if it served America's "national interest." Berger attempted to make the case that it did, arguing satellite technology would give remote Chinese villagers access "to people and ideas in democratic societies." For its part, Loral had no greater cause than its bottom line. "If a decision is not forthcoming in the next day or so, we stand to lose the contract," Loral lobbyist Thomas Ross wrote Berger. "In fact, even if the decision is favorable, we will lose substantial amounts of money with each passing day."[72]

So much for the national interest.

On March 8, 1996, Chinese military forces launched one of the largest exercises in the communist regime's history. The exercise kicked off with test firings of M-9 short-range mobile missiles into "impact areas" north and south of the island of Taiwan. Exercise Strait 961, as it was called, lasted for seventeen more days. "This was the latest and largest of what the Office of Naval Intelligence (ONI) assesses to be a series of rehearsals of a contingency scenario for the invasion of Taiwan," the ONI said in a report on the maneuvers.[73]

On May 23, 1996, President Clinton called for renewal of MFN for China, saying that renewal would not be "a referendum on all China's policies," but "a vote for America's interests." That same day, the Clinton administration announced that China would not be sanctioned for transferring the ring magnets to Pakistan, saying that there is no evidence that the Chinese government had "willfully aided or abetted" Pakistan's nuclear weapons program.[74]

On May 23, 1996, Wang Jun ran into problems of his own when CNN reported "the largest seizure of smuggled automatic weapons in U.S. history." The San Francisco Bureau of Alcohol, Tobacco, and Firearms had infiltrated a smuggling ring and confiscated two thousand fully automatic AK-47 rifles imported from China. The weapons were found on board a COSCO ship, the enterprise that had been trying to secure the Long Beach Naval Station. CNN traced the rifles to Wang Jun's Poly Technologies.[75] Wang Jun, however, had not wasted his investment. Someone in the know did the arms merchant a large favor by leaking the news of the BATF gun smuggling investigation well before it was wrapped up. The Bay-area bust was premature. The BATF was not able to nail the operation's ringleaders.[76]

On June 1, 1996, in Hong Kong, Clinton donor Johnny Chung met with China Aerospace Corp. Executive Liu Chaoying, a lieutenant colonel in the People's Liberation Army who attended counterintelligence school. Her company built satellites and rockets and provides equipment for China's nuclear tests. The company also owned China Great Wall Industry Corp., which was sanctioned by the United States in 1991 and 1993 for selling missiles to Pakistan. Her father, Gen. Liu Huaquing, was, at the time, the top commander of the Chinese military, specifically in charge of directing China's efforts to acquire Western military technology. He was also a member of the Standing Committee of the Politburo of the Communist Party, which controls China's Communist government.[77]

From July 19 to July 26, 1996, Johnny Chung helped Lieutenant Col. Liu Chaoying obtain a visa to the United States and visit the home of Democratic fund-raiser Eli Broad. He also brought her to meet President Clinton at two events, for which Chung contributed $45,000. She shook Mr. Clinton hand and took a picture with him. Liu and Johnny Chung incorporate Marswell Investment, Inc., similar to a Hong Kong company that is a front for the political department of the Chinese People's Liberation Army (PLA). Deposits to Marswell accounts reportedly travelled from the PLA to U.S. Democratic Party causes.[78]

Chung told the Justice Department that Liu gave him most of the $100,000 he contributed to the DNC in the latter part of 1996, and that she told him the source of the money was China's People's Liberation Army (PLA), which Liu's father commanded. The Chinese government–owned company for which Liu worked, admitted to the *Christian Science Monitor* on May 19, 1998 that Liu did indeed give Chung $300,000, but claimed that the donation "was done by Liu Chaoying acting as an individual."[79]

On August 8, 1996, President Clinton met again with Long Beach officials to push for Chinese government–owned COSCO to be given the Long Beach Naval Station.[80]

After President Clinton won reelection on November 5, 1996, Dorothy Robyn, a Clinton administration official from the National Economic Council, placed a series of phone calls to Long Beach officials urging them to push the COSCO deal through. The key phone call occurred the day before the election, when Robyn held a conference call with eight Long Beach officials and said that the "national interest would be best served if the re-use [COSCO] plan proceeds." Such high-level intervention was quite unusual, and one official said that the call made clear that leasing the port to COSCO was "the preference of the White House."[81]

On December 9, 1996, President Clinton rolled out the red carpet for Chi Haotian, the Butcher of Beijing, during an official visit. Chi was the Communist Chinese military leader who was in operational command of the army forces that massacred an estimated thirty-seven hundred unarmed dissidents during a 1989 pro-democracy demonstration in Tiananmen Square. During his visit, the Chinese leader brazenly insisted that "not a single person" had been killed in the 1989 incident at Tiananmen Square.[82]

On December 12, 1996, President Clinton and Attorney General Janet Reno, just the two of them, sat down for a meeting at the White House. It appeared Reno sold out. In return for four more years as attorney general, she went along with a secret program to ensure that the heir apparent, Albert Gore, would be protected and that those who had benefitted from the most successful foreign penetration of the American government would not be prosecuted. Unfortunately, Reno held up her end of the bargain.[83]

In January 1997, the Panamanian government awarded the contract to operate the Atlantic and Pacific ports of the Panama Canal to a Hong Kong company, Hutchison Whampoa. Six months later, China took control of Hong Kong. The United States, which was set to relinquish control of the canal the following year, did not bother to protest.[84]

In the summer of 1997, Gordon Oehler, the CIA's top proliferation expert, delivered a report to Congress that said: "During the last half of 1996, China was the most significant supplier of weapons of mass destruction-related goods and technology to foreign countries."[85]

Oehler would be proven correct. It was later disclosed that China was exporting WMD technology to Iran, Syria, Libya, Pakistan and North Korea. The White House, amazingly, objected to Oehler's claims. When he returned from vacation in the fall of 1997, Oehler found his authority at the CIA curtailed. He retired soon thereafter.[86]

The timing of Dr. Oehler's problems at the CIA was quite interesting. He departed just as Chinese President Jiang Zemin arrived for the first-ever visit by a Chinese Communist leader. Highlighting the Jiang visit was the announcement that the United States planned to transfer American nuclear technology to China. Obviously, his CIA reports of continuing sales to terrorist countries would not have been welcomed by the visiting Chinese Communist leader.[87]

In September 1997, FBI Director Louis Freeh told DOE officials that the Los Alamos investigation had stalled and, that lacking the evidence to arrest the suspected spy, he should be fired. DOE allowed the suspect to retain his security clearance and sensitive job for over a year after that meeting.[88]

On October 29, 1997, President Clinton stated that he would approve exports to China of advanced U.S. nuclear technology after a written Chinese pledge to forswear new nuclear dealings with Iran was made in a confidential letter to Secretary of State Madeleine K. Albright from Foreign Minister Qian Qichen.[89]

In December 1997, a Taiwanese-born scientist working in a U.S. nuclear weapons lab, Peter Lee, pleaded guilty to giving the Chinese the secrets of a highly specialized laser plasma system used to test nuclear weapons. The system is considered crucial to maintaining the viability of the U.S. nuclear weapons stockpile. Until the invention of the laser system, the U.S. had to actually detonate nuclear weapons from the stockpile to ensure that they worked. "This system gives China the means to test new weapons and to validate their designs, without anyone having a clue to what they are doing," a former U.S. intelligence officer told the *American Spectator*. For his crime, Peter Lee received a minor sentence: He was fined $20,000 and sentenced to twelve months in a halfway house.[90]

On January 15, 1998, after China promised that it would no longer aid Iran's nuclear program, President Clinton certified that China is a reliable partner for nuclear technology exchange.[91] The next month, despite opposition from the Justice Department, President Clinton quietly signs a waiver approving the launch of a Loral satellite from a Chinese rocket and reportedly authorizing the transfer of the same type of missile technology to China that Loral reportedly was being investigated for allegedly illegally transferring in 1996. On April 4, 1998, "officials said the criminal investigation was dealt a serious blow two months ago when President Clinton quietly approved the export to China of similar technology by one of the companies under investigation."[92]

On March 14, 1998, President Clinton announced that, after backing it since the Tiananmen Square massacre, the United States would no longer sponsor a UN resolution denouncing China's human rights practices.[93]

At a May 17, 1998 press conference in Birmingham, England, President Clinton responded in lawyerly language to allegations that Chinese campaign funds affected American foreign policy.[94]

> **REPORTER:** "Mr. President, there's new evidence that the Chinese government funneled money into the American election campaign. Did you or anybody in your administration make decisions based on the influence of Chinese money?"
> **CLINTON:** "No."
> **REPORTER:** "And what do you feel about that evidence?"
> **CLINTON:** "For one thing, first of all, I understand there's a new allegation about that. I have two things to say about it. First of all, all the foreign policy decisions we made were based on what we believed—I and the rest of my administration—were in the interests of the American people. Now, if someone tried to influence them, that's a different issue and there ought to be an investigation into whether that happened. And I would support that. I have always supported that. But I can tell you that the decisions we made, we made because we thought they were in the interests of the American people."[95]

On May 20, 1998, the House voted 412 to 6 to ban missile technology exports to China, 364 to 54 to ban satellite exports to China, and 417 to

4 to condemn Clinton's February 1998 decision to sign a waiver allowing Loral Space & Communications to launch a satellite in China and transfer missile technology to China. White House Counsel Charles F.C. Ruff and White House Press Secretary Michael McCurry both denied that the administration's decision in February to issue the waiver was influenced by campaign donations or that the transfer of satellite technology had compromised national security.[96]

Bill Clinton repeatedly had overruled his security and defense establishments by letting U.S. companies sell sensitive technology to China. Classified reports indicated he compromised Americans' safety in the bargain. As Mr. Clinton's poll numbers slipped, this forced his spinners to resort to their old tricks.[97]

Clinton's handlers claimed that everybody does it. The Clinton White House said the Reagan and Bush administrations also let China get ahold of sensitive technology, and had produced a list of "waivers" in which each president set aside rules prohibiting the sale of products that might permit a potential enemy to acquire the means with which to destroy us.[98]

Here's the difference. The Reagan and Bush White House used a "nine-point template" in assessing technology transfers. If a proposed sale could enhance a country's capabilities in one of the nine specified areas—which included such things as anti-jam capabilities, encryption devices, propulsion systems, radiation protection and pointing accuracy—the administrations would send the application to the State Department for review. State rejected more than two-thirds of all such requests.[99]

Those and other safeguards vanished with the Clintons. The president rejected the advice of the interagency task force and handed final export-decision authority to the Commerce Department, which by statute favored sales over security.[100]

On May 25, 1998, Bernard Schwartz appeared on ABC's *This Week* and denied that contributions he made to the DNC had any connection with a foreign satellite-launch waiver his company received from President Clinton and said any insinuation of a quid pro quo was "just untrue.[101] I have never spoken to the President of the United States about my business," he said. "I never once raised any issue that would be favorable to us, and I have never sought favor nor gotten favor."[102]

On May 29, 1998, the ground shook in a remote region of southwestern Pakistan. The underground nuclear test marked the culmination of a covert weapons development program that had begun in the early 1970s. It was the beginning of a new arms race in Southwest Asia, and it happened only because the Clinton administration chose to ignore China's sales of nuclear weapons technology to Islamabad. Clinton administration policymakers, presented with solid intelligence information of a dangerous sale of nuclear technology, closed their eyes to the evidence and then lied to protect the Chinese from the consequences of blatantly violating the Nuclear Non-Proliferation Treaty, which barred signatories from exporting nuclear weapons-related know-how.[103]

On June 9, 1998, President Clinton denied responsibility that he signed a waiver allowing Loral Space & Communications Systems to export a satellite while the firm was under investigation by the Justice Department for helping China's ballistic missile program. Mr. Clinton said he wasn't warned off the waiver by government agencies. "I took the advice of the National Security Council, the Defense Department, the State Department and the Arms Control and Disarmament Agency," he said. Mr. Clinton also called it a "pretty routine decision." However, the president ignored the advice of the Justice Department, which opposed the waiver.[104]

On June 11, 1998, Gordon Oehler, former director of the CIA's Nonproliferation Center, told the Senate Foreign Relations Committee that administration policy-makers used "almost any measure" to block intelligence judgments confirming that China transferred 34 M-11 missiles to Pakistan in November 1992. These sales automatically required economic sanctions to be imposed under U.S. anti-proliferation laws. The administration used "loopholes" in U.S. law to avoid sanctions by requiring unrealistic standards of proof of the missile transfer, Mr. Oehler said.[105]

When asked on Monday, June 8, 1998, about the presence of the M-11s, State Department spokesman James P. Rubin told reporters: "It is the position of the United States government that we have not determined that Pakistan has received M-11 missiles from China." In addition to ignoring the M-11 transfers, the administration declared that Chinese sales of C-802 cruise missiles to Iran were not "destabilizing" even though the missiles threaten U.S. ships in the Persian Gulf. The declaration avoided mandatory sanctions under U.S. law.[106]

On June 24, 1998, Eric Schmitt of the *New York Times* reported a congressional hearing had revealed China stole a secret circuit board from the crash of an American satellite. "For five hours, American officials said,

Chinese authorities barred them from the crash site, saying it was for their own safety. When the Americans finally reached the area and opened the battered but intact control box of the satellite, a super-secret encoded circuit board was missing."[107]

On June 30, 1998, while visiting China, President Clinton rattled Taiwan with his declaration that the United States opposes Taiwan's quest for greater international recognition. Mr. Clinton's declaration was made at a roundtable discussion. In his talks with Chinese President Jiang Zemin, he said, "I had a chance to reiterate our Taiwan policy, which is that we don't support independence for Taiwan, or two Chinas, or one Taiwan, one China. And we don't believe that Taiwan should be a member in any organization for which statehood is a requirement." This was the first time an American president had openly expressed opposition to Taiwan's efforts to upgrade its standing through membership in international organizations, including the United Nations, and through high-level visits to foreign countries.[108]

Predictably, the administration officials claimed that there was nothing new in what Clinton had said. But no matter how offhandedly or casually his remarks were delivered, Clinton had changed America's diplomatic posture. Richard Halloran, a former *New York Times* reporter, was perhaps the first to note that, "Fundamentally, Mr. Clinton was the first United States president to accept Beijing's concept on the issue of sovereignty over Taiwan, the island nation of 21 million people who consider themselves independent, but that Beijing claims is a province of China."[109] Shortly after Clinton returned to Washington, the Senate, properly alarmed repudiated Clinton's new policy by voting 92 to 0 for a resolution reaffirming support for Taiwan. It was a clear slap at the president.[110]

In July 1998, House Intelligence Committee requests an update on Los Alamos. Notra Trulock forwarded this request to Elizabeth Moler, then acting energy secretary. She reportedly ordered Trulock not to brief the committee for fear that his testimony would be used to attack Clinton's China policy.[111]

On July 1, 1998, China conducted a ground test of its latest ICBM, the DF-31. This came just three days after the Clinton-Jiang summit in Beijing. The DF-31 is a single-warhead missile that could be deployed on a road-mobile launcher, which was powered by solid fuel. It has a range in excess of forty-five hundred miles, making it capable of hitting targets in the

American Midwest. Prior to the test, conducted at the Wuzhai Missile and Space Test Center some 250 miles south of Beijing, the U.S. intelligence community thought it would take China five to ten years to deploy the new missile. Instead it appeared that assistance from U.S. aerospace firms and satellite makers allowed China to "dramatically shorten the timetable," sources familiar with the highly classified intelligence reports said.[112]

In November 1998, the Pentagon detected another alarming development. Chinese military forces conducted a large-scale missile exercise along the Pacific Coast that included mock missile firings against Taiwan. They also, for the first time, demonstrated simulated nuclear missile attacks against the thousands of U.S. troops based in Japan and South Korea. The exercise began in late November 1998 and ended in early December 1998, according to a secret Defense Intelligence Agency report of December 2, 1998. The targeting of U.S. forces had contradicted the pledge made by Chinese President Jiang Zemin only months earlier, during his summit with President Clinton, when he promised that China would not target nuclear missiles at the United States. The CIA had reported earlier in the year that 13 of China's 18 long-range nuclear missiles were targeted on the United States.[113]

Following the revelations of unauthorized transfers of satellite technology to China, the House Select Committee on U.S. National security and Military/Commercial Concerns with the People's Republic of China, chaired by Rep. Christopher Cox (R-Calif.), began an investigation into the matter. On December 31, 1998, the committee unanimously approved its final report, finding that China had acquired more than just our satellite and missile technology. The committee issued a summary of the highlights but agreed not to release the full report until the White House had a chance to review it and comment upon it. After the Cox Committee submitted its report to the Clinton administration, the White House sat on it for some five months while saying it was reviewing it for security purposes.[114]

When the report eventually became public, one item that stood out was the absence of procedures to detect and prevent the movement of sensitive information from secure computers to less secure computers at the nuclear labs. This enabled Wen Ho Lee to download some of our most classified nuclear secrets to a computer that was not secure.

So who is Wen Ho Lee? In 1982, the FBI had information suggesting that Dr. Lee had contacted a suspected spy. Given that Lee was a mechanical engineer helping to develop nuclear bombs at the Los Alamos National Laboratory in New Mexico, that information alone was alarming, but it was only the beginning of the trail. Later, the FBI learned that Lee, who was Chinese born, had failed to report a possible relationship with a key figure in China's nuclear program.[115] The *New York Times* reported that Lee began downloading classified files into his unclassified computer in 1983, but that most of the files had been downloaded in 1994 and 1995. According to a special intelligence report delivered to President Clinton in November 1998, the Energy Department had recorded 324 attacks on the unclassified computer system in Los Alamos between October 1997 and June 1998. Unfortunately, Attorney General Janet Reno let stand a decision originally made by the Justice Department's Office of Intelligence Policy and Review (OIPR), and affirmed by Deputy Attorney General Eric Holder, in August 1997, that denied the FBI permission to apply to a special federal court for a warrant to monitor the computer and tap the phones of Wen Ho Lee. This fell under the 1978 federal statute known as the Foreign Intelligence Surveillance Act (FISA).[116]

If Justice had approved the FBI's application—and if that application had been approved by the court—the FBI would have found on Lee's computer more than one thousand of the most highly classified files on this nation's nuclear arsenal. It also means the FBI would have found them in a period just before more than three hundred individuals or foreign governments broke into that computer system and were in position to steal the files Lee had deposited there.[117]

In 1998, he told the FBI that he also had been approached by nuclear scientists from China. Furthermore, he had gone to extraordinary lengths to download, copy, and remove materials from a secure national laboratory: forty hours of work stretching over seventy days. Even after Lee's security clearances were stripped at Los Alamos, he made attempts to reenter the weapons design area, including one try at 3:30 a.m. on Christmas Eve of 1998.[118]

On March 8, 1999, after the Los Alamos espionage story borke in the *New York Times*, Energy Department fires Wen Ho Lee. A fifty-nine-count indictment was eventually returned against Lee, and at the FBI's urging, he was held nine months in solitary confinement due to the odds of Lee trying to flee to China.[119]

Lee admitted in 1993, 1994 and 1997, he erased classified markings on documents, which were then shifted from secure computers to open, accessible computers, where the information was then copied onto ten portable computer tapes, seven of which were still missing. Altogether, he copied nearly four hundred computer files, the equivalent of four hundred thousand pages of data, including the mathematical approximation of the designs of nuclear weapons, their exact dimensions, information about testing problems, actual and simulated testing results and computer programs required to design and test weapons. It is also worth noting that China has a long history of using Chinese-Americans, including emigres from Taiwan such as Lee, as spies.[120]

On September 11, 2000, Wen Ho Lee pled guilty on one felony count of unlawfully retaining nuclear-weapon secrets, be sentenced to time already served (nine months). He also agreed to cooperate with federal investigators concerning the seven missing computer tapes with data on nuclear-weapons design and testing.[121]

On March 17, 1999, the Senate voted 97 to 3 to approve a national missile defense system. Interestingly, it was the same bill that Senate Democrats had filibustered twice during the 105th Congress. The next day, the House voted 317 to 105 to approve a national missile defense system. "Even though I have opposed it in the past, I will vote for a missile defense system today," said Rep. Jim Traficant (D.-Ohio). "The first reason is the Russian spy who defected to America, warned us that China is determined to destroy America. Since then, China has stolen our military secrets and China has missiles aimed at America. . . . North Korea has missiles that could reach America. . . . But the main reason for my vote here today is very simple: our misdirected foreign policy."[122]

On March 19, 1999, in his first press conference since early 1998, President Clinton said no one had informed him of any Chinese espionage at U.S. energy labs, such as the one at Los Alamos, that had occurred during his administration—at least as far as he could remember: "To the best of my knowledge, no one has said anything to me about any espionage which occurred by the Chinese against the labs during my presidency," said Clinton. Further, "if I have misstated this in any way because I don't remember something, then I will tell you that. But I don't believe that I have forgotten."[123]

On April 12, 1999, Notra Trulock, a career public servant who was in charge of counterintelligence for the Energy Department from 1994-1998, testified before the Senate Armed Services Committee that the Clinton administration actively sought to prevent Congress from learning about Chinese espionage at U.S. weapons labs in order to protect Clinton's policy of engagement with China. His immediate target was Elizabeth Moler, a longtime Democratic staffer on the Senate Energy Committee, whom President Clinton appointed deputy energy secretary and later made acting secretary of energy.[124]

> * In the years before Moler began overseeing security, Trulock had briefed Congress regularly. In the summer of 1996, for example, his DOE counterintelligence shop briefed the House and Senate about some of the espionage it was beginning to uncover. After Moler took charge, DOE counterintelligence didn't brief the Congress about the problems at the labs until the select House committee on Red Chinese activities headed by Rep. Chris Cox (R.-Calif.) began probing that specific question.
> * In his sworn testimony, Trulock said he tried several times to get approval from Moler to brief congressional intelligence committee members and staff about Chinese penetration of the lab. Finally, he says, he confronted Moler and told her that Congress had to be told. He says she told him to keep quiet about the investigation because members of the House Intelligence Committee were interested only in embarrassing Clinton and his policy of engagement with China.
> * Beginning in 1997, Trulock's, direct supervisors began urging him to hush up the espionage case that came to be code-named "Kindred Spirit." Trulock says he began to experience a pattern of "harassment, intimidation and retaliation" from his superiors because of his zeal in trying to inform Congress about problems at the labs.
> * In May 1998, after making a third trip to the DOE inspector general to report flack from his superiors, Trulock was demoted and was being forced to "compete" for the position of deputy director of counterintelligence.
> * On July 21, 1998, Trulock documented these requests in a memo to Moler, then acting secretary. Trulock recommended that Rep. Porter Goss (R.-Fla), chairman of the House Intelligence Committee and the Senate Intelligence Committee be given a briefing on the "Kindred Spirit" investigation.

* Trulock's deputy hand-carried the memo to Moler's deputy, Paul Richenback. A week later at a meeting, Trulock huddled with Moler and Richenback to discuss the classified briefing. He said Moler denied the briefing. "I can only tell you that Secretary Moler told me that she believed that they—and by 'they' I believe she was referring to the House Permanent Select Committee on Intelligence—were only interested in harming the President on China policy," he said.
* "The original of this memo was subsequently found in Deputy Secretary Moler's personal two-drawer office safe after she left the department, and was returned to us by the department's executive secretariat with a notation to the effect that no action had been taken on the memo," said Trulock.
* When the committee questioned her about the tell-tale memo, Moler followed what has become a familiar pattern in the Clinton administration. She said she couldn't remember. Why was the document found in your safe? She was asked. "I have no knowledge of having received this document. I have no knowledge of it having been in my safe when I left the department," she said.
* Moler's aide Richenback echoed his boss's story. He was listed as having been carbon-copied on the "Kindred Spirit" memo. Had he seen it? Asked Sen. Carl Levin (D.-Mich). "I have no recollection of ever receiving or seeing that document until recently."[125]

On May 23, 1999, Tim Russert of NBC's *Meet the Press* ripped apart President Clinton's claim on March 19, 1999, that "no one has reported to me that they suspect" espionage had occurred at America's national laboratories. Enclosed is the transcript with Russert, Notra Trulock, head of intelligence at the Energy Department, and Rep. Chris Cox (R-CA), chairman of the select committee that investigated the espionage:[126]

> **Tim Russert:** "Do you have any doubt that there has been Chinese espionage at our nuclear labs?"
> **Notra Trulock:** "I am convinced there has been Chinese nuclear espionage at our laboratories, yes sir."
> **Russert:** "Congressman Chris Cox . . . are you convinced that there has been Chinese espionage at our nuclear labs?"
> **Chris Cox:** "Indeed, that is one of the principal findings of the select committee's bipartisan and unanimous report. That espionage didn't

begin last week either. It has been occurring now for some decades. But importantly, it continues, we state in our report, to this very day. . . . We presented that report on January 3rd [1999] to the president."
Russert: "Mr. Trulock, let me help the public here and clear up some details on the chronology. In April of 1996, you briefed National Security Adviser to the President Sandy Berger."
Trulock: "Yes, I did."
Russert: "In March of this year [1999], on this program, he talked about that briefing. He said it was very general. Was it general or specific?"
Trulock: "I attempted to communicate to him as explicitly as I could the findings of our efforts to date, which I have mentioned to you already—the fact of the espionage, the scope, and magnitude of the problem at that time, and the fact that we had also identified a number of suspects."
Russert: "He then said that he briefed the President after that April '96 briefing from you."
Russert: "You again briefed National Security Adviser Berger in July of '97."
Trulock: "That's correct."
Russert: "So Mr. Berger on this program you acknowledged he was briefed by you in April of '96 and then briefed the president. He was briefed by you in July of '97 and briefed the president. And in January of this year [1999], you sent a report to the White House outlining your findings."

Let me put on the screen what the president of the United States said in March of this year [1999]. Question: "Can you assure the American people that under your watch, no valuable nuclear secrets were lost?" President Clinton: "Can I tell you there has been no espionage at the labs since I've been president? I can tell you that no one has reported to me that they suspect such a thing has occurred."

Later in the press conference, "To the best of my knowledge, no one has said anything to me about any espionage which occurred by the Chinese against the labs during my presidency."

Mr. Cox, that would suggest that Mr. Berger did not speak to the president ever in '96, '97 or '98, or the president never saw the report you sent him in January?

Cox: "Well, I would be very concerned if the latter were the case . . ."[127]

Two days later, on May 25, 1999, the Cox Report was released and listed the following concerns:

1. The People's Republic of China (PRC) has stolen classified design information on the United States' most advanced thermonuclear weapons.

* The stolen information includes classified information on seven U.S. thermonuclear warheads, including every currently deployed thermonuclear warhead in the U.S. ballistic missile arsenal.

* The stolen information also includes classified design information for an enhanced radiation weapon (commonly known as the "neutron bomb"), which neither the United States, nor any other nation, has yet deployed.

* The PRC has obtained classified information on the following U.S. thermonuclear warheads, as well as a number of associated reentry vehicles (the hardened shell that protects the thermonuclear warhead during reentry).

* In addition, in the mid-1990s, the PRC stole from a U.S. national weapons laboratory, classified thermonuclear weapons information that cannot be identified in this unclassified Report.

* The W-88, a miniaturized, tapered warhead, is the most sophisticated nuclear weapon the United States has ever built. In the U.S. arsenal, it is mated to the D-5 submarine-launched ballistic missile carried aboard the Trident nuclear submarine. The United States learned about the theft of the W-88 Trident D-5 warhead information, as well as about the theft of information regarding several other nuclear weapons, in 1995.

2. The PRC has stolen U.S. design information and other classified information for neutron warheads.

* The PRC stole classified U.S. information about the neutron bomb from a U.S. national weapons laboratory. The U.S. learned of the theft of this classified information on the neutron bomb in 1996.

* The PRC acquired this and other classified U.S. nuclear weapons information as the result of a 20-year intelligence collection program to develop modern thermonuclear weapons, continuing to this very day, that includes espionage, review of unclassified publications, and extensive interactions with scientists from the Department of Energy's national weapons laboratories.

* The Select Committee has found that the primary focus of this long-term, ongoing PRC intelligence collection effort has been on the following national weapons laboratories:
  - Los Alamos
  - Lawrence Livermore
  - Oak Ridge
  - Sandia

3. The Select Committee judges that the PRC will exploit elements of the stolen design information on the PRC's next generation of thermonuclear weapons.

* The PRC plans to supplement its silo-based CSS-4 ICBMs targeted on U.S. cities with mobile ICBMs, which are more survivable because they are more difficult to find than silo-based missiles.

* The PRC has three mobile ICBM programs currently underway—two road-mobile and one submarine-launched program—all of which will be able to strike the United States. The first of these new People's Liberation Army (PLA) mobile ICBMs, the DF-31, may be tested in 1999, and could be deployed as soon as 2002.

* The United States did become fully aware of the magnitude of the counterintelligence problem at the Department of Energy national weapons laboratories until 1995. In 1995, the United States received a classified PRC document from a PRC national. This individual approached the CIA outside the PRC and turned over a number of documents. The PRC document included, among other matters, stolen U.S. design information on the W-88 thermonuclear warhead used on the Trident D-5 missile, as well as U.S. technological information on half a dozen other U.S. thermonuclear warheads and associated reentry vehicles.

* Currently deployed PRC ICBMs targeted on U.S. cities are based on 1950s-era nuclear weapons designs. With the stolen U.S.

technology, the PRC has leaped, in a handful of years, from 1950s-era strategic nuclear capabilities to the more modern thermonuclear weapons designs. These modern thermonuclear weapons took the United States decades of effort, hundreds of millions of dollars, and numerous nuclear tests to achieve.

4. The Select Committee judges that elements of the stolen information on U.S. thermonuclear warhead designs will assist the PRC in building its next generation of mobile ICBMs, which may be tested this year.

* The stolen U.S. design information will assist the PRC in building smaller nuclear warheads—vital to the success of the PRC's ongoing efforts to develop survivable, mobile missiles. Current PRC ICBMs, which are silo-based, are more vulnerable to attack than mobile missiles.

5. The Select Committee judges that, if the PRC, were successful in stealing nuclear test codes, computer models, and data from the United States, it could further accelerate its nuclear development.

* By using such stolen codes and data in conjunction with High Performance Computers (HPCs) already acquired by the PRC, the PRC could diminish its need for further nuclear testing to evaluate weapons and proposed design changes.

* The possession of the stolen U.S. test data could greatly reduce the level of HPC performance required for such leaks. For these reasons, the Select Committee judges that the PRC has and will continue to aggressively target for theft our nuclear test codes, computer models, and data.

6. In the near term, a PRC deployment of mobile thermonuclear weapons, or neutron bombs, based on stolen U.S. design information, could have a significant effect on the regional balance of power, particularly with respect to Taiwan.

* PRC deployments of advanced nuclear weapons based on stolen U.S. design information would pose greater risks to U.S. troops and interests in Asia and the Pacific. In addition, the PRC's theft of information on our most modern nuclear weapons designs enables the PRC to deploy modern forces much sooner than would otherwise be possible.

* At the beginning of the 1990s, the PRC had only one or two silo-based ICBMs capable of attacking the United States. Since then, the PRC has developed up to two dozen additional silo-based ICBMs capable of attacking the United States; has upgraded its silo-based missiles; and has continued development of three mobile ICBM systems and associated modern thermonuclear warheads.

* If the PRC is successful in developing modern nuclear forces, as seems likely, and chooses to deploy them in sufficient numbers, then the long-term balance of nuclear forces with the United States could be adversely affected.

7. Counterintelligence programs at the national weapons laboratories today fail to meet even minimum standards.

* Repeated efforts since the early 1980s have failed to solve the counterintelligence deficiencies at the National Laboratories. While one of the Laboratories had adopted better counterintelligence practices than the others, all remain inadequate.

* Even though the United States discovered in 1995 and the PRC had stolen design information on the W-88 Trident D-5 warhead and technical information on a number of other U.S. thermonuclear warheads, the White House has informed the Select Committee, in responsive to specific interrogatories propounded by the Committee, that the President was not briefed about the counterintelligence failures until early 1998.

8. In the late 1990s, the PRC stole or illegally obtained U.S. developmental and research technology that, if taken to successful conclusion, could be used to attack U.S. satellites and submarines.

* During the late 1990s, U.S. research and developmental work on electromagnetic weapons technology has been illegally obtained by the PRC as a result of successful espionage directed against the United States. Such technology, once developed, can be used for space-based weapons to attack satellites and missiles.

* In 1997, the PRC stole classified U.S. developmental research concerning very sensitive detection techniques that, if successfully concluded, could be used to threaten U.S. submarines.

9. In the aftermath of three failed satellite launches since 1992, U.S. satellite manufacturers transferred missile design information and know-how to the PRC without obtaining the legally required licenses. This information has improved the reliability of PRC rockets useful for civilian and military purposes. The illegally transmitted information is useful for the design and improved reliability of future PRC ballistic missiles, as well.

* In 1993 and 1995, Hughes showed the PRC how to improve the design and reliability of PRC rockets. Hughes' advice may also be useful for design and improved reliability of future PRC ballistic missiles. Hughes deliberately acted without seeking to obtain the legally required licenses.

* In 1996, Loral and Hughes showed the PRC how to improve the design and reliability of the guidance system used in the PRC's newest Long March rocket. Loral's and Hughes' advice may also be useful for design and improved reliability of elements of future PRC ballistic missiles. Loral and Hughes acted without the legally required license, although both corporations knew that a license was required.

* Loral and Hughes provided valuable additional information that exposed the PRC to Western diagnostic processes that could lead to improvements in the reliability of all PRC ballistic missiles.

10. The PRC requires high performance computers (HPCs) for the design, modeling, testing, and maintenance of advanced nuclear weapons based on the nuclear weapons design information stolen from the United States. The United States relaxed restrictions on HPC sales in 1996; and the United States has no effective way to verify that HPC purchases reportedly made for commercial purposes are not diverted to military uses. The Select Committee judges that the PRC has in fact used HPCs to perform nuclear weapons applications.[128]

Other points in the Cox Report included:

* Virtually no domestic supercomputer industry existed in the PRC, and that the PRC had almost no supercomputers as of 1996. But the Clinton administration changed the export control regulations in January 1996—at the beginning of the 1996 presidential

campaign—and by the end of 1998, the PRC had more than six hundred American supercomputers.[129]

* There were seventeen significant major technology breaches.
* Sixteen of the seventeen most significant major technology breaches were discovered after 1994—more than two years after Clinton took office. With the lone exception of the breach of the initial design information of the W-70 warhead (the so-called neutron bomb)—which was discovered during the Carter administration—everything else was first discovered during the Clinton administration.
* Of the sixteen technology breaches discovered during the Clinton years, only one definitely occurred during the Reagan administration: the theft of the design for the W-88 Trident D-5 warhead.
* Seven other breaches occurred at some undetermined date before 1995.[130]

These are the eight security breaches that we know with certainty happened during Clinton's watch:
1. The transfer of the so-called Legacy Codes containing data on fifty years of U.S. nuclear weapons development including over one thousand nuclear tests;
2. The sale and diversion to military purposes of hundreds of high-performance computers enabling China to enhance its development of nuclear weapons, ballistic missiles, and advanced military aviation equipment;
3. The theft of nuclear warhead simulation technology enhancing China's ability to perfect miniature nuclear warheads without actual testing;
4. The theft of advanced electromagnetic weapons technology useful in the development of anti-satellite and anti-missile systems;
5. The transfer of missile nose cone technology enabling China to substantially improve the reliability of its intercontinental ballistic missiles;
6. The transfer of missile guidance technology (by President Clinton to China) enabling China to substantially improve the accuracy of its ballistic missiles—these same missiles that are targeting U.S. cities;

7. The theft of space-based radar technology giving China the ability to detect our previously undetectable submerged submarines; and
8. The theft of some other "classified thermonuclear weapons information" which "the Clinton administration" (not the Cox committee) "has determined cannot be made public."[131]

On May 26, 1999, then-Secretary of Energy Bill Richardson was quoted in *USA Today*: "Americans can be reassured our nation's nuclear secrets are today safe and secure." The following events occurred at the Los Alamos lab after his quote:

* In early January 2000, hard drives containing information on U.S. and nuclear bombs last officially seen.

* On March 28, 2000, hard drives reportedly disappeared on or around this date.

* On May 7, 2000, Los Alamos workers notice hard drives are missing.

* On May 11, 2000, fires sweep through area around Los Alamos. Bill Richardson declares, "All our nuclear materials are safe."

* On June 1, 2000, Department of Energy learns of missing hard drives.

* On June 13, 2000, hard drives discovered behind copy machine.

* On June 14, 2000, Bill Richardson attends National Press Club function, leaving a seat empty in the Senate Intelligence Committee. Chairman Richard Shelby (R.-Ala.) says: "Perhaps if the secretary would spend more time ensuring the safety of our nation's nuclear treasures and less time trying to get the Vice President elected President, we would not be here today."[132]

So where do we go from here. According to reporter and author Bill Gertz: "America must treat China as a rival for power and not as a strategic partner. Dismissing current and future threats posed by China is dangerous and could lead to devastating miscalculation and war. The 1995 threat by Communist Chinese General Xiong Guangkai to use nuclear weapons against Los Angeles if the United States came to the military defense of Taiwan should be taken as a clear warning of things to come."[133]

CHAPTER 31

TERRORISM

*When people see a weak horse and a strong horse,
by nature they will like the strong horse.*

—Osama bin Laden

YEMEN 1992

Osama bin Laden's first strike against Americans began in the port city of Aden, Yemen. This largely unknown attack was the start of a deadly pattern. President-elect William Jefferson Clinton's first face-off with bin Laden was December 29, 1992.[1]

Bin Laden's men had trained and fought together in Afghanistan. Their targets were two skyscrapers at opposite ends of the harbor, the Goldmore and Aden Hotels. Not only were they the only international five-star hotels in the city, these hotels were temporary homes to almost one hundred U.S. Marines.[2] The terrorists detonated bombs in both hotels, killing three and wounding five. In addition, a strike team carrying RPG-7 rocket launchers was caught near the fences of the Aden airport getting ready to launch at U.S. Air Force transport planes.[3]

The hunt for the terrorists was on, at least on the Yemeni side. A few days after the attack, Yemen's Ministry of Interior publicly blamed "hirelings of foreign elements." But in private, they knew who was responsible. The Ministry of Interior, which supervises Yemen's police and intelligence services, contacted Interpol, an international body that coordinates efforts to capture trans-national criminals and terrorists. Yemen wanted help tracking down Osama bin Laden.[4]

Unfortunately, over the next few weeks and months, no assistance ever came from the Clinton administration. If Clinton had decided to assist Yemen's efforts to arrest those responsible for the attack, bin Laden might have been stopped years before September 11, 2001. And thousands of lives could have been saved.[5]

The terrorists had failed to kill or wound a single American. It was not a miscalculation that bin Laden would make again.[6]

In the end, bin Laden won anyway. Within hours of the blasts, all American military personnel were immediately evacuated from Aden. By midnight, most Americans had been airlifted out. A spokesman for the U.S. Naval Forces Central Command told the Associated Press that the evacuation was ordered "because of concern about the security situation." Not only was this a victory for bin Laden, but his allies also took note of how he handled the situation as well as his use of his own personal assets to get the job done.[7]

Since the attack occurred towards the end of the Bush administration, some would say that Bush should have responded. Usually, outgoing administrations will brief incoming ones extensively and defer to the incoming administration before taking any action. Since it is a tradition of presidential courtesy, ultimately, the decision was Clinton's not Bush's. [8]

WORLD TRADE CENTER 1993

On Friday morning, February 26, 1993, Mohammed Salameh drove a rented yellow one-ton Ford F-350 Econoline van through the Holland Tunnel toward lower Manhattan. Behind the seat was fifteen hundred pounds of ammonium nitrate, three tanks of hydrogen gas, four cylinders of nitroglycerin, blasting caps, and four twenty-foot long fuses. The first foreign terrorist attack on American soil was about to occur.[9]

Besides Salameh, the plot involved the leader of their cell, master bomb maker Rashid the Iraqi. Investigators later called him Ramzi Yousef. Mahmud Abouhalima followed behind in the getaway car, a blue Lincoln Town Car sedan.[10]

The bomb detonated in the van parked on the second level of the World Trade Center parking basement. The explosion radiated outward from the south wall of Trade Tower Number One, displacing an estimated sixty-eight hundred tons of material. Despite having occurred in an area of the building made of steel-reinforced concrete, twelve to fourteen inches thick, the blast left a crater 150 feet in diameter and five floors deep.[11]

Six people died and 1,042 were injured. Fifty thousand people had to be evacuated from the surrounding area and it took 750 firefighters an entire month to get the damage under control. According to U.S. District Court Judge Kevin Duffy, who would later preside over the trial of the terrorists responsible, the explosion caused "more hospital casualties than any other event in domestic American history other than the Civil War."[12]

Once the investigation began, inspectors realized that both the World Trade Center buildings and the nearby Vista Hotel were in danger. The hotel might have collapsed within days had steel supports not been carefully placed to reinforce the structure. The structure of Trade Tower Number One was also undergirded with steel supports as well.[13]

New York Governor Mario Cuomo telephoned President Clinton while the Twin Towers were still being evacuated. Cuomo told Clinton that a bomb had most likely caused the World Trade Center blast. Clinton, though, considered that pure "speculation." After discussing the situation with his aides, Clinton asked his press secretary to put out the cautious line that the New York authorities "have reason to believe it was a bomb but are not definite." This allowed Clinton time to decide how and whether to act.[14]

Clinton decided to take the politically safe path by treating the bombing as a criminal matter rather than the terrorist attack that it really was. As a result, he shut the CIA out of the investigation. Administration blundering enabled Khalid Shaikh Mohammed, a top bin Laden aide who eight years later would coordinate the September 11 attacks, escape capture in Qatar.[15] By downplaying the national importance of the bombing, it appeared that Clinton was incapable of dealing with terrorism, so he tried to keep Americans from focusing on it. After the February 26, 1993, bombing of the World Trade Center, President Clinton never visited the site and only alluded to it once in his regular Saturday radio address right after the bombing. Visiting New Jersey shortly after the attack, he urged Americans not to "overreact."[16]

Columnist Andrew Sullivan best summarized the Clinton administration nonresponse:

"Did the Clinton administration overhaul its intelligence and defense priorities in response to the 1993 warning? No. No effort was made to coordinate the mess of agencies designed to counter terrorism—the FBI, the CIA, the Pentagon, the State Department, the airlines, local law enforcement, and the Coast Guard. No effort was made to recruit more spies who would speak Arabic or go undercover to pre-empt such attacks." Mr. Sullivan also quotes Clinton aide George Stephanopoulos as saying that the Clinton administration ignored the implications of the WTC attack because "it wasn't a successful bombing."[17]

SOMALIA

Though information of bin Laden operations in Somalia is limited, numerous interviews with American, Sudanese, and other intelligence sources reveal the details of bin Laden's combat with American forces. Author Richard Miniter independently translated Sudanese intelligence documents on a 2002 visit to Khartoum that reveal bin Laden's second plot to kill American soldiers. (The first was in Aden, Yemen in December 1992.)[18]

The Somalia operation began when bin Laden met with a man variously known as Mohammed Atef and Abu Hafs al Masry, known to his terrorist comrades as "the commander."[19] Bin Laden dispatched Atef to Somalia on a scouting mission sometime in early 1993, according to a Sudanese intelligence source. There he observed U.S. military operations and met with local members of Al Itihaad al Islamiya. Through that terrorist network, Atef met with several Somali warlords, including Mohammed Farrah Aideed. Aideed would emerge as a major nemesis of the United States.[20]

Atef was an Egyptian who had fought in Afghanistan in the 1980s and had co-founded al Qaeda. By 1993, he was the head of the military committee of bin Laden's organization, and he became one of bin Laden's most-trusted subordinates. Atef was designated to be bin Laden's successor, in the event of his death or capture.[21]

Shortly after Atef's first expedition to Somalia, bin Laden began to supply arms and training for the Somali warlord Aideed. Bin Laden sent a team of bomb makers and guerilla-warfare specialists to help the Somali warlord.[22] The team was led by Mohammed Ibrahim Makawi. Also known as Saif al-Adl al-Maduni, Makawi was another veteran of the Afghan war and longtime bin Laden associate. A former Egyptian army officer, Makawi was also linked to Zawahiri's Egyptian Islamic Jihad. This suggested that the operational coordination between the two terror groups, al Qaeda and Egyptian Islamic Jihad, is much older and much closer than what had been previously reported.[23]

Sudanese intelligence, which observed Makawi talking with bin Laden on several occasions, believes that he was designated to be Atef's successor. In his trips to Somalia, Makawi would transit through Nairobi, using a Yemeni passport. Most interestingly, he is believed to have been in Aden during the bombing of hotels frequented by U.S. troops in December 1992. He may, in fact, have been the operation's field commander.[24]

In mid-1993, with the escalation in Mogadishu looming, bin Laden moved a total of three thousand Yemeni "Afghans," their weapons—which included high explosives, sophisticated remote-control bombs, booby-trapped dolls, and a few Stingers—plus their terrorist equipment from Yemen to Somalia in a quick airlift. He would later tell an Egyptian interviewer that this operation cost him $3 million of his own money.[25]

President Bush had already concluded the American mission in Somalia when Bill Clinton gave some of the best troops in the United States Army a new mission—without proper support. The result was tragic: Mohammed Farah Aideed's militiamen, who were trained by al Qaeda, killed eighteen American soldiers and dragged their bodies through the streets of Mogadishu. Another seventy-three were injured. Mr. Clinton's response was to end the U.S.-led humanitarian mission to Somalia and send diplomat Robert Oakley to negotiate surrender terms.[26]

Osama bin Laden saw the Somalia disaster for what it was. As with the Aden bombing ten months earlier, bin Laden's "holy warriors" had driven the world's sole superpower from a poor, Muslim land with a single night of attacks. The outcome of the battle would only confirm his view that Allah had granted him a triumph. He called Somalia his "greatest victory."[27]

Bin Laden was still exultant and confident in his vision of American weakness when he sat for an interview with an ABC News camera crew five years later, on May 28, 1998:[28]

> It cleared from Muslim minds the myth of superpowers. After leaving Afghanistan, the Muslim fighters headed for Somalia and prepared for a long battle, thinking that the Americans were like the Russians. The youth were surprised at the low morale of the American soldiers and realized more than before that the American soldier was a paper tiger and after a few blows ran in defeat.[29]

He plainly saw Clinton as a weak giant, and America as more feckless and less fearsome than the old Soviet Union. This is what bin Laden learned from Clinton's strategy of carefully calibrated attacks followed by rapid retreats.[30]

MANILA 1995

At about 10:30 p.m. on January 6, 1995, a security guard at the Dona Josefa apartment building in Manila was told that black smoke was billowing from the building. He ran upstairs and saw two men trying to wave the smoke out of the sixth-floor hallway.[31]

"Don't worry," one of them told the security guard, "it was just some firecrackers."[32]

The guard entered Apartment 603 and saw the fire expiring. When he went outside, both men were gone. A team of firemen soon arrived, followed by officers from the Philippine National Police. Leading the police was Aida Farsical, police block commander responsible for that part of Manila. The police found pipe bombs and components—including chemicals and laboratory equipment—for making explosives.[33]

While the police were looking through the apartment, one of the tenants returned. He was Abdul Hakim Murad, a Pakistani national, member of a secret cell of terrorists belonging to al Qaeda, and the mixer of the chemicals. Murad offered the police two thousand dollars in cash not to take him to police headquarters, but the police turned him down.[34]

By 2:30 a.m., senior Philippine police officials were on the scene. Chief Inspector Nap Taas, who was in charge of intelligence for the police, confiscated a Toshiba computer. It held an amazing series of documents. One document revealed that the International Relations and Information Center, a nongovernmental organization operating in the Philippines, was a front to fund al Qaeda activities. Its leader was Mohammed Jamal Khalifa, a Filipino Muslim and brother-in-law of Osama bin Laden.[35]

More shocking was a document that outlined a plot to assassinate Pope John Paul II during his visit to the Philippines, a visit that was only a week away. Murad's apartment was two hundred yards from the residence of the Vatican's ambassador to the Philippines, which was where the pope would be staying. The terrorists planned a suicide mission, dressing one of their number as a priest and getting close enough to the pope to set off a homemade chemical bomb that would kill the disguised terrorist and the Pope.[36]

Murad's roommate turned out to be Ramzi Yousef, the mastermind behind the 1993 terrorist bombing of the World Trade Center. Yousef walked away from the apartment before police could arrest him, but was apprehended in Pakistan on February 7, 1995, and a day later shipped to the United States to stand trial on charges related to the 1993 bombing.[37]

The police used a Philippine computer expert to crack the coded information found on Yousef's computer hard drives. "This is where we found most of the evidence of the projects that were being funded by Osama bin Laden in the Philippines," Garcia said.[38]

Another plot revealed on the computer was a major terrorist campaign against U.S. airliners. It was called Project Bojinka.[39]

PROJECT BOJINKA

Bojinka means "loud bang" in Serbo-Croatian. Project Bojinka was plot to detonate small explosive devices aboard eleven U.S. airliners flying from Asia to the United States. Yousef had designed small bombs operated by nine-volt batteries. The batteries were to be concealed in the hallowed-out heels of a terrorist's shoes. The bomb itself was designed to pass undetected through airport screening machines. The plan was for eleven airliners to explode simultaneously after the terrorists changed shoes during stopovers and left the bomb shoes beneath their seats. It was to have been Ramzi Yousef's terrorist spectacular.[40]

Yousef carried out several attacks in 1994. The deadliest was a bomb planted on Philippine Airlines (PAL) Boeing 747 flying from Cebu to Narita, Tokyo, on December 11, 1994. Traveling with fake Italian documents, Yousef personally planted the bomb onboard before disembarking safely at a stopover in Manila. The bomb exploded above Okinawa, which killed a Japanese passenger, but the aircraft was not destroyed because it was too low and the bomb was too small. The jet managed to successfully land on Okinawa.[41]

According to Lt. Col. Robert "Buzz" Patterson the Clinton administration

> knew that terrorists were plotting to use commercial airliners as weapons. The president received a Presidential Daily Brief, or PDB,

every morning. It was a document encased in a smart leather folder, and emblazoned with the presidential seal, that contained the president's daily intelligence update from the NSC. A senior NSC representative normally delivered it to the president. On weekends, at Camp David, and on vacations, the military aide was responsible for delivering and retrieving the brief.[42]

On a Saturday in the last summer of 1996, the president asked Patterson to pick up some PDBs that had accumulated in the Oval Office. "He gave them to me with handwritten notes stuffed inside the folders," Patterson said "and asked that I deliver them back to the NSC. I opened the PDB to rearrange the notes and noticed the heading 'Operation Bojinka.' I keyed on a reference to a plot to use commercial airliners as weapons and another plot to put bombs on U.S. airliners. Because I was a pilot, this naturally grabbed my attention. I can state for a fact that this information was circulated within the U.S. intelligence community, and that in late 1996 the president was aware of it."[43]

U.S. CONSULATE WORKERS KILLED IN PAKISTAN

On March 8, 1995, two U.S. consulate workers were killed in Karachi, Pakistan. Their van, with diplomatic license plates, was sprayed with bullets from men armed with AK-47 assault rifles. Speculation pointed to retaliation for the arrest and extradition of Ramzi Yousef. Pakistani Prime Minister Benazir Bhutto called it "part of a well-planned campaign of terror." President Clinton called the attack a "cowardly act" and sent an FBI team to Pakistan to investigate. Again, the administration chose to treat the latest act of terrorism as a law enforcement issue.[44]

U.S. MILITARY TRAINING CENTER IN SAUDI ARABIA

On November 13, 1995, dozens of Americans were eating lunch in the snack bar at the Military Cooperation Program building in Riyadh, a military training center run by the United States for the Saudi National Guard. At approximately 11:40 a.m., a car bomb exploded in the parking lot in front of the three-story building. The explosion blew off one side of the building, destroyed more than forty-five cars, and shattered windows more than a mile away. After a few minutes, a secondary antipersonnel bomb exploded in the parking lot, inflicting additional casualties among the people rushing to help those injured in the first explosion.[45]

Six people died from the two bombs, five of them Americans. More than sixty people were wounded, more than half of them Americans, some critically. The main bomb, which had been installed in a white van, was constructed of between 200 and 225 pounds of most likely high explosive SEMTEX. The Mitsubishi 81 van was professionally "cleaned," with all serial and identification numbers thoroughly erased, even from the chassis. The bomb was activated by a sophisticated timing device with a possible remote-control back-up system. The second antipersonnel bomb was also expertly constructed, placed, and timed to cause maximum casualties despite its small size.[46]

The National Security Agency uses intelligence satellites to intercept virtually any wireless phone call on earth. Less than an hour before the blast in Saudi Arabia, bin Laden had given his final approval by satellite telephone. The call had come from his modest farm, some twenty miles south of Khartoum.

Later that day the NSA intercepted an ominous call to bin Laden.[47] When bin Laden came on the line, the caller gave what seemed to be pre-arranged coded reference to a forthcoming attack. Bin Laden became emotional, implored God to bless the caller, and declared, "This is not the first or the last. The rain starts with one drop and it soon becomes a downpour. Things will be ready."[48]

Over the next few days, the Clinton administration learned that the Riyadh bombing was the work of Osama bin Laden. The satellite evidence was overwhelming. The pattern was clear. Bin Laden had declared war on the United States in December 1992. He had ordered the bombing of hotels housing American troops in Aden, financed the 1993 World Trade Center bombing, underwritten savage attacks in Mogadishu in the summer and fall of 1993, and authorized Project Bojinka in 1994. Ramzi Yousef worked for him, and with the U.S. presidential campaign heating up, bin Laden had murdered Americans in Saudi Arabia.[49]

President Clinton reacted angrily to the news. He promised that the United States would "devote an enormous effort" to bring the attackers to justice. The FBI sent a team of agents to investigate, but the agents soon became bogged down to Saudi bureaucracy. The Saudis eventually arrested four militants and beheaded them before the FBI could interrogate them.[50]

SUDAN

Trusting Sudan to watch or imprison bin Laden didn't seem plausible. Osama bin Laden enjoyed friendly relations with scores of senior Sudanese officials. Those friendly relations started to change in 1996 when Sudan's strategic planners, which included Minister of Information Ghazzi Selehedin Attaboni and then-Foreign Minister Ali Osman Mohammed Taha, put into action a plan to overthrow their onetime mentor, Sudan's speaker of the assembly, Hassan al-Turabi. The ouster of bin Laden and his "undesirable factions" was vital to their plan to topple Turabi. But the Clinton administration, especially its Africa expert on the National Security Council, Susan Rice, had not paid sufficient attention to the internal shifts in Sudan's politics and was intensely suspicious of anything Sudan offered to do.[51]

The encouraging sign that Sudan was changing came on the night of February 6, 1996. U.S. ambassador to Sudan, Timothy M. Carney, with David Shinn, director of East African Affairs at the State Department, who was visiting Sudan at the time, were invited to dinner at the home of Sudan's then-Foreign Minister Ali Osman Mohammed Taha. The conversation quickly turned to terrorism. Carney reminded Taha that Washington was increasingly nervous about the presence of bin Laden, who seemed to be financing Egyptian Islamic Jihad and many other terrorist groups across the Middle East. Taha said that Sudan was very concerned about its poor relations with the United States. "If you want bin Laden," Taha said, "we will give you bin Laden." A month later, bin Laden was formally offered to the Clinton administration through the CIA.[52]

President Clinton's opportunity to get Osama bin Laden came late in the afternoon of March 3, 1996, in an Arlington, Virginia, hotel suite. It lasted less than thirty minutes.[53] Sudan's then-Minister of State for Defense Elfatih Erwa flew in for the secret meeting with Tim Carney and David Shinn. Also present was a middle-aged man who was a member of the CIA's Directorate of Operations (African division).[54] The CIA believed, and its representative told Erwa at the time, that some two hundred al Qaeda terrorists were holed up in Sudan. The actual number, according to author Richard Miniter, was as high as 583.[55]

Five days later, Erwa met with the CIA operative. This time, the two State Department officials, Carney and Shinn, were not present. Erwa and the CIA officer were alone as they decided the fate of Osama bin Laden.

Sudan offered to arrest and turn over bin Laden at this meeting, according to Erwa. He brought up bin Laden directly. "Where should we send him?" he asked. This was the key question. When Sudan turned over the infamous terrorist Carlos the Jackal to French intelligence in 1994, the CIA covertly provided satellite intelligence that allowed Sudanese intelligence to capture him on a pretext and escort him to the VIP lounge at the Khartoum airport. There, he was met by armed members of French intelligence and flown to Paris in a special plane. Would the CIA pick up bin Laden in Khartoum and fly him back to Washington, D.C.? Or would bin Laden go to a third country?[56]

The CIA officer was silent. It was obvious to Erwa that a decision had not yet been made. Or perhaps his offer was not quite believed. Yet, the Sudanese official was still hoping for a repeat of the French scenario. Finally, the CIA official spoke.[57] "We have nothing we can hold him on," he carefully said.[58]

Erwa was surprised by this, but he didn't let on. He was still hoping for a repeat of the French scenario, a silent and quick operation to seize bin Laden and bring him to justice. He explained that three Sudanese intelligence services, the Mukhabarat (external intelligence), Internal Security, and Military Intelligence, had been watching bin Laden since he had settled in Sudan in 1991.[59]

Sudan's files on bin Laden and his network were extensive. Sudan had dossiers on all of bin Laden's financial transactions, every fax he sent (the Mukhabarat had even bugged his fax machines), every one of bin Laden's terrorist associates, and his dubious visitors. If Sudan's surveillance was as good as Erwa claimed, bin Laden's entire global terrorist network would be laid bare. And the CIA would be able to track the movements of his foot soldiers and lieutenants across the Middle East.[60]

There were good reasons to believe that Sudan was serious about taking action against bin Laden. His terror activities had isolated Sudan from the United States and much of the developed world. Sudan's internal politics were moving against the terror master too. President Bashir was in the midst of a power struggle against Hassan al-Turabi, the Islamist leader. Bin Laden supported Turabi with cash and a potential armed cadre of Muslim militants. If Bashir could rid himself of bin Laden, he could simultaneously restart Sudan's relationship with the United States and vanquish his chief internal political rival.[61]

Over the next few months and years, Sudan would repeatedly try to provide its voluminous intelligence files on bin Laden to the CIA, the FBI, and senior Clinton administration officials, but they repeatedly were rebuffed through both formal and informal channels. The most puzzling, and in the end disastrous, part of this was that the CIA's own intelligence on bin Laden was shockingly poor.[62]

Human intelligence on al Qaeda was virtually nonexistent. *Washington Times* investigative reporter Bill Gertz uncovered a memo written only a few months after Sudan offered its intelligence on bin Laden. The July 1, 1996, CIA memo was marked "TOP SECRET UMBRA," meaning only the case officers, analysts, and officials specifically cleared to read the documents marked "UMBRA" could have access to this sensitive document. (Very few CIA officials and National Security Council staffers have access to all top-secret documents; most who have security clearances can read documents from only a handful of passwords.) The July 1996 memo revealed how ignorant the United States was about its emerging nemesis. "We have no unilateral sources close to bin Laden, nor any reliable way of intercepting his communications," the report said. "We must rely on foreign intelligence services to confirm his movements and activities."[63]

In March and April 1996, the Clinton administration repeatedly tried to get Saudi Arabia to accept bin Laden from Sudan, but the Saudis repeatedly refused to take custody of the wealthy terrorist. They didn't want him. They just wanted him to go away. But because the Saudis would not take bin Laden into custody, he was America's problem now.[64]

Since the Clinton administration was locked into the law-enforcement mode of fighting terrorism, its inability to indict bin Laden made it impossible in their eyes to take him into custody. What seemed, to the Clinton administration, like a logical and safe decision would ultimately make the world far more dangerous for Americans.[65]

When explaining the administration's failure to act, Sandy Berger, among other Clinton officials, repeatedly argued from a law-enforcement rationale—and also indulged some very Clintonian blame-shifting. "The FBI did not believe we had enough evidence to indict bin Laden at that time," Berger said, "and therefore opposed bringing him to the United States."[66]

Finally, only one option remained: Asking Sudan to expel bin Laden. When General Erwa asked Ambassador Carney where the U.S. wanted bin

Laden sent, Carney gave him the official line from Washington: "Anywhere but Somalia."[67]

Bin Laden later told *Al-Quds al-Arabi*, the London-based Arabic language newspaper that is generally pro-Islamist, what his options were in 1996: "Iraq is out of the question. I would rather die than live in a European state. I have to live in a Muslim country and so the choice is between Yemen and Afghanistan."[68]

Yemen made it quite clear that bin Laden would not be welcome in their desert republic, despite his family ties to the country. Afghanistan beckoned. For bin Laden, it was like starting over. He was returning to the land that made him a legend.[69]

KHOBAR TOWERS

Shortly before 10:00 p.m. local time on June 25, 1996, a Datsun driven by Hani al-Sayegh, a prominent member of the Saudi branch of Hezbollah, "Party of God," pulled into the far corner of a parking lot adjacent to Building 131 at the King Abdul Aziz Airbase in Dharan, Saudi Arabia. The eight-story apartment structure was part of a housing complex collecting as Khobar Towers, then home to more than two thousand American, British, French, and Saudi troops. Building 131 was occupied almost exclusively by members of the U.S. Air Force enforcing the no-fly zone that had been in effect over southern Iraq ever since the end of the first Gulf War. A few minutes later, a white, four-door Chevrolet Caprice entered the parking lot and waited for the Datsun to blink its lights. It was the all-clear signal. When it did, a tanker truck followed the Chevy into the lot. After the truck backed up to a fence just in front of the north side of Building 131, the driver and his passenger leaped from the cab, raced to the Chevy, and drove off, followed by the Datsun.[70]

Then the tanker truck exploded, ripping a crater thirty-five feet deep and eighty-five feet wide and shearing off the north face of the apartment building. The bomb was a sophisticated directional charge constructed with five thousand pounds of military-class high explosives reinforced by tanks of incendiary material that created a secondary blast and also shock and heat waves. The bomb was constructed by expert bomb makers who not only knew how to shape the explosives and incendiary materials to achieve maximum effect but also were able to perfectly place and install a very sophisticated electronic fuse system.[71]

The blast killed nineteen Americans and wounded 372 U.S. military personnel. Khobar was the deadliest attack on American citizens abroad in thirteen years, since the October 1983 explosion at a U.S. Marine barracks in Beirut, Lebanon, which killed 241 Marines.[72]

Hezbollah was active in the Sunni-dominated Eastern Province of Saudi Arabia, where the bombing had occurred. Although Hezbollah is based in Lebanon, it takes its orders and draws financial and logistic support from Tehran, particularly Iran's two security services: the Islamic Revolutionary Guards Corps (IRGC) and the Intelligence and Security Ministry (MOIS). That raised the specter that the Iranian government had known of and backed the bombing of Khobar Towers. For Iran to officially sanction an attack in the Saudi kingdom would be very serious.[73]

The day after the Khobar Towers bombing, Secretary of State Warren Christopher promised, "We will not rest until these terrorists are brought to justice. We will hunt them down." The president was also quite aggressive in his words: "The cowards who committed this murderous act must not go unpunished," said Clinton. "Let me say again: We will pursue this. America takes care of our own. Those who did it must not go unpunished." The following day, en route to an economic summit in France, Clinton had more to say. "Let me be very clear . . . we will not rest in our efforts to find who is responsible for this outrage, to pursue them and to punish them."[74]

Despite all the rhetoric there was no immediate response. Though the FBI concluded that Iran was behind the attack, Clinton administration officials suppressed the report in hope to pursue secret diplomatic initiatives to restore ties with Iran, which ultimately failed.[75]

In the summer of 1999, President Clinton sent a secret cable to the newly elected president of Iran, Mohammad Khatami and said in part:

> The United States Government has received credible evidence that members of the Iranian Revolutionary Guard Corps. (IRGC) along with members of Lebanese and Saudi Hezbollah were directly involved in the planning and execution of the terrorist bombing in Saudi Arabia of the Khobar Towers military resident complex. The United States views this in the gravest terms. We acknowledge that the bombing occurred prior to your election. Those responsible, however, have yet to face justice for this crime. And the IRGC may be involved in planning for further terrorist attacks against American

citizens. . . . The involvement of the IRGC in terrorist activity and planning aboard remains a cause of deep concern to us.[76]

It appears that there was no response to the cable and the Clinton administration turned the other cheek.[77]

EMBASSY BOMBINGS

On August 7, 1998, two bombs exploded simultaneously outside U.S. embassies in Nairobi, Kenya, and Dar-es-Salaam, Tanzania, 450 miles apart. In Nairobi, all windows within a quarter-mile splintered, the doors were blown off the embassy, people were blown out of buildings, and a seven-story building next to the embassy collapsed. In Dar-es-Salaam the bomb blew off one side of the embassy. Altogether more than 250 people died and more than 5,500 were injured, mostly Africans.[78]

President Clinton promised to do whatever was necessary to deliver justice to the perpetrators: "These acts of terrorist violence are abhorrent; they are inhuman. We will use all means at our disposal to bring those responsible to justice, no matter what or how long it takes."[79]

On August 9, 1998, Sudanese authorities detained two bin Laden operatives thought to be complicit in the attacks. FBI Director Louis Freeh wanted them extradited. Secretary of State Madeleine Albright nixed the deal.[80] According to a chronology published by the *New York Times* of the White House activities leading to the August 20 strike, the president was notified on August 12 about the evidence connecting Osama bin Laden to the bombing of the U.S. embassies in Kenya and Tanzania and of the essence of the planned retaliatory missile strikes. U.S. intelligence had already proposed August 20 as the strike date based on knowledge that a high-level terrorist gathering was planned for that day.[81]

However, on August 12, 1998, when the strike plan was originally presented to the president, both U.S. intelligence and the national decision makers should have questioned the validity of the information. Starting on August 8, U.S. intelligence had learned of unusual movements at terrorist bases and camps throughout Afghanistan. There was "a [dispersal] of people from bin Laden's bases of operations within Afghanistan in the aftermath of the explosions," a U.S. official told CNN on August 13.[82]

A reliable military source in Islamabad confirmed that "State Department officials had informed their Pakistani counterparts of their plans for a military strike" several days beforehand. Several Pakistani military and intelligence sources confirmed that President Clinton had briefed Prime Minister Nawaz Sharif about the U.S. plans by August 14. The *New York Times* chronology of activities in Washington identified August 14 as the date "Clinton [met] with his foreign policy advisers to begin planning military action." On August 18, according to this chronology, "Clinton called Berger to confirm that the military actions were in place."[83] Also, Madeleine Albright contacted Nawaz Sharif on the eve of the attack, and Punjab chief minister Shahbaz Sharif, who is Nawaz Sharif's brother and confidant, held talks in Washington with senior U.S. officials in the White House, State Department, and other parts of government.[84]

When military action was finally taken against bin Laden, it proved to be ineffective and even counterproductive. On August 20, 1998, five U.S. warships in the Arabian Sea fired sixty Tomahawk cruise missiles at four suspected terrorist training camps located about ninety-four miles south of Kabul, the Afghan capital. As a supposed exclamation point, two Navy warships in the Red Sea fired another twenty missiles at the Sudanese Al-Shifa pharmaceutical plant suspected of making a precursor chemical unique to the VX nerve agent.[85]

The bombing of the terrorist training camps was carried out even though bin Laden was known to have left the area. Worse, Defense Secretary William Cohen stated that bin Laden was *not* a target. Instead, the strikes "were targeting these facilities and his infrastructure." General Hugh Shelton, then chairman of the Joint Chiefs of Staff, said, "We were not going directly after Osama bin Laden. It was an attack on his network of terrorist groups, as I think you can see from the targets. We will continue to go after that if we feel like it's appropriate and if the threats to Americans or American interests continue."[86]

Somehow, the missiles managed to miss every single one of the suspects. Instead, they killed Pakistani intelligence officers who were equipping Kashmir guerrillas. Pakistani leaders were so outraged, they released two suspects they had arrested in connection with the bombing of the embassies.[87] To make matters worse, a day before the attacks on the Sudanese pharmaceutical factory, George Tenet, director of Central Intelligence, took part in a video conference that included Rear Admiral Thomas Wilson, the Joint Staff senior intelligence official known as the J-2.[88] Wilson said, "We don't have the evidence that that factory is involved in producing nerve agent," Wilson said during the secret video meeting.[89]

"You will make it a target," ordered Tenet.[90]

The CIA later claimed that the factory was targeted by demand of White House National Security Council staff, specifically Richard Clarke, its specialist on terrorism. This rash action embarrassed the State Department, which had the Treasury Department release assets it had seized from the plant's owner, quietly paying him $1 million dollars in interest.[91]

The Clinton administration was criticized on the timing of the strike because it appeared it was an attempt to distract attention from the Lewinsky scandal. Wag the Dog? Some Republicans raised this possibility, as did some left-wing demonstrators. "No blood for blow jobs," read one protest sign. Top FBI officials had the same suspicion, and some of them referred to the cruise missiles used in the attacks as "Monica's missiles."[92]

President Clinton never attempted to strike back at Osama bin Laden again. This one attempt at hurting Al Qaeda amounted to little more than an empty gesture. It was a lesson to the terrorists that the United States was incompetent and was not able to deal with them. Ultimately, they could strike without fear of any real retribution.[93]

USS *SULLIVANS*

Following the lunar calendar of traditional Islam, bin Laden planned his next attack on January 3, 2000, a date of religious significance during that year's Ramadan holiday. Like most al Qaeda attacks, it had been planned for years. Yemeni intelligence would later learn that bin Laden began preparations for the attacks in 1997.[94]

On that night, in the harbor of Aden, Yemen, a few men in a small fiberglass skiff pushed off from a deserted dock. The skiff was loaded with explosives.[95] Their target was an American destroyer, anchored a few miles away. The USS *Sullivans*, a warship named to commemorate the five Sullivan brothers who had died simultaneously when their U.S. Navy cruiser was surprised by the Japanese during World War II, was about to face a surprise attack of its own.[96] But as the men approached, their boat began to sink. The explosives were too heavy and the cheap craft too flimsy to float the load.[97]

As always, bin Laden's men would learn from their mistakes. The next time they targeted an American naval vessel in Aden harbor, it would not escape unscathed.[98] American intelligence would not learn about the attempted attack on the night of January 3, 2000, for almost a year. And by that time, it would be too late to do any good.[99]

USS COLE

On October 7, 2000, the final act of terrorism during the Clinton presidency occurred. The USS *Cole*, a 505-foot-long, 8,400-ton, Arleigh Burke-class guided missile destroyer with a complement of 249 men and 44 women was in Aden harbor. It was eighteen hundred feet off shore in a body of water known as the Bander al-Tawahi and attached to a floating refueling station. It wouldn't take long. At 2,200 gallons per minute, the entire fueling would take less than six hours. The fueling began at 10:30 a.m.[100]

Forty-seven minutes later, at 11:18 a.m. local time, disaster struck. A small craft headed toward the *Cole*. The two men aboard seemed to be aiming dead center between the two towers that rose from the deck of the destroyer. On board the speeding boat was Abd al-Muhsin al-Taifi, a Yemeni man wanted in connection with the 1998 bombing of the U.S. embassy in Nairobi, Kenya.[101]

The bomb had been carefully prepared for weeks. It was made from C-4, a plastic explosive long used by the U.S. military. The bomb was equivalent of seven hundred pounds of TNT. The C-4 was packed in heavy steel to direct the blast and magnify its force.[102] When the bomb exploded, it smashed its way through the half-inch reinforced steel plating and ripped a forty-by-forty-foot hole in the hull. Within minutes, seventeen sailors were dead or mortally wounded and another thirty-nine severely injured. The *Cole* was taking on water and began to list four degrees to port.[103]

Petty Officer John Washak immediately trained his M-60 machine gun on a second craft that was approaching the *Cole's* fantail to defend the ship from another surprise attack. Unbelievably, a senior chief petty officer waved him off and told him to stand down! Even "with blood still on my face," Washak said, we couldn't shoot "unless we're shot at."[104] The irony wasn't missed by Petty Officer Jennifer Kudrick, a sonar technician aboard the *Cole*. She said, "We would have gotten in more trouble for shooting two foreigners than losing 17 American sailors."[105] By midnight on October 10, 2000, after three days of struggle, the USS *Cole* was saved. It was the most devastating attack on an American warship since World War II.[106]

Many questions followed. Why was the dinghy allowed to approach the *Cole* when the ship was operating under Threat Condition Bravo—the second highest of four security warnings? Why were the sentries on the deck required to bear unloaded weapons? Why did the destroyer's rules of engagement require permission from the *Cole's* captain or another officer before firing?[107]

Admiral Vern Clark, chief of naval operations for the Navy under Bill Clinton, said you can't have weapons that fire. The Pentagon-approved rules of engagement for the destroyer basically said you mustn't show any hostility, especially not to our Arab brethren. Even though they approached the ship from Yemen, a known terrorist stronghold, you just never know about their true intentions.[108]

President Clinton promised that his administration would do something about the attack. "We will find out who was responsible and hold them accountable. If their intention was to deter us from our mission of promoting peace and security in the Middle East, they will utterly fail." But President Clinton did not respond to the terrorist attack as Byron York wrote for *National Review*:[109]

> Clinton's reaction to the Cole terrorism was more muted than his response to the previous attacks . . . He seemed more concerned that the attack might threaten the administration's work in the Middle East (the bombing came at the same time as a spate of violence between Israelis and Palestinians) . . . The next day, the *Washington Post's* John Harris, who had good connections inside the administration, wrote, "While the apparent suicide bombing of the *U.S.S. Cole* may have been the more dramatic episode for the American public, the escalation between Israelis and Palestinians took the edge in preoccupying senior administration officials yesterday. This was regarded as the more fluid of the two problems, and it presented the broader threat to Clinton's foreign policy aims."[110]

ABLE DANGER

Able Danger was a classified military planning effort led by the U.S. Special Operations Command (SOCOM) and the Defense Intelligence Agency (DIA). It was created as a result of a directive by Chairman of the Joint Chiefs of Staff Gen. Hugh Shelton to develop an information operations campaign plan against transnational terrorism.[111]

Then-Major Tony Shaffer got involved in Able Danger in September 1999 when he was based at SOCOM headquarters in Tampa, Florida. Capt. Scott Phillpott, who managed the project, brought him into the select group.[112] Shaffer had used the U.S. Army's Land Information Warfare Activity (LIWA) unit to support two other black operations and he was impressed with its results. Based in Fort Belvoir, Virginia, and led by then-Major Erik Kleinsmith, who was chief of intelligence in 1999 and 2000, LIWA was using the then-novel capabilities of data mining to help locate al Qaeda cells around the world.[113]

Over six months in 1999, LIWA had acquired a vast four-terabyte database and had assembled all these scattered pieces of information into a global map of al Qaeda using only open-source data. Its model was based in targeting methodology developed by J.D. Smith, an analyst for Orion Scientific Systems (a LIWA contractor), who deconstructed every individual involved in the 1993 World trade Center bombing into basis data points—the year they were born, their associates, tribal affiliation, mosque memberships, and so on—and built an algorithm. It was then used to examine immense amounts of publicly available data and identify other potential terrorists by comparing them to the original '93 World Trade Center terrorists.[114]

In January 2000, Shaffer brought charts produced by LIWA to Able Danger's operations in Tampa. They were two-dimensional representations of the large open-source database containing between three and four terabytes of information on known and suspected al Qaeda operatives, enablers, and affiliates. The charts had hundreds of photos (from passports, visas, and other sources) and names (including aliases). Some photos were grouped on the chart by terrorist affiliation, others by suspected geographic location.[115]

One Brooklyn cell stood out. They had only a grainy but sinister photo. There were several names under the photo. One was "Atta."[116] Able Danger linked Mohammed Atta and three other September 11 hijackers to the Brooklyn cell: Khalid al-Mihdhar, Nawaf al-Hazmi and Marwan al-Shehhi.[117] Able Danger was able to identify a total of five "nodes" of al Qaeda activity. Besides the one identified in Brooklyn, N.Y., there was another in the port of Aden in Yemen where the USS *Cole* would be attacked ten months later in October 2000. "It shocked us how entrenched a presence al Qaeda had in the United States," Mr. Kleinsmith said.[118]

In the summer of 2000, the Able Danger team was prepared to share the chart that included the visa photographs of the four 9/11 hijackers to the Federal Bureau of Investigation, to Congressman Curt Weldon (R.-Pa.), and to a former intelligence official. The recommendation was rejected and the information was not shared. Mr. Shaffer would later testify that he tried three times to have Able Danger data on the Brooklyn cell presented to the FBI, but on each occasion the Army's Special Operations Command (SOCOM) lawyers forbade the meeting.[119] It was a huge roadblock, but SOCOM lawyers feared a public-relations blowback and decided to withhold the information from the FBI. They concluded that Atta and others were in the country legally and, despite the fact that they were linked with terrorist organizations, they had the same legal protections as U.S. citizens. "If something went wrong, SOCOM felt it could get blamed." Shortly after that, the Army got cold feet because of the "U.S. persons" issue and determined that it wasn't in compliance with DOD intelligence oversight policies. They began to shut down all Army support.[120]

In March 2000, Maj. Kleinsmith was ordered to stop all work on Able Danger and later, on orders from Tony Gentry, general counsel of the Army Intelligence and Security Command, to delete all the information collected. Special Operations Command didn't want to lose the capability, so it transferred Able Danger to private contractor Raytheon.[121]

Able Danger was ordered to terminate its activities sometime in late January 2001. Then came the attack on September 11, 2001. Because of the bureaucracy, if Able Danger had not been stopped, they might have played a role in stopping the 9/11 attacks.[122]

Hearings began in 2005. During one of those hearings in the House Armed Services Committee, Congressman Weldon disclosed to Stephen Cambone, then-undersecretary of defense for intelligence, that he had an affidavit from a retired intelligence officer who said he was told by one of Mr. Cambone's aides that they were going to "get" recently promoted Lt. Col. Shaffer for having told Rep. Weldon what Able Danger had found. When Lt. Col. Shaffer was interviewing to become an intelligence officer, he admitted that at age thirteen he had taken a box of pens from the embassy where his father worked. The Defense Intelligence Agency tried to use that, $180 in disputed travel expenses, and $67 in disputed telephone charges as grounds for firing him. He was eventually fired in 2006.[123]

Shafer has told the story of the CIA's opposition to Able Danger prior to 9/11 based on the view that Able Danger was encroaching on its turf. According to Shaffer, the CIA representative said, "I clearly understand. We're going after the leadership. You guys are going after the body. But it doesn't matter. The bottom line is, CIA will never give you the best information from Alex Base or anywhere else. CIA will never provide that to you because if you were successful in your effort to target Al Qaeda, you will steal our thunder. Therefore, we will not support this."[124]

Finally, it became unclear why the George W. Bush administration was covering this up, since the suppression of Able Danger occurred on President Clinton's watch. Unfortunately, it became clear that there was a cover up.[125]

CHAPTER 32

TWA FLIGHT 800

Our citizens may be deceived for awhile, and have been deceived, but as long as the presses can be protected, we may trust them for light.
—Thomas Jefferson wrote in 1799[1]

On July 17, 1996, at 8:19 p.m., TWA flight 800 left JFK Airport bound for Paris. At 8:31 p.m., the plane exploded ten miles off the Long Island shore. The mid-air disintegration killed the jumbo jet's 230 passengers and crew. Those involved in the TWA probe included FBI Assistant Director James Kallstrom; Andrew Vita, assistant director of field operations for the Bureau of Alcohol, Tobacco, and Firearms and Explosives (ATF); and Jim Hall, chairman of the National Transportation Safety Board (NTSB).[2]

The summer of 1996 was tense at the White House. In the weeks leading up to the July 17 explosion of TWA 800, Ramzi Yousef, mastermind of the World Trade Center bombing and architect of a plot to blow up eleven U.S. jumbo jetliners on a single day, was on trial in New York.[3]

As the Atlanta Summer Olympics neared, the government's counterterrorist apparatus went on high alert. Richard Clarke, terrorism coordinator for the National Security Council, had reviewed an escalated number of terrorist threats. The NSC briefed the Transportation Department's aviation security team about the threats. Alarmed at the danger, the Federal Aviation Administration pressed for extraordinary security measures on airplanes and at airports. The FBI terrorism task force was placed on ready standby for immediate deployment.[4]

The TWA 800 destruction was the kind of crisis that President Clinton feared most. He had given it a generic name, Greg Norman. Clinton and golfer Greg Norman were buddies. A few months earlier, in April 1996, Norman took a six-stroke lead into the final round of the Masters and blew it. Clinton worried that his reelection campaign might suffer a similar fate. He and Hillary had spent sixteen months scrambling out of the crater left by the disastrous 1994 mid-term elections. With a lead in the polls seemingly as solid as Norman's at the Masters, Clinton left nothing to chance. "We could have a major crisis go bad on us," he worried. "Greg Norman," he reminded his staff over and over. "Greg Norman."[5]

By 3:00 a.m., July 18, the Clintons had settled on a strategy. Evidence strongly suggested that a trusted source in the U.S. Navy received orders to secure the plane's black boxes and to silence his colleagues. CIA documents showed that the White House had recruited the agency, not to hunt for international terrorists but to suppress missile speculation. In a July 20 internal memo, a CIA analyst reported "no evidence of a missile" in the radar data. In no memo was there any mention of a possible naval misfire even though one memo acknowledged the Navy was "reportedly conducting an exercise in the area." If it came out that it was a Navy missile that took down TWA 800, there goes President Clinton's reelection.[6]

The NTSB should have been exclusively responsible for the investigation *until* evidence of sabotage was found. Instead, Deputy Attorney General Jamie Gorelick directed the FBI to take over the TWA 800 investigation. Heading up the Justice's operation on the ground in Long Island was United States Attorney Valerie Caproni. Gorelick and Caproni knew the FBI was the subordinate agency. They also knew the NTSB could not legally be restricted in its pursuit of information. They simply ignored the law. The FBI reported to the Department of Justice. The NTSB did not. Also, it was understood that while Attorney General Janet Reno contented herself with "policy issues," Gorelick ran the department and would also influence the investigation along the way.[7]

So began a contentious, three-year, $35-million government-wide probe carried out under White House oversight by the FBI, the NTSB, the Defense Department, the Central Intelligence Agency, the Transportation Department, the Coast Guard, the Defense Intelligence Agency, the Federal Aviation Administration, the ATF, and numerous state and local agencies and law enforcement organizations.[8]

From the beginning, James Kallstrom thought terrorists were responsible. The sudden halt to voice transmissions from the cockpit before the explosion was consistent with the pattern of Pan Am 103. So was the mid-air disintegration of the aircraft. Then there were the eyewitness reports, eventually 270, which seemed to the FBI agents who collected them in the hours and days following the explosion to confirm a missile hit. About ninety-six of them all described it the same way: a red tip, a plume trail after it, gray, and then it gets near the plane, arcs over, zigzags, hits the plane, and blows up. Below are some of the FBI eyewitness reports:[9]

1. Sandy—not her real name—was at the beach near the Moriches Inlet on the South Shore of Long Island. She observed an aircraft climbing in the sky, traveling from her right to left. While keeping her eyes on the aircraft, she observed a 'red streak' moving up from the ground toward the aircraft at an approximately 45-degree angle. The red streak' was leaving a light gray colored smoke trail. The 'red streak' went past the right side and above the aircraft before arcing back toward the aircraft's right wing." Sandy described the arc's shape "as resembling an upside down NIKE swoosh logo. The smoke trail, light gray in color, widened as it approached the aircraft.
2. Mike Wire was working late with several engineers and electricians to open a new bridge on Beach Lane. Needing a breather, he leaned out over the rail and saw a white light travel upwards. It zigzagged as it rose. And at the apex of its travel, it arched over and disappeared.
3. Witness 73, a travel agent, said she was looking at TWA 800 as the object approached it and "never took her eyes off the aircraft during this time." She continued: "At the instant the smoke trail ended at the aircraft's right wing, she heard a loud sharp noise which sounded like a firecracker had just exploded at her feet. She then observed a fire at the aircraft followed by one or two secondary explosions which had a deeper sound. She then observed the front of the aircraft separate from the back. She then observed burning pieces of debris falling from the aircraft."

4. Witness 88 was fishing with friends in Moriches Inlet facing south out over the ocean. At first he heard an explosion. He then saw to the southeast what looked like a "firework ascending." The object "a wispy white smoke trail." At the peak of its ascent, the object, now flaming red at its tip, arced from the east to the west. He then saw the airplane come into the field of view. The bright red object "ran into the airplane and upon doing so both exploded into a huge plume of flame." He believed the object hit the plane near the cockpit.
5. Witness 129 was fishing with a friend off a jetty in the Moriches Inlet, when he saw to his southeast a "flare rising upwards." He followed it for about five seconds as it lifted from his eye level and curved southeast and slightly downward. He then saw a small flash, followed by a large explosion. A huge fireball then fell to the ocean in two pieces.
6. Witness 144 was walking around the track at Mastic Beach High School with a friend when she noticed a plane, traveling west to east, the direction TWA 800 was heading She then "saw an object to the right with a bright orange glow with a white streak behind it." She described the streak as "taking off like a rocket."
7. At Bayshore, Long Island, Witness 145 was looking out the window of a friend's house when she "saw a plane and noticed an object spiraling towards the plane." She described the object as having "a glow at the end of it and a grey/white smoke trail." She watched "the object hit the plane" but was not sure where.
8. Witness 166, a veteran of the Polish Army with missile experience, was at a park in Lindenhurst with his wife when he "noticed something ascending . . . like white, yellow fire, trailed by black smoke." He heard a "shhh" sound. The object arched slightly at top. He then observed an explosion.
9. Witness 282, a master sergeant with the New York Air National Guard, had just parachuted into his base at Gabreski Airport as part of an exercise. He was on the ground, looking

south, "when he saw what looked like a flare at about three thousand feet traveling from west to east. The object was orange with a pink center. It also had a very faint grayish white plume." The flare then erupted into a fireball and the fireball fell straight down and broke into two."

10. Witness 364, a former helicopter crew chief, saw an object ascend vertically. He watched for thirty seconds as the object "rose from the east to the west on a steep angle." He told the FBI he thought he had seen "a missile hitting the airplane."

11. Witness 649 (a.k.a. Joseph Delgado) had just finished exercising on the track at Westhampton High School and was walking to his vehicle when he observed "an object ascending from behind the trees." He described the bright white light object as "elongated." More specifically, it had a reddish pink aura around it and a grey tail. It ascended vertically, moving in a "squiggly" pattern, and arced off to the right in a southwesterly direction. Had he not been tracking "object number one," Delgado would not likely have seen "object number two," which "glittered" with the reflection of the sun. That first object, said Delgado, "appeared like it was going to slightly miss object number two unless it made a dramatic correction." This, it apparently did.

12. Vassilis Bakounis, a veteran Olympic Airlines Greek pilot, was flying along the south shore of Long Island at about two thousand feet when he saw a light coming out of the sea. "I followed that light for many seconds before it makes, kind of veers to the right," said Bakounis using his hands to illustrate the turn. The gesture, in fact, looked like an upside down Nike swoosh. "Then I see an explosion," Bakounis said.

13. Senior Navy NCO Dwight Brumly saw a streak from his window seat thousands of feet above TWA 800 on US Air Flight 217. The streak rose up towards his plane before leveling off and heading north towards Long Island on a course perpendicular to TWA 800's.

14. Engineer Paul Angelides tracked the southbound streak from his Westhampton deck and then watched in awe as the northbound streak rose off the horizon.

15. Air National Guard pilot Major Fritz Meyer had little doubt what caused the airplane to explode. "It was definitely a rocket motor," he said. "What I saw was definitely ordnance. I have enough experience. I saw one, two, three, four explosions before the fireball." No one was in a better position to see. Meyer was in the helicopter over the Long Island shore facing southbound.
16. Captain Christian Baur was the Air National Guard helicopter co-pilot flying with Major Fritz Meyer. Baur reported seeing a flare-like object moving from left to right, towards JFK. He saw enough of it to ask the flight engineer, "Is that a pyro?" Baur then saw a succession of explosions followed by a "huge fireball."
17. Charles Le Brun, an assistant fire chief for the Air National Guard was heading south by boat in Moneybogue Bay when he saw a flare-like object ascend. Given his location, the FBI reported, "Le Brun knew it originated from the ocean." The object ascended vertically for about fifteen seconds, then burst into a yellow flash slightly larger than the light of the flare. This yellow flash remained illuminated and descended. It then burst into a huge fireball "about twenty times the size of the yellow flash" and fell toward the sea.[10]

Despite the salt-water immersion, traces of military high explosives components PETN and RDX were found on the plane's wreckage. Kallstrom thought he had the evidence he'd been searching for, especially after his agents checked the aircraft logs for TWA 800 and found no sign of recent use of the plane to transport explosives or conduct canine bomb-detection tests.[11]

At first, the probability that TWA 800 was struck by such a missile seemed remote. The plane's altitude of 13,700 feet was at the outer limit of a MANPAD "footprint," the necessary flight path the missile would have taken to hit the plane. But it was a possibility that Kallstrom took seriously.[12]

Two days after the crash, July 19, the NTSB's Bruce Magladry formed a witness group that included accident investigators from TWA, Airline Pilots Association (ALPA), and the Federal Aviation Administration (FAA). On that same day, the FBI informed Magladry that no outside investigator could have any access to witness information. Two days later, Assistant United States Attorney, Valerie Caproni told Magladry he could review FBI witness statements only that "no notes [be] taken and no copies made." A day later, he was told he could not even take notes during an interview and could only interview a witness in the presence of an FBI agent. Two days later, he gave up and went back to Washington.[13]

The same day, July 19, 1996, the *New York Times* published the president's remarks on the crash. "We do not know what caused this tragedy," said Clinton. "I want to say that again: We do not know as of this moment what caused this tragedy." To drive home a lie, Clinton had the habit of repeating an assertion as if repetition signaled sincerity.[14] In a separate article on July 19, the *New York Times'* David Johnston introduced the possibility of a missile strike. "In public, investigators were talking about an 'accident,' but 'in private' they hinted at a terrorist's missile."[15]

It took seven days after the crash before two Navy divers finally went in the water to search for the black boxes. Within a very short time, both boxes were easily found 120 feet beneath the surface.[16] When the NTSB agents examined the recordings, they found no useful information. The last words out of the cockpit were "power set," a casual acknowledgment of an air traffic control order to continue ascending. This was said nearly a minute before the tape ended. According to former NTSB member Vernon Grose, this complete lack of information was unusual to the point of extraordinary. Some people believe that the boxes were recovered immediately after the crash, edited, and then put back in the water.[17]

At this point, one would hope that a Navy whistleblower would come forward to expose this episode, but President Clinton made sure that wouldn't happen. On March 11, 1997, he quietly signed Executive Order 13039 effectively removing all federal whistleblower protection from anyone, civilian or military, associated with U.S. Navy "special warfare" operations. This would include any Navy divers charged with removing black boxes. Coincidently, the following day, March 12, the *New York Times* reported that government officials had "unleashed a pre-emptive strike" to neutralize an upcoming fifty-seven-page article in the *Paris Match*. That article explored in depth the Navy's role in the destruction of TWA 800.[18]

The *New York Times* also noted that on the day before, March 11, the same day as Clinton's executive order, the Riverside *Press-Enterprise* broke the story of James Sanders' residue test. (Sanders had tested material and found exhaust residue of a solid-fuel missile.) Having cause to fear the collapse of the cover-up, Clinton, for the first time, left his fingerprints on the investigation.[19]

On August 2, 1996, President Clinton shared his thoughts on TWA 800 with Taylor Branch, a Pulitzer Prize-winning historian. "Unless some telltale chemical survived the brine," Clinton told Branch, "[the investigators] must try to reassemble the plane to determine the cause." Clinton also told Branch that the FBI was "rechecking" its interviews with "some fifteen ground witnesses who saw a bright streak in the sky near the plane." If corroborated, Branch added, this "could suggest a missile rather than a bomb."[20]

On August 14, 1996, the *New York Times* offered the first detailed account of the plane's break-up sequence. The most salient revelation was that the center fuel tank caught fire as many as twenty-four seconds after the initial blast. This meant that the "only good explanation remaining" were either a bomb or missile.[21]

On August 22, 1996, government officials in Washington called Kallstrom to meet with Deputy Attorney General Jamie Gorelick. This meeting reversed the momentum of the investigation.[22]

What followed in the next several weeks was the most ambitious and successful cover-up in American peacetime history. At the center was Gorelick. With the help of a complicit media, she and her cronies transformed a transparent missile strike into a mechanical failure of unknown origin. In January 1997, Gorelick left the DOJ to become vice chairman of Fannie Mae, despite having no financial or housing experience. She made $877,573 in that first half year alone. In January 2004, the *New York Times* reported that Jamie Gorelick had resigned from Fannie Mae "to spend more time on the national commission investigating the Sept. 11 terrorist attacks and to pursue other interests." What the *Times* did not report is that during her five-plus years, she earned $26,466,834 in salary, bonuses, performance pay, and stock options.[23]

On Friday, August 23, 1996, Don Van Natta wrote an article titled, "Prime Evidence Found That Device Exploded in Cabin of TWA 800." In the article, investigators had found "scientific evidence" of an explosive device, specifically traces of PETN, or pentaerythritol tetranitrate, a component found in bombs and missiles.[24]

There was another August 23 headline that read, "Clinton Signs Bill Cutting Welfare; States in New Roll." The signing of this bill three days before the start of the Democratic National Convention in Chicago was hardly a coincidence. Clinton hoped to sell the party's peace and prosperity message. Front page headlines about explosives devices destroying an American airliner, by a bomb or especially by a missile, would remind America of what Clinton was not—namely, a trustworthy wartime leader.[25]

Back from Washington on the day the article appeared, on Friday, August 23, an apparently chastened Kallstrom reversed direction and returned to the FBI's lab at Calverton, a changed man. Based on his subsequent performance, he seemed to have no more urgent task than to negate the *New York Times* reporting on explosive residues. By mid-September 1996, Kallstrom had ended all serious talk of a missile and pushed through the administration's "mechanical failure" narrative.[26]

On August 31, 1996, the *New York Times'* Don Van Natta complicated matters for the White House. He reported that investigators had found "additional traces of explosive residue" on the interior of the aircraft near where the ring wing met the fuselage. For the record, Witness 73 had also identified "the aircraft's right wing" as the initial point of contact.[27]

On September 19, 1996, the U.S. government went public with its change of direction. The news came from NTSB Chairman Jim Hall from its headquarters in Washington. "Convinced that none of the physical evidence recovered from TWA 800 proves that a bomb brought down the plane, the NTSB was now planning tests to show that the explosion could have been caused by a mechanical failure alone."[28]

In October 1996, Terry Stacey, the TWA senior manager who worked on the investigation through the NTSB, noticed a subtle shift in FBI behavior. He relayed this to James Sanders, an investigative reporter. Stacey knew there was a cover-up in progress. Stacey believed the initial blast outside the right wing appeared to leave a reddish-orange residue trail across two rows of nearby seats. In late August 1996, the FBI had the residue tested but refused to share the results with Stacey and others working with the NTSB. Stacey decided to cut out a few square inches of material and sent it by FedEx to Sanders. Sanders had the material tested at an independent lab on the West Coast, and its elements were found to be consistent with elements present in the exhaust residue of a solid-fuel missile. After Sanders went public with his findings in March 1997, the FBI counter-claimed that the material was simply glue. Then, the FBI felt compelled to arrest Terry Stacey and James and Elizabeth Sanders.[29]

In November 1996, to quell the mounting doubt, Kallstrom came out and insisted there was no Navy involvement in TWA 800's destruction. "We have looked at this thoroughly and we have absolutely not one shred of evidence that it happened or it could have happened." The pressure seemed to get to him.[30]

On another occasion, Kristina Borjesson, then a CBS producer, attended a press conference and watched in horror as Kallstrom exploded at a reporter who asked how the U.S. Navy could be involved in the investigation when it was a possible suspect. "Remove him." Kallstrom shouted. Two men promptly grabbed the reporter by the arms and dragged him out of the room. Wrote Borjesson, "Right then and there, the rest of us had been put on notice to be on our best behavior."[31]

On November 6, 1996, two days after the presidential election, former Kennedy press secretary and veteran ABC correspondent Pierre Salinger came forward with a claim that TWA 800 was the victim of friendly fire from a U.S. Navy vessel. His source was the French intelligence services. Soon, Salinger came under assault by the FBI, the White House, and the Navy. Then the media joined in. In November 1996 alone, the *New York Times* ran four articles with headlines that mocked Salinger. Salinger was unprepared to respond, and the issue went away.[32]

In March 1997, the White House rewarded George Tenet for his faithful service by naming him the director of the Central Intelligence Agency. He had served as acting director from nearly the beginning of the TWA 800 crash. According to the *New York Times*, "The rise of Mr. Tenet is proof of the rewards of being loyal and obedient servant to one's boss, be he a senator, a spymaster, or the President of the United States."[33]

On November 18, 1997, the CIA produced an animated video simulating TWA 800's final flight. The video explains the 244 eye-witness accounts, many of which suggested that a missile was fired into the aircraft, as mistaken. Because light travels faster than sound, the CIA concluded that witnesses actually saw a flame trail from burning jet fuel before they heard the sound of the plane's explosion, and naturally were convinced that the streak of light leading to the plane occurred before the explosion.[34]

What the CIA did not explain in November 1997 was that its video was altered after consultation with the NTSB. In a letter from CIA Director

George Tenet to Rep. James Traficant (D-Ohio) dated January 13, 1998, Tenet acknowledged that more than forty changes were made to the video animation at the NTSB's suggestion. After the changes were made, Tenet says the CIA showed the video to "NTSB managers" who approved its release to the general public.[35]

On May 10, 1999, Sen. Charles Grassley (R-Iowa) held a one-day hearing with witnesses offering damaging testimony about the FBI's role in the TWA 800 probe. Andrew Vita, assistant director of field operations for the ATF, testified that several months into the investigation the ATF concluded there was no evidence that high explosives caused TWA 800's mid-air disintegration. In late January 1997, Vita put the ATF's views in an unsolicited, written report to be submitted to the NTSB. But Vita testified, he "met resistance" from the FBI. Also, there was senior NTSB investigator Hank Hughes who complained about the FBI's failure to respect the evidence and honor the chain of custody. He was alarmed by a "disappearance of parts from the hanger." Whole seats were missing and other evidence was disturbed. At one point, he set up an overnight video surveillance that recorded two FBI agents in the hangar without authorization at 3:00 a.m. On another occasion, he saw an FBI agent trying to flatten out a piece of metal with a hammer.[36]

Hughes was not alone. Jim Speer, representing ALPA watched the FBI skew the investigation. With twenty-five years of experience as an Air Force fighter pilot and additional experience with TWA, Speer brought a rich experimental knowledge into his work. None of this impressed the FBI. On one occasion, he brought a suspicious-looking part from the right wing to the FBI's field lab at Calverton to test it. The part tested positive for nitrates. This threw the testers into a panic. One of them picked up the phone, made a call, and in "nanoseconds" three agents in suits came running in. The agents huddled with the testers before informing Speer the machine had frequent false positives. They ran the tests several times without letting Speer watch. When finished, the lead agent turned to Speer and said, "All the rest of the tests were negative. We will declare the overall test negative and the first one you saw, we'll call it a false positive."[37]

By 1999, three years after the TWA 800 crash, NTSB chairman Jim Hall could not find the answer to the mystery of the center fuel tank's ignition. Also, Hall was never pressed to answer questions on his and Vice President Al Gore's roles in raising more than $500,000 in soft-money contributions from the airline industry for the 1996 Clinton-Gore reelection effort. This was at a time when the White House Commission on Aviation Safety and Security was considering security measures which would have cost the airline industry $1 billion.[38] Coincidentally, those tough safety airline recommendations were eventually rejected by the White House because of "racial profiling."[39]

By the time James Kallstrom retired in December 1997, he had closed the book on the TWA 800 case. He would also sell the CIA's duplicitous video to a credulous media, and he would block all eyewitness testimony at the NTSB hearing that was scheduled for the following year. Kallstrom would later take an executive position with the MBNA Bank before assuming New York's top security post in response to 9/11.[40] On the tenth anniversary of the crash, in July 2006, Lisa Michelson, a parent who lost her son on TWA 800, got in Kallstrom's face at the memorial service on Long Island. "I can't believe you're still sticking to this story," she said to him. "How can you lie to people's faces?" He dropped his head and said nothing.[41]

So what caused the fuel tank to explode? I do not believe it was a spark from faulty wiring which caused the plane's center fuel tank to explode. Let us explore the things we know:

After TWA 800 went down, the FBI received reports from four witnesses claiming to have seen a similar "surface-to-air something" launched on July 7, 1996. That same night, a guy and his buddy were trying to master a new video camera. Then, sure enough, a small trail emerged from the horizon zigzagging its way up at about a seventy-five-degree angle in an east to west direction. "It must be a rocket or something going up," said one of the men matter-of-factly.[42]

On July 12, 1996, five days *before* the crash, a fellow with his friend on Long Island were attempting to videotape the sunrise when they recorded "a grey trail of smoke ascending from the horizon at an angle of approximately 75 [degrees]." So compelling was the sight that the fellow commented to his friend, "They must be testing a rocket."[43]

Five days later, on July 17, 1996, MSNBC, on the air for just two days, secured an amateur video showing an object approaching the plane. The network was airing the video in regular rotation until "three men in suits" came to the editing suite. They demanded every copy of the video that the network had and cautioned the employees that there could be serious consequences if they chose to talk about the video, let alone air it again.

Although the government and the media would scramble to change the storyline, CNN was still reporting on July 19, that "radar records reviewed by military officials showed a mystery blip in the vicinity of the TWA flight path."[44]

Jim Holtsclaw knew something about radar. He graduated from the U.S. Air Force Air Traffic Control School and the FAA Air Traffic School, served as LAX Control Tower manager and ATC manager with American Airlines before moving on to the Air Transport Association. After reviewing a copy of the radar tape recorded at the New York Terminal Radar Approach Control (TRACON) he commented that "a primary target at the speed of approximately 1,200 knots was converging with TWA 800, during the climb out phase of TWA 800." "Target" was controller speak for "unknown object."[45]

Witness 150 tracked an "unusual object traveling at high speed north to south." She described it as "cylindrical, tubular, and bullet shaped" with no wings, no vapor trail, and a slight trajectory. She followed the object for several seconds when she saw it approach a "large commercial airliner" traveling at roughly the same altitude. The object headed toward the side of the plane. She saw a puff of smoke, and then the plane simply seemed to "just stop." Fissures developed throughout the plane, and it broke like a toy.[46]

Linda Kabot was taking photographs for her boss at a fund-raising party. The event was held outdoors at Docker's, an East Quogue restaurant with a deck that overlooks Shinnecock Bay. A few days later, she picked up the developed photos. In one, she saw what the *New York Times* described as a "long cylindrical object high in the sky," its left end tilted downward, its right end was "brightly lighted." The *Times* did not use the word "drone," but a drone was likely what Kabot captured on film.[47]

There was one other bit of evidence that the FBI chose not to discuss. Long Island resident Dede Muma received a fax from an employee at San Diego's Teledyne Ryan Aeronautical in May 1997. The employee had intended to send the fax to his superior on assignment at Calverton but transposed the last two numbers. The object in the fax was a Teledyne Ryan BQM-34 Firebee I, a target drone about twenty-three-foot-long capable of flying more than seven hundred miles an hour.[48]

Then you had the NTSB conceding in its final report that FAA radar had picked up four unidentified ships within six miles of the TWA 800 explosion. After the plane went down, three of the four left the scene at between twelve and twenty knots and then disappeared. The fourth vessel, which was less than three miles away, instead of heading back to the site to look for survivors, fled the scene at a speed the FBI estimated at between twenty-five and thirty-five knots. That captain has never been held to account.[49]

This is where all of the pieces seem to come together. On the evening of July 17, 1996, Captain Ray Ott and his crew on a Navy surveillance plane, the P-3 Orion, with its transponder turned off, were flying about seven thousand feet above TWA 800 when it exploded. At the same time, there were approximately four Navy vessels in the immediate vicinity below the P-3 aircraft: Cruiser USS *Normandy* and three submarines: the USS *Trepang*, the USS *Wyoming*, and the USS *Albuquerque*.[50]

After circling for a half hour and shooting video of the debris field, the plane headed south two hundred miles on a routine sub-hunting exercise. No entity in the military arsenal was as capable of hunting down any suspected terrorists as the P-3, but Ott had orders to do otherwise.[51]

There is also evidence of a fifth ship in the area. Witness 150 and her friend noticed about two hours before the crash near the coast of Fire Island and heading east a large (453 feet) gray military ship with lots of equipment and an ID number on the front. "The ship was so big and close," said the woman, "that you couldn't capture the entire profile in one glance."[52]

The naval vessel appears to have been the USS *Carr*, a guided missile frigate. In 1995, the ship underwent extensive combat system upgrades which led to "two highly successful dual missile firing exercises" in early 1996. The ship's official history is oddly silent on where the ship operated between April 1996 and November 1996 when it headed for the Mediterranean.[53]

With a drone in the mix, the U.S. Navy would have had all the "combatants" needed for a Cooperative Engagement Capability (CEC) missile test. In 1996, the Navy was in the process of introducing this enormously complex system. The CEC was created to integrate the information from each of the combatant's sensors—range, bearing, elevation, Doppler updates—and feed the integrated picture back to the individual combatants. The P-3's role was to relay data among the various units involved.[54]

Based on available evidence, it appears that at least two missiles detonated near TWA in quick order, one at the No. 3 engine on the right side, and a second and fatal blast at the lower left side of the aircraft. If there were a drone in the mix, it seems to have been destroyed.[55]

The International Association of Machinists and Aerospace Workers (IAMAW), a participant in the NTSB investigation, stated in its final report: "A high pressure event breached the fuselage and the fuselage unzipped due to the event. The explosion [of the center fuel tank] was a result of this event." In layman's terms, a blast—"outside of the aircraft in close proximity to the aircraft"—ripped open the center fuel tank and caused the fuel to vaporize and explode. Thus, the center fuel tank was not the primary contributor to this incident.[56]

The Navy could not have—and would not have—concealed its responsibility unless authorized to do so. Nor would the FBI and CIA have intervened on their own initiative. These authorizations could only have come from the White House. This was the rare White House in American history reckless enough to have authorized a cover-up this bold.[57]

CHAPTER 33

PAULA JONES PART II

Well, I'm pleased about it [the April 1, 1998 dismissal of the Paula Jones lawsuit], because the judge ruled as a matter of law the case had no merits. And that exposed the raw political nature of this whole situation.

—President Clinton
responding to a question from a *Time* magazine reporter[1]

After President Clinton's six-hour deposition, on Saturday, January 17, 1998, the first couple planned to go out for dinner. The dinner was apparently meant to counteract any impression that the President's forced deposition had shaken up their lives.[2]

The Clintons never made it. Except for a visit to church on Sunday, they remained in seclusion until Monday. The wind had been knocked out of Bill Clinton. But it was Hillary who almost immediately went into full battle mode. She granted several interviews on Monday, January 19. Although Hillary was wearing a bold plaid suit, she was pale, her voice was nasally, and her eyes seldom met those of the interviewer.[3]

Reporter Peter Mayer: "Can I ask you, uh, how difficult a day Saturday was for you and your family?
Clinton: "It wasn't difficult for me. On Saturday, I just hunkered down and went through my household tasks. Then my husband came home and we watched a movie and we had a—[she paused while searching for the appropriately innocuous phrase]—a good time that evening."

Mayer: "And Sunday?"
Clinton: "Oh, we just stayed home and cleaned closets."[4]

In another interview that Monday Hillary Clinton was asked in an interview with Mutual-NBC radio whether the notoriety of the case [Paula Jones sexual misconduct lawsuit] had affected her life? Mrs. Clinton said: "Not really; we do box it off, because there's no way that you can let people with their own agendas, whatever they might be, interfere with your private life or your public duties, and that's what my husband does every single day," she said.[5]

On January 26, 1998, Bill Clinton expressed his support for the Secret Service's motion for a protective order, to keep the Secret Service agents from testifying in the Paula Jones case. Mr. Clinton's motion objecting to subpoenas from Mrs. Jones attorneys said permitting the testimony "sets a precedent which could significantly jeopardize the Secret Service's ability to perform its vital duty of protecting the physical safety of the president, vice president, their families and visiting heads of state."[6]

On February 17, 1998, Clinton's lawyer Robert Bennett made a last-ditch effort to prevent the Paula Jones case from going to trial, asking, in a motion filed with U.S. District Judge Susan Weber Wright in Little Rock, to dismiss her sexual harassment lawsuit because of "a total lack of proof."[7]

Ten days later Donovan Campbell, Paula Jones' lead attorney, filed a motion that President Clinton engaged in a "vast pattern of suppression of evidence and obstruction of justice" and enlisted a wealthy Maryland Democratic contributor—Nathan Landow—to silence a woman [Kathleen Willey] who says the president sexually groped her. Mr. Campbell wanted them to explain why they discussed Mrs. Willey's testimony before her deposition in the Jones case.[8]

On March 10, 1998, Kathleen Willey testified before a grand jury that President Clinton kissed her and put his hand on her breast and placed her hand on his crotch in a hallway adjacent to the Oval Office on November 29, 1993. Willey also alleged that Nathan Landow talked with her about her testimony in the Jones case. Within weeks of the encounter between Clinton and Willey, Ms. Willey received a paid job at the White House. This would bolster the premise that Bill Clinton used his elected office to reward or punish women based on their sexual encounters.[9]

The next day the *Washington Times* reported that the White House legal team had ballooned to thirty-three lawyers, paralegals, and researchers—up from four employees in early 1993. The annual taxpayer cost for the office was $2.36 million. On March 25, 1998, the *Times* followed up that the White House actually had eighty-four taxpayer-funded lawyers. I wonder how many of those taxpayer-funded lawyers were conducting personal legal work for the Clintons?[10]

On March 12, 1998, the *Washington Times* reported that former Arkansas Secretary of State William J. McCuen had told one of Mrs. Jones attorneys that he witnessed an oral sex episode in his own office between Mr. Clinton and a young state worker.

On March 15, 1998, CBS's *60 Minutes* broadcasted their interview of Kathleen Willey with Ed Bradley. That night, an America that had been skeptical of Paula Jones's claim that Clinton was a sexual harasser was jarred to a new reality by another witness who not only sounded more credible but whose story also meant that Clinton continued to accost women even after he'd reached the White House.[11]

In halting tones, Willey's revelations to Bradley would, for the first time, begin to unravel Clinton's support with that all-important Democratic Party demographic—women:

> **Willey:** And then he—then he—and then he kissed me on my mouth and pulled me closer to him. And I remember thinking, I just remember thinking: "What in the world is he doing?" I—it—I just thought: "What is he doing?" And I pushed back away from him and he—he—he - he- he's a big man. And he—he had his arms—they were tight around me, and he—he—he—he touched me.
> **Bradley:** "Touched you how?"
> **Willey:** "Well, he—he—he touched my breast with his hand, and I—I—I—I was—I—I was just startled."
> **Bradley:** "This wasn't just an accidental, grazing touch?"
> **Willey:** "No, no. And then he whispered, he said in my ears that "I've wanted to do this ever since I laid eyes on you." And—and I remember saying to him, "Aren't you afraid that somebody's going to walk in here?" The—and he said, "No, no, I'm not." And then—and—and then he took my hand and he put it on him. And that's when I pushed away from him and decided it was time to get out of there."

Bradley: "When you say he took your hand and put it on him—where on him"
Willey: "On—on his genitals."
Bradley: "Was he aroused?"
Willey: "Uhm-hum."[12]

As Willey's story exploded on the front page of nearly every newspaper across the United States the next day, no reporter dared to question Hillary Rodham Clinton, who only six years earlier had warned, "We must never again shy away from raising our voices against sexual harassment." In fact, the woman whom she had praised for stepping forward with her own harassment claim against Supreme Court justice Clarence Thomas took to the op-ed pages of the *New York Times* to justify Clinton's Oval Office sex attack.[13]

The next morning, the White House promptly produced fifteen letters and notes she wrote to the president. The White House also provided a detailed compendium of all her telephone calls and contacts with the Oval Office. Clinton personally approved the release of the records, which aides at the time said were compiled the previous weekend. Yet, on December 15, 1997, the Jones legal team directed Clinton to turn over any documents related to Willey, including personal records, appointment calendars and "all documents (such as logs, telephone records, security videotapes, or lists) reflecting any communications, meetings, or visits involving Defendant Clinton and Ms. Willey, especially within the White House." A January 15, 1998, response prepared by the president's attorneys said, "President Clinton has no documents responsive to this request."[14]

Mrs. Jones' attorneys charged that the release was a "gross suppression" of records that had specifically been requested and constituted an obstruction of justice. The White House denied it was ever asked for such documents. That was a lie.[15] It ended up releasing the letters, which prompted another lawsuit by *Judicial Watch*. It argued that the White House had violated the Privacy Act. In March 2000, a federal judge agreed, finding that President Clinton had committed a crime.[16]

Although Hillary Rodham Clinton was not named in the finding, her role in the White House's Kathleen Willey smear was obvious from the testimony of her top aide Sidney Blumenthal, whose lawyer explained in court documents: "Mr. Blumenthal recalls that he and Mrs. Clinton discussed Ms. Willey's letters to the President, and that the letters were inconsistent with what Willey had told *60 Minutes*. Both Mrs. Clinton and Mr. Blumenthal agreed that the letters should be released." The same court documents noted that Blumenthal moved quickly to act on Mrs. Clinton's decision: "That same day, March 16, 1998, Mr. Blumenthal telephoned Ms. Jill Abramson, a reporter for the *New York Times*" to tip the paper off to the Willey letters.[17]

With the Kathleen Willey and Paula Jones stories, there were now two compelling accounts suggesting that Bill Clinton's sexual proclivities weren't always consensual. That allegations of these two women would grow. Author Roger Morris's "young woman lawyer in Little Rock" would make three. The woman who told Arkansas Republican gubernatorial candidate Sheffield Nelson that she was raped while drunk would be number four. Former Miss America Liz Ward Gracen had said, "it was rough sex and Clinton got so carried away that he bit my lip." Later Gracen insisted the episode was consensual, yet the "young woman lawyer in Little Rock" had also described biting during the forced encounter. That made five. A sixth woman had privately alleged yet another Oval Office attack in a story remarkably similar to Willey's, but has declined to go public to this day.[18]

There was another incident in which a female administration official (a seventh woman) confided that Clinton had slipped "his hands up her leg." She, too, refused to go public with details of the assault.[19]

There was a story about an eighth woman reported by the *Washington Times*. She was an airline stewardess who claimed the then-presidential candidate invited her into his campaign plane lavatory in 1992, made crude references to oral sex, and fondled her breasts for forty minutes as Hillary slept in a nearby seat.[20]

Amazingly, as Mrs. Clinton was deciding her political options in the early days of January 1999, a ninth woman was deciding whether to go public with her own story. Having been beseeched for nearly a year by NBC investigative reporter Lisa Myers, Arkansas businesswoman Juanita Broaddrick finally decided to step into the public square and tell her story. On January 20, Broaddrick sat down with Myers to give her account of a brutal rape by Bill Clinton twenty years earlier. The network had already thoroughly vetted her story, hiring private investigators to go through every aspect of her life. NBC producers had managed to turn up four witnesses who corroborated different aspects of her allegations, including a friend,

Norma Rogers Kelsay, who discovered Broaddrick bruised and bleeding moments after the attack. Ms. Broaddrick was interviewed by NBC for eight hours, five of which, she was told, yielded usable videotape where she went through every conceivable detail of her life that could have been relevant to the attack.[21]

NBC clearly recognized how explosive its Broaddrick exclusive was and decided to delay its broadcast past the end of Clinton's Senate trial. Apparently NBC feared the revelation would tip what looked like a sure acquittal into a guilty verdict that would remove Mr. Clinton from office. A month earlier, MSNBC's Chris Matthews had revealed that it was a rape allegation and other secret evidence stored in Washington, D.C.'s Ford Building that had persuaded up to forty wavering House Republicans to vote for Clinton's impeachment. In a very real sense, it was Broaddrick's account, and not the Lewinsky scandal, that catalyzed the first impeachment of an elected president in U.S. history.[22]

Meanwhile, NBC's delays made Broaddrick nervous. Word was out on the *Drudge Report* that she had sat down with Myers. Knowing that she was the most damaging of all the whistleblowers, Broaddrick feared retaliation without the protection of having the American people know her story. On January 26, 1999, six days after her session with Myers, NBC told Broaddrick her story would be broadcast on the network's prestigious *Dateline* within three days. In her first comments to any media outlet since her sit-down with Myers, Broaddrick told *Newsmax* that day she was concerned about the network's foot-dragging, especially after Myers passed along the comments of network higher-ups. "The good news is, you're credible," Myers told the Clinton rape whistleblower. "The bad news is, you're very, very credible."[23]

Broaddrick was forced to turn to another mainstream outlet before NBC would broadcast her account. After *Newsmax* tipped the *Wall Street Journal* to Broaddrick's frustration over the network's delays, the *Journal* sent its Pulitzer Prize–winning reporter Dorothy Rabinowitz to Arkansas in a bid to win Broaddrick's trust. Finally, on February 19, 1999, the story exploded on the *Journal's* editorial page under the headline "Juanita Broaddrick Meets the Press," a subtle slap at NBC's premier Sunday news broadcast headed up by Tim Russert. The show's host was caught between his bosses' apparent desire to protect Clinton and his own reporter's bombshell scoop—the biggest exclusive NBC ever had—which he had to throw away.[24]

The *Journal* reported the basics of the ugly encounter: How Clinton first put his arms around her, startling her. Broaddrick recalled, "He told me, 'We're both married people,'" whereupon she responded that she was deeply involved with another man. The "argument failed to persuade Mr. Clinton, who, she says, got her onto the bed, held her down forcibly and bit her lips."[25]

"The sexual entry itself was not without some pain because of her stiffness and resistance," Rabinowitz recounted on the basis of Broaddrick's comments. "When it was over, she says, he looked at her and said not to worry, he was sterile. He had the mumps when he was a child."[26]

"I felt paralyzed and was starting to cry," Broaddrick said. Clinton turned before leaving, she recalled. "This is the part that always stays in my mind—the way he put on his sunglasses. Then he looked at me and said, 'You better put some ice on that.' And then he left." Minutes later her friend Norma Rogers Kelsay, "a nurse who had accompanied her on the trip," came into the room and found her still on the bed. Broaddrick was, Kelsay told the *Journal*, "in a state of shock—lips swollen to double their size, mouth discolored from the biting, her pantyhose torn in the crotch. She just stayed on the bed and kept repeating, 'I can't believe what happened.'"[27]

Five days later, on February 24, 1999, its big scoop preempted, NBC finally relented and broadcast its Broaddrick report to little fanfare. *NBC Nightly News* anchor Tom Brokaw refused to cover Myer's bombshell on his own newscast. The network, meanwhile, prompted other *Dateline* segments that night instead of the explosive rape account. Still, Broaddrick's video presentation was significant. Even without any promotion, 24 million people tuned in to hear her level an accusation never before made against any sitting president:[28]

> **Myers:** "Is there any way at all that Bill Clinton could have thought this was consensual?"
> **Broaddrick:** "No, not with what I told him and with how I tried to push him away. It was not consensual."
> **Myers:** "You're saying that Bill Clinton sexually assaulted you, that he raped you?"
> **Broaddrick:** "Yes."

Myers: "And you have no—there's no doubt in your mind that that's what happened?"
Broaddrick: "No doubt whatsoever."[29]

Within days, polls suggested that those who watched the *Dateline* broadcast believed Juanita, with 54 percent telling a Fox News Dynamic/*New York Post* survey that they found her charges credible. Just 23 percent disagreed. In an unscientific online poll taken by *MSNBC*, immediately after the broadcast, 83 percent said they believed the president of the United States was a rapist.[30]

Broaddrick herself suspected Hillary knew, recalling what she remembered as a direct effort to keep her from going public with a rape accusation against Bill as his political career was just getting off the ground. "Hillary sought me out," Broaddrick told author Christopher Andersen. "And when somebody told her where I was, she came straight for me and cornered me and grabbed my hand very forcefully." The bizarre encounter between Hillary and her husband's victim took place just three weeks after the attack, at a fund-raiser for Mr. Clinton's first gubernatorial bid. "I can't explain why I went," Broaddrick said. "I was still sort of in a state of denial, a state of shock. I didn't know what to think, what to do."[31]

Broaddrick recalled Mrs. Clinton's words verbatim, as well as her demeanor: "I want you to know how grateful we all are for all you've done for Bill," Hillary said, eyes glaring as if to underline another message. "We are so grateful for all you've done for Bill, and all you'll keep doing." Broaddrick remembered that Hillary's grasp lingered before she let go.[32] "She was looking at me straight in the eye, and I understood perfectly what she was saying. I knew exactly what she meant, that I was to keep my mouth shut," the Arkansas businesswoman said. "That meant she knew [what had happened] almost from the beginning . . . . But apparently it was something she was willing to overlook." Broaddrick said she was so shaken by the encounter that she exited the gathering because she felt "sick to [her] stomach."[33]

President Clinton refused to answer any questions about Broaddrick's explosive charge. All Clinton would say at a press conference was that "my counsel has made a statement . . . and I have nothing to add to it." What lawyer David Kendall had said on behalf of the President was: "Any allegation that the President assaulted Mrs. Broaddrick more than twenty years ago is absolutely false. Beyond that, we are not going to comment."[34]

On April 1, 1998, U.S. District Judge Susan Webber Wright stunned everyone by throwing out Paula Jones' sexual misconduct lawsuit against President Clinton: "Although the governor's alleged conduct, if true, may certainly be characterized as boorish and offensive, even a most charitable reading of the record in this case fails to reveal a basis for a claim of criminal sexual assault," U.S. District Judge Susan Webber Wright wrote in her thirty-nine-page ruling. "The plaintiffs' allegations fall short of the rigorous standards for establishing a claim of outrage under Arkansas law. It is adjudged that this case be, and hereby is, dismissed."[35]

Mrs. Jones attorney T. Wesley Holmes revealed that upon hearing the news of the ruling Paula Jones was "very upset. She started crying. She asked, 'How could this happen?'" He told her there were possibilities for an appeal to the Eighth Circuit Court of Appeals, but he would first have to study the decision.[36]

White House Press Secretary Michael McCurry said that when Bob Bennett told Mr. Clinton (he was overseas in Senegal at the time) of the ruling, he asked if it was an April Fool's joke. Once the reality set in, an uninhibited Clinton celebrated the news by chewing a cigar and beating on an African drum.[37]

On April 16, 1998, Paula Jones announced that she would appeal the decision to the Eighth U.S. Court of Appeals in St. Louis, which had three times reversed Little Rock judges who had ruled in Mr. Clinton's favor in Whitewater-related litigation.[38] On September 30, 1998, Paula Jones' attorneys filed a final brief asking the Eighth U.S. District Court of Appeals in St. Louis to reinstate her sexual misconduct lawsuit against President Clinton. They said their case would be helped by independent counsel Ken Starr's conclusion that Mr. Clinton lied under oath in Jones' lawsuit about his relationship with Monica Lewinsky.[39]

On October 9, 1998, the *Washington Times* reported that presidential attorney Robert Bennett formally asked to Judge Susan Webber Wright, in a September 30 letter, to disregard the affidavit he submitted from Monica Lewinsky denying a sexual relationship despite Mr. Clinton's January 17 testimony that it was "absolutely true."[40]

On October 14, 1998, Abe Hirschfeld, a New York real estate tycoon and friend of Clinton's, gave Paula Jones two days to accept a $1 million offer to settle her claims against President Clinton. Mr. Clinton also offered $700,000 to settle the case. The offer came six days before oral arguments were scheduled in the Eighth U.S. Circuit Court of Appeals.[41] Three days later Jones announced that she wanted $2 million in exchange for dropping all claims against President Clinton. Half would come from President Clinton and the other half from Abe Hirschfeld.[42]

On October 31, 1998, Abe Hirschfeld gave Paula Jones a check for $1 million that would become part of the overall settlement of her lawsuit. Her name and that of her lawyers, past and present, were on the check, which was held in escrow. The payment was contingent on her reaching a settlement with President Clinton.[43]

On November 9, 1998, the U.S. Supreme Court refused on a 7 to 2 vote to hear the Clinton administration's appeal in allowing the Secret Service to testify in the Paula Jones case and for the independent counsel.[44]

Oral argument before the federal court of appeals seemed to favor Paula Jones, particularly since Clinton's public *mea culpa* suggested that his deposition for the Jones case contained possibly perjurious statements. Not wanting to risk the appellate court reinstating the Jones lawsuit, Clinton settled with Jones out of court on November 13, 1998. She dropped her appeal, and he paid her $850,000 (more than she originally requested in her complaint).[45]

On January 12, 1999, President Clinton mailed Paula Jones an $850,000 check to settle the 1994 lawsuit that set the Monica Lewinsky investigation in motion. A Chubb Group insurance policy against civil liability paid $475,000, while Bill dipped into Hillary's million-dollar-plus blind trust for the remaining $375,000.[46]

What Paula Jones' sexual-misconduct lawsuit cost President Clinton was substantial:

- Settled the Jones lawsuit for $850,000
- Impeached by the House of Representatives on two counts
- Fifty senators voted to convict on one charge
- Held in contempt of court and fined by Judge Susan Webber Wright for intentional lying and attempting to obstruct justice.

- Agreed to a suspension of his Arkansas law license and conceded the falsity of some testimony in exchange for the independent counsel's closure of an outstanding criminal investigation.[47]

CHAPTER 34

MONICA LEWINSKY

*I want to say one thing to the American people. I want you to listen to me.
I did not have sexual relations with that woman, Miss Lewinsky.
I never told anybody to lie. Not a single time. Never.
These allegations are false and I need to go back to work for the American people.*

—President Clinton while wagging his finger denying the
Lewinsky affair, January 26, 1998[1]

On January 21, 1998, all hell broke loose as the *Washington Post, Los Angeles Times,* and ABC News reported on President Clinton's alleged relationship with a twenty-one-year-old former intern, Monica Lewinsky and on independent counsel Kenneth Starr's probe of allegations that Bill Clinton and Vernon Jordan encouraged her to lie. What events led up to this?

In the summer of 1995, Hillary's office received a phone call from Walter Kaye, a wealthy New York insurance mogul and a Democratic donor who was especially close to the first lady. Walter Kaye was calling to ask Hillary for a favor. A family friend named Marcia Lewis was trying to line up a summer job for her daughter, Monica Lewinsky. Monica was graduating from Lewis and Clark, a small college in Oregon, and was looking for a job in Washington, D.C.[2]

Just shy of her twenty-second birthday, Monica Samille Lewinsky arrived in Washington, D.C. in July 1995 to start an internship in the White House. Living with her mom and younger brother, Michael, in the Watergate Hotel, Monica interned for Leon Panetta, then Clinton's chief of staff, answering phones and preparing correspondence.[3]

On August 9, 1995, Bill Clinton was moving down the rope line of White House guests, when a dark-haired beauty thrust herself into his sight line. The President gave the girl "the full Bill Clinton," undressing her with his eyes. It's the way he flirts with women, as the intern was to discover. On that day, on their first encounter, Lewinsky was completely taken in: "When he came to shake my hand, the smile disappeared, the rest of the crowd disappeared, and we shared an intense but brief sexual exchange."[4] Their flirtation continued from a distance the next day at a birthday celebration for Clinton to which interns were invited. For a few months they exchanged only brief greetings on a handful of occasions.[5]

The first sexual encounter took place on the same day that Clinton signed a "Family Week" proclamation. On that day, November 15, 1995, which was the second day of the government shutdown, Monica Lewinsky, while talking alone to President Clinton in the Chief of Staff's office, raised her jacket in the back and showed him the straps of her thong underwear, which extended above her pants. Hillary's husband was intrigued and invited the intern back to his office later in the evening. They met again, and she performed oral sex while President Clinton was speaking to two members of Congress. President Clinton spoke with Rep. Jim Chapman from 9:25 p.m. to 9:30 p.m. and Rep. John Tanner from 9:31 p.m. to 9:35 p.m. from the Oval Office.[6]

Immediately, Clinton realized that being sexually serviced by an intern could be a political problem. He pulled on her intern pass and told her so. Yet, the good times continued.[7]

Clinton's next intimate rendezvous with the young woman was two days later on November 17, 1995. President Clinton asked Monica to bring him some slices of pizza. Again, Monica Lewinsky performed oral sex while President Clinton was speaking to a member of Congress, Rep. H. L. "Sonny" Callahan.[8]

On Sunday afternoon, January 7, 1996, Clinton called Monica at her Watergate apartment for the first time. She told prosecutors that was "the first time he called me at home . . . . And I asked him what he was doing." The President of the United States told his twenty-two-year-old intern that he was "going into the office soon." She replied, "Oh, do you want some company?" Said the president, "Oh, that would be great."[9]

The two met that afternoon at the door of the Oval Office. They got past Secret Service Uniformed Officer Lew Fox and reposed for a brief chat on a sofa in the Oval Office before repairing to the lavatory. As the *Starr Report* put it, "she and the president kissed and he touched her breasts with his hands and mouth. The president 'was talking about performing oral sex on me,' according to Ms. Lewinsky. But she stopped him because she was menstruating, and he did not. Miss Lewinsky did perform oral sex on him." There is more. They engaged in oral-anal contact as well.[10]

On January 16, 1996, Mrs. Clinton left on her book tour to support the sales of *It Takes a Village*. Clinton took advantage of the situation that evening to call Monica for their first round of phone sex.[11] Five days later, Clinton and Lewinsky had a genuinely accidental meeting near the Oval Office, and the president invited her in. Before he ushered her into the private office, Lewinsky asked him, "[I]s this just about sex . . . or do you have some interest in me as a person?" Clinton, she said, assured her that "he cherishes the time that he had with me." A short time later, the president got word that his next appointment, Jim and Diane Blair, friends from Arkansas had arrived. In order to avoid being seen, Lewinsky tried to sneak out through the office of Betty Currie, but the door was locked. When Lewinsky came back to tell the president that she would have to find another exit, she found him in the office of Nancy Hernreich, Currie's boss, masturbating. Lewinsky wound up leaving through the Rose Garden.[12]

On Sunday afternoon, February 4, 1996, Clinton again telephoned Lewinsky to arrange another "accidental" encounter at the White House. They walked back to his private study and she performed oral sex.[13] Two weeks later President Clinton telephoned Monica to come to the White House. In the Oval Office, Mr. Clinton told Ms. Lewinsky that he no longer felt right about their intimate relationship, and he had to put a stop to it. She was welcome to continue coming to visit him, but only as a friend. This was breakup day, but it didn't last long.[14]

On Sunday afternoon, March 31, 1996, Clinton telephoned Monica at her desk and suggested that she come to the Oval Office on the pretext of delivering papers to him. In the hallway by the study President Clinton began foreplay with Ms. Lewinsky and then inserted a cigar into her vagina. He then put the cigar in his mouth and said: "It tastes good."[15]

Despite Bill's attempts at being stealth, Hillary had eyes and ears everywhere in the White House. Her main watchdog was Deputy Chief of Staff Evelyn Lieberman, whom she met in the 1980s when they served together at the Children's Defense Fund. Hillary assigned her loyal friend the task of monitoring the sexual activity of Bill Clinton in the White House. Her nickname was Mother Superior.[16]

Soon, Evelyn Lieberman and other White House officials expressed concern that Monica Lewinsky had developed an apparent crush on Bill Clinton and was overly eager to spend time in his presence. They wanted her out of the White House. On Friday, April 5, 1996, Lewinsky was fired from the White House staff and transferred to the Defense Department where she was hired as a $32,736-a-year confidential assistant working for press spokesman Kenneth Bacon with the promise that she could return to the White House after Clinton's reelection was clinched.[17]

Two days after her transfer, on Easter Sunday, April 7, 1996, President Clinton telephoned Monica at her home. She told him of the job transfer to the Pentagon and asked to see him. At the White House, he told her, "I promise you if I win in November, I'll bring you back like that." Clinton continued, "You can have whatever you want." Then Monica made a joke: "Well, can I be the assistant to the president for blow jobs?" And the President said, "I'd like that." Then in the hallway, Monica performed oral sex.[18]

Interestingly, during the encounter, someone called out from the Oval Office that the president had a phone call. He went to the Oval Office for a moment, then took the call in the study. The president indicated that Monica should perform oral sex while he talked on the phone, and she obliged. White House records showed that the president had one telephone call during Ms. Lewinsky's visit. It was from Dick Morris.[19]

Their session though, was soon interrupted. Clinton's aide Harold Ickes arrived in the Oval Office to see the president. Lewinsky left out a side door. They didn't see each other privately for the rest of 1996.[20]

At the Pentagon, Lewinsky was given a Top Secret security clearance to go with her job as a "confidential assistant" to Defense Department spokesman Kenneth Bacon. But, that was only part of the truth. According to Terence Jeffrey in *Human Events*:

> Lewinsky not only held a Top Secret clearance, a Pentagon spokesman, Col. Dick Bridges, confirmed to me [Jeffrey], but also a Sensitive Compartmented Information (SCI) clearance, the highest security clearance granted by the U.S. Government. The Secretary of Defense, the national security advisor, and the chairman of the House and

Senate Intelligence Committees did not have higher clearances than that woman, Miss Lewinsky.[21]

Shortly after she started at the Pentagon, Monica noticed that one of her colleagues in the public affairs office had decorated her work space with "jumbos" of President Clinton. They are the large-format photographs that are displayed throughout the White House. Lewinsky wondered if the owner of the photographs had also worked at the White House. As Tripp later testified in the grand jury, "I had the jumbos and she begged me for one of the jumbos." So on the basis of this aspect of their shared past, Monica Lewinsky and Linda Tripp began their friendship.[22]

At first Lewinsky would say only that she had had an affair with "someone" at the White House. She initially called him "Handsome." Eventually, she admitted her lover was the president.[23]

In August 1996, Monica traveled to New York to attend a gala fundraiser on the occasion of Clinton's fiftieth birthday. At this event, Lewinsky was able to place herself near the president, and then, in the words of one of her FBI debriefings, "Lewinsky reached behind herself to fondle and squeeze the President's penis."[24]

In early November 1996, Monica managed to gain entry to a fundraiser for Senate Democrats that was attended by Clinton. She walked up to the president and had her picture taken with him. This time, he was wearing one of her neckties. "Hey, Handsome," she told him, "I like your tie."[25] That same night, Clinton telephoned Monica for some phone sex, and she mentioned that she planned to be at the White House on Pentagon business the next day.[26] "Stop by the Oval Office," the president said. But when Monica showed up at the White House the following day, she spotted Evelyn Lieberman standing near the Oval Office. Monica decided to leave without seeing Clinton.[27]

Once Clinton defeated Bob Dole in the '96 presidential election, he never delivered on his promise of a White House job. But he did agree to see Lewinsky again. After she left the White House, she began cultivating the president's personal secretary, Betty Currie, who came to serve as Lewinsky's conduit for messages to, and occasionally from, Clinton.[28] On February 28, 1997, Betty Currie invited Lewinsky to watch the taping of the president's weekly radio address. After the speech, they retreated to his private office. Clinton gave Monica a pair of belated Christmas gifts: A blue glass hat pin and an edition of Walt Whitman's *Leaves of Grass*. For the first time in nearly eleven months, Monica began performing oral sex on the president, but this time their encounter would end differently from all the others. As Lewinsky later testified to Starr's prosecutors, "I finished."[29]

Monica was wearing a navy blue Gap dress that came into contact with "biological" proof of the tryst. She told Linda Tripp about the dress and that she suspected some of Clinton's semen might be on it. Tripp encouraged her to keep it and not have it cleaned.[30]

There was only one more sexual contact between them. On March 29, 1997, with the president still on crutches from his knee injury at golfer Greg Norman's house in Florida, Lewinsky once again performed oral sex "to completion" while, as she put it to Starr's prosecutors, Clinton "manually stimulated me" to four orgasms. Afterwards, according to Ms. Lewinsky, she and the President had a lengthy conversation. He told her that he suspected a foreign embassy—he did not specify which one—was tapping his telephones. He proposed several cover stories. If ever questioned, she should say that the two of them were just friends. If anyone ever asked about their phone sex, she should say that they knew their calls were being monitored all along, and the phone sex was just a put-on.[31]

In April or May 1997, according to Lewinsky, the president called her to ask if she had told her mother about their intimate relationship. She responded, "No. Of course not." (In truth, she had told her mother.) The president indicated that Ms. Lewinsky's mother possibly had said something about the nature of the relationship to Walter Kaye, who had mentioned it to Marsha Scott, who in turn had alerted the president.[32]

On May 24, 1997, Betty Currie telephoned Monica to come to the White House. When President Clinton met with her privately, he told her that they had to end their intimate relationship. Monica was devastated by the news and the sexual relationship was over. This was officially known as "dump day."[33]

On July 3, 1997, Monica was very frustrated over her inability to get in touch with President Clinton to discuss her job situation. She wrote a letter with the opening, "Dear Sir" taking him to task for breaking his promise to get her another White House job. Monica also obliquely threatened to disclose their relationship. If she was not going to return to work at the White House, she wrote, then she raised the possibility of a job outside Washington. If returning to the White House was impossible, she asked in this letter if he could get her a job at the United Nations in New York?[34]

On July 4, 1997, they met again. Lewinsky said Clinton was "the most affectionate with me as he'd ever been." She told the grand jury that while he stroked her hair and kissed her neck, "I made some remarks to him about his relationship with Mrs. Clinton. And he, he remarked a little bit later that he wished he had more time with me. And so I said, well, maybe you will have more time in three years. And I was sort of thinking just when he wasn't president, he was going to have more time on his hands. And he said, well, I don't know. I might be alone in three years."[35]

On July 14, 1997, Lewinsky had just returned from an overseas trip with the Pentagon when she received a call from Betty Currie asking her to meet with the president that evening. Since Paula Jones's lawyers were on to Kathleen Willey, Clinton asked Lewinsky to please convince Tripp to call Bruce Lindsey, presumably to find out exactly what Tripp was prepared to say publicly about Willey. Lewinsky complied with Clinton's request. In the same conversation Clinton asked Lewinsky if she had said anything to Tripp about her relationship with him. Lewinsky said (falsely) that she had not.[36]

Lewinsky was still hoping that she might be given a job at the White House. She remained hopeful until the morning of October 6, 1997, when she had a conversation with Linda Tripp. Tripp said she had spoken to a friend at the National Security Council, where Lewinsky had applied for a job. "She has heard that you will not be placed over there.... And she said, 'I promise you that if they wanted to have her placed, they would have done it by now. And the last thing on earth that they want is her in this White House.'"[37]

Lewinsky was stunned. "This is just—I'm going to vomit," she told Tripp. "You know what? I'm going to call Betty and I'm going to tell her to go fuck herself. That's what I'm going to do. I don't care. I don't care anymore... It's like, wake up. This thing is over. It's over."[38]

Lewinsky was so upset, she left work for the day. At home, she decided that she was going to forget the White House, leave Washington, and get a job in New York. And she was going to make the president find her one. That evening, Monica wrote a letter to Clinton. As she wrote, she talked each line over with Tripp. "I'd like to ask you to secure a position for me," Lewinsky read aloud. "Or how about, 'Help me secure?'" Tripp thought "help me obtain" might be better. "But you know," Lewinsky answered, "maybe I'm being an idiot. I don't want to have to work for this position. I want it to be given to me."[39]

"Right," Tripp responded. "You don't want to go through the whole interview process."[40]

"Right," Lewinsky said.[41]

Lewinsky sent her letter to Clinton by courier the next day, on October 7. She didn't hear back from the president that day or the next. But on Friday morning, October 10 at 2:00 a.m., Clinton called, and he was furious.[42]

"He just yelled at me," Lewinsky told Tripp later in the day. "And I'm not kidding you . . . . I mean, Linda, he got so mad at me, he must have been purple." By her own account, Lewinsky wanted a job and she "wanted to make the president pay for fucking up my life." For his part, Clinton feared Lewinsky might one day reveal their sexual relationship.[43]

Lewinsky was so upset that she called in sick on Friday, October 10, spending much of the day talking to Tripp. Early Saturday morning Lewinsky's phone rang. It was Currie, who said Clinton wanted her to come to the White House.[44] Lewinsky rushed to the White House, arriving a little after 9:30 a.m. Meeting alone in the Oval Office study, Lewinsky and Clinton talked about having Vernon Jordan help with her New York job search. Lewinsky later told the grand jury that she thought Jordan "would be a good person who is a close friend of the president and who has a lot of contacts in New York."[45]

Secret Service records showed that Monica left the White House at 10:54 a.m. At that moment Jordan was miles away, in Manassas, Virginia, at the Robert Trent Jones Golf Club. Jordan was then the president of the club and had gone there that morning to attend a board of directors meeting.[46]

On Sunday, the president flew to Venezuela, the start of a weeklong visit to Latin America. Back home, Lewinsky was preparing to send Clinton a "wish list" of jobs she would be willing to accept in New York. She wrote that she wanted to be an assistant producer at any of the networks, do news/political segments at MTV, work at one of several public relations firms, or do "anything at *George* magazine." At the bottom of the list she added a final note:[47] "I do not have any interest in working [at the U.N.]. As a result of what happened in April '96, I have already spent a year and a half at an agency in which I have no interest. I want a job where I feel challenged, engaged and interested. I don't think the U.N. is the right place for me."[48]

On October 16, 1997, Lewinsky sent the note to Clinton, when he was still in Latin America. But by then it was too late. Clinton was already working the U.N. angle. Shortly before leaving for Latin America, the president told Currie to have a chat with John Podesta, at the time a top Clinton aide. As Podesta later testified, Currie "reminded me who Miss Lewinsky was . . . that she wanted to move to New York." According to Podesta, Currie asked "whether I could give her any referrals of any people she could talk to about getting a job in New York." As it turned out, Podesta was traveling with the president, as was Bill Richardson. Podesta brought up the topic of Lewinsky with Richardson. Podesta, as he later remembered the conversation, told Richardson that Currie had "a friend who was moving to New York, who was a low-level, entry-level public affairs person, and could he take a look at her?" Podesta said Richardson responded "that he might have something at the U.N., that they had some positions in their public affairs office. And I said to him, 'Why don't I have Betty get you a resume of the young woman.'"[49]

Richardson soon began a series of rapid moves to accommodate Lewinsky's job wishes. He returned from Latin America on Sunday October 19. It was an extremely busy time. Richardson's schedule called for him to return to the office on Monday for three days and then fly to the Congo on Thursday, October 23. Nevertheless, when Richardson got to work on Monday, October 20, he told his longtime assistant, Isabelle Watkins, to "keep an eye out" for a resume coming from Podesta's office. By the next day, Watkins told Richardson that she not received the resume. He asked her to get in touch with Podesta's office to see what was going on. At that point Betty Currie arranged for the resume to be faxed to the United Nations office. Records obtained by Starr show it was faxed a little after three o'clock in the afternoon on Tuesday, October 21.[50]

Richardson examined Lewinsky's resume the same afternoon it appeared on the fax machine. Phone records obtained by Starr's investigators show that someone using Richardson's office telephone extension called Lewinsky at home that very night, October 21, at seven o'clock. But there is conflicting testimony over who spoke to whom. Lewinsky testified that she spoke to Richardson himself. Richardson denied it.[51]

Lewinsky told Starr's prosecutors that she specifically remembered the phone ringing and a secretary telling her, "Hold for Ambassador Richardson." She was surprised that Richardson was calling. According to notes of a Lewinsky interview with prosecutors, she "was upset because [she] did not want to work at the United Nations. No one told her Richardson would be calling, and she did not want to get stuck working there with no other opportunities."[52]

Whoever made the call, the evidence shows that Richardson tried to set up the interview as quickly as possible, perhaps even for the next day, which would have been the eve of his trip to the Congo. That didn't work out, and on Thursday, October 23, Richardson left the country, not to return until the next Wednesday, October 29. But he was still moving quickly on Lewinsky. When he returned from the Congo, Richardson made room for Monica on his second day back. The job interview was set up for Friday morning, October 31, at a suite at the Watergate Hotel.[53]

Lewinsky was surprised and dismayed at how rapidly Richardson was moving. Since he had already decided she didn't want to work at the U.N., she was placing her hopes on Vernon Jordan's private sector job search. But Jordan was away from Washington for much of this time period, while Richardson was a sure thing. She didn't want to turn him down flat, but she didn't want to say yes, either.[54]

She sent word through Currie that she needed to talk to the president. Two days after the phone call from Richardson, Clinton called her. Lewinsky revealed the job search situation and the call from Richardson to her friend Linda Tripp:

> **Tripp:** "Did he know that?"
> **Lewinsky:** "I—Okay, no, but yeah," Lewinsky said. "He didn't know, but I'm not—I think—he had put—he kind of had put Podesta on it. Or maybe he put Betty. You know, you never know the real truth."
> **Tripp:** "I know."
> **Lewinsky:** "And he wants the U.N. to be my insurance policy . . . . He wants me to have options. Vernon's been out of town —"
> **Tripp:** "Did he understand about your not wanting to go to the U.N.?"
> **Lewinsky:** "Yes, he did. But what he also said was, 'Look, I want you to—I want you to think about it, I want you to spend some time and think about . . . what kinds of things you could—what you could do there.' You know, [Richardson's] a good guy, he's flexible, he's, you

know, he's willing to kind of create a position. You know, 'Maybe he might be able to create a position, what you want to do.' "[55]

The president's words seemed to assure Lewinsky. The interview was set for 7:30 a.m. at the Watergate Hotel in Washington.[56]

On Sunday, November 2, 1997, Lewinsky wrote in a letter to Currie, just two days after the interview: "As you know, the U.N. is supposed to be my back-up, but because VJ [Vernon Jordan] has been out of town, this is my only option right now. What should I say to Richardson's people this week when they call? . . . If you feel it's appropriate, maybe you could ask 'the big guy' what he wants me to do. Ahhhhh . . . anxiety!!!!!"[57]

Lewinsky was right to be nervous. At 11 o'clock Monday morning, November 3, the first business day after the Friday interview, the phone rang at her Pentagon desk. It was Richardson's office. She was offered a job as a U.N. staffer.[58]

At the end of her conversation, Lewinsky said she needed some time to consider the job offer. Richardson's office said that was okay. Of course, Lewinsky had no intention of accepting the position, but she wanted to keep it on the table while she waited to see what Jordan could come up with. Fortunately for her, Richardson's offer had no time limit.[59]

From October 7 to December 8, 1997, Lewinsky sent nine packages to the White House addressed to Betty Currie, containing letters and, in one case, a sexually provocative audiotape for the president.[60]

On November 4, 1997, Monica informed her bosses at the Pentagon that she intended to resign. She told them "her mother had moved to New York and she wanted to be near her."[61] The next day Monica met with Vernon Jordan for twenty minutes. No action followed, no job interviews were arranged, and there were no further contacts with Mr. Jordan. It was obvious that Mr. Jordan made no effort to find a job for her.[62]

Lewinsky was unhappy that Jordan had yet to produce any results. "I am not a moron," Lewinsky wrote in a letter to Clinton sent by courier on November 11. "I know what is going on in the world takes precedence, but I don't think what I have asked you for is unreasonable . . . . I need you now not as president, but as a man. PLEASE be my friend," she wrote. Clinton and Lewinsky talked the following evening, and he proposed she stop by briefly on November 13.[63]

On November 13, 1997, Lewinsky met with Clinton and gave him an antique paperweight and showed him an e-mail describing the effects of chewing Altoid mints before performing oral sex. "Ms. Lewinsky was chewing Altoids at the time," the *Starr Report* noted, "but the President replied that he did not have enough time for oral sex." He hurried off to a state dinner.[64]

Towards the end of November 1997, Lewinsky travelled to California to visit her family. She was waiting to hear from Vernon Jordan, who was traveling during the last three weeks of November. The day before Thanksgiving, she called Betty Currie at the White House. Later that day, Jordan called Currie, and a few minutes later Currie paged Lewinsky with the message, "Please call Vernon Jordan. Betty Currie."[65]

Lewinsky told Starr's investigators that she got the page and called Currie from a pay phone at the Wilshire Courtyard Marriott in Los Angeles. Currie told her to call Jordan, who told Lewinsky that he was working on her job search, but that he was leaving on a business trip to China. He told Lewinsky to call him when he got back in the first week of December. An hour and a half later, Jordan called the White House. Jordan would later tell the grand jury he couldn't remember any of the calls.[66]

Jordan came back from China on Thursday, December 4. The next day, he flew to Dallas for the day. He returned to Washington and escorted his wife to the white-tie Symphony Ball held at the National Building Museum in Washington.[67] That Friday Secret Service Director Lewis Merletti issued a directive to thirty-two hundred current and five hundred former Secret Service personnel reminding them of an unwritten code of silence that prohibits agents from talking to anyone about "any aspect of the personal lives of [their] protectees." Agents' commitment to remain silent "should continue forever," Mr. Merletti wrote.[68] On the same day, Monica asked Betty Currie if the president could see her the next day, but Ms. Currie said that the president was scheduled to meet with his lawyers all day. Later that Friday, Lewinsky spoke briefly to the president at a Christmas party.[69]

At 5:40 p.m., on Friday, December 5, 1997, Paula Jones legal team faxed their witness list to Robert Bennett in Washington. Many of the names were unfamiliar to Bennett and his team, so they had an informal agreement with David Pyke, one of Jones' attorneys, to give a capsule summary of each potential witness testimony. Bennett's partner, Mitch Ettinger, called Pyke for the rundown. As Ettinger read a name, Pyke would say, "He slept with that one," "He raped that one," "He harassed that one." Monica Lewinsky's name was also on that list, but she didn't find out until the president told her nearly two weeks later, on December 17.[70]

After her conversation with Ms. Currie and seeing the president at the Christmas party the previous evening, Monica drafted a letter to the president terminating their relationship. The next morning, Saturday, December 6, 1997, Monica went to the White House to deliver the letter and some gifts for the president to Ms. Currie. These included a sterling silver antique cigar holder, a mug from Starbucks, a tie, "a little box that's called hugs and kisses," and an antique book on Theodore Roosevelt that she had purchased at a New York flea market.[71]

When she arrived at the Northwest Gate of the White House, Lewinsky spoke to several Secret Service officers, and one of them told her that the president was not with his lawyers as she thought, but rather he was meeting with Eleanor Mondale. Lewinsky was livid. She stormed off to a nearby bar, telephoned Currie, and began screaming at her. Then she went home. After that phone call, Ms. Currie was shaking and ready to cry when she approached several Secret Service officers. She told them that the president was "irate" that someone told Lewinsky with whom he was meeting. According to the *Starr Report* Currie told Sergeant Keith Williams, a supervisor, that if he "didn't find out what was going on, someone could be fired." She also told the watch commander, Captain Jeff Purdie, the president was "so upset he wants somebody fired over this."[72]

On Saturday, December 6, 1997, at 12:05 p.m., records demonstrate that Ms. Currie paged Bruce Lindsey with the message: "Call Betty ASAP." Around the same time, according to Ms. Lewinsky, while she was back at her apartment, Lewinsky and the president spoke on the telephone. The president was very angry. He told her that no one had ever treated him as poorly as she had. Nevertheless, in a sudden change of mood, he invited her to visit him at the White House that afternoon.[73]

Monica went to the White House for the second time that day and was cleared to enter at 12:52 p.m. Although, in her words, the president was "very angry" with her during their recent telephone conversation, he was "sweet" and "very affectionate" during the visit. He also told her that he would talk to Vernon Jordan about her job situation.[74]

After Clinton's meeting with Lewinsky, Bob Bennett arrived at the White House to discuss the witness list. When Monica Lewinsky's name came up, the Jones team claimed Clinton had an affair with her. He responded, "Bob, do you think I'm fucking crazy? Hey, look, let's move on. I know the press is watching me every minute. The right has been dying for this kind of thing from day one. No, it didn't happen." Yet, Clinton had talked to Lewinsky on the phone and in person for a total of nearly two hours immediately prior to his denial to Bennett.[75]

The next day, Vernon Jordan went to the White House to see Clinton. Four days later, on December 11, Mr. Jordan met with Monica and gave her a list of contact names. The two also discussed the president. Jordan remembered placing calls to two prospective employers. Later in the afternoon, he even called the president to give him a report on his job search efforts. Clearly, Mr. Jordan and the president were now *very* interesting in helping Monica find a good job in New York. That's because, on the morning of December 11 Judge Susan Weber Wright ordered that Paula Jones was entitled to information regarding any state or federal employee with whom the president had sexual relations or proposed or sought to have sexual relations. To keep Monica on their team was now of critical importance.[76]

On December 16, 1997, Clinton received a request from the Jones lawyers to turn over "documents that related to communications between the president and Monica Lewinsky." In the middle of the night Clinton called Monica.She told the grand jury: "The phone rang unexpectedly at about maybe 2:00 or 2:30." It was the president with the news that her name was on the Jones witness list. "He told me it broke his heart," she recalled. Monica asked him what she could do if she receives a subpoena. He told her she might be able to sign an affidavit to avoid testifying. It was then that he made his now well-known suggestion that Lewinsky could "always say you were coming to see Betty or that you were bringing me letters." Clinton also told Lewinsky to contact Betty Currie immediately if she received a subpoena.[77]

After talking with Clinton, Monica called Linda Tripp. Tripp had been subpoenaed in the Jones case and Monica had been pressuring her to be a team player. She wanted her to deny the suggestion that anything sexual had ever happened between Clinton and Willey, and especially between Clinton and her. That night, Monica wanted Tripp to know that if she lied about knowing anything concerning her and Clinton, it would be okay because she and the others would make the same denials. Everyone could provide a "unified front" and the problem might just disappear.[78]

On December 19, 1997, Monica received a subpoena to testify in a deposition on January 23, 1998, in the Jones case. The subpoena called not just for her testimony, but also for her to produce "each and every gift" she had received from the president, including "jewelry and or hat pins."[79] Monica was very upset, and she immediately called Vernon Jordan. She called Jordan instead of Currie because her brother had recently died, and she did not want to bother her. Jordan invited Lewinsky to his office, and Jordan called Clinton to tell him Monica had been subpoenaed. During the meeting with Lewinsky, which Jordan characterized as "disturbing," she talked about her infatuation with Clinton. Jordan decided to get Monica a lawyer. That evening, Jordan met with Clinton and relayed his conversation with Monica. He told the president again that she had been subpoenaed and that he was concerned about her fascination with him. Jordan also asked Clinton if he had sexual relations with Lewinsky.[80]

After meeting with Lewinsky one more time on December 22, 1997, Jordan arranged for her to meet her new lawyer, Frank Carter. Lewinsky told Carter there was no way she should have received this subpoena and that the Paula Jones's case was "bunk." Lewinsky also said she would be willing to sign an affidavit denying a sexual relationship with Clinton and/or explaining away her frequent visits and correspondence to the White House by saying she was just over there visiting Betty Currie.[81]

On December 26, 1997, Monica Lewinsky left the Department of Defense.[82]

On Sunday, December 28, 1997, nine days after she had been served with a subpoena, Monica went to the White House and met with Clinton. He gave her a throw rug, a pin, and an Alaskan stone carving, which was odd given he knew about the subpoena.[83]

Their conversation turned to her subpoena in the Jones case—another critical moment in the case against Clinton. Clinton believed that it was Linda Tripp, or, as he called her, "that woman from the summer, with Kathleen Willey," who was cooperating with the Jones lawyers. Lewinsky and Clinton arranged for Betty Currie to retrieve a box of gifts that she was not going to turn over to the Jones lawyers.[84]

Clinton gave her a "physically intimate" kiss, she testified later. After a while, he walked her to the door and almost in passing said to her the unforgettable words "My life is empty." This marked Lewinsky's final encounter with the president. Three weeks later in the Paula Jones deposition, Clinton testified, "I don't remember a single gift."[85]

A few hours after Lewinsky and Clinton met, Currie showed up at her house and said something like, "The President said you have something to give me." Lewinsky gave Currie a sealed box that contained the subpoenaed gifts. Currie hid the box under her bed.[86]

On December 30, 1997, Lewinsky called Vernon Jordan. She was concerned about the mention of a "hat pin" in the Jones subpoena. Jordan suggested they meet the next morning for breakfast at the Park Hyatt. At the Park Hyatt, seated at Jordan's customary corner table, Lewinsky "fessed up." She later testified:

> **Lewinsky:** "I told him that I had had this friend, Linda Tripp, who was sort of involved in the Paula Jones case. And I said that she was my friend, that I didn't really trust her. I used to trust her, but I didn't trust her anymore and I was a little bit concerned because she had spent the night at my house a few times and I thought, I told Mr. Jordan, I said, well, maybe she's heard some, you know, I mean, maybe she saw some notes lying around."
> **Jordan:** "Notes from the president to you?"
> **Lewinsky:** "No, notes from me to the president."
> **Jordan:** "Go home and make sure they're not there."[87]

"What did you understand him to mean?" prosecutors asked.[88]

"I thought that meant that—to go home and search around and if there are copies of notes or anything that I sent or drafts, to throw them away." Lewinsky told investigators she did just that, throwing away as much as fifty pages of letters to Clinton and implicating Jordan in a possibly criminal act of obstruction of justice.[89]

On January 3, 1998, Monica's access to the White House was cut off. She had visited the White House thirty-seven times from April 1996, when she left the White House to work at the Pentagon, to December 28, 1997.[90] The next day, Monica created a scene at the White House gate when uniformed Secret Service officers refused to admit her. "Do you know who I am?" Lewinsky is said to have screamed when she was denied entry. The president was vacationing out of town.[91]

The next afternoon Monica met with her lawyer, Frank Carter, to discuss the affidavit. After the meeting, she called Betty Currie and said that she wanted to speak to the president before she signed anything. Lewinsky and the president discussed the issue of how she would answer under oath if asked about how she got her job at the Pentagon. The president told her, "Well, you could always say that the people in Legislative Affairs got it for you or helped you get it." That was a lie.[92]

On January 6 Lewinsky picked up a draft of the affidavit from Mr. Carter's office. She delivered a copy to Mr. Jordan's office because she wanted him to look at the affidavit in the belief that if Vernon Jordan gave his approval, Clinton would also approve. Lewinsky and Jordan conferred about the contents and agreed to delete a paragraph inserted by Carter that might open a line of questions concerning whether she had been alone with the president.[93]

Interestingly, Vernon Jordan would later testify that he had nothing to do with the details of the affidavit. He admitted, though, that he spoke with the president after conferring with Ms. Lewinsky about the changes made to her affidavit. The next day, January 7, 1998, Monica Lewinsky signed the false affidavit. She showed the executed copy to Jordan which allowed him to report to Clinton that it had been signed.[94]

Later that day, Lewinsky flew to New York for her job interview. On the following day, January 8, she had an interview with MacAndrews & Forbes. The interview went badly. Lewinsky complained to Vernon Jordan, who then called company chairman Ronald Perelman on Monica's behalf to "make things happen if they could happen." Mr. Jordan called Monica back and told her not to worry. That evening, MacAndrews & *Forbes* called Lewinsky and told her she would be given more interviews the next morning.[95]

The next morning, January 9, 1998, Monica received her reward for signing the false affidavit. After a series of interviews with MacAndrews & Forbes personnel, she was informally offered a $40,000 salaried position in their public relations department. She accepted. When Monica called Vernon Jordan's office to tell him, he passed the good news on to Betty Currie: Tell the president, "Mission Accomplished." Later, Mr. Jordan called the president and told him personally.[96]

On January 12, 1998, Francis Carter informed Paula Jones's attorneys that Lewinsky had denied having a sexual relationship with the president, although the affidavit remained unfiled. Carter shared the information in hopes of persuading Jones's lawyers not to depose her because she could not help them establish that Clinton had shown a pattern of sexual misconduct.[97]

That same day, Linda Tripp contacted independent counsel Ken Starr after Monica Lewinsky asked her to deny the relationship. Tripp had seventeen audiotapes, some as long as two hours, with Lewinsky describing sex with the president in a room near the Oval Office, late-night phone sex conversations she had with Mr. Clinton, and assertions by the president that he did not believe oral sex legally constituted adultery. The tapes also appeared to document an effort by President Clinton and Vernon Jordan to persuade Monica Lewinsky to lie about the affair in giving testimony in the Paula Jones sexual misconduct lawsuit.[98]

That evening, Office of the Independent Counsel (OIC) prosecutors, Jackie Bennett, Sol Wisenberg, and Steve Binhak and FBI agent Steve Irons traveled to Columbia, Maryland, to meet Linda Tripp and listen to her story.[99]

The next day, on January 13, 1998, Lewinsky stopped by Jordan's office for a brief visit and gave him a tie and a pocket square as a thank-you gift. It was their last meeting.[100] Following her visit with Jordan, Lewinsky made her way to the Ritz-Carlton Hotel in Pentagon City for a late lunch with Linda Tripp. The FBI had wired Tripp, and for the first time, Starr's investigators heard firsthand Lewinsky discuss her relationship with Clinton.[101] One item stood out: "I told [Mr. Jordan] that I wouldn't sign the affidavit unless I got the job."[102]

On January 14, 1998, Tripp and Lewinsky saw each other again, and Lewinsky delivered a set of "talking points" to her confidante, urging Tripp to lie in testimony in the Jones case.[103] It described how she could deny claims Mr. Clinton acted improperly with Kathleen Willey, including instructions on how to dodge questions on sexual misconduct and contained a legal affidavit that Tripp could copy to deny the accusations. It also urged Tripp to say Willey smeared her own lipstick and untucked her own blouse in order to discredit the president. The document also suggested Tripp might lose her job if she refused to lie about her knowledge of Clinton's suspected affairs.[104] "It's important to you that [Clinton administration officials] think you're a team player," the document said. "After all, you are a political appointee."[105]

On January 14, 1998, the president's lawyers called Frank Carter and left a message, presumably to find out if he had filed Lewinsky's affidavit with the court. The next day the president's attorneys called him twice. When they finally reached him, they requested a copy of the affidavit and asked him, "Are we still on time?" To have its full effect, the affidavit had to be filed with the court and provided to the president's attorneys in time for his deposition on the seventeenth. Carter called the court in Arkansas twice on January 15 to ensure that the affidavit could be filed on Saturday, January 17. He then faxed a copy of the affidavit on January 15. The president's counsel was aware of its contents and used it to their full advantage at the deposition. Obviously, the president needed that affidavit to be filed with the court to support his plans to mislead Paula Jones's attorneys in the deposition.[106]

On January 15, 1998, Ken Starr's deputy Jackie Bennett contacted Deputy Attorney General Eric Holder to update him of the situation. Once he learned about the new details, Holder had no choice but to expand Starr's authority to deal with the case. With *Newsweek* close to publishing an article on the affair, Holder said, "It was pretty clear to us—there wouldn't be time to get somebody else in there," and if the opportunity had been lost to move against Clinton and Jordan before they were aware of the investigation, "we would've been criticized justifiably."[107]

On January 16, 1998, three major events occurred: First, a three-judge panel that oversees independent counsels approved Attorney General Janet Reno's request to expand Starr's mandate.[108] Second, Frank Carter filed Monica's affidavit with the court with the motion to quash the subpoena Miss Lewinsky received from Paula Jones's attorneys. By the end of the day, Lewinsky fired Carter.[109] Finally, on instructions from the OIC, Tripp set up a meeting with Lewinsky, at 11:30 a.m., at the food court in the Pentagon City Mall, near where the two women had had lunch three days earlier.[110]

At 12:45 p.m., as Tripp went down the escalator, she signaled to FBI agents Steve Irons and Patrick Fallon, Jr., who were assigned to Starr, and who were anxiously waiting. They descended on Lewinsky and told her that she was wanted for questioning in connection with an investigation of the president of the United States for obstruction of justice. The two agents quickly escorted Lewinsky to Room 1012 of the adjoining Ritz-Carlton Hotel. Tripp trailed behind and joined them in the hotel room.[111]

From the moment Lewinsky arrived at 1:05 p.m., she was questioned by OIC agents Michael Emmick, Jackie Bennett, and Bruce Udolf. They told her she might be prosecuted and face a long prison sentence and encouraged her to cooperate. At around 3:00 p.m., Lewinsky asked to call her mother, and Emmick reluctantly allowed Monica to leave the room and make the call from a pay phone.[112] When Monica returned her mother, Marcia Lewis, called the room from New York. On the spot Emmick decided to offer immunity to both Monica and her mother. Obviously stalling, Lewinsky asked if her mother could join the negotiations in person. Emmick agreed, and Marcia, who feared air travel, got the next train to DC.[113]

As they were waiting for Marcia Lewis's arrival that evening, Ms. Tripp left the hotel room and went home where she spoke with Jones's lawyers for two hours, discussing what Miss Lewinsky had said in some twenty hours of secretly recorded conversations. Ms. Tripp had already given those tapes to Mr. Starr's investigators.[114]

Ms. Lewis finally arrived at 10:16 p.m. and spoke to her daughter alone. At that point, everyone in the room was tired from the combination of boredom and tension. They called Bernie Lewinsky, Monica's father, in Los Angeles. A lawyer friend of Bernie's, named William Ginsburg, called to speak to Monica and then to Emmick to disclose that he was her new lawyer. Clearly Lewinsky would not be answering any questions. At 12:45 a.m., the agents escorted Lewinsky and her mother to Monica's car in the mall parking lot.[115]

The next day, Ginsburg flew to Washington, and Monica picked him up at the airport. From there they drove to the Hay-Adams Hotel, across the street from the White House, where they spent three hours discussing her situation. The one thing Ginsburg knew for sure was that Monica shouldn't talk to anyone, not the president, not Betty Currie, and not the prosecutors until he obtained immunity for her.[116]

Ginsburg went to Starr's office that night, Saturday, January 17, 1998. The prosecutors, Jackie Bennett, Bob Bittman, and Mike Emmick, still wanted Lewinsky to make controlled phone calls to Currie, Jordan, and perhaps the president. Ginsburg said no. He didn't believe Lewinsky was in any state of mind to become an undercover operative. Ginsburg promised that his client would tell prosecutors everything she knew, but she wouldn't go to work for them.[117]

Soon realizing he was in over his head, Ginsburg placed a late-night phone call to an old acquaintance, Nathaniel Speights, an experienced Washington criminal lawyer, to assist him with the legal work. On Sunday, January 18, 1998, Ginsburg and Monica spent most of the day at Speight's house in Chevy Chase, and Lewinsky again explained her relationship with Clinton. Speights called Mike Emmick at the OIC to say that if his office was considering prosecuting Monica, they could forget about any kind of cooperation. He wanted immunity for her or there would be no further discussions. Emmick called back and said that immunity was a possibility, but they needed to hear more of Monica's story before they decided.[118]

On Monday afternoon, January 19, 1998, Ginsburg, Speights, and Lewinsky met with the OIC agents at the independent counsel's offices. While negotiations were going on, the prosecutors were called away to study some important news that just arrived. It was the *Drudge Report*, which contained the first public reference to Lewinsky's name. "It's too late now," Jackie Bennett announced. "She's radioactive." Suddenly Monica's value as a covert operative dropped to zero.[119]

Newsweek reporter Michael Isikoff also had details about Lewinsky and knowledge that the Justice Department had authorized independent counsel Kenneth Starr to examine links between the president and accusations of suborning, perjury, obstructing justice, and making false statements. Unfortunately, *Newsweek* decided to kill the story. Their excuse was: "Because it's sex, it's Vernon Jordan, it's [Bill] Clinton, and it makes people nervous."[120]

The Monica Lewinsky post on the *Drudge Report* actually occurred at 11:32 p.m., Saturday evening, January 17, 1998. Matt Drudge had posted a "World Exclusive" item on his Web site. He revealed that the editors at *Newsweek* magazine, after considerable internal debate, had decided to kill a story that was "destined to shake official Washington to its foundation."[121]

On Sunday morning, January 18, 1998, the White House was rapidly losing control of the situation. Clinton called Betty Currie to the White House. At 5:00 p.m., Currie met with Clinton. Clinton said that he had just been deposed and that the attorneys asked several questions about Monica Lewinsky. This, incidentally, was a violation of Judge Wright's gag order prohibiting any discussions about the deposition testimony. He then made a series of statements to Ms. Currie:[122]

1. "I was never really alone with Monica, right?"
2. "You were always there when Monica was there, right?"
3. "Monica came on to me, and I never touched her, right?"
4. "You could see and hear everything, right?"
5. "She wanted to have sex with me, and I cannot do that."[123]
6. Very soon after his Sunday meeting with Betty Currie, at 5:12 p.m., Ms. Currie began an intensive search for Monica Lewinsky.[124]

* Currie paged Lewinsky at 5:12 p.m. on January 18, 1998: "PLEASE CALL KAY AT HOME."

* Currie paged Lewinsky at 6:22 p.m.: "PLEASE CALL KAY AT HOME."

* Currie paged Lewinsky at 7:06 p.m.: "PLEASE CALL KAY AT HOME."

* Currie paged Lewinsky at 8:28 p.m.: "CALL KAY."

* Currie received a phone call from President Clinton at 11:02 p.m.

* Currie paged Lewinsky at 7:02 a.m. on Monday, January 19, 1998: "PLEASE CALL KAY AT HOME AT 8:00 THIS MORNING."

* Currie paged Lewinsky at 8:08 a.m.: "PLEASE CALL KAY."

* Currie tried to call Lewinsky at 8:29 a.m.

* Currie paged Lewinsky at 8:33 a.m.: "PLEASE CALL KAY AT HOME."

* Currie paged Lewinsky at 8:37 a.m.: "PLEASE CALL KAY AT HOME. IT'S A SOCIAL CALL. THANK YOU."

* Currie paged Lewinsky at 8:41 a.m.: "KAY IS AT HOME. PLEASE CALL."

* Currie called Clinton at 8:43 a.m.

* Currie paged Lewinsky again at 8:44 a.m.: "PLEASE CALL KATE RE: FAMILY EMERGENCY."

* Currie called Clinton again at 8:50 a.m.

* Currie paged Lewinsky again at 8:51 a.m.: "MSG FROM KAY. PLEASE CALL, HAVE GOOD NEWS."[125]

* Clinton called Jordan at his home at 8:55 a.m., and the two spoke for ten minutes. Jordan then went to his office and began a day-long frenzy of phone calls.[126]

* Jordan called the White House at 10:29 a.m.

* Jordan paged Lewinsky at 10:33 a.m.: "PLEASE CALL MR. JORDAN AT [His Number]."
* Jordan paged Lewinsky again at 10:34 a.m.
* Jordan called Nancy Hernreich at 10:35 a.m.
* Jordan called Erskine Bowles at 10:44 a.m.
* Jordan called Frank Carter at 10:53 a.m.
* Jordan called the White House at 10:58 a.m.
* Jordan called Bruce Lindsey at 11:04 a.m.
* Jordan paged Lewinsky again at 11:16 a.m.: "PLEASE CALL MR. JORDAN AT [His Number]."
* Jordan called Lindsey again at 11:17 a.m.
* Jordan called the White House at 12:31 p.m.
* Jordan called the White House at 2:29 p.m.[127]

The afternoon of January 19 things really went downhill for the president. At 4:54 p.m., Vernon Jordan called Frank Carter. Mr. Carter relayed that he had been told he longer represented Monica Lewinsky. Mr. Jordan then made feverish attempts to reach the president or someone at the White House to tell him the bad news, as represented by the six calls between 4:58 p.m. and 5:22 p.m. Mr. Jordan called Mr. Carter back at 5:14 p.m. to go over what they had already talked about. Mr. Jordan finally reached the President at 5:56 p.m. and told him that Mr. Carter had been fired. Enclosed are the records of the phone calls:[128]

* Jordan called Lindsey at 4:58 p.m.
* Jordan called Mills at 4:59 p.m.
* Jordan called Lindsey's number and then the number of White House Counsel Charles Ruff.
* Jordan called Lindsey two more times at 5:05 p.m.
* Jordan called Mills at 5:09 p.m.
* Jordan called Frank Carter again at 5:14 p.m.
* Jordan called Lindsey and Mills at 5:22 p.m. (Still no luck).
* Jordan called Betty Currie at home at 5:55 p.m.
* Jordan called Clinton at 5:56 and spoke for seven minutes.
* Jordan called Currie again at 6:04 p.m.[129]

The negotiations continued until the dispute between the two men centered on a single issue. Bennett demanded an oral proffer before they gave Monica immunity. Ginsburg wanted the immunity deal before she said anything to them. Finally, at around 10:30 p.m., Bennett tried one last gambit to shake up the Lewinsky team. "I'd like you to accept service of a subpoena for her mother," said Bennett, handing Ginsburg the document summoning Marcia Lewis to the grand jury. Ginsburg accepted it.[130]

As part of the negotiations, Ginsburg and Speights had agreed to allow Starr's investigators to search Monica's apartment at the Watergate the following day. The agents arrived at Lewinsky's apartment Tuesday morning and collected Lewinsky's computer, most of her dresses, and gifts. They were, of course, looking for the semen-stained dress that Tripp had told them about, but Monica had moved it to her mother's new apartment in New York. The gifts included a brooch and a signed book of poetry, Walt Whitman's *Leaves of Grass*. It contains the poem "Sons of Myself," a tale of erotic love with allusions to oral sex.[131]

At around 9:00 p.m., on Tuesday, January 20, 1998, a White House lawyer named Lanny Breuer received a call from Wolf Blitzer, of CNN. "Have you heard anything about an intern?" Unlike many people at the White House, Breuer did not read the *Drudge Report*. Breuer couldn't help Blitzer. Then, about ten minutes later, Breuer's pager nearly overheated with calls.[132]

As Tuesday night wore on, Lanny Breuer figured the news was big enough to summon his boss, Charles Ruff, back to the office for an emergency conference with the scandal management team: John Podesta, Bruce Lindsey, Cheryl Mills, and Lanny Davis. Ruff, who had attended Clinton's deposition, said he thought the questions about Lewinsky "came out of left field." David Kendall was brought in by speakerphone, and they decided to take the safest course and say as little as possible.[133]

Clinton himself spoke to both Kendall and Bennett on Tuesday evening and continued his denial of any sexual relationship with Lewinsky, just as he had in the deposition. Ruff said the White House spokesman could repeat the denial in the morning, but no one should go into any detail, not until they knew more about the whole story.[134]

Later that night, the White House learned the substance of the *Washington Post's* story to run in the morning entitled "Clinton Accused of Urging Aide to Lie; Starr Probes Whether President Told Woman to Deny

Alleged Affair to Jones' Lawyers." After the President knew of the existence of the story, he made a series of telephone calls. At 12:08 a.m., according to the Starr referral, he called his attorney, Robert Bennett. The next morning, Mr. Bennett was quoted in the *Post* stating: "The President adamantly denies he ever had a relationship with Ms. Lewinsky and she confirmed the truth of that. This story seems ridiculous and I frankly smell a rat."[135]

The *Starr Report* laid out the chronology. After his conversation with Bennett, the president had a half-hour conversation with Bruce Lindsey. At 1:16 a.m., the president called Betty Currie and spoke to her for twenty minutes. He then called Bruce Lindsey again. At 6:30 a.m., the president called Vernon Jordan. After that, the president again spoke with Lindsey. This flurry of activity was a prelude to the stories that the president would soon inflict upon his top White House aides and advisors.[136]

On the morning of January 21, 1998, the president met with White House Chief of Staff Erskine Bowles and his two deputies, John Podesta and Sylvia Matthews. Bowles recalled entering the president's office at 9:00 a.m. He then recounted to the grand jury the president's immediate words as he and two others entered the Oval Office: "He looked up at us and he said the same thing he said to the American people. He said, 'I want you to know I did not have sexual relationships with this woman, Monica Lewinsky. I did not ask anybody to lie. And when the facts come out, you'll understand.'"[137]

Clinton had planned interviews on January 21, to tout the upcoming State of the Union address to Congress. Instead, they were dominated by the story about Monica Lewinsky, with Mr. Clinton using lawyerly language to deny any improper relationship with her.[138]

These are the excerpts of the interview with Clinton on PBS' *The NewsHour with Jim Lehrer*:

> **Lehrer:** "The news of this day is that Kenneth Starr, independent counsel, is investigating allegations that you suborned perjury by encouraging a 24-year-old woman, former White House intern, to lie under oath in a civil deposition about her having had an affair with you. Is that true?"
> **Clinton:** "That is not true. That is not true. I did not ask anyone to tell anything other than the truth. There is no improper relationship. And I intend to cooperate with this inquiry. But, that is not true."

Lehrer: " 'No improper relationship'—define what you mean by that."

Clinton: "Well, I think you know what it means. It means that there is not a sexual relationship, an improper sexual relationship, or any other kind of improper relationship."

Lehrer: "You had no sexual relationship with this young woman?"

Clinton: "There is not a sexual relationship; that is accurate. We are doing our best to cooperate here, but we don't know much yet. And that's all I can say now. What I'm trying to do is to contain my natural impulses and get back to work. It's important that we cooperate. I will cooperate, but I want to focus on the work at hand."

Lehrer: "Just for the record, make sure I understand what your answer means and there is no ambiguity about it—"

Clinton: "There is no ambiguity."

Lehrer: "You had no conversations with this woman, Monica Lewinsky, about her testimony, before—in giving a deposition?"

Clinton: "I did not urge anyone to say anything that was untrue. That's my statement to you."[139]

Soon, every twenty-four-hour cable news channel was carrying the story of how Monica Lewinsky had given Bill Clinton blow jobs in the Oval Office. Radio talk show hosts were referring to the Oval Office as the Oral Orifice and people were e-mailing each other with Hillary jokes. "After Monica admitted to an affair with the president, Hillary phoned her up and asked her, 'What was it like?' "[140]

That same day (January 21), Revlon Corp. withdrew its job offer to Monica Lewinsky.[141] The next day, Mr. Starr's office serves the White House with subpoenas seeking Secret Service records documenting Ms. Lewinsky's visits and telephone records.[142] The audiotapes reminded the public of the embarrassing audiotapes with Gennifer Flowers. Mrs. Flowers, without Bill Clinton's knowledge, had recorded conversations about her twelve-year romance with Mr. Clinton, pregnancy by him, and subsequent abortion.[143]

On Friday, January 23, 1998, forty-eight hours after the story broke, senior White House officials decided on the "rules of the road" going forward. This was a legal matter and only a select few people would deal with the strategy and the details: David Kendall, Kendall's partner Nicole

Seligman, Cheryl Mills, and Hillary. "Hillary was in all the meetings," the official said. "She had done this before, and she was going to do it again."[144]

On Saturday, January 24, 1998, ABC had independently confirmed through other sources what Goldberg had fed to Drudge earlier in the week. It was a bombshell statement: "Lewinsky says she saved, apparently as a kind of souvenir, a navy blue dress with the president's semen stain on it."[145]

The White House responded to the news the next day (January 25), by changing its strategy on discrediting Monica Lewinsky. She was initially portrayed as the star-struck intern fantasizing about the president who was on the verge of being fired for sneaking into events featuring the president and for doing shoddy work. The story was that the White House instead decided to assign her to a job at the Pentagon.[146]

On Monday, January 26, 1998, after an event to promote child care, President Bill Clinton, with Hillary Rodham Clinton looking on from behind, made the following statement about Monica Lewinsky:[147]

> I want to say one thing to the American people. I want you to listen to me. I'm going to say this again. I did not have sexual relations with that woman, Miss Lewinsky. I never told anybody to lie. Not a single time. Never. These allegations are false, and I need to go back to work for the American people.[148]

Mr. Clinton, looking weary, wagged his finger at the media when he spoke. He refused to take questions and stormed out of the room, with Hillary in his wake.[149]

It took President Clinton just twenty seconds and fifty words to tell one of the most blatant lies in the annals of modern presidential history. And there was Hillary, nodding in approval, even though she knew he was lying.[150]

According to George Stephanopoulos: "This was Clinton at his cold-blooded worst. Gone were the guilty tics of his past denials—the downcast eyes, the stutter, the dry throat and pale face that displayed a sense of shame and sorrow and vulnerability. Now, full of self-righteous fury, he was lying with true conviction. All that mattered was his survival. Everyone else had to fall in line: his staff, his cabinet, the country, even his wife."[151]

On February 9, 1998, George Stephanopoulos, on ABC's *This Week*, described how the White House was going to defend itself in the Lewinsky scandal:

Stephanopoulos: "There's a different, long-term strategy . . . . White House allies are already starting to whisper about I'll call the 'Ellen Rometsch strategy.' 'Rometsch,' was a girlfriend of John F. Kennedy, who also happened to be an East German spy. And Robert Kennedy was charged with getting her out of the country and also getting John Edgar Hoover to go to the Congress and say, don't you investigate this, because if you do, we're going to open up everybody's closets . . . ."

Sam Donaldson: "Are you suggesting for a moment that what they're beginning to say is that if you investigate this too much, we'll put all your dirty linen right on the table? Every member of the Senate? Every member of the press corps?"

Stephanopoulos: "Absolutely. The President said he would never resign, and I think some around him are willing to take everybody down with him."[152]

At the time that Stephanopoulos made these comments, he was an ABC News analyst, having resigned as White House communications chief in early 1997. He was thus able to pose as an impartial journalist, innocently "reporting" what his White House sources told him. Behind the mask of objectivity, however, Stephanopoulos was still doing the Clintons' dirty work, using his platform as an ABC analyst to deliver the Clintons' threat.[153]

On February 18, 1998, the Justice Department decided that it would not represent President Clinton in his claim of executive privilege in the matter of Monica Lewinsky. This was a virtually unprecedented step that prompted Clinton to hire outside counsel to defend the claim before U.S. District Judge Norma Holloway Johnson. Clinton hired private attorney Neil Eggleston to make the legal argument for his claims of executive privilege concerning conversations that Hillary Rodham Clinton, White House Deputy Counsel Bruce Lindsey, and adviser Sidney Blumenthal may have had among themselves or with others about the president's relationship with former White House intern Monica Lewinsky.[154]

On March 13, 1998, with President Clinton teetering on the brink of impeachment, the Department of Defense (DOD) broke a federal law by leaking information taken from a Privacy Act–protected personnel document to Jane Mayer of the *New Yorker* magazine. Tripp had answered that she had not ever been arrested. And Mayer used that answer to create a brief mini-scandal because, twenty-nine years earlier, Tripp had indeed been arrested as the result of a teenage prank pulled off by some of her friends. Once a judge had sorted things out, however, he had informed Tripp that, in the eyes of the law, she had never actually been arrested. So years later, when applying for a government job, Tripp felt justified in answering no.[155] (Later the, the *Washington Post* quoted Pentagon's chief spokesman Ken Bacon apologizing for releasing the information about Tripp, saying, "In retrospect, I'm sorry the incident occurred.")[156]

On April 30, 1998, President Clinton held his first news conference since the Lewinsky sex-and-lies scandal broke, and in a combative mood, lashed out at his accusers, charging that independent counsel Kenneth Starr heads a "hard, well-financed, vigorous effort" to undercut his moral authority but declaring it has failed. But he repeatedly declined to elaborate on his relationship with the former White House intern.[157]

On June 2, 1998, Monica Lewinsky and her family concluded that Ginsburg had poisoned relations with Starr and dumped him in favor of Plato Cacheris and Jacob A. Stein, two longtime, well-connected Washington criminal attorneys.[158]

On July 17, 1998, President Clinton was subpoenaed by independent counsel Ken Starr to appear before the Lewinsky grand jury.[159] On July 27, 1998, a three-judge panel on the U.S. Court of Appeals for the D.C. Circuit voted 2-1 to allow conversations President Clinton had with government lawyers to be submitted as evidence.[160] That same day, Monica Lewinsky struck the immunity deal with prosecutors, sparing her a federal perjury indictment. The deal was met with grim resignation at the White House, where spokesman Michael McCurry tried to put a happy face on the announcement: "I think that he's pleased that things are working out for her," Mr. McCurry said of Mr. Clinton's reaction.[161]

The next day, as she prepared to appear before the grand jury, she turned over what would become the case's most important piece of evidence—a size 12 navy blue dress. The dress was then sent to the FBI lab for forensic tests.[162]

On July 29, 1998, Mr. Clinton decided to testify August 17, ending twelve days of tense negotiations over a grand jury subpoena demanding the president's appearance. The agreement called for the withdrawal of the July 17 grand jury subpoena and allowed his attorney, David Kendall, and other lawyers to be present.[163] It also allowed for the president's question-and-answer session to be broadcast inside the grand jury room through live, close-circuit video transmission. And it would be videotaped, just in case a member of the grand jury was absent that day. This meant that Clinton wouldn't have to endure the indignity of walking into a federal courthouse.[164]

With Monica Lewinsky now cooperating with prosecutors, the president's lawyers were anxious to know what Ken Starr knew. A day after Clinton agreed to testify, David Kendall got his answer when Starr informed him that prosecutors needed to draw a vial of the president's blood. For months, there had been rumors and then press reports of a semen-stained dress. Such a request could only mean that Starr was going to use a DNA test to unravel seven months of the president's lies.[165]

Then, according to Jeff Gerth and Don Van Natta, in their book, *Her Way*, it happened. On August 3, 1998, in the Map Room of the White House, the president, his face flushed with anger, rolled up his left shirt sleeve. The White House physician, Dr. E. Connie Mariano, drew a vial of the president's blood, while an FBI agent, one of Starr's prosecutors, and David Kendall watched this first-ever event. For Bill, this episode was the ultimate indignity in a long year of humiliation. "When they took the blood from his arm," one of Bill's closest friends said later, "that's when it really hit home."[166]

If the DNA sample had not matched the DNA on Monica's dress, Bill might still be telling the same lie. But unfortunately for him and Hillary, the DNA odds against him turned out to be 7.87 trillion to one.[167]

On August 6, 1998, Monica Lewinsky made her first appearance before the grand jury. She testified that she engaged in oral sex with Mr. Clinton and then discussed cover stories to deflect questions about their relationship. Clinton knew he was trapped.[168]

On August 17, 1998, Bill Clinton was confronted by Sol Wisenberg and Robert Bittman, prosecutors from Starr's office, in the Map Room of the White House on Monday. Members of the grand jury watched live at the federal courthouse on closed-circuit television. Kendall was with the president. Wisenberg began the proceedings by reminding Bill that he was under oath. If he provided false or misleading answers, Wisenberg reminded him, "you could be prosecuted for perjury and/or obstruction of justice."[169]

"I believe that's correct," the president said.[170]

Bill gave them nothing. When asked directly whether he was "physically intimate with Monica Lewinsky," he read a written statement acknowledging "inappropriate intimate contact," but he repeatedly said that this "did not consist of sexual intercourse," nor did it "constitute sexual relations" under the three-pronged definition he had been given during the Jones deposition back in January.[171]

The president devoted much of the four hours allotted for the grand jury session to bitterly ripping his accusers and even the prosecutors. He seemed to be purposefully running out the clock. He seethed that the Jones case was less about alleged sexual harassment and more about a concerted effort to harass him for political gain. "They just thought they would take a wrecking ball to me and see if they could do some damage," he said.[172]

Bittman pointed to a passage in Bill's Jones deposition when his lawyer, Robert Bennett, had assured everyone that "there is no sex of any kind in any matter, shape, or form" between the president and Lewinsky. Bittman asked the president whether he agreed that this "was an utterly false statement."[173]

With a wan smile, the president said, "It depends on what the meaning of 'is' . . . is." That smile seemed to suggest that Bill knew the line was preposterous. "If 'is' means is, and never has been, that is one thing." He continued. "If it means, there is none; that was a completely true statement." The quotation came to symbolize Bill's hairsplitting obfuscation and infuriated Starr's prosecutors and strengthened their resolve to send a report on the matter to Congress, which they felt was their obligation under the independent counsel law.[174]

The president also told the jurors that he "also had *occasional* telephone conversations with Monica Lewinsky that included sexual banter." Actually, the word *occasional* was misleading. The two had at least fifty-five phone conversations, many in the middle of the night, and in seventeen of these calls, Monica and the president of the United States engaged in phone sex.[175]

Starr's prosecutors left the White House that evening believing Clinton had lied under oath not only in the Paula Jones deposition but also that afternoon to the grand jury. Meanwhile, Clinton left the Map Room at 6:35 p.m., burning with rage. After a quick meal and shower, he carried that anger into the White House Solarium, where his top advisers were waiting. They included Charles Ruff, the White House counsel, his lawyers, David Kendall and Mickey Kantor, his strategists, Rahm Emmanuel, Paul Begala, and James Carville, and his old friends Harry and Linda Thomason. The president's task was to prepare a brief statement to deliver to the nation that evening at ten o'clock eastern standard time. Chelsea was also in the Solarium, but Hillary was not there.[176]

On August 17, 1998, at 10:00 p.m., the leader of the free world appeared on national television to admit getting at least partially naked with a lovesick twenty-one-year-old. He never uttered the phrases people wanted to hear: "I'm sorry" and "forgive me." His "confession" lasted four minutes, and he spent half that time ranting about Starr. Bill Clinton came to Washington in 1993 to represent the "Most Ethical Administration in the History of the Republic." Instead, he gave us the American Caligula, a man who proposes to escape the law by claiming he had non-sex sex with Monica Lewinsky. It also appears that the tie Clinton wore for the speech was given to him by Monica Lewinsky.[177]

Within minutes, the media's reaction to Bill's speech poured in, and it was negative. The political strategists who had pleaded with Clinton to be more apologetic were proven right. The media wanted to hear a confession and an apology. Instead it was another attack on Ken Starr. After his performance, a growing number of the American people wanted Clinton to resign.[178]

On August 18, 1998, the Clintons left Washington for their summer vacation on Martha's Vineyard. Bill and Hillary spent most of their stay in seclusion, avoiding the usual rounds of golf, boating, and dinner parties. Clinton did, eventually, venture out to speak before friendly audiences. He seemed little changed. According to one witness who declined to be identified, he even made a pass at an attractive woman during one of his appearances, unfazed by the reactions of witnesses, who were shocked and amazed.[179]

On August 20, 1998, Monica Lewinsky made her second appearance before the grand jury, ironically finishing only minutes before President Clinton announced that the U.S. bombed terrorist targets in Afghanistan and Sudan. The timing of the attack became suspect since it came three days after he admitted that he lied for seven months about an "inappropriate relationship" with Monica Lewinsky and the same day that Ms. Lewinsky was making her second appearance before the federal grand jury.[180]

The results of the raids were that they "knocked the scandal out of the lead story, and gave the Sunday talk shows something else to talk about," according to Republican pollster Frank Luntz. And it worked. For example, ABC News devoted the first twenty-four minutes of their August 20 broadcast half-hour evening broadcast to the bombing attacks, mentioning Monica Lewinsky's testimony in the sex-and-lies scandal with just five minutes left.[181]

On September 3, 1998, Sen. Joseph I. Lieberman (D-Conn.) spoke on the Senate floor condemning President Clinton's actions in misleading the nation about his relationship with a White House intern. Sen. Daniel Patrick Moynihan (D-N.Y.) also expressed on the Senate floor his dissatisfaction with Clinton's speech.[182]

The next day, while overseas in Dublin, Ireland, President Clinton used the word *sorry* for the first time. While standing with Irish Prime Minister Bertie Ahern during a planned photo session, President Clinton said to a reporter's question: "I've already said that I made a bad mistake, it was indefensible, and I'm sorry about it."[183]

Clinton's sincerity only went so far. Even after the Lewinsky scandal made headlines, two past military aides, a retired Secret Service agent, and two permanent White House employees reported that Clinton would continue to be "consoled" by two other White House interns. During the Lewinsky scandal, R. Emmett Tyrrell Jr.'s researchers at the *American Spectator* gathered a list of seven White House staffers, five of them interns, whom Clinton used as comfort women. None would go public. One of them, Mary Mahoney, was shot dead at the Starbucks in Georgetown (Washington, D.C.).[184]

The same day that President Clinton said he was "sorry," House Minority Leader Richard A. Gephardt asked House Majority Leader Newt Gingrich for a private meeting the following week to discuss the process of impeachment.[185]

CHAPTER 35

IMPEACHMENT

I think it's plain that the president should resign and spare the country the agony of this impeachment ... [There is] no question that an admission of making false statements to government officials . . . is an impeachable offense.
—Bill Clinton on President Nixon's resignation, August 8, 1974[1]

Vice President Al Gore was at the center of the Democratic Party's fund-raising efforts for the 1996 election. Both he and President Clinton received weekly reports of the DNC fund-raising meetings. Both men micromanaged strategies to acquire more funds. Clinton personally reviewed "mind-numbing campaign budget minutia on a weekly, and sometimes daily basis." Clinton and Gore were also well aware that their activities were illegal. In a memo from Harold Ickes reporting that the DNC would have to set aside $1.5 million for audit costs and another $1 million for potential fines from the Federal Election Commission, Clinton scribbled in the margin, "Ugh"—clearly revealing his awareness that they were breaking the law.[2]

Gore made personal phone calls, soliciting big donations in what was described as a heavy handed and offensive manner. It was unprecedented for a vice president to inject himself into direct solicitation. Unfortunately for Gore, Clinton didn't like to make the calls, so the calls were defaulted for Gore to make. One person commented that Gore sounded more like the DNC finance director than the vice president of the United States. In at least one case, Democrats admitted there was an uncomfortable connection between the solicitation of funds and government action. After Secretary of Commerce Ron Brown helped a Texas telecommunications company acquire a $36 million contract in Mexico, the firm contributed $100,000 to the Democratic National Committee. Gore personally called the executive at the company to thank him for the donation.[3]

In addition to his phone solicitation, Gore made many personal appearances at fund-raising events during the campaign. He participated in thirty-nine events outside the White House that raised $8.74 million for the DNC. He was the principal attraction at twenty-three White House coffees, accompanied Clinton at eight more such gatherings, and opened up the vice president's residence for other fund-raising parties. Altogether, Gore was responsible for raising $40 million of the DNC's $180 million take during the election cycle.[4]

Unfortunately, Gore didn't always display a charming demeanor in his solicitation of campaign cash. In fact, some of Gore's targets were offended by his high-pressure approach. One longtime friend and supporter described his tactics as "revolting." Another donor who wrote a $100,000 check to the DNC under pressure by Gore, said, "There were elements of a shakedown in the call. It was very awkward. For a vice president, particularly this vice president who has real power and is the heir apparent, to ask for money gave me no choice. I have so much business that touches on the federal government—the telecommunications act, tax policy, regulations galore."[5]

Gore spokeswoman Lorraine Voles vigorously disputed the notion that there was anything untoward about Gore's direct participation in the process. "There is nothing inappropriate about the vice president calling people for money."[6]

After four months of silence—and after watching White House press secretary Mike McCurry fumbling to explain Gore's level of involvement in the mounting fund-raising scandals—Gore, on March 3, 1997, admitted in a nationally televised press conference that he solicited campaign contributions by telephone from his White House office for the Clinton-Gore campaign in 1996, but he denied it was illegal. He insisted he had broken any laws but said he would no longer make fund-raising calls from his office. Gore said that he was "very proud" of the millions of dollars he had raised through his fund-raising efforts. During the twenty-four-minute conference, Gore resorted seven times to answering allegations of illegality with the statement: "My counsel advises me, let me repeat, that there is 'no controlling legal authority' that says that any of these activities violated any law." He protested that he had used a Democratic National

Committee credit card when making his phone solicitations, presumably to demonstrate that his calls were for soft money and not hard money, the latter of which would have been illegal.[7]

Yet, in April 1995, White House Counsel Abner J. Mikva sent a memo to Vice President Al Gore and President Clinton which stated: "Campaign activities of any kind are prohibited in or from government buildings. . . . [A]lso no fundraising phone calls or mail may emanate from the White House or any other federal buildings."[8]

When confronted with the Mikva memo ordering White House employees not to make fund-raising calls or mail solicitations from the White House or other federal buildings, Gore said, "There is an exemption for the President and Vice President." Gore also denied reports that his solicitation calls had amounted to a shakedown of donors. "Well, I cannot explain to you what some anonymous sources want to say," Gore said. "I can tell you this, that I never, ever said or did anything that would have given rise to a feeling like that on the part of someone who was asked to support our campaign. I never did that, and I never would do that." Gore added, "I never did anything that I thought was wrong. If there had been a shred of doubt in my mind that anything I did was a violation of law, I assure you I would not have done that."[9]

A couple years before Gore's weird denial, then-White House Counsel Bernard Nussbaum, sent a memo on July 12, 1993, to, among others, Bill Clinton and Al Gore, clearly stating at least four times that fund-raising may not be done on federal property. Nussbaum's memo says:

> Soliciting or receiving campaign contributions on Federal property or in Federal buildings [is a federal crime for any federal employee, whether or not "hatched"]. This means that fund-raising events may not be held in the White House; that no fund-raising phone calls or mail may emanate from the White House or any other Federal buildings; and that no campaign contributions may be accepted at the White House or any other Federal building.[10]

Federal law prohibits campaign fund-raising in government office buildings, including the business spaces of the White House. According to U.S. Code, Title 18, Section 607:

> It shall be unlawful for any person to solicit or receive any (campaign) contribution in any room or building occupied in the discharge of official duties . . . Any person who violates this section shall be fined under this title or imprisoned not more than three years, or both.[11]

It appears that in the beginning, Clinton and Gore treated their own campaign funds and DNC funds as one giant pot that, in itself, had legal ramifications because, when the Clinton-Gore campaign decided to accept $62 million in public funds for the 1996 campaign, it expressly agreed to abide by the proposed spending limits. Gore denied the funds were mixed, saying, "No, there was a clear distinction" between the DNC and the Clinton-Gore campaign. "There was a separate message. There were separate legal requirements," said Gore.[12]

The new line held until September 1997, when Bob Woodward reported in the *Washington Post*, that more than $120,000 of the money Gore solicited had in fact been funneled into the DNC's "hard money" accounts. "Hard money is a contribution made under strict federal limits and regulations that can be used directly to support a federal election campaign; "soft" money is any contribution not used to directly support a federal election campaign. Though soft money must be reported, there are no contribution limits on it. Hard money is subject to limits and other regulations and cannot be solicited from federal property. Some of the calls were made on a DNC charge card, and some of the calls were charged to government phones at the White House. When this became public knowledge, the DNC reimbursed the U.S. Treasury $24.20. But Gore raised another problem for himself with the language he used in some of the thank-you letters he sent to contributors. In one typical letter Gore wrote, "President Clinton and I thank you . . . . We appreciate your dedication to our Administration." If a solicitation contains a reference to a federal candidate or a federal election, the money is subject to federal election laws.[13]

Gore maintained that he had not expressly solicited hard-money contributions and was unaware that any money from his phone calls had ended up in hard-money accounts. Amy Weiss Tobe, a spokeswoman for the Democratic National Committee, explained that the soft money was inadvertently placed in the hard-money account. A review of the records, however, indicated that something was going on. Usually, when a contribution exceeded $20,000—the legal limit for a hard-money contribution—the excess was placed into a soft-money account.[14]

Despite Gore's frank admission that he was raising money for the 1996 reelection campaign, Attorney General Janet Reno initially decided an independent counsel investigation was not needed in the case, because Gore had raised only "soft," not "hard" money through his White House phone calls. This is disputed by the following examples:[15]

1) Ice Tea Defense Did Not Hold Water:
Gore attended campaign meetings in the White House, particularly a documented Nov. 21, 1995, meeting, where the Democratic National Committee's (DNC) media fund was a principle topic— including the fact that the president and vice president needed to raise more "hard" money for this fund. According to the FBI, in an August 8, 1998, interview with investigators, "The vice president said he did not recall such (hard money—soft money fundraising) conversations or memos . . . . The vice president . . . observed that he drank a lot of ice tea during the meetings, which could have necessitated a restroom break" thus causing him to miss important discussions.[16]
But former Deputy White House Chief of Staff Harold Ickes, who coordinated the meetings, told the FBI that the proceedings were routinely interrupted whenever the president or the vice president left the room precisely so that they would not miss relevant discussions.[17]

2) Panetta Saw Gore "Attentively Listening":
According to the *Los Angeles Times*, then-White House Chief of Staff Leon Panetta told the FBI he remembered Gore "attentively listening" to discussions about the need to raise hard money at the Nov. 21, 1995, meeting.[18]

3) Gore Aide Noted Hard Money Discussion:
Gore Deputy Chief of Staff David Strauss wrote these notes at the November 21, 1995, meeting: 65 percent soft / 35 percent hard; Corporate or everything over $20,000 from an individual; VP: Is it possible to do a reallocation for me to take more of the events and calls? VP: Count me in on the calls."[19]

Strauss also jotted down a definition of soft money as "corporate or anything over $20,000 from an individual."[20]

4). Ickes Sent Gore Thirteen Memos:
Harold Ickes sent Gore at least thirteen memos reminding him of the urgent need to raise hard money. In one June 3, 1996, memo, for example, Ickes wrote, "Of the approximately $8.4 million in cash on hand, only approximately $1.6 million is hard money. As described below, this is beginning to present a very serious problem . . . . Thus, the remainder of the fundraising efforts between now and the end of October will have to focus very much on increasing the amount of federal [hard] dollars raised."[21]

In the June 3 memo, Ickes pointedly defined "hard money"—or what he referred to as "federal" dollars—as "the first $20,000 in *individual* contributions to federal political activity for the calendar year." He reiterated this definition in memos sent to Gore on July 15 and July 28, 1996.[22] On July 24, 1996, Ickes sent another memo to Clinton, Gore, and senior White House and DNC officials stressing the need for the president and vice president to *continue* raising hard money. Wrote Ickes:

> Attached are two documents, the first captioned "Federal dollars," dated 7/18/96. The second is captioned "Summary of DNC estimated expenditures calendar 1996 (January-October); Fundraising to date (7/9/96); and federal dollars needed," dated 7/14/96.
> The short of these documents is that in order to meet the $128 million fundraising goal for all DNC budgets for calendar 1996 (January-October), an additional $47 million needs to be raised (from major donors during the less than 4 months period of 7/9/96-10/31/96, of which $28 million (59.4%) must be "federal" dollars."[23]

For Gore to claim to Justice Department investigators that he did not know that the contributions that he had solicited from individuals had been accounted as hard money by the DNC would mean that he paid no attention to repeated, explicit, urgent messages from Ickes. In addition to receiving these memos from Ickes, Gore attended regularly Wednesday political strategy meetings at the White House, as did Ickes. Is it possible that Ickes never reiterated the subject of his urgent memos at these meetings?[24]

On March 7, 1997, four days after Gore's statement, President Clinton held his own White House press conference. Referring to Gore's campaign-solicitation tactics, a reporter asked: "Mr. President, your press secretary this week left open the possibility that you, too, had made calls like the vice president did. Did you ever make those calls?"[25]

"I'm not sure, frankly," said Clinton. "I don't like to raise funds that way . . . . But I can't say over all the hundreds and hundreds and maybe thousands of phone calls I've made in the last four years that I never said to anybody while I was talking to them, 'Well, we need your help or I hope you'll help us.' . . . But I don't believe the vice president did anything wrong in making the calls . . . . [And] I don't want to flat-out say I never did something that I might, in fact, have done just because I don't remember it."[26]

Yet two weeks later, Paul Bedard and Warren Strobel of the *Washington Times* reported that, the previous day, White House officials had revealed that, while Clinton did not remember on March 7 whether he had made fund-raising calls, he then recalled that, if he made such calls, he had not made them from the Oval Office, but from the residential area of the White House, a legally safe zone for fund-raising. "That's right, he said he can remember no calls were made from the Oval [Office]," an administration official told the *Washington Times*.[27]

Interestingly, according to top presidential advisor Dick Morris in his book, *Behind the Oval Office*, "Clinton complained bitterly at having to raise this much money. 'You don't know, you don't have any remote idea,' he said to me, 'how hard I have to work, how hard Hillary has to work, how hard Al [Gore] has to work to raise this much money.'"[28]

Once, Clinton told Morris, "I can't think. I can't act. I can't do anything but go to fund-raisers and shake hands. You want me to issue executive orders; I can't focus on a thing but the next fund-raiser. Hillary can't, Al can't—we're all getting sick and crazy because of it."[29]

Also, during the March 7 White House press conference, President Clinton tried to explain why Hillary Clinton's Chief of Staff, Margaret Williams, who received a $50,000 contribution in the First Lady's White House office from a Chinese-American businessman named Johnny Chung, did not violate the law against "soliciting" or "receiving" a contribution in the White House: "If you receive a contribution and all you do is pass it on, and you've been involved in no way in any solicitation on public property and you're just passing it through, that is what the regulation provides for."[30]

On March 11, 1997, Rep. Bob Barr, Georgia Republican, in a three-page letter to Henry J. Hyde, chairman of the House Judiciary Committee, made a request to begin an impeachment inquiry of President Clinton and Vice President Al Gore amid accusations that a growing campaign-finance scandal had compromised national-security interests and corrupted the country's foreign-policy decisions.[31]

The Constitution gives a simple majority of the House of Representatives the power to "impeach" or bring charges for removal from office, against officials of the executive branch. The Senate is given the sole power to try officials who have been "impeached" by the House. A two-thirds vote of the Senate is necessary to remove an impeached official from office. When the House of Representatives approves Articles of Impeachment against the president, the Constitution requires that the Chief Justice of the United States preside over the trial in the Senate.[32]

> **Article I, Section 3:** The Senate shall have the sole Power to try all Impeachments. When sitting for that Purpose, they shall be on Oath or Affirmation. When the President of the United States is tried, the Chief Justice shall preside. And no Person shall be convicted without the Concurrence of two-thirds of the Members present. Judgement in Cases of Impeachment shall not extend further than to removal from Office, and disqualification to hold and enjoy any Office of honor, Trust or Profit under the United States: but the Party convicted shall nevertheless be liable and subject to Indictment, Trial, Judgement and Punishment, according to Law.
> **Article II, Section 4:** The President, Vice President and all civil Officers of the United States, shall be removed from Office on Impeachment for, and Conviction of, Treason, Bribery, or other high Crimes and Misdemeanors.

President Andrew Johnson (1865-1869) was the only President impeached by the House and then tried in the Senate. He was accused of seeking to remove Secretary of War Edwin Stanton from office. His opponents fell one vote short of mustering the two-thirds majority necessary to remove him from office.[33]

President Richard Nixon (1969-1974) avoided a trial of impeachment in the U.S. Senate by resigning the presidency on August 9, 1974.[34]

On October 10, 1973, Vice President Spiro T. Agnew pleaded "no contest" to tax-evasion charges and resigned the vice presidency of the United States.[35]

Several House members began to review a 1974 Watergate report, coincidently, a report that then-Hillary Rodham helped research, to determine if impeachment articles could be drawn up against President Clinton and Vice President Al Gore including Article II, Section 4 of the U.S. Constitution, which says, "treason, bribery or other high crimes and misdemeanors" could include efforts to use the White House for improper purposes or personal gain.[36]

Next, you had the following questions which made the case for impeachment:

Question #1: Did Vice President Gore or President Clinton commit felonies by soliciting campaign contributions in the White House?

Vice President Gore's admission that he solicited contributions from his White House office is a patent felony. It is a federal felony to solicit campaign contributions on federal property. President Clinton, however, "did not recall" making such calls, but if he did, he had not made them from the Oval Office, but from the residential area of the White House.[37]

Interestingly, on June 26, 1997, an Associated Press story revealed a newly discovered White House memo that credited President Clinton with raising $500,000 for his campaign through phone calls placed "from" the Oval Office. Clinton previously claimed "memory loss" as to whether he made such illegal calls. Given the amount of cash he did, in fact, raise, it's obvious he's been caught lying . . . again.[38]

Question #2: Did the President sell access to the presidency and other high offices through coffees, dinners, overnights in the Lincoln Bedroom, and rides on Air Force One, in exchange for campaign contributions for the purpose of staying in power?

Between November 1995 and November, the Clinton administration and the Democratic National Committee (DNC), organized 103 "coffees" for 358 guests. These meetings, which generated $27 million for the Democratic Party (about $75,000 per attendee), were usually held at the White House. These White House "coffees" featured two distinct groups of people: Clinton political appointees who had control over federal regulatory policy, and wealthy businessmen whose interests could be dramatically impaired or advanced by the actions of these appointees. The "coffees" were arranged by Alexis Herman, director of the White House Office of Public Liaison.[39]

Documents released by the White House confirmed that the "coffees" were fund-raisers. Some of the documents, for example, read: "Coffee w/Top 20 fund-raisers," "donor events," and campaign "trustee service dinners" for those who donate at least $100,000. Other points are as follows:

Clinton-Gore campaign Finance Chairman Terry McAuliffe wrote a January 5, 1995, memo to presidential aide Nancy Hernreich asking for three days to be scheduled that month for Clinton to meet 20 "major supporters" for breakfast, lunch or coffee. Another 10 people, wrote McAuliffe, could be invited on golf outings or morning jogs with the President. "This will be an excellent way to energize our key people for the upcoming year." Hernreich passed the memo on to Clinton with the query, "Do you want me to pursue?" Clinton, in his own handwriting replied: "Yes, pursue all 3 promptly. And get other names at 100,000 [dollars] or more, 50,000 [dollars] or more. Cc H. Ickes, L. Panetta, B. Webster. Ready to start overnights right away. Give me the top 10 list back, along w/the 100, 50,000."[40]

On February 25, 1997, the White House released a list of 938 first-term visitors who were invited to sleep in the Lincoln and Queen's bedrooms. The list, which the White House refused to make available on two occasions, showed a large number of political supporters, fund-raisers. and potential campaign donors. More than one in three White House guests gave money to the president or the Democratic National Committee during the previous two years, a computer analysis by the *Washington Post* showed. How about before 1995-1996?[41]

Former usher Chris Emery, who worked at the White House from 1986 to 1994, read from his personal records as usher and said the Lincoln and Queen's bedrooms on the second floor, where the Clintons reside, and four spare guest rooms on the third floor were used 911 times in 1993. "Guests were treated like royalty," Emery said. "Each bedroom received a package of morning newspapers, which in the beginning included the *Washington Times*. In the end, the guests poured $10 million into the Clinton reelection campaign and the Democratic National Committee.[42]

The White House was not the only Democrats' only bed-and-breakfast. White House sources told the *American Spectator* that Blair House, a private White House residence just across Pennsylvania Avenue, was also rented out to potential donors. "People would sleep at Blair House, be served breakfast there and then escorted over the Old Executive Office Building for tours and briefings in the White House," said one White House source. "Many of the Blair guests were donors to the DNC in the $35,000-$50,000 range."[43]

On October 5, 1997, the White House released videotapes to journalists showing President Clinton greeting major Democratic party donors at forty-four coffees in 1995 and 1996. In one footage from one reception, Don Fowler, then the Democratic Party chairman, could be heard refusing five checks from a donor who offered them inside the White House."[44]

Finally, President Clinton told reporters on March 7, 1997 that the "coffees" were held to allow people to "talk about things" and "share their convictions." "I almost wish that one of you [reporters] had been in all these coffees, because they were, frankly, fairly pedestrian events in the sense that nothing very juicy was discussed," said Clinton. If that were true, why were none of the coffees ever listed on his public schedule and why were reporters never invited?[45]

Question #3: Did President Clinton allow foreign agents of influence to penetrate the government of the United States and thus compromise U.S. security for campaign cash?

China Resources Holding Company was a Beijing-government-owned corporation known to provide cover for Chinese intelligence gathering. It owned part of the Hong Kong Chinese Bank, which was a subsidiary of James Riady's Lippo Group. Raidy was a big Clinton campaign supporter.

Newsweek, in February 1997, reported that "according to U.S. intelligence sources, China Resources is routinely used as a front by Beijing to run spy operations" and that "U.S. investigators have identified 'nearly 1,000' American companies that are used by the Chinese either for espionage activities or to illegally acquire American technology."[46]

On September 23, 1993, Lippo executive John Huang signed two checks totaling $30,000 to the Democratic National Committee (DNC). The money was drawn "against accounts at Lippo Bank held in the name of two subsidiaries of James Riady's Lippo Group, for which Huang still worked." The subsidiaries were Hip Hing Holdings, Ltd., and Toy Center Holdings of CA, Inc., both of which were in the red financially. On the day of the meeting, September 27, 1993, Huang signed an additional check for $15,000 to the DNC— also illegal—on the account of a third Lippo subsidiary, San Jose Holdings, Inc.[47]

The next day, September 24, 1993, John Huang escorted Shen Jueren, chairman of China Resources Holding Co. and his assistant Miss Liang, to the White House for a meeting with Vice President Gore's top adviser, his then-chief of staff Jack Quinn.[48]

Three days later, on September 27, 1993, Vice President Al Gore attended a reception in an office building at 100 Wilshire Boulevard in Santa Monica, Calif. The reception was attended by John Huang, Shen Jueren, Maria Hsia, a Democrat fund-raiser and a small group of other Asian-Americans. Was there a direct connection between these contributions from Lippo and the vice president's meeting with a Communist Chinese official?[49]

On April 29, 1996, John Huang organized a fund-raiser at the His Lai Buddhist Temple close to Los Angeles. The featured speakers were Vice President Al Gore, Don Fowler and Rep. Robert Matsui (D.-Ca.). Hank Tseng videotapes the speeches, as does temple official Man Chin. Despite the fact that the monks and nuns had taken vows of poverty, the DNC raised $140,000 at the temple, not counting the unreported $15,000 cost the temple absorbed in sponsoring the event.[50]

On October 21, 1996, during an interview on National Public Radio, Mr. Gore claimed that he "did not know" that the [Buddhist

Temple] event was a fund-raiser. That was a lie. Memoranda written to Vice President Gore by then-Deputy White House Chief of Staff Harold Ickes in January, February and April 1996 read: "Democratic National Committee proposed calendar 1996 budget . . . VPOTUS [Vice President of the United States] Los Angeles 200K . . . . 29-April VPOTUS Los Angeles $250,000 [and] other DNC events . . . April 29th—LA/San Jose—DNC event—all proceeds to DNC."[51]

What Clinton Got from Lippo & Friends

Worthen campaign loan	$3,500,000
Huang's fundraising dinner	$1,000,000
Arief and Sonya Wiriadinata contributions	$425,000
Entergy contributions	$283,463
Payments to Webster Hubbell	$250,000
Cheong Am contributions	$250,000
James Riady contributions	$175,000
John Huang contributions	$162,494
Joe Giroir contributions	$83,250
Lippo America contributions	$74,500
Charles De Queljoe contributions	$70,500

What Lippo Got from Clinton

Access to President Clinton

Appointment of John Huang to Commerce Dept.

Nine hundred thousand dollars in Export-Import Bank Credits

Eased foreign banking regulations

Renewed MFN status for China

Priority administration backing of Asian-American deals

Ambassadorial meeting with President Clinton

Ignoring East Timor human rights abuses

De Queljoe placed on trade advisory committee

Question #4: Did President Clinton provide favors to foreign nationals in return for campaign contributions?

Yah Lin (Charlie) Trie, was born in Taichung, Taiwan, on August 15, 1949. He came to the United States and settled in Little Rock, Arkansas in the early 1970s to join his older sister, Dailan Outlaw, in the restaurant business. Ms. Outlaw was well known for her Fu Lin restaurant near the state capitol. She turned it over to her brother in 1984. Trie had known Bill Clinton for nearly twenty years.[53]

In 1991, Trie started the Daihatsu International Trading Co., which reportedly operated out of offices in Little Rock, Shanghai, Beijing and a four-thousand-dollars-a-month apartment at the Watergate in Washington, D.C. Trie also ran the U.S. branch of the Hong Kong-based San Kin Yip Trading Corp. with Ng Lap Seng, a Chinese real-estate developer. Former Lippo executive Antonio Pan was another business partner of Trie. Until October 1996, Trie served as a DNC finance board member.[54]

What Trie Gave Clinton
- Through the 1996 election cycle, Trie gave or solicited $320,000 in contributions to the DNC. These contributions included $142,000 from his family members, $70,000 in corporate donations through Daihatsu, and $15,000 through San Kin Yip Trading Corp. The latter corporate donation was returned, the *Washington Post* reported on December 18, 1996, because it came from a foreign source.[55]
- On March 21, 1996, Trie delivered a large Manila envelope containing $460,000, mostly in checks and money orders for $500 and $1,000 in questionable contributions to Michael Cardozo, the executive director of the Presidential Legal Defense Trust (PLET).[56]

- On April 24, 1996, Trie visits the legal defense fund again and tried to contribute an additional $179,000. Cardozo refused the money but did not ask Trie any questions.[57]
- On April 1, 1997, the *Wall Street Journal* reported that at the same time Trie was making campaign contributions, he received numerous wire transfers, in increments of $50,000 to $100,000, from the Chinese-government-owned Bank of China.[58]

What the Clinton Administration Gave Trie
- According to administration records released December 18, 1996, Trie visited the White House 23 times in Clinton's first term. He had six meetings with the president, two with the vice president, and nine with Mark Middleton—a former Clinton fund-raiser and top aide to former Chief of Staff Mack McLarty. (Middleton pleaded the Fifth Amendment in refusing to cooperate with congressional investigators.)
- Trie was allowed access to top-level trade meetings. In November 1994, at the Asian-Pacific Economic Conference in Jakarta, Trie was invited to a reception hosted by then-Commerce Secretary Ron Brown and attended by U.S. business officials and foreign trade ministers.
- On February 6, 1996, Trie was allowed to bring Wang Jun, a Chinese official, to meet President Clinton at a White House breakfast. Jun was chairman of the China International Trust and Investment Corp. (CITIC), the largest Chinese-government owned conglomerate, and also of Poly Technologies, Inc.—a company owned by the People's Liberation Army (PLA) and used for exporting Chinese weapons and acquiring military and dual-use technology for China.[59]

Interestingly, just four days before the February 6, 1996, White House breakfast the ATF suddenly approved a waiver of the ban on importing semi-automatic weapons, which Clinton himself had signed into law, thus allowing Poly Technologies to bring more than 100,000 AK-47 rifles into the United States. After the Wang visit came to public attention, President Clinton said he remembered "literally nothing" about the meeting, but he conceded it was "clearly inappropriate."[60]

Even more amazing, on March 18, 1996, just a month after the coffee, federal agents posing as Miami Mafia, confiscated two thousand fully automatic AK-47s, not covered by the waiver, that U.S. representatives of Poly Technologies tried to bring in secretly on a ship owned by another Chinese state company, the China Ocean Shipping Co. (COSCO). The guns and four thousand clips to go with them, reported the *Chicago Tribune*, had a value of $4 million. Robert Ma, the president of Poly Technologies' U.S. subsidiary (called PTK International) fled the country.[61]

Also, on the day of the coffee, Democratic fund-raiser Ernest G. Green, another Arkansas friend of the President's, delivered a $50,000 donation to the Democratic National Committee . . . . Mr. Green, a managing director at Lehman Brothers, had never before given such a large contribution to the Democratic Party. Mr. Wang used a letter of invitation written by Green to obtain a visa for Mr. Wang's trip to the White House for coffee. After delivering the check, Mr. Green met with Mr. Wang before Mr. Wang went to the White House.[62]

- On February 14, 1996, the White House counsel's office approved Yah Lin (Charlie) Trie for a confidential security clearance that qualified Trie to see classified information. A source familiar with the security clearance procedures said that those procedures were the hands-on responsibility of then-Director of White House Personnel Security Craig Livingstone.[63]
- On April 17, 1996, Clinton appointed Trie to the Commission on U.S. Pacific Trade and Investment Policy, which reviews U.S. commercial policies in Asia. Clinton reportedly expanded the commission to up to 20 people in early 1996 in part to make room for Trie. At this point, Trie had contributed $177,000 to the Democratic National Committee (DNC), at a time when his net income was only about $30,000 per year. He had also pledged to raise an additional $350,000 for the DNC.[64]

On February 3, 1998, Trie surrendered to FBI agents at Washington Dulles International Airport. He faced a fifteen-count felony indictment. In May 1999, he pleaded guilty to a felony count of making false statements to the Federal Election Commission and a misdemeanor charge of making political donations in the names of others. In exchange for probation, he agreed to cooperate in the government's campaign finance probe.[65]

What Chung Gave Clinton
Johnny Chung, like Huang and Trie, was a friend of Bill and Hillary Rodham Clinton. According to a report in the March 3, 1997 issue of *Time*, Chung (a Taiwanese-born U.S. citizen) met the Clintons in 1992 when he walked up to the then-Gov. Clinton's mansion in Arkansas, knocked on the door, and introduced himself to Mrs. Clinton.[66]

In the 1996 election cycle, Johnny Chung and his company, Automated Intelligence Systems, an office fax supply firm in California, gave a total of $366,000 to the DNC. As Chung would later describe it, "I see the White House is like a subway: You have to put in coins to open gates." Between July 1995 and September 1996, Chinese military intelligence passed $300,000 to Chung via Lieutenant Colonel Liu Chaoying. Colonel Liu was the vice president of China Aerospace, a company that deals in satellite and supercomputer technology, as well as the daughter of General Liu Huaqing, one of the most powerful members of the politburo of the Chine Communist Party. At least $100,000 of Colonel Liu's money found its way to the Democratic National Committee.[67]

- On March 8, 1995, Chung showed up at DNC headquarters in Washington, D.C. carrying what the *Los Angeles Times* called "an ambitious wish list. He wanted a White House tour, a meeting with Hillary Rodham Clinton, lunch in the White House mess, and admission to the taping of President Clinton's Saturday morning radio address." Former DNC Finance Director Richard Sullivan told the committee in a sworn deposition: "Johnny had showed up at the DNC and . . . said that he would contribute $50,000 if I would get him and five members of his entourage into a radio address with the President."[68]

On March 8, 1995, after the meeting with Sullivan, Chung took his donation-for-access offer directly to First Lady Hillary Rodham Clinton's White House office. He asked Mrs. Clinton's aide Evan Ryan if he and his friends could meet the First Lady and eat in the White House mess, also inquiring about how he could help the White House. According to Chung, as reported by the *Los Angeles Times*, "Ryan left for about 15 to 20 minutes and returned, saying he had spoken with [Mrs. Clinton's then-Chief of Staff Maggie] Williams. Then he said: 'Maybe you can help us.' The aide told Chung that 'the First Lady had some debts with the DNC' from expenses associated with White House Christmas parties. Chung believes Ryan mentioned a figure of around $80,000. Chung said, 'I said I will help for $50,000.'"[69]

The next day, Chung returned to Mrs. Clinton's office, handing Ryan an envelope. "Ryan lifted the flap and examined the contents. Inside was his check [to the DNC]," reported the *Los Angeles Times*. Then Maggie Williams appeared, took the envelope, and called to reserve a lunch table for Chung and his Chinese friends at the White House mess. Just before lunch, Chung was told that he and his friends could have their pictures taken with Hillary Rodham Clinton that afternoon. At 4:00 p.m., Mrs. Clinton met the group in a White House reception room, greeting Chung, "Welcome to the White House, my good friend." Chung told the *Los Angeles Times* that while waiting for Mrs. Clinton to arrive, he asked Ryan if the first lady knew about his donation. Ryan said, "Yes, she definitely knows." By accepting the check, Ms. Williams violated federal law preventing White House staffers from soliciting or accepting donations on government property.[70]

Interestingly, according to bank records released by the Senate Governmental Affairs Committee, Johnny Chung received a $150,000 wire transfer from the Chinese-government-owned Bank of China on March 6, 1995. Before the transfer, Chung's balance had been just over $20,000. Three days after the transfer, on March 9, he wrote a check for $50,000 to the Democratic National Committee (DNC).[71]

- On March 10, 1995, Chung returned to the First Lady's office and asked Ryan about getting his Chinese acquaintances into the next day's radio address. He called the DNC and spoke to Carol Khare, an assistant to DNC Chairman Don Fowler. "Chung got what he wanted, with the DNC's assistance, said the *Los Angeles Times*.⁷²

The next day, Chung and his friends, including the COSCO advisor, Hongye Zheng, attended the taping of President Clinton's radio address in the Oval Office. They had their pictures taken with President Clinton. Following the radio address, Chung wanted the resulting photographs, a request that raised issues for the NSC. Clinton also wanted Chung's friends to get the photos, even if the $50,000 contribution was illegal. Clinton just didn't want the photos widely circulated.⁷³

In the end, Chung got the photographs. He was demonstrably capable at arranging both access and visible evidence of access. So Lieutenant Colonel Liu and her associates picked him to channel their contributions, arrange their photo ops, and help them square the administration on issues of concern to COSCO, thus giving China the time and opportunity it needed to pursue its goal of naval expansion. They picked the right intermediary, and from their point of view, the right administration to do business.⁷⁴

* On April 7, 1995, National Security Council (NSC) official Marcy Darby memoed NSC official and Asia expert Robert Suettinger that the President "wasn't sure we'd want photos of him with these people [Chung's Chinese friends] circulating around." That same day Suettinger wrote a memo to then-NSC Director Anthony Lake saying: "My impression is he's [Chung's] a hustler and appears to be involved in setting up some kind of consulting operation that will thrive by bringing Chinese entrepreneurs into town for exposure to high-level U.S. officials." Chung was subsequently cleared into the White House a total of seventeen times—eight times after another memo by Suettinger to Lake in July 1995 recommending that "we be very careful about the kinds of political favors he [Chung] is granted."⁷⁵ The next day Chung gave Sullivan a check for $125,000 at a Hollywood fund-raising dinner with Clinton, held at Steven Spielberg's home.⁷⁶

Between 1994 and 1996, Johnny Chung gave the Democratic Party $366,000. In 1997, the DNC returned Chung's contributions as suspect. On May 18, 1998, it was reported that Chung had told the Justice Department that $300,000 of his dirty money came from Liu Chaoying, the daughter of senior People's Liberation Army commander Gen. Liu Huaqing, and herself an executive with the China Aerospace Corp.[77]

What Clinton Gave Chung

According to Secret Service records released to the Senate Governmental Affairs Committee, Chung was admitted to the White House twenty times "after" the NSC declared him a "hustler." All told, Chung had visited the White House at least fifty-one times in Clinton's first term.[78]

On December 24, 1994, Johnny Chung brought Chen Shizeng, the president of a Chinese beer company, Haoman, to meet the Clintons at the White House Christmas party. After the meeting, Chung brought his Chinese guest over to the Commerce Department to discuss how to facilitate the sale of Haoman beer in the United States. Interestingly, a picture of one of them taken with the Clintons, showed up in a Chinese beer ad, to the embarrassment of the White House.[79]

In September 1995, Clinton met Long Beach, California, officials at the White House to discuss leasing Long Beach Naval Station to COSCO, reported the *Los Angeles Times*. "Participants said Clinton shook hands and encouraged his subordinates to do what they could do to assist Long Beach."[80]

On August 8, 1996, Clinton went back to Long Beach to lobby for the COSCO deal, the *Los Angeles Times* reported March 9, 1997. The COSCO deal never underwent a national security review. However, after briefings by the CIA and Naval Intelligence on April 9, 1997, Rep. Duncan Hunter (R-Calif.) stated that COSCO "is totally controlled by the Chinese government," linked to the PLA, and guilty of smuggling "components of weapons of mass destruction" to anti-U.S. entities. Also, according to a June 1997 *American Spectator* article, "U.S. shipping companies reported they were shut out from bidding on Long Beach by the Maritime Administration, the federal agency that was in charge of determining the fate of the former naval station, because the China fix was in."[81]

What Kanchanalak Gave Clinton

Thai-born Pauline Kanchanalak ran Ban Chang International, which brokers joint-venture deals between U.S. and Thai companies. She helped organize and was a lobbyist for the U.S.-Thai Business Council. She was also a friend of John Huang.[82]

Between 1992 and 1996, Kanchanalak donated $650,000 to the DNC. About $235,000 of which was later returned because the actual source of the money was not revealed, reported the *Los Angeles Times* on January 3, 1997.[83]

On July 29, 1998, Pauline Kanchanalak, pleaded not guilty to a twenty-four-count indictment that she illegally channeled $679,000 in campaign contributions to the Democratic National Committee and various party candidates. Two years later, in July 2000, Kanchanalak agreed to plead guilty to a plan to funnel illegal foreign campaign contributions to the Democratic Party in exchange for access to President Clinton and other administration officials. As part of the plea deal, Kanchanalak agreed to cooperate with the Justice Department in its investigation.[84]

What Clinton Gave Kanchanalak

- Kanchanalak visited the White House at least twenty-six times in Clinton's first term, meeting with the President at least ten times, according to Secret Service records released December 26, 1996.
- In September 1994, Kanchanalak telephoned John Huang at Commerce. That same day, Huang "wrote a memo urging a senior Commerce Department official to support" the establishment of the U.S.-Thai Business Council—Kanchanalak's pet project.
- On October 6, 1994, Kanchanalak and members of the U.S.-Thai Business Council met with President Clinton and Thailand's prime minister, who stopped in to congratulate the group at the White House. "Clinton's tacit endorsement of the council gave it extra clout in Thailand." John Huang arranged the meeting. Twelve days later, Kanchanalak visited Huang at Commerce and two days later, donated $32,500 to the DNC.

- On June 18, 1996, Kanchanalak attended a John Huang-arranged coffee at the White House. Kanchanalak donated $85,000 that day and the DNC noted it as being contributed at a "WH coffee," reported the January 3, 1997, *Los Angeles Times*. President Clinton and DNC Chairman Don Fowler attended this coffee and Kanchanalak brought along four U.S.-Thai Business Council members, three of them executives of the multi-national Bangkok-based Charoen Pokphand Group, which has extensive business interests in China. At this "coffee" discussion with "the President centered on U.S.-China relations and economic policy."[85]

On March 8, 1997, Sen. Daniel Patrick Moynihan (D-N.Y.) appeared on CNN's *Evans & Novak* and said he believed the U.S. political system came under attack during the last [1996] election "from Asia, from Indochina and mainland China, and as well as perhaps from Taiwan." Moynihan continued: "The system was attacked, and some of the people penetrated."[86]

Despite Moynihan's concern, by late 1997, Attorney General Janet Reno refused to appoint an independent counsel to investigate Clinton or Gore and instead had placed in motion a secret program to control, limit and obstruct justice any true investigation of Chinese fund-raising abuses.[87]

On December 1, 1997, House Rules Committee Chairman Jerry Solomon (R.-N.Y.) took the first formal step toward impeachment of President Clinton when he sent the president a letter officially notifying him that the committee would be reviewing proposed legislation designed to initiate a congressional impeachment inquiry.[88]

On March 26, 1998, House Judiciary Committee Chairman Henry J. Hyde named David P. Schippers, a former federal prosecutor and a registered Democrat, as his chief counsel to investigate why Attorney General Janet Reno did not appoint an independent counsel to investigate charges of campaign finance violations. The investigation could expand into impeachment proceedings against President Clinton.[89]

Enclosed is an analysis by Edward Timperlake and William C. Triplett II that shows the cascades of money that went into the Clinton/Gore coffers. The record of campaign-finance abuses is staggering.

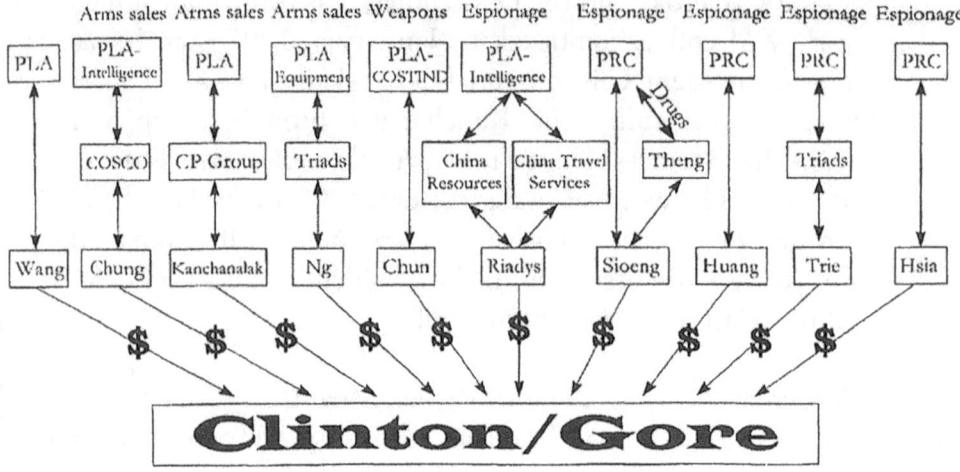

*Copyright © 1998 by Edward Timperlake and William Triplett II.
From the book, Year of the Rat (Washington, DC: Regnery Publishing, 1998).
Used by permission.*

On July 16, 1998, Charles LaBella, the Justice Department lawyer that Reno picked to investigate the campaign finance charges, filed his final report strongly recommending that she seek an independent counsel. Like FBI Director Louis Freeh, Mr. LaBella concluded that his investigation had satisfied both the provisions of the independent counsel law. Both also concluded that it was a conflict of interest for Ms. Reno to investigate the matters. In the end, Reno refused to appoint an independent counsel.[90]

Coincidently, on July 16, 1998, shortly after LaBella submitted his report, he learned that he would not receive the job of U.S. attorney for the Southern District of California, even though he had already been given the post on an acting, interim basis. Was this "payback" for his report. Shortly after that, he left the Justice Department after seventeen years of service.[91]

Now, the Congressional impeachment inquiry turned to the Paula Jones sexual harassment lawsuit and President Clinton's testimony. Defenders of the president claimed that even if he lied under oath and in fact did have a sexual relationship with Monica Lewinsky, "everybody lies about sex" and therefore such a lie should not be an impeachable offense. The legal history of lying under oath in civil cases are as follows:

- Judge Harry Claiborne was impeached in July 1986 because he "did willfully and knowingly" file a false return with the IRS, a form of lying under oath since he signed a statement swearing the information he provided was true.
- Judge Alcee Hastings was impeached in 1988 for making false statements in a case involving bribery and reductions in sentences.
- Judge Walter Nixon was impeached on May 10, 1989, for lying about interfering with the criminal prosecution of his business partner's son, who had been accused of drug smuggling.[92]

In 1998, *Human Events* reported on an *Arkansas Democrat* article from August 6, 1974, in which Clinton commented on the release of the smoking-gun tape recording of President Richard Nixon made in the Oval Office six days after the 1972 Watergate break-in. "There's nothing left to say. There's not any point now in putting the country through an impeachment since he isn't making any pretense of innocence now." Clinton said he believed the president should have stayed in office and resisted resignation if Nixon thought himself innocent. But now that the President has admitted wrongdoing, he should resign.[93]

On September 6, 1998, Sen. Daniel Patrick Moynihan (D-N.Y.) appeared on ABC-TV's *This Week* and said, "Congress ought to get on with . . . an impeachment procedure in the sex-and-lies scandal that threatens the presidency." "Perjury in a civil case, lying to a grand jury and lying to the American people are all impeachable offenses," he said, "and Congress should stay in session until it addresses President Clinton's actions."[94]

At 3:45 p.m. on Wednesday, September 9, 1998, Jackie Bennett announced that the report and its supporting material were being placed in vans for delivery to the Ford building. There were two copies of everything—one for the Democrats, one for the Republicans. The report itself totaled 452 pages, with 1,660 footnotes, and 18 boxes of supporting material—FBI interviews, grand jury testimony, and other evidence.[95]

On September 11, 1998, the House of Representatives voted 363-63 to release the report submitted by the Office of the Independent Counsel (OIC). The report contented that there were eleven possible grounds for impeachment. They included:

1. President Clinton lied under oath in his civil case when he denied a sexual affair, a sexual relationship, or sexual relations with Monica Lewinsky.
2. President Clinton lied under oath to the grand jury about his sexual relationship with Ms. Lewinsky.
3. In his civil deposition, to support his false statement about the sexual relationship, President Clinton also lied under oath about being alone with Ms. Lewinsky and about the many gifts exchanged between Ms. Lewinsky and him.
4. President Clinton lied under oath in his civil deposition about his discussions with Ms. Lewinsky concerning her involvement in the Jones case.
5. During the Jones case, the President obstructed justice and had an understanding with Ms. Lewinsky to jointly conceal the truth about their relationship by concealing gifts subpoenaed by Ms. Jones's attorneys.
6. During the Jones case, the President obstructed justice and had an understanding with Ms. Lewinsky to jointly conceal the truth of their relationship from the judicial process by a scheme that included the following means: (i) Both the President and Ms. Lewinsky understood that they would lie under oath in the Jones case about their sexual relationship; (ii) the President suggested to Ms. Lewinsky that she prepare an affidavit that, for the President's purposes, would memorialize her testimony under oath and could be used to prevent questioning of both of them about their relationship; (iii) Ms. Lewinsky signed and filed the false affidavit; (iv) the President used Ms. Lewinsky's false affidavit at his deposition in an attempt to head off questions about Ms. Lewinsky; and (v) when that failed, the President lied under oath at his civil deposition about the relationship with Ms. Lewinsky.

7. President Clinton endeavored to obstruct justice by helping Ms. Lewinsky obtain a job in New York at a time when she would have been a witness harmful to him were she to tell the truth in the Jones case.
8. President Clinton lied under oath in his civil deposition about his discussions with Vernon Jordan concerning Ms. Lewinsky's involvement in the Jones case.
9. The President improperly tampered with a potential witness by attempting to corruptly influence the testimony of his personal secretary, Betty Currie, in the days after his civil deposition.
10. President Clinton endeavored to obstruct justice during the grand jury investigation by refusing to testify for seven months and lying to senior White House aides with knowledge that they would relay the President's false statements to the grand jury—and did thereby deceive, obstruct, and impede the grand jury.
11. President Clinton abused his constitutional authority by (i) lying to the public and the Congress in January 1998 about his relationship with Ms. Lewinsky (ii) promising at that time to cooperate fully with the grand jury investigation; (iii) later refusing six invitations to testify voluntarily to the grand jury; (iv) invoking Executive Privilege; (v) lying to the grand jury in August 1998; and (vi) lying again to the public and Congress on August 17, 1998—all as part of an effort to hinder, impede, and deflect possible inquiry by the Congress of the United States.[96]

On September 18, 1998, the House Judiciary Committee voted to make the videotape and other evidence public, and set the release for Monday September 21 at 9:00 a.m.[97]

On September 22, 1998, former president Jimmy Carter, in a speech at Emory University, said that the Clinton scandal has done "a lot of damage" to the presidency and that "I have deplored and been deeply embarrassed about what has occurred." Carter predicted that the House would vote to impeach but expected that the Senate will not be able to muster the two-thirds vote to remove Clinton from office.[98]

On September 30, 1998, Rep. Henry Hyde, chairman of the House Judiciary Committee, proposed a draft resolution for impeachment of President Clinton that he said follows "word for word" the committee's 1974 resolution for the impeachment of President Nixon.[99]

On October 4, 1998, Larry Flynt, the publisher of *Hustler* magazine, had taken out a full-page advertisement in the *Washington Post* to announce that he would pay as much as $1 million to any woman who was willing to go public about her affairs with government officials. Flynt later said that his offer drew about two thousand calls to his 800 number. Flynt hired private investigators, who narrowed the original list down to forty-eight possibilities, and then took a closer look at about a dozen. Some of these tales concerned Republican Congressman Bob Livingston.[100]

On October 8, 1998, the House of Representatives voted 258 to 176, with 31 Democrats breaking ranks, to authorize the Judiciary Committee to launch an inquiry to determine whether President Clinton committed impeachable offenses.[101]

On November 5, 1998, Rep. Hyde, on behalf of his Judiciary Committee, sent President Clinton 81 questions to admit or deny their truthfulness under oath. The questions, which were drawn up by committee counsel David Schippers and his staff, were "for purposes of the inquiry of impeachment only" and that the responses Clinton provides "shall not be considered to have any bearing or effect on any subsequent or prospective action by the executive or judicial branches of the United States that may be related to this matter."[102]

On November 10, 1998, the House Judiciary Committee legal staff concluded that the crimes independent counsel Kenneth Starr charged to President Clinton are impeachable offenses.[103]

On November 19, 1998, the impeachment hearings began with the arrival of Judge Kenneth Starr before the committee. Hyde called the hearing to order. Starr's opening statement gave the history of the investigation, described the manner in which it was conducted, and then offered an analysis and explanation of the charges.[104]

The House Judiciary Committee Counsel David Schippers charged President Clinton with fifteen felony allegations. They were as follows:

1. The President Led a Conspiracy to Obstruct Justice
2. The President Solicited a False Affidavit from a Federal Witness
3. The President Aided a Witness in Obstructing Justice by Filing a False Affidavit
4. The President Sustained Lewinsky's Perjury in Court
5. The President Lied Under Oath to a Federal Court about His Relations with Lewinsky
6. The President Lied Under Oath to a Federal Grand Jury About His Relations with Monica Lewinsky
7. The President Lied Under Oath to a Federal Court About Being Alone with Lewinsky and About Gifts He Gave Her
8. The President Lied Under Oath about His Conversations with Lewinsky Concerning the Paula Jones Lawsuit
9. The President Obstructed Justice by Hiding Evidence That Had Already Been Subpoenaed by a Federal Court
10. The President Obstructed Justice by Agreeing to a Cover Story and then Securing a False Affidavit and Committing Perjury to Back Up the Cover Story
11. The President Obstructed Justice by Helping a Potentially Adverse Witness Find a Job
12. The President Lied Under Oath to a Federal Court Concerning His Conversations with Vernon Jordan About Monica Lewinsky
13. The President Obstructed Justice and Tampered with a Witness by Coaching the Testimony of Betty Currie
14. The President Tampered with Witnesses by Narrating Elaborate and False Stories to White House Aides He Thought Would Be Subpoenaed
15. The President Lied Under Oath to the Grand Jury About His Knowledge of Monica Lewinsky's False Affidavit[105]

On December 11 and 12, 1998, the House Judiciary Committee approved four articles of impeachment against President Clinton. They were as follows:

Article I: The President "willfully provided perjurious, false and misleading testimony" to the grand jury on August 17 regarding the Paul Jones case and his relationship with Monica Lewinsky. (Approved 21-16).

Article II: The President "willfully provided perjurious, false and misleading testimony" in the Jones case in sworn, written answers December 23, 1997, and in his videotaped deposition, Jan. 17, 1998. (Approved 20-17).

Article III: The President "prevented, obstructed and impeded the administration of justice" in an effort "to delay, impede, cover up and conceal the evidence and testimony" related to the Jones case. (Approved 21-16).

Article IV: The President "engaged in conduct that resulted in misuse and abuse of his high office" by making "perjurious, false and misleading sworn statements" in his written responses to some of the 81 questions posed to him by the Judiciary Committee. (Approved 21 to 16).[106]

For only the second time in U.S. history, the Judiciary Committee of the House of Representatives had voted for the impeachment of an elected president. The feeling of accomplishment was short lived. Immediately the attacks from the Democrats and the president's supporters began. The spin was that Clinton-haters had forced the Republicans to be stampeded into an ill-advised move.[107]

The plan was to have the articles debated and voted on by the full House the week of December 14, 1998. The day before the scheduled debate, Hyde had a morning meeting of Republican committee members. The meeting was in progress when Steve Buyer (R-IN) entered the room. Buyer, who was also on the House Armed Services Committee, said, "We just learned that Clinton is bombing Iraq tonight."[108]

There was stunned, unbelieving silence. Hyde blurted, "My God!—*Wag the Dog*," referring to the popular film in which the White House staged a phony war to distract the public's attention from a breaking scandal. The new Speaker-designate, Bob Livingston, called a Republican caucus to discuss the impeachment schedule given this manufactured foreign crisis. The immediate cry from the Democrats was, "How can you impeach the Commander in Chief when our armed services are engaged in foreign combat?"[109]

The debate was postponed for a couple of days. The delay allowed the House managers to invite all House members to examine the secure room evidence. They showed videos, played tapes, and provided transcripts, statements, reports, and any other material needed. In all, some sixty-five members came in a four-day period. In reviewing the sign-in sheets, David Schippers found out later that *all* the visitors were Republicans. *Not one Democrat saw fit to examine the evidence.* Interestingly, the visitors were ambivalent or leaning against impeachment. Yet of those sixty-five who actually examined the evidence and asked us questions, *sixty-four* voted to impeach. President Clinton's bombing gambit had backfired. It had given the House managers time to convince enough Republicans to ensure impeachment.[110]

Rep. Hyde began the proceedings in the well of the House on Friday, December 18. "Mr. Speaker," he said, "I call up a privileged resolution . . . and ask for its immediate consideration. The clerk [Paul Hays] will read the resolution, as follows: "Resolved," Hays said, "that William Jefferson Clinton is impeached for high crimes and misdemeanors, and that the following articles be exhibited to the United States Senate . . . ." It took him five minutes to read through all four articles. Such words had not been uttered in the House of Representatives in 130 years, since the impeachment of President Andrew Johnson.[111]

On December 19, 1998, the House of Representatives impeached President Clinton for grand jury perjury and obstructing justice, and for the first time in 130 years, asked the Senate to remove a president from office. The historic vote, which in the words of one congressman would leave the president's legacy "indelibly stained," occurred at 1:25 p.m. when the House adopted the first article of impeachment by a 228-206 vote. William Jefferson Clinton became the first elected U.S. President ever impeached.[112]

"Wherefore, William Jefferson Clinton, by such conduct, warrants impeachment and trial, and removal from office and disqualification to hold and enjoy any office of honor, trust, or profit under the United States," declared H.R. 611, the official impeachment resolution.[113]

Article two, perjury in the Jones deposition, which was rock-solid and was the basis of Clinton's perjury before the grand jury, lost 229 to 205. Article three, obstruction of justice, passed 221 to 212. Article 4, ultimately based on Clinton's written answers to the Judiciary Committee, failed 285 to 148.[114]

After the vote, President Clinton said in a brief White House speech that resignation was not in his plans. He vowed to continue in office "for two more [years] until the last hour of the last day of my term." Interestingly, a few hours after the speech, Clinton abruptly announced he was suspending the bombing of Iraq that he had abruptly initiated only seventy hours before.[115]

At 1:00 p.m., on the afternoon of Thursday, January 14, 1999, with Chief Justice William H. Rehnquist presiding, the formal Senate impeachment trial of William Jefferson Clinton began. Thursday, Friday, and Saturday were taken up with opening statements by each of the thirteen managers.[116]

On Saturday, January 16, 1999, Rep. Hyde concluded the managers' opening statements with an oration of his own. "One hundred and thirty-six years ago," Hyde began, "at a small military cemetery in Pennsylvania, one of Illinois's most illustrious sons asked a haunting question: whether a nation conceived in liberty and dedicated to the proposition that all men are created equal can long endure."[117]

On Thursday, February 4, 1999, at 1:00 p.m., the managers began the "evidence" phase of the impeachment trial. Nobody connected with the managers was shocked or even surprised when the Senate opted for the deposition testimony in place of live testimony. The full deposition of Monica Lewinsky was not shown, just excerpts. Lewinsky's testimony was followed by the depositions of Vernon Jordan and Sidney Blumenthal. That was the extent of the "evidence" the managers were permitted to present. With full knowledge that they were running in a rigged race, the president's lawyers neither cross-examined the prosecution witnesses nor produced any factual evidence in defense of the charges. Instead, they chose to play excerpts from the same depositions.[118]

The "testimony" was followed, on Monday, February 8, 1999, by the final arguments. Then the Senators went into Executive Session to debate the articles. On Friday, February 12, 1999, the United States Senate, in a foreordained and actually anticlimactic vote, perfunctorily acquitted William Jefferson Clinton on both articles. The House Managers didn't even achieve a simple majority.[119]

By a vote of 45 to 55, the Senate fell far short of the two-thirds majority required to convict President Clinton of making "perjurious, false and misleading testimony." Ten Republicans joined all forty-five Senate Democrats in acquitting the president. The Senate then voted 50 to 50 to clear him of Article II obstruction of justice allegations. Again, a two-thirds vote was needed to convict. Five Republicans joined with Democrats in voting to exonerate the president. Bill Clinton survived.[120]

On March 31, 1999, in an interview with Dan Rather on CBS's *60 Minutes II*, an amazingly unrepentant President Clinton insisted that all the charges leveled against him during his presidency have been "false," and that he never considered resigning because he had a duty to fight impeachment for the sake of the American people, the Framers, and the Constitution.[121]

Clinton's bitterness continued. On April 2000, sixteen months after William Jefferson Clinton attained the dubious distinction of being only the second American president in more than two hundred years to be impeached, he had the unmitigated nerve to blame the House of Representatives for its adversity. He said: "On the impeachment, let me tell you, I am proud of what we did there because I think we saved the Constitution of the United States. I am not ashamed of the fact that they impeached me. That was their decision, not mine. And it was wrong. As a matter of law, the Constitution, and history, it was wrong. And I am glad I didn't quit, and I'm glad we fought it."[122]

CHAPTER 36

DISBARMENT

I don't have any control over that, and I don't spend much time thinking about it. I don't believe I should be charged, I don't want that. If that's what they want, I'll be happy to stand and fight.
—President Clinton on disbarment, December 2000[1]

In September 1998, the Southeastern Legal Foundation filed a complaint to the ethics committee of the Arkansas Supreme Court and charged that President Clinton obstructed justice and lied under oath in the Paula Jones case. The foundation cited the American Legal Association's code of conduct that prohibits lawyers from engaging in "conduct involving dishonesty, fraud, deceit or misrepresentation" or conduct that is prejudicial to the administration of justice." That same month, the Landmark Legal Foundation petitioned U.S. District Judge Susan Weber Wright to hold President Clinton in contempt.[2]

On April 12, 1999, Judge Susan Webber Wright, in a scathing thirty-two-page opinion, lambasted President Clinton for "undermining the integrity of the judicial system" with his "false, misleading and evasive answers that were designed to obstruct the judicial process." Mr. Clinton became the first U.S. president to be held in contempt of court. Judge Wright also fined President Clinton $90,686. Her ruling, in part, is as follows:

> The record demonstrates by clear and convincing evidence that the president responded to plaintiff's questions by giving false,

misleading and evasive answers that were designed to obstruct the judicial process. The president acknowledged as much in his public admission that he 'misled people.' . . . there simply is no escaping the fact that the president violated this court's discovery orders and thereby undermined the integrity of the judicial system. Sanctions must be imposed, not only to redress the President's misconduct, but to deter others who might themselves consider emulating the President of the United States. . . .[3]
Accordingly, the court adjudges the President to be in civil contempt of court pursuant to Federal Rule of Civil Procedure 37(b)(2) for his willful failure to obey this court's discovery orders . . . [and] the court will refer this matter to the Arkansas Supreme Court's Committee on Professional Conduct for review and any action it deems appropriate."[4]

It was a bitter pill to swallow. President Clinton also chose not to appeal Judge Wright's ruling, which he could have done. Part of the reason might have been that Judge Wright explicitly held in reserve her right to hold Mr. Clinton in criminal contempt.[5]

On February 15, 2000, President Clinton was served notice of the disciplinary complaints via certified mail. On March 16, 2000, President Clinton asked the Arkansas Supreme Court disciplinary unit to delay disbarment hearings over his conduct in the Paula Jones case until a month after he leaves office.[6] On March 17, 2000, the Arkansas Committee on Professional Conduct rejected President Clinton's request to delay the disbarment proceedings. The committee, an arm of the Arkansas Supreme Court, ordered Mr. Clinton to file within five weeks his response to a court finding that he lied under oath and obstructed justice in the Jones case and the grand jury investigation triggered by the Lewinsky scandal.[7]

On May 22, 2000, the Arkansas Supreme Court Committee on Professional Conduct recommended that President Clinton be disbarred from law practice for lying under oath, the most severe punishment sought to date for his misconduct. Arkansas is among the many states that allows a disbarred lawyer to petition after five or more years for reinstatement based on good behavior. While a lawyer is disbarred, other states that know of the case, honor that order. This includes federal courts in which the lawyer is admitted to practice, including the U.S. Supreme Court.[8]

On June 17, 2000, Marie B. Miller was hired by the Arkansas Supreme Court's Committee on Professional Conduct to argue for stripping President Clinton of his law license for lying in a deposition in the Paula Jones sexual harassment case.[9] Nearly two weeks later, on June 30, 2000, the same Arkansas Committee filed an unprecedented five-page lawsuit against President Clinton seeking to confiscate his law license for lying under oath in the Paula Jones sexual misconduct case. The suit, which accuses the president of "dishonesty, deceit, fraud and misrepresentations," asked a court to find that Mr. Clinton "conducted himself in a manner that violates the model rules of professional conduct as adopted by the Arkansas Supreme Court." The suit stated that Mr. Clinton's conduct "damages the legal profession and demonstrates a lack of overall fitness to hold a license to practice law." It said the president's misstatements were "motivated by a desire to protect himself from the embarrassment of his own conduct."[10]

On July 11, 2000, Judge Leon Johnson agreed to preside over the disbarment case against President Clinton. Unfortunately, Judge Johnson resisted for months hearing the disbarment case. On January 2, 2001, Judge Johnson was replaced by Pulaski County Circuit Judge William Proctor Jr. to begin the case.[11]

Prosecutor Marie B. Miller said that she and the Bar were deeply offended by Clinton's offenses and wanted him fined and denied his law license, all before he left office. Clinton wanted to settle for a two-year suspension and to delay an agreement until after leaving office. On the morning of January 19, an agreement was forced on him. Clinton accepted a $25,000 fine and a five-year suspension of his law license. He also agreed that he had given false testimony about Monica Lewinsky.[12]

On November 9, 2001, former President Bill Clinton submitted his resignation from the Supreme Court Bar hours before the deadline to disbar him. The October 1 suspension of Mr. Clinton's privilege to practice law before the high court began the mechanism toward virtually automatic disbarment. That forty-day process, in which Mr. Clinton was ordered to "show cause," ended on November 9.[13]

Bill Clinton thus went down in history as the first president in American history to lose his law license while in office, a punishment that was not even visited upon Richard Nixon, who surrendered his law license after he left the White House. Disbarment became a lifetime stigma and a definitive verdict for history.[14]

CHAPTER 37

PARDONS

On the merits, I don't think it was a wrong decision; I regret all the political flap.
—President Clinton on Marc Rich pardon, February 2, 2001[1]

The Constitution (Article II, Section 2) gives presidents "power to grant reprieves and pardons for offenses against the United States, except in cases of impeachment." Pardons nullify a conviction, block prosecutions and erase remaining penalties, except impeachment. A reprieve commutes a sentence to more lenient terms but lets convictions stand.[2]

Bill Clinton's first mention of the pardon came when he said Gerald Ford's pardon of Richard Nixon in 1974 "undermined respect for law and order" and "prejudiced pending trials." The comments were made during Mr. Clinton's unsuccessful 1974 congressional race against Arkansas Republican Rep. John Hammerschmidt. So how would Clinton do with the power of the pardon?[3]

Records showed that Governor Clinton, a week after his 1990 re-election to a fifth term, pardoned Dan Lasater, who was convicted of cocaine distribution on 180 occasions and who contributed thousands of dollars to several of his gubernatorial campaigns in Arkansas.[4]

Then there was the quiet pardon of Jack Pakis that was unearthed by the *Washington Times*' Frank J. Murray. Pakis was an Arkansas gambling king and betting pal of presidential mom Virginia Kelley and father of Roger Clinton's best friend. Pakis was convicted in 1972 of operating a gambling business. Though his two-year sentence was suspended and he never spent a day in jail, Mr. Pakis was disturbed that he couldn't vote or own a gun. Mr. Clinton came through with the pardon in April 1995.[5]

On August 7, 1999, on the one-year anniversary of the U.S. embassy bombings in East Africa that killed 257 people and injured 5,000, President Bill Clinton reaffirmed his commitment to the victims of terrorism, vowing that he "will not rest until justice is done." Four days later, while Congress was on summer recess, the White House quietly issued a press release announcing that the president was granting clemency to sixteen imprisoned members of the terrorist group FALN. What began as a simple paragraph on the AP wire exploded into a major controversy.[6]

FALN, the *Fuerzas Armadas de Liberacion Nacional* (Armed Forces of National Liberation), was a Marxist group responsible for a reign of terror that included over 130 bombing attacks in five major U.S. cities from 1974 to 1983. All told, the terrorists racked up five deaths, eighty-four wounded, and $3.5 million in property damage in their pursuit of independence for Puerto Rico.[7]

The first bombing was in January 1975 at the historic Fraunces Tavern in lower Manhattan. Timed to go off during the lunch-hour rush, the explosion decapitated one of the four people killed and injured another sixty. FALN bragged about the bloodbath, calling the victims "reactionary corporate executives" and threatening: "You have unleashed a storm from which you comfortable Yankees can't escape."[8] More bombings followed:

* On February 18, 1977, powerful bombs rocked the Chrysler Building and Gulf & Western Building, also in New York. The next day, the FALN demanded independence for Puerto Rico and that a grand jury halt its investigation of the group. By then, the FALN had taken credit for 49 bombings.
* On March 22, 1977, the FALN bombed the American Note Co. as well as an FBI office in New York City.
* On April 9, 1977, the FALN set fires at Macy's, Gimbel's, and Bloomingdale's.
* On August 3, 1977, a worker found a bomb in a purse outside a Defense Department office in a Madison Avenue skyscraper. The building was safely evacuated. An hour later, a FALN-planted bomb exploded in the personnel office of the Mobil One Building at ground level, blowing glass across Forty-second Street. One person

was killed, several injured. Bomb threats emptied the World Trade and Empire State Building. The mayor of New York City demanded that terrorism be made a capital offense.

* On October 19, 1979, the FALN detonated six bombs in Chicago. The targets included the Republican Central Committee, a city government building, the Great Lakes Naval Training Center and the Ted Kennedy for President Campaign.

* In 1980, armed FALN members stormed the George H. W. Bush for President and Carter/Mondale campaign headquarters, where they tied up and gagged campaign workers. At the Carter campaign, they also took a list of Democratic National Convention delegates. Investigators told the *New York Times* that the FALN maintained files on more than fifty top executives who could be kidnapped and held for ransom. At trial, volunteers from the Carter Campaign identified the terrorists. They offered no defense, declaring themselves to be "prisoners of war" under international law. FALN supporters turned court appearances into a raucous circus.

* On New Year's Eve 1982, FALN was responsible for the bombing at One Police Plaza in New York. The explosion ripped the lower leg off of Police Officer Rocco Pascarella, as well as destroying the entrance of the building. Moments later, Detective Anthony Senft and his partner, Richard Pastorella, "were blown fifteen feet in the air as they knelt in protective gear to defuse another bomb. Detective Senft was blinded in one eye, his facial bones shattered, his hip severely fractured. Detective Pastorella was blinded in both eyes and lost all the fingers of his right hand." There were four bombs that New Year's Eve night. In an hour, in addition to the two explosions at One Police Center, FBI headquarters in Manhattan and Brooklyn's federal courthouse were attacked.

* In 1983, the group robbed an armored car of $7.5 million in West Hartford, Conn.[9]

The FALN's Adolfo Matos made it clear that he and his terrorist colleagues were not ashamed of what they had done and saw no need to ask forgiveness. As a matter of fact, he stated that he wanted to continue their personal war against the United States and its innocent civilians.[10]

Mr. Clinton justified the clemencies by asserting that the sentences were disproportionate to the crimes. None of the petitioners, he stated, had been directly involved in crimes that caused bodily harm to anyone. That was an absolute lie.[11]

The prisoners were convicted on a variety of charges that included conspiracy, sedition, murder, armed robbery, and illegal possession of weapons and explosives. This included large quantities of C-4 plastic explosive, dynamite, and huge caches of ammunition.[12]

The Justice Department, FBI Director Louis Freeh, and the U.S. attorneys' offices in Illinois and Connecticut all opposed the release of the FALN terrorists. In addition, Clinton also ignored the Bureau of Prisons. Testifying before the House Government Reform and Oversight Committee, Michael B. Cooksey of the Bureau of Prisons said that Clinton never contacted the bureau before releasing the terrorists. The FALN members, Cooksey said, had an "extreme propensity to violence or escape."[13]

Clinton also had not bothered to consult with relatives of the victims of the FALN terrorism. In fact, the survivors of those murdered and those whose lives had otherwise been destroyed by the terrorists were not even informed that their attackers were being released. The White House, with opposition rising against the pardons, tried to claim that the late John Cardinal O'Connor backed clemency for the FALN terrorists. That statement was subsequently denied by the archbishop of New York.[14]

Usually, a pardon is granted only after a prisoner applies for clemency and expresses remorse. Yet, Clinton offered clemency without it being requested. The FALN prisoners refused to send letters of contrition even though the Justice Department had urged them to do so. Instead they issued a statement saying, "innocent victims were on all sides." Then, the White House approached former president Carter and recruited him to recommend clemency for the FALN terrorists. Also, notes obtained by the House Government Reform Committee during its investigation of the matter revealed that White House aides planned to identify "liberal supporters in key media outlets" in an effort to drum up more support for clemency.[15]

One fact that Bill Clinton surely had considered was the emerging senatorial campaign of his wife, Hillary. She was in the midst of her state-wide "listening tour" in anticipation of her run for the U.S. Senate seat in New York. There were more than two million Puerto Ricans in the

United States, and approximately 1.3 million Puerto Ricans in New York. As a group, Puerto Ricans tend to vote Democratic. Also, three members of the Congressional Hispanic Caucus, Luis V. Gutierrez (D-Ill.), Jose E. Serrano, (D-N.Y.) and Nydia M. Velazquez, (D-N.Y.), along with local Hispanic politicians and leftist human-rights advocates, had been agitating for years on behalf of the FALN cases directly to the White House and the first lady.[16]

The immediate question was: "Did the White House commute the sentences to win Puerto Rican votes for Hillary Clinton's senatorial campaign?" Before this, President Clinton had granted clemency in only three cases and ignored the 3,226 clemency petitions that had piled up on his desk over the years. Now he suddenly reached into the stack and pulled out these sixteen meritless cases? The *New York Times* ran a column with the headline "Bill's Little Gift."[17]

Initial reports stated that Mrs. Clinton supported the clemencies, but when public reaction went negative she quickly reversed course and stated her opposition to the pardons, trying to recover ground by seeming to be independent from her husband. The Puerto Ricans knew that they had been beneficiaries of Hillary's political ambitions. But Hillary was able to claim to opponents of the clemency that she not only had not been responsible, but that she would have opposed the actions.[18]

Meanwhile, Puerto Rican politicians in New York who'd been crowing to their constituents about the impending release of these "freedom fighters" were enraged and insulted when Hillary Rodham Clinton eventually withdrew her support. "It was a horrible blunder," said State Sen. Olga A. Mendez. "She needs to learn the rules." Mrs. Clinton called her failure to consult the Puerto Rican political establishment before assessing the issue a mistake "that will never happen again."[19]

On September 9, 1999, just one day before those pardoned were set to walk, President Clinton said, "She [Hillary] didn't know anything about it until—as far as I know—until someone from her office called and asked her for comment, because I did not discuss it with her."[20]

The House and Senate then went into action. Each chamber quickly passed resolutions condemning the pardons. The House vote was 311-41, and the Senate vote was 95-2. The Senate resolution stated that, "making concessions to terrorists is deplorable, and that President Clinton should not have offered or granted clemency to the FALN terrorists."[21]

When the FBI gave its position on the FALN clemencies, which the White House temporarily succeeded in keeping out of news coverage, it said: "The release of these individuals will psychologically and operationally enhance the ongoing violent and criminal activities of terrorist groups, not only in Puerto Rico, but throughout the world." The White House then spun into action, claiming that its clemencies were a sign of the president's universal commitment to "peace and reconciliation."[22]

President Clinton's use of his constitutional power to pardon the FALN terrorists apparently showed him that he could use the pardon power for personal and political ends, ignore the Department of Justice, and get away with it. All Clinton had to do was to say that a pardon had nothing to do with politics, that his actions were based strictly on the facts and merits of the case and claim that the sentence commutation served the interests of justice.[23]

The FALN incident was the first time a president had used his pardon power to grant clemency to terrorists. Clinton would return to this theme again at the end of his presidency.[24]

On December 22, 2000, President Clinton pardoned fifty-nine people, including Dan Rostenkowski, former House Ways and Means Committee Chairman who pleaded guilty to two counts of mail fraud in a corruption scandal. The investigation that sent Mr. Rostenkowski to federal prison began with a probe of abuses at the House post office, first reported by the *Washington Times* in 1992. The Illinois Democrat admitted to using office funds to buy gifts for friends and cronies. Clinton also pardoned Archie Schaffer III, chief spokesman for Arkansas-based Tyson Foods who was convicted for giving illegal gratuities to former Agriculture Secretary Mike Espy and trying to influence agricultural policy by arranging for Mr. Espy to attend a Tyson birthday party in Arkansas in 1993.[25]

On January 20, 2001, with just two hours left in his presidency, Bill Clinton granted 140 pardons and 36 commutations. Unfortunately, Mr. Clinton violated his own pledge by granting more than thirty pardons directly.[26] As the details of the last-minute pardons and commutations became public, there was outrage and disbelief. One television commentator said, "Not since the opening of the gates of the Bastille have so many criminals been liberated on a single day."[27]

A couple other standouts who were pardoned were Marc Rich and Pincus Green. According to the U.S. Department of Justice, Mr. Rich conspired in April 1980 with Iran to purchase more than 6 million barrels of oil in violation of the trade embargo imposed by the United States during the hostage crisis. In 1983, federal prosecutors, led by Rudy Giuliani, put together a compelling tax evasion case against Marc Rich, accusing him of pulling off the biggest tax fraud scheme in U.S. history.[28]

Mr. Rich fled to Switzerland in 1983 after the U.S. government indicted him on sixty-five counts of tax fraud, racketeering and evading more than $48 million in taxes. The charges carried a maximum 325 years in jail.[29]

Denise Rich visited the White House about 100 times, just during 2000. Most of the Oval Office rendezvous took place while Mrs. Clinton was campaigning in New York. Ms. Rich, with Beth Dozoretz, a Democratic fund-raiser, were also at the White House on January 19, 2001, just hours before President Clinton signed the Rich pardon. Both women denied being at the White House that day, but Secret Service logs showed Rich and Dozoretz checking into the executive mansion at 5:29 p.m. and 5:30 p.m. on January 19, 2001.[30]

Then, in August 2001, in an unguarded moment of conversation with Congresswoman Nancy Pelosi, a Capitol Hill police officer standing two feet away heard Hillary Rodham Clinton snap, "Bill f***ed" Denise."[31]

Interestingly, the pardon was favored by Clinton's former White House counsel, Jack Quinn and Deputy Attorney General Eric Holder. According to investigators for the House Government Reform Committee, Holder was working as "a willing participant in the plan to keep the Justice Department from knowing about and opposing" the pardon. The investigators went on to note that "Eric Holder's support of the Rich pardon played a critical role." Apparently compassion for a tax-evasion fugitive was not Eric Holder's motive. Investigators found that he "was seeking Jack Quinn's support to be appointed as attorney general in a potential Al Gore administration."[32]

On January 21, 2001, when he was asked about the Rich pardon, Bill Clinton said: "I spent a lot of personal time . . . because it's an unusual case, but Quinn made a strong case, and I was convinced he was right on the merits." Five days later, Mr. Clinton told reporters that the American people would support the pardon "if they take a look at the record."[33]

The *New York Times*, though, looked at the record and did not support it. The *Times* described the Rich pardon as "a shocking abuse of presidential power and a reminder of why George W. Bush's vow to restore integrity to the Oval Office resonated with millions of Americans who otherwise disagreed with the new president's politics."[34]

Then, there was Carlos Vignali, a drug kingpin, whom the first lady's brother, Hugh Rodham, lobbied for, received a last-minute presidential pardon. He was convicted on narcotics charges for his role in a drug ring that transported more than eight hundred pounds of cocaine from Los Angeles to Minnesota. There the traffickers converted the drug to crack for sale on the streets. His father, Horacio, whom investigators also suspected of drug trafficking, spread hundreds of thousands of dollars throughout the Democratic Party in California to expedite his son's commutation. Interestingly, the $200,000 Horacio paid Hugh Rodham was not deposited until three days after his son's pardon.[35]

Another of Hugh Rodham's clients was Glenn Braswell. He had been convicted of tax evasion and mail fraud but was pardoned after paying Hugh Rodham $230,000. While his pardon was being pursued he was under federal investigation for still more criminal acts, a condition that in itself should have denied him a pardon. In the end, Braswell got his pardon. When word spread of Hugh Rodham's payment from Braswell, Rodham returned the payment. He also agreed to return the money he got from Vignali, though investigators reported that he returned only $50,000.[36]

President Clinton also shaved some prison time off the sentences of four Hasidic Jews, Kalmen Stern, David Goldstein, Benjamin Berger, and Jacob Elbaum, who were charged with stealing more than $40 million in education grants, small business loans, and housing grants by creating a fake parochial school. Representatives for these men met with then New York senatorial candidate Hillary Rodham Clinton in August 2000. During the election, New Square voted 1,400 to 12 in favor of her in her 2000 Senate campaign. Then, on December 22, 2000, Bill Clinton and Sen-elect Clinton met with Grand Rabbi David Twersky from the New Square Hasidim, a Jewish Orthodox community in New York that lobbied for release of the four Hasidic Jews during a forty-five-minute meeting at the White House Map Room. Should we connect the dots here?[37]

President Clinton also commuted the sentence of Susan Rosenberg, a member of the Weather Underground, one of the most violent of the left-wing militias that disrupted the nation from the 1960s through the 1980s. The Weather Underground was part of an interlocking directorate that included the May 19 Communist Organization (May 19 is the birthday of both Ho Chi Minh and Malcolm X), the Black Liberation Army, the Red Guerilla Resistance, and others, together known as "The Family." One of their objectives was to establish the "Republic of New Afrika" in the American South. It was a vision that was part of the Communist Party policy that did not view blacks or Jews as genuine Americans.[38]

In October of 1981, Rosenberg and her "Family" held up a Brink's truck in Nanuet, New York, killing guard Peter Paige and two police officers, Edward O'Grady and Waverly Brown. She drove the getaway car and managed to escape. The Family's other targets included the United States Capitol, the National War College at Fort McNair, the Washington Navy Yard's computer center and its officers club, the FBI office in Staten Island, New York, the Israeli Aircraft Industries Building in New York, the South African consulate in New York, and the Patrolmen's Benevolent Association in New York.[39]

In 1984, police caught Susan Rosenberg at a warehouse in Cherry Hill, New Jersey, where she was unloading 640 pounds of explosives, what she called "combat material." That amount of explosive was enough to create a massacre of Oklahoma City proportions. She also possessed fourteen firearms, including an Uzi submachine gun, and fake identification.[40]

Some other notable pardons included:

1. Henry Cisneros, former secretary of Housing and Urban Development under Clinton who pleaded guilty in 1999 to lying to the FBI about payments he made to a former mistress, Linda Medlar. The misrepresentations came during background checks while he was waiting for confirmation as Housing and Urban Development secretary.
2. Linda (Medlar) Jones, who accepted payoffs to cover up her affair with Clinton's HHS Secretary Henry Cisneros and pleaded guilty to fraud and obstruction of justice.
3. Roger Clinton, President Clinton's half-brother who served two years in prison after pleading guilty to distributing cocaine.
4. John Deutch, former director of the Central Intelligence Agency under Clinton who had agreed to plead guilty to keeping government secrets on unsecured home computers.

5. Susan McDougal, partner of the Clintons in their Whitewater real estate deal who was convicted of fraud in the Whitewater case and contempt of court for refusing to say whether Clinton had committed perjury.
6. Robert Palmer, former Madison Guaranty land appraiser whose actions made possible a $300,000 loan to the Whitewater case and pleaded guilty to conspiracy in falsifying and backdating Whitewater loans.
7. Melvin Reynolds, former Democratic member of the U.S. House from Chicago who was convicted of sex with a teenager and of illegal diversions of campaign monies for personal use.
8. Alvarez Ferrouillet, who managed the congressional campaign of Democrat Henry Alvarez, brother of Clinton Agriculture Secretary Mike Espy, and was convicted of bank fraud and money laundering.
9. Steven A. Smith, who served as Governor Clinton's executive assistant and Whitewater figure who pleaded guilty in 1995 to one misdemeanor count of conspiracy to misapply the funds of a Small Business Administration loan.
10. Chris Wade, who pleaded guilty to bankruptcy fraud and submitting false applications in the Whitewater case.
11. Jack L. Williams, Tysons Food executive who was convicted of making false statements to the FBI to conceal his knowledge of illegal gifts to former Agriculture Secretary Mike Espy.
12. Richard Riley, Jr., son of Clinton's Secretary of Education, Richard Riley, who pleaded guilty to conspiracy to sell cocaine and marijuana.
13. Philip J. Grandmaison, former New Hampshire Democratic Party official and Clinton delegate in 1992, was found guilty of mail fraud in connection with a local bribery scandal.
14. Ronald Blackley, who received a twenty-seven-month prison sentence for making false statements about outside income he got as an aide to Secretary of Agriculture Mike Espy.
15. Mitchell Couey Wood, who was found guilty of conspiracy to possess and to distribute cocaine in 1986 Arkansas. Wood once bought cocaine from Bill's brother Roger.

16. Almon Glenn Braswell, an herbal remedy marketer who was under criminal investigation for possible tax evasion and money laundering. "No one knew of any ongoing criminal investigation" at the time of the pardon, Mr. Clinton's office said in a statement.
17. Dorothy Rivers, who pled guilty in April 1997 to a forty-count theft and tax evasion indictment. Rivers pocketed $1.3 million in federal HUD grants and moneys from the Illinois and Chicago governments.
18. Arnold Paul Prosperi, a Palm Beach attorney, who evaded taxes on $3 million he embezzled from clients. President Clinton commuted his three-year sentence before Prosperi, free on bond, spent even a night in jail. Clinton's old college pal donated $45,000 to the preservationist White House Historical Association. Prosperi is suspected of embezzling this sum too.
19. Harvey Weinig, a Manhattan attorney and Clinton fundraiser in 1992, who pled guilty in September 1995 to laundering $100 million in cash for the Cali cocaine cartel.
20. Charles Wilfred Morgan III, an Arkansan who spent three years in jail for cocaine distribution in the 1980s. Morgan's lawyer was former Clinton White House counsel William Kennedy III. Morgan's stepfather, George Billingsley, donated $42,200 to Democrats in the 1990s.[41]

As former FBI Director Louis Freeh looked back on the 177 pardons and commutations Clinton issued as his final act of office, he is still stunned by the fact that neither the FBI nor the attorney general of the Department of Justice was ever consulted about a single one of them.[42]

In February 2001, we learned that it wasn't just Hugh Rodham trying to benefit from the pardons. Witnesses emerged with canceled checks claiming that first brother Roger Clinton, himself a convicted drug dealer, also got into the act, shaking down a Texas family for $235,000 in exchange for a presidential pardon. The Clinton sibling began stonewalling probers.[43] And then on February 5, 2001, Rep. Dan Burton, (R-IN) and chairman of the Government Reform Committee, sent a two-page letter to Denise

Rich's lawyers requesting answers to fourteen questions. She also began stonewalling.[44]

Three days later, Denise Rich refused to testify, asserting her Fifth Amendment privilege not to be a witness against herself. Her attorney, Carol Elder Bruce, wrote that Mrs. Rich "will not answer any questions of the chairman or the committee."[45]

Soon, Democratic fund-raiser Beth Dozoretz, along with numerous other top Democrats, began taking the Fifth Amendment. "A total of 26 witnesses either invoked their Fifth Amendment rights or refused to be interviewed," according to the House Government Reform Committee report. And there were other difficulties that by now have become staples of a Clinton scandal: "A number of document requests issued by the Committee," investigators wrote in their report, "have not been complied with by their recipients, either because of an invocation of Fifth Amendment rights or an invocation of attorney-client privilege. In some cases the invocation of privilege has been spurious."[46]

On Sunday, February 11, 2001, Mr. Clinton turned to the *New York Times* op-ed page to spin his side of the pardon, that he made his decision based on the merits of each case. "The suggestion that I granted the pardons because Mr. Rich's former wife, Denise, made political contributions and contributed to the Clinton library foundation is utterly false. There was absolutely no quid pro quo."[47]

Mr. Clinton also wrote that three Republicans had "advocated" or "reviewed and advocated" the pardons. In fact all three denied they had done so. Clinton aides confirmed their denials were accurate.[48] On Thursday, February 15, 2001, former president Bill Clinton turned to Geraldo Rivera, a longtime Clinton sycophant, to complain about being victimized yet again by Republicans. "I have no infrastructure to deal with this, no press person," Mr. Clinton lamented to Mr. Rivera, according to the talk show host's notes. "I just wanted to go out there and do what past presidents have done. But the Republicans had other ideas for me," Mr. Clinton complained.[49]

Two distinct Wednesday events apparently precipitated Mr. Clinton's outburst to Mr. Rivera. The first was the announcement by senior government officials that Mary Jo White, the Clinton-appointed U.S. attorney in New York, where Mr. Rich was indicted, had initiated a preliminary investigation into the circumstances of the pardon, which reportedly left Ms. White "livid." The investigation sought to determine if anyone acting on behalf of Mr. Rich had attempted to purchase his pardon or otherwise illegally obtain it.[50]

The second pivotal event on Wednesday was the testimony before the Senate Judiciary Committee by U.S. Pardon Attorney Roger C. Adams, who was the Justice Department official responsible for reviewing pardon applications. Mr. Adams told the committee that "none of the regular procedures were followed." On Inauguration Day, Mr. Adams had told the *Washington Post*, "I've never seen anything like this." Indeed, Mr. Adams recounted for the committee how he received a telephone call after midnight on January 20 from the White House counsel's office. With less than twelve hours remaining in the Clinton presidency, it was the first time he had learned of the pending pardon. Interestingly, Marc Rich's pardon request was filed on November 21, 2000 with the White House. And the White House failed to inform him that Marc Rich and Pincus Green were fugitives. Instead, he was told that "they had been living abroad for several years."[51]

On February 21, 2001, former president Jimmy Carter accused Bill Clinton of selling his presidential powers with his "disgraceful" pardon of fugitive tax-evader Marc Rich:

> I think President Clinton made one of his most serious mistakes in the way he handled the pardon situation the last few hours he was in office . . . I don't think there is any doubt that some of the factors in [the Rich] pardon were attributable to his large gifts. In my opinion, that was disgraceful . . . . I never pardoned anyone whose pardon was not recommended to me after a complete investigation by the Justice Department.[52]

On that same day, former White House chief of staff, Hamilton Jordan, attacked the Clinton pardons in the *Wall Street Journal*: "It is difficult for the average citizen to comprehend how outrageous Bill Clinton's pardons are to those of us who have worked in the White House. . . . If I had suggested to Mr. Carter that he grant a pardon to someone who contributed generously to our campaign and even promised to contribute to the Carter presidential library, he would have thrown me out of the Oval Office and probably fired me on the spot," Jordan wrote.[53]

Mr. Jordan accused the Clintons of being calculating, self-absorbed, arrogant people, driven by "their own egos, appetites and ambitions," who "developed a feeling of invincibility . . . after his impeachment trial." He compared them to "grifters," a term used in the Great Depression to describe "fast-talking con artists who roamed the country-side, profiting at the expense of the poor and the uneducated, always one step ahead of the law, moving on before they were held accountable for their schemes and half-truths."[54]

Out of office, Clinton's disregard for the law continued. Nearly two years after issuing a pardon to Marc Rich, a source reported that Clinton actually had a brief meeting with Rich. On December 14, 2002, Clinton was speaking in Geneva, Switzerland, at a meeting of the United Israel Appeal. This group had also received large contributions from Marc Rich. The log of the Secret Service shows a brief private meeting took place prior to Clinton's joining the general reception. The log does not indicate with whom Clinton met, but sources close to the Secret Service say it was Rich. A retired senior bodyguard to Rich confirmed the meeting to R. Emmett Tyrrell's researcher.[55]

Despite the compelling evidence of bribery in the Clinton pardon mess, more than two years of investigations, from 2001-2003, yielded not a single indictment, and the Bush Justice Department abandoned the case against Mrs. Clinton altogether. Some like Fox News Channel's Bill O'Reilly, suspected a deal. In fact, the popular cable host told his *Radio Factor* audience in June 2002 that he had evidence President George W. Bush had made a background deal to keep prosecutors muzzled. "A very highly placed source—and I mean this guy knows what's going on in the Bush administration—told me about a month ago that when President Bush took office he had meetings with all of the Democratic leadership . . . one-on-one meetings in the Oval Office," O'Reilly said. "The Democratic leadership made it quite clear to Mr. Bush that he would not get any cooperation—zero—on the part of the Democrats in the Senate and in the House if he pursued any kind of a criminal investigation against Bill Clinton.[56]

"Basically, they said, look, if you embarrass us—by us we mean the Democratic Party—if you, Bush-Ashcroft, indict Clinton on bribery or go after Hillary or any of this—we're gonna shut you down," O'Reilly explained. "We're not gonna do anything. You're not going to get any legislation passed in four years." The Fox News host never indicated who his source might be beyond describing him as "very highly placed."[57]

CHAPTER 38

THE FINAL DAYS
HILLARY'S BOOK DEAL/WHITE HOUSE THEFT/ VANDALISM

As have other presidents and their families before us, we received gifts over the course of our eight years in the White House and followed all of the gift rules.

—President Clinton, on gifts received just before leaving the White House[1]

In mid-December 2000, just weeks before she became a senator, Hillary stirred up an ethical storm by signing a controversial book contract with Simon & Schuster. She was paid a record advance of $8 million to tell her story. The deal shocked even her most enthusiastic supporters. It was, according to the *New York Times*' editorial page, "an affront to common sense. No lawmaker should accept a large, unearned sum from a publisher whose parent company, Viacom, is vitally interested in government policy on issues likely to come before Congress—for example, copyright or broadcasting legislation."[2]

Greed seemed to be the only explanation for the book deal. And greed was a motivating factor behind two other rather tasteless moves by Hillary. She registered like a bride for supporters to purchase gifts for her newly acquired homes in Chappaqua, New York, and Washington, D.C., and to strip the White House of hundreds of thousands of dollars worth of furniture.[3]

Two weeks after closing the book deal, Hillary and Bill paid $2,850,000 to buy a large brick colonial in northwest Washington, D.C. The house, near the British Embassy, is named for the cul-de-sac it sits on, Whitehaven. Hillary would later spend more than $1 million to remodel the house, adding an elevator and a new pool house and expanding the residence from 6,260 square feet to 7,218 square feet.[4]

Then, unknown to the public, and in the waning days of his presidency, Bill Clinton sent out an APB (All Points Bulletin) to Democratic fundraisers outlining his post-office home-furnishing needs. He and Mrs. Clinton wanted to pack their new homes with the finest in tables, chairs, sofas, rugs, silver, linens, crystal, lighting, painting, window treatments, armoires, cabinets, televisions, sculptures, and so on. Word had it that the couple put together a weird variation of a bridal registry, establishing password-protected sites in which contributors could pledge to purchase specific items selected in advance by the Clintons' design teams for his 'n' her homes. All of the gifts had to be wrapped up, so to speak, before January 3, 2001, when Senate gift rules would have limited her to $100 per year, per donor.[5]

The donors were solicited by friends of the Clintons, mainly Beverly Hills contributor Rita Pynoos, and urged to send money—$5,000 was frequently suggested—so that items could be purchased from Hillary's "wish list" on file at Borsheim's, an upscale Omaha store.[6] Then, at a minimum, the Clintons marched out of the White House with $200,000 worth of furnishings.[7]

On Sunday, January 21, 2001, the *Washington Post* revealed that the Clintons, "faced with multimillion-dollar houses to furnish here and in suburban New York, left the White House . . . with an unprecedented $190,027 worth of gifts received over the last eight years." Within hours the news media carried additional reports, this time of the damage done to the White House and of the petty theft on Air Force One.[8]

The Clintons were eventually forced to return twenty-five of the forty-four pieces of furniture that had been given to the White House or the president as gifts during their presidency. This was because the government had in its files thank-you letters from the National Park Service (NPS) to the gift-givers. As soon as the NPS sends a thank-you note to a benefactor, the gift that benefactor has given becomes U.S. government property.[9]

What had yet to be reported was that Mrs. Clinton's late-mother, Dorothy Rodham, was involved in the theft, and the pilfering that had begun the previous January 2000.[10]

On January 4, 2000, the Clintons began trucking furniture to their $1.7 million home in Chappaqua, New York. The day before the items were shipped out, White House chief usher Gary J. Walters asked whether the Clintons should be taking the furnishings because he believed they were government property donated as part of a White House redecoration project in 1993. Walters blamed himself for not raising any questions when the rest of the furnishings were taken from the White House in January 2001. He said Hillary Clinton aide, Eric Hothem, had told him they were the Clintons' personal property. "I should have asked for specifics on these items," Walters said. "I shoulder the blame for not saying, 'Hey, wait a minute.'"[11]

In interviews, Walters said that Kaki Hockersmith, a Little Rock designer who redecorated the White House in 1993, told the late Vincent Foster, then the White House deputy counsel, that the furnishings she was soliciting for the 1993 redecoration project were meant for the White House collection, not the Clintons personally. Walters said that Foster directed him and the Park Service in a March 24, 1993, memo to begin accepting the gifts with formal acknowledgment, thereby making the furnishings government property.[12]

"I can only say that all gifts were appropriately dealt with," Hillary explained to reporters, "and we followed the same procedures that all presidents have followed."[13]

Soon, longtime supporters in the media, such as the *New York Times* and the *Washington Post*, began criticizing Hillary. There was also another newspaper that asked her to step down from Congress. According to the *New York Observer*, "Hillary Rodham Clinton is unfit for elective office. Had she any shame, she would resign." Of her husband, the *Observer* wrote, "the image that presents itself is terrifyingly close to the caricature his enemies drew of him."[14]

On February 2, 2001, the Clintons announced that they would pay $85,966 of the $190,027 spent on china, furniture, and other finery that they had originally planned to accept from friends and supporters. Thus, by their actions on the gifts, the Clintons were essentially bowing to critics who said it was questionable on grounds of ethics and taste for the Clintons to accept such a bounty at a time when both remain important figures in public life. Public watchdog groups and GOP lawmakers also questioned the propriety of Hillary Clinton accepting a rash of presents just before she joined the Senate and became covered by strict ethics rules that prohibit all but very small gifts.[15]

Five days later, on February 7, 2001, they returned $28,000 worth of donated sofas, rugs and other furnishings they took from the White House. That brought the total value of items the Clintons decided to either pay for or return to $114,000.[16]

Next, we had the trashing of the White House. Following a 6:00 p.m. champagne engagement party hosted by Hillary for one of her staffers in the Roosevelt Room, staffers suggested to the first lady the possibility of leaving a few practical jokes in the offices of the incoming Bush administration. Hillary reportedly had a great idea: "Wouldn't it be hysterical if someone just happened to remove all the Ws from the computer keyboards?" When the champagne party was over, the rampage began. In the end, sixty computer keyboards were disabled, desks were glued shut, file cabinets vandalized, a lewd message was left on an answering machine, doorknobs were stolen, and a presidential seal disappeared.[17]

On the following day, Inauguration Day 2001, when the General Services Administration (GSA) workers entered the White House at noon—just after the Clintons left—they found the presidential residence and its neighboring Old Executive Office Building (OEOB) in shambles. One estimate of the damage was $200,000. Including the damaged already mentioned, there was also shattered glass, broken furniture, and rotting food that was found in the offices that the Bush administration would arrive later that day to occupy.[18]

Eyewitnesses to the wreckage reported to *Human Events* that certain offices in the Old Executive Office Building, where many presidential aides worked, were littered with empty beer, wine. and champagne bottles. The desktops were littered with old files, papers, pens, staplers, and miscellaneous junk, as if the previous occupants had left simply dumped out their desk drawers.[19]

Glass plates were shattered across the floor in some rooms. The extension numbers were removed from many phones or crossed out, causing communication problems in the first days of the new administration, problems that were made worse by sabotage done to some of the voice mail and e-mail systems. Also, someone apparently slashed a number of phone chords.[20]

Desks and chairs lay inexplicably overturned, including one sofa with broken legs. Computers, copying machines, and other office equipment were missing. Locked file cabinets with missing keys stood uselessly amid the wreckage, and when the Bush people tried to move the desks in some offices, they found that they were booby-trapped with a goo on the underside of tops.[21]

The mess was so overwhelming, both to the Bush administration officials and to the maintenance crews, that one cleaning lady was found in tears, wondering how the former employees could have been so thoughtless. Not surprisingly, career White House workers told the Bush employees who arrived in the building they were just plain glad that the Clintons were gone.[22]

To add insult to injury, the Clintons wanted to leave Washington in style. The Clintons boarded a Marine helicopter on the White House lawn and waved goodbye to staff and the waiting bank of television cameras. After an agonizingly endless televised orgy of goodbyes at Andrews Air Force Base, President George W. Bush graciously loaned Air Force One and flew the Clintons into New York's John F. Kennedy International Airport.[23]

Once Air Force One landed, it headed towards TWA Hangar No. 12, where approximately three thousand people waited to greet the Clintons. A high school marching band performed, and a big-screen television beamed the now-former president's image to those in the audience. Questions soon arose as to who paid for it. When Jim McTague of *Barron's* decided to look into it, he found that the Democratic Party hadn't paid for it. None of the national Democratic organizations paid for it either. Clinton spokeswoman Julia Payne disclosed that "friends" of Bill Clinton had paid for it. I wonder if Denise Rich was one of those "friends?"[24]

Unfortunately, when the loaned aircraft returned to its hangar at Andrews Air Force Base, it looked as if it had been stripped by a skilled band of thieves. Gone were the porcelain dishes bearing the presidential seal, along with silverware, salt and pepper shakers, pillows, blankets, candles, and even toothpaste.[25]

Think of it as Clinton class. James Carville once tried to suggest that dragging a $100 bill through a trailer park would flush out all manner of Clinton critics interested in the prospect of easy money. To judge what happened on Air Force One, traveling under the guise of a "Special Air Mission," Mr. Carville was in no position to criticize the ethics of anyone living in a trailer park. Let's drag some salt and pepper shakers through Chappaqua or Whitehaven and see what turns up there.[26]

In February 2002, the New York *Daily News* reported that the Bush administration requested that the GAO expand its probe into vandalism in the White House complex done by outgoing Clinton aides to include damage to offices that Hillary and her staff used. When CNN's Paula Zahn asked the senator what she thought of this, she was apparently caught off guard and began dissembling: "Well, I was curious as anyone when I read it. I'll have to wait and see what the real story on that is . . . I can't understand why they're spending their time, you know, chasing red herrings and false trails, but maybe they can tell us."[27]

When Zahn asked Sen. Clinton if she could "categorically deny that anybody vandalized anything in your offices before you and your husband left Washington?" Hillary stumbled around for a bit, avoiding the question, until she finally said, "I can't even imagine, you know. There was no such—as far as I know, there was no such action. Certainly, no one's brought it to my attention and I just don't believe it happened."[28]

Unfortunately, it was the taxpayers who paid the bill to replace and repair the broken and missing equipment in the White House and on Air Force One. Furthermore, none of the thieves or vandals were ever prosecuted, although clearly some laws were broken.[29]

CHAPTER 39

BILL CLINTON (LEGACY)

*I may not have been the greatest president,
but I've had the most fun in eight years.*

—Bill Clinton[1]

After the 1996 presidential election, Bill Clinton had run for public office for the last time. He was no longer subject to judgment by voters; he was now accountable only to history, or at least to the historians who will write the history books. They will write about his "legacy."[2]

"No president obsessed over his 'legacy' as much as Bill Clinton did," observes the *National Review Online*. "He sometimes complained that he had no enormous national crisis to contend with, meaning that he didn't have a fair shot at attaining historic greatness. "The first thing I had to start with was, you know, we don't have a war," he told the *New York Times* in 1997. "We don't have a depression; we don't have a Cold War."[3]

Bill Clinton once told Vice President Al Gore, whenever he was making a major decision, "I'm risking my presidency on this." To Clinton, everything felt like a risk, because he was so afraid of losing. That is why he feared taking on big things. Instead, he took refuge in small, politically popular measures to keep his poll numbers up. They ensured public approval and reelection.[4]

Speaking of polls, former Clinton strategist Dick Morris wrote: "For Bill Clinton, positive poll results are not just tools—they are vindication, ratification, and approval—whereas negative poll results are a learning process in which the pain of the rebuff to his self-image forces deep introspection."⁵

Author Bill Gertz wrote: "President Clinton's most important legacy will not be his comic sex scandals, but his dead serious disarmament of the United States and his self-serving appeasement of powerful and determined foreign enemies. His flower-child 'can't we all just get along' approach to global power politics has left the nation weakened and vulnerable in a dangerous and hostile world."⁶

Gertz continued: "The president and his adversaries knowingly placed economic prosperity—and campaign contributions—above national security interests and the damage will be felt for years to come. The administration's policies have endangered not only the United States, but the peace and security of the entire world. A significant part of the Clinton legacy will be the dominance of 'spin' over substance, a practice perfected during his tenure. No matter how disastrously a presidential decision or action turned out, White House spin-meisters managed to seduce most of the press and public into believing that the action taken was, all things considered, for the best."⁷

Author James Bovard wrote:

The principle of government supremacy is Clinton's clearest legacy. Clinton did more than any recent president to place the federal government above all laws—above the Constitution—and beyond any effective restraint. Clinton ignored federal and Supreme Court decisions limiting his power and Congress rarely had the gumption to check his abuses. Clinton exploited and expanded the dictatorial potential of the U.S. presidency.

Clinton was the Nanny State champion incarnate—the person who taught tens of millions of Americans to look to government for relief from every irritation of daily life—from child safety car seats to unpasteurized cider to leaky basements. Clinton's perennial message was that people should trust political action far more than the voluntary efforts of individuals to improve their own lives. Clinton sought to continually remind people of the greatest of the State and the helplessness of the citizen.

Another Clinton legacy is a two-class system in America: those whom the law fails to restrain, and those whom it fails to protect;

those above the law, and those below it; those for whom there is 'no controlling legal authority,' in Vice President Gore's famous words, and those for whom there are few, if any, constitutional protections. The notion that 'the king can do no wrong' permeated the Clinton administration's legal and public relations defense strategies. The Clinton administration perennially invoked sovereign immunity to protect wrongdoing feds—from the FBI sniper who killed Vicki Weaver in the doorway of her Idaho cabin; to IRS agents who wantonly seized people's property and disrupted their lives; to Treasury Department employees who shredded 162 cartons of documents detailing how the government robbed hundreds of thousands of Indians who relied on Bureau of Indian Affairs trust fund accounts; and to the FBI agents involved in the final attack at Waco. Clinton sought to raise the reputation of government to lofty new heights—at the same time that Justice Department lawyers argued that individual federal agents are exempt from liability for wrongdoing other Americans.[8]

Bill Clinton's political legacy will include the fact that he was the first Democratic president to serve two terms since Franklin Delano Roosevelt. However, history will also record the fact that in four congressional elections held while Mr. Clinton was president, the Republican Party first won and then retained effective majorities in both chambers of Congress. This was an astounding feat. After all, during the sixty-two years between Franklin Roosevelt's 1932 election and the 1994 congressional midterm election, the Democratic Party controlled the U.S. House of Representatives for fifty-eight years and the U.S. Senate for fifty-two years.[9]

The Clinton political legacy is further diminished by the fact that it has been nearly half a century since Republicans controlled the White House and both bodies of the U.S. Congress at the same time. In the eighth year of the Clinton presidency, however, voters not only declined to return the Democratic Party to majority status in either house of Congress; they also dislodged the Democratic Party from power in the White House. Republicans had not gained control of so much federal power since Dwight Eisenhower was elected president in 1952.[10]

While Mr. Clinton basked in the glow of a 57 percent job approval rating when he left the White House, little has been said of the widespread electoral damage to the Democratic Party he has left behind.[11]

In 1992, the year Mr. Clinton clawed his way to the White House, Democrats enjoyed a 102-seat advantage—268-166 with one independent—in the House of Representatives. On Election Day in 1992, in a foreshadowing of much worse things to come two years later, Democrats actually lost ten seats. In the 1994 election, their majority collapsed. The 1994 midterm election represented a repudiation of Mr. Clinton's policies, although only his fellow Democrats felt the voters' wrath. The GOP achieved control of the House for the first time in forty years by gaining fifty-two seats, winning a twenty-six-seat majority. The victory was overwhelming. The authoritative, nonpartisan *Congressional Quarterly* described the Republican triumph with such phrases as "Elephant Romp," "Heartland Collapse" and "Dixie Debacle." No GOP incumbent was defeated, while thirty-four Democratic incumbents lost, including House Speaker Tom Foley. Republican House candidates, who captured a majority of the total House vote for the first time since 1946, received nearly 9 million more votes in 1994 than they received in 1990, the previous midterm election. It was the largest gain between midterm elections that any party ever achieved in history.[12]

During 1992, Democrats enjoyed a 57-43 advantage in the U.S. Senate. Unlike the 1980 presidential victory of Ronald Reagan, who helped defeat nine incumbent Democrats and added three open seats to the GOP caucus without a loss of a single Republican seat, Mr. Clinton's 1992 election failed to add a single Democrat to his party's Senate roll. Two years later, the 1994 election produced a devastating defeat for Mr. Clinton's party in the Senate. Without losing a single incumbent, the GOP defeated two Democratic senators, swept all nine open seats and emerged from the November 8 election with a 52-48 majority. The next day Democratic Sen. Richard Shelby of Alabama switched parties, giving the GOP a 53-47 majority in the 104th Congress. Several months later, Colorado Democratic Sen. Ben Nighthorse Campbell joined the GOP as well.[13]

While Mr. Clinton's tenure in the White House has had a devastating effect on his party in the U.S. Congress, it has been even worse for Democratic gubernatorial candidates. When Mr. Clinton arrived in Washington in January 1993, Democrats controlled the governorships of thirty-one states, including four of the largest six states: Texas, New York, Florida and Pennsylvania. On his departure, in 2001, each of those four states was run by a Republican. Indeed, eight of the largest nine states in 2001 had GOP governors. Only Gray Davis of California was a Democrat within that group. Altogether, there were, in 2001, twelve fewer Democratic governors than when Mr. Clinton swore his first presidential oath.[14]

Democrats in state legislatures didn't fare any better. In 1992, Democratic state legislators outnumbered Republicans by 1,469. The Democratic advantage declined by nearly 100 on the day he was elected to his first term. By 2001, that advantage was less than 350. That is a loss of more than 1,100 state legislators.[15]

As bad as the Clinton years were to other Democratic candidates running for state and federal office, there was a good reason for Democrats to fear that the future would not be much better. The reason is redistricting, a process in which boundaries are redrawn after each ten-year census. In most states, redistricting is controlled by state legislatures, with the governor generally exercising veto power. It very much matters how many state legislatures and governor mansions a party controls. In 1991, Republicans controlled both legislative bodies of only six states, while Democrats exercised control of roughly half the states' legislatures. Control of the legislatures in the remaining states was divided. By 2001, Republicans controlled both bodies of seventeen state legislatures, compared to sixteen controlled by the Democrats. And the GOP gubernatorial advantage was 29-19, with two independents.[16]

Specifically, there were Republican governors in thirteen of the seventeen states in which the GOP controlled both bodies of the legislature. There were Democratic governors in only eight of the sixteen states in which the Democrats controlled both bodies of the state legislature. Granted, the redistricting process varies state by state, but one conclusion is beyond dispute: Compared to the redistricting process that was based on the 1990 census, the Republican Party in 2001 was in a vastly improved position.[17]

In terms of our military, just three years after America's spectacular victory in the Gulf War, at a time when America was enjoying unprecedented prosperity, our finest young men and women, active-duty members of the United States military and their families, were surviving on food stamps and other forms of welfare. Bill Clinton's self-professed loathing of the military manifested itself in a rapid manner.[18]

In less than three years as commander in chief, Clinton and his subordinates, while increasing the number of overseas deployments, reduced the total active-duty force from 2.1 million to 1.6 million men and women. The Army was reduced from eighteen full-strength light and mechanized divisions to a vulnerable twelve (ten fortified divisions had been used in the Gulf War alone). The Navy was reduced from 546 to 380 ships, toward a targeted reduction of 300—the smallest naval force since the pre-World War II period. And the Air Force was reduced from seventy-six flight squadrons down to fifty.[19]

As the resources dwindled, the number of military interventions increased. From 1946 to 1991, the United States deployed military troops in eight foreign campaigns. During the Clinton years, we deployed troops to at least forty separate foreign locations. The Clinton administration called these "unanticipated missions." According to Lt. Col. Robert "Buzz" Patterson, "My peers, fellow pilots, and aircrew members called them 'channel surfing.' Somalia, Rwanda, Haiti, Macedonia, Bosnia, Ecuador, East Timor, Kuwait, Liberia, Albania, Congo, Gabon, Sierre Leone, Afghanistan, Sudan, and Iraq were countries that saw direct U.S. military intervention of one sort or another."[20]

The military was forced to rely on increasingly hollowed-out units. It also had to do without significant modernization, as it lived off defense systems acquired in the 1970s and 1980s. Spending to acquire new weapons went from more than $100 billion in 1987 to $44 billion in 1998 (a loss of $56 billion). By the end of the decade, the Congressional Budget Office reported that the military was underfunded by $50 billion a year.[21]

As the Clinton administration decimated the military, so too did it cripple the nation's first line of defense: its unequaled electronic intelligence services. At a time when China's espionage operations against the United States were growing rapidly, the National Security Agency's research and development budget was slashed by 90 percent. Unfortunately, the ensuing personnel reductions saw the loss of many of the most highly skilled intelligence officers. The timing could not have been worse.[22]

The Energy Department was staffed at the highest levels largely by antinuclear activists appointed during the Clinton administration. As a result, U.S. nuclear weapons programs were severely undermined. Clinton's decision to halt underground testing threatened the viability of our strategic nuclear deterrent. Combined with Bill Clinton's ideological aversion to strategic defense, this increased the danger that the United States might be attacked by miscalculation, by accident, or by a power that thinks it can get away with it, because our deterrent capability had seriously eroded.[23]

While women and gays were welcomed into the military, veterans were handed their pink slips. When Vice President Al Gore was given the task of "reinventing government," he and the White House took credit for removing 305,000 people from the government payroll. What they didn't tell you was that 286,000 of those cuts, approximately 90 percent, came from employees of the Department of Defense.[24]

Bill Clinton also crushed morale. He immediately froze military pay at a time when it had already fallen behind the private sector by almost 20 percent. The pay freeze was especially harmful when approximately 80 percent of the force was earning less than $30,000 annually and more than twenty thousand enlisted personnel were eligible for food stamps.[25]

The Association of the U.S. Army coined a new phrase, "the military poor." It described the growing numbers of enlisted personnel throughout the Clinton presidency who were forced to depend on food stamps and other forms of public assistance to support their families. Both the Army and the Marine Corps reported dangerously low reenlistment rates for their enlisted ranks, while overseas deployments were escalating. "Too many good, young Marines are leaving," said First Marine Expeditionary Force Sergeant Major Michael Magraw. "Many lance corporals and corporals are bailing out after their first hitch, because our operational commitments have been burning them out. And the pay they receive isn't enough to take care of their families."[26]

A 1994 service-wide state study by *Parade* magazine of the U.S. Department of Agriculture's Women, Infants, and Children (WIC) supplemental food aid program found the number of enlisted military families living beneath the poverty line and using WIC services average between 12 and 20 percent of the total population of major military bases. Out of 5,400 sailors stationed at King's Bay, Georgia, there were 1,370 WIC families. Some 4,700 families were among 14,000 soldiers and Air Force members in the San Antonio, Texas area. Out of 35,000 Marines in North Carolina, some 4,500 were WIC recipients.[27]

A good barometer of the Clinton-Gore team and its views toward military men and women can be summed up in its actions during the presidential campaign of 2000. With the race down to the hotly disputed electoral votes in Florida, the Gore campaign attempted to disallow the votes of military personnel stationed overseas who had voted via absentee ballot. While the Democrats screamed disenfranchisement on the part of minority and elderly voters in Palm Beach, they were attempting to disenfranchise the men and women whose lives were on the line serving their country outside the United States. The Gore campaign's lawyers asked the court to throw away the service members' votes, claiming, on a technicality, that the absentee ballots needed postmarks.[28]

Lt. Col. Robert "Buzz" Patterson" summarized how foreign policy decisions were made under Bill Clinton: "Over his two terms, President Clinton's decisions to deploy his armed forces mimicked the way a squirrel crosses the road—darting halfway across, stopping and looking up into headlights, becoming confused, and finally returning whence it came.[29]

In a world where nuclear weapons are proliferating and missile threats from North Korea and other rogue states are growing, perhaps the most serious concern to the American people was the nation's vulnerability to enemy missiles, thanks to the president's stubborn refusal to expedite an anti-missile defense system that was started under Ronald Reagan. For years Clinton denied the existence of any foreign missile threat. Once the missile threat could no longer be ignored, he switched gears and claimed that U.S. technology wasn't capable of knocking out incoming missiles with other missiles. This claim has been contradicted by numerous specialists who say the know-how could be carried out easily from either space or the ground, given the political will and leadership to do so.[30]

As former President Clinton lamented (in public, of course) about his lack of a positive legacy, evidence kept rolling in that he failed to stop terrorism while in the Oval Office. Former Clinton pollster and strategist Dick Morris wrote that, at two separate White House meetings, advisers urged Clinton to cut off aid to domestic Hamas fund-raisers. Clinton refused out of fear it would look like "profiling" of Islamic charities. As columnist Morris put it, "While Clinton was politically correct, the Hamas flourished."[31]

Morris also wrote that Clinton's dedication to political correctness doomed another internal recommendation: Requiring that driver's licenses and visas for non-citizens expire simultaneously. Under such a system, illegal aliens pulled over in traffic stops could be identified and deported. Liberal advisers such as George Stephanopoulos prevailed, and Clinton took the politically safe, but ultimately deadly, position of killing yet another idea for quelling terrorist operations.[32]

On February 26, 1993, when Egyptian and Palestinian terrorists blew a hole six stories deep under the North Tower of the World Trade Center, President Clinton had been in office thirty-eight days. Eight months after President Clinton left office, al-Qaeda terrorists flew hijacked U.S. commercial airliners into the North and South Towers of the World trade Center and into the Pentagon. The towers came down and the terrorists finished the job begun eight years earlier. From 1993 to 2001, the Islamic terrorists brought their war to the United States.[33]

Unfortunately, the Clinton administration never responded decisively, even when given the opportunity, with its own "war against terrorism." The Clinton administration had an obligation in the name of our national security to deploy and use the military resources necessary to deal with al-Qaeda as its deadly presence became known and its declared war on America became public and costly. That it did not respond is a consequence for which the Clinton administration is extremely culpable. In the span of just eight years, Bill Clinton not only inflamed the passions of America's enemies, but left America unprotected from their weapons of vengeance. By failing to answer the threat as it should have, the Clinton administration was guilty of gross negligence and dereliction of duty to the safety of our country, which the president was sworn to defend.[34]

Legacy highlights (Criminal Statistics):[35]

47	Number of individuals and businesses associated with the Clintons who had been convicted of or pleaded guilty to crimes.
33	Number of these convictions during Clinton's presidency.
61	Number of indictments/misdemeanor charges.
122	Number of congressional witnesses who had pleaded the Fifth Amendment, fled the country to avoid testifying, or in the case of foreign witnesses, refused to be interviewed.

BIBLIOGRAPHY

This book is based principally on my research on Bill Clinton and to some degree Hillary Rodham Clinton. Since I began writing this biography, I encountered a real reluctance among some, who came in contact with the Clintons, to talk about their experiences; fearing retaliation from them . . . even to this day. Thus, I drew my research primarily from the books written about Bill Clinton and his presidency, which are an extraordinary resource. I also drew heavily from newspaper and magazine articles as well as the internet for this book. Besides the books listed below, I am especially grateful to the print media coverage, including the *Washington Times*, the *Washington Post* the *New York Times* and the *Wall Street Journal*.

BOOKS

Aldrich, Gary. *Unlimited Access: An FBI Agent Inside the Clinton White House*. Washington, D.C.: Regnery Publishing, 1996.

Alexander, Yonah and Michael S. Swetnam. *Usama bin Laden's al Qaeda: Profile of a Terrorist Network*. Ardsley, NY: Transnational Publishers, 2001.

Andersen, Christopher. *American Evita*. New York: HarperCollins, 2004.

Andersen, Christopher. *Bill and Hillary: The Marriage*. New York: William Morrow and Company, 1999.

Barnett, Michael N. *Eyewitness to Genocide*. Ithaca, NY: Cornell University Press, 2002.

Bernstein, Carl. *A Woman in Charge: The Life of Hillary Rodham Clinton*. New York: Alfred A. Knopf, 2007.

Bodansky, Yossef. *Bin Laden: The Man Who Declared War on America*. Roseville, CA: Prima Forum, 1999.

Borjesson, Kristina. *Into the Buzzsaw: Leading Journalists Expose the Myth of a Free Press*. New York: Prometheus Books, 2004.

Bossie, David N. *Intelligence Failure: How Clinton's National Security Policy Set the Stage For 9/11*. Nashville: WND Books, 2004.

Bovard, James. *Feeling Your Pain: The Explosion and Abuse Of Government Power in the Clinton-Gore Years.* New York: St. Martin's Press, 2000.

Bowden, Mark. *Black Hawk Down.* New York: Penguin Books, 1999.

Breault, Marc and Martin King. *Inside the Cult.* New York: Signet, 1993.

Brock, Alan. *Ambush at Ruby Ridge: How Government Agents Set Randy Weaver Up and Took His Family Down.* Brown, Floyd G., *"Slick Willie": Why America Cannot Trust Bill Clinton* (Annapolis, Maryland: Annapolis-Washington Book Publishing, Inc., 1993).

Irvine, CA: Dickins Press, 1995.

Brock, David. *The Seduction of Hillary Rodham.* New York: Free Press Paperbacks, 1997.

Brown, Floyd. *Slick Willie.* Annapolis: Annapolis Publishing Company, 1992.

Brown, Tracey. *The Life and Times of Ron Brown: A Memoir by His Daughter.* New York: William Morrow and Company, 1998.

Campbell, Tom. *The Clintons Of Arkansas*, ed. Ernest Dumas. Little Rock, 1993.

Carpenter, Amanda B. *A Vast Right-Wing Conspiracy's Dossier on Hillary Clinton.* Washington, D.C.: Regnery Publishing, 2006.

Cashill, Jack. *Ron Brown's Body: How One Man's Death Saved the Clinton Presidency and Hillary's Future.* Nashville: WND Books, 2004.

Cashill, Jack. *TWA 800: The Crash, The Cover-Up, and the Conspiracy.* Washington, D.C.: Regnery History, 2016.

Dempsey, Gary T. with Roger W. Fontaine. *Fools Errands.* Washington, D.C.: The Cato Institute, 2001.

Diehl, Alan. *Silent Knights: Blowing the Whistle on Military Accidents and Their Cover-Ups.* Washington: Brassey's, 2002.

Drew, Elizabeth. *On the Edge: The Clinton Presidency.* New York: Touchstone, 1994.

Evans-Pritchard, Ambrose. *The Secret Life of Bill Clinton: The Unreported Stories.* Washington, D.C.: Regnery Publishing, 1997.

Fleitz, Jr., Frederick H. *Peacekeeping Forces of the 1990s.* Westport, CT: Praeger, 2002.

Freeh, Louis J. *My FBI: Bringing Down the Mafia, Investigating Bill Clinton, and Fighting the War on Terror.* New York: St. Martin's Press, 2005.

Gallen, David. *Bill Clinton as They Know Him: An Oral Biography.* New York: Marlowe & Co., 1996.

Gerth, Jeff and Don Van Natta Jr. *Her Way: The Hopes and Ambitions of Hillary Rodham Clinton.* New York: Little, Brown and Company, 2007.

Gertz, *Betrayal: How the Clinton Administration Undermined American Security*. Washington, D.C. Regnery Publishing, 1999.

Gertz, Bill. *Breakdown: How America's Intelligence Failures Led to September 11*. Washington, D.C.: Regnery Publishing, 2002.

Goldman, Peter and Thomas M. DeFrank, Mark Miller, Andrew Murr and Thomas Mathews. *Quest For The Presidency*. College Station, TX: Texas A&M University Press, 1994.

Halberstam, David. *War in a Time of Peace*. New York: Touchstone, 2002.

Hitchens, Christopher. *No One Left to Lie To: The Triangulations of William Jefferson Clinton*. London: Verso, 2000.

Holmes, Steven A. *Ron Brown: An Uncommon Life*. New York: John Wiley & Sons, 2000.

Hubbell, Webb. *Friends in High Places*. New York: William Morrow and Company, 1997.

Isikoff, Michael. *Uncovering Clinton*. New York: Three Rivers, 1999.

Jackson, Candice E. *Their Lives: The Women Targeted by The Clinton Machine*. Los Angeles: World Ahead, 2005.

Johnson, Haynes and David S. Broder. *The System*. New York: Little, Brown and Company, 1996.

Kagan, Donald and Frederick W. Kagan. *While America Sleeps*. New York: St. Martin's Press, 2000.

Kengor, Paul. *God and Hillary Clinton: A Spiritual Life*. New York: HarperCollins, 2007.

Kessler, Ronald. *Inside the White House*. New York: Pocket Books, 1996.

Klein, Edward. *The Truth About Hillary*. New York: Sentinel, 2005.

Kopel, David B. and Paul H. Blackman, *No More Wacos: What's Wrong with Federal Law Enforcement and How to Fix It*. Amherst, NY: Prometheus Books, 1997.

Levin, Robert E. *Bill Clinton: The Inside Story*. New York, NY, 1992.

Limbaugh, David. *Absolute Power: The Legacy of Corruption in the Clinton-Reno Justice Department*. Washington, D.C.: Regnery Publishing, 2001.

Limbacher, Carl. *Hillary's Scheme: Inside the Next Clinton's Ruthless Agenda to Take the White House*. New York: Crown Forum, 2003.

Lowry, Rich. *Legacy: Paying the Price for the Clinton Years*. Washington, D.C.: Regnery Publishing, 2003.

Maraniss, David. *First in His Class: The Biography of Bill Clinton*. Touchstone, 1996.

Matalin, Mary and James Carville. *All's Fair: Love, War and Running for President*. New York: Simon & Schuster, 1994.

Mazarr, Michael. *North Korea and the Bomb*. New York: St. Martin's Press, 1995.

McDougal, Jim and Curtis Wilke. *Arkansas Mischief: The Birth of a National Scandal*. New York: Henry Holt and Company, 1998.

Miller, John and Michael Stone with Chris Mitchell, *The Cell: Inside the 9/11 Plot, and Why the FBI and CIA Failed to Stop It*. New York: Hyperion, 2002.

Milton, Joyce. *The First Partner: Hillary Rodham Clinton*. New York: William Morrow and Company, 1999.

Miniter, Richard. *Losing Bin Laden: How Bill Clinton's Failures Unleashed Global Terror*. Washington, D.C.: Regnery Publishing, 2003.

Morris, Dick. *Behind the Oval Office: Getting Reelected Against All Odds*. Los Angeles: Renaissance, 1999.

Morris, Roger. *Partners in Power: The Clintons and Their America*. Washington, D.C.: Regnery Publishing, 1996.

Morton, Andrew. *Monica's Story*. New York: St. Martin's Press, 1999.

Oakley, Meredith. *On the Make: The Rise of Bill Clinton*. Washington, D.C.: Regnery Publishing, 1994.

Olson, Barbara. *Hell to Pay: The Unfolding Story of Hillary Rodham Clinton*. Washington, D.C.: Regnery Publishing, 1999.

Olson, Barbara. *The Final Days: The Last, Desperate Abuses of Power by the Clinton White House*. Washington, D.C. Regnery Publishing, 2001.

Oppenheimer, Jerry. *State of a Union: Inside the Complex Marriage of Bill and Hillary Clinton*. New York: HarperCollins, 2000.

Patterson, Lt. Col. Robert "Buzz." *Dereliction of Duty: The Eyewitness Account of How Bill Clinton Compromised America's National Security*. Washington, D.C.: Regnery Publishing, 2003.

Peterson, Scott. *Me Against My Brother: At War in Somalia, Sudan and Rwanda*. London: Routledge, 2000.

Petrie, John N. (ed.) Essays in Strategy 12. Diane Publishing, 1996.

Poe, Richard. *Hillary's Secret War: The Clinton Conspiracy to Muzzle Internet Journalists*. Nashville: WND Books, 2004.

Reavis, Dick. *The Ashes of Waco: An Investigation*. New York: Simon & Schuster, 1995.

Ruddy, Christopher. *The Strange Death of Vincent Foster: An Investigation*. New York: The Free Press, 1997.

Savage, Michael. *Liberalism Is a Mental Disorder*. Nashville: Nelson Current, 2005.

Schippers, David P. *Sellout: The Inside Story of President Clinton's Impeachment*. Washington, D.C.: Regnery Publishing, 2000.

Shaffer, Lt. Col. Anthony. *Operation Dark Heart: Spycraft and Special OPS on the Frontlines Of Afghanistan—And The Path To Victory*. New York: St. Martin's Press, 2010.

Sheehy, Gail. *Hillary's Choice*. New York: Ballantine Books, 1999.

Smith, I.C. *Inside: A Top G-Man Exposes Spies, Lies and Bureaucratic Bungling in the FBI*. Nelson Current, 2004.

Starr, Kenneth. *The Starr Report*. Pocket Books, 1998.

Steele, Shelby. *A Dream Deferred: The Second Betrayal of Freedom in Black America*. New York: HarperCollins, 1998.

Stephanopoulos, George. *All Too Human: A Political Education*. Boston: Little, Brown and Company, 1999.

Stewart, James B. *Blood Sport*. New York: Simon and Schuster, 1996.

Thibodeau, David and Leon Whiteson. *A Place Called Waco: A Survivor's Story*. New York: Public Affairs, 1999.

Timperlake, Edward and William C. Triplett II. *Year of the Rat*. Washington, D.C.: Regnery Publishing, 1998.

Toobin, Jeffrey. *A Vast Conspiracy*. New York: Touchstone, 1999.

Trulock, Notra. *Code Name Kindred Spirit: Inside the Chinese Nuclear Espionage Scandal*. San Francisco: Encounter Books, 2002.

Tyler, Patrick. *A Great Wall, Six Presidents and China: An Investigative History*. New York: A Century Foundation Books, 1999.

Tyrrell Jr., R. Emmett. *Boy Clinton: The Political Biography*. Washington, D.C.: Regnery Publishing, 1996.

Tyrrell Jr., R. Emmett with Mark W. Davis. *Madame Hillary: The Dark Road to the White House*. Washington, D.C.: Regnery Publishing, 2004.

Tyrrell Jr., R. Emmett Tyrrell. *The Clinton Crack-Up: The Boy President's Life After the White House*. Nashville: Thomas Nelson, 2007.

Weigel, George. *Witness to Hope: The Biography of Pope John Paul II*. New York: HarperCollins, 2001.

Wickam, DeWayne. *Bill Clinton and Black America*. New York: Ballantine Books, 2002.

Woodward, Bob. *Shadow: Five Presidents and the Legacy of Watergate*. New York: Touchstone, 1999.

Woodward, Bob. *The Agenda: Inside the Clinton White House*. New York: Simon & Schuster, 1994.

ENDNOTES

INTRODUCTION
1. Paul Bedard, "Clinton Denies Lewinsky Allegations," *Washington Times*, January 27, 1998.
2. (*Associated Press*) "More Legal Woes Await Citizen Clinton," *Washington Times,* January 15, 2001.

ONE: BILL CLINTON (FAMILY ORIGIN)
1. John McCaslin, "Chasing Clinton," *Washington Times,* Inside The Beltway, June 6, 2001
2. Alan McConagha, "President Scion of Confederate Troops," *Washington Times*, May 31, 1993.
3. R. Emmett Tyrrell, Jr., *Boy Clinton: The Political Biography* (Washington, D.C.: Regnery Publishing, 1996), 147; Gene Weingarten, "The First Father," *Washington Post*, June 20, 1993.
4. David Maraniss, *First in His Class: The Biography of Bill Clinton* (New York: Touchstone, 1996), 26.
5. Roger Morris, *Partners in Power: The Clintons and Their America* (Washington, D.C.: Regnery Publishing, 1996), 19-20.
6. Ibid, 20.
7. Morris, *Partners in Power*, 20; (*Associated Press*), "Another Seat at the Clinton Family Reunion?" *Washington Times*, August 6, 1993.
8. Morris, *Partners in Power*, 20.
9. Morris, *Partners in Power*, 20-21; Meredith Oakley, *On the Make: The Rise of Bill Clinton* (Washington, D.C.: Regnery Publishing, 1994), 19.
10. Morris, *Partners In Power*, 21.
11. Morris, *Partners In Power*, 21; Oakley, *On The Make*, 21.
12. Maraniss, *First In His Class*, 27-28; Tyrrell, *Boy Clinton*, 145; Joyce Milton, *The First Partner: Hillary Rodham Clinton* (New York: William Morrow and Company, 1999), 71.
13. Gail Sheehy, *Hillary's Choice* (New York: Ballantine Books, 1999), 95.
14. Author Gail Sheehy interview with Wilma Booker, 1998; Sheehy, *Hillary's Choice*, 95.
15. Tyrrell, *Boy Clinton*, 148.
16. Weingarten, "The First Father."
17. Maraniss, *First in His Class*, 30; Oakley, *On the Make*, 22.
18. Maraniss, *First in His Class*, 31; Oakley, *On the Make*, 24.
19. Morris, *Partners in Power*, 31; Maraniss, *First in His Class*, 31-32.
20. Morris, *Partners in Power*, 34; Oakley, *On the Make*, 26.
21. Morris, *Partners in Power*, 35.
22. Oakley, *On the Make*, 28.
23. Morris, *Partners in Power*, 49.
24. Sheehy, *Hillary's Choice*, 103.
25. Complaint in Equity, *Clinton v. Clinton*, April 14, 1962; Oakley, *On the Make*, 29; Morris, *Partners in Power*, 51.
26. Oakley, *On The Make*, 31.
27. Ibid.

28 Morris, *Partners In Power*, 52; Tyrrell, *Boy Clinton*, 149-150.
29 Oakley, *On The Make*, 37.

TWO: BILL CLINTON (EARLY YEARS)
1 R. Emmett Tyrrell, Jr., "Georgetown Classmates," *Washington Times*, July 4, 2008.
2 R. Emmett Tyrrell, Jr., *Boy Clinton: The Political Biography* (Washington, D.C.: Regnery Publishing, 1996), 152.
3 David Maraniss, *First In His Class: The Biography of Bill Clinton* (New York: Touchstone, 1996), 11-12.
4 Roger Morris, *Partners In Power: The Clintons and Their America* (Washington, D.C.: Regnery Publishing, 1996), 57.
5 Maraniss, *First In His Class*, 75, 90.
6 Maraniss, *First In His Class*, 81-82; Jim McDougal and Curtis Wilke, *Arkansas Mischief: The Birth of a National Scandal* (New York: Henry Holt and Company, 1998), 100.
7 Maraniss, *First In His Class*, 85.
8 Maraniss, *First In His Class*, 85; Bill Clinton, interview with Bob Lancaster, *Arkansas Democrat*, August 25, 1977, Oakley, *On The Make*, 53.
9 Maraniss, *First In His Class*, 93; Morris, *Partners In Power*, 75.
10 Maraniss, *First In His Class*, 106.
11 Ibid, 108.
12 Ibid, 114.
13 R. Emmett Tyrrell, Jr., *The Clinton Crack-Up: The Boy President's Life After the White House* (Nashville: Thomas Nelson, 2007), 36.
14 Ibid.
15 Maraniss, *First In His Class*, 128.
16 Ibid, 136.
17 Meredith Oakley, *On The Make: The Rise Of Bill Clinton* (Washington, D.C.: Regnery Publishing, 1994), 70; Maraniss, *First In His Class*, 149; Wesley Pruden, "The *Post* Discovers Mr. Clinton's Past," *Washington Times*, February 10, 1995.
18 Maraniss, *First In His Class*, 149.
19 Ibid, 154.
20 Ibid, 162.
21 Ibid, 164.
22 Russ Vaughn, "The Clinton Honor Roll: Those Bill and Hill Call Liars," *American Thinker*, January 2, 2016; Tyrrell, *Boy Clinton*, 64.
23 Author Meredith Oakley interview with Cliff Jackson, July 12, 1993; Oakley, *On The Makethe Make, 69*; Maraniss, First In Hisin His Class, 165.
24 Oakley, *On The Make*the Make, 70.
25 Maraniss, First In Hisin His Class, 168.
26 Tom Campbell, The Clintons of Arkansas, ed. Ernest Dumas (Little Rock, 1993), 42; Oakley, *On The Make*, 77.
27 Morris, *Partners In Power*, 88.
28 Maraniss, *First In His Class*, 172.
29 Morris, *Partners In Power*, 88.
30 Maraniss, *First In His Class*, 173.
31 Maraniss, *First In His Class*, 173; Morris, *Partners In Power*, 89.
32 Morris, *Partners In Power*, 89-90.
33 David Mixner, quoted by Robert E. Levin, Bill Clinton: The Inside Story (New York, N.Y., 1992), 77; Oakley, *On The Make*, 73-74.

34   Oakley, *On The Make*, 74.
35   Mixner, quoted by Levin, Bill Clinton, 77; Oakley, *On The Make*, 74.
36   Ibid, 75.
37   Maraniss, *First In His Class*, 180-181.
38   Maraniss, *First in His Class*, 186; Oakley, *On the Make*, 80; Tom Williamson, *The Sunday Times*, October 25, 1992.
39   Floyd Brown, Slick Willie (Annapolis: Annapolis Publishing Company, 1992), 23-26; Morris, *Partners in Power*, 92.
40   Morris, *Partners in Power*, 92.
41   Maraniss, *First in His Class*, 190-193.
42   Ibid, 198.
43   Maraniss, *First in His Class*, 199-204.
44   Holmes affidavit, September 7, 1992; Oakley, *On The Make*, 82.
45   Ibid.
46   Maraniss, *First in His Class*, 204.
47   Morris, *Partners in Power*, 100.
48   Ibid, 102-103.
49   Ibid, 103-104.
50   Morris, *Partners In Power*, 104; Tyrrell, *Boy Clinton*, 64.
51   Oakley, *On The Make*, 84.
52   Charlie Daniels, *The Sunday Times*, October 25, 1992; Oakley, *On The Make*, 84.
53   Maraniss, *First In His Class*, 213-214.
54   Ibid, 215.
55   Maraniss, *First In His Class*, 223; Interview by author R. Emmett Tyrrell, Jr. on August 14, 2004 with Stefan Halper, who studied with Clinton during a stay at Oxford from 1967 to 1971; Tyrrell, *The Clinton Crack-Up*, 9

THREE: BILL AND HILLARY AT YALE

1   Joyce Milton, *The First Partner: Hillary Rodham Clinton* (New York: William Morrow and Company, 1999), 59.
2   Carl Bernstein, *A Woman in Charge: The Life Of Hillary Rodham Clinton* (New York: Alfred A. Knopf, 2007), 77.
3   Roger Morris, *Partners in Power: The Clintons and Their America* (Washington, D.C.: Regnery Publishing, 1996), 144; Edward Klein, *The Truth About Hillary* (New York: Sentinel, 2005), 70-71.
4   Author Edward Klein interview with Yale Law School classmate who requested anonymity, May 18, 2004; Klein, *The Truth About Hillary*, 71.
5   Ibid, 71-72.
6   Author Edward Klein interview with Yale Law School classmate who requested anonymity, May 18, 2004; Klein, *The Truth About Hillary*, 72.
7   David Maraniss, *First in His Class: The Biography of Bill Clinton* (New York: Touchstone, 1996), 226-227; Bernstein, *A Woman in Charge*, 77.
8   Bernstein, *A Woman in Charge*, 77.
9   Jeff Gerth and Don Van Natta Jr., *Her Way: The Hopes and Ambitions of Hillary Rodham Clinton* (New York: Little Brown, 2007), 47.
10 Authors Jeff Gerth and Don Van Natta Jr. interviews with Leon Panetta and former Clinton administration official in 2006; Jeff Gerth and Don Van Natta Jr. interviews with Ann Crittenden and John Henry in 2007; Gerth and Van Natta, *Her Way*, 9.
11 Gail Sheehy, *Hillary's Choice* (New York: Ballantine Books, 1999), 84; Maraniss, *First in His Class*, 263.

12   Meredith Oakley, *On the Make: The Rise of Bill Clinton* (Washington, D.C.: Regnery Publishing, 1994), 107.
13   Maraniss, *First in His Class*, 269, 275; Sheehy, *Hillary's Choice*, 84.
14   Gerth and Van Natta, *Her Way*, 48; Oakley, *On the Make*, 118.
15   Maraniss, *First in His Class*, 283-284.
16   Joyce Milton, *The First Partner: Hillary Rodham Clinton* (New York: William Morrow and Company, 1999), 60; Bernstein, *A Woman in Charge*, 89.
17   Milton, *The First Partner*, 60-61.
18   Ibid, 61.
19   Bernstein, *A Woman in Charge*, 91-92.
20   Ibid, 92.
21   Ibid, 93-94.
22   Bernstein, *A Woman in Charge*, 94; Sheehy, *Hillary's Choice*, 88.
23   Bernstein, *A Woman in Charge*, 94.
24   Ibid.
25   Bernstein, *A Woman in Charge*, 95; Sheehy, *Hillary's Choice*, 89.

FOUR: BACK IN ARKANSAS

1   David Maraniss, *First in His Class: The Biography of Bill Clinton* (New York: Touchstone, 1996), 288.
2   David Maraniss, *First In His Class: The Biography of Bill Clinton* (New York: Touchstone, 1996), 288-290.
3   Carl Bernstein, *A Woman In Charge: The Life of Hillary Rodham Clinton* (New York: Alfred A. Knopf, 2007), 97.
4   Jeff Gerth and Don Van Natta Jr., *Her Way: The Hopes and Ambitions of Hillary Rodham Clinton* (New York: Little Brown, 2007), 53.
5   Bernstein, *A Woman In Charge*, 97-98; Maraniss, *First In His Class*, 319.
6   Bernstein, *A Woman In Charge*, 98.
7   Maraniss, *First In His Class*, 319.
8   Maraniss, *First In His Class*, 319-320; Edward Klein, *The Truth About Hillary* (New York: Sentinel, 2005), 83.
9   Klein, *The Truth About Hillary*, 84.
10   Author Gail Sheehy interviews with Paul Fray, 1999; Gail Sheehy, *Hillary's Choice* (New York: Ballantine Books, 1999), 113.
11   Barbara Olson, *Hell To to Pay: The Unfolding Story of Hillary Rodham Clinton* (Washington, D.C., Regnery Publishing, 1999), 87.
12   David Brock, *The Seduction of Hillary Rodham* (New York: Free Press Paperbacks, 1997), 53-54.
13   Ibid, 54.
14   Brock, *The Seduction of Hillary Rodham*, 55; Oakley, *On The Make*, 134.
15   Author Roger Morris confidential interview; Roger Morris, *Partners In Power: The Clintons and Their America* (Washington, D.C.: Regnery Publishing, 1996), 181.
16   Maraniss, *First In His Class*, 333-334.
17   Brock, *The Seduction of Hillary Rodham*, 57.
18   Joyce Milton, *The First Partner: Hillary Rodham Clinton* (New York: William Morrow and Company, 1999), 80; Maraniss, *First in His Class*, 336.
19   Maraniss, *First in His Class*, 336.
20   Maraniss, *First in His Class*, 337; Olson, *Hell To Pay*, 94; Jerry Oppenheimer, *State of a Union: Inside The Complex Marriage of Bill and Hillary Clinton* (New York: HarperCollins, 2000), 153-156.

21 Oppenheimer, *State of a Union*, 153-156; *Human Events*, July 28, 2000, 3.
22 Ibid; Ibid.
23 Klein, *The Truth About Hillary*, 87.
24 Ibid.
25 Bernstein, *A Woman In Charge*, 121.
26 Morris, *Partners In Power*, 187.
27 Ibid, 187-188.
28 Christopher Andersen, *Bill and Hillary: The Marriage* (New York: William Morrow and Company, 1999), 150; Carl Limbacher, *Hillary's Scheme: Inside the Next Clinton's Ruthless Agenda to Take the White House* (New York: Crown Forum, 2003), 161.
29 Milton, *First Partner*, 86; Morris, *Partners in Power*, 188.
30 Meredith Oakley, *On the Make: The Rise of Bill Clinton* (Washington, D.C.: Regnery Publishing, 1994), 152-153.
31 Maraniss, *First in His Class*, 349.
32 Ibid, 350.
33 Milton, *The First Partner*, 86-87.
34 Author Roger Morris confidential interviews; Morris, *Partners In Power*, 204; Bernstein, *A Woman In Charge*, 128.
35 Author Roger Morris confidential interviews; Morris, *Partners In Power*, 204; Milton, *The First Partner*, 95.
36 Ibid, 132.
37 Oakley, *On The Make*, 161; Bernstein, *A Woman In Charge*, 132.
38 Milton, *The First Partner*, 93-94.
39 Morris, *Partners In Power*, 205.

FIVE: THE GOVERNORSHIP
1 Webb Hubbell, *Friends in High Places* (New York: Signet, 1993), 86.
2 David Maraniss, *First in His Class: The Biography of Bill Clinton* (New York: Touchstone, 1996), 352; Dick Morris, *Behind the Oval Office: Getting Reelected Against All Odds* (Los Angeles: Renaissance, 1999), 46.
3 Maraniss, *First in His Class*, 353.
4 Ibid, 354.
5 Meredith Oakley, *On the Make: The Rise of Bill Clinton* (Washington, D.C.: Regnery Publishing, 1994), 179.
6 David Brock, *The Seduction of Hillary Rodham* (New York: Free Press Paperbacks, 1997), 74.
7 Oakley, *On the Make*, 186.
8 Oakley, *On the Make*, 186.
9 Morris, *Partners in Powers*, 209.
10 Morris, *Partners in Powers*, 209.
11 Oakley, *On the Make*, 187.
12 Oakley, *on the Make*, 188.
13 Ibid, 200.
14 Author Gail Sheehy interview with Bobby Roberts, 1999; Gail Sheehy, *Hillary's Choice* (New York: Ballantine Books, 1999), 125; "Uneasy Rider," Charlie Daniels, 1973.
15 Sheehy, *Hillary's Choice*, 134-135, 142-143.
16 Maraniss, *First in His Class*, 361.
17 Brock, *The Seduction of Hillary Rodham*, 131.
18 *Arkansas Gazette*, March 31, 1979; Oakley, *On the Make*, 212.
19 Oakley, *On the Make*, 212; Brock, *The Seduction of Hillary Rodham*, 130.

20 Author Edward Klein interview with an anonymous source who was with the Clintons in Bermuda; Klein, *The Truth About Hillary*, 91.
21 Brock, *The Seduction of Hillary Rodham*, 132.
22 Roger Morris, *Partners in Power*, 237-38.
23 Barbara Olson, *Hell to Pay: The Unfolding Story of Hillary Rodham Clinton* (Washington, D.C.: Regnery Publishing, 1999), 185.
24 Brock, *The Seduction of Hillary Rodham*, 130-131.
25 Oakley, *On the Make*, 238.
26 Ibid, 238-39.
27 Maraniss, *First in His Class*, 377.
28 Bernstein, *A Woman in Charge*, 158; Maraniss, *First in His Class*, 379.
29 Maraniss, *First in His Class*, 380.
30 Oakley, *On the Make*, 246.
31 Paul Greenberg, "Like Old *Times*," *Washington Times*, July 6, 2004.
32 Ibid.
33 Ibid.
34 Milton, *The First Partner*, 117-18.
35 Maraniss, *First in His Class*, 384.
36 Brock, *The Seduction of Hillary Rodham*, 132.
37 Maraniss, *First in His Class*, 384-385.
38 Ibid, 385.
39 Milton, *The First Partner*, 120.
40 Maraniss, *First in His Class*, 387-388; Morris, *Partners in Power*, 247.
41 Ibid, 388.
42 Author R. Emmett Tyrrell, Jr. interview with retired FBI agent I.C. Smith, December 2004. Smith served during the Clinton administration as Special Agent for Arkansas and had two sources for this story; R. Emmett Tyrrell, Jr., *The Clinton Crack-Up: The Boy President's Life After the White House* (Nashville: Thomas Nelson, 2007), 28.
43 Klein, *The Truth About Hillary*, 96.
44 Authors Jeff Gerth and Don Van Natta Jr. interview with Jim McDougal in 1992; Jeff Gerth and Don Van Natta Jr., *Her Way: The Hopes and Ambitions of Hillary Rodham Clinton* (New York: Little, Brown and Company, 1998), 68.
45 Maraniss, *First In His Class*, 392; Oakley, *On The Make*, 262.
46 Milton, *The First Partner*, 122.
47 Klein, *The Truth About Hillary*, 98-99.
48 Morris, *Partners in Power*, 268-269; Brock, *The Seduction of Hillary Rodham*, 135-136.
49 Morris, *Partners in Power*, 271.
50 Maraniss, *First in His Class*, 397-398.
51 Deposition of George Locke, "Investigation of Whitewater Development Corporation and Related Matters," Senate Report 104-869, Report of the Special Committee to Investigate Whitewater Development Corporation, administered by the Committee on Banking, Housing and Urban Affairs, 104 Cong. First Session (hereafter D'Amato Committee), Vol. XVII, pp. 5251-52; Milton, *The First Partner*, 122.
52 Ibid, 122-123.
53 Morris, *Partners in Power*, 275.
54 Brock, *The Seduction of Hillary Rodham*, 147.
55 Ibid, 148-49.
56 Ibid, 141.
57 Maraniss, *First in His Class*, 399.
58 Sheehy, *Hillary's Choice*, 145.

59	Maraniss, *First in His Class*, 400.
60	Oakley, *On the Make*, 269-270.
61	Ibid, 271.
62	Author Roger Morris confidential interview with prominent African American attorney; Morris, *Partners in Power*, 289.
63	Morris, *Partners in Power*, 290.
64	Maraniss, *First in His Class*, 405-406, 409, 411.
65	Ibid, 416.
66	Oakley, *On the Make*, 295-96.
67	Maraniss, *First in His Class*, 419.
68	Ambrose Evans-Pritchard, *The Secret Life of Bill Clinton: The Unreported Stories* (Washington, D.C.: Regnery Publishing, 1997), 241. The tape is hard to make out because of background noise, but Detective Bunn was traveling with Roger Clinton in the car and insists that he heard the words clearly at the time
69	Two-hour surveillance tape filmed at the apartment of Rodney Myers, viewed by author Ambrose Evans-Pritchard; transcripts; Evans-Pritchard, *The Secret Life of Bill Clinton*, 239.
70	Author Meredith Oakley interview with Tommy Goodwin, January 10, 1994; Oakley, *On The Make*, 296-297.
71	Evans-Pritchard, *The Secret Life of Bill Clinton*, 242.
72	Ibid.
73	Ibid.
74	Author Ambrose Evans-Pritchard interview with a confidential source; Evans-Pritchard, *The Secret Life of Bill Clinton*, 242.
75	Evans-Pritchard, *The Secret Life of Bill Clinton*, 242.
76	*Arkansas Gazette*, August 3, 1984; Oakley, *On the Make*, 296.
77	*Arkansas Democrat*, August 15, 1984; Oakley, *On the Make*, 297-298.
78	Roger decided to cooperate with authorities, who said they had "plenty of video" of his drug transactions with undercover agents; Oakley, *On the Make*, 299.
79	Oakley, *On the Make*, 309-310.
80	Oakley, *On the Make*, 302; Evans-Pritchard, *The Secret Life of Bill Clinton*, 241.
81	*Arkansas Democrat*, March 2, 1985; Oakley, *On the Make*, 310-311.
82	Oakley, *On the Make*, 310.
83	Morris, *Partners in Power*, 330-333.
84	Oakley, *On the Make*, 294.
85	Ibid, 320, 325.
86	Ibid, 323-326
87	Ibid, 431.
88	*Arkansas Gazette*, April 19, 1987; Roger Morris, *Partners in Power*, 432.
89	Author Roger Morris confidential interviews with participants, journalists, and law enforcement officials; *Miami Herald*, May 4, 1987; Roger Morris, *Partners in Powers*, 432-433.
90	Brock, *The Seduction of Hillary Rodham*, 217-218.
91	Morris, *Partners in Power*, 436.
92	Sheehy, *Hillary's Choice*, 174.
93	Maraniss, *First in His Class*, 440-441.
94	Ibid, 441.
95	Morris, *Partners in Power*, 436.
96	Ibid, 437.
97	Maraniss, *First in His Class*, 445-446.
98	Maraniss, *First in His Class*, 446; Milton, *The First Partner*, 187.
99	Morris, *Partners in Power*, 439.

100 Ibid, 439.
101 Maraniss, *First in His Class*, 448.
102 Maraniss, *First in His Class*, 451, 455; Oakley, *On the Make*, 406.
103 Morris, *Partners in Power*, 457.
104 Morris, *Partners in Power*, 458; Oakley, *On the Make*, 421.
105 Oakley, *On the Make*, 420.
106 Ibid, 420-421.
107 Oakley, *On the Make*, 419.
108 Ibid.
109 Bernstein, *A Woman in Charge*, 189; Oakley, *On the Make*, 423-424.
110 Maraniss, *First in His Class*, 457; Morris, *Partners in Power*, 459.
111 Milton, *The First Partner*, 209.
112 Ibid, 209-210.
113 Morris, *Partners in Power*, 460; Limbacher, *Hillary's Scheme*, p.13.
114 Milton, *The First Partner*, 209.

SIX: MENA AIRPORT

1   R. Emmett Tyrrell, Jr., "Arkansas Drug Diggings," *Washington Times*, October 14, 1994.
2   Ibid.
3   Ibid.
4   Ibid.
5   R. Emmett Tyrell, Jr., *Boy Clinton: The Political Biography* (Washington, D.C.: Regnery Publishing, 1996), 13.
6   Tyrrell, *Boy Clinton*, 12; R. Emmett Tyrrell, Jr., "The Arkansas Shuttle," *American Spectator*, August 1995, 18.
7   Tyrrell, *Boy Clinton*, 1, 12.
8   Brown deposition, Reed v. Young; Ambrose Evans-Pritchard, *The Secret Life of Bill Clinton: The Unreported Stories* (Washington, D.C.: Regnery Publishing, 1997), 333.
9   Tyrrell, "The Arkansas Drug Shuttle," 17.
10 Evans-Pritchard, *The Secret Life of Bill Clinton*, 334.
11 Roger Morris, *Partners in Power: The Clintons and Their America* (Washington, D.C.: Regnery Publishing, 1996, 407; Evans-Pritchard, *The Secret Life of Bill Clinton*, 334-335.
12 Morris, *Partners in Power*, 407; Tyrrell, "The Arkansas Drug Shuttle," 17.
13 DEA agent Ernest Jacobsen in a deposition to the House Subcommittee on Crime, March 11, 1988; Evans-Pritchard, *The Secret Life of Bill Clinton*, 318; Ronald Koziol, "Informant's Murder Puts Heat on Authorities," *Chicago Tribune*, April 13, 1986, 5; Tyrrell, *Boy Clinton*, 1.
14 Testimony of Billy Bottoms to the House Subcommittee on Crime, June 20, 1988; Evans-Pritchard, *The Secret Life of Bill Clinton*, 318-319.
15 Evans-Pritchard, *The Secret Life of Bill Clinton*, 319.
16 Ibid, 320.
17 Jacobsen deposition; Evans-Pritchard, *The Secret Life of Bill Clinton*, 320-321.
18 Morris, *Partners in Power*, 396-397.
19 Ibid, 407-408.
20 Morris, *Partners in Power*, 408; Tyrrell, *Boy Clinton*, 4.
21 Jacobsen deposition; Tyrrell, *Boy Clinton*, 4.
22 Tyrrell, *Boy Clinton*, 4-5.
23 Evans-Pritchard, *The Secret Life of Bill Clinton*, 337.
24 Morris, *Partners in Power*, 409.
25 Tyrrell, *Boy Clinton*, 8.

26 Morris, *Partners in Power*, 410.
27 Ibid, 410-411.
28 Tyrrell, *Boy Clinton*, 14.
29 Tyrrell, *Boy Clinton*, 14.
30 Morris, *Partners in Power*, 397; Jacobsen deposition; Evans-Pritchard, *The Secret Life of Bill Clinton*, 329.
31 Evans-Pritchard, *The Secret Life of Bill Clinton*, 329.
32 Ibid, 342.
33 Ibid, 343.
34 Ibid.
35 Tyrrell, *Boy Clinton*, 16.
36 Ibid
37 Tyrrell, *Boy Clinton*, 17; Evans-Pritchard, *The Secret Life of Bill Clinton*, 347.
38 There is extensive police documentation of suspicious activities at Nella, e.g. DEA October 28, 1986; Evans-Pritchard, *The Secret Life of Bill Clinton*, 348-349.
39 Ibid.
40 Ibid, 351.
41 DEA file GJ-83-Z001, dated March 12, 1984; FBI 302 report, statement of State Senator George Locke, October 10, 1986; Evans-Pritchard, *The Secret Life of Bill Clinton*, 291-293.
42 Author Roger Morris confidential interviews; Morris, *Partners in Power*, 417-418.
43 Morris, *Partners in Power*, 418.
44 Ibid.
45 Ibid, 419.
46 The contact was Maurice Rodriguez. Roger had requested $16,000 to $20,000, but Lasater told the FBI he only paid $8,000. Roger then pocketed half the money for himself; FBI 302 report, statement of Dan Lasater; Evans-Pritchard, *The Secret Life of Bill Clinton*, 292.
47 Author Roger Morris confidential interviews; Morris, *Partners in Power*, 422.
48 Author Ambrose Evans-Pritchard interview with a confidential informant, June 1994; Evans-Pritchard, *The Secret Life of Bill Clinton*, 298.
49 Morris, *Partners in Power*, 421.
50 Ibid, 422-423.
51 *Arkansas Gazette*, October 26-30, 1986; Morris, *Partners in Power*, 425-426; Evans-Pritchard, *The Secret Life of Bill Clinton*, 297.
52 *Arkansas Gazette*, September 18-19, 1986; Morris, *Partners in Power*, 425.
53 Morris, *Partners in Power*, 325, 442.
54 Author Ambrose Evans-Pritchard interview with Gary Martin, DEA agent, Little Rock, June 1994; Evans-Pritchard, *The Secret Life of Bill Clinton*, 259, 262.
55 Evans-Pritchard, *The Secret Life of Bill Clinton*, 262..
56 Ibid, 257, 262-263.
57 Ibid, 263.
58 Ibid, 259, 263.
59 Ibid.
60 Ibid, 263-264.
61 Ibid, 264.
62 Tyrrell, *Boy Clinton*, xvi; Evans-Pritchard, *The Secret Life of Bill Clinton*, 238-239.
63 Ibid, 239.
64 Evans-Pritchard, *The Secret Life of Bill Clinton*, 243.
65 Ibid.
66 Ibid.
67 Evans-Pritchard, *The Secret Life of Bill Clinton*, 243; Tyrrell, *Boy Clinton*, xvii-xviii.

68   Tyrrell, *Boy Clinton*, xix.
69   Morris, *Partners in Power*, 426.
70   Ibid, 402.
71   Ibid.

SEVEN: ELECTION 1992

1   Clinton, *Arkansas Democrat-Gazette*, January 18, 1992; Meredith Oakley, *On The Make: The Rise of Bill Clinton* (Washington, D.C.: Regnery Publishing, 1994), 506.
2   David Maraniss, *First in His Class: The Biography of Bill Clinton* (New York: Touchstone, 1996), 462.
3   Meredith Oakley, *On the Make: The Rise of Bill Clinton* (Washington, D.C.: Regnery Publishing, 1994), 477.
4   R. Emmett Tyrrell, "Divisiveness Duplicity," *Washington Times*, April 28, 1995.
5   Oakley, *On the Make*, 478.
6   *Newsweek*, April 11, 1994; *National Journal*, May 9, 1992; Roger Morris, *Partners in Power: The Clintons and Their America* (Washington, D.C.: Regnery Publishing, 1996), 462.
7   Ibid.
8   Mary Matalin and James Carville, *All's Fair: Love, War and Running for President* (New York: Simon & Schuster, 1994), p.243; Richard Poe, *Hillary's Secret War: The Clinton Conspiracy to Muzzle Internet Journalists* (Nashville: WND Books, 2004), 31.
9   Ruth Marcus and Howard Schneider, "Media Control Was Legacy of '92 Campaign: 'War Room' Tactics Backfire in Office," *Washington Post*, July 29, 1994, A21; Poe, *Hillary's Secret War*, 31-32.
10   Interview with Michael Cook, campaign aide, by Stephen Engelberg of the *New York Times* in 1994; Jeff Gerth and Don Van Natta Jr., *Her Way: The Hopes and Ambitions of Hillary Rodham Clinton* (New York: Little, Brown and Company, 2007), 91-92.
11   Memorandum from Loretta Lynch to Segal, Wright and Lyons, March 25, 1992, RE: Issues Facing the Defense Team; Gerth and Van Natta, *Her Way*, 92.
12   Authors Jeff Gerth and Don Van Jr. interview with David Ifshin in 1994. Ifshin died in 1996; Gerth and Van Natta, *Her Way*, 92.
13   Byron York, "The Truth About Bill's Lies," *American Spectator*, March 1998, 28.
14   Steve Daley, "Clinton Challenging Long-*Time* Party Ideals," *Chicago Tribune*, October 6, 1991; David Maraniss, "Image Questions Bewilder Clinton, Longtime Friends; Allies Describe Candidate's 'Constancy,'" *Washington Post*, April 12, 1992; Candice E. Jackson, *Their Lives: The Women Targeted by the Clinton Machine* (Los Angeles: World Ahead, 2005), 66.
15   Joyce Milton, *The First Partner: Hillary Rodham Clinton* (New York: William Morrow and Company, 1999), 236-237.
16   Poe, *Hillary's Secret War*, 34.
17   George Stephanopoulos, *"Betrayal,"* *Newsweek*, August 31, 1998; Milton, *The First Partner*, 227.
18   York, "The Truth About Bill's Lies," 28.
19   Maraniss, *First in His Class*, 460-461..
20   York, "The Truth About Bill's Lies," 28.
21   Oakley, *On the Make*, 511.
22   Ibid.
23   York, "The Truth About Bill's Lies," 28-29.
24   Milton, *The First Partner*, 221.
25   Barbara Olson, *Hell to Pay: The Unfolding Story of Hillary Rodham Clinton* (Washington, D.C.: Regnery Publishing, 1999), 214.
26   Ibid.
27   York, "The Truth About Bill's Lies," 29.
28   Ibid.

29 *Vanity Fair*, May 1992; Olson, *Hell To Pay*, 215.
30 Sheehy, *Hillary's Choice*, 205.
31 York, "The Truth About Bill's Lies," 29.
32 Authors Jeff Gerth and Don Van Natta Jr. interview with former campaign aide in 2006; Gerth and Van Natta, *Her Way*, 92-93.
33 Rebecca Borders, "Bill's Mary Poppins," *American Spectator*, August 1996, 42.
34 Carl Limbacher, *Hillary's Scheme: Inside the Next Clinton's Ruthless Agenda to Take the White House* (New York: Crown Forum, 2003), 149.
35 Seth Rosenfeld, "Watching the Detective," *San Francisco Examiner*, January 31, 1999; Sheehy, *Hillary's Choice*, 201.
36 The *Washington Post*, July 26, 1992; Sheehy, *Hillary's Choice*, 201.
37 Dick Morris in *San Francisco Examiner*, January 31, 1999, op cit.; Sheehy, *Hillary's Choice*, 201-202.
38 The *Washington Post*, July 26, 1992. Palladino was originally hired through Jim Lyons, a Denver attorney whose firm performed legal work for the Clinton campaign. About $28,000 in payments to Lyons' firm, included on Clinton's May report to the Federal Elections Commission, were actually payments to Palladino. Thereafter, fees and expenses for the private investigator were simply reported to the FEC as "legal fees"; *Gannett News Service*, August 13, 1992; Sheehy, *Hillary's Choice*, 202.
39 Federal Election Commission released, March 1, 1993, and March 19, 1993; Morris, *Partners in Power*, 463-464.
40 Morris, *Partners in Power*, 464.
41 Jack Cashill, *Ron Brown's Body: How One Man's Death Saved the Clinton Presidency and Hillary's Future* (Nashville: WND Books, 2004), 99.
42 Bob Woodward, *The Agenda: Inside the Clinton White House* (New York: Simon & Schuster, 1994), 40-41; Cashill, *Ron Brown's Body*, 99.
43 DeWayne Wickam, *Bill Clinton and Black America* (New York: Ballantine Books, 2002), 49. Cashill, *Ron Brown's Body*, 100.
44 Tyrrell, *Boy Clinton*, 43.
45 Governor Bill Clinton, Remarks at Georgetown University, Washington, D.C., October 23, 1991; Tyrrell, *Boy Clinton*, 43-44.
46 Tyrrell, *Boy Clinton*, 44-45.
47 Milton, *The First Partner*, 240.
48 Albert Gore, Speech at the 1992 Democratic National Convention, New York, July 16, 1992; Tyrrell, *Boy Clinton*, 48.
49 Tyrrell, *Boy Clinton*, 46-47.
50 Richard L. Berke, "Perot Says He Quit in July to Thwart G.O.P. 'Dirty Tricks,' " *New York Times*, October 26, 1992; Gwen Ifill, "With No Break, Clinton Initiates Campaign Tour," *New York Times*, July 18, 1992; Rich Lowery, *Legacy: Paying The Price For The Clinton Years* (Washington, D.C.: Regnery Publishing, 2003), 349.
51 Oakley, *On the Make*, 490, 545.
52 Linda Burnett, *Arkansas Democrat-Gazette*, September 19, 1992; Oakley, *On the Make*, 490.
53 Clinton, *Arkansas Democrat-Gazette*, September 19, 1992; Oakley, *On the Make*, 490-491.
54 *New York Times* News Service, *Arkansas Democrat-Gazette*, September 19, 1992; Clinton, *Arkansas Democrat-Gazette*, September 19, 1992; Oakley, *On the Make*, 491.
55 Jerry Seper, "From Women to Whitewater, Scandals Never Seem To Stop," *Washington Times*, August 30, 1996.
56 *Washington Times*, October 20, 1992.
57 Major Garrett, "Stockdale Blames Vietnam Protests," *Washington Times*, October 20, 1992.
58 Donald Lambro, "Dealings, Profits Shatter Image ff Populist Couple," *Washington Times*, April 23, 1994.

59 York, "The Truth About Bill's Lies," 26.
60 Ibid.
61 *Arkansas Democrat-Gazette*, October 30, 1992; Limbacher, *Hillary's Scheme*, 44.
62 Lead Editorial, "Sentencing in Little Rock," *Washington Times*, August 21, 1996.
63 *Boston Globe*, October 31, 1992; Limbacher, *Hillary's Scheme*, 44.
64 Limbacher, *Hillary's Scheme*, 45.
65 *Minneapolis Star-Tribune*, October 31, 1992; Limbacher, *Hillary's Scheme*, 45.
66 Tyrrell, *Boy Clinton*, 282-283.

EIGHT: INAUGURATION DAY

1 Joel Achenbach, "Another Failed Presidency, Already?" *Washington Post*, May 27, 1993.
2 Roger Morris, *Partners in Power: The Clintons And Their America* (Washington, D.C.: Regnery Publishing, 1996), 7.
3 Elizabeth Drew, "The Arrival of Overdue Bill," *Washington Post*, January 17, 1993.
4 Barbara Olson, *Hell To Pay: The Unfolding Story of Hillary Rodham Clinton* (Washington, D.C.: Regnery Publishing, 1999), 65.
5 *Time*, October 26, 1996; Olson, *Hell To Pay*, 65-66.
6 Chuck Conconi, ed., "Capital Comment," *Washingtonian*, July 1993, 7; R. Emmett Tyrrell, Jr., *Boy Clinton: The Political Biography* (Washington, D.C.: Regnery Publishing, 1996), 25.
7 Tyrrell, *Boy Clinton*, 25-26.
8 Gary Aldrich, *Unlimited Access: An FBI Agent Inside the Clinton White House* (Washington, D.C.: Regnery Publishing, 1996), 11.
9 Aldrich, *Unlimited Access*, 11; Author Gail Sheehy interviews with two knowledgeable sources who were present; Gail Sheehy, *Hillary's Choice* (New York: Ballantine Books, 1999), 223.
10 Aldrich, *Unlimited Access*, 11.
11 R.W. Apple, Jr., "The Inauguration: A Grand Beginning," *New York Times*, January 18, 1993, A1; Tyrrell, *Boy Clinton*, 28.
12 Carl Bernstein, *A Woman in Charge: The Life of Hillary Rodham Clinton* (New York: Alfred A. Knopf, 2007), 232.
13 Paul M. Rodriguez, "TVs, VCRs Taken As Souvenirs,'" *Washington Times*, May 17, 1993.
14 Ibid.

NINE: 1993 STUMBLES PART I

1 Joel Achenbach, "Another Failed Presidency, Already?" *Washington Post*, May 27, 1993.
2 Barbara Olson, *Hell to Pay: The Unfolding Story of Hillary Rodham Clinton* (Washington, D.C.: Regnery Publishing, 1999), 248.
3 Robert D. Novak and Zelda Novak, "Oh, What a Tangled Webb ...," *American Spectator*, June 1994, p.24; David Brock, *The Seduction of Hillary Rodham* (New York: Free Press Paperbacks, 1997), 309.
4 Ruth Marcus, "Attorney General-Designate Baird Fined For Undocumented Workers," *Washington Post*, January 17, 1993, A4.
5 Ibid.
6 Ibid.
7 Jerry Knight, "Nannies and Zoe," *Washington Post*, January 17, 1993.
8 Ibid.
9 Ruth Marcus and David S. Broder, "President Takes Blame For Pushing Baird Selection," *Washington Post*, January 23, 1993.

10 Brock, *The Seduction of Hillary Rodham*, 309.
11 Ruth Marcus, "Babysitter Problems Sink Second Clinton Prospect," *Washington Post*, February 6, 1993; Elizabeth Drew, *On the Edge: The Clinton Presidency* (New York: Touchstone, 1994), 53.
12 Marcus, "Babysitter Problems Sink Second Clinton Prospect"; R. Emmett Tyrrell, Jr., *Boy Clinton: The Political Biography* (Washington, D.C. Regnery Publishing, 1996), 184.
13 Jerry Seper and Paul Bedard, " 'Baird Problem' Forces Out Wood," *Washington Times*, February 6, 1993.
14 Ruth Marcus, "Babysitter Problems Sink Second Clinton Prospect," *Washington Post*, February 6, 1993; Tyrrell, *Boy Clinton*, 184.
15 Olson, *Hell To Pay*, 249.
16 Ibid, 249-250.
17 Drew, *On The Edge*, 42.
18 George Weigel, *Witness To Hope: The Biography Of Pope John Paul II* (New York: HarperCollins, 2001), 715; Paul Kengor, *God And Hillary Clinton: A Spiritual Life* (New York: HarperCollins, 2007), 99.
19 Drew, *On The Edge*, 42.
20 Byron York, "Clinton's Phony War," *American Spectator*, February 1994, 41.
21 Ibid.
22 Drew, *On the Edge*, 42.
23 Gary Lee, "Gays Get Reassurance on Military," *Washington Post*, March 27, 1993.
24 "Gays-Military Chronology," (*Associated Press*), December 22, 1993; Lt. Col. Robert "Buzz" Patterson, *Dereliction of Duty: The Eyewitness Account of How Bill Clinton Compromised America's National Security* (Washington, D.C.: Regnery Publishing, 2003), 100-101.
25 Drew, *On the Edge*, 43.
26 Ibid, 43,45-46.
27 Patterson, *Dereliction Of Duty*, 101.
28 Ronald A. Taylor and Bill Gertz, "Gay-Ban Policy Moves Out of The Closet," *Washington Times*, July 17, 1993.
29 Drew, *On the Edge*, 87.
30 Michael Hedges and J. Jennings Moss, "300,000 March to Celebrate Rites with Demand for Rights," *Washington Times*, April 26, 1993.
31 Rowan Scarborough, "Court-Martials of Gays Usually for Sex Assaults," *Washington Times*, June 4, 1993.
32 Ibid.
33 J. Jennings Moss, "President Feels Heat from Both Sides," *Washington Times*, July 20, 1993; Drew, *On the Edge*, 250.
34 "Address to the Nation on the Economic Program," *Public Papers of the Presidents*, February 15, 1993, 207; James Bovard, *Feeling Your Pain: The Explosion and Abuse of Government Power in the Clinton-Gore Years* (New York: St. Martin's Press, 2000), 189.

TEN: WACO
1 Frank J. Murray, "Clinton Defends Waco Strategy," *Washington Times*, April 24, 1993.
2 David Limbaugh, *Absolute Power: The Legacy of Corruption in the Clinton-Reno Justice Department* (Washington, D.C.: Regnery Publishing, 2001), 2.
3 Ibid, 1, 8.
4 Jerry Seper and Laurie Kellman, "Waco Slaughter Comes Under Scrutiny of House," *Washington Times*, July 17, 1995; Limbaugh, *Absolute Power*, 12.
5 House of Representatives, *Investigation into the Activities of Federal Law Enforcement Agencies Toward the Branch Davidians*, House Report 104-749, August 2, 1996; James Bovard, *Feeling Your*

Pain: The Explosion and Abuse of Government Power in the Clinton-Gore Years (New York: St. Martin's Press, 2000), 269.

6 Limbaugh, *Absolute Power*, 14.
7 U.S. Department of the Treasury, *Report of the Department of the Treasury on the Bureau of Alcohol, Tobacco, and Firearms, Investigation of Vernon Wayne Howell also known as David Koresh* (Washington, D.C., 1993), 37. Hereinafter, *Treasury Report*; David B. Kopel and Paul H. Blackman, *No More Wacos: What's Wrong With Federal Law Enforcement and How to Fix It* (Amherst, N.Y.: Prometheus Books, 1997, 53, Limbaugh, *Absolute Power*, 14; Jerry Seper, "Waco-Raid Whistleblower Arrested on Lying Charge," *Washington Times*, November 10, 2000.
8 U.S. House of Representatives, Committee on Government Reform and Oversight in conjunction with the Committee on the Judiciary, *Investigation into the Activities of Federal Law Enforcement Agencies Toward the Branch Davidians*, Report 104-179, 104th Cong., 2nd sess. (Washington, D.C., 1996), 14. Hereinafter, *Committee Report*; Marc Breault and Martin King, *Inside the Cult* (New York: Signet, 1993), 299-300; Limbaugh, *Absolute Power*, 15.
9 Sue Ann Pressley and John F. Harris, "House Republicans Suggest ATF Deceived Military to Get Equipment, Training," *Washington Post*, July 21, 1995.
10 Bovard, *Feeling Your Pain*, 270.
11 Kopel and Blackman, *No More Wacos*, 64; Limbaugh, *Absolute Power*, 15-16.
12 Bureau of Alcohol, Tobacco and Firearms: "Synopsis of Surveillance—February 19, 1993," internal memo from Davy Aguilera, approved by Phillip J. Chojnacki, February 24, 1993. This report was uncovered in 1999 by a FOIA request by David Hardy, an Arizona investigator; Bovard, *Feeling Your Pain*, 270.
13 Kopel and Blackman, *No More Wacos*, 64; Limbaugh, *Absolute Power*, 16.
14 Limbaugh, *Absolute Power*, 16.
15 David Wattenberg, "Gunning for Koresh," *American Spectator*, August 1993, 38.
16 Ibid, 39.
17 Ibid.
18 Limbaugh, *Absolute Power*, 16.
19 Dick Reavis, *The Ashes of Waco: An Investigation* (New York: Simon and Schuster, 1995), 32; Limbaugh, *Absolute Power*, 17.
20 *Committee Report*, 14; Limbaugh, *Absolute Power*, 17
21 *Committee Report*; Scott Parks, "Military Role In Davidian Siege Cloudy," *Dallas Morning News*, September 26, 1999; Bovard, *Feeling Your Pain*, 270-271; Wattenberg, "Gunning For Koresh," 38.
22 Sue Ann Pressley, "Agent Says ATF Bosses Knew Koresh Was Warned Of Raid," *Washington Post*, July 25, 1995.
23 Pressley, "Agent Says ATF Bosses Knew Koresh Was Warned Of Raid"; *Treasury Report*, 89; Limbaugh, *Absolute Power*, 19.
24 *Treasury Report*, 91; Limbaugh, *Absolute Power*, 19.
25 Pressley, "Agent Says ATF Bosses Knew Koresh Was Warned Of Raid."
26 *Committee Report*, Bovard, *Feeling Your Pain*, 271.
27 Quoted in "Hearing of the Senate Judiciary Committee Subject Federal Raid at Waco," Federal News Service, November 1, 1995; Bovard, *Feeling Your Pain*, 272; Wattenberg, "Gunning for Koresh," 40.
28 Jennifer Autrey, "Critics of Raid Demand Inquiry into Helicopters," *Fort Worth Star Telegram*, September 25, 1999, Bovard, *Feeling Your Pain*, 272; Wattenberg, "Gunning For Koresh," 40.
29 Wattenberg, "Gunning For Koresh," 40.
30 Ibid.
31 Ibid.

32 Ibid.
33 Limbaugh, *Absolute Power*, 23-24.
34 Federal News Service, "Bentsen Insists Siege Was Justices Responsibility," *Washington Times*, July 22, 1995; Bovard, *Feeling Your Pain*, 272.
35 Kopel and Blackman, *No More Wacos*, 229; Limbaugh, *Absolute Power*, 24.
36 James Bovard, "Hear No Evil," *American Spectator*, January 1996, 43.
37 Pierre Thomas, "Waco Probe Faults ATF In Raid," *Washington Post*, September 30, 1993; Limbaugh, *Absolute Power*, 25.
38 Waco: The Inside Story, *Frontline*, 1995.
39 "Joint Hearing of the Crime Subcommittee of the House Judiciary Committee and the National Security, International Affairs and Criminal Justice Subcommittee of the House Government Reform and Oversight Committee, Subject: Review of Siege of Branch Davidians' Compound in Waco, Texas," Federal News Service, July 25, 1995; David Wise and Lorraine Adams, "FBI Produces New Waco Documents; Logs Detail Aggressive Federal Tactics," *Washington Post*, October 8, 1999; Bovard, *Feeling Your Pain*, 273.
40 Limbaugh, *Absolute Power*, 26.
41 Ibid.
42 Kopel and Blackman, *No More Wacos*, 137; Limbaugh, *Absolute Power*, 27-28.
43 Ibid, 138; Ibid, 28.
44 Jerry Seper and Laurie Kellman, "Waco Slaughter Comes Under Scrutiny of House," *Washington Times*, July 17, 1995.
45 Reavis, *The Ashes Of Waco*, 256; Limbaugh, *Absolute Power*, 29.
46 Lee Hancock, "Koresh Vowed Not To Give In," *Dallas Morning News*, April 21, 1993; Limbaugh, *Absolute Power*, 30.
47 Jerry Seper, "White House Supports Call For Outside Probe of Waco," *Washington Times*, September 2, 1999.
48 Seper and Kellman, "Waco Slaughter Comes Under Scrutiny Of House."
49 David Thibodeau and Leon Whiteson, *A Place Called Waco: A Survivor's Story* (New York: Public Affairs, 1999), 247; Limbaugh, *Absolute Power*, 31.
50 Kopel and Blackman, *No More Wacos*, 162; Limbaugh, *Absolute Power*, 31-32.
51 Memo quoted in "Joint Hearing of the Crime Subcommittee of the House Judiciary Committee and the National Security, International Affairs and Criminal Justice Subcommittee of the House Government Reform and Oversight Committee, Subject: Review of Siege of Branch Davidians' Compound in Waco, Texas," Federal News Service, July 31, 1995. Hereinafter, *House Report*; Bovard, *Feeling Your Pain*, 274-275, 277; Seper and Kellman, "Waco Slaughter Comes Under Scrutiny Of House"; Gary Aldrich, "An FBI Man's View Of Waco," *Human Events*, December 10, 1999, 7; Reavis, *The Ashes of Waco*, 277; Limbaugh, *Absolute Power*, 32.
52 Jerry Seper, "FBI Used Chemical Banned for War, Cult's Children Faced Hell," *Washington Times*, April 22, 1993; Thibodeau and Whiteson, A Place Called Waco. At the end of this well-reviewed book, survivor Thibodeau lists the names and ethnicity of all eighty-six victims.; Jack Cashill, *Ron Brown's Body: How One Man's Death Saved the Clinton Presidency and Hillary's Future* (Nashville: Thomas Nelson Pubilshers, 2004), 106.
53 Seper, "FBI Used Chemical Banned for War, Cult's Children Faced Hell."
54 Kopel and Blackman, *No More Wacos*, 226-227; Bovard, *Feeling Your Pain*, 278.
55 Ann Devroy, "Clinton Says He Bears 'Full Responsibility' For The Outcome," *Washington Post*, April 21, 1993, A15; R. Emmett Tyrrell, Jr., *Boy Clinton: The Political Biography* (Washington, D.C.: Regnery Publishing, 1996), 250.
56 "Waco: What Went Wrong?" Transcript, ABC News, Nightline, April 19, 1993. (Emphasis added); Bovard, *Feeling Your Pain*, 278-279.

57   Paul Craig Roberts, "Above the Smoke and Stir," *Washington Times*, April 22, 1993; Elizabeth Drew, *On The Edge: The Clinton Presidency* (New York: Touchstone, 1994), 132.
58   Michael Hedges, FBI Used Chemical Banned For War, Search For Corpses Starts, *Washington Times*, April 22, 1993; (*Associated Press*), "White House, FBI Differ on Evidence of Abused Children," *Washington Times*, April22, 1993.
59   Drew, *On the Edge*, 133.
60   "President Bill Clinton, News Conference, White House Rose Garden," Federal News Service, April 20, 1993; Stephen Labaton, "Reno Contradicted in New Report on Decision to Attack Waco Cult," *New York Times*, October 9, 1993; Bovard, *Feeling Your Pain*, 280.
61   Jerry Seper, "Tragedy Blamed On Cult," *Washington Times*, October 9, 1993; Michael Isikoff, "FBI Clashed Over Waco Report Says; Attack On Davidians Draws No Criticism," *Washington Post*, October 9, 1993; *Treasury Report*, Bovard, *Feeling Your Pain*, 280.
62   Robert Jackson and Lianne Hart, "Trial Begins For 11 Davidians Charged In Waco Murder Conspiracy," *Los Angeles Times*, January 10, 1994; Bovard, *Feeling Your Pain*, 280-281.
63   Lee Hancock, "Judge Cautions Cult Lawyers about Self-Defense Claims," *Dallas Morning News*, January 11, 1994; Kopel and Blackman, *No More Wacos*, 238; Bovard, *Feeling Your Pain*, 281.
64   Hugh Aynesworth, "All Davidians Acquitted of Murder Counts, *Washington Times*, February 27, 1994; Sam Howe Verhovek, "11th In Texas Sect Are Acquitted of Key Charges," *New York Times*, February 27, 1994; Bovard, *Feeling Your Pain*, 282.
65   Paul Craig Roberts, "Cover Up from Idaho to Waco? Role for Congress," *Washington Times*, January 18, 1995.
66   Paul Bedard, "Criticism of Federal Cops Riles Clinton, *Washington Times*, July 21, 1995. "Transcript of President Clinton's Remarks on 60 Minutes," U.S. Newswire, April 24, 1995; Bovard, *Feeling Your Pain*, 283.
67   James Bovard, "Not So Wacko," New Republic, May 15, 1995; Joyce Price, "Rubin Fires Early Shot at Waco Hearings," *Washington Times*, July 6, 1995; Bovard, *Feeling Your Pain*, 283-284.
68   Editorial, "Janet Reno, Torchbearer," *Washington Times*, May 1, 1997; Suzanne Fields, "The Unlearned Lessons of the Waco Tragedy," *Washington Times*, May 4, 1995; Bovard, *Feeling Your Pain*, 285.
69   Rowan Scarborough, "Former Officials Clear Commandos at Waco," *Washington Times*, September 2, 1999; James Bovard, "Waco Returns," *American Spectator*, December 1999/January 2000, 76-77.
70   Bovard, "Waco Returns, 77.
71   Jerry Seper, "2nd Infrared-Evidence Expert Attests to FBI Gunfire at Waco," *Washington Times*, October 7, 1999.
72   Ibid.
73   " 'Chinagate' Fundraiser Feared Clintons Would Murder Him," www.*worldnetdaily.com*, February 23, 2017.
74   Jerry Seper, "Danforth Clears Government in Raid on Davidians," *Washington Times*, July 21, 2000.
75   Bovard, *Feeling Your Pain*, 289.

ELEVEN: *RUBY RIDGE*

1   "Remarks on the Assault Weapons Ban," *Public Papers of the Presidents*, April 6, 1998; James Bovard, *Feeling Your Pain: The Explosion and Abuse of Government Power in the Clinton-Gore Years* (New York: St. Martin's Press, 2000), 291.
2   Ibid.
3   Jerry Seper, "Freeh Again Clears FBI of Misconduct in Siege," *Washington Times*, February 15, 1995; Senate Committee on the Judiciary, "*Ruby Ridge* Report of the Subcommittee on Terrorism,

Technology and Government Information," Report 95-S522-4, December 1995; Bovard, *Feeling Your Pain*, 291-292.
4   Alan W. Bock, "Ambush at *Ruby Ridge*: How Government Agents Set Randy Weaver Up and Took His Family Down," *Reason.com*, October 1, 1993.
5   Jerry Seper, "Waco Plan Almost Used in Idaho," *Washington Times*, August 24, 1995.
6   Editorial, "The Senate *Ruby Ridge* Hearings," *Washington Times*, September 6, 1995; "Department of *Justice Report* Regarding Internal Investigation of Shootings at *Ruby Ridge*, Idaho, During Arrest of Randy Weaver," Released Through Lexis Counsel Connect/*American Lawyer* Media, June 1995. Hereinafter *Justice Report*; Bovard, *Feeling Your Pain*, 292.
7   Ibid; Ibid; (*Associated Press*), "FBI Admits Photos of Idaho Scenes Were Staged," *Los Angeles Times*, May 28, 1993.
8   Laurie Kellman, U.S. to Pay $3.1 Million to Weavers," *Washington Times*, August 16, 1995; Jim Fisher, "Weaver Case: More comeuppance For The FBI," *Lewiston (Idaho) Morning Tribune*, November 1, 1993, Bovard, *Feeling Your Pain*, 292.
9   Kellman, "U.S. to Pay $3.1 Million to Weavers"; *Justice Report*; David Johnston, "U.S. Won't Charge FBI's Sniper in Siege," *New York Times*, December 8, 1994; Author James Bovard interview with investigative journalist Greg Rushford, November 7, 1999. Rushford wrote about a number of OPR cover-ups while working for the *Legal Times* from 1986 to 1994. See also, U.S. General Accounting Office, "Department of Justice: Office of Professional Responsibility's Case Handling Procedures," March 1995; Bovard, *Feeling Your Pain*, 292-293.
10 Federal Bureau of Investigation National Press Office, "FBI Director Disciplines FBI Employees in Connection With *Ruby Ridge* Incident," U.S. Newswire, January 6, 1995; Bovard, *Feeling Your Pain*, 293.
11 Federal Bureau of Investigation National Press Office," FBI Director Disciplines FBI Employees in Connection With *Ruby Ridge* Incident," U.S. Newswire, January 6, 1995; David Johnston, "FBI Chief Reprimands Officials On Their Role in a 1992 Idaho Raid," *New York Times*, January 7, 1995; Jerry Seper, "Freeh Again Clears FBI Of Misconduct In Siege," *Washington Times*, February 15, 1995; Bovard, *Feeling Your Pain*, 293.
12 Federal Bureau of Investigation National Press Office, "FBI Director Disciplines FBI Employees in Connection with *Ruby Ridge* Incident," U.S. Newswire, January 6, 1995; Author James Bovard interview with Chuck Peterson, January 9, 1995; Author James Bovard interview Dean Miller; Bovard, *Feeling Your Pain*, 294.
13 James Bovard, "No Accountability At The FBI," *Wall Street Journal*, January 10, 1995; James Bovard, letter to the editor, *Wall Street Journal*, February 27, 1995; *Ruby Ridge*, Senate Judiciary Committee, Senate Report 95-S522-4, December 1995; Michael Sniffen, "FBI's No. 2 Official Among 12 Disciplined In Idaho Shootout," (*Associated Press*), January 6, 1995; Bovard, *Feeling your Pain*, 294.
14 Sniffen, "FBI's No. 2 Official Among 12 Disciplined in Idaho Shootout."Bovard, *Feeling Your Pain*, 294.
15 Bovard, *Feeling Your Pain*, 294.
16 Editorial, "*Ruby Ridge* And Waco," *Washington Post*, January 9, 1995; Editorial, "The Guns Of Waco And *Ruby Ridge*," *New York Times*, July 14, 1995; Bovard, *Feeling Your Pain*, 294-295.
17 *Justice Report*; Bovard, *Feeling Your Pain*, 295-296.
18 Pierre Thomas and Serge F. Kovaleski, "Justice Dept. Pledges Thorough Probe of FBI Conduct in 1992 Idaho Siege," *Washington Post*, July 14, 1995; Bovard, *Feeling Your Pain*, 296.
19 Kellman, "U.S. to Pay $3.1 Million to Weavers."
20 Jerry Seper, "Hill Panel Opens Hearings Today on Idaho Siege," *Washington Times*, September 6, 1995.
21 "Hearing of the Terrorism, Technology and Government Information Subcommittee of the Senate Judiciary Committee, Subject: *Ruby Ridge*," Federal News Service, September 7, 1995; Bovard, *Feeling Your Pain*, 297.

22 Senate Judiciary Committee, *Ruby Ridge*, Senate Report 95-S522-4, December 1995; Bovard, *Feeling Your Pain*, 298.
23 James Bovard, "Another Justice Cover-Up: *Ruby Ridge* Goes the Way of the Fundraising Scandals," *American Spectator*, December 1997, p.59; Bovard, *Feeling Your Pain*, 301.
24 Jerry Seper, "FBI Man Gets 18 Months in Prison," *Washington Times*, October 11, 1997.
25 "Feds Pay $380,000 to *Ruby Ridge* Victim, *Washington Times*, September 23, 2000.
26 David Limbaugh, *Absolute Power: The Legacy of Corruption in the Clinton-Reno Justice Department* (Washington, D.C.: Regnery Publishing, 2001), 34.

TWELVE: TRAVEL OFFICE FIRINGS

1 David R. Sands, "Senate Democrats Unable to Block Legal Fees For Dale," *Washington Times*, September 13, 1996.
2 David Brock, "The Travelgate Cover-Up," *American Spectator*, June 1994, 30.
3 Toni Locy, "For the White House Travel Office, a Two-Year Trip of Trouble," *Washington Post*, February 27, 1995.
4 Brock, "The Travelgate Cover-Up," 31.
5 Ibid.
6 Ibid.
7 Ibid.
8 Susan Schmidt and Toni Locy, "Papers Detail Clinton Friend's Contract Push." *Washington Post*, October 25, 1995; Brock, "The Travelgate Cover-Up," 31.
9 Ibid, 32.
10 Lead Editorial, "The Travel Office Hearings," *Washington Times*, November 3, 1995.
11 Brock, "The Travelgate Cover-Up," 32.
12 Ann Devroy and Ruth Marcus, "Clinton Friend's Memo Sought Business," *Washington Post*, May 22, 1993.
13 Brock, "The Travelgate Cover-Up," 32.
14 Ibid.
15 (*Associated Press*), "Partner Urged Clinton Friend to Seek Business with White House," *Washington Times*, January 13, 1996; David Brock, *The Seduction of Hillary Rodham* (New York: Free Press Paperbacks, 1997), 369.
16 Brock, "The Travelgate Cover-Up," 32.
17 Carl Bernstein, *A Woman in Charge: The Life of Hillary Rodham Clinton* (New York: Alfred A. Knopf, 2007), pp. 324-325; Brock, "The Travelgate Cover-Up," 32.
18 Devroy and Marcus, "Clinton Friend's Memo Sought Business."
19 Brock, "The Travelgate Cover-Up, 33.
20 Ibid.
21 David Limbaugh, *Absolute Power: The Legacy of Corruption in the Clinton-Reno Justice Department* (Washington, D.C.: Regnery Publishing, 2001), 67.
22 Ann Devroy and Ruth Marcus, "Clinton Friend's Memo Sought Business," *Washington Post*, May 22, 1993; Brock, *The Seduction of Hillary Rodham*, 373.
23 Ibid, 374.
24 (*Associated Press*), "Clinton Had Knowledge of Travelgate, Papers Say," *Washington Times*, January 12, 1996.
25 Rebecca Borders, "Bill's Cousin Cornelius?" *American Spectator*, May 1996, 27; Joyce Milton, *The First Partner: Hillary Rodham Clinton* (New York: William and Morrow and Company, 1999), 289.
26 Borders, "Bill's Cousin Cornelius?" 27.
27 Locy, "For White House Travel Office, a Two-Year Trip of Trouble; Brock, "The Travelgate Cover-Up," 34.

28   Locy, "For White House Travel Office, a Two-Year Trip of Trouble."
29   Mark Levin, "Travelgate and the FBI," *Washington Times*, January 26, 1996; Brock, "The Travelgate Cover-Up," 34.
30   Mark Levin, "From Watergate to Travelgate," *Washington Times*, November 17, 1995; Brock, "The Travelgate Cover-Up," 34.
31   Brock, "The Travelgate Cover-Up," 34.
32   Ibid, 34-35.
33   Ann Devroy, "Clinton Apologizes For 'Glitches' in White House Handling of Events," *Washington Post*, May 28, 1993; Brock, "The Travelgate Cover-Up," 35.
34   Brock, "The Travelgate Cover-Up," 35-36.
35   Ibid, 36.
36   Byron York, "Have GAO Will Travel," *American Spectator*, December 1994, 21.
37   Lead Editorial, "A Textbook on the Abuse of Power," *Washington Times*, September 21, 1996; Brock, "The Trravelgate-Cover-Up, 36.
38   Locy, "For White House Travel Office, a Two-Year Trip of Trouble."
39   Bernstein, *A Woman in Charge*, 326.
40   Brock, "The Travel Office Cover-Up," 36.
41   Ibid.
42   Ibid.
43   Mark Levin, "Anyone Remember Travelgate?" *Washington Times*, March 11, 1994; Brock, "The Travelgate Cover-Up," 36.
44   Brock, "The Travelgate Cover-Up," 36.
45   Laurie Kellman, "Travelgate Signs Point to Hillary," *Washington Times*, October 25, 1995.
46   Brock, "The Travelgate Cover-Up," 36.
47   Ibid, 36-37.
48   Brock, The Seduction of Hillary Clinton, 378.
49   Locy, "For White House Travel Office, a Two-Year Trip of Trouble"; Brock, "The Travelgate Cover-Up," 37; Toni Locy, "Foster Journal Shows Worry About Travel Office," *Washington Post*, July 29, 1995.
50   Frank J. Murray and Ronald A. Taylor, "Hillary Tied to Firings," *Washington Times*, July 3, 1993.
51   Brock, *The Seduction of Hillary Rodham*, 379.
52   Ibid.
53   Locy, "For White House Travel Office, a Two-Year Trip of Trouble"; Lead Editorial, "The Travel Office Seven," *Washington Times*, January 26, 1996.
54   Ann Devroy, "Clinton Apologizes for 'Glitches' in White House Handling Of Events," *Washington Post*, May 28, 1993.
55   Frank J. Murray, "White House Travel Staff Fired for Bad Accounting," *Washington Times*, May 20, 1993; Byron York, "Travelgate Survivors," *American Spectator*, November 1995, 23.
56   Bernstein, *A Woman in Charge*, 328.
57   Ann Devroy, "Volunteer Travel Aide Got $1,400; White House Calls Fee a 'Mistake,' " *Washington Post*, June 2, 1993.
58   Frank J. Murray, "Travel Firm Sent Packing," *Washington Times*, May 22, 1993; Devroy and Marcus, "Clinton Friend's Memo Sought Business."
59   Byron York, "The Truth about Bill's Lies," *American Spectator*, March 1998, 30.
60   (*Associated Press*), "Clinton Had Knowledge of Travelgate, Papers Say," *Washington Times*, January 12, 1996.
61   Paul Bedard, "Treasury Probes 'Travelgate' Affair," *Washington Times*, July 16, 1993; Brock, "The Travelgate Cover-Up," 78; Dale McFeatters, "Travel Office Encore Pending?" *Washington Times*, November 29, 1995.
62   Milton, *The First Partner*, 291.

63 Bernstein, *A Woman in Charge*, 329.
64 Brock, "The Travelgate Cover-Up," 80; Paul Bedard, "Treasury Probes 'Travelgate' Affairs," *Washington Times*, July 16, 1993.
65 Murray and Taylor, "Hillary Tied to Firings."
66 Paul Bedard, "White House To Hire Back 'Travelgate 5,' " *Washington Times*, August 5, 1993; Editorial, "The Clerk in the Travel Office Case," *Washington Times*, November 2, 1995.
67 Lead Editorial, "A Travel Office Bombshell," *Washington Times*, June 6, 1996; Milton, *The First Partner*, 292.
68 Paul Bedard, "Travelgate Jury Quickly Finds Dale Not Guilty," *Washington Times*, November 17, 1995.
69 Toni Locy, "Fired Travel Office Director Acquitted of Embezzlement; Dale Charged after Ouster from White House," *Washington Post*, November 17, 1995; Limbaugh, *Absolute Power*, 81.

THIRTEEN: FOREIGN POLICY STUMBLES

1 Paul Bedard, "Bush Aides Rebut Bragging On Foreign Policy," *Washington Times*, October 15, 1993.
2 Ibid.
3 Rich Lowry, *Legacy: Paying the Price for The Clinton Years* (Washington, D.C.: Regnery Publishing, 2003), 216.
4 Frank J. Murray, "Aristide Said To Be Angry About Terms," *Washington Times*, September 20, 1994; Jack Cashill, *Ron Brown's Body: How One Man's Death Saved the Clinton Presidency and Hillary's Future* (Nashville: Thomas Nelson, 2004), 31-32.
5 Cashill, *Ron Brown's Body*, 32.
6 "Human Rights Section of the "1992 Democratic Party Platform: A New Covenant with the American People"; Cashill, *Ron Brown's Body*, 32.
7 DeWayne Wickam, *Bill Clinton and Black America* (New York: Ballantine Books, 2002), 103; Cashill, *Ron Brown's Body*, 32.
8 R. Emmett Tyrrell, Jr., *Boy Clinton: The Political Biography* (Washington, D.C.: Regnery Publishing, 1996), 244.
9 Murray, "Aristide Said to Be Angry about Terms."
10 Ibid.
11 Harry G. Summers Jr., "Pitfalls of Persistence in Haitian Policy," *Washington Times*, September 15, 1994.
12 Ed McCullough (*Associated Press*), "Haitian Mob Blocks Docking of U.S. Ship," *Washington Times*, October 12, 1993.
13 Ibid.
14 Elizabeth Drew, *On the Edge: The Clinton Presidency* (New York: Touchstone, 1994), 334; Ed McCullough (*Associated Press*), "Haitian Militants Force U.S. Troops to Retreat," *Washington Times*, October 13, 1993.
15 Drew, *On The Edge*, 334.
16 Murray, "Aristide Said to Be Angry about Terms."
17 Kevin Merida, "Hill's Black Caucus Faults U.S. Policy on Haiti, Pressed for Aristide Return," *Washington Post*, March 24, 1994.
18 Summers, "Pitfalls of Persistence in Haitian Policy."
19 Frank J. Murray, " 'Your *Time* Is Up,' Clinton Tells Haitian Junta; TV Speech Sets No Deadline," *Washington Times*, September 16, 1994.
20 Philip Smucker, "Haitians Flee As Carter Arrives," *Washington Times*, September 18, 1994.
21 Frank J. Murray, "Carter Bargained with Cedras' Wife to Throw in Towel," *Washington Times*, September 20, 1994; Rowan Scarborough, "Carter's Action in Haiti Not What Clinton Expected," *Washington Times*, September 20, 1994.

22 Scarborough, "Carter's Actions in Haiti Not What Clinton Expected."
23 Frederick H. Fleitz, Jr., *Peacekeeping Fiascos of the 1990s* (Westport, CT: Praeger, 2002), 131; Donald Kagan and Frederick W. Kagan, *While America Sleeps* (New York: St. Martin's Press, 2000), 328; Lowry, Legacy, 250.
24 Terrence P. Jeffrey, "Gore's 'Ill-Considered' Somalia Story," *Human Events*, October 20, 2000, 7.
25 Gary T. Dempsey with Roger W. Fontaine, *Fools Errands* (Washington, D.C.: The Cato Institute, 2001), 25, 32; Lowry, Legacy, 250-251.
26 Author Rich Lowry interview with Tony Lake; Kagan and Kagan, *While America Sleeps*, 329-331; Lowry, Legacy, 251.
27 Jeffrey, "Gore's 'Ill –Considered' Somalia Story," 7; Lt. Col. Robert "Buzz" Patterson, *Dereliction of Duty: The Eyewitness Account of How Bill Clinton Compromised America's National Security* (Washington, D.C.: Regnery Publishing, 2003), 113.
28 Drew, *On the Edge*, 158.
29 Jeffrey, "Gore's 'Ill-Considered' Somalia Story," 7.
30 Patterson, *Dereliction of Duty*, 113-114.
31 Drew, *On the Edge*, 238-239.
32 Richard Miniter, *Losing Bin Laden: How Bill Clinton's Failures Unleashed Global Terror* (Regnery Publishing, 2003), 59.
33 Ibid.
34 Mark Bowden, *Black Hawk Down* (New York: Penguin Books, 1999), 96, Lowry, Legacy, 252.
35 Drew, *On the Edge*, 324.
36 Yossef Bodansky, *Bin Laden: The Man Who Declared War on America* (Roseville, CA: Prima Forum, 1999), 81.
37 Ibid, 82.
38 Ibid.
39 Jeffrey, " 'Ill-Considered Somalia Story," 7; Bill Gertz, "Aspin's Decision on Tanks Was Political," *Washington Times*, October 3, 1995.
40 Gertz, "Aspin's Decision on Tanks Was Political."
41 Ibid.
42 Bodansky, *Bin Laden*, 82.
43 Ibid.
44 Ibid, 83.
45 Ibid, 84-85.
46 Ibid, 85.
47 Miniter, *Losing Bin Laden*, 68.
48 Drew, *On the Edge*, 335.
49 Dempsey with Fontaine, Fool's Errand, 25, 41; Lowry Legacy, 254.
50 Patterson, *Dereliction of Duty*, 135-136.
51 Ibid, 115-116.
52 Lowry, Legacy, 267.
53 Dempsey with Fontaine, *Fools Errands*, 137; David Halberstam, *War in a Time of Peace* (New York: Touchstone, 2002), Lowry, Legacy, 267-268.
54 Bodansky, *Bin Laden*, 297.
55 Boris Johnson, "Cold War Warriors Scorns 'New Minority,' " *The Daily Telegraph* (London), June 28, 1999.
56 "Remarks Announcing Airstrikes Against Serbian Targets in the Federal Republic of Yugoslavia (Serbia and Montenegro)," *Public Papers of the Presidents*, March 24, 1999, p.513; John Pilger, "Revealed: The Amazing NATO Plan, Tabled at Rambouillet, To Occupy Yugoslavia," *New Statesman*, May 17, 1999; Bovard, *Feeling Your Pain*, 327.
57 Terence Jeffrey, "Anti-terrorism Acts Ignored?" *Washington Times*, January 21, 2006.

58   "Support Troops, Deplore War," *Human Events*, April 2, 1999, 8.
59   Richard Boudreaux, "Civilian Deaths in Airstrikes Erode NATO Credibility," *Los Angeles Times*, May 31, 1999; Bovard, *Feeling Your Pain*, 329-330.
60   "Civilian Deaths in the NATO Air Campaign, *Human Rights Watch*, February 7, 2000; Bovard, *Feeling Your Pain*, 330.
61   Alberto R. Coll, "Kosovo and the Moral Burdens of Power," in *War Over Kosovo*, ed. Andrew J. Bacevich and Eliot A. Cohen (New York: Columbia University Press, 2001), 131; Lowry, Legacy, 270.
62   Conservative Forum, George E. Rubin, New York, N.Y., *Human Events*, April 23, 1999, 25.
63   Rep. Christopher Cox, "U.S. Taxpayers Are Financing North Korea's Nuclear Nightmare, *Human Events*, November 26, 1999, 8.
64   Charles Krauthammer, "Capitulation in Korea," *Washington Post*, January 7, 1994.
65   Gertz, *Betrayal*, 114.
66   Kagan and Kagan, *While America Sleeps*, 355; Michael J. Mazarr, *North Korea and the Bomb* (New York: St. Martin's Press, 1995), 150; Lowry, Legacy, 239.
67   Kagan and Kagan, *While America Sleeps*, 357-358; Lowry, Legacy, 239.
68   Krauthammer, "Capitulation in Korea."
69   Ibid.
70   Gertz, *Betrayal*, 114.
71   Ibid, 115.
72   Ibid, 115-116.
73   James Sterngold, "South Korea President Lashes Out at U.S.," *New York Times*, October 8, 1994.
74   Scott Park, "Clinton's Dollars Haven't Changed North Korea," *Human Events*, July 16, 1999, 4.
75   Ibid.
76   Cox, "U.S. Taxpayers are Financing North Korea's Nuclear Nightmare," 26.
77   Gertz, *Betrayal*, 109.
78   Ibid, 117.
79   Ibid.
80   Ibid.
81   Ibid.
82   Philip Sehon, "Suspected North Korean Atom Site is Empty, U.S. Finds," *New York Times*, May 28, 1999; Nicholas Eberstadt, "U.S. Aid Feeds North Korean's Nuclear Designs," AEI *On the Issues*, April 1999, Lowry, Legacy, 417.
83   Cox, "U.S. Taxpayers are Financing North Korea's Nuclear Nightmare," 8.
84   Gertz, *Betrayal*, 109.
85   Rep. Chris Cox, "End Clinton's Aid to North Korea," *Human Events*, October 28, 2002, 6.
86   Ibid.
87   Scott Park, "Clinton's Dollars Haven't Changed North Korea," *Human Events*, July 16, 1999, 4.
88   Kenneth R. Timmerman, "Bill Perry's Asian Portfolio," *American Spectator*, November 1997, 56.
89   Ibid.
90   "Clinton's North Korea Legacy," *The Limbaugh Letter*, August 2006, 13.
91   Ibid.
92   Gertz, *Betrayal*, 79.
93   Fleitz, *Peacekeeping Fiascos of the 1990s*, 150-151; Lowry, Legacy, 255-256.
94   Ibid, 151; Ibid, 256.
95   John Corry, "A Formula for Genocide," *American Spectator*, September 1998, 26.
96   Fleitz, *Peacekeeping Fiascos of the 1990s*, 152; Lowry, Legacy, 256.
97   Michael N. Barnett, *Eyewitnesses to Genocide* (Ithaca, NY: Cornell University Press, 2002), 98-99; Lowry, Legacy, 257.
98   Corry, "A Formula for Genocide," 26.

99 Corry, "A Formula for Genocide," 26; Barnett, *Eyewitness to Genocide*, 144; Lowry, Legacy, 258-259.
100 Corry, "A Formula for Genocide," 26.
101 Clarence Page, "Rwanda's Lesson: 'Never Again,' " *Washington Times*, April 10, 2004.
102 Ibid.

FOURTEEN: HEALTH CARE REFORM

1 Rich Lowry, *Legacy: Paying the Price For the Clinton Years* (Washington, D.C.: Regnery Publishing, 2003), 108.
2 Elizabeth Drew, *On the Edge: The Clinton Presidency* (New York: Touchstone, 1994), 190.
3 Haynes Johnson and David S. Broder, *The System* (New York: Little, Brown and Company, 1996), 105; Drew, *On the Edge*, 190.
4 Drew, *On the Edge*, 191.
5 Johnson and Broder, *The System*, 90; Rich Lowry, *Legacy: Paying the Price for the Clinton Years* (Washington, D.C.: Regnery Publishing, 2003), 107.
6 David Brock, *The Seduction of Hillary Rodham*, (New York: Free Press Paperbacks, 1997), 360.
7 Ibid.
8 Judi Hasson and Judy Keen, "First Lady Trying to Minimize Rift in Health Reform," *USA Today*, June 24, 1993.
9 Carl Bernstein, *A Woman in Charge: The Life of Hillary Rodham Clinton* (New York: Alfred A. Knopf, 2007), 346.
10 Bernstein, *A Woman in Charge*, 394; Drew, *On the Edge*, 302-303.
11 Joyce Milton, *The First Partner: Hillary Rodham Clinton* (New York: William Morrow and Company, 1999), 305.
12 Frank J. Murray, "First Lady Blasts Insurance Firms' Attack on Plan," *Washington Times*, November 2, 1993; Milton, *The First Partner*, 307.
13 Grace-Marie Arnett, "Cops and Doctors: It May Take a National Police Force to Monitor the Clinton Health Plan," *Washington Post*, December 19, 1993; Milton, *The First Partner*, 308.
14 Mona Charen, "Beyond Spin Control ... Rhetoric Gaposis," *Washington Times*, March 11, 1994.
15 Bayer, "Hill Figures Tough Way Ain't No Way to Treat a First Lady"; Barbara Olson, *Hell to Pay: The Unfolding Story of Hillary Rodham Clinton* (Washington, D.C.: Regnery Publishing, 1999), 255.
16 Elizabeth McCaughey, "Health Plan's Devilish Details," *Wall Street Journal*, September 30, 1993.
17 Clay Chandler, "Health Care Costs a Long-Term Headache," *Washington Post*, October 17, 1993.
18 Arnett, "Cops and Dollars: It May Take a National Police Force to Monitor the Clinton Health Plan."
19 Milton, *The First Partner*, 274.
20 Karen Riley, "Chamber Deserts Clinton," *Washington Times*, February 4, 1994; Donald Lambro, "Cost of Clinton Health Plan Put at 2 Million Jobs," *Washington Times*, February 23, 1994.
21 "Flashback: The 1994 Healthcare 'Debate'" *Sweetness & Light*, July 23, 2009.
22 Ibid.
23 Drew, *On the Edge*, 434.
24 "Flashback: The 1994 Healthcare 'Debate.'"
25 Ibid.
26 Paul Bedard, "Clinton Hides Behind Truman," *Washington Times*, July 31, 1994.
27 Ibid.
28 "Flashback: The 1994 Healthcare 'Debate.' "
29 Ibid.
30 Ibid.

31 J. Jennings Moss and Major Garrett, "Health Reform is Dead," *Washington Times*, September 27, 1994.
32 (*Associated Press*), "Hillary Out as Health Care Coordinator," *Washington Times*, November 3, 1994.

FIFTEEN: 1993 STUMBLES PART II

1   William Raspberry, "First Things First," *Washington Post*, May 28, 1993.
2   Lance Gay (Scripps Howard News Service), "Air Base Stands by Clinton-Bashing General," *Washington Times*, June 10, 1993; John Lancaster, "Accused of Ridiculing Clinton, General Faces Air Force Probe," *Washington Post*, June 8, 1993.
3   Lancaster, "Accused of Ridiculing Clinton, General Faces Air Force Probe."
4   Gay, "Air Base Stands by Clinton-Bashing General."
5   (Reuters News Agency), "Ridicule Story Backed Up by Military Probe," *Washington Times*, June 19, 1993; John Lancaster, "General Who Mocked Clinton Set to Retire," *Washington Post*, June 19, 1993.
6   Bill Gertz, "General Who Ridiculed Clinton Fined, Forced Out," *Washington Times*, June 19, 1993.
7   Laura A. Kiernan, "Running on TV: Clinton Makeup Job," *Boston Globe*, May 27, 1993; R. Emmett Tyrrell, Jr., *Boy Clinton: The Political Biography* (Washington, D.C.: Regnery Publishing, 1996), 257-258.
8   Ibid, Ibid.
9   Janet Naylor, "Many Veterans Refuse to Hail the Chief," *Washington Times*, June 1, 1993.
10 David Clayton Carrad, "Hill 1969," *American Spectator*, August 1993, 46-47.
11 Ibid.
12 Ibid.
13 Ruth Marcus, "Jeers, Cheers Greet Clinton at the Wall," *Washington Post*, June 1, 1993.
14 Paul Greenberg, "Watching, Wondering and Wincing," *Washington Times*, June 4, 1993.
15 Paul Bedard, "Clinton Surge to Center Leaves the Skeptics Cold," *Washington Times*, June 6, 1993; Tyrrell, *Boy Clinton*, 260.
16 Tyrrell, *Boy Clinton*, 260.
17 Paul Kengor, *God and Hillary Clinton: A Spiritual Life* (New York: HarperCollins, 2007), 122.
18 George Weigel, *Witness to Hope: The Biography of Pope John Paul II* (New York: HarperCollins, 2001), 681; Kengor, *God and Hillary Clinton*, 122.
19 Transcript of August 12, 1993, remarks by Pope John Paul II. Also see: Weigel, *Witness to Hope*, 681; Kengor, *God and Hillary Clinton*, 122-123.

SIXTEEN: VINCE FOSTER

1   From Combined Dispatches, "Key Clinton Aide, Friend Kills Self," *Washington Times*, July 21, 1993.
2   From Combined Dispatches, "Key Clinton Aide, Friend Kills Self," *Washington Times*, July 21, 1993; Frank J. Murray, "Close Aide's Suicide Leaves President, Staff Puzzled," *Washington Times*, July 22, 1993.
3   Statement of Elizabeth Braden Foster, May 9, 1994, 29 D-LR-35063: Federal Bureau of Investigation; also Office of the Independent Counsel, Kenneth W. Starr, "Report on the Death of Vincent Foster, Jr.," October 31, 1997; Joyce Milton, *The First Partner: Hillary Rodham Clinton* (New York: William Morrow and Company, 1999), 301-302.
4   Christopher S. Bond, "Why is Foster's Death Still a Mystery?" *Washington Times*, August 1, 1994; Milton, *The First Partner*, 294.
5   Carl Bernstein, *A Woman in Charge: The Life of Hillary Rodham Clinton* (New York: Alfred A. Knopf, 2007), 292.

6. Susan Schmidt and Charles R. Babcock, "Foster Worried About Audit on Whitewater," *Washington Post*, July 14, 1995.
7. Webb Hubbell, *Friends in High Places* (New York: William Morrow and Company, 1997), 193; Bernstein, *A Woman in Charge*, 293.
8. Rebecca Borders, "Hell to Pay," *American Spectator*, January 1997, 35.
9. (*Associated Press*), "Foster Widow Certain He Took His Life," *Washington Times*, September 4, 1995; Milton, *The First Partner*, 294-295.
10. (*Associated Press*), "Top Court Gets Plea in Foster Notes," *Washington Times*, January 7, 1998; Byron York, "The Last Testimony of Vincent Foster," *American Spectator*, June 1998, 30.
11. Michael Isikoff, "Foster Was Shopping For Private Lawyer, Probers Find," *Washington Post*, August 15, 1993.
12. Milton, *The First Partner*, 295.
13. "GOP: White House Guilty of Highly Improper Conduct," *Washington Times*, June 19, 1996.
14. Author Ambrose Evans-Pritchard confidential interview with family member; Evans-Pritchard, *The Secret Life of Bill Clinton*, 231.
15. FBI 302 report, statement of Dr. Hedaya, May 17, 1994. In the handwritten notes of the interview there are multiple references to Top Secret issues; Evans-Pritchard, *The Secret Life of Bill Clinton*, 231.
16. Evans-Pritchard, *The Secret Life of Bill Clinton*, 219.
17. SWSC deposition of Webster Hubbell, July 13, 1995; FBI 302 report, statement of Lisa Foster, April 12, 1994; Evans-Pritchard, *The Secret Life of Bill Clinton*, 223.
18. Ibid; Ibid.
19. Evans-Pritchard, *The Secret Life of Bill Clinton*, 128.
20. Jerry Seper, "Rose Staffers Say Hillary Ordered Papers Shredded," *Washington Times*, March 7, 1994.
21. Evans-Pritchard, *The Secret Life of Bill Clinton*, 247.
22. Ibid, 246.
23. Ibid, 248.
24. Ibid.
25. Evans-Pritchard, *The Secret Life of Bill Clinton*, 248; John McCaslin, "Keeping a Rumor Alive," Inside The Beltway, *Washington Times*, March 25, 1994.
26. Evans-Pritchard, *The Secret Life of Bill Clinton*, 249.
27. Richard Poe, *Hillary's Secret War: The Clinton Conspiracy to Muzzle Internet Journalists* (Nashville: WND Books, 2004), 91.
28. Author Ambrose Evans-Pritchard interview with Jane Parks, April 1994, Evans-Pritchard, *The Secret Life of Bill Clinton*, 233.
29. Evans-Pritchard, *The Secret Life of Bill Clinton*, 233, 236.
30. Poe, *Hillary's Secret War*, 92.
31. Evans-Pritchard, *The Secret Life of Bill Clinton*, 249
32. Milton, *The First Partner*, 301.
33. Lisa Foster went through the accounts later and claimed that the credit union had made a mistake with every withdrawal. The sums were actually $35 each. This does not pass the smell test. Foster had $292 in cash in his wallet when he died; Evans-Pritchard, *The Secret Life of Bill Clinton*, 223-224.
34. Evans-Pritchard, *The Secret Life of Bill Clinton*, 231.
35. David Von Drehle, "The Crumbling of a Pillar in Washington," *Washington Post*, August 15, 1993.
36. Author Ambrose Evans-Pritchard interview with Alice Sessions, February 1995; Evans-Pritchard, *The Secret Life of Bill Clinton*, xii, 129; Michael Hedges, "Sessions Says White House 'Compromised' Foster Probe," *Washington Times*, February 4, 1994.

37 Evans-Pritchard, *The Secret Life of Bill Clinton*, 129.
38 FBI 302 report, statement of Marsha Scott, June 9, 1994; Evans-Pritchard, *The Secret Life of Bill Clinton*, 224.
39 FBI 302 report, statement of Linda Tripp, April 12, 1994; Evans-Pritchard, *The Secret Life of Bill Clinton*, 224.
40 Evans-Pritchard, *The Secret Life of Bill Clinton*, 224.
41 SWSC ancillary documents; Evans-Pritchard, *The Secret Life of Bill Clinton*, 224.
42 Frank J. Murray, "Clinton Called Foster Day Before His Suicide," *Washington Times*, July 28, 1993; Ambrose Evans-Pritchard, "A Death That Won't Die," *American Spectator*, November 1995, 35.
43 Von Drehle, "The Crumbling of a Pillar in Washington."
44 Park Police interview with Lisa Foster, July 29, 1993; Evans-Pritchard, *The Secret Life of Bill Clinton*, 227.
45 Ambrose Evans-Pritchard confidential interview with a family member; Evans-Pritchard, *The Secret Life of Bill Clinton*, 227.
46 Reed Irvine/Joe Goulden, "Unremitting Trail of Clues in the Foster Suicide," *Washington Times*, December 11, 1993; Von Drehle, "The Crumbling of a Pillar in Washington."
47 Jerry Seper, "Subdued Foster Spent Final Days Tidying Affairs," *Washington Times*, July 1, 1994.
48 Seper, "Subdued Foster Spent Final Days Tidying Affairs"; Milton, *The First Partner*, 301.
49 Evans-Pritchard, "A Death That Won't Die," p.35; Evans-Pritchard, *The Secret Life of Bill Clinton*, 129.
50 "Here Lies Kenneth Starr: Executive Summary," *AIM Report*, vol. xxvi, no. 19, October 1997, p.2; Poe, *Hillary's Secret War*, 104.
51 Christopher Ruddy, "Foster Case: Park Witness to Appear Before Starr's Grand Jury," *Pittsburgh Tribune-Review*, October 29, 1995; Ambrose Evans-Pritchard, "Death in the Park: Is This the Killer?" *The Sunday Telegraph*, October 22, 1995.
52 Ruddy, "Foster Case: Park Witness to Appear Before Starr's Grand Jury."
53 Michael Hedges, "Foster Letter Disputed," *Washington Times*, February 5, 1994.
54 John McCaslin, "No Smoking Gun," Inside the Beltway, *Washington Times*, April 5, 1994; Evans-Pritchard, *The Secret Life of Bill Clinton*, 120.
55 Evans-Pritchard, *The Secret Life of Bill Clinton*, 120.
56 McCaslin, "No Smoking Gun"; Evans-Pritchard, *The Secret Life of Bill Clinton*, 120.
57 McCaslin, "No Smoking Gun."
58 Christopher Ruddy, "Foster's Death Site Strongly Disputed," *Pittsburgh Tribune-Review*, January 25, 1995.
59 Christopher Ruddy, "Foster Eyewitnesses Ignored," *Pittsburgh Tribune-Review*, June 14, 1995; Evans-Pritchard, "Death in the Park: Is This the Killer?"
60 Ruddy, "Foster Eyewitnesses Ignored."
61 Evans-Pritchard, *The Secret Life of Bill Clinton*, 155; Evans-Pritchard, "Death in the Park: Is This the Killer?"
62 Fiske Report, p.11: Exhibit I, FBI documents; Evans-Pritchard, *The Secret Life of Bill Clinton*, 157.
63 Evans-Pritchard, *The Secret Life of Bill Clinton*, 156.
64 Evans-Pritchard, *The Secret Life of Bill Clinton*, 155-156.
65 Poe, *Hillary's Secret War*; 104.
66 "Here Lies Kenneth Starr: Executive Summary"; Poe, *Hillary's Secret War*, 104.
67 Evans-Pritchard, *The Secret Life of Bill Clinton*, 124.
68 Green Books: Deposition of Kevin Fornshill, July 12, 1994; Evans-Pritchard, *The Secret Life of Bill Clinton*, 124.
69 Evans-Pritchard, *The Secret Life of Bill Clinton*, 124; Jerry Seper, "Park Police Officer Files Suit Over Article on Foster's Death," *Washington Times*, September 1, 1994.

70	Evans-Pritchard, *The Secret Life of Bill Clinton*, 179.
71	Evans-Pritchard, *The Secret Life of Bill Clinton*, 124-125; Christopher Ruddy, "Other Witnesses Still Unexplained," *Pittsburgh Tribune-Review*, June 14, 1995.
72	Ruddy, "Other Witnesses Still Unexplained."
73	Ibid.
74	Paul Craig Roberts, Lying Reprise … as the Plot Thickens," *Washington Times*, August 8, 1994; Evans-Pritchard, *The Secret Life of Bill Clinton*, 125.
75	Evans-Pritchard, *The Secret Life of Bill Clinton*, 125.
76	Michael Hedges, "Questions Cloud Ruling of Suicide in Foster's Death," *Washington Times*, January 28, 1994.
77	Ibid.
78	Green Books, p.871: Senate deposition of Richard Arthur, July 14, 1994; Evans-Pritchard, *The Secret Life of Bill Clinton*, 127.
79	Robert Bryant, "FBI Special Agent in Charge," Washington Metropolitan Office, August 10, 1993; Evans-Pritchard, *The Secret Life of Bill Clinton*, 128.
80	Evans-Pritchard, *The Secret Life of Bill Clinton*, 134.
81	Ibid, 184.
82	Christopher Ruddy, "Missing Briefcase Could Be Key in Solving Vince Foster Mystery," *Pittsburgh Tribune-Review*, June 13, 1995; Evans-Pritchard, *The Secret Life of Bill Clinton*, 184.
83	Ruddy, "Missing Briefcase Could Be Key in Solving Vince Foster Mystery."
84	Green Books, p.2517: Park Police evidence receipt; Senate deposition of Rolla; FBI 302 report, statement of Lisa Foster; Evans-Pritchard, *The Secret Life of Bill Clinton*, 180.
85	Christopher Ruddy, "Police Failed to Find Keys to Foster's Car at Park," *Pittsburgh Tribune-Review*, September 20, 1995.
86	Christopher Ruddy, "Make-Up Artist Links Clinton to Possible Cover-Up," *Pittsburgh Tribune-Review*, February 26, 1996; Evans-Pritchard, *The Secret Life of Bill Clinton*, 184-185.
87	Evans-Pritchard, *The Secret Life of Bill Clinton*, 185.
88	SWSC deposition of Betsy Pond, p.51; Evans-Pritchard, *The Secret Life of Bill Clinton*, 195.
89	SWSC deposition of Patsy Thomasson, July 25, 1995; Evans-Pritchard, *The Secret Life of Bill Clinton*, 195-197.
90	SWSC deposition of Lisa Caputo, July 10, 1995; SWSC deposition of Maggie Williams, July 7, 1995; Evans-Pritchard, *The Secret Life of Bill Clinton*, 194-195.
91	FBI 302 report, statement of Corey Ashford, April 27, 1994; Evans-Pritchard, *The Secret Life of Bill Clinton*, 144.
92	FBI 302 report, second statement of Corey Ashford, April 27, 1994; Evans-Pritchard, *The Secret Life of Bill Clinton*, 144.
93	FBI 302 report, statement of Roger Harrison, March 11, 1994; Evans-Pritchard, *The Secret Life of Bill Clinton*, 144.
94	Green Books, p.891 Arthur deposition, July 14, 1994; Evans-Pritchard, *The Secret Life of Bill Clinton*, 144.
95	Green Books, p.885 Arthur deposition, July 14, 1994; Evans-Pritchard, *The Secret Life of Bill Clinton*, 144.
96	Green Books, p.996, deposition of Sgt. George Gonzalez, July 20, 1994; Evans-Pritchard, *The Secret Life of Bill Clinton*, 144.
97	Evans-Pritchard, *The Secret Life of Bill Clinton*, 145.
98	Christopher Ruddy, "Police Failed to Find Keys to Foster's Car," *Pittsburgh Tribune-Review*, September 20, 1995.
99	Ibid.
100	Evans-Pritchard, *The Secret Life of Bill Clinton*, 170.

101	Author Ambrose Evans-Pritchard interview with Orenstein, May 1995; Evans-Pritchard, *The Secret Life of Bill Clinton*, 145.
102	"Foster Probe in Perspective," *Washington Times*, July 18, 1995.
103	Deposition of Detective John Rolla, July 21, 1994; Evans-Pritchard, *The Secret Life of Bill Clinton*, 228.
104	Green Books, p.2153: interview with Lisa Foster, July 29, 1993, Supplemental Criminal Incident Record; Evans-Pritchard, *The Secret Life of Bill Clinton*, 114-115, 130.
105	Ann Devroy and Michael Isikoff, "Handling of Foster Case is Defended," *Washington Post*, July 30, 1993; Evans-Pritchard, "A Death That Won't Die," p.36.
106	"Foster Probe in Perspective."
107	Barbara Olson, *Hell to Pay*: The Unfolding Story of Hillary Rodham (Washington, D.C.: Regnery Publishing, 1999), 267-269; Edward Klein, *The Truth About Hillary*, New York: Sentinel, 2005), 23.
108	Olson, *Hell to Pay*, 269.
109	Milton, *The First Partner*, 297.
110	"Foster Probe in Perspective."
111	Ruddy, "Make-Up Artist Links Clinton to Possible Cover-Up."
112	"Foster Probe in Perspective."
113	Evans-Pritchard, *The Secret Life of Bill Clinton*, 197.
114	Jerry Seper, "Justice Was Wary of Foster Probe," *Washington Times*, July 26, 1995.
115	"Foster Probe in Perspective"; Frank J. Murray, "White House Confirms Search of Foster's Office," *Washington Times*, December 21, 1993.
116	Milton, *The First Partner*, 298; Jerry Seper, "Hillary's Top Aide Took Foster Files, Lawman Testifies," *Washington Times*, July 27, 1995.
117	Seper, "Hillary's Top Aide Took Foster Files, Lawman Testifies."
118	Ibid.
119	Brock, *The Seduction of Hillary Rodham*, 391-392.
120	Jerry Seper, "Police Not told of Foster Office Search: Officers Kept Out, Wanted Room Sealed," *Washington Times*, July 21, 1995.
121	"GOP: White House Guilty of Highly Improper Conduct," *Washington Times*, June 19, 1996.
122	Laurie Kellman, "Clinton Pal Denies Calling About Papers," *Washington Times*, August 9, 1995.
123	Ibid.
124	"Foster Probe in Perspective."
125	John McCaslin, "202/628-7087," Inside the Beltway, *Washington Times*, November 15, 1995; Jerry Seper, "Hillary's Mystery Phone Call Apparently Routed to McLarty," *Washington Times*, December 8, 1995.
126	Jerry Seper, "Hillary: 'I Do Not Recall' Call Made to White House the Night Foster Died," *Washington Times*, December 9, 1995.
127	Susan Schmidt, "Probe Into Handling of Foster Files May Highlight Some Discrepancies," *Washington Post*, July 10, 1995; "GOP: White House Guilty of Highly Improper Conduct."
128	Frank J. Murray and Michael Hedges, "Close Aide's Suicide Leaves President, Staff Puzzled," *Washington Times*, July 22, 1993.
129	Jerry Seper, "Clinton 'Fixer' at Foster's Desk," *Washington Times*, July 20, 1995.
130	Jerry Seper, "No. 2 Justice Official Saw 'Disaster' in Foster Probe," *Washington Times*, August 3, 1995.
131	Editorial, "All Roads Lead to Hillary?" *Washington Times*, October 26, 1995.
132	Brock, *The Seduction of Hillary Rodham*, 393.
133	Milton, *The First Partner*, 299.
134	Jerry Seper, "Hearing Yield New Foster Note Tale," *Washington Times*, July 28, 1995.
135	Michael Hedges, "Foster Letter Disputed," *Washington Times*, February 5, 1994.

136 Sharon LaFraniere and Ruth Marcus, "Nussbaum Staff Monitored Foster Probe Interviews," *Washington Post*, February 5, 1994.
137 Laurie Kellman, "Clinton Pal Denies Calling About Papers," *Washington Times*, August 9, 1995.
138 Ronald A. Taylor, "President Buries Lifelong Pal," *Washington Times*, July 24, 1993; Milton, *The First Partner*, 302.
139 SWSC deposition of Deborah Gorham, July 31, 1995. Foster's secretary said that he did not usually rip his notes for the burn bag. He rolled up the paper and tossed it; Evans-Pritchard, *The Secret Life of Bill Clinton*, 214.
140 Brock, *The Seduction of Hillary Rodham*, 395.
141 Evans-Pritchard, *The Secret Life of Bill Clinton*, 215; Lead Editorial, "The Foster Note: What We've Learned So Far," *Washington Times*, August 9, 1995.
142 SWSC deposition of Louis Hupp, July 14, 1995. Brett Cavanaugh from the OIC was present. He left the room to consult with Mark Tuohey and was told that the witness was not to answer; Evans-Pritchard, *The Secret Life of Bill Clinton*, 214.
143 Brock, *The Seduction of Hillary Rodham*, 397.
144 Ibid, 397-398.
145 Michael Hedges, "Questions Cloud Ruling of Suicide in Foster's Death," *Washington Times*, January 28, 1994.
146 Ibid.
147 Ibid.
148 Paul Craig Roberts, "Whitewater Travail," *Washington Times*, February 11, 1994.
149 Paul M. Rodriguez, "Hill Republicans Open Investigation Into Foster's Death," *Washington Times*, February 25, 1994.
150 Poe, *Hillary's Secret War*, 97.
151 From Combined Dispatches, "Photo of Foster Death Scene on TV," *Washington Times*, March 12, 1994.
152 From Combined Dispatches, "Photo of Foster Death Scene on TV"; Poe, *Hillary's Secret War*, 98.
153 Ibid, 98.
154 Poe, *Hillary's Secret War*, 98; Ruddy, *The Strange Death of Vincent Foster*, 32-33, 57-58; Evans-Pritchard, *The Secret Life of Bill Clinton*, 208-209.
155 Ibid.
156 Paul Craig Roberts, "Cover-Up Ramifications," *Washington Times*, March 11, 1994.
157 Ibid.
158 Western Journalism Center Ad, *Washington Times*, October 24, 1995.
159 Ibid.
160 Bernstein, A Woman Charge, 386.
161 Jerry Seper, "Subdued Foster Spent Final Days Tidying Affairs," *Washington Times*, July 1, 1994.
162 Western Journalism Center, "Vincent Foster's Death: Was it a Suicide?"; Ruddy, "Police Failed to Find Keys to Foster's Car at Park"; Christopher Ruddy, "Grand Jury Examines Foster Matter," *Pittsburgh Tribune-Review*, June 28, 1995; John Corry, "Burton in the Snake Pit," *American Spectator*, June 1997, 22.
163 Paul Craig Roberts, "Muzzled on Foster," *Washington Times*, August 8, 1994.
164 Poe, *Hillary's Secret War*, 102.
165 Christopher Ruddy, "Kenneth Starr-The Clintons' Accomplice," *NewsMax.com*, July 1, 1999; Poe, *Hillary's Secret Scheme*, 102-103.
166 Poe, *Hillary's Secret War*, 103.
167 Ibid.
168 Christopher Ruddy, "Ex-Prosecutor Can Show Apparent Cover-Up in Foster Probe," *Pittsburgh Tribune-Review*, June 19, 1995.

169 Author Ambrose Evans-Pritchard interview with a confidential source at OIC; Evans-Pritchard, *The Secret Life of Bill Clinton*, 138.
170 Evans-Pritchard, *The Secret Life of Bill Clinton*, 149.
171 Ruddy, "Ex-Prosecutor Can Show Apparent Cover-Up in Foster Death Probe."
172 Ibid.
173 Ibid.
174 Ibid.
175 Ibid.
176 Christopher Ruddy, *The Strange Death of Vincent Foster*, 214-216; Poe, *Hillary's Secret War*, 108.
177 Evans-Pritchard, *The Secret Life of Bill Clinton*, 149.
178 Evans-Pritchard, "A Death That Won't Die," 38.
179 Evans-Pritchard, *The Secret Life of Bill Clinton*, 140.
180 Ibid.
181 Ibid, 141.
182 Ibid, 112.
183 Ibid, 149.
184 Art Moore, "Tape of U.S. Attorney: Foster Probe a Fraud," *WorldNetDaily.com*, July 17, 2003; Poe, *Hillary's Secret War*, 108.
185 Christopher Ruddy, "Policy Dispute Led to Shakeup in Foster Probe," *Pittsburgh Tribune-Review*, May 3, 1995.
186 Poe, *Hillary's Secret War*, 108.
187 Ibid, 111.
188 Editorial, "*The Starr Report* on Vince Foster," *Washington Times*, October 14, 1997.
189 Poe, *Hillary's Secret War*, 91.
190 John F. Kennedy, Jr., "Who's Afraid of Richard Mellon Scaife," *George Magazine*, January 1999; Poe, *Hillary's Secret War*, 91.
191 Roger Morris, *Partners in Power: The Clintons and Their America* (Washington, D.C.: Regnery Publishing, 1996), 445.

SEVENTEEN: THE TROOPERS TALK

1 David Brock, "Living with the Clintons," *American Spectator*, January 1994.
2 David Brock, "Living with the Clintons," *American Spectator*, January 1994, 20.
3 Ibid, 21.
4 R. Emmett Tyrrell, Jr., *Boy Clinton: The Political Biography* (Washington, D.C.: Regnery Publishing, 1996), 267-268; Brock, "Living with the Clintons," 20, 22.
5 James Stewart, *Blood Sport* (New York: Simon & Schuster, 1996), 320-324, 351-352; Rich Lowry, *Legacy: Paying the Price for the Clinton Years* (Washington, D.C.: Regnery Publishing, 2003), 154; Brock, "Living with the Clintons," 22-23.
6 Brock, "Living with the Clintons," 22-23.
7 Ibid, 24.
8 Ibid, 25.
9 Ibid, 26.
10 Ibid.
11 Ibid.
12 Ibid, 28.
13 Ibid, 27.
14 Ibid.
15 Ibid, 26.
16 Ibid.
17 Ibid, 28.

18 Ibid.
19 Author Roger Morris confidential interviews; Roger Morris, *Partners in Power: The Clintons and Their America* (Washington D.C.: Regnery Publishing, 1996), 444.
20 Gail Sheehy, *Hillary's Choice* (New York: Ballantine Books, 1999), 220.
21 Ibid, 220-221.
22 Ibid, 221.
23 Morris, *Partners in Power*, 443.
24 Elizabeth Drew, *On the Edge: The Clinton Presidency* (New York: Touchstone, 1994), 380-381.
25 Drew, *On the Edge*, 381.
26 Ibid, 382-383.
27 Ibid, 383.
28 Lois Romano, "The Reliable Source," *Washington Post*, December 23, 1993; Carl Bernstein, *A Woman In Charge: The Life of Hillary Rodham Clinton* (New York: Alfred A. Knopf, 2007), 361-362.
29 William C. Rempel and Douglas Frantz, "Troopers Say Clinton Sought Silence on Personal Affairs," *Los Angeles Times*, December 21, 1993, A1; Tyrrell, *Boy Clinton*, 274.
30 Byron York, "The Truth About Bill's Lies," *American Spectator*, March 1998, 30.
31 David Brock, *The Seduction of Hillary Rodham*, (New York: Free Press Paperbacks, 1997), 399.
32 York, "The Truth About Bill's Lies," 30; Drew, *On the Edge*, 389.
33 Jerry Seper, "White House Denies Effort to Silence Trooper," *Washington Times*, October 21, 1994.
34 Michael Hedges, "Another Trooper Says He Found Women for Clinton," *Washington Times*, April 12, 1994; Michael Hedges, "State Trooper's Demotion Captures Attention of FBI," *Washington Times*, May 5, 1994.

EIGHTEEN: WHITEWATER

1 Howard Schneider and Charles Babcock, "Clintons' Arkansas Land Venture Losses Disputed," *Washington Post*, December 19, 1993.
2 Jim McDougal and Curtis Wilkie, *Arkansas Mischief: The Birth of a National Scandal* (New York: Henry Holt and Company, 1998), 149-151.
3 James Ring Adams, "Beyond Whitewater," *American Spectator*, February 1994, 53.
4 Roger Morris, *Partners in Power: The Clintons and Their America* (Washington, D.C.: Regnery Publishing, 1996), 213-214.
5 Ibid.
6 Editorial, "Passive Investors?" *Washington Times*, August 25, 1995; Byron York, "Fool for Bill," *American Spectator*, October 1996, 39.
7 Editorial, "Passive Investors?"
8 York, "Fool for Bill," 39-40.
9 Editorial, "Passive Investors?"; Morris, *Partners in Power*, 362.
10 Martin Gross, "Did Clintons Lose on Whitewater," *Washington Times*, January 24, 1995; Jerry Seper, "What Were the Clinton Stakes in Land Scheme?" *Washington Times*, November 4, 1993.
11 McDougal and Wilkie, *Arkansas Mischief*, 179.
12 Editorial, "Passive Investors?"
13 Howard Schneider and Charles Babcock, "Clintons' Arkansas Land Venture Losses Disputed," *Washington Post*, December 19, 1993.
14 Editorial, "Passive Investors?"
15 Ibid.
16 Ibid.
17 Editorial, "Passive Investors?"
18 Morris, *Partners in Power*, 369.

19   Editorial, "Passive Investors?"
20   Morris, *Partners in Power*, 370.
21   Author Roger Morris confidential interviews; Morris, *Partners in Power*, 370.
22   Editorial, "Passive Investors?"
23   Morris, *Partners in Power*, 371.
24   Ibid.
25   Ibid.
26   Editorial, "Passive Investors?"
27   Brock, *The Seduction of Hillary Rodham*, 203.
28   Editorial "Passive Investors?"; Morris, *Partners in Power*, 372.
29   Jerry Seper, "Fiske Probe Focuses on Four Suspect Checks," *Washington Times*, July 22, 1994.
30   Morris, *Partners in Power*, 373-374.
31   Brock, *The Seduction of Hillary Rodham*, 203; Jerry Seper, "Clinton's Office Got Madison Warning," *Washington Times*, January 26, 1996.
32   Brock, *The Seduction of Hillary Rodham*, 204; Adams, "Beyond Whitewater," 55-56.
33   Joyce Milton, *The First Partner: Hillary Rodham Clinton* (New York: William Morrow and Company, 1999), 176; Jerry Seper, "Questions on Ozarks Venture Arose Early in Campaign," *Washington Times*, November 4, 1993.
34   Editorial, "Passive Investors?"; Seper, "What Were the Stakes in Land Scheme?"
35   James Ring Adams and R. Emmett Tyrrell, Jr., "The Case Against Hillary," *American Spectator*, February 1996, 25.
36   Editorial, "Passive Investors?"
37   (*Associated Press*), "Trooper Confirms Clinton-Hale Chat," *Washington Times*, October 20, 1994.
38   Adams and Tyrrell, "The Case Against Hillary," 25.
39   Morris, *Partners in Power*, 380.
40   Ibid, 381.
41   Ibid, 382.
42   Ibid, 381.
43   Jerry Seper, "Clinton's Office Got Madison Warning," *Washington Times*, January 26, 1996; Brock, *The Seduction of Hillary Rodham*, 212.
44   Seper, "Clinton's Office Got Madison Warning."
45   Brock, *The Seduction of Hillary Rodham*, 212; Charles R. Babcock, "Ex-Regulator Remembers '85 Call Differently," *Washington Post*, January 26, 1996.
46   Seper, "Clinton's Office Got Madison Warning."
47   Editorial, "Passive Investors?"
48   "Your Guide to Whitewater," *Washington Times*, January 14, 1994.
49   Seper, "What Were the Clinton Stakes in Land Scheme?"
50   Susan Schmidt and Michael Isikoff, "Arkansas Probe Sensitive from Start," *Washington Post*, January 5, 1994; Jerry Seper, "RTC Critical of Hillary's Former Law Firm," *Washington Times*, August 5, 1995
51   David Brock, "Where Was Hillary?" *American Spectator*, September 1994, 24.
52   Morris, *Partners in Power*, 385; Milton, *The First Partner*, 213.
53   Milton, *The First Partner*, 213-214.
54   James B. Stewart, *Blood Sport* (New York: Simon & Schuster, 1996), 177-178; McDougal and Wilkie, *Arkansas Mischief*, 231-240; Milton, *The First Partner*, 214.
55   Morris, *Partners in Power*, 387.
56   Elizabeth Drew, *On the Edge: The Clinton Presidency* (New York: Touchstone, 1994), 366-367.
57   Jerry Seper, "Rose Staffers Say Hillary Ordered Papers Shredded," *Washington Times*, March 7, 1994.
58   James Ring Adams, "The Obstructionists," *American Spectator*, April/May 1994, 27.
59   Ibid.

60 Adams and Tyrrell, "The Case Against Hillary," 26.
61 Susan Schmidt and Serge F. Kovaleski, "Hubbell Says Nussbaum Kept Probers from Files," *Washington Post*, July 20, 1995.
62 McDougal and Wilkie, *Arkansas Mischief*, 251-252.
63 Adams and Tyrrell, "The Case Against Hillary," 26.
64 Editorial, "Republicans and the RTC," *Washington Times*, March 29, 1994; Ruth Marcus, "Hill Hearings Reveal a White House Obsessed with Whitewater," *Washington Post*, August 8, 1994.
65 Susan Schmidt, "Aides Say SBA Shared Data on Clinton Foe," *Washington Post*, November 29, 1995.
66 Adams, "The Obstructionists," 27.
67 Ibid.
68 Ibid.
69 Ibid, 24.
70 Excerpts from the draft report on the Washington phase of the special Senate Whitewater committee investigation, "White House Responses Risked 'Obstruction of Justice,'" *Washington Times*, June 17, 1996.
71 Ibid, 25.
72 Ibid.
73 Adams, "The Obstructionists," 25; James Ring Adams, "Beyond Whitewater," *American Spectator*, February 1994, 57.
74 Adams, "The Obstructionists," 28-29.
75 Jerry Seper, "White House Knew Aim of RTC Inquiry," *Washington Times*, November 14, 1995; Paul Bedard, "Hottest Seat at Hearings for Altman," *Washington Times*, July 27, 1994.
76 Seper, "White House Knew of RTC Inquiry."
77 Major Garrett and Jerry Seper, "On Capitol Hill, a Chorus of Denials," *Washington Times*, July 29, 1994.
78 Paul Bedard, "White House Discloses More Talk with Probers," *Washington Times*, March 9, 1994.
79 Jerry Seper, "Lawmakers Look into Two Clinton-Tucker Meetings," *Washington Times*, August 15, 1994; Seper, "White House Knew Aim of RTC Inquiry."
80 Seper, "White House Knew Aim of RTC Inquiry."
81 Seper, "White House Knew Aim of RTC Inquiry,"; Robert D. Novak and Zelda Novak, "Oh, What a Tangled Webb …," *American Spectator*, June 1994, 28.
82 Seper, "What Were the Clinton Stakes in Land Scheme?"
83 Susan Schmidt and Charles R. Babcock, "Whitewater Notes Sketchy on Meeting," *Washington Post*, December 23, 1995; Excerpts from the draft report on the Washington phase of the Senate Whitewater committee investigation, "White House Responses Risked 'Obstruction of Justice.'"
84 Ibid.
85 Seper, "White House Knew Aim of RTC Inquiry,"; Brock, *The Seduction of Hillary Rodham*, 398.
86 Adams and Tyrrell, "The Case Against Hillary," 27; (*Associated Press*), "Lawyer Had Whitewater Documents," *Washington Times*, November 13, 1995.
87 Drew, *On the Edge*, 391.
88 Bernstein, *A Woman in Charge*, 481-482.
89 George Stephanopoulos, *All Too Human: A Political Education* (Boston: Little, Brown and Company, 1999), 226.
90 Jerry Seper, "Hillary's Role with Foster Papers Scrutinized," *Washington Times*, July 24, 1995.
91 Martin Gross, "Did Clintons Lose on Whitewater?" *Washington Times*, January 24, 1995.
92 Ibid.
93 Jerry Seper and Frank J. Murray, "Clinton to Release Real Estate Documents," *Washington Times*, December 24, 1993.

94 Nancy E. Roman, " 'A Good Strategy' By Clinton Lawyer," *Washington Times*, January 7, 1994; Howard Schneider and Charles R. Babcock, "An Ever-Growing Paper Trail," *Washington Post*, January 8, 1994.
95 Donald Lambro, "Clinton Insensitive to Conflicts," *Washington Times*, August 4, 1994; Marcus, "Hill Hearings Reveal a White House Obsessed with Whitewater."
96 David Brock, "Lloyds of Clinton," *American Spectator*, October 1994, 28.
97 York, "The Truth About Bill's Lies," 30.
98 Jerry Seper, "Dole Charges Conspiracy in Whitewater Land Probe," *Washington Times*, January 7, 1994.
99 Jerry Seper and Major Garrett, "RTC Worker on Madison Probe Likely to be Hearings' Key Witnesses," *Washington Times*, July 25, 1994.
100 J. Jennings Moss and Frank J. Murray, "7 Democrats Join the Call for Whitewater Counsel," *Washington Times*, January 12, 1994.
101 J. Jennings Moss, "Dole Demands Investigation by Select Congressional Panel," *Washington Times*, January 13, 1994.
102 York, "The Truth About Bill's Lies," 30.
103 Jerry Seper, "Fiske Says He Wants Clintons to Give Testimony Under Oath," *Washington Times*, January 21, 1994; Excerpts from Rep. Jim Leach, Iowa Republican, on the House floor, "'In a Nutshell, Whitewater is About Arrogance of Power,'" *Washington Times*, March 25, 1994.
104 Drew, *On the Edge*, 379.
105 Susan Schmidt and Charles R. Babcock, "Senior Official Steps Aside in Probe of S&L Linked to Clintons' Venture," *Washington Post*, February 26, 1994.
106 Jerry Seper, "House Panel Awaits the Crucial Witness," *Washington Times*, August 3, 1995.
107 Ibid
108 Ibid.
109 Ibid.
110 Ibid.
111 R. Emmett Tyrrell, Jr., "Little Rock Labyrinth," *Washington Times*, February 11, 1994.
112 Novak and Novak, "Oh, What a Tangled Webb …," 28.
113 George J. Church and Michael Kramer, "Into the Line of Fire," *Time*, April 4, 1994, 23.
114 Ibid.
115 Brock, "Lloyds of Clinton," 29, 82.
116 Ibid, 82.
117 Ibid.
118 Ibid.
119 Jerry Seper, "Hillary Received Reports on Probes," *Washington Times*, August 2, 1994.
120 Ibid.
121 Major Garrett and Jerry Seper, "GOP Cites Whitewater Leaks," *Washington Times*, August 3, 1994.
122 Frank J. Murray, "Is He Really Angry or Just Acting? Clinton's Composure Confounds," *Washington Times*, March 16, 1994.
123 Ronald A. Taylor, "Clintons' Partner Pleads for Records," *Washington Times*, March 14, 1994.
124 Murray, "Is He Really Angry or Just Acting? Clinton's Composure Confounds."
125 From Combined Dispatches, "Fiske Notes Benefit to Probe as Hale Pleads Guilty," *Washington Times*, March 23, 1994.
126 James Ring Adams, "A New Lasater Connection," *American Spectator*, September 1997, 56.
127 Ibid.
128 Jerry Seper, "Dash Joins Whitewater Investigators," *Washington Times*, October 6, 1994.
129 Susan Schmidt, "Ex-Solicitor General Starr to Take Over Probe," *Washington Post*, August 6, 1994; Mark R. Levin, "Honest Scrutiny of Starr's Record Smashes Clinton's Smear Campaign," *Human Events*, February 13, 1998, 1, 8.

130   Jerry Seper, "Hanson Follows Altman in Exit from Treasury Department," *Washington Times*, August 19, 1994.
131   R. Emmett Tyrrell, Jr., "The Continuing Crisis," *American Spectator*, May1995, 8; (*Associated Press*), "Whitewater Figure Sentenced," *Washington Post*, April 15, 1995; Jerry Seper, "Plea Gives Starr Fifth Conviction in Whitewater Probe," *Washington Times*, May 3, 1995; Jerry Seper, "Indictment Covers Loans to Clinton Campaign," *Washington Times*, March 1, 1995; Jerry Seper, "Ex-Clinton Aide Takes Whitewater Plea Deal," *Washington Times*, June 9, 1995; Jerry Seper, "No Jail For Appraiser in Whitewater Case," *Washington Times*, June 17, 1995.
132   Jerry Seper, "Senate Sets Up Special Panel on Whitewater," *Washington Times*, May 18, 1995.
133   Jerry Seper, "Whitewater-Notes Subpoena Passes in Party-Line Vote," *Washington Times*, December 21, 1995; Jerry Seper, "White House Gives in, Agrees to Release Notes," *Washington Times*, December 22, 1995.
134   (*Associated Press*), "Whitewater Panel Issues 16 New Subpoenas," *Washington Post*, December 29, 1995.
135   Jerry Seper, "U.S. Deadline for Claims Against Rose Extended," *Washington Times*, February 29, 1996.
136   Jerry Seper, "Hillary Billing Papers 'Just Appeared,'" *Washington Times*, January 19, 1996; Lead Editorial, "The Trouble With Mrs. Clinton," *Washington Times*, January 10, 1996.
137   Warren P. Strobel, "Hillary's Ethics Get Sharp Defense," *Washington Times*, January 10, 1996.
138   Ibid.
139   Jerry Seper and Paul Bedard, "Hillary Faces Jurors Today," *Washington Times*, January 26, 1996.
140   Paul Bedard, "In Video Testimony, Clinton Denies Loan Pressure," *Washington Times*, April 29, 1996.
141   "Which One's Lying?" *Human Events*, May 2, 1997, 3.
142   Ibid.
143   Jerry Seper, "FBI Finds Hillary's Fingerprints on Recently Rediscovered S&L Papers," *Washington Times*, April 29, 1996.
144   Hugh Aynesworth, "Arkansas Governor Clintons' Partners Are Found Guilty in Whitewater Trial," *Washington Times*, May 29, 1996; Lead Editorial, "Sentencing in Little Rock," *Washington Times*, August 21, 1996.
145   McDougal and Wilkie, *Arkansas Mischief*, 3.
146   Editorial, "Whitewater Under the Bridge," *Washington Times*, September 22, 2000.

NINETEEN: STATE DEPARTMENT FILE SEARCH
1   Michael Hedges, "2 Cited for File Searches on Bush Aides," *Washington Times*, February 3, 1994.
2   George Archibald, "Clinton Threat of Firing Didn't Stop Searches," *Washington Times*, June 11, 1996.
3   Ibid.
4   Michael Hedges, "2 Cited for File Searches on Bush Aides," *Washington Times*, February 3, 1994.
5   Michael Hedges, "Criminal Probe Opens in Searches of State Files," *Washington Times*, November 4, 1993.
6   Hedges, "Criminal Probe Opens in Searches of State Files"; Mike Mitchell, "Justice Delayed and Justice Denied in the File Search Case," *Washington Times*, September 21, 1994.
7   Hedges, "2 Cited for File Searches on Bush Aides"; Mitchell, Justice Delayed and Justice Denied in the File Search Case."
8   Mitchell, "Justice Delayed and Justice Denied in the File Search Case."
9   Hedges, "2 Cited for File Searches on Bush Aides"; Hedges, "Justice Rankles Bush-Era State Officials, Won't Charge Clinton-Era File Searches."
10   Hedges, "Justice Rankles Bush-Era State Officials, Won't Charge Clinton-Era File Searchers."
11   Hedges, "2 Cited for File Searches on Bush Aides."

12 Archibald, "Clinton Threat of Firing Didn't Stop Searches."
13 Ibid.
14 Hedges, "Criminal Probe Opens in Searches of State Files"; Mitchell, "Justice Delayed and Justice Denied in the File Search Case."

TWENTY: VIETNAM

1   Frank J. Murray, "Clinton Revises Views on the Draft," *Washington Times*, May 30, 1993.
2   Editorial, "Their Man in Washington, *Washington Times*, October 30, 1996.
3   John Corry, "The MIA Cover-Up," *American Spectator*, February 1994, 26.
4   Ibid.
5   Ibid.
6   Ibid, 27.
7   Ibid.
8   Ibid.
9   Reed Irvine and Joe Goulden, "How the POW 'Hysteria' Game is Being Played," *Washington Times*, June 7, 1993; Susan Katz Keating, "Down This Road Before," *Washington Times*, May 4, 1993.
10 Keating, "Down This Road Before."
11 Irvine and Goulden, "How the POW 'Hysteria' Game is Being Played."
12 Francis Loewenheim, "Fragment of the Record," *Washington Times*, May 4, 1993.
13 Corry, "The MIA Cover-Up," 29.
14 Ibid, 31.
15 Ibid, 33.
16 Ibid.
17 Ibid.
18 Ibid.
19 Ibid.
20 Irvine and Goulden, "How the POW 'Hysteria' Game is Being Played."
21 Ibid.
22 Ibid.
23 Ibid.
24 Ibid.
25 Ibid.
26 Bill Gertz, "Second Vietnamese Document Claims U.S. POWs Left Behind," *Washington Times*, September 9, 1993.
27 Ibid.
28 Loewenheim, "Fragment of the Record."
29 Ibid.
30 Editorial, "Their Man in Washington."
31 David Fields, "Oil Drilling, Consumer Goods Still Off Limits," *Washington Times*, December 24, 1993.
32 Corry, "The MIA Cover-Up," 26.
33 Andrew Quinn (Reuters), "Mobil in on Deal with PetroVietnam," December 24, 1993.
34 Quinn (Reuters), "Mobil in on Deal with PetroVietnam"; Fields, "Oil Drilling, Consumer Goods Still Off Limits."
35 Fields, "Oil Drilling, Consumer Goods Still Off Limits."
36 Jim Adams (AP), "Senate Urges End of Hanoi Embargo," *Washington Times*, January 28, 1994.
37 Frank J. Murray, "Clinton Lifts Trade Embargo on Vietnam After 30 Years," *Washington Times*, February 4, 1994.

38 Paul Bedard, "Clinton's Move Angers Many Vets, Republicans," *Washington Times*, July 12, 1995.
39 Joyce Price and Jerry Seper, "Clinton Says Book Vindicates His Dodging Vietnam War Draft," *Washington Times*, April 15, 1995.
40 Bedard, "Clinton's Move Angers Many Vets, Republicans"; Martin Sieff, "Vietnam and U.S. Establish Full Ties," *Washington Times*, August 6, 1995.
41 Al Santoli, "Unanswered Questions," *Washington Times*, July 11, 1995; David R. Sands, "President Urges New Vietnamese Partnership," *Washington Times*, November 18, 2000.
42 Martin Sieff, "U.S. Quietly Opens Embassy in Vietnam," *Washington Times*, August 7, 1995.

TWENTY-ONE: PAULA JONES PART I

1 "The President Bums Out," *Washington Times* Lead Editorial, December 17, 1997.
2 Michael Hedges, "Woman Accuses Clinton of Sexual Advances in '91," *Washington Times*, February 12, 1994.
3 Michael Isikoff, Charles E. Shepard and Sharon LaFraniere, "Former State Employee in Arkansas Alleges Improper Advance in 1991," *Washington Post*, May 4, 1994.
4 Ibid.
5 Ibid.
6 Michael Hedges, "Sexual Harassment Suit Filed Against President," *Washington Times*, May 7, 1994; Isikoff, Shepard and LaFraniere, "Former State Employee in Arkansas Alleges Improper Advance in 1991."
7 Hedges, "Sexual Harassment Suit Filed Against President."
8 Isikoff, Shepard and LaFraniere, "Former State Employee in Arkansas Alleges Improper Advance in 1991."
9 Ibid.
10 Ibid.
11 Ibid.
12 Hedges, "Sexual Harassment Suit Filed Against President."
13 Isikoff, Shepard and LaFraniere, "Former State Employee in Arkansas Alleges Improper Advance in 1991."
14 Debra Ballentine on what Jones told her on May 8, 1991. Quoted by Stuart Taylor *American Lawyer*, November 1996, *Human Events*, June 13, 1997, 3.
15 Isikoff, Shepard and LaFraniere, "Former State Employee in Arkansas Allege Improper Advance in 1991."
16 Ibid.
17 Ibid.
18 Ibid.
19 Frank J. Murray, "Clinton's Sex Life Probed in Jones Suit," *Washington Times*, October 14, 1997; Isikoff, Shepard and LaFraniere, "Former State Employee in Arkansas Alleges Improper Advance in 1991."
20 Isikoff, Shepard and LaFraniere, "Former State Employee in Arkansas Alleges Improper Advance in 1991."
21 Hedges, "Woman Accuses Clinton of Sexual Advances in 1991."
22 Ibid.
23 R. Emmett Tyrrell, Jr., "Getting to the Heart of an Accusation," *Washington Times*, February 18, 1994.
24 George Stephanopoulos, *All Too Human: A Political Education* (Boston: Little, Brown and Company, 1999), 267.
25 Carl Bernstein, *A Woman in Charge: The Life of Hillary Rodham Clinton* (New York: Alfred A. Knopf, 2007), 385.

26 Hedges, "Woman Accuses Clinton of Sexual Advances in 1991."
27 Rod Dreher, "*Post* Sex Story About Clinton Gets the Spike," *Washington Times*, March 25, 1994; (Accuracy in Media), "Censored By The *Post*," *Washington Times*, April 4, 1994.
28 Martin Schram, "When Sex Accusations Become News," *Washington Times*, April 16, 1994.
29 "Who Is Paula Jones and Why is the *Post* Suppressing Her Charge of Sexual Harassment?" *Washington Times*, Ad, April 4, 1994; Richard Cohen, "Bill Clinton's Anita Hill," *Washington Post*, May 4, 1994.
30 Bernstein, *A Woman in Charge*, 383-384.
31 "Jones' Harassment Suit Is Well-Drawn and Plausible," *Human Events*, May 20, 1994.
32 Joe Conason and Gene Lyons, "Impeachment's Little Elves," *Salon.com*, March 4, 2000.
33 Andy Thibault, "Clinton Accuser Gives Nod to Schedule," *Washington Times*, February 17, 1996.
34 Ibid.
35 Jeffrey Toobin, *A Vast Conspiracy* (New York: Touchstone, 1999), 44.
36 Ibid.
37 Ibid.
38 Hedges, "Sexual Harassment Suit Filed Against President."
39 Joyce Price, "Feminists Got Behind Hill, But Not Jones," *Washington Times*, May 7, 1994; Hedges, "Sexual Harassment Suit Filed Against President."
40 Price, "Feminists Got Behind Hill, But Not Jones."
41 Hedges, "Sexual Harassment Suit Filed Against President."
42 Hedges, Sexual Harassment Suit Filed Against President"; Paul M. Rodriguez, "Bennett Claims Profit Underlies Woman's Suit," *Washington Times*, May 7, 1991.
43 Joyce Milton, *The First Partner: Hillary Rodham Clinton* (New York: William Morrow and Company, 1999), 314.
44 Hedges, "Sexual Harassment Suit Filed Against President."
45 Toobin, *A Vast Conspiracy*, 52.
46 Bill Sammon, "Decisions Ensures Trail Won't Occur During Presidency," *Washington Times*, April 2, 1998.
47 Ruth Marcus, "Clinton Asks Unprecedented Immunity," *Washington Post*, August 11, 1994.
48 Rowan Scarborough, "Appeals Court Clears Jones Suit to Move Forward," *Washington Times*, January 10, 1996.
49 Thomas L. Jipping, "Presidential Immunity Anyone?" *Washington Times*, January 12, 1996.
50 Paul Bedard, "Clinton Was Insured For Sexual Lawsuits," *Washington Times*, February 9, 1996.
51 Frank J. Murray, "Jones Suit on Way to Top Court," *Washington Times*, May 9, 1996.
52 Brian Blomquist, "Clinton Dodges Suit, Says He's in the Military," *Washington Times*, May 22, 1996.
53 Lt. Col. Robert "Buzz" Patterson, *Dereliction of Duty: The Eyewitness Account of How Bill Clinton Compromised America's National Security* (Washington, D.C.: Regnery Publishing, 2003), 94.
54 Frank J. Murray, "Clinton Won't Face Jones Suit Before Election," *Washington Times*, June 25, 1996.
55 Frank J. Murray, "High Court Urged to Let Trial Go on Without President," *Washington Times*, January 14, 1997.
56 Frank J. Murray, "Justices Order Jones Case to Proceed," *Washington Times*, May 28, 1997.
57 Julia Duin and Joyce Price, "Feminists Chilly Toward Decision," *Washington Times*, May 28, 1997. Cartoon *Washington Times* (Garner)
58 Maggie Gallagher, "Harassers, Hypocrites … and Lechers," *Washington Times*, June 6, 1997.
59 Ibid.
60 Jerry Seper, "Jones' Attorneys Want Former Staffer Deposed," *Washington Times*, July 31, 1997.
61 Toobin, *A Vast Conspiracy*, 118-119.
62 Ibid, 119.

63. Frank J. Murray, "Judge Lets Jones' Lawyers Quit, Hold to Schedule For Trial," *Washington Times*, September 10, 1997.
64. Frank J. Murray, "Jones, Husband Audited By IRS," *Washington Times*, September 14, 1997.
65. Ibid.
66. Jerry Seper and Bill Sammon, "White House Denies Role in Audit of Jones," *Washington Times*, September 16, 1997.
67. (*Associated Press*), "Jones' Attorney Agrees to Be Mum with Media," *Washington Times*, September 17, 1997.
68. Frank J. Murray, "Clinton Demands Exposure Evidence," *Washington Times*, September 27, 1997; Toobin, *A Vast Conspiracy*, 136.
69. Toobin, *A Vast Conspiracy*, 137-138.
70. Frank J. Murray, "Jones Hires Six Texas Lawyers to Pursue Case Against Clinton," *Washington Times*, October 2, 1997.
71. Michael Isikoff, *Uncovering Clinton* (New York: Three Rivers, 1999), 216; Rich Lowry, *Legacy: Paying the Price for the Clinton Years* (Washington D.C.: Regnery Publishing, 2003), 158.
72. Inside Politics, "Harassment Hot Line," *Washington Times*, October 1, 1997.
73. Frank J. Murray, "Jones Legal Fund Reports to Judge on Harassment," *Washington Times*, October 12, 1997.
74. Bob Woodward, *Shadow: Five Presidents and the Legacy of Watergate* (New York: Touchstone, 1999), 373-374; Lowry, Legacy, 160-161.
75. *Human Events*, February 27, 1998, 15.
76. Toobin, *A Vast Conspiracy*, 215.
77. Ibid.
78. Ibid, 216.
79. Warren P. Strobel, "Clinton Quizzed For 6 Hours in Jones' Lawsuit," *Washington Times*, January 18, 1998.
80. Jeff Gerth and Don Van Natta Jr., *Her Way: The Hopes and Ambitions of Hillary Rodham Clinton* (New York: Little, Brown and Company, 2007), 173.
81. Gerth and Van Natta, *Her Way*, 173, Gail Sheehy, *Hillary's Choice* (New York: Ballantine Books, 1999), 10.
82. Excerpts from President Clinton's Jan. 17 Deposition in the Paula Jones Lawsuit, "I've Never Had an Affair with Her," *Washington Times*, August 17, 1998.
83. Toobin, *A Vast Conspiracy*, 221.
84. Excerpts from President Clinton's Jan. 17 Deposition in the Paula Jones Lawsuit."; Toobin, *A Vast Conspiracy*, 221.
85. Toobin, *A Vast Conspiracy*, 222.
86. Excerpts From President Clinton's Jan.17 Deposition in the Paula Jones Lawsuit, "I've Never Had an Affair with Her."
87. Toobin, *A Vast Conspiracy*, 223.
88. Excerpts from President Clinton's Jan. 17 Deposition in the Paula Jones Lawsuit, "I've Never Had an Affair with Her."
89. Ibid.
90. Toobin, *A Vast Conspiracy*, 225.
91. Excerpts from President Clinton's Jan. 17 Deposition in the Paula Jones Lawsuit, "I've Never Had an Affair with Her."
92. Toobin, *A Vast Conspiracy*, 226.
93. Kenneth Starr, *The Starr Report* (New York: Public Affairs, 1998), 159; Lowry, Legacy, 173.
94. Peter Baker, "Linda Tripp Briefed Jones Team on Tapes," *Washington Post*, February 14, 1998.
95. Strobel, "Clinton Quizzed For 6 Hours in Jones' Lawsuit"; Toobin, *A Vast Conspiracy*, 229.
96. George Stephanopoulos, *All Too Human*, 436.

TWENTY-TWO: 1994 STUMBLES

1. " 'Chinagate' Fundraiser Feared Clintons Would Murder Him," www.wnd.com, February 23, 2017.
2. John McCaslin, Inside the Beltway, *Washington Times*, March 29, 1994.
3. Ibid.
4. Ibid.
5. "Clinton Death List: 33 Most Intriguing Cases," www.*worldnetdaily.com*, August 21, 2016; " 'Chinagate' Fundraiser Feared Clintons Would Murder Him," www.*worldnetdaily.com*, February 23, 2017.
6. " 'Chinagate' Fundraiser Feared Clintons Would Murder Him," www.wnd.com, February 23, 2017.
7. John McCaslin, "R-E-L-I-E-F," *Washington Times*, Inside the Beltway, March 23, 1994.
8. Philip Terzian, "A Deal To Try On Your Banker," *Washington Times*, July 27, 1994; Matt Labash, "Buy George," *American Spectator*, October 1994, 30.
9. Labash, "Buy George," 31.
10. "Clinton Donation Isn't First Ethical Misstep For Stephanopoulos," *Washington Times*, May 21, 2005; Labash, "Buy George," 32.
11. Labash, "Buy George," 32.
12. Ibid, 33.
13. Terzian, "A Deal To Try On Your Banker." Labash, "Buy George," 33-34.
14. Ibid, 34.
15. Ibid.
16. Mona Charen, "Dignity Yields to Vulgarity," *Washington Times*, April 25, 1994.
17. Ibid.
18. Ibid.
19. Doug Jehl, "Clinton Calls Show to Assail Press, Falwell and Limbaugh," *New York Times*, June 25, 1994, A1; R. Emmett Tyrrell, *Boy Clinton: The Political Biography* (Washington, D.C.: Regnery Publishing, 1996), 162.
20. Patrick J. Buchanan, "Clintons Reignite the Culture War," *Human Events*, June 17, 1994, 9.
21. (*Associated Press*), "President and Pope Discuss Differences," *Chicago Tribune*, June 2, 1994, 1; Tyrrell, *Boy Clinton*, 158-159.

TWENTY-THREE: ELECTION 1994

1. George Anne Geyer, "Clueless After The Earthquake," *Washington Times*, November 16, 1994.
2. Rhodes Cook (Congressional Quarterly), "Midterm Elections Provide Danger for Democrats," *Washington Times*, February 18, 1994.
3. Cook, "Midterm Elections Provide Danger For Democrats"; Maureen Grope (Congressional Quarterly), "GOP '94 Tactic: Rush to an 800 Number," *Washington Times*, April 18, 1994.
4. Grope, "GOP '94 Tactic: Rush to an 800 Number."
5. (*Associated Press*), "Clinton Set to Battle 'Right Wing,'" *Washington Times*, May 4, 1994.
6. Donald Lambro, "GOP Victories Shock Democrats," *Washington Times*, May 26, 1994.
7. Jeff Gerth and Don Van Natta Jr., *Her Way: The Hopes and Ambitions of Hillary Rodham Clinton* (New York: Little, Brown and Company, 2007), 141.
8. (Reuters), "Clinton Cuts Press Contact to Better Control Message," *Washington Times*, August 19, 1994.
9. Donald Lambro, "Hearing Bolster Public Disaffection with White House," *Washington Times*, August 7, 1994.
10. Kevin Merida, "Many Democratic Candidates Are Steering Clear of Clinton," *Washington Times*, August 21, 1994.

11   Jeffrey Hart, "GOP Contract for a Political Mandate," *Washington Times*, September 27, 1994.
12   Rod Dreher, "GOP's 'Contract' Proffers a New Life for Gipper's Ideas," *Washington Times*, October 9, 1994.
13   Ralph Z. Hallow, "Perot Buoys GOP Hopes for Nov. 8," *Washington Times*, October 6, 1994.
14   Major Garrett, "Republicans Plan Takeover of House," *Washington Times*, October 8, 1994.
15   David S. Broder, "Democrats Run a Risk in Running Against '80s," *Washington Post*, October 12, 1994.
16   John R. Kasich, "Rekindling Reagan's Revolution," *Washington Times*, October 12, 1994.
17   Kasich, "Rekindling Reagan's Revolution"; George F. Will, "Punctured Moral Vanity," *Washington Post*, March 10, 1994.
18   Kasich, "Rekindling Reagan's Revolution."
19   Paul Bedard, "Clinton Raises Money but Stays Out of Sight," *Washington Times*, October 14, 1994.
20   Ibid.
21   Rod Dreher, "White House Disclosures Redden Faces," *Washington Times*, October 24, 1994.
22   Ibid.
23   (*Associated Press*), "Foley Avoids Appearance with Clinton," *Washington Times*, October 24, 1994.
24   Donald Lambro, "Clinton a Drag Wherever He Goes," *Washington Times*, October 23, 1994.
25   Paul Bedard, "Clinton Out of Gas on Trip's Second Day," *Washington Times*, October 28, 1994.
26   Dick Morris, *Behind the Oval Office: Getting Reelected Against All Odds* (Los Angeles: Renaissance, 1999), 15-16.
27   Ibid.
28   David S. Broder, "Naked Punditry," *Washington Post*, November 6, 1994.
29   R. Emmett Tyrrell, Jr. with Mark W. Davis, *Madame Hillary: The Dark Road to the White House* (Washington, D.C.: Regnery Publishing, 2004), 183.
30   Major Garrett, "Voters' Anger Puts GOP Back in Charge," *Washington Times*, November 9, 1994; Elizabeth Drew, *On the Edge: The Clinton Presidency* (New York: Touchstone, 1994), 440-441.
31   Morris, *Behind the Oval Office*, 33.
32   Major Garrett, "Stunned by Defeat, He Backs a Tax Cut," *Washington Times*, November 10, 1994.
33   Ibid, Tyrrell with Davis, *Madame Hillary*, 108, 183.
34   Tyrrell with Davis, *Madame Hillary*, 183.
35   Edward Klein, *The Truth About Hillary* (New York: Sentinel, 2005), 122.

TWENTY-FOUR: RON BROWN

1   Jack Cashill, *Ron Brown's Body: How One Man's Death Saved The Clinton Presidency and Hillary's Future* (Nashville: NelsonCurrent, 2004), 209.
2   Jack Cashill, *Ron Brown's Body: How One Man's Death Saved the Clinton Presidency and Hillary's Future* (Nashville: NelsonCurrent, 2004), 56.
3   Cashill, *Ron Brown's Body*, 56-57; Tom Maely, "Remembering Ron Brown: Honoring a Consummate Advocate for Asian Pacific American's," *Asia Week*, April 12, 1996.
4   Cashill, *Ron Brown's Body*, 54; Byron York, "Michael Brown Goes Free," *American Spectator*, November 1997, 24.
5   York, "Michael Brown Goes Free," 25.
6   Ibid.
7   Ibid.
8   Ibid.
9   Ibid.
10   Jason DeParle, "Businessman Details Case Involving Commerce Chief," *New York Times*, October 4, 1993; Cashill, *Ron Brown's Body*, 87.

11   Author Jack Cashill interview with Nolanda Hill; Cashill, *Ron Brown's Body*, 87.
12   Cashill, *Ron Brown's Body*, 87-88.
13   Jerry Seper, "Brown Allegations Lead to Hill Request for Papers, Answers," *Washington Times*, October 13, 1993.
14   DeParle, "Businessman Details Case Involving Commerce Chief"; Cashill, *Ron Brown's Body*, 88.
15   Don Philips, "High-Profile Party Insider at Commerce," *Washington Post*, December 13, 1992.
16   Seper, "Brown Allegations Lead to Hill Request For Papers, Answers."
17   Cashill, *Ron Brown's Body*, 88.
18   Ibid, 88-89.
19   Jerry Seper, "Haitian Woman Key in Probe of Brown; She Lives in Posh House He Bought," *Washington Times*, October 21, 1993; Cashill, *Ron Brown's Body*, 89.
20   Jerry Seper, "FBI Questions Commerce Secretary in Vietnam Probe," *Washington Times*, October 15, 1993; Cashill, *Ron Brown's Body*, 89.
21   DeParle, "Businessman Details Case Involving Commerce Chief"; Cashill, *Ron Brown's Body*, 89.
22   The affidavit was reprinted in William P. Hoar, "Ron Brown's Hanoi Kickback," *New American*, November 15, 1993; Cashill, *Ron Brown's Body*, 89-90.
23   Seper, "Brown Allegations Lead to Hill Request For Papers, Answers."
24   Tracey Brown, *The Life and Times of Ron Brown: A Memoir By His Daughter* (New York: William Morrow and Company, 1998), 246; Cashill, *Ron Brown's Body*, 90.
25   Marcy Gordon, "Vietnam Veterans Group Demands U.S. Commerce Secretary Resign," (*Associated Press*), October 1, 1993; Cashill, *Ron Brown's Body*, 90.
26   Cashill, *Ron Brown's Body*, 90.
27   Michael Kranish, "U.S. Probe of Brown Near End; Secretary Denies Influence Peddling," *Boston Globe*, October 24, 1993; Cashill, *Ron Brown's Body*, 90.
28   Seper, "FBI Questions Commerce Secretary in Vietnam Probe."
29   DeParle, "Businessman Details Case Involving Commerce Chief"; Cashill, *Ron Brown's Body*, 90-91.
30   (*Associated Press*), "Brown Denies $700,000 Influence Peddling," *Washington Times*, August 14, 1993.
31   Seper, "FBI Questions Commerce Secretary in Vietnam Probe"; Cashill, *Ron Brown's Body*, 92.
32   (*Associated Press*), "Commerce Secretary Linked to Vietnam Deal," *Washington Times*, September 27, 1993.
33   From News Services, "Brown Predicts Exoneration, Clashes With GOP Lawmakers," *Washington Post*, September 30, 1993.
34   Cashill, *Ron Brown's Body*, 109.
35   (*Associated Press*), "Brown 'Pleased' By Exoneration in Vietnam Probe," *Washington Times*, February 3, 1994.
36   "Mystery Woman," *Prime Time Live*, ABC News, June 18, 1997; Author Jack Cashill interview with Nolanda Hill; Cashill, *Ron Brown's Body*, 109.
37   Steven A. Holmes, *Ron Brown: An Uncommon Life* (New York: John Wiley & Sons, 2000), 258; Cashill, *Ron Brown's Body*, 122.
38   Mary Ann Akers, "Ex-DNC Chief Ignored CIA Warnings," *Washington Times*, September 10, 1997.
39   Charles Smith, "Clinton Export Policy Helped India Hide the Bomb," *WorldNetDaily*, August 4, 1998. The actual documents dated February 10, 1994 and obtained through the Freedom of Information Act can be viewed at www.us.net/softwar/tamraz.html; Cashill, *Ron Brown's Body*, 123-124.
40   Author Gail Sheehy interviews with James Jenkins, 1999; Gail Sheehy, *Hillary's Choice* (New York: Ballantine Books, 1999), 251.
41   *Investor's Business Daily*, July 9, 1997; Sheehy, *Hillary's Choice*, 251.

42	Byron York, "Who is Bruce Hegyi?" *American Spectator*, October 1997, 24; "Ron Brown and the Roots of Indogate," *Human Events*, November 8, 1996, 4.
43	Author Jack Cashill interview with Nolanda Hill; Cashill, *Ron Brown's Body*, 131.
44	Cashill, *Ron Brown's Body*, 131.
45	Ibid, 133.
46	Ibid, 134.
47	Author Jack Cashill interview with Nolanda Hill; Cashill, *Ron Brown's Body*, 134-135.
48	Cashill, *Ron Brown's Body*, 135.
49	Charles Smith, "Indonesian Power Deal Blows Financial Fuse," NewsMax, January 27, 2001; Cashill, *Ron Brown's Body*, 136.
50	Cashill, *Ron Brown's Body*, 137.
51	Wolf Blitzer, "Clinton Declares Utah Canyons a National Monument, " *CNN.com*, September 18, 1996; Cashill, *Ron Brown's Body*, 137-138.
52	Cashill, *Ron Brown's Body*, 138.
53	Ibid.
54	Jerry Seper, "Watchdog Group Seeks Records of Brown's Travel," *Washington Times*, January 20, 1995.
55	(*Associated Press*), "Senators Seek Probe of Commerce Chief," *Washington Times*, January 25, 1995.
56	(*Associated Press*), "Brown Protests GOP Hit About Business Dealings," *Washington Times*, February 7, 1995.
57	(*Associated Press*), "Clinton Supports Commerce Chief," *Washington Post*, February 19, 1995.
58	(*Associated Press*), "Slum Apartments in PG Gave Brown Huge Tax Write-Off," *Washington Times*, April 10, 1995.
59	Arlo Wagner, "Out of Sight, Out of Mind?" *Washington Times*, April 12, 1995.
60	Michael Hedges, "Independent Counsel Sought for Brown Probe," *Washington Times*, May 18, 1995.
61	Ibid.
62	Cashill, *Ron Brown's Body*, 169.
63	Ibid.
64	Michael Kirk and Peter J. Boyer, "The Fixers," *Frontline*, #1511, Public Broadcasting Service, April 14, 1997.
65	Benjamin Wittes, "The Browns' Oklahoma Connection," *Legal Times*, October 16, 1995; Cashill, *Ron Brown's Body*, 170.
66	Cashill, *Ron Brown's Body*, 170.
67	Wittes, "The Browns' Oklahoma Connection"; Cashill, *Ron Brown's Body*, 170-171.
68	Wittes, "The Browns' Oklahoma Connection"; Cashill, *Ron Brown's Body*, 171.
69	Cashill, *Ron Brown's Body*, 172.
70	Affidavit of Nolanda Butler Hill, C.A. No. 95-0133 (RCL), *Judicial Watch, Inc. Plaintiff v. United States Department of Commerce, Defendant*, in the United States District Court for the District of Columbia; Cashill, *Ron Brown's Body*, 166.
71	Cashill, *Ron Brown's Body*, 176.
72	Andy Thibault, "Brown Probe Looks at Payments to Son," *Washington Times*, February 15, 1996.
73	Cashill, *Ron Brown's Body*, 184-185.
74	Ibid, 185.
75	Ibid, 185-186.
76	Ibid, 182.
77	Part III, CommerceGate/ChinaGate, "*Judicial Watch* Interim Report on Crimes and Other Offenses Committed by President Clinton Warranting His Impeachment and Removal from Elected Office."; Cashill, *Ron Brown's Body*, 186.

78	Charles Smith, "Red Money Inside American Politics," *WorldNetDaily.com*, September 20, 2000; Charles Smith, "How China Took the White House," *WorldNetDaily.com*, June 1, 1998; Cashill, *Ron Brown's Body*, 187.
79	Andy Thibault, "Up to 20 Are Subpoenaed in Criminal Probe of Brown, *Washington Times*, March 29, 1996.
80	Cashill, *Ron Brown's Body*, 187-188.
81	Brown, *The Life and Times of Ron Brown*, 6; Cashill, *Ron Brown's Body*, 188.
82	Cashill, *Ron Brown's Body*, 188.
83	Brown, *The Life and Times of Ron Brown*, 7; Cashill, *Ron Brown's Body*, 188.
84	Cashill, *Ron Brown's Body*, 188-189.
85	Brown, *The Life and Times of Ron Brown*, 11-12; Cashill, *Ron Brown's Body*, 189-190.
86	"A Chronology of Events as Logged by Personnel at Embassy Zagreb in Connection with Secretary Brown's Plane Crash," as summarized in Carl Limbacher, "Documents Reveal Two May Have Survived Initial Impact of Ron Brown Plane Crash," NewsMax, September 24, 1999; Alan Diehl, *Silent Knights: Blowing the Whistle on Military Accidents and Their Cover-Ups* (Washington: Brassey's, 2002); Accident Investigation Board Report pp. v 193, 215, 393-398, 761, 1157, 2581; Cashill, *Ron Brown's Body*, 191-198.
87	Cashill, *Ron Brown's Body*, 198.
88	"Ron Brown and the Roots of Indogate," *Human Events*, November 8, 1996, 4.
89	Cashill, *Ron Brown's Body*, 198.
90	Brown, *The Life and Times of Ron Brown*, 24-25, Cashill, *Ron Brown's Body*, 199.
91	Brown, *The Life and Times of Ron Brown*, 25; Cashill, *Ron Brown's Body*, 199.
92	White House Press Release, "Remarks By the President About Secretary of Commerce Ron Brown," The White House Office of the Press Secretary, April 3, 1996; Cashill, *Ron Brown's Body*, 200.
93	Editorial, "The Ron Brown Conspiracy," *Washington Times*, January 10, 1998; Byron York, "Ron Brown's Body," *American Spectator*, February 1998, 51.
94	Cashill, *Ron Brown's Body*, 203-204.
95	Christopher Ruddy, "Second Officer: Wound Appeared to Be from Gunshot," *Pittsburgh Tribune-Review*, December 9, 1997; Cashill, *Ron Brown's Body*, 204.
96	*BET Tonight*, Black Entertainment Television, December 11, 1997. Transcript was included as attachment with *Judicial Watch*'s petition in order continuation of the independent counsel's investigation into matters related to former Secretary of Commerce, Ronald H. Brown (In re Ronald H. Brown, Division No. 95-2); Cashill, *Ron Brown's Body*, 204.
97	Cashill, *Ron Brown's Body*, 204.
98	Ibid, 204-205.
99	Christopher Ruddy, "Experts Differ on Ron Brown's Head Wound," *Pittsburgh Tribune-Review*, December 9, 1997, Cashill, *Ron Brown's Body*, 205.
100	Ibid; Ibid.
101	Tony Smith, "Airport's Navigations System Maintenance Chief Kills Himself," (*Associated Press*), April 8, 1996. The AP calls him "Jerkic." Other accounts say "Junic." The most frequently cited is "Jerkuic." Cashill, *Ron Brown's Body*, 205, 264.
102	Author Jack Cashill interview with Tony Campolo, September 5, 2003; Cashill, *Ron Brown's Body*, 206.
103	The video clip is still widely available on the internet; Cashill, *Ron Brown's Body*, 206.
104	Cashill, *Ron Brown's Body*, 207.
105	Richard Poe, *Hillary's Secret War: The Clinton Conspiracy to Muzzle Internet Journalists* (Nashville: NelsonCurrent, 2004), 160.
106	Ibid.
107	Ibid.

108 Ibid.
109 Christopher Ruddy and Hugh Sprunt, "Questions Linger About Ron Brown Plane Crash," *Pittsburgh Tribune-Review*, November 24, 1997; Poe, *Hillary's Secret War*, 160.
110 Poe, *Hillary's Secret War*, 160-161.
111 Ruddy and Sprunt, "Questions Linger About Ron Brown Plane Crash"; Poe, *Hillary's Secret War*, 161.
112 "Police Investigating Death at Commerce Department," November 29, 1996. (Credit here to Missy Kelly for assembling the timeline.); Cashill, *Ron Brown's Body*, 217.
113 Author Jack Cashill interview with Nolanda Hill; Cashill, *Ron Brown's Body*, 217-218.
114 Cashill, *Ron Brown's Body*, 218.
115 Paul Roderiquez, on the *Mary Matalin Radio Show*, August 21, 1997; Cashill, *Ron Brown's Body*, 218-219.
116 "Commerce Department Employee Found Dead in Office," (*Associated Press*), November 29, 1996; Cashill, *Ron Brown's Body*, 220-221.
117 Cashill, *Ron Brown's Body*, 221.
118 "Female Commerce Worker Found Dead," (*Associated Press*), November 30, 1996; Cashill, *Ron Brown's Body*, 221.
119 "Natural Causes Probable Explanation for Commerce Department Death," (*Associated Press*), December 6, 1996; Cashill, *Ron Brown's Body*, 222.
120 "Ron Brown's Son Gets Probation," CNN, November 21, 1997; Cashill, *Ron Brown's Body*, 231.
121 York, "Michael Brown Goes Free," 22.
122 Ibid, 23.
123 "Ron Brown's Son Gets Probation"; Cashill, *Ron Brown's Body*, 232.
124 Cashill, *Ron Brown's Body*, 232.
125 Christopher Ruddy, "Experts Differ on Ron Brown's Head Wound," *Pittsburgh Tribune-Review*, December 3, 1997; Poe, *Hillary's Secret War*, 167.
126 Cashill, *Ron Brown's Body*, 234-235.
127 Letters to Families of Victims, reprinted in *Newsmax.com*, December 27, 1997; Cashill, *Ron Brown's Body*, 236; Christopher Ruddy, "Gag Order Issued in Cause of Brown Death," *Pittsburgh Tribune-Review*, December 11, 1997.
128 Christopher Ruddy, "Pathologists Dispute Claim in Brown Probe," *Pittsburgh Tribune-Review*, December 11, 1998; Cashill, *Ron Brown's Body*, 236-237, 241.
129 Christopher Ruddy, "Wecht: Autopsy Needed in Brown Case," *Pittsburgh Tribune-Review*, December 17, 1997; Cashill, *Ron Brown's Body*, 237.
130 Ruddy, "Wecht: Autopsy Needed in Brown Case"; Cashill, *Ron Brown's Body*, 237-238.
131 Brown, *The Life and Times of Ron Brown*, 299; Cashill, *Ron Brown's Body*, 238.
132 Hurley Green III, "Pastor Demands Investigation into Late Ron Brown's Death," *Chicago Independent Bulletin*, December 11, 1997; James Wright, "Brown Head Injury Suspected Bullet Wound: At Second Chance," *Baltimore Afro-American*, December 13, 1997; Cashill, *Ron Brown's Body*, 238.
133 Poe, *Hillary's Secret War*, 170.
134 *BET Tonight*, Black Entertainment Television, December 11, 1997; The law is sometimes unofficially referred to as the "presidential assassination statute."; Cashill, *Ron Brown's Body*, 238-239.
135 George Archibald, "Was Brown Dead Before His Plane Went Down?" *Washington Times*, December 17, 1997.
136 Cashill, *Ron Brown's Body*, 240.
137 Paul Shephard, "Jesse Jackson Calls for Investigation of Ron Brown's Death," (*Associated Press*), January 5, 1998; Cashill, *Ron Brown's Body*, 240.
138 "Officials Back Up Brown Crash Findings," *Air Force News Service*, January 5, 1998, Cashill, *Ron Brown's Body*, 240.

139 Michael Fletcher, "Justice Dept. Declines to Probe Death of Brown," *Washington Post*, January 9, 1998.
140 James Wright, "Brown's Death Botched, Fourth Expert Says," *Washington Afro-American*, January 17, 1998.
141 Cashill, *Ron Brown's Body*, 245-246.
142 Ibid, 242.
143 Ibid, 242-243.
144 Jon Dougherty, "'The Other Jesse' Blasts Jackson Says News of Civil Rights Leader's Affair 'No Surprise,'" *WorldNetDaily*, January 24, 2001; Cashill, *Ron Brown's Body*, 243.
145 *Judicial Watch*, In re Ronald H. Brown, Division No. 95-2, Petition to Order Continuation of the Independent Counsel Counsel's Investigation into Matters Related to Secretary of Commerce, Ronald H. Brown; Cashill, *Ron Brown's Body*, 247.
146 Cashill, *Ron Brown's Body*, 248.
147 George Archibald, "Commerce Trips Called Fund-Raisers," *Washington Times*, March 24, 1998.
148 Cashill, *Ron Brown's Body*, 251-252.
149 Ibid, 252.
150 George Lardner Jr., "Judge Sets 10-Month Term in Political Donations Case," *Washington Post*, September 10, 1997; Cashill, *Ron Brown's Body*, 252-253.

TWENTY-FIVE: FBI FILES

1 George Archibald, "Livingstone Informed Superiors of File Plans," *Washington Times*, October 8, 1996.
2 Byron York, "Contempt of Congress," *American Spectator*, November 1999, 30; *Human Events*, February 27, 1998, 15.
3 Tony Snow, "Explanations That Don't Hold Water," *Washington Times*, June 14, 1996; James Bovard, *Feeling Your Pain: The Explosion and Abuse of Government Power in the Clinton-Gore Years* (New York: St. Martin's Press, 2000), 319.
4 Snow, "Explanations That Don't Hold Water."
5 Byron York, "Contempt of Congress," *American Spectator*, November 1999, 30.
6 Cal Thomas, "The Price Colson Paid," *Washington Times*, June 21, 1996.
7 Sean Piccoli, "ACLU Keeps Close Eye on FBI Files Scandal," *Washington Times*, June 6, 1996.
8 Nancy E. Roman and Ruth Larson, "Deposition Bares Past of Clinton Operative," *Washington Times*, June 27, 1996.
9 Paul Bedard, "Army Security Aide Was Recruited Twice," *Washington Times*, June 19, 1996.
10 Gary Aldrich, *Unlimited Access: An FBI Agent Inside the Clinton White House* (Washington, D.C.: Regnery Publishing, 1996), 36.
11 Bedard, "Army Security Aide Was Recruited Twice."
12 Piccoli, "ACLU Keeps Close Eye on FBI Files Scandal."
13 Ibid.
14 Jerry Seper, "Clinton Apologizes, Denounces Idea of 'Enemies List,'" *Washington Times*, June 13, 1996.
15 George Lardner, "Clinton Vows File Incident Will Never Happen Again," *Washington Post*, June 13, 1996.
16 Jerry Seper and Warren P. Strobel, "Freeh Slams White House, Rewrites Files Rules," *Washington Times*, June 15, 1996.
17 Editorial, "Filegate: The Invisible Scandal," *Investor's Business Daily*, June 20, 1997; James Bovard, *Feeling Your Pain: The Explosion And Abuse of Government Power in the Clinton-Gore Years* (New York: St. Martin's Press, 2000), 319.

18 George Lardner, "Many Notified After FBI 'Heads-Up,'" *Washington Post*, August 2, 1996; Bovard, *Feeling Your Pain*, 319; "The FBI Has Become an FOB," *Human Events*, October 25, 1996, 5.
19 Paul Bedard, "FBI Ordered to Probe Files Case," *Washington Times*, June 19, 1996.
20 Mark R. Levin, "Honest Scrutiny of Starr's Record Smashes Clinton's Smear Campaign," *Human Events*, February 13, 1998.
21 George Archibald, "Livingstone Quits Before Panel," *Washington Times*, June 27, 1996.
22 Brian Blomquist, Papers Point to Hillary in Hiring," *Washington Times*, July 26, 1996.
23 Wesley Pruden, "Let's Blame the Dead for the Scary Stuff," *Washington Times*, July 2, 1996.
24 Ibid.
25 Joyce Price, "FBI Files Scandal May Reach Higher Than Livingstone," *Washington Times*, July 8, 1996.
26 Ibid.
27 George Archibald, "Stephanopoulos Appears Before House Committee," *Washington Times*, July 12, 1996.
28 Ruth Larson, "Probe of Secret Service Men Who Testified on Hill Questioned," *Washington Times*, October 26, 1996.
29 Editorial, "The Abuse of Filegate Witnesses," *Washington Times*, October 28, 1996.
30 George Lardner Jr. and Anne Farris, "Ex-White House Investigator Continues to Invoke Fifth Amendment," *Washington Post*, July 19, 1996.
31 Joyce Milton, *The First Partner: Hillary Rodham Clinton* (New York: William Morrow and Company, 1999), 323-324.
32 George Archibald, "Livingstone Case Agent Quits FBI," *Washington Times*, August 3, 1996.
33 Ibid.
34 Andy Thibault, "White House Sued By Five Whose Files Were Obtained," *Washington Times*, September 13, 1996.
35 "Former White House Assistant Contradicts Livingstone and Marceca on FBI Files," *Human Events*, October 18, 1996, 3.
36 Ibid.
37 Byron York, "Where Starr Stands," *American Spectator*, April 1998, 29.
38 Ibid, p.25.
39 Jerry Seper, "Clinton Aides Accused of Snooping in Files," *Washington Times*, January 8, 2000.
40 Ibid.
41 Ibid.
42 Lead Editorial, "Closing Filegate?" *Washington Times*, March 21, 2000.
43 Ibid.
44 Jerry Seper, "No Evidence to Back 'Filegate' Prosecution, Report Says," *Washington Times*, July 29, 2000.
45 Ibid.

TWENTY-SIX: 1995 THROUGH 2000 STUMBLES

1 Lt. Col. Robert "Buzz" Patterson, *Dereliction of Duty: The Eyewitness Account of How Bill Clinton Compromised America's National Security* (Washington, D.C.: Regnery Publishing, 2003), 52.
2 R. Emmett Tyrrell, Jr., "The Continuing Crisis," *American Spectator*, June 1995, 8.
3 Wesley Pruden, "The Patriotic Snub of a Tribute to Heroes," *Washington Times*, May 9, 1995.
4 Ibid.
5 R. Emmett Tyrrell, Jr., "The Continuing Crisis," *American Spectator*, November 1995, 11.
6 John McCaslin, "Above the Law," Inside The Beltway, *Washington Times*, September 20, 1995; Tyrrell, "The Continuing Crisis, 11.

7   On the Prowl, "Pope Vetoes White House Visit," *American Spectator*, December 1995, 14.
8   Paul Kengor, *God and Hillary Clinton: A Spiritual Life* (New York: HarperCollins, 2007), 310.
9   Author Paul Kengor interview with Rob Schenk, November 6, 2006; Kengor, *God and Hillary Clinton*, 213.
10 Rowan Scarborough, "Press Avoids Kerry Take on Clinton as 'Good Liar,'" *Washington Times*, February 6, 1996.
11 Brock Yates, "The NASCAR Red State," *American Spectator*, April 2005, 15.
12 Gary Aldrich, *Unlimited Access: An FBI Agent Inside the Clinton White House* (Washington, D.C.: Regnery Publishing, 1996), 137.
13 Ibid.
14 Ibid.
15 Christopher Woody, "Bill Clinton Once Lost the Nuclear Codes for Months, and a 'Comedy of Errors' Kept Anyone from Finding Out," *Business Insider*, January 3, 2018.
16 Patterson, *Dereliction of Duty*, 55.
17 Ibid.
18 Ibid, 56.
19 Ibid.
20 Ibid.
21 Ibid.
22 Ibid, 56-57.
23 Ibid, 57.
24 Ibid, 57-58.
25 Woody, "Bill Clinton Once Lost the Nuclear Codes for Months, and a 'Comedy of Errors' Kept Anyone From Finding Out."
26 Ibid.
27 Ibid.
28 Ibid.
29 Ibid.
30 Bill Sammon, "Clinton Implores Blacks to Pick 'Outstreched Hands' Instead of 'Clenched Fists,'" *Washington Times*, October 30, 2000; Wesley Pruden, "Gods Gets a Hard *Time* on the Hustings," *Washington Times*, October 31, 2000.
31 Lead Editorial, "Win One for the Groper," *Washington Times*, November 1, 2000.
32 Sammon, "Clinton Implores Blacks to Pick 'Outstretched Hands' Instead of 'Clenched Fists,'"; Bill Sammon, "Clinton Miffed Remarks Released Before Election," *Washington Times*, October 31, 2000.
33 Sammon, "Clinton Miffed Remarks Released Before the Election."
34 Ibid.
35 Ibid.

TWENTY-SEVEN: ELECTION 1996

1   Jennifer Harper, "Networks Deflated, Polls Berated and Viewers Sedated," *Washington Times*, November 7, 1996.
2   Donald Lambro, "President's Team on the Lookout For Potential Primary Challengers," *Washington Times*, May 10, 1994.
3   Ibid.
4   Edward Walsh, "Democrats to Return to Chicago in '96," *Washington Post*, August 5, 1994.
5   Dick Morris, *Behind the Oval Office: Getting Reelected Against All Odds* (Los Angeles: Renaissance, 1999), 23; Jeff Gerth and Don Van Natta Jr., *Her Way: The Hopes and Ambitions of Hillary Rodham Clinton* (New York: Little, Brown and Company, 2007), 146.

6   Gerth and Van Natta, *Her Way*, 146.
7   Morris, *Behind the Oval Office*, 24.
8   Gerth and Van Natta, *Her Way*, 146.
9   Morris, *Behind the Oval Office*, 25.
10 George Stephanopoulos, *All Too Human: A Political Education* (Boston: Little, Brown and Company, 1999), 334, 336.
11 James Ring Adams, "The Once and Future Scandal," *American Spectator*, May 1998, 44.
12 Ibid.
13 Morris, *Behind the Oval Office*, 149.
14 Deposition of Donald L. Fowler, 290-292, in Thompson Report at 61; Edward Timperlake and William C. Triplett II, *Year of the Rat*: Washington, D.C.: Regnery Publishing, 1998), 64.
15 Deposition of Bruce Lindsey, p.1118, in Thompson Report at 1660; Timperlake and Triplett, *Year of the Rat*, 64.
16 Thompson *Committee Report*, Chapter 15: Timperlake and Triplett, *Year of the Rat*, 66; Jack Cashill, *Ron Brown's Body: How One Man's Death Saved the Clinton Presidency and Hillary's Future* (Nashville: WND Books, 2004), 164-165.
17 Dick Morris, *Behind the Oval Office*, 150.
18 Ibid, 152.
19 Ibid, 153.
20 Warren P. Strobel, "Clinton Puts All-Stars on Campaign Team," *Washington Times*, January 15, 1996.
21 John McCaslin, "Four More Years?" *Washington Times*, Inside the Beltway, January 17, 1996.
22 Morris, *Behind the Oval Office*, 277.
23 (*Associated Press*), "Nowhere to Go but the White House or Home," *Washington Times*, May 16, 1996.
24 Lead Editorial, "A Vivid Clinton Memory at Last," *Washington Times*, June 11, 1996.
25 John Corry, "Network Meanness," *American Spectator*, October 1996, 42.
26 Rowan Scarborough, "Morris Hooked by Prostitute," *Washington Times*, August 30, 1996.
27 Carl Bernstein, *A Woman in Charge: The Life of Hillary Rodham Clinton* (New York: Alfred A Knopf, 2007), 465.
28 Paul Bedard, "Clinton Sets Off on Rocky Ride," *Washington Times*, August 31, 1996.
29 "No *Time* for Timidity," *Human Events*, November 15, 1996, 1.
30 Grover G. Norquist, "House Sweet It Is," *American Spectator*, January 1997, 49.

TWENTY-EIGHT: OKLAHOMA CITY

1   Ambrose Evans-Pritchard, *The Secret Life of Bill Clinton: The Unreported Stories* (Washington, D.C.: Regnery Publishing, 1997), 3.
2   Ibid.
3   Howard Kurtz and Dan Balz, "Clinton Assails Spread of Hate Through Media," *Washington Post*, April 25, 1995.
4   Evans-Pritchard, *The Secret Life of Bill Clinton*, 4-5.
5   Jayna Davis, *The Third Terrorist: The Middle East Connection to Oklahoma City Bombing* (Nashville: Nelson Current, 2004), pp.256-258, 262-263, 266, 317-318.
6   Ibid, 24-25, 171-172, 179-181.
7   "The Oklahoma City Bombing 20 Years Later, https://stories.fbi.gov/oklahoma-bombing/, April 19, 2015
8   Davis, *The Third Terrorist*, 27-32, 34-35, 40-42, 181-183.
9   "The Oklahoma City Bombing, 20 Years Later."
10 Ibid.

11 Davis, *The Third Terrorist*, 32, 48-52.
12 Evans-Pritchard, *The Secret Life of Bill Clinton*, 11.
13 Ibid, 12.
14 "The Oklahoma City Bombing 20 Years Later."
15 Ibid.
16 Evans-Pritchard, *The Secret Life of Bill Clinton*, 5.
17 Writ of Mandamus, Timothy McVeigh defense team; Evans-Pritchard, *The Secret Life of Bill Clinton*, 6.
18 Inspector General's report. It noted that the blast might have been an ANFO bomb but it was also consistent with a dynamite explosion. Residue of nitroglycerine was found at the crime scenes, and so was a dynamite wrapper. Yet the FBI failed "to address the possibility that the main charge consisted of dynamite." Evans-Pritchard, *The Secret Life of Bill Clinton*, 6.
19 Evans-Pritchard, *The Secret Life of Bill Clinton*, 6-7.
20 There was no science to back any of this up. The FBI labs never measured "the radius of the curvature of the fragments" so it was "virtually impossible" to know where the plastic came from; Evans-Pritchard, *The Secret Life of Bill Clinton*, 7.
21 Evans-Pritchard, *The Secret Life of Bill Clinton*, 7-8.
22 Ibid, 8.
23 Davis, *The Third Terrorist*, 299.
24 Ibid.
25 Ibid, 300.
26 "Incendiary Charges," *Washington Times*, February 16, 2003.
27 Ibid.
28 Jack Kelly, "Oklahoma City Loose Ends," *Washington Times*, January 4, 2007.
29 "Incendiary Charges."

TWENTY-NINE: FUND-RAISING SCANDALS
1   Robert Suro, "Chung Makes Deal With Prosecutors," *Washington Post*, March 6, 1998.
2   Byron York, "Al Gore's Loyalty Problem," *American Spectator*, August 1999, 75.
3   *Human Events*, August 8, 1997, 3.
4   White House press release, January 21, 1993; Edward Timperlake and William C. Triplett II, *Year of the Rat* (Washington, D.C.: Regnery Publishing, 1998), 216-217.
5   Timperlake and Triplett, *Year of the Rat*, 217, emphasis added.
6   Ibid.
7   Ibid.
8   Donald Lambro, "Oiling the Moneygate," *Washington Times*, February 3, 1997.
9   Ibid.
10 Ibid.
11 Charles G. LaBella, Interim Report for Janet Reno, Attorney General, July 16, 1998; David Limbaugh, *Absolute Power: The Legacy of Corruption in the Clinton-Reno Justice Department* (Washington, D.C.: Regnery Publishing, 2001), 170-171.
12 Limbaugh, *Absolute Power*, 171.
13 Timperlake and Triplett, *Year of the Rat*, 218,220.
14 Ibid, 221.

THIRTY: CHINA
1   R. Emmett Tyrrell, Jr., *The Clinton Crack-Up: The Boy President's Life After the White House* (Nashville: Thomas Nelson, 2007), 118.

2   Charles Smith, "Dead Men Tell No Tales—Part 2," *WorldNetDaily.com*, March 23, 1999; Richard Poe, *Hillary's Secret War: The Clinton Conspiracy to Muzzle Internet Journalists* (Nashville: WND Books, 2004), 161-162.
3   Tyrrell, *The Clinton Crack-Up*, 112.
4   Ibid, 118.
5   John N. Petrie (ed.), *Essays in Strategy 12* (Diane Publishing, 1996), 15; Tyrrell, *The Clinton Crack-Up*, 112.
6   Kenneth R. Timmerman, "The DNC's Chinese Money Laundry," *American Spectator*, November 1998, 18; Tyrrell, The Clinton-Crack-Up, 112-113.
7   Kenneth R. Timmerman, "Partners In Crime," *American Spectator*, August 1999, 30.
8   Ibid.
9   Ibid.
10 Ibid, 31.
11 Kenneth R. Timmerman, "Red Star Over Washington," *American Spectator*, May 1999, 31.
12 Carl Limbacher, "Clinton Wants to be Boss of U.N.," *NewsMax.com*, October 3, 2000; David Horowitz, "Spy Stories: The Wen Ho Lee Cover-Up," *FrontPageMagazine.com*, Poe, *Hillary's Secret War*, 162.
13 Timmerman, "Red Star Over Washington," 30-31.
14 Timmerman, "Red Star Over Washington," 31; Kenneth R. Timmerman, "Casualties of China Connection," *Washington Times*, February 24, 2000, A16; Tyrrell, *The Clinton Crack-Up*, 119-120; Jeff Gerth and David E. Sanger, "Aircraft Deal with Chinese is Questioned," *New York Times*, October 30, 1996, A1.
15 Timmerman, "Red Star Over Washington," 31.
16 Ibid.
17 Timmerman, "Partners in Crime," 28; Kenneth Timmerman, "PNTR Will Only Boost Transfer of U.S. Technology to China," *Human Events*, June 2, 2000, 12.
18 Editorial, "Clinton Renews MFN For China" Voice of America, June 14, 1993; Jack Cashill, *Ron Brown's Body: How One Man's Death Saved the Clinton Presidency and Hillary's Future* (Nashville: WND Books, 2004), 115-116.
19 Patrick Tyler, *A Great Wall, Six Presidents and China: An Investigative History* (New York: A Century Foundation Book, 1999), 399; Cashill, *Ron Brown's Body*, 116. In January 1994, Clinton partially lifted the ban on satellite launches by transferring the export licenses for some satellites from State to the ever-friendly Commerce Department. One of those so transferred belong to Hughes. *New York Times*, April 13, 1998; Edward Timperlake and William C. Triplett II, *Year of the Rat* (Washington, D.C.: Regnery Publishing, 1998), 180.
20 Timperlake and Triplett, *Year of the Rat*, 180-181, emphasis added.
21 John Mintz, "How Hughes Got What It Wanted on China," *Washington Post*, June 25, 1998; *Human Events*, May 29, 1998, 3.
22 *New York Times*, October 2, 1995; Timperlake and Triplett, *Year of the Rat*, 144; *Weekly Standard*, September 8, 1997.
23 Timmerman, "Red Star Over Washington," 31.
24 Ibid.
25 *Human Events*, May 29, 1998, 3.
26 Lead Editorial, "Quid Pro Quo? A China Chronology," *Washington Times*, May 22, 1998.
27 "President Clinton's Visit to China in Context," *Human Rights Watch*, last updated December 8, 1998; Cashill, *Ron Brown's Body*, 117.
28 Cashill, *Ron Brown's Body*, 117.
29 Ibid.
30 *Human Events*, May 29, 1998, 3.

31 President Clinton's Visit to China in Context," *Human Rights Watch*, last updated December 8, 1998; Cashill, *Ron Brown's Body*, 118, *Human Events*, May 29, 1998, 3.
32 Lead Editorial, "Quid Pro Quo? A China Chronology"; Lt. Col. Robert "Buzz" Patterson, *Dereliction of Duty: The Eyewitness Account of How Bill Clinton Compromised America's National Security* (Washington D.C.: Regnery Publishing, 2003), 168.
33 Lead Editorial, "Quid Pro Quo? A China Chronology."
34 Paul Klebnikov, "What He Wants, Bernie Gets," *Forbes*, October 7, 1996, Cashill, *Ron Brown's Body*, 125.
35 Juliet Eilperin, "GOP Says U.S. Gave China Nuclear Edge," *Washington Post*, May 6, 1998; Cashill, *Ron Brown's Body*, 125-126; *New York Times*, May 28, 1998; Timperlake and Triplett, *Year of the Rat*, 173.
36 Timperlake and Triplett, *Year of the Rat*, 173.
37 MSNBC, May 21, 1998; Timperlake and Triplett, *Year of the Rat*, 173-174.
38 *New York Times*, July 18, 1998; Timperlake and Triplett, *Year of the Rat*, 174.
39 Eilperin, "GOP Says U.S. Gave China Nuclear Edge"; Cashill, *Ron Brown's Body*, 126.
40 *Human Events*, May 29, 1998, 3.
41 Statement on the Occasion of the U.S.-North Korean Nuclear Agreement, October 14, 1994, *Public Papers of the Presidents*; Timperlake and Triplett, *Year of the Rat*, 136; Patterson, *Dereliction of Duty*, 169.
42 Patterson, *Dereliction of Duty*, 169.
43 *Human Events*, May 29, 1998, 3.
44 The Bellows Report has redacted all references to the memo other than the date of its submission to Notra Trulock. Bellows Report, ch. 6, 238; Cox Report, vol. 1, 72; Notra Trulock, Code Name Kindred Spirit: Inside the Chinese Nuclear Espionage Scandal (San Francisco: Encounter Books, 2002), 72.
45 "China Story: Money, Maneuvering and Missiles," *Human Events*, March 26, 1999, 3; Sen. James Inhofe, "Clinton Stonewalled Senate on Chinese Espionage Case," *Human Events*, March 26, 1999, 17.
46 *Human Events*, May 29, 1998, 3.
47 "Cancel the Kowtow Summit," *Human Events*, May 29, 1998, 8.
48 *Human Events*, May 29, 1998, 4.
49 Ibid.
50 "China Story: Money, Maneuvering and Missiles," *Human Events*, March 26, 1999, 3.
51 "Cancel the Kowtow Summit," 8.
52 Cashill, *Ron Brown's Body*, 177.
53 Ibid.
54 Eric Schmitt and Jeff Gerth, "White House Memos to President Reveal Strategy to Shift Purview Over Satellite Sales," *New York Times*, July 18, 1998; Cashill, *Ron Brown's Body*, 177.
55 *Washington Post*, January 26, 1997; Timperlake and Triplett, *Year of the Rat*, 182.
56 Timperlake and Triplett, *Year of the Rat*, 182.
57 *Human Events*, May 29, 1998, 4.
58 Charles Smith, "Smoking Gun: Made in China," *WorldNetDaily*, February 9, 2000; Cashill, *Ron Brown's Body*, 178.
59 Cashill, *Ron Brown's Body*, Patterson, *Dereliction of Duty*, 172-173.
60 Byron York, "The End of the Scandal: The Final Gasps of the Campaign Finance Investigation," *National Review* Online, January 8, 2002.
61 *Human Events*, May 29, 1998, 4.
62 Patterson, *Dereliction of Duty*, 172-173.
63 Volume II, Chapter 6, U.S. House of Representatives, Select Committee on U.S. National Security and Military/Commercial Concerns with the People's Republic of China. *House Report*

105-851, January 3, 1999. Also known as the Cox Committee; Cashill, *Ron Brown's Body*, 179-180; Jerusalem Channel 2 Television Network, February 16, 1996; Timperlake and Triplett, *Year of the Rat*, 170-171; Hong Kong Standard, March 26, 1996.

64 Review & Outlook, "Why China Hates NMD," *Wall Street Journal* Interactive Edition, July 11, 2000; Cashill, *Ron Brown's Body*, 180.
65 Eric Schmitt and Jeff Gerth, "White House Memos to President Reveal Strategy to Shift Purview Over Satellite Sales," *New York Times*, July 18, 1998; Cashill, *Ron Brown's Body*, 180.
66 Ibid; Ibid.
67 Aviation Week, February 26, 1996; Timperlake and Triplett, *Year of the Rat*, 171.
68 "It's Not Sex, It's National Security," *Human Events*, April 24, 1998, 8; Bill Gertz, *Betrayal: How the Clinton Administration Undermined American Security* (Washington, D.C.: Regnery Publishing, 1999, 85.
69 Gertz, *Betrayal*, 85.
70 "Text of Correspondence on Waiver to Permit Satellite Export," *New York Times*, May 23, 1998; Cashill, *Ron Brown's Body*, 180-181.
71 Cashill, *Ron Brown's Body*, 181.
72 "Text of Correspondence on Waiver to Permit Satellite Export"; Cashill, *Ron Brown's Body*, 181.
73 Gertz, *Betrayal*, 82.
74 *Human Events*, May 29, 1998, 4; Patterson, *Dereliction of Duty*, 174.
75 "Sting Nabs Alleged Chinese Arms Smugglers: Seizure Billed as Largest in U.S. History," *CNN.com*, May 23, 1996; Cashill, *Ron Brown's Body*, 181-182.
76 Cashill, *Ron Brown's Body*, 182.
77 Patterson, *Dereliction of Duty*, 175; "Cancel the Kowtow Summit," 8.
78 Ibid; Ibid.
79 "Cancel the Kowtow Summit," 8.
80 Ibid.
81 *New York Times*, May 9, 1997; Timperlake and Triplett, *Year of the Rat*, 197.
82 Steven A. Schwalm, "Clinton Caters to Butcher of Beijing," *Human Events*, December 20, 1996, 4.
83 Timperlake and Triplett, *Year of the Rat*, 247.
84 *Human Events*, May 29, 1998, 4.
85 "The Acquisition of Technology Relating to Weapons of Mass Destruction and Advanced Conventional Munitions," report by the CIA to Congress, June 1997, at 5; Timperlake and Triplett, *Year of the Rat*, 139-140.
86 Tyrrell, The Clinton-Crack-Up, 120.
87 Timperlake and Triplett, *Year of the Rat*, 140.
88 "China Story: Money, Maneuvering and Missiles," *Human Events*, March 26, 1999, 3.
89 R. Jeffrey Smith, "China's Pledge to End Iran Nuclear Aid Yields U.S. Help," *Washington Post*, October 30, 1997.
90 Timmerman, "Red Star Over Washington," 28.
91 *Human Events*, May 29, 1998, 4.
92 "Cancel the Kowtow Summit," 8; *Human Events*, May 29, 1998, 4.
93 *Human Events*, May 29, 1998, 4.
94 "Cancel the Kowtow Summit," 8; *Human Events*, May 29, 1998, 4.
95 "Cancel the Kowtow Summit," 8.
96 Nancy E. Roman and Bill Gertz, "House Slams Clinton on China Waiver," *Washington Times*, May 21, 1998; *Human Events*, May 29, 1998, 1.
97 Tony Snow, "Patterns of Presidential Perfidy," *Washington Times*, May 29, 1998.
98 Ibid.
99 Ibid.

100   Ibid.
101   "LaBella's Memo Called For Bribery Investigation of President Clinton," *Human Events*, May 12, 2000, 1.
102   Ibid.
103   Gertz, *Betrayal*, 136.
104   Paul Bedard, "Clinton Defends Visit to Tiananmen: Decision to Let China Launch U.S. Satellite 'Routine,' He Says," *Washington Times*, June 10, 1998.
105   Bill Gertz, "CIA Analyst Says U.S. Winked At Cheating," *Washington Times*, June 12, 1998.
106   Ibid.
107   L. Brent Bozell, "Espionage Gap in the China Coverage," *Washington Times*, July 1, 1998.
108   Warren Strobel, "Clinton Clarifies U.S. Position on Taiwan's Status," *Washington Times*, July 1, 1998.
109   Richard Halloran, Global Beat Issue Brief No. 40, July 14, 1998. Center for War, Peace and the News Media; Tyrrell, *The Clinton Crack-Up*, 125.
110   Tyrrell, *The Clinton Crack-Up*, 126.
111   "China Story: Money, Maneuvering and Missiles," *Human Events*, March 26, 1999, 3.
112   Bill Gertz, "White House Plays Down Test of Rocket Motor By Chinese," *Washington Times*, July 23, 1998; Kenneth R. Timmerman, "Long Beach Missile Transfers," *American Spectator*, September 1998, 49.
113   Gertz, "White House Plays Down Test of Rocket Motor By Chinese"; Gertz, *Betrayal*, 102.
114   David Limbaugh, *Absolute Power: The Legacy of Corruption in the Clinton-Reno Justice Department* (Washington, D.C.: Regnery Publishing, 2001), 260.
115   Louis J. Freeh, *My FBI: Bringing Down the Mafia, Investigating Bill Clinton, and Fighting the War on Terror* (New York: St. Martin's Press, 2005), 219.
116   Terence P. Jeffrey, "Reno and Holder Both Involved in Decision Not to Tap Wen Lee," *Human Events*, May 14, 1999, 1, 8..
117   Freeh, *My FBI*, 219.
118   Ibid.
119   "China Story: Money, Maneuvering and Missiles," 3, Freeh, *My FBI*, 220-221.
120   From Combined Dispatches, "Spy-Case Nuclear Scientist Lee Freed," *Washington Times*, September 14, 2000; Lead Editorial, "Wen Ho Lee, No Martyr," *Washington Times*, September 27, 2000.
121   Richard Benke, "Lee Plea Bargain To Win Release For Nuclear Scientist," *Washington Times*, September 11, 2000.
122   *Human Events*, April 2, 1999, 30-31.
123   Scott Park, "Security Experts Doubt Clinton on Espionage Case," *Human Events*, April 2, 1999, 4.
124   Scott Park, "Energy Officials 'Have No Recollection' of Covering Up Espionage," *Human Events*, April 23, 1999, 6.
125   Ibid.
126   "More Evidence That Clinton Lied About Espionage," *Human Events*, June 4, 1999, 3.
127   Ibid.
128   "Chinese Espionage Puts U.S. National Security at Risk," *Human Events*, June 4, 1999, 17.
129   "Red China's People's Liberation Army Knows U.S. Is Vulnerable," *Human Events*, December 3, 1999, 21.
130   Sen. James M. Inhofe, "End Chinagate Cover-Up," *Human Events*, July 16, 1999, 1.
131   Ibid.
132   "The Decline and Fall of Bill Richardson," *Human Events*, June 30, 2000, 5.
133   Gertz, *Betrayal*, 214.

THIRTY-ONE: TERRORISM

1. Richard Miniter, *Losing Bin Laden: How Bill Clinton's Failures Unleashed Global Terror* (Washington, D.C.: Regnery Publishing, 2003), 1.
2. According to a news report from Yemen's state-run television, which was cited in French and American reports; Miniter, *Losing Bin Laden*, 1.
3. Yossef Bodansky, *Bin Laden: The Man Who Declared War on America* (Roseville: Prima Forum, 1999), 71.
4. Abbas Ghalib, "Yemen Blast Kills Janitor, Austrian Tourist," (*Associated Press*), December 30, 1992; Miniter, *Losing Bin Laden*, 4.
5. Miniter, *Losing Bin Laden*, 4.
6. Ibid.
7. Nabila Megalli, "U.S. Military Slips Out of Bomb-Plagued Yemen," *Associated Press*, January 2, 1993; Miniter, *Losing Bin Laden*, 4-5; David N. Bossie, *Intelligence Failure: How Clinton's National Security Policy Set the Stage for 9/11* (Nashville: WND Books, 2004), 150.
8. Miniter, *Losing Bin Laden*, 16.
9. Tom Robbins, "The Lesson: Incident at the Towers, 1993," *New York Daily News*, December 9, 1998; Miniter, *Losing Bin Laden*, 19.
10. Miniter, *Losing Bin Laden*, 19-20.
11. Dave Williams, "The Bombing of the World Trade Center in New York City," *International Criminal Police Review*, No. 469-471 (1998). Available at Interpol.com; Bossie, *Intelligence Failure*, 133.
12. Dick Morris, "Why Clinton Slept," *New York Post*, January 2, 2002; Bossie, *Intelligence Failure*, 133.
13. Bossie, *Intelligence Failure*, 133.
14. Malcolm Gladwell, "At Least Five Died, 500 Hurt as Explosion Rips Garage Under World Trade Center; Bomb Suspected in Midday Blast; Thousands Flee," *Washington Post*, February 27, 1993; Miniter, *Losing Bin Laden*, 27.
15. Lead Editorial, "Clinton's Failed War On Terror," *Washington Times*, November 19, 2004.
16. Dick Morris, "While Clinton Fiddled," *Wall Street Journal*, February 5, 2002; Bossie, *Intelligence Failure*, 142.
17. Andrew Sullivan, "The Damage Clinton Did," *Sunday Times*, September 30, 2001; Bossie, *Intelligence Failure*, 143; Lead Editorial, "Demagoguing September 11, *Washington Times*, May 21, 2002.
18. Miniter, *Losing Bin Laden*, 50.
19. According to the sworn statement of Jamal al-Fadl (Southern District Court of New York), February 6, 2001; Miniter, *Losing Bin Laden*, 50.
20. Miniter, *Losing Bin Laden*, 50.
21. This assertion appears in numerous places. See, for example, Yonah Alexander and Michael S. Swetnam, *Usama bin Laden's al Qaida: Profile of a Terrorist Network* (Ardsley, New York: Transnational Publishers, 2001), 7; Miniter, *Losing Bin Laden*, 50-51.
22. Author Richard Miniter interview with a Sudanese intelligence source; Miniter, *Losing Bin Laden*, 51.
23. Miniter, *Losing Bin Laden*, 51.
24. Ibid.
25. Bodansky, *Bin Laden*, 74.
26. Paul Greenberg, "The Ghosts of Mogadishu," *Washington Times*, August 16, 2002; Lead Editorial, "Demagoguing September 11," *Washington Times*, May 21, 2002.
27. Scott Peterson, *Me Against My Brother: At War in Somalia, Sudan and Rwanda* (London: Routledge, 2000), 151; Miniter, *Losing Bin Laden*, 70.
28. Miniter, *Losing Bin Laden*, 70.

29 John Miller and Michael Stone, with Chris Mitchell, *The Cell: Inside the 9/11 Plot, and Why the FBI and CIA Failed to Stop It*. (New York: Hyperion, 2002), 188; Rich Lowry, *Legacy: Paying the Price for the Clinton Years* (Washington, D.C.: Regnery Publishing, 2003), 300.
30 Miniter, *Losing Bin Laden*, 70.
31 Bill Gertz, *Breakdown: How America's Intelligence Failures Led to September 11* (Washington, D.C.: Regnery Publishing, 2002), 21.
32 Ibid.
33 Ibid.
34 Ibid.
35 Ibid, 22.
36 Ibid.
37 Ibid.
38 Ibid.
39 Ibid.
40 Ibid, 22-23.
41 Bodansky, *Bin Laden*, 113.
42 Lt. Col. Robert "Buzz" Patterson, *Dereliction of Duty: The Eyewitness Account of How Bill Clinton Compromised America's National Security* (Washington, D.C.: Regnery Publishing, 2003), 139.
43 Ibid.
44 Sam Vincent Meddis, "Terrorism Brushes U.S. Again," *USA Today*, March 9, 1995; Patterson, *Dereliction of Duty*, 136.
45 Bodansky, *Bin Laden*, 135.
46 Ibid, 136-137.
47 Miniter, *Losing Bin Laden*, 97-98.
48 Gertz, *Breakdown*, 7; Miniter, *Losing Bin Laden*, 98.
49 In 1998, *Bin Laden* told *Time* magazine that he had been at war with America "for ten years." ; Miniter, *Losing Bin Laden*, 98.
50 Patterson, *Dereliction of Duty*, 137.
51 Miniter, *Losing Bin Laden*, 110.
52 Ibid.
53 Ambassador Shinn told author Richard Miniter; Miniter, *Losing Bin Laden*, 99.
54 Miniter, *Losing Bin Laden*, 99.
55 According to a deputy director of the Mukhabarat, Sudan's external intelligence agency; Miniter, *Losing Bin Laden*, 100-101.
56 While the first of these secret meetings is now publicly acknowledged, what exactly was discussed is controversial. In the months following the September 11 attacks, three senior Clinton administration officials have essentially denied that Sudan ever offered to turn over *bin Laden* in May 1996. Clinton's last National Security Advisor, Sandy Berger, asserted that he knew nothing of Sudan's offer to turn over *bin Laden*, in a phone interview with Richard Miniter, in January 2002. Berger's denial doesn't track with President Clinton's own acknowledgement of the Sudanese offer. In the weeks after the September 11 attacks, the president was dining in a Manhattan restaurant roughly one mile north of Ground Zero. He told several dinner companions that turning down Sudan's offer to seize *bin Laden* in May 1996 was "The biggest mistake of my presidency."; Miniter, *Losing Bin Laden*, 101-102.
57 Ibid, 102.
58 According to Erwa's recollection to author Richard Miniter; Miniter, *Losing Bin Laden*, 102.
59 Miniter, *Losing Bin Laden*, 102.
60 Ibid, 102-103.
61 Ibid, 103.
62 Ibid, 104.

63 Gertz, *Breakdown*, 10-11; Miniter, *Losing Bin Laden*, 104.
64 Miniter, *Losing Bin Laden*, 109-110.
65 Ibid, 122.
66 Barton Gellman, "U.S. Foiled Multiple *Times* in Efforts to Capture *Bin Laden* or Have Him Killed; Sudan's Offer to Arrest Militant Fell Through After Saudis Said No," *Washington Post*, October 3, 2001; Miniter, *Losing Bin Laden*, 122-123.
67 Miniter, *Losing Bin Laden*, 123.
68 "Part one of a series of reports on *bin Laden*'s life in Sudan," No byline given, *Al-Quds Al-Arabi*, (London: November 24, 2001). Richard Miniter relied on a translation from the Foreign Broadcast Information Service, a U.S. government agency; Miniter, *Losing Bin Laden*, 124.
69 Miniter, *Losing Bin Laden*, 124.
70 Louis J. Freeh, *My FBI: Bringing Down the Mafia, Investigating Bill Clinton, and Fighting the War on Terror* (New York: St. Martin's Press, 2005), 1-2.
71 Freeh, *My FBI*, 2; Bodansky, *Bin Laden*, 124.
72 Freeh, *My FBI*, 2.
73 Ibid, 9.
74 Sioban Roth, "Khobar Towers: A Case of Futility," *Legal Times*, September 17, 2001; Bossie, *Intelligence Failure*, 165; Byron York, "Clinton Has No Clothes: What 9/11 Revealed About the Ex-President," *National Review*, November 30, 2001.
75 Patterson, *Dereliction of Duty*, 138.
76 John Solomon, "Clinton White House Suppressed Evidence of Iranian's Terrorism," *Washington Times*, October 6, 2015.
77 Ibid.
78 Bodansky, *Bin Laden*, 231.
79 Remarks by the president, Office of the Press Secretary, The White House, August 7, 1998. Available at http://usinfo.state.gov/topical/pol/terror/98080704.htm; Bossie, *Intelligence Failure*, 178.
80 Oliver North, "How Could This Possibly Happen?" *Human Events*, October 15, 2001, 11.
81 Bodansky, *Bin Laden*, 285.
82 Ibid.
83 Ibid, 287.
84 Ibid.
85 Gertz, *Breakdown*, 18; Patterson, *Dereliction of Duty*, 140.
86 Gertz, *Breakdown*, 18.
87 Transcript: Clinton Oval Office remarks on antiterrorist attacks; Bossie, *Intelligence Failure*, 182.
88 Gertz, *Breakdown*, 19.
89 Ibid.
90 Ibid.
91 Gertz, *Breakdown*, 19; Bill Sammon, "*Bin Laden* Blamed in New York's Plots," *Washington Times*, May 18, 2000.
92 Christopher Hitchens, *No One Left To Lie To* (London: Verso, 2000), 87; Author Rich Lowry interview with a former FBI official; Lowry, Legacy, 320.
93 Bossie, *Intelligence Failure*, 183.
94 According to an interview with an Arab intelligence source with author Richard Miniter in Cairo, in March 2002; Miniter, *Losing Bin Laden*, 194.
95 Miniter, *Losing Bin Laden*, 195.
96 Ibid, 195.
97 Steven Lee Myers, "Failed Plan to Bomb a U.S. Ship is Reported," *New York Times*, November 10, 2000; Miniter, *Losing Bin Laden*, 195.
98 Miniter, *Losing Bin Laden*, 195.

99	"The Road to Ground Zero," *The Sunday Times* (of London), January 6, 2002; Miniter, *Losing Bin Laden*, 195.
100	Miniter, *Losing Bin Laden*, 216-217.
101	Ibid, 217.
102	John F. Burns, "How a Mighty Power Was Humbled by a Little Skiff," *New York Times*, October 28, 2000; Miniter, *Losing Bin Laden*, 216.
103	Miniter, *Losing Bin Laden*, 217-218; "U.S. Vows to Find Terrorist Attackers of Navy Destroyer," *CNN.com*, October 12, 2000.
104	"Cole Guards Told Not to Fire First," *NewsMax.com*; Michael Savage, *Liberalism is a Mental Disorder* (Nashville: Nelson Current, 2005), 14.
105	"Standing Guard with No Ammunition?" *CBSNews.com*, November 14, 2000; Savage, *Liberalism is a Mental Order*, 14.
106	Miniter, *Losing Bin Laden*, 217-218.
107	Savage, *Liberalism is a Mental Disorder*, 13.
108	Ibid, 13-14.
109	Bossie, *Intelligence Failure*, 195-196.
110	Byron York, "Clinton Has No Clothes: What 9/11 Revealed About the Ex-President," *National Review*, December 17, 2001; Bossie, *Intelligence Failure*, 196.
111	Https://en.wikipedia.org/wiki/Able_Danger.
112	Lt. Col. Anthony Shaffer, *Operation Dark Heart: Spycraft and Special OPS on the Frontlines of Afghanistan and the Path to Victory* (New York: St. Martin's Press, 2010), 166.
113	Shaffer, *Operation Dark Heart*, 168; Jack Kelly, "Able Danger's Muzzled Mission," *Washington Times*, February 20, 2006.
114	Shaffer, *Operation Dark Heart*, 169.
115	Ibid, 169-170.
116	Ibid, 170.
117	Douglas Jehl, "4 in 9/11 Plot Are Called Tied to Qaeda in '00," *New York Times*, August 9, 2005.
118	Kelly, "Able Danger's Muzzled Mission."
119	Ibid.
120	Audrey Hudson, "Fears of Backlash Kept Pre-9/11 Data From FBI," *Washington Times*, August 16, 2005; Shaffer, *Operation Dark Heart*, 172-173.
121	Kelly, "Able Danger's Muzzled Mission"; "Data-Mining Offensive in the Works," Government Computer News, October 7, 2005 (http://www.gcn.com/Articles/2005/10/07/Datamining-offensive-in-the-works.aspx?Page=2).
122	Shaffer, *Operation Dark Heart*, 175-176.
123	Kelly, "Able Danger's Muzzled Mission."
124	Jacob Goodwin, "Inside Able Danger—The Secret Birth, Extraordinary Life and Untimely Death of a U.S. Military Intelligence," Government Security News, September 2005. See http://www.gsnmagazine.com/sep_05/shaffer_interview.html.
125	Kelly, "Able Danger's Muzzled Mission."

THIRTY-TWO: TWA FLIGHT 800

1	Thomas Jefferson to Archibald Stuart, 1799, http://famguardian.org/Subjects/Politics/thomasjefferson/jeff1600.htm. ; Jack Cashill, *TWA 800: The Crash, The Cover-Up, and the Conspiracy* (Washington, D.C.: Regnery History, 2016), 222.
2	John B. Roberts II, "The Ongoing Dissent Over *TWA 800*," *American Spectator*, August 1999, 41.
3	Ibid, 42.
4	Ibid.

5	Robert Woodward, *The Choice: How Clinton Won* (New York: Touchstone, 1997), 367; Jack Cashill, *TWA 800: The Crash, The Cover-Up, And The Conspiracy* (Washington, D.C.: Regnery History, 2016), 6.
6	CIA documents cached at TWA Flight 800: The Impossible Zoom Climb, raylahr.entryhost.com, "CIA records released to Tom Stalcup," records 26-50; Cashill, *TWA 800*, 96.
7	Roberts, "The Ongoing Dissent Over *TWA 800*," 43; Cashill, *TWA 800*, 154-155.
8	Roberts, "The Ongoing Dissent Over *TWA 800*," 42.
9	Roberts, "The Ongoing Dissent Over *TWA 800*," 42-43; Cashill, *TWA 800*, 192.
10	Cashill, *TWA 800*, 2, 26, 31-32, 44-45, 54, 59, 68, 190, 202-203.
11	Roberts, "The Ongoing Dissent Over *TWA 800*," 43.
12	Ibid, 44.
13	NTSB Witness Group Factual Report, Docket No. SA-516, Exhibit No. 4A, October 16, 1997, http://twa800.com/4a/exhibit4a.html.; Cashill, *TWA 800*, 65.
14	Cashill, *TWA 800*, 94-95.
15	David Johnston, "Explosion Aboard T.W.A. 800: The Theories," *New York Times*, July 19, 1996; Cashill, *TWA 800*, 95.
16	Cashill, *TWA 800*, 141.
17	CVR transcript TWA Flight 800, Aviation Safety Network, http://aviation-safety.net/investigation/cvr/transcripts/cvr_tw800.php; Cashill, *TWA 800*, 142.
18	Matthew Purdy, "Missile Theory Rebutted in T.W.A. Flight 800 Crash," *New York Times*, March 12, 1997; Cashill, *TWA 800*, 143.
19	Cashill, *TWA 800*, 143.
20	Ibid, 98.
21	Don Van Natta, "Fuel Tank's Condition Makes Malfunction Seem Less Likely," *New York Times*, August 14, 1996; Cashill, *TWA 800*, 99-100.
22	Cashill, *TWA 800*, 101.
23	Michelle Cottie, "Nice Work if You Can Get it: How Fannie Mae Became Washington's Biggest Power Player," *Washington Monthly*, June 1, 1998; Cashill, *TWA 800*, 155-156, 160.
24	Don Van Natta, "Prime Evidence Found That Device Exploded in Cabin of *TWA 800*," *New York Times*, August 23, 1996; Cashill, *TWA 800*, 102.
25	Cashill, *TWA 800*, 103.
26	Ibid, 104.
27	Don Van Natta, "More Traces of Explosive in Flight 800," *New York Times*, August 31, 1996; Cashill, *TWA 800*, 113-114.
28	Matthew Wald, "New Focus on Malfunctions in Inquiry on T.W.A. Crash," *New York Times*, September 19, 1996; Cashill, *TWA 800*, 118.
29	Cashill, *TWA 800*, 116-117.
30	Jocelyn Noveck, "Pierre Salinger's TWA Flight 800 Missile News Conference," (*Associated Press*), November 8, 1996; Cashill, *TWA 800*, 135.
31	Kristina Borjesson, Into the Buzzsaw: Leading Journalists Expose the Myth of a Free Press (New York: Prometheus Books, 2004), 291; Cashill, *TWA 800*, 134.
32	Roberts, "The Ongoing Dissent Over *TWA 800*," 43; Noveck, "Pierre Salinger's TWA Flight 800 Missile News Conference"; Cashill, *TWA 800*, 22-23.
33	Tim Weiner, "For 'the Ultimate Staff Guy,' a *Time* to Reap the Rewards of Being Loyal," *New York Times*, March 20, 1997; Cashill, *TWA 800*, 157.
34	Roberts, "The Ongoing Dissent Over *TWA 800*," 44.
35	Ibid.
36	Roberts, "The Ongoing Dissent Over *TWA 800*," 41; Cashill, *TWA 800*, 115.
37	Author Jack Cashill interview. Jack Cashill and James Sanders, *Silenced*, 2001; Cashill, *TWA 800*, 115-116.

38 Roberts, "The Ongoing Dissent Over *TWA 800*," 42.
39 Lead Editorial, "Democrats Target the White House," *Washington Times*, May 18, 2002.
40 Cashill, *TWA 800*, 158-159, 178.
41 Cashill, *TWA 800*, 178-179.
42 CIA documents cached at TWA Flight 800: The Impossible Zoom Climb, raylahr.entryhost.com, "CIA released to Tom Stalcup," records 26-50; Cashill, *TWA 800*, 213.
43 Cashill, *TWA 800*, 180.
44 "What Happened to TWA Flight 800," *CNN.com*, July 19, 2015; Cashill, *TWA 800*, 21, 84.
45 Affidavit, James Allan Holtschlaw, October 25, 2012; Cashill, *TWA 800*, 21.
46 Cashill, *TWA 800*, 68, 215.
47 TWA Flight 800, NTSB docket materials, DCA-96-MA070, August 2000, Exhibit 4A, appendix C: Cashill, *TWA 800*, 215.
48 Michael Pitcher, "Fax Gives Glimpse of Crash Investigation," Southampton Press, July 24, 1997; Cashill, *TWA 800*, 218.
49 Cashill, *TWA 800*, 138-139.
50 Ibid, 5, 138.
51 TWA Flight 800, NTSB docket materials, DCA-96-MA070, August 2000, Exhibit 4A, appendix M, Cashill, *TWA 800*, 5.
52 Cashill, *TWA 800*, 136, 175.
53 Ibid, 175.
54 Ibid, 219.
55 Ibid, 220.
56 "Analysis and Recommendations Regarding T.W.A. Flight 800," https://twa800.sites.usa.gov/files/twa800/DCA96MA070/50470.pdf; Cashill, *TWA 800*, 220-221.
57 Cashill, *TWA 800*, 221.

THIRTY-THREE: PAULA JONES PART II
1 Joyce Howard Price, "Jones Likely To Appeal Dismissal of Case," *Washington Times*, April 6, 1998.
2 Gail Sheehy, *Hillary's Choice* (New York: Ballantine Books, 1999), 10-11.
3 Ibid, 11.
4 Author Gail Sheehy interview with Hillary Rodham Clinton, CBS Radio, January 19, 1998; Sheehy, *Hillary's Choice*, 11.
5 (Reuters), " 'You Have to Box it Off,' Says Hillary of Paula Jones' Suit," *Washington Times*, January 20, 1998.
6 (*Associated Press*), "Clinton Lawyers Sought to Muzzle Secret Service Agents in Jones Suit," *Washington Times*, November 10, 1998.
7 Bill Sammon, "Clinton Asks Judge to Dismiss Jones Suit," *Washington Times*, February 18, 1998.
8 Bill Sammon, "Lawyer Details 'Pattern' of Clinton Obstruction," *Washington Times*, March 14, 1998.
9 Peter Baker and Susan Schmidt, "Willey Testifies Before Grand Jury," *Washington Post*, March 11, 1998; Bill Sammon, "Grand Jury Hears Willey," *Washington Times*, March 11, 1998.
10 "Scandal at a Glance," *Washington Times*, March 16, 1998.
11 Carl Limbacher, *Hillary's Scheme: Inside the Next Clinton's Ruthless Agenda to Take the White House* (New York: Crown Forum, 2003), 163-164.
12 Excerpts from 60 Minutes interview with Kathleen Willey and CBS correspondent Ed Bradley, "It Was Just Horrible Behavior on the Part of the President," *Washington Times*, March 16, 1998.
13 Limbacher, *Hillary's Scheme*, 165.

14	Peter Baker, "Clinton Didn't Yield Letters When Asked in Jones Case," *Washington Post*, March 29, 1998.
15	Jerry Seper, "Clinton Obstructed Justice, Lawyers Say," *Washington Times*, March 29, 1998.
16	Limbacher, *Hillary's Scheme*, 182.
17	Ibid, 182-183.
18	Ibid, 166.
19	Ibid, 167.
20	Lead Editorial, "The Tabloid President …, *Washington Times*, March 30, 1998.
21	Limbacher, *Hillary's Scheme*, 167-168.
22	Ibid, 168.
23	Carl Limbacher, "Broaddrick Blockbuster Set to Run Friday—Before NBC Panicked," *NewsMax.com*, January 29, 1999; Limbacher, *Hillary's Scheme*, 168-169.
24	Limbacher, *Hillary's Scheme*, 170-171.
25	Ibid, 171.
26	Ibid.
27	Ibid.
28	Ibid, 172.
29	Juanita Broaddrick, interviewed on NBC's *Dateline*, NBC News transcript; Limbacher, *Hillary's Scheme*, 172.
30	Limbacher, *Hillary's Scheme*, 172.
31	Ibid.
32	Ibid.
33	Christopher Andersen, Bill and Hillary: The Marriage (New York: William Morrow and Company, 1999), 164; Limbacher, *Hillary's Scheme*, 174.
34	Capital Briefs, "Clinton Demurs," *Human Events*, March 5, 1999, 2.
35	Jerry Seper, "Judge Throws Out Suit Against Clinton," *Washington Times*, April 2, 1998.
36	Ibid.
37	Seper, "Judge Throws Out Suit Against Clinton"; John F. Harris, "The White House Feeling Relieved, Resentful, *Washington Post*, April 2, 1998.
38	Joyce Howard Price, "Jones Likely to Appeal Dismissal of Case," *Washington Times*, April 6, 1998.
39	(*Associated Press*), "Jones' Attorneys File Final Brief in Appeal," *Washington Times*, October 1, 1998.
40	Frank J. Murray, "Bennett's Admission Could Hurt President," *Washington Times*, October 9, 1998.
41	(*Associated Press*), "Legal Fees Hurdle in Settling Jones' Harassment Suit," *Washington Times*, October 15, 1998.
42	(*Associated Press*), "Jones Adviser Demand of $2 Million For Settlement," *Washington Times*, October 18, 1998.
43	Joyce Howard Price, "Jones Given Incentive to Settle Her Lawsuit," *Washington Times*, November 1, 1998.
44	Peter Baker, "President Sought to Shield Officers," *Washington Post*, November 10, 1998.
45	Peter Baker, "Appeals Court Hears Arguments in Jones Harassment Case," *Washington Post*, October 21, 1998; Peter Baker, "Clinton, Jones Reach Settlement; President to Pay $850,000 to End Harassment Suit, Without Admission or Apology," *Washington Post*, November 14, 1998; Candice E. Jackson, *Their Lives: The Women Targeted By the Clinton Machine* (Los Angeles: World Ahead, 2005), 122.
46	Capital Briefs, "Paula Gets Paid Off," *Human Events*, January 22, 1999, 2; Hillary Watch, *Human Events*, February 5, 2001, 15.
47	Bruce Fein, "The Court Vindicated?" *Washington Times*, July 17, 2001.

THIRTY-FOUR: MONICA LEWINSKY

1. Paul Bedard, "Clinton Denies Lewinsky Allegations," *Washington Times*, January 27, 1998.
2. Edward Klein, *The Truth About Hillary* (New York: Sentinel, 2005), 105.
3. Candice E. Jackson, *Their Lives: The Women Targeted By The Clinton Machine* (Los Angeles: World Ahead, 2005), 190.
4. Andrew Morton, *Monica's Story* (New York: St. Martin's Press, 1999), 58; Gail Sheehy, *Hillary's Choice* (Ballentine Books, 1999), 270.
5. Jackson, *Their Lives*, 190.
6. "Text Lists 'Acts That May Constitute Grounds For Impeachment,'" *Washington Times*, September 12, 1998.
7. Kenneth Starr, *The Starr Report* (Pocket Books, 1998), 54; Rich Lowry, *Legacy: Paying the Price for the Clinton Years* (Washington, D.C.: Regnery Publishing, 2003), 161.
8. "Text Lists 'Acts That May Constitute Grounds for Impeachment.' "
9. Referral to the U.S. House of Representatives Pursuant to Title 28, U.S.C. S595 @ Appendix, sub'd by the Office of the Independent Counsel, September 9, 1998 (hereafter *"Appendix to Starr Report"*), 1297; R. Emmett Tyrrell, Jr., *The Clinton Crack-Up: The Boy President's Life After the White House* (Nashville: Thomas Nelson, 2007), 67.
10. Starr, *The Starr Report*, 80, 414; Author R. Emmett Tyrrell, Jr. interview with a former member of Congress who requests anonymity, June 2005; Tyrrell, *The Clinton Crack-Up*, 68.
11. Jeffrey Toobin, *A Vast Conspiracy* (New York: Touchstone, 1999), 89.
12. Toobin, *A Vast Conspiracy*, 90; Kara Hopkins, "The President Preyed on a Young Girl's Emotions," *Human Events*, 4; "Text Lists 'Acts That May Constitute Grounds For Impeachment.' "
13. Ibid.
14. Ibid.
15. Ibid.
16. Klein, *The Truth About Hillary*, 4.
17. Dana Priest and Rene Sanchez, "Kindred Spirits' Pentagon Bond," *Washington Times*, January 22, 1998; Toobin, *A Vast Conspiracy*, 108.
18. "Text Lists 'Acts That May Constitute Grounds For Impeachment' "; Toobin, *A Vast Conspiracy*, 109.
19. "Text Lists 'Acts That May Constitute Grounds For Impeachment.' "
20. Toobin, *A Vast Conspiracy*, 109.
21. Terence P. Jeffrey, "Lewinsky's SCI Clearance Could Land Her in the Clink," *Human Events*, February 13, 1998, 6.
22. Toobin, *A Vast Conspiracy*, 110.
23. Ibid, 110-111.
24. Ibid, 110.
25. "The Testing of the President: Lewinsky's Testimony on Love, Friend and Family," *New York Times*, September 22, 1998; Klein, *The Truth About Hillary*, 5.
26. "The Testing of the President: Lewinsky's Testimony on Love, Friend and Family"; Klein, *The Truth About Hillary*, 5.
27. Klein, *The Truth About Hillary*, 5-6.
28. Toobin, *A Vast Conspiracy*, 111.
29. Ibid.
30. "Lewinsky's Aug. 6 Grand Jury Testimony, Part 3" available at http://www.washingtonpost.com/wp-srv/politics/special/clinton/stories/mltest080698_3.htm#TOP; Jackson, *Their Lives*, 193.
31. Toobin, *A Vast Conspiracy*, 111; Starr, *The Starr Report*, 116-117; Tyrrell, *The Clinton Crack-Up*, 71-72.
32. "Text Lists 'Acts That May Constitute Grounds For Impeachment.' "

33 Ibid.
34 Ibid.
35 Hopkins, "The President Preyed on a Young Girl's Emotions," 4.
36 "Lewinsky's Aug. 6 Grand Jury Testimony, Part 6" available at http://www.washingtonpost.com/wp-srv/politics/special/clinton/stories/mltest080698_6.htm; "Text List 'Acts That May Constitute Grounds For Impeachment.' "
37 Byron York, "Slick Billy," *American Spectator*, December 1998, 49.
38 Ibid.
39 Ibid, 49-50.
40 Ibid, 50.
41 Ibid.
42 Ibid.
43 Ibid.
44 Ibid.
45 Byron York, "*False Witness, American Spectator*, February 1999, 26.
46 Ibid.
47 York, "Slick Billy," 50.
48 Ibid.
49 Ibid, 50-51.
50 Ibid.
51 Ibid.
52 Ibid.
53 Jerry Seper, "Richardson Recalls Lewinsky Job Meeting," *Washington Times*, July 23, 1998; York, "Slick Billy," 52.
54 York, "Slick Billy," 52.
55 Ibid.
56 Ibid.
57 Ibid, 53.
58 Editorial, "Intern Employment Inc.," *Washington Times*, August 12, 1998; York, "Slick Billy," 53.
59 York, "Slick Billy," 54.
60 Warren Strobel, "Clinton's Most Loyal Friends Aren't Going on the Attack," *Washington Times*, January 23, 1998.
61 Amy Goldstein and John Mintz, "Was Career Help Intended to Silence Lewinsky?" *Washington Post*, January 28, 1998.
62 David P. Schippers, *Sellout: The Inside Story of President Clinton's Impeachment* (Washington, D.C.: Regnery Publishing, 2000), 211.
63 Toobin, *A Vast Conspiracy*, 162-163.
64 Ibid, 163.
65 York, "*False Witness*," 29.
66 Ibid, 30.
67 Ibid.
68 Stewart M. Powell, "Clinton May Fight to Stop Testimony of Secret Service," *Washington Times*, January 30, 1998.
69 Schippers, *Sellout*, 208.
70 Toobin, *A Vast Conspiracy*, 166; Schippers, *Sellout*, 208.
71 Schippers, *Sellout*, 208; Toobin, *A Vast Conspiracy*, 168.
72 Schippers, *Sellout*, 208-209; Scott Park, "Clinton Contradicts Secret Service Agents' Testimony," *Human Events*, September 25, 1998, 3.
73 Schippers, *Sellout*, 209.
74 Ibid.

75   Lowry, Legacy, 146.
76   Schippers, *Sellout*, 211-212.
77   York, "*False Witness*," 32.
78   Jackson, *Their Lives*, 195-196.
79   Schippers, *Sellout*, 216; Toobin, *A Vast Conspiracy*, 179.
80   Schippers, *Sellout*, 216-217.
81   "Lewinsky's Aug. 6 Grand Jury Testimony, Part 10" available at http://www.washingtonpost.com/wp-srv/politics/special/clinton/stories/mltest080698_10htm; See also "Lewinsky's Aug. 6 Grand Jury Testimony, Part 11" available at http://www.washingtonpost.com/wp-srv/politics/special/clinton/stories/mltest080698_11.htm; Jackson, *Their Lives*, 196.
82   Warren P. Strobel, "Clinton's Most Loyal Friends Aren't Going on the Attack," *Washington Times*, January 23, 1998.
83   Peter Baker, "President Testified to Late Gifts to Lewinsky," *Washington Post*, August 22, 1998.
84   Toobin, *A Vast Conspiracy*, 182; York, "*False Witness*", 33.
85   Roger Morris, *Partners in Power: The Clintons and Their America* (Washington, D.C.: Regnery Publishing, 1996), xiv; Hopkins, "The President Preyed on a Young Girl's Emotions," 4.
86   Joseph A. D'Agostino, "Currying Favors: How the President Abused His Secretary," *Human Events*, October 2, 1998, 5.
87   York, "*False Witness*," 34-35.
88   Ibid, 35.
89   Ibid.
90   Jerry Seper, "Lewinsky Visits Get Intense Scrutiny," *Washington Times*, February 4, 1998.
91   Frank J. Murray, "Lewinsky Excluded from Jones Case," *Washington Times*, January 30, 1998.
92   Schippers, *Sellout*, 222.
93   Ibid, 222-223.
94   Ibid, 223.
95   York, "*False Witness*," 38; Schippers, *Sellout*, 223.
96   Schippers, *Sellout*, 223.
97   Amy Goldstein, "N.Y. Job Offer Coincides with Lewinsky Affidavit," *Washington Post*, January 31, 1998.
98   Peter Baker, "For Clinton, Long-Delayed Words and Painful What-Ifs," *Washington Post*, January 20, 2001.
99   Toobin, *A Vast Conspiracy*, 194.
100 York, "*False Witness*," 38.
101 Amy Goldstein, "N.Y. Job Offer Coincides with Lewinsky Affidavit," *Washington Post*, January 31, 1998.
102 Lead Editorial, "A Job for Monica," *Washington Times*, February 8, 1998.
103 Amy Goldstein, "N.Y. Job Offer Coincides with Lewinsky Affidavit."
104 Jerry Seper, "Ex-Intern Tells Starr She'll Admit Denial of Clinton Trysts Was a Lie," *Washington Times*, January 27, 1998; Jerry Seper and Bill Sammon, "Lindsey Must Talk, Starr Tells Judges," *Washington Times*, June 30, 1998.
105 Seper and Sammon, "Lindsey Must Talk, Starr Tells Judges."
106 Schippers, *Sellout*, 225-226.
107 Author Rich Lowry interview with Eric Holder; Lowry. Legacy, 171.
108 "From White House Intern to Vortex of Controversy," *Washington Post*, February 1, 1998.
109 Goldstein, "N.Y. Job Offer Coincides with Lewinsky Affidavit."
110 Toobin, *A Vast Conspiracy*, 203.
111 Ibid.
112 Ibid, 204-205.
113 Ibid, 205.

114 (*Associated Press*), "Prosecutors Irking Her, Lewinsky's Lawyer Says," *Washington Times*, February 15, 1998.
115 Toobin, *A Vast Conspiracy*, 206, 237.
116 Ibid, 236, 238.
117 Ibid, 265.
118 Ibid.
119 Ibid, 267.
120 Jennifer Harper, "Leaks Finally Forced Story from Whispers to Page One," *Washington Times*, January 22, 1998.
121 Matt Drudge, *Drudge Report*, January 17, 1998.
122 Schippers, *Sellout*, 230.
123 Ibid.
124 Ibid, 234.
125 York, *"False Witness,"* 39; "Desperately Seeking Monica Lewinsky," *Human Events*, October 2, 1998, 3.
126 York, *"False Witness,"* 39.
127 York, *"False Witness,"* 39; "Desperately Seeking Monica Lewinsky," 3.
128 Schippers, *Sellout*, 236.
129 York, *"False Witness,"* 41.
130 Toobin, *A Vast Conspiracy*, 268.
131 Toobin, *A Vast Conspiracy*, 269; Frank J. Murray, "Ex-Intern Has Tuesday Date With Federal Grand Jury," *Washington Times*, January 24, 1998.
132 Toobin, *A Vast Conspiracy*, 239.
133 Ibid, 239-240.
134 Ibid, 240.
135 Schippers, *Sellout*, 179-180.
136 Ibid, 180.
137 Ibid.
138 *Human Events*, January 30, 1998, 4.
139 Ibid.
140 Louise Branson, "The Truth About HRC," *Scotsman*, August 12, 1998; Klein, *The Truth About Hillary*, 104.
141 "From White House Intern to Vortex of Controversy," *Washington Post*, February 1, 1998.
142 Warren P. Strobel, "Clinton's Most Loyal Friends Aren't Going On The Attack," *Washington Times*, January 23, 1998.
143 John Lang (Scripps Howard News Service), "Intern Tapes Seem to Echo Maneuvers in Flowers Case," *Washington Times*, January 26, 1998.
144 Authors Jeff Gerth and Don Van Natta Jr. interview with former Clinton official in 2007; Gerth and Van Natta, *Her Way*, 180.
145 Toobin, *A Vast Conspiracy*, 250.
146 Paul Bedard, "Intern Has a New Look with a Shift in the Spin," *Washington Times*, January 26, 1998.
147 Paul Bedard, "Clinton Denies Lewinsky Allegations," *Washington Times*, January 27, 1998.
148 *Associated Press*, "'Never' Clinton Says to Charges, *Washington Times*, January 27, 1998.
149 Bedard, "Clinton Denies Lewinsky Allegations."
150 Klein, *The Truth About Hillary*, 130.
151 George Stephanopoulos, *All Too Human: A Political Education* (Boston: Little Brown and Company, 1999), 436.
152 *Human Events*, February 27, 1998, 28.

153 Richard Poe, *Hillary's Secret War: The Clinton Conspiracy to Muzzle Internet Journalists* (Nashville: WND Books, 2004), xiv.
154 Michael Chapman, "Reno Won't Defend Clinton's Executive Privilege Claim," *Human Events*, April 24, 1998, 7.
155 Scott Park, "Defense Department Appears to Stonewall Tripp-Gate Report," *Human Events*, March 10, 2000, 5.
156 Sen. James Inhofe, "Colson Served *Time* for Same Act Ken Bacon Committed," *Human Events*, May 5, 2000, 5.
157 Warren Strobel, "Clinton Takes Aim at Starr, Maintains Silence on Lewinsky," *Washington Times*, May 1, 1998.
158 Peter Baker and Susan Schmidt, "Lewinsky Gets Immunity For Her Testimony," *Washington Post*, July 29, 1998.
159 "Scandal at a Glance," *Washington Times*, August 3, 1998.
160 Jerry Seper, "Clinton Renews Lindsey Appeal," *Washington Times*, August 22, 1998.
161 Jerry Seper, "Lewinsky Gets Full Immunity to Testify," *Washington Times*, July 29, 1998.
162 Jerry Seper and Bill Sammon, "Lewinsky Dress Going to FBI For DNA Tests," *Washington Times*, July 31, 1998; Gerth and Van Natta, *Her Way*, 188.
163 "Scandal at a Glance."
164 Authors Jeff Gerth and Don Van Natta Jr. interview with OIC official in 1998; Gerth and Van Natta, *Her Way*, 188.
165 Ibid, 188-189.
166 Authors Jeff Gerth and Don Van Natta interview with two Clinton confidants in 1998; Authors Jeff Gerth and Don Van Natta Jr. interview with Bill Clinton confidant in 1998; Gerth and Van Natta, *Her Way*, 189.
167 Klein, *The Truth About Hillary*, 137-138.
168 Paul Bedard, "Clinton Won't Dodge Questions About His Sex Life," *Washington Times*, August 13, 1998.
169 Gerth and Van Natta, *Her Way*, 191.
170 Starr, *The Starr Report*, Text of Bill Clinton's Grand Jury Testimony, August 17, 1999. See http://www2.jsonline.com/news/president/0921fulltestimony.asp; Gerth and Van Natta, *Her Way*, 191.
171 Ibid; Ibid.
172 Ibid, Ibid.
173 Gerth and Van Natta, *Her Way*, 192.
174 Authors Jeff Gerth and Don Van Natta Jr. interview with two OIC officials in 1998; Gerth and Van Natta, *Her Way*, 192,
175 Schippers, *Sellout*, 237.
176 Authors Jeff Gerth and Don Van Natta Jr. interview with two OIC officials in 1998; Authors Jeff Gerth and Don Van Natta Jr. interview with one of the meeting's attendees; Gerth and Van Natta, *Her Way*, 192.
177 Tony Snow, "Fakery in a Gift Tie," *Washington Times*, August 21, 1998.
178 Gerth and Van Natta, *Her Way*, 193.
179 Joyce Milton, *The First Partner: Hillary Rodham Clinton* (New York: William Morrow and Company, 1999), 400-401.
180 Jennifer Harper, "Lewinsky Making Transition From Bimbo to 'Credibility,'" *Washington Times*, August 21, 1998; Paul Bedard and August Gribbin, "Questions Arise About Timing of Retaliatory Raids," *Washington Times*, August 21, 1998.
181 Bedard and Gribbin, "Questions Arise About Timing of Retaliatory Raids."
182 Sean Scully, "Clinton Ally Condemns His 'Misconduct,'" *Washington Times*, September 4, 1998.
183 Warren P. Strobel, "Clinton 'Sorry' as Rebuke Rises in His Own Party," *Washington Times*, September 5, 1998.

184 Report from investigator who seeks anonymity, September 2004; *American Spectator* researcher whose name is confidential; Tyrrell, *The Clinton Crack-Up*, 69.
185 Strobel, "Clinton 'Sorry' as Rebuke Rises in His Own Party."

THIRTY-FIVE: IMPEACHMENT

1. Bill Sammon, "Flip-Flops: Clinton vs. Lott," *Washington Times*, October 1, 1998.
2. Susan Schmidt and John Harris, "Ickes' Papers Offer Insight into Clinton Fund-Raising; President Frequently Reviewed Details of Campaign Money Efforts, Files Indicate," *Washington Post*, April 3, 1997; David Limbaugh, *Absolute Power: The Legacy of Corruption in the Clinton-Reno Justice Department* (Washington, D.C.: Regnery Publishing, 2001), 205-206.
3. Limbaugh, *Absolute Power*, 206.
4. Ibid.
5. Ibid, 206-207.
6. Bob Woodward, "Gore Was 'Solicitor-in-Chief,'" *Washington Post*, March 2, 1997; Limbaugh, *Absolute Power*, 207.
7. Limbaugh, *Absolute Power*, 207; Michael Chapman, "A Case For Impeachment?" *Human Events*, May 23, 1997, S4.
8. "Al Gore Broke the Law," *Human Events*, March 14, 1997, 7.
9. Limbaugh, *Absolute Power*, 207-208; Terence P. Jeffrey, "FBI Gore Spoke Falsely," *Human Events*, June 9, 2000, 1.
10. Chapman, "A Case for Impeachment?" S5.
11. Ibid.
12. John F. Harris, "Gore: Calls Broke No Law," *Washington Post*, March 4, 1997; Limbaugh, *Absolute Power*, 208.
13. Bob Woodward, "Gore Donors' Funds Used as 'Hard Money,'" *Washington Post*, September 3, 1997; David Limbaugh, *Absolute Power*, 222.
14. Ibid; Ibid.
15. "The Case Against Gore," *Human Events*, August 4, 2000, S3.
16. Ibid.
17. Ibid.
18. Ibid.
19. Ibid.
20. Scott Park, "Incriminating Memos Force New Investigation of Gore," *Human Events*, September 4, 1998, 7.
21. "The Case Against Gore," S3.
22. Scott Park, "Ickes Memos Raise Question: Did Gore Lie to Investigators?" *Human Events*, September 18, 1998, 7.
23. Ibid.
24. Ibid.
25. Chapman, "A Case for Impeachment?" S4.
26. Ibid.
27. Ibid, S5.
28. "Reno Violated Her Own Criteria in Refusing an Independent Counsel to Investigate Vice President Gore's White House Fundraising Calls," *Human Events*, December 19, 1997, 4.
29. Ibid.
30. "Spinning Themselves into a Corner," *Human Events*, March 21, 1997, 3.
31. Jerry Seper, "Hyde Asked to Begin Impeachment Inquiry," *Washington Times*, March 14, 1997.
32. Chapman, "A Case for Impeachment?" S2.
33. Ibid.
34. Ibid.

35   Ibid, S6.
36   Jerry Seper, "Hyde Asked to Begin Impeachment Inquiry," *Washington Times*, March 14, 1997.
37   Chapman, "A Case for Impeachment?" S4-5.
38   *Human Events*, July 25, 1997, 14.
39   Steven A. Schwalm, "The Clinton Koffee Klatch Club," *Human Events*, February 14, 1997, 3.
40   Warren P. Strobel, "For Rent Sign Was Out at White House, Documents Prove," *Washington Times*, February 26, 1997.
41   Charles R. Babcock and Sharon LaFraniere, "Hundreds of Contributors Enjoyed an Overnight Stay at White House," *Washington Post*, February 26, 1997.
42   Paul Bedard, "Mansion Run Like Royal Hotel," *Washington Times*, February 27, 1997.
43   "Blair Force One," *American Spectator*, On the Prowl, April 1997, 14.
44   Joyce Price, "Clinton On Video Hosting Coffees At White House," *Washington Times*, October 6, 1997; Chapman, "A Case for Impeachment?" S7
45   Chapman, "A Case for Impeachment?" S7.
46   "Huang Contributed $45,000 Before Gore Met Chairman of Reputed Espionage Front," *Human Events*, August 1, 1997, 7.
47   "Huang Contributed $45,000 Before Gore Met Chairman of Reputed Espionage Front," 1; Michael Chapman, "Al Gore Dodges Questions About Chinese Intelligence Connection," *Human Events*, March 13, 1998, 1.
48   "Huang Contributed $45,000 Before Gore Met Chairman of Reputed Espionage Front," 1, 7.
49   Chapman, "Al Gore Dodges Questions About Chinese Intelligence Connection," 1, 8; "Huang Contributed $45,000 Before Gore Met Chairman of Reputed Espionage Front," 1.
50   Ruth Marcus and R.H. Melton, "DNC Donor Controversy Widens as Republicans Step Up Criticism," *Washington Post*, October 18, 1996.
51   "The Hard Evidence: Even Gore Himself Called It a 'Fundraiser,'" *Human Events*, September 19, 1997, 5.
52   "A Presidential Quid Pro Quo?" *Human Events*, October 5, 1996, 3.
53   James Ring Adams, "The Once and Future Scandal," *American Spectator*, May 1998, 47.
54   Chapman, "A Case for Impeachment?" S10.
55   Ibid.
56   Joseph A. D'Agostino, "Is Clintonan Innicent Victim of Charlie Trie?" *Human Events*, February 27, 1998, 3.
57   Ibid.
58   Chapman, "A Case for Impeachment?" S10.
59   Chapman, "A Case for Impeachment?"
60   "Hyde Committee to Reno: Was Clinton Bribed?" *Human Events*, September 19, 1997, 3; Jeffrey, "White House Counsel Gave Charlie Trie Security Clearance," 1.
61   Joseph A. D'Agostino, "Hyde Committee: Did Communist Chinese Official Bribe President Bill Clinton?" *Human Events*, October 17, 1997, 5.
62   "Hyde Committee to Reno: Was Clinton Bribed?" 3.
63   Jeffrey, "White House Counsel Gave Charlie Trie Security Clearance," 1.
64   "Fugitive Clinton Friend Laundered Money, Aroused Suspicions, Won Presidential Appointment," *Human Events*, August 8, 1997, 5; Jeffrey, "White House Counsel Gave Charlie Trie Security Clearance," 1.
65   "Trie Snagged," Capital Briefs *Human Events*, February 13, 1998, 2; Jerry Seper, "Trie Apologizes to Clinton, Calls Fund Raising Naïve," *Washington Times*, March 2, 2000.
66   Chapman, "The Case For Impeachment?", S10
67   Chapman, "A Case for Impeachment?" S10; Joyce Milton, *The First Partner: Hillary Rodham Clinton* (New York: William Morrow and Company, 1999), 373.

68	"Clinton Sold Access to NSC-Declared 'Hustler,' Did He Sell Foreign Policy, Too?" *Human Events*, August 8, 1997, 3.
69	Ibid.
70	Ibid.
71	Ibid.
72	Ibid.
73	Edward Timperlake and William C. Triplett II, *Year of the Rat* (Washington, D.C.: Regnery Publishing, 1998), 202.
74	Ibid, 202-203.
75	"Clinton Sold Access to NSC-Declared 'Hustler,' Did He Sell Foreign Policy, Too?" 3; Chapman, "A Case For Impeachment?" S11.
76	"Clinton Sold Access to NSC-Declared 'Hustler,' Did He Sell Foreign Policy, Too?" 3.
77	Michael Kelly, "The Clinton Standard," *Washington Post*, May 27, 1998.
78	"Clinton Sold Access to NSC-Declared 'Hustler,' Did He Sell Foreign Policy, Too?" 3.
79	Milton, *The First Partner*, 370; Kenneth R. Timmerman, "While America Sleeps," *American Spectator*, June 1997, 36.
80	Chapman, "A Case for Impeachment?" S11.
81	Chapman, "A Case for Impeachment?" S11; "Clinton Sold Access to NSC-Declared 'Hustler,' Did He Sell Foreign Policy, Too?" 3.
82	Chapman, "A Case for Impeachment?" S11.
83	Ibid.
84	Bill Miller, "Thai Woman Pleads Innocent to Campaign Rap," *Washington Post*, July 30, 1998; Limbaugh, *Absolute Power*, 248.
85	Chapman, "A Case for Impeachment?" S11.
86	Joyce Price, "Burton Probes for Evidence of Donations-For-Secrets Deal," *Washington Times*, March 9, 1997.
87	Timperlake and Triplett, *Year of the Rat*, 248.
88	"Solomon Takes First Formal Step Toward Impeachment," *Human Events*, December 12, 1997, 4.
89	Mary Ann Akers, "Hyde Taps Democrat for Probe of Justice," *Washington Times*, March 27, 1998.
90	Editorial, "Charles LaBella Speaks," *Washington Times*, July 27, 1998.
91	"LaBella Passed Over," *Human Events* Capital Briefs, August 14, 1998, 2; "LaBella's Memo Called for Bribery Investigation of President Clinton," *Human Events*, May 12, 2000, 8.
92	Cal Thomas, "Judicial Benchmarks for Impeachment," *Washington Times*, August 12, 1998.
93	"Resign, Mr. President," *Human Events*, August 28, 1998, 8.
94	Joyce Howard Price, "Moynihan Seeks Quick Action on Impeachment," *Washington Times*, September 7, 1998.
95	Toobin, *A Vast Conspiracy*, 329-330.
96	Ruth Marcus and Roberto Suro, "Report Gives the House Host of Difficult Issues," *Washington Post*, September 12, 1998.
97	"Scandal at a Glance," *Washington Times*, September 21, 1998.
98	Capital Briefs, "Carter Slams Clinton," *Human Events*, October 2, 1998, 2.
99	Mary Ann Akers, "Resolution Echoes Nixon's in '74," *Washington Times*, October 1, 1998.
100	Toobin, *A Vast Conspiracy*, 364.
101	Limbaugh, *Absolute Power*, 116.
102	"Judiciary's 81 Impeachment Questions for Bill Clinton," *Human Events*, November 27, 1998, 12.
103	Frank J. Murray, "Judiciary Staff Finds Basis For Impeachment," *Washington Times*, November 11, 1998.
104	Schippers, *Sellout*, 149.
105	*Human Events*, December 11, 1998, 5-19.

106 "In Historic Vote, Judiciary Committee Approves Four Articles of Impeachment," *Human Events*, December 25, 1998, 12.
107 Schippers, *Sellout*, 252.
108 Ibid, 253.
109 Ibid.
110 Ibid, 254-255.
111 Toobin, *A Vast Conspiracy*, 365.
112 Frank J. Murray, "2 Out Of 4 Articles Approved By House," *Washington Times*, December 20, 1998.
113 Ibid.
114 Toobin, *A Vast Conspiracy*, 367.
115 Murray, "2 Out Of 4 Articles Approved by House"; "Dump Dick Gephardt," *Human Events*, September 15, 2000, 1.
116 Schippers, *Sellout*, 263.
117 Toobin, *A Vast Conspiracy*, 375.
118 Schippers, *Sellout*, 280.
119 Ibid.
120 Ibid.
121 "Clinton: I Defended the Constitution Against Defamers," *Human Events*, April 16, 1999, 7.
122 Schippers, *Sellout*, 3.

THIRTY-SIX: DISBARMENT

1 *Associated Press*, "More Legal Woes Await Citizen Clinton," *Washington Times*, January 15, 2001.
2 Frank J. Murray, "Clinton Asks Arkansas Court to Delay Disbarment Hearing," *Washington Times*, March 17, 2000; Mark R. Levin, "In Contempt," *Washington Times*, May 25, 2000.
3 "Court Adjudges the President to be in Contempt," *Washington Times*, May 23, 2000; Jeffrey Toobin, *A Vast Conspiracy* (New York: Touchstone, 1999), 398.
4 "Court Adjudges the President to be in Contempt."
5 Levin, "In Contempt."
6 Murray, "Clinton Asks Arkansas Court to Delay Disbarment Hearing."
7 Frank J. Murray, "Arkansas Panel Gives Clinton 5 Weeks to Defend Law License," *Washington Times*, March 18, 2000.
8 Murray and Cain, "Court Panel Urges Clinton Disbarment."
9 (Reuters), "Ex-Nun to Prosecute Clinton Disbarment Case," *Washington Times*, June 18, 2000.
10 Seper, "Arkansas Panel Moves to Disbar 'Unfit' Clinton."
11 (*Associated Press*), "Judge Gives Nod to Case on Clinton," *Washington Times*, July 12, 2000; (*Associated Press*), "Judge with Clinton Ties May Hear Case," *Washington Times*, January 3, 2001.
12 R. Emmett Tyrrell, Jr., *The Clinton Crack-Up: The Boy President's Life after the White House* (Nashville: Thomas Nelson, 2007), 15.
13 Frank J. Murray, "Clinton Resigns from Bar, Beats Deadline for Disbarment By Court," *Washington Times*, November 10, 2001.
14 Lead Editorial, "Bill Clinton's Nightmare," *Washington Times*, September 12, 2000.

THIRTY-SEVEN: PARDONS

1 John F. Harris, "Clinton Will Pay For Half Of Gifts," *Washington Times*, February 3, 2001.
2 "Pardons Are Grounded in History," *Washington Times*, September 25, 1996.
3 Jerry Seper, "Democrats Stall Vote on Clinton Pardons," *Washington Times*, September 28, 1996.
4 Seper, "Democrats Stall Vote on Clinton Pardons"; Morton C. Blackwell, "Protecting the Clinton Mafia," *Washington Times*, October 29, 1996.

5   Lead Editorial, "The Rose Garden of Pardon," *Washington Times*, October 2, 1996.
6   Debra Burlingame, "The Clintons' Terror Pardons," *Wall Street Journal*, February 12, 2008.
7   Barbara Olson, *The Final Days: The Last, Desperate Abuses of Power by the Clinton White House* (Washington, D.C.: Regnery Publishing, 2001), 16; Scott Park, "Clinton Frees Anti-American Terrorists," *Human Events*, September 17, 1999, 4.
8   Burlingame, "The Clintons' Terror Pardons."
9   Park, "Clinton Frees Anti-American Terrorists," 4; Jeffrey Lord, "Obama and the Bombmaker's Church," www.americanspectator.org, March 18, 2008.
10 Olson, *The Final Days*, 17.
11 Burlingame, "The Clintons' Terror Pardons."
12 Ibid.
13 Olson, *The Final Days*, 18; Scott Park, "FBI Vehemently Opposed Clemency For terrorists," *Human Events*, October 1, 1999, 4.
14 Olson, *The Final Days*, 18-19.
15 U.S. House of Representatives Committee on Government Reform, *The FALN and Macheteros, Executive Summary*, 3; Olson, *The Final Days*, 19; David Limbaugh, *Absolute Power: The Legacy of Corruption in the Clinton-Reno Justice Department* (Washington, D.C.: Regnery Publishing, 2001), 296.
16 Olson, *The Final Days*, 15-16; Burlingame, "The Clintons' Terror Pardons."
17 Burlingame, "The Clintons' Terror Pardons."
18 Olson, *The Final Days*, 19-20.
19 Burlingame, "The Clinton's Terror Pardons."
20 Ron Kolb, "Hillary, Terrorism and the FALN," www.realclearpolitics.com, May 29, 2008.
21 Ibid.
22 Burlingame, "The Clintons' Terror Pardons."
23 Olson, *The Final Days*, 20.
24 Ibid.
25 Andrew Cain and Jerry Seper, "Clinton Pardons Rostenkowski," *Washington Times*, December 23, 2000.
26 Jerry Seper, "McDougal, Deutch Get Clinton Pardons," *Washington Times*, January 21, 2001.
27 John McLaughlin, *John McLaughlin's One on One*, January 26, 2001; Olson, *The Final Days*, 10.
28 Joseph Curl, "Was a Pardon a Quid Pro Quo?" *Washington Times*, January 22, 2001; Bill O'Reilly, "*Post*-Clinton Dilemma," *Washington Times*, February 2, 2001.
29 Curl, "Was a Pardon a Quid Pro Quo?"
30 Jerry Seper, "Rich Refuses to Testify About Pardon," *Washington Times*, February 28, 2001; Hillary Watch, "She Just Keeps Giving and Giving and Giving," *Human Events*, February 19, 2001.
31 Disclosed to R. Emmett Tyrrell, Jr. by the officer during a September 2004 interview with anonymous interviewer; Tyrrell, *The Clinton Crack-Up*, 78.
32 Alison Leigh Cowan, "Panel Says Top Justice Department Aide Held Information on Rich's Pardon," *New York Times*, March 13, 2002, A1; U.S. House of Representatives, Committee on Government Reform, "Executive Summary," *Justice Undone: Clemency Decisions in the Clinton White House*, 107th Cong., 2nd Sess., 2002, H. Rpt.,5; Tyrrell, *The Clinton Crack-Up*, 87-88.
33 Curl, "Was a Pardon a Quid Pro Quo?"; Jerry Seper, "Pardon Made Behind Democrats' Backs," *Washington Times*, January 27, 2001.
34 Steve Chapman, "Scandalous Farewell," *Washington Times*, January 30, 2001.
35 Lead Editorial, "Who's Sorry Now?" *Washington Times*, February 14, 2001; Tyrrell, *The Clinton Crack-Up*, 93.
36 Tyrrell, *The Clinton Crack-Up*, 93-94.

37	O'Reilly, "*Post*-Clinton Dilemma"; Jerry Seper, "Probe Targets Commutations of Hasidic Men," *Washington Times*, February 24, 2001.
38	Olson, *The Final Days*, 21.
39	Ibid.
40	Ibid.
41	"When Crime Pays …," *Human Events*, January 29, 2001, 3; Jerry Seper, "McDougal, Deutch Get Clinton Pardons," *Washington Times*, January 21, 2001; Jerry Seper, "Clinton Broke Vow in Pardon of Rich," *Washington Times*, February 2, 2001; Clinton Granted 47 Clemencies Without Following Standard Procedures," *Human Events*, March 5, 2001, 3; Deroy Murdock, "Drug Dealers, Embezzlers, Contributors: Clinton's Other Pardons," *Human Events*, February 26, 2001, 9.
42	Louis J. Freeh, *My FBI: Bringing Down the Mafia, Investigating Bill Clinton, and Fighting the War on Terror* (New York: St. Martin's Press, 2005), 269.
43	Carl Limbacher, *Hillary's Scheme: Inside the Next Clinton's Ruthless Agenda to Take the White House* (New York: Crown Forum, 2003), 60.
44	"Why the Lady Took the Fifth," *Human Events*, February 26, 2001, 3.
45	Jerry Seper, "Clinton Told DNC of His Intent to Pardon Rich," *Washington Times*, February 9, 2001.
46	House Government Reform Committee, Justice Undone, Introduction, 13; Tyrrell, *The Clinton Crack-Up*, 89.
47	Lead Editorial, "Woe is Clinton," *Washington Times*, February 19, 2001.
48	Donald Lambro, "Playing the Blame Game," *Washington Times*, February 22, 2001.
49	Lead Editorial, "Woe is Clinton."
50	Ibid.
51	Ibid.
52	Donald Lambro, "Carter Calls Clinton's Rich Pardon 'Disgraceful,'" *Washington Times*, February 22, 2001.
53	Ibid.
54	Ibid.
55	Bodyguard interviewed by R. Emmett Tyrrell, Jr.'s researcher, August 2004; Tyrrell, *The Clinton Crack-Up*, 102-103.
56	Carl Limbacher, "O'Reilly: Bush Insider Claims Clinton Deal Torpedoed Pardongate," *NewsMax.com*, June 21, 2002; Limbacher, *Hillary's Scheme*, 61.
57	Ibid.

THIRTY-EIGHT: *THE FINAL DAYS* HILLARY'S BOOK DEAL/WHITE HOUSE THEFT/VANDALISM

1	John F. Harris, "Clintons Will Pay For Half Of Gifts," *Washington Times*, February 3, 2001.
2	"Mrs. Clinton's Book Deal," *New York Times*, December 22, 2000; Edward Klein, *The Truth About Hillary* (New York: Sentinel, 2005), 202.
3	Klein, *The Truth About Hillary*, 202-203.
4	Building permits on file with District of Columbia Department of Consumer and Regulatory Affairs; Jeff Gerth and Don Van Natta Jr., *Her Way: The Hopes and Ambitions of Hillary Rodham Clinton* (New York: Little, Brown and Company, 2007), 221.
5	Ibid.
6	Hillary Watch, *Human Events*, February 5, 2001, 15.
7	Snow, "Trashing the White House."
8	Thomas B. Edsall, "Clintons Take Away $190,000 in Gifts," *Washington Post*, January 21, 2001, A18; R. Emmett Tyrrell, Jr., *The Clinton Crack-Up: The Boy President's Life After the White House* (Nashville: Thomas Nelson, 2007), 22.
9	"The Clinton Heist," *Human Events*, February 18, 2002, 3.

10 Author R. Emmett Tyrrell Jr. interview with then-current White House staffer who wishes to remain anonymous, June 2004; "On the Prowl," *American Spectator*, March 2000, 14.
11 George Lardner Jr., "Clintons Shipped Furniture Year Ago," *Washington Post*, February 10, 2001.
12 Ibid.
13 Scott Shifrel, "Hillary Defends Self on Gift Raps," *New York Daily News*, February 12, 2001, 4; Barbara Olson, *The Final Days: The Last, Desperate Abuses of Power by the Clinton White House* (Washington, D.C.: Regnery Publishing, 2001), 73.
14 "Clinton Corruption Plays Us for Fools—We Won't Forget," *New York Observer*, March 25, 2001; R. Emmett Tyrrell, Jr. with Mark W. Davis, *Madame Hillary: The Dark Road to the White House* (Regenery Publishing, 2004), 95-96.
15 John H. Harris, "Clintons Will Pay for Half of Gifts," *Washington Post*, February 3, 2001.
16 (*Associated Press*), "Clinton Returns Some Gifts," *Washington Times*, February 8, 2001.
17 Christopher Andersen, *American Evita* (New York: HarperCollins, 2004), 5; Tyrrell, *The Clinton Crack-Up*, 16-17.
18 Timothy Carney, "Clintonites Left White House in Shambles," *Human Events*, January 29, 2001; Hillary Watch, *Human Events*, February 5, 2001, 15.
19 Carney, "Clintonites Left White House in Shambles," 6.
20 Ibid.
21 Ibid.
22 Ibid.
23 Snow, "Trashing the White House"; Olson, *The Final Days*, 74.
24 Olson, *The Final Days*, 74-75.
25 Snow, "Trashing the White House."
26 Editorial, "Anyone Seen the Silverware?" *Washington Times*, January 26, 2001.
27 Hillary Watch, "Vandals at the Gate," *Human Events*, February 18, 2002, 15.
28 Ibid.
29 Carney, "Clintonites Left White House in Shambles," 6.

THIRTY-NINE: BILL CLINTON (LEGACY)

1 Quoted in "International Perspectives," *Newsweek*, December 11, 2000; Rich Lowry, *Legacy: Paying the Price for the Clinton Years* (Washington, D.C.: Regnery Publishing, 2003) ,1
2 Doug Bandow, "Presidents and the Judgment of History," *Washington Times*, January 5, 1997.
3 Jennifer Harper, "Bill, Bill, Bill," Inside Politics, *Washington Times*, February 1, 2001.
4 Bob Woodward, *The Choice* (New York: Simon & Schuster, 1996), Lowry, *Legacy*, 2
5 Dick Morris, *Behind the Oval Office: Getting Reelected Against All Odds* (Los Angeles: Renaissance, 1999), 11.
6 Bill Gertz, *Betrayal: How the Clinton Administration Undermined American Security* (Washington, D.C.: Regnery Publishing, 1999), 211.
7 Ibid.
8 James Bovard, *Feeling Your Pain: The Explosion and Abuse of Government Power in the Clinton-Gore Years* (New York: St. Martin's Press, 2000), 341-42, 346.
9 Lead Editorial, "Bill Clinton vs. Democratic Party, *Washington Times*, January 28, 2001.
10 Ibid.
11 Ibid.
12 Ibid.
13 Ibid.
14 Ibid.
15 Ibid.
16 Ibid.
17 Ibid.

18 (Al Santoli, Foreword), Lt. Colonel Robert "Buzz" Patterson, *Dereliction of Duty: The Eyewitness Account of How Bill Clinton Compromised America's National Security* (Washington, D.C.: Regnery Publishing, 2003), 3-4.
19 Patterson, *Dereliction of Duty*, 4.
20 Geoff Metcalf, "The Excrement of Propaganda," *WorldNetDaily*, March 29, 1999; Patterson, *Dereliction of Duty*, 112.
21 John Hillen, "Kicking the Can Down the Road," *Washington Times*, May 29, 1997; Andy Dworkin, "Defense Firms Set Sights on the World; Firms Exporting Expands Trade, Keeps Jobs; "Critics Say U.S Policy Increases Chances of War," *Dallas Morning News*, October 19, 1997; Leslie Wayne, "The Shrinking Military Complex; After the Cold War, the Pentagon is Just Another Customer," *New York Times*, February 27, 1998, Lowry, Legacy, 248-249.
22 Gertz, *Betrayal*, 212.
23 Ibid.
24 J. Michael Waller, "Policy Disaster," *Insight on the News*, November 13, 2000; Patterson, *Dereliction of Duty*, 106.
25 David Hackworth, "Clinton Can Undo the Damages in Military Morale," *Newsweek*, June 28, 1993, 24-25; Patterson, *Dereliction of Duty*, 107.
26 Patterson, *Dereliction of Duty*, 107-108.
27 Al Santoli, "They're Fighting to Stay Above the Poverty Line," *Parade*, May 28, 1995; Patterson, *Dereliction of Duty*, 108.
28 Patterson, *Dereliction of Duty*, 108.
29 Ibid, 111-112.
30 Gertz, *Betrayal*, 212-213.
31 Capital Briefs "Clinton's Real Legacy," *Human Events*, January 7, 2002, 2.
32 Ibid.
33 Patterson, *Dereliction of Duty*, 131.
34 Alan Dowd, "Legacy of Weakness," *Washington Times*, January 15, 2001; Patterson, *Dereliction of Duty*, 131-132.
35 John Leo, "Words from the Comeback Champion," *Washington Times*, January 24, 2001.

INDEX

A

Abbott, Bruce, **186**
ABC News, **192**, **271**, **298**, **345**, **354**, **407**, **451**, **477**, **478**, **483**
Abernethy, Bob, **272**
Able Danger:
    al Qaeda and, **422-423**
    "Alex Base," **424**
    Brooklyn cell (Mohammed Atta, Khalid al-Mihdhar, Nawaf al-Hazmi and Marwan al-Shehhi), **422-423**
    cover up in, **424**
    Central Intelligence Agency (CIA), **424**
    Federal Bureau of Investigation (FBI), **423**
    Defense Intelligence Agency (DIA), **421**, **423-424**
    House Armed Services Committee, **423**
    Land Information War Activity (LIWA), **422**
    Orion Scientific Systems, **422**
    Raytheon (Garland, TX), **423**
    U.S. Special Operations Command (SOCOM), **421-423**
Abortion, **29**, **88-89**
Abramson, Jill, **444**
Absolute Power (Limbaugh), **364-365**
Acapulco, **27**
Accuracy in Media, **258**
Acosta, Manuel, **351-353**
Adams, Roger C., **188**, **531**
Addington, Ron, **24**

Advertising Associates, Inc. (Ark.), **120**
Aetna Life and Casualty, **86**
Afghanistan, **379**, **415**, **417**, **482**
Agnew, Spiro T., **492**
Agreed Framework, **151**
Aguilera, Davy, **94**
Ahern, Bertie, **483**
Ainley, Neil, **234**
Air Contra, **57-59**
"Air Elvis," **123**
Air Force One, **365**, **534**, **536**
Air Force Two, **365**
Air National Guard, **11**
Al Qaeda, **406-408**, **412**, **414**, **419-423**, **547**
Al-Shifa pharmaceutical plant (Sudan), **418**
Al-Zawahiri, Ayman, **144**, **146**, **349-350**
Al-Zawahiri, Muhammad, **144**
Al Qaeda,
Albania, **146**
Albright, Madeleine:
    China in, **385**
    embassy bombing in, **417**
    North Korea in, **152-155**
    Rwanda in, **157**
    Somalia in, **140**
    Sudan in, **418**
Alcohol, Tobacco, and Firearms Bureau, U.S.,
Aldrich, Gary, **326**, **336**

Alexander, Wanetta, **1-2**
Alfond, Dolores, **252**
Alfred P. Murrah Federal Building, **348-359**
All Our Children, **86**
Allard, Edward F., **110**
Alpha Phi Omega Fraternity, **7**
Altman, Roger, **221, 223, 229, 231, 234**
AK-47s, **498-499**,
American Airlines, **356**
American Banker, **282**
American Embassy (London, England), **13**
American Federation of Government Employees, **329**
American Legion, **252**
American Legion's Boy State summer camp, **6**
American Note Co., **520**
American Spectator, **39, 47, 205-206, 256, 335, 368, 370-371, 385, 483, 494, 503**
Americans for Democratic Action, **12**
Andersen, Christopher, **27, 447**
Anderson, Bob, **95**
Anderson, Larry, **201**
Anderson, Mari, **331**
Anderson, Ronnie, **201**,
Anderson, Sam, Jr., **46**
Andrews Air Force Base, **537**
Angelides, Paul, **429**
ANGLE, **89**
Annan, Kofi, **156**
Anthony, Beryl F., Jr., **171**
Anthony, Sheila, **172**,
Antiwar activities:
    Clinton's participation, **12-13**
Antonucci, Mike, *The Right Mind*, **272**
Antoinette, Marie, **161**
Apple, Howard, **126**
Aristide, Jean Bertrand, **136-139**
Arkansas:

education reform, **42-43**
National Guard of, **36**
State troopers, **36, 55-56, 200-207, 254-257, 260, 266, 280**
taxes raised, **32-33**
Arkansas Democrat, **41, 52, 507**
Arkansas Democrat-Gazette, **28, 345**
Arkansas Gazette, **5, 13, 31, 33, 35**
Arkansas Group, the, **173**
Arkansas-Louisiana Gas Company (Arkla), **28, 120**
Arkansas Retired Officers Group, **31**
Arkansas Supreme Court, **517-518**
Arlington National Cemetery, **313**
Armed Forces Institute of Pathology (AFIP), **313, 319, 321**
Armey, Dick, **161**
Armstrong, Michael, **371-372**
Armstrong, William S., **8**
Arnold, Philip, **101**
Arsenio Hall Show, **78**
Arthur, Richard, **180, 183**
Arusha Agreement, **155-156**
Ashe, John, **279**
Ashton, Marc (Gourmet Fresh Foods), **294-296**
Asian Pacific Advisory Council, **293, 306**
Asian Development Bank, **301**
Asian Pacific Economic Cooperation (APEC), **373, 498**
Ashford, Corey, **183**
Ashton, Marc,
Aspin, Les:
    gays in the military, **90**
    Somalia, **140-143**
    Vietnam, **250**
Atlanta Journal-Constitution, **198**
Atta, Mohammed, **361, 422**
Ausen, Lee, **233**
Automated Intelligence Systems, **500**

B

Bacon, Kenneth, **454**, **479**
Baird, Zoe, **86-87**
Bajac, Vitomir, **311**
Bakounis, Vassilis, **429**
Ballantine, Debra, **256-257**
Bang Chang International, **504**
Bank of Cherry Valley, **213**
Banks, Charles, **220-221**
Banks, Ken, **350**
Barbash, Fred, **257**
Barley, William S., Jr., **280**
Barling, Ark., **36**
Barr, Bob, **491**
Barrister's Union Prize Trial, **19-20**
Barron's, **537**
Bassett, Beverly, **213-214**, **216-217**
Bassett, Woody, **213**
Bastille, The, **524**
Baugh, Gandy, **275**
Baur, Capt. Christian, **430**
Bedard, Paul, **490**
Begala, Paul:
    election of **1992** and, **70**, **77**
    election of **1996** and, **344**
    Lewinsky and, **482**
Behind the Oval Office (Morris), **289-290**, **490**
Ben-Veniste, Richard, **57**
Bender, John, **55**
Bennett, Jackie, **468-470**, **474**, **507**
Bennett, Robert S.:
    Dale and, **134**
    Jones and, **258-259**, **261-264**, **266-267**, **270**, **441**, **448**, **462**
    Lewinsky and, **463**, **474-475**, **481**
Bentsen, Lloyd:
    health care reform and, **163**
    resignation, **234**
Berger, Benjamin, **526**
Berger, Samuel R. "Sandy,":
    bin Laden and, **414**
    China and, **378**, **380-382**, **395**
    Hogan and Hartson law firm, **379**
Betrayal (Gertz), **148**
Bhutto, Benazir, **410**
Biamby, Philippe, **139**
Biden, Joe, **70**
Bill Clinton and Black America (Wickam), **78**
Billingsley, George, **529**
"Bimbo eruptions," **76**, **78**
Bin Laden, Osama:
    Aden Hotel bombing and, **403**
    Afghanistan, **406-407**, **415**
    Goldmore Hotel bombing and, **403**
    Kenya embassy bombing and, **417**
    Kosovo, **146**, **148**
    Manila (**1995**) and, **408-409**
    Somalia and, **406-408**
    Sudan and, **412-415**
    Tanzania embassy bombing and, **417**
    U.S. Military Training Center (Saudi Arabia) and, **411**
    U.S.S. *Cole* and, **420-421**
    U.S.S. *The Sullivans*, and, **419-420**
    view of Bill Clinton, **408**
    World Trade Center bombing (**1993**) and, **404-406**
    World Trade Center bombing (**2001**) and, **547**
    Yemen, **406**, **415**
Binhak, Steve, **468**
Bittman, Bob, **480**
Black Dog store (Martha's Vineyard), **269**
Black Hawk Down, **145**, **156**
Blackard, Pamela, **255-257**
Blair, Diane, **453**
Blair, James, **453**
Black Liberation Army, **527**
Blackley, Ronald, **528**
Blaylock, Louis, **312**
Blitzer, Wolf, **252**, **301-302**, **474**
Blix, Hans, **149**

Blood Sport (Stewart), **207**
Bloomingdale's (department store), **520**
Blumenthal, Sidney, **443-444**, **478**, **514**
Blythe, Henry Leon, **1**
Blythe, Sharron Lee, **2**
Blythe, Virginia Dell Cassidy, **1-5**, **27**, **69**
Blythe, William Jefferson III:
    birth of, **1**
    courtship of Virginia, **2**
    death, **4**
    marriages, **1-3**
    World War II service, **3**
Boorda, Adm. Jeremy Michael, **328-329**
Bodansky, Yossef, **349-350**
Booker, Wilma, **3**
Booth, Larry, **377**
Borjesson, Kristina, **434**
Borsheim's, **534**
Boston Globe, **198**
Bottoms, Billy, **57**
Bourke, Jim, **126**
Bovard, James, **99**, **117**, **540**
Bowie, David, **128**
Bowles, Crandall, **271**
Bowles, Erskine, **271**
    election of **1996** and, **343**
    Lewinsky and, **475**
    Whitewater and, **221**
Bowman, John, **224**
Boy Clinton (Tyrrell), **3**, **59**
Boys Nation, **6**
Bradley, Bill, **228**
Bradley, Ed, **442-443**
Branch, Taylor, **432**
Brantley, Max, **48**
Brasseaux, Barney, **132**, **134**
Braswell, Glenn, **526**, **529**
Bratton, Sam, **217**
Braun, Cheryl, **181**, **183-184**, **187**
Breault, Marc, **94**
Breslaw, April, **229-230**
Breuer, Lanny, **474**

Breyer, Stephen, **88**
Bridges, Col. Dick, **454**
Bridges, Daryl (a.k.a. Timothy McVeigh), **358**
Brinkley, David, **341**
Britt, Henry, **8**
Broad, Eli, **383**
Broaddrick, Juannita, **444-448**
Brock, David, **24**, **41**
    Troopergate, **205**
Brokaw, Tom, **49**, **446**
Brosnahan, James, **81-82**
Brown, Alma, **307**, **313**
Brown, Jerry, 77, **90**
Brown, Larry Douglas (L.D.):
    Mena airport and, **55-62**
    Troopergate and, **207**
    Whitewater and, **215**
Brown, Lee Patrick, **89**
Brown, Michael, **292**, **294-295**, **304**, **307**, **312-313**, **323**
    Greenberg, Traurig, Hoffman, Lipoff, Rosen & Quentel, **294**
    guilty of, **318**
    independent counsel, **304**
Brown, Ron,
    Armed Forces Institute of Pathology (AFIP), **313**, **319**, **321**
    Asian Development Bank, **301**
    Asian involvement of, **293-297**
    bagman and, **300**, **305**
    Baltimore African-American, **320**
    Banque Indosuez, **296**
    Belle Haven Apartments, **303**
    Black Entertainment Television (BET), **320**
    BET Tonight, **320**
    bullet wound to the head, **313-314**, **318**
    business ventures, **294-295**
    Chicago Independent Bulletin, **320**
    China, **369**, **373-376**, **378-381**
    Cilipi Airport, **308**, **311**, **314**
    death of, **276**, **312**

INDEX 631

death inquiry, **313-316, 318-321**
Department of Commerce career, **295-300, 302, 484-485, 498**
DNC career, **292**
Dynamic Energy Resources (formerly Gage Corporation), **293**
flight of, **308-310**
funeral of, **313, 315**
Hrvatska Radiotelevizija (HRT), **312**
on inauguration day (**1993**), **84**
independent counsel investigation of, **302**
Kolocep Island, **309, 311**
Matteo's Restaurant (Hawaii), **292**
Paiton project, **301**
Patton Boggs, **295-296**
St. John's Chapel (Washington, D.C.), **315**
St. John's Peak (Sveti Ivan), **310-311, 314**
Vietnam Development Corp. (VDC)., **294**
Washington Afro-American, **321**
Brown, Sam, **12**
Brown, Tracey, **307, 320**
Brown, Waverly, **527**
Bruce, Carol Elder, **530**
Brumly, NCO Dwight, **429**
Bryson, John, **301**
Buck, Brantley, **171**
Budahn, Phil, **252**
Bumpers, Dale, **26, 46, 48, 213**
Bunch, James, **275**
Bunn, Travis, **44-45**
Bureau of Alcohol, Tobacco and Firearms (ATF):
  Oklahoma City bombing and, **361**
  Ruby Ridge and, **113, 118-119**
  TWA Flight 800 and, **425-426, 435**
  Waco and, **93-100, 105-106, 108-110**
Burnett, Linda, **80**
Burton, Bill, **190**
Burton, Dan, **529**
Bush, Barbara, **75, 84, 346**

Bush, George H. W. Bush, **50, 52, 56, 75, 80-82, 84, 136-137, 219, 292, 329, 346, 407**
Bush, George W., **525, 537**
Busters (bar), **37**
Butera, Eric, **277**
Butzner, John, **195**
Buyer, Steve, **512**
Byerly, Herb, **118**

C

C-123K airplane, **58**
Cabe, Gloria, **50**
Cacheris, Plato, **479**
Cajun's Wharf (Little Rock, Ark.), **56**
Callahan, H.L. "Sonny," **452**
Cammarata, Joseph, **258, 264**
Cambone, Stephen, **423**
Camelot Hotel (Little Rock, Ark.), **29**
Camp Robinson (Ark.), **62**
Camp Shelby, (Mississippi), **3**
Campbell, Ben Nighthorse, **542**
Campbell, Charles, **215**
Campbell, Donovan, **441**
Campbell, Maj. Gen. Harold N., **166**
Campolo, Rev. Tony, **315**
Canavan, Brig. Gen. Michael, **313**
Cannistraro, Vincent, **354**
Cannon, Craig, **51**
Capital-Management Services Company, **220**
Capitol Hill Police, **84**
Caproni, Valerie, **426, 431**
Caputo, Lisa, **206**
Cargile, Ken, **56**
Carl, Tom, **127-128**
Carlos the Jackal, **413**
Carney, Betta, **120-121, 125, 130**
Carney, Timothy N., **412, 414**
Caproni, Valerie,
Cardozo, Michael, **172, 497-498**
Cardozo, Harolyn, **172**

Carney, Betta,
Carpenter-McMillan, Susan, **264-265**, 271
Carr, Bob, **288**
Carson, Johnny, **49-50**
Carter, Ashton, **369**
Carter, Frank, **465, 467, 469, 473**
Carter, Jimmy:
    Clinton and, **28, 36, 39, 509, 531**
    Cuban refugees, **35-36**
    Haiti, **139**
    North Korea, **150**
    primary challenge, **341**
    Somalia, **141**
Carter administration, **29, 136**
Carver, Allen, **227**
Carville, James, **537-538**
    election of 1992, **70, 74, 76**
    election of 1996, **344**
    Jones and, **261**
    Lewinsky and, **482**
Casey, Albert, **221, 231**
Casey, Paula, **222-225**
Casolaro, Danny, **274**
Cassidy, Edith, **4**
Cassidy, Eldridge, **4**
Castle Grande development, **215**
Cato Institute, **326**
Cavanaugh, James, **97, 100**
CBS News, **228, 345**
Cedras, Raoul, **137-139**
Central High School (Little Rock, Ark.), **345**
Central Intelligence Agency (CIA):
    Able Danger, **424**
    Barry Seal and, **56-60**
    bin Laden and, **412-414**
    China and, **385, 390, 503**
    Clinton's ties to, **16**
    gun running
    L.D.Brown and, **56, 58-62**
    Mena airport and, **68**
    Operation Chaos and, **16**
    Parks murder and, **174**
    TWA Flight 800 and, **426, 434, 436, 439**
    Waco and, **110**
    World Trade Center bombing (1993), **405**
Cerda, Clarissa, **122, 134**
Chapman, Jim, **452**
Charity Hospital, **4**
"Chelsea Morning," **34**
Chen Shizeng, **503**
Cheney, Richard B., **96**
Cheong Am, **496**
Chi Haotian (Butcher of Beijing), **384**
Chicago Tribune, **499**
Children's Defense Fund, **21-22, 453**
China, **155**
    CATIC, **370**
    Chi Haotian (Butcher of Bejing), **384**
    China Milky Way, **368**
    China's Great Wall Industries Corp. (CGWIC), **371, 381, 383**
    China International Trust and Investment Corp. (CITIC), **498**
    China Resources Holding Company, **494-495**
    "China Shops" article, **370**
    Commission of Science Technology and Industry for National Defense (COSTIND), **368-369, 371, 380**
    Coordinating Committee on Export Controls (CoCom), **369, 374**
    China Ocean Shipping Co. (COSCO), **383-384, 499, 502-503**
    Defense News, **372**
    "Democracy Wall" movement, **374**
    Export Administration Act (EAA), **373**
    Hip Hing Holdings, Ltd., **495**
    Hong Kong Chinese Bank, **494**
    Hua Mei (Galaxy New Technology), **368-369**
    Hutchison Whampoa, **384**

Iran and, **372**, **376**, **385**, **388**
"Kindred Spirit," **393-394**
La Stampa, **372**
Li Peng, **374**
Libya and, **385**
Lippo America, **496**
Long Beach Naval Station, **377**, **383-384**, **503**
Marswell Investment Inc., **383**
McDonald-Douglas aerospace plant, **370**
Motorola, **371**
North Korea and, **385**
Pakistan and, **371-372**, **377**, **380**, **383**, **385**, **387-388**
People's Liberation Army (PLA), **379**, **383-384**, **397**, **498**
Poly Technologies, **379**, **383**, **498-499**
Qian Qichen, **376**
San Jose Holdings, Inc., **495**
supercomputers, **368**, **372-373**, **377**, **400-401**
Syria and, **372**, **385**
Taiwan and, **389-390**
Tiananmen Square, **384**
Toy Center Holdings of CA, Inc., **495**
Wang Jun, **379-380**, **383**
Wuzhai Missile and Space Test Center, **390**
Claiborne, Harry, **507**
The Choice (Woodward), **364**
Chojnacki, Phillip, **97**, **100**, **108**
Christian, Randy, **351**, **361**
Christian Science Monitor, **73**, **384**
Christopher, Warren:
　China and, **374**, **376**, **378**, **381**
　Haiti, **139**
　Khobar Towers bombing and, **416**
　North Korea, **150**
　Somalia, **140**
　State Department file search and, **241**
　Vietnam and, **253**
Chrysler Building (NY), **520**

Chubb Group Insurance, **262**, **449**
Chung, Johnny, **363**, **383-384**, **490**, **500-503**
Cisneros, Henry, **329**, **527**
Clark, Adm. Vern, **421**
Clarke, Floyd, **104**, **175**
Clarke, Richard, **419**, **425**
Clements, William, **247**
Clinger, William:
　Brown and, **298**
　Filegate and, **324**
　Foster and, **185**
Clinton, Chelsea, **42**, **52**, **69**, **114**, **169**
　birth of, **34**
Clinton, Hillary Diane Rodham:
　60 *Minutes* interview, **73-74**
　abortion, **88-89**
　aftermath of **1988** Democratic Convention Clinton speech, **50**
　anger, temper, and hurt of, **84**, **201-203**, **205**
　aspirations, **19-21**, **27**
　attorney general search, **86-88**
　bar exams taken by, **20-21**
　in Bermuda, **33-34**
　billing records found, **236**
　board of directors Wal-mart, **121**
　book contract, **533**
　Broaddrick and, **447**
　Brown and, **300**, **306**, **312-313**, **315-317**, **320-322**
　the "bunker," **71**
　in Carter campaign, **28**
　Children's Defense Fund, **21-22**
　church-going, **41**
　Clinton's alleged cocaine overdose, **67**
　Clinton's complex relationship with, **24**
　Clinton's first meeting with, **18**
　Clinton's fights and marital problems, **34**, **203**
　Clinton's gubernatorial campaigns and, **38-40**, **42**

Clinton's House campaign, **24-27**
Clinton's loss and comeback and, **38-39**
Clinton's presidential campaigns and, **52-53, 69-82**
courtship, **18-21, 27**
the "Defense Team," **71**
dependency relationship (views of), **18**
education of:
Yale Law School, **18**
election of **1974, 23-27**
election of **1976, 27-29**
election of **1978, 30-32**
election of **1980, 38**
election of **1982, 41-43**
election of **1990, 51-52**
election of **1992, 52-53, 69-82**
election of **1994, 291**
election of **1996, 342-344, 346**
Filegate and, **326, 328-329, 331-333**
Foster affair with, **189, 204**
Foster and, **170-174, 182, 185, 187, 190, 199**
Fray and, **26-27**
fund-raising scandal and, **490, 500-501**
grand jury appearance, **237**
health care reform and, **158-165**
home furnishing needs, **534, 536**
honeymoon, **27**
on Inauguration day, **84**
It Takes a Village, **453**
John Paul II and, **168-169, 283, 335**
Jones and, **258, 271, 440-441, 443-444, 447**
Legal Services Corporation (LSC), **38**
Lewinsky and, **453-454, 457, 477-478**
pregnancy and childbirth, **33-34**
private investigators use of, **40, 76**
Rich and, **525**
at Rose Law Firm, **28**
as Senate candidate, **522-523, 526**
shredding documents, **192**
Secret Service, **336**
Travelgate and, **124, 126, 128-130, 133**
Troopergate and, **200-207**
twenty-year project, **19**
war room, **70**
Watergate investigative committee work of, **21-22, 492**
wedding, **27**
White House theft and, **534-535**
White House vandalism, **536-538**
Whitewater and, **192, 208-214, 216-219, 223, 225-227, 229, 232, 235-238**
Willey and, **443-444**
Yale Law Review and Social Action, **18**
Clinton, Ina Mae Murphy, **4**
Clinton, Raymond G., **8,9**
Clinton, Roger, Sr.., **4**
abusiveness of, **4**
arrests, **4**
Buick agency, **4**
death of, **5**
divorces, **4,5**
drinking and alcoholism, **4,5**
extramarital affairs, **4**
finances of, **4**
gambling of, **4**
marriages, **4,5**
Virginia's divorce from, **5**
Virginia's remarriage to, **5**
Clinton, Roger Cassidy:
aid from Lasater, **63**
arrests of, **43-45**
Bill Clinton's congressional campaign, **19,26**
birth of, **4**
Dealer's Choice, **65**
drug activities, **26, 35, 37, 43-44, 65-67**
drug use trial, **45-46**
employment by Lasater and Company, **63**
indictment, **45**
influence on granting pardon, **529**
pardon of, **527**
sentencing of, **46**

INDEX

traffic violations, **43**
Clinton, William Jefferson Blythe IV:
    1993 World Trade Center bombing, **404-406**
    2001 World Trade Center bombing, **547**
    Able Danger, **421-424**
    abortion, **29, 88-89, 283, 335**
    accused of inappropriate behavior, **35**
    accused of rape (Oxford), **10**
    Aden Hotel Bombing, **403**
    affairs, **64, 67, 72**
    Air Force One petty theft, **534, 537**
    anger of, **11, 84**
    antiwar demonstrations, **10, 13, 80**
    antiwar movement, **12-13, 17**
    appeasement,
    arrested for speeding, **37**
    as attorney general, **29**
    attorney general search, **86-88**
    bar exam, **20**
    in Bermuda, **33-34**
    Beta Club, **6**
    birth of, **1,3**
    black churches burning (supposedly), **345**
    blue dress (Lewinsky), Introduction ix, **456, 474, 479-480**
    bombing of Iraq, **512, 514**
    Broaddrick and, **444-448**
    Brown and, **292, 295, 297-303, 305-307, 312-313, 315-318, 320-321**
    in Carter campaign, **28**
    Central Intelligence Agency (Operation Chaos), **16**
    China and, **367-402**
    church-going, **41**
    college years, **7-8**
    Congressional House race of **1974, 23-27**
    courtship of Hillary, **18-21, 27**
    dating and womanizing, **24,27**
    denial of Lewinsky relationship, Introduction ix, **463-464, 475-477**
    denial of Mena operations, **54, 68**
    Dissidents File, **15**
    "distinguishing characteristic" in Jones affair, **259-260, 265**
    disbarment and, **516-518**
    DNA testing, **480**
    "doomsday list," **49**
    draft, **7-11, 14-15**
    draft dodging, **8-12, 14-15, 25**
    draft dodging allegations against, **31, 72-73**
    drinking by, **35**
    drug overdose alleged, **67**
    drug trafficking in Arkansas, **46**
    drug use issue, **72**
    drugs, **10, 26, 35, 38, 44, 54, 64-68**
    Duffy campaign and, **19**
    education of:
    high school, **6,7**
    Georgetown University, **6-8**
    Oxford University, **7, 9-11, 17**
    Yale Law School, **14, 17-18**
    embassy bombings, **417-419**
    Esquire magazine interview, **339-340**
    European grand tour taken by, **15-17**
    Excelsior announcement, **49**
    extramarital affairs, **34, 49, 69, 202-206, 266, 299**
    felony allegations, **510-511**
    Filegate and, **325, 327-328, 330, 331**
    firing William Sessions, **175**
    foreign policy, **136-157**
    Foster and, **170-171, 176**
    Foster death, **170, 185, 187-188**
    fund-raising scandals and, **363-366, 386**
    as Fulbright intern, **7**
    gays in the military, **89-91**
    Goldmore Hotel bombing, **403**
    Hamas, **546**
    Hart scandal and, **48**
    heath care reform and, **158-165**
    home furnishing needs, **534, 536**
    honeymoon, **27**

houses purchased, **27, 29, 41**
impeachment and, **484-515**
on Inauguration day, **83-85**
Iran and, **416-417**
John Paul II, **168-169, 283, 335**
Jones and, **254-271, 440-450**
Kennedy handshake, **6**
Key Club, **6**
Khobar Towers bombing, **415-417**
Larry King Live appearance, **185**
legacy, **539-547**
Lewinsky and, **267-271, 452-469, 471, 474-483**
Marriott Hotel (Washington, D.C.), **336**
marriage strains, **27, 29, 34**
McGovern campaign, **20, 25**
media flop, **168**
Mena operations and, **54-62**
middle class tax cut, **91-92**
MTV, **282-283**
NASCAR, **336**
National Cathedral, **335**
North Korea and, **148-155**
nuclear codes lost, **337-339**
obstruction of justice, **471-472**
Oklahoma city bombing and, **348, 362**
Pardongate and, **519-532**
Park Avenue (Ark.), **1, 5**
personal property taxes owed, **33**
philanderer reputation, **34**
presidential candidacy (**1992**), **52-53, 69-82**
presidential candidacy (**1996**), **341-347**
presidential immunity, **261**
"Project Bojinka," **409-410**
Rhodes scholarship, **7, 10**
ROTC program, **11-15, 31, 80**
Ruby Ridge and, **113-119**
Rwanda and, **155-157**
"Saturday-Night Bill," **35**
saxophone playing, **64, 78**
Somalia, **144, 406-408**

speech to **1988** convention, **49**
State Department file search and, **239-241**
Sudan and, **412-414**
Taiwan and, **389**
talk radio, **283**
term limits, **284**
Travelgate and, **123-126, 130-132, 135**
Troopergate and, **200-207**
TWA Flight **800** and, **425-439**
twenty-year project, **19**
University of Arkansas Medical Center, **67**
University of Arkansas Law School professor, **23**
"unusually good liar," **335-336**
U.S. Consulate (Pakistan), **410**
U.S. Military Training Center (Saudi Arabia), **410-411**
USS *Cole*, **420-421**
USS *Sullivans*, **419-420**
Vantage Point, **66-67**
V-E Day, **334**
Vietnam and, **245, 251**
Vietnam Memorial Wall and, **167-168**
Vietnam War and, **9-10, 17**
Waco and, **93-112**
wagging his finger (Lewinsky), Introduction ix, **477**
wedding, **27**
White House Map Room incident, **185**
White House theft, **533-535**
White House vandalism, **536-537**
Whitewater and, **208-210, 212-221, 223-224, 226-230, 232-233, 235-238**
Willey and, **441-443**
Clinton, William Jefferson Blythe IV campaigns:
    for attorney general in **1976**, **27-29**
    for governorship in **1978**, **30-32**
    for governorship in **1980**, **35-38**
    for governorship in **1982**, **39-43**
    for governorship in **1984**, **46-47**

INDEX 637

for governorship in **1986**, **47**
for governorship in **1990**, **50-52**
for the House in **1974**, **23-25**, **27**
for the presidency in **1992**, **52-53**, **69-82**
for the presidency in **1996**, **341-347**
CNN, **205**, **207**, **252**, **301**, **354**, **356**, **437**, **474**, **505**, **538**
Coast Guard and, **426**
Cobb, Charles, **87**
Cogswell, Lt. Col. Steve, **314-318**
Cohen, William:
    nuclear codes lost, **339**
    Sudan, **418**
Coleman, Randy, **222**
Coleman, Susan, **273**
Collingwood, John, **131**
Collins, Gregory, **273**
Collins, Judy, **34**
Collins, Locke and Lasater brokerage, **41**
Colombell, William, **196**
Colson, Charles, **325**
The Comeback Kid, **39**
Commision on U.S. Trade and Investment Policy, **499**
Compromised (Reed), **61**
Congressional Black Caucus, **137-138**, **321**
Congressional Hispanic Caucus, **523**
Coney, Keith, **273**
Congressional Budget Office (CBO), **544**
Congressional Quarterly, **542**
"Contract With America," **286-289**
Conroy, Edward, **100**
Contras:
    Air Contra, **61**
    gun running, **57-59**
    Mena scandal, **54-68**
    pilot training, **61**
Conway, George T., III, **258**
Conway, Michael, **19**
Cooksey, Michael B., **522**
Cornelius, Catherine, **121-122**, **124-127**, **129-130**, **134**
Corridor Broadcasting Corp., **302**
Coulson, Danny, **104**, **126-127**
Coulter, Anne, **258**
Cox, Chris:
    China and, **390**, **393-396**
    North Korea and, **154**
Cox Report and, **396-401**
Craig, Greg, **19**
Cuba:
    Cuban refugees, **35-36**
    incident at Fort Chaffee, **35-36**
Cuomo, Mario,
Currie, Betty,
    Lewinsky and, **268-270**, **453**, **455-467**, **470-473**, **475**, **509**
Curtis, Glion, **224**
Cummins, Jim, **353**
Cuomo, Mario, **48**
    nominating speech **1992**, **79**
    World Trade Center bombing (**1993**), **405**
Czechoslovakian Party, **17**

D

D'Amato, Alfonse:
    Whitewater and, **235**
Daihatsu International Trading Co., **497**
Dale, Billy, **120**, **123-124**, **131**, **134-135**
Daley, Richard M., **70**
Dallas Morning News, **109-110**, **355**
Danforth, John C., **111-112**
Daniels, Charlie, **16**
Darby, Marcy, **502**
Dateline NBC, **445**, **447**
Davis, Capt. Ashley J., **309-310**
Davis, Gilbert K., **258-259**, **264**
Davis, Gray, **543**
Davis, Jayna, **348**, **357**, **361-362**
Davis, Lanny,
    Lewinsky and, **266**, **474**
Davison, Steve, **121**

Dayton Accords, **307**
De Queljoe, Charles, **496-497**
Decaro, Ann (Witness **144**), **428**
Defense Inteligence Agency (DIA), **153**, **247-249, 421, 423-424, 426**
Defense News, **372**
Defense Readiness Council, **91**
Degan, William, **114-115**
DeGuerin, Dick, **102**
Delgado, Joseph (Witness **649**), **429**
Dellinger, William, **263**
Democrat Leadership Conference, **52**
Democrat Leadership Council, **52, 70**
Democratic National Committee, **484-485, 487-488, 493-497, 499-502, 504**
Democratic National Convention, 1972, **20**
Democratic National Convention, 1980, **35-36**
Democratic National Convention, 1988, **49**
Democratic National Convention, 1992, **78**
Democratic National Convention, 1996, **346, 433**
Dennis, Edward, **107**
Densberger, William, **280**
Department of Commerce, **370, 376, 378-379, 381, 387**
Department of Energy, **369, 391-392, 397, 402, 544**
Department of Transportation, **426**
Dereliction of Duty (Patterson), **145**
Desler, Jim, **297**
Dessalines, Jean-Jacques, **138**
Deutch, John, **527**
Disbarment:
    American Legal Association, **516**
    Arkansas Committee on Professional Conduct, **517-518**
    Arkansas Supreme Court, **517-518**
    Landmark Legal Foundation, **516**
    Southeastern Legal Foundation, **516**
Djurkovic, Ivo, **311**
Doar, John, **20-21**
Dole, Bob, **28, 228, 345-346**
Donaldson, Sam, **478**
Donilon, Thomas, **241**
Dozoretz, Beth, **525-530**
Dresch, Stephen, **298**
Dreylinger, John, **131, 134**
Drudge, Matt, **477**
Drudge Report, **445, 471, 474**
Drug Czar, **89**
Drug Enforcement Agency (DEA), **57, 303**
Drummond, James E., **35**
Duda, Ivan, **40**
Duffey, Rev. Joseph P., **12**
Duffy, Joseph, **19**
Duffy, Kevin, **405**
Dukakis, Michael, **50, 82**
    Clinton endorsement of Dukakis, **49**
    Clinton's nominating speech, **49**
Dupleix, Jean Francois, **311**
Durant, Michael, **144**
Dutko, Daniel, **278**
Duvalier, Jean-Claude "Baby Doc," **295**
Dwire, George J. "Jeff," **5, 11**
Dwire Welch, Diane, **5**
Dynamic Energy Resources, **293**

E

Easley, Charles, **195**
The Economist, **273**
Edelman, Marian Wright, **21-22, 88**
Edison International, **301**
Education Standards Committee (Ark.), **43**
Egan, Wesley W., **289**
Eggleston, Neil:
    Lewinsky and, **478**
    Whitewater and, **225-226, 232**
Eisenhower, Dwight, **541**

Elbaum, Jacob, **526**
Election of **1968**, **8**
Election of **1972**, **20**, **25**
Election of **1974**, **19**, **23-27**
Election of **1976**, **27**
Election of **1978**, **30-32**
Election of **1980**, **35-38**
Election of **1982**, **39-43**
Election of **1984**, **46-47**
Election of **1986**, **47**
Election of **1988**, **47-49**
Election of **1990**, **50-52**
Election of **1992**, **52-53**, **69-82**
Election of **1994**, **284-291**
Election of **1996**, **341-347**
Eller, Jeff, **125**, **129**, **134**
Ellis, Opal, **11**
Ellis, Trice, Jr., **8**, **9**
Elmore, David, **351**
Embassy bombings, **417-419**
    Clinton reaction, **417**
    Nawaz Shariff, **418**
    Shahbaz Shariff, **418**
    Vx nerve agent, **418**
    "Wag the Dog," **419**
Emery, Chris, **493-494**
Emmanuel, Rahm:
    election of **1992**, **70**
    Lewinsky and, **482**
Emmick, Michael, **470-471**
Emory University, **509**
Empire State Building (NY), **521**
Engstrom, Steve, **45**
Entergy Corporation, **299**, **496**
Esposito, Jennifer, **328**
Espy, Mike, **524**
Esquire magazine, **335**, **339**
Estrich, Susan, **263**
Ettinger, Mitch, **264**, **270**, **462-463**
Evans & Novak, **505**
Evans-Pritchard, Ambrose, **45**, **54**, **61-62**, **183-184**, **198**

Evans, Sharon Ann, **10**
Excelsior Hotel (Little Rock, Ark.), **49**
    Jones and, **204**, **254**, **267**
Export-Import Bank, **496**
Eye Gotcha optical shop, **280**

F

Fabiani, Mark,
Fadley, Kenneth (a.k.a. Gus Magisono)
Fairmont Hotel, (San Francisco, Ca.), **144**
Fallon, Patrick, Jr., **49**
FALN, *the Fuerzas Armadas de Liberacion Nacional*, **520-524**
Fat Lady and **58**,
Faubus, Orval E., **7**, **28**
    campaign for governorship in **1986**, **47**
Federal Aviation Administration, **425-426**, **430**
Federal Bureau of Investigation (FBI):
    Able Danger, **423**
    bin Laden, **414**
    Brown and, **314**
    China, **378**
    FALN terrorists,
    Filegate and, **326-328**
    Foster death cover-up, **176**, **178**, **180-181**
    Foster office search, **188**
    Hale and, **222**
    Khobar Towers bombing, **416**
    Lums and, **304**
    Ly Tranh Binh, **297**
    Oklahoma City bombing and, **352-362**
    Parks murder, **171**
    Ruby Ridge and, **114-119**
    terrorism and, **349**
    Travelgate and, **126-131**, **133**
    TWA Flight **800**, **426-427**, **430**, **435**, **439**
    Waco and, **100-112**
    Wen Ho Lee, **391**
Federal Deposit Insurance Corporation

(FDIC), **218**, **232**, **236**
Federal Election Commission (FEC), **500**
Federal Home Loan Bank Board (FHLB), **217**
Feeling Your Pain (Bovard), **117**
Feingold, Russell, **228**
Ferguson, Danny:
    Jones and, **254-256**, **260**, **266-267**
    Troopergate and, **201**, **205-206**
Ferguson, Kathy, **275**
Ferraro, Geraldine, **325**
Ferrouillet, Alvarez, **528**
Filegate, **324-333**
First International Communications, **302-303**
First United Methodist Church (Little Rock, Ark.), **41**
Fisher, George, **32**
Fisher, James, **267-271**
Fiske, Robert, **193**, **195**, **222**, **229**, **233**
Fiske Report, **193**, **196**
Fitzhugh, Davis, **213**
Fitzhugh, Eugene, **234**, **236**
Fleetwood Mac, **70**
Flynt, Larry, **510**
Flowers, Gennifer:
    Clinton affair with, **29**, **73**, **476**
    tape recorded conversations, **74-75**, **476**
Foley, Thomas, **289**, **542**
"Football" the, **83**, **337**
Ford, Gerald R., **28**, **345**, **519**
Foreign Intelligence Surveillance Act (FISA),
Foren, Pat, **126**
Foren, Wayne, **221**
Fornshill, Kevin, **179-180**
Fort Chaffee, Ark., **35-36**, **38**
Fort Marcy Park crime scene:
    Asman Custom Photo, **197**
    confidential witness and, **177-178**
    Fairfax County Emergency Medical Services, **179**
    Fairfax County Fire and Rescue Department, **183**
    Fairfax County Hospital morgue, **183**
    gun, absence of, **178-179**
    gun, appearance of, **180**
    gun in hand, **180**
    lack of blood, **177**, **179**, **183**
    McLean Fire Service, Company One, **179**
    missing keys, **181**
    neck wound, **197-198**
    photos, **191-192**, **197**
    Special Forces (U.S. Park Police), **181-182**
    U.S. Park Police, **178-180**
Fort Marcy Park parking lot:
    confidential witness story, **177-178**
    Josie's and Duncan's story, **178-179**
    Patrick Knowlton's story, **177**
Fort Riley, Kansas, **357**
Fort Smith (Ark.), **23**, **25**, **44**
Fortier, Michael, **358**
Fortune **500**, **159**
Foster, Lisa, **171-173**, **176**, **184**
Foster, Vincent, **4**, **51**
    affair with Hillary Rodham Clinton, **189**, **204**
    credit union visit, **174-175**
    death of, **170**, **177**, **222**, **521**
    Desyrel, **174**, **176**
    files removed from office of, **185-186**
    "In the Line of Fire" (Clint Eastwood movie), **176**
    keys found, **183**
    Livingstone hiring, **329**
    missing keys, **181**
    office alarm system, **182**
    office safe, **182**
    Parks and **173**
    purported depression, **172**
    Randolph Towers ("the flat"), **173-174**
    Rose Law Firm income, **174-175**
    as Rose Law Firm partner, **28**
    Senate Whitewater Committee

investigation, **235**
special counsel investigation, **190**
St. Andrew's Roman Catholic Cathedral (Little Rock, Ark.), **189**
Tidewater Inn (Easton, Md.), **172**
Travelgate and, **126-127, 129-131, 133**
Waco and, **103**
White House redecoration project, **535**
Whitewater and, **171**
Foster family:
Brugh, **176**
Lee Bowman, **184**
Mary Bowman, **176**
Sharon Bowman, **176**
Sheila Anthony, **172**
Vincent III, **176**
Foster's Honda Accord:
briefcase discrepancies, **177, 181**
color discrepancies, **177-179**
search, **181**
Foucart, Brian, **129**
Foust, Kevin, **354**
Fowler, Don:
election of **1996** and, **343**
fund-raising scandal, **494, 502, 505**
Fox, Lew, **452-453**
Fox News, **532**
Fox News Sunday, **329**
Francis, James B., Jr., **109**
Francois, Michel, **139**
Fraunces Tavern (lower Manhattan), **520**
Fray, Mary Lee Saunders, **7, 26**
Fray, Paul, **7, 11,**
Freeh, Louis J.:
Chinagate and, **385**
Embassy bombings and, **417**
FALN terrorists, **522**
Filegate, **327-328**
Oklahoma City bombing and, **355**
Pardongate, **529**
Ruby Ridge, **116-117**
Freedom Hall (Louisville, Ky.), **81**

Freedom of Information Act (FOIA), **182, 228, 299, 302, 306**
Freeman, Charles, **380**
Freeman, Woody, **47**
Friday, Hershell, **275**
Fu Lin restaurant, **497**
Fulbright, J. William, **7-9, 20**
Funk, Sherman M., **240**
Furioso, George, **282**

G

Gage Corporation, **293**
Galbraith, Peter, **308-310**
Gangloff, Joseph E., **127, 298**
Garland County Chancery Court, **5**
Garrett, Benjamin C., **105-106**
Gas Lite (bar), **25**
Gash, Adele, **1**
Gays in the military issue, **89-91**,
Gearan, Mark:
Jones and, **257**
Gejdenson, Sam, **370**
General Services Administration (GSA), **536**
Gentry, Tony, **423**
George magazine, **199, 458**
Georgetown University, **78**
Foreign Service School of, **7**
Gephardt, Dick, **70, 164, 483**
Gergen, David:
Clinton media flop, **168**
Troopergate and, **205, 207**
Geren, Lt. Col. Billy G., **31**
Gerth, Jeff, **71, 219, 223, 376, 480**
Gertz, Bill, **148, 150, 152, 154, 371, 402, 414, 540**
Gewirtz, Paul, **86**
Ghigliotti, Carlos, **111, 278**
Gibbs, Robert, **44**
Gimbel's (department store), **520**
Gingrich, Newt, **164, 228, 287, 483**
Ginsburg, William, **470-471, 474, 479**

Giroir, C.J. "Joe," Jr., **343**, **496**
Giuliani, Rudy, **525**
Gluhan, Lenadra, **310**
Goldberg, Fred, **265**
Goldberg, Lucianne, **267**, **477**
Goldstein, David, **526**
Golden Corral Steakhouse (Little Rock area), **257**
Gomez, Max (real name Felix Rodriguez), **60-61**
Gone with the Wind, **288**
Gonzalez, George, **179-180**, **183**
Good Morning America, **132**
Goodwin, Col. Tommy, **44**, **207**
Gordon, Shep, **84**
Gore, Al, Jr., **50**, **384**, **525**, **539**
    election of **1988**, **326**
    election of **1992**, **78**
    election of **1994**, **286**
    election of **1996**, **343**
    election of **2000**, **339**
    fund-raising scandal, **363-366**, **484-490**, **492**, **495**
    health care reform and, **164**
    "reinventing government," **545**
    TWA Flight **800**, **435-436**
Gore, Mary Elizabeth "Tipper," **164**
Gorelick, Jamie,
    Fannie Mae and, **432**
    Foster and, **191**
    TWA Flight **800** and, **426-432**
Gorham, Deborah, **182**, **189**
Gormley, Col. William, **314**, **319-320**
Goss, Porter, **393**
Governors Island Agreement, **137**
Gracen, Elizabeth Ward, **444**
Granger, David, **340**
Grand Escalante Canyons, **301-302**
Grandmaison, Philip J., **528**
Grassley, Charles, **435**
Great Lakes Naval Training Center, **521**
The Green Berets, **9**

Green, Ernest G., **380**, **499**
Green, Pincus, **524**, **531**
Greenberg, Paul, **37**
Greenberg, Stanley, **285**, **344**
Greer, Frank, **49**
Gregg, Donald, (alias Dan Magruder), **56**
Gregory, Dick, **321**
Gridiron Club (Little Rock, Ark.), **50**
Grober, Paula, **274**
Grose, Vernon, **431**
Gubernatorial campaigns:
    of **1978**, **30-32**
    of **1980**, **35-38**
    of **1982**, **39-43**
    of **1984**, **46-47**
    of **1986**, **47**
    of **1990**, **51-52**
Gulf & Western Building (NY), **520**
Gulf of Tonkin, **7**
Gurley, Steven, **297**
Gutierrez, Luis V., **523**

H

Haiti,
    Clinton in, **137-139**
    Resolution **940**, **139**
    U.S.S. *Harland County*, **138**
Hale, David:
    indictment of, **223**, **233**
    Whitewater and, **176**, **215-216**, **220-223**, **225**
Hall, Arsenio, **78**
Hall, Jim, **425**, **433**, **435**
Hall, Sheryl, **332**
Hall, Todd, **179-181**
Halloran, Richard, **389**
Hamas, **148**, **350**, **356**, **546**
Hamilton, James:
    Foster and, **171**, **176**, **184**
Hamilton, Lee, **280**
Hamilton, Maxine, **1**
Hammerschmidt, John Paul, **261**

campaign in **1974**, **23**, **25**
career assessment, **23**, **25**
Handley, Charles, **213**
Hanger, Charlie, **352**
Hanley, Brian, **280**
Haoman beer company, **503**
Hansen, Nanette, **167**
Hanson, Jean, **223-224**, **231**, **234**
Harmon, Don:
    drug use, **65**
    Henry murder, **66**
    Ives murder, **66**
Harnett, Dan, **100**
Harriman, Pamela, **307**
Harrington, David, **255-256**
Harris, John, **421**
Harris, Kevin, **114-115**, **117**, **119**
Harris, Oren, **46**
Harrison, Roger, **183**
Hart, Gary, **20**, **48**, **77**, **325-326**
Hart, Peter, **38**
Hartford Seminary, **19**
Hartwell, Jack, **99**
Hastert, Dennis, **154**
Hastings, Alcee, **507**
Hatch, Orrin, **120**, **232**
Hatfield-McGovern amendment, **17**
Hause, Lt. Col. David, **314**, **319**
Havens, Mike (a.k.a. Terry Nichols), **358**
Hawk, David, **12**
Hawkins, Paul, **38**
Hay-Adams Hotel (Washington, D.C.), **470**
Hays, Cindy
Hays, Paul, **513**
Health Care Reform:
    American Academy of Pediatricians, **160**
    bus caravan, **164**
    Catalyst Institute, **159**
    Harry and Louise ads, **160-161**, **163**, **165**
    Health Insurance Association of America (HIAA), **160**, **163**
    Health Security Act, **162**
    protests and, **164**
    single-payer plan, **159**
Heard, Stanley, **275**
Hedaya, Charles, **172**
Hedges, Jeremy, **192**
Helsinki, Finland (Clinton trip), **16**
Henley, Don, **48**, **273**
Henry, Don, **66**
Hernreich, Nancy, **453**, **493**
Henry, Morris, **27**
Henson, Robby, **377**
Hentoff, Nat, **379**
Her Way (Gerth and Van Natta), **480**
Herman, Alexis, **493**
Herman, Larry, **128-129**
Heuer, Sam, **219**, **237**
Hewitt, Don, **73**
Heymann, Philip, **188**, **191**
Hezbollah, **356**, **416**
Higgins, Stephen, **94**, **108**
Hill, Anita, **263**
Hill, Nolanda:
    Brown's death, **312**
    Brown's relationship with, **294**, **298**, **300-301**, **305-307**
    Drug Enforcement Agency (DEA), **303**
    Foster and, **195**
    incarceration of, **323**
    independent counsel and, **302-303**
    payments to Brown, **302**
Hillary's Choice (Sheehy), **3**
Hillyer, John, **276**
Hilton Hotel (Dallas, TX), **56**
Hirschfeld, Abe, **449**
His Lai Buddist Temple (Los Angeles, CA), **495**
Ho Chi Minh, **527**
Hoar, Joseph, **142**
Hockersmith, Kaki, **535**
Holder, Eric,
    Lewinsky and, **469**

pardon and, **525**
Wen Ho Lee and, **391**
Holmes, Eugene J., **12**, **14-16**, **31**, **72**, **79-80**
Holmes, T. Wesley, **448**
Holt, Frank, **7**
Holtsclaw, Jim, **437**
Hongye Zheng, **502**
Hoover, John Edgar, **478**
Horiuchi, Lon:
Ruby Ridge and, **114-116**
Waco and, **110**
Horizons Hotel (Bermuda), **33**
Hot Springs, Ark., **3,4,5**
draft board, **8-10**, **14**
Hotel Playa Conchas Chinas, **61**
Hothem, Eric, **535**
House Appropriations Committee, **152**
House Armed Services Committee, **423**, **512**
House Committee on Government Operations, **298**
House Foreign Operations Appropriations Committee, **153**
House Government Operations Committee, **191**
House Government Reform and Oversight Committee, **293**, **324**, **333**, **522**
House Intelligence Committee, **356**, **389**, **393**
House International Relations Committee, **153**, **362**
House Judiciary Committee,
articles of impeachment and, **511-512**
impeachment inquiry and, **491**
Justice Department stonewalling and, **505**
Starr's referral and, **508-509**
Watergate and, **507**
House Managers,
impeachment process, **513**
House Rules Committee, **505**

Howard, Ed, **13**, **15**
Howard, George, Jr., **234-235**, **238**
Howell, Vernon (a.k.a. David Koresh), **93**
Hsia, Maria, **495**
Huang, John, **293**, **317**, **343-344**, **495-496**, **504-505**
Hubbell, Susie
Hubbell, Webb, **30**, **51**, **86**, **88**, **192**
Brown and, **298**, **300**
Foster and, **171-172**, **176**, **190**
fund-raising scandal, **496**
Lums and, **298**
resignation, **234**
Waco and, **103-104**
Whitewater and, **218**, **220**, **222**, **224**, **226**, **230**, **232**
Huber, Carolyn, **236**
Huddleston, Vicki, **138**
Huggins, Stanley, **276**
Hughes Electronics, **372**, **377**, **381**, **400**
Hughes, Hank, **435**
Hughes, Lt. Gen. Patrick, **153**
Hulser, Raymond, **318**
Human Events, **154**, **454-455**, **507**, **536**
Human Rights Watch, **148**, **374**
Hunter, Duncan, **503**
Hupp, Louis, **190**
Hussman media empire, **28**
Hustler magazine, **510**
Hutchinson, Asa, **44**
Hyde, Henry J., **491**, **505**, **510**, **512-514**

I

Ickes, Harold M.., **17**
China and, **375**
election of **1996** and, **342-344**
fund-raising scandal, **484**, **488-490**, **493**, **496**
Lewinsky and, **454**
Stephens and, **231**
Travelgate and, **125**
Whitewater and, **229**, **232**

INDEX 645

Ifshin, David M., **71**
Immanuel Baptist Church (Little Rock, Ark.), **41**
Immigration and Naturalization Service (INS), **86**, **354**
Impeachment articles:
    House Judiciary Committee and, **512**
    House vote and, **513-514**
    Senate trial and, **514**
    Senate vote on, **514-515**
Impeachment inquiry:
    House of Representatives and, **508-509**
    Hyde and, **510**
    obstruction of justice and, **508-509**
    Starr and, **508**
Indyk, Martin, **289**
Ingraham, Laura, **258**
Insight magazine, **317**
Internal Revenue Service (IRS), **126**, **133**, **174**, **264**
International Atomic Energy Agency (IAEA), **149**
Iorio, Richard, **233**
Iran and, **151**, **154-155**, **372**, **376**, **379**, **385**, **388**, **416**, **525**
International Defense Review, **372**
Intourist tourist board (Soviet Union), **16**
Iraq and, **379**, **512**, **514**
Ireland, Patricia, **263**
Irons, Steve, **219**, **221-222**, **468-469**
Irvine, Reed, **258**
Isikoff, Michael:
    election of 1992, **76**
    Jones and, **257**, **266-267**
    Lewinsky and, **471**
Israeli Aircraft Industries Building (NY), **527**
It Takes a Village, **453**
Ives, Kevin, **66**, **273**

J
Jackson, Cliff, **11**

Clinton's draft avoidance and, **11**
Clinton's relationship with,
Jackson, Jesse,
    Brown inquiry and, **321**
    Clinton's relationship with, **52**, **77**
    Lewinsky and, **322**
    Karin Stanford and, **322**
    Rainbow/PUSH, **322**
    Southern White Boys Club, **52**
Jacobsen, Ernest, **57**
Jamar, Jeff, **100**, **102-103**
Janoski, Kathleen, **313-314**, **319**, **321**
Jaworski, Leon, **325**
Jeffrey, Terrance, **454-455**
Jenkins, Marilyn Jo, **205**, **266**, **299**
Jerkuic, Niko, **314**
Jiang Zemin, **367**, **373**, **385**, **389**
John Paul II, **168-169**, **283**, **335**, **408**
Johnson, Andrew, **491**
Johnson, Don, **286**
Johnson, Jim, **7**
Johnson, Leon, **518**
Johnson, Lyndon B., **7**, **341**
Johnson, Michael (a.k.a. L.D. Brown), **61**
Johnson, Norma Holloway, **478**
Johnson, William H., **94**
Johnston, Bennett, **181**
Johnston, Bill, **100**, **108**
Johnston, David, **431**
Johnston, Lt. Gen. Robert, **140-141**
Jones, Clinton D., **73**
Jones, David, **97**
Jones, Paula Corbin, **204**
    apology and, **257**
    Arkansas Quality Management Governor's Conference, **254**
    attempt to dismiss, **261-263**
    Broaddrick and, **444-448**
    Campaign for Victims of Sexual Harassment, **265-266**
    Clinton's false testimony regarding, **469**
    Clinton's "genital defect," **259-260**, **265**

Conservative Political Action Conference (CPAC), **254**
delaying filing of lawsuit, **262-263**
deposition of, **471**
elves (Jerome Marcus, George T. Conway III, Richard Porter, Laura Ingraham and Anne Coulter), **258**
Industrial Development Commission, **254**
Internal Revenue Service (IRS) audit, **264**
Jones legal defense fund, **264**
Lewinsky's false affidavit in, **271, 448**
Lewinsky's job situation and, **458-461, 463-464**
Lewinsky and, **267-270**
NOW Legal Defense Fund, **258**
Old Ebbit Grill, **271**
Pacific Indemnity (Chubb Group Insurance), **262, 449**
Paula's coming forward, **254, 256-257**
Paula's fear of retribution, **257**
Paula's story, **254-256**
presidential immunity, **261**
Privacy Act, **443**
Rader, Campbell, Fisher & Pyke, **265**
settlement, **449**
sexual misconduct lawsuit filed, **260**
Soldiers' and Sailors' Relief Act of **1940**, **262**
State Farm, **262**
Tripp and, **267, 271, 470**
Willey and, **267**
Jones, Perry, **98**
Jones, Stephen, **271**
Jordan, Hamilton:
  Clinton and, **531**
Jordan, Vernon:
  Brown and, **306**
  Lewinsky and, **451, 458, 460-469, 472-473, 475, 509, 514**
Juanita's restaurant (Little Rock, Ark.), **62**
Judicial Watch, **299-300, 305-306, 321-322, 330, 443**
Julia Chester Hospital, **1**
Justice Department:
  Brown and, **298, 318, 321**
  China and, **382, 386, 388**
  FALN terrorists, **522**
  Foster death, **180, 188, 191**
  fund-raising scandal, **489, 503-504, 506**
  Hill and, **322**
  Lewinsky and, **478**
  Pardongate, **529**
  Rich and, **524-525**
  Ruby Ridge, **115-119**
  State Department file search, **241**
  Travelgate and, **127, 134**
  Waco and, **99, 105, 107, 111-112**
  Wen Ho Lee, **391**
  Whitewater and, **212, 221, 227**

K

Kabot, Linda, **437**
Kahoe, Michael, **118-119**
Kaiparowitz Plateaus, **301-302**
Kaiser, Robert, **258**
Kallstrom, James:
  MBNA Bank, **436**
  TWA Flight 800, **425, 427, 430, 432-433, 436**
Kamen, Al, **240-241**
Kanchanalak, Pauline, **301, 504-505**
Kantor, Mickey:
  Brown and, **316-317**
  election of **1992, 53, 70**
  Lewinsky and, **482**
Kaye, Walter, **451, 456**
Keeny, Jack, **127**
Kellee Communications, Inc., **302**
Kelley, Dick, **46**
Kelly, Robert, **280**
Kelly, Shelly, **311-312**
Kelsay, Norma Rogers, **445-446**
Kemp, Jack, **345**

INDEX

Kendall, David:
    Broaddrick and, **447-448**
    Foster and, **191**, **193**
    Lewinsky and, **474**, **476**, **480**, **482**
    Troopergate and, **205**
    Whitewater and, **220**, **225-227**, **235**
Kennedy, Edward, **28**, **318**, **341**
Kennedy, John F., **6**, **334**, **348**, **478**
    Jones and, **262**
Kennedy, John F., Jr. (*George* magazine), **199**
Kennedy, John F., School of Government (Harvard), **75**
Kennedy, Robert, **8**, **12**, **478**
Kennedy, Weldon, **355**
Kennedy, William H., III, **192**, **529**
    Filegate and, **326**
    Foster and, **183**
    resignation, **234**
    Travelgate and, **126-130**, **134**
    Whitewater and, **225**, **235**
Kenya embassy bombing, **417**
Kerrey, Bob, **335-336**
    election of **1992**, **75**
    health care, **158**
    Whitewater and, **228**
Kerry, John F., **249-252**
Kesey, Ken, **18**
Kessler, Gladys, **134**
Kettleson, Jordan, **274**
Kevorkian, Dr. Jack, **161**
Khare, Carol, **502**
Khobar Towers bombing, **415-417**
    casualties, **416**
    Clinton reaction, **416**
    Hani al-Sayegh, **415**
    Hezbollah, **415-416**
    Intelligence and Security Ministry (MOIS), **416**
    Iran and, **416**
    Islamic Revolutionary Guards Corp (IRGC), **416**

King Abdul Aziz Airbase (Saudi Arabia), **415**
    Mohammad Khatami, **416**
Khrushchev, Nikita, **248**
Kilbane, Navy Cmdr. Edward, **314**
King Hussein, **289**
King, John, **73**
King, Martin Luther, **313**
Kissinger, Henry:
    Vietnam and, **245-247**
Klayman, Larry, **299**, **302**, **321**
Klein, Edward, **33**, **40**
Kleinsmith, Maj. Erik, **422-423**
Knight, Jerry, **87**
Knight-Ridder, **232**
Knowlton, Patrick, **177**
Kopold, Bedrich, **17**
Kopold, Jan, **17**
Kopoldova, Jirina, **17**
Koppel, Ted, **106**
Koresh, David (a.k.a Vernon Howell,), **93-95**, **97-102**, **104-106**
Kosovo, **145-148**
Kosovo Liberation Army (KLA), **145-146**, **148**
KPMG Peat Marwick, **128-130**
Kramer, Michael, **88**
Kristol, William, **288**
Kroft, Steve, **74**
Kuca, Lawrence, **236**
Kudrick, Petty Officer Jennifer, **420**,
Kulka, Ellen, **229**

L

L'Osservatore Romano, **89**
LaBella, Charles:
    Chinagate and, **506**
    Justice Department stonewalling and, **506**
    report of, **506**
Lader, Philip, **124**
Lake, Celinda, **287**
Lake, Anthony, **502**

Lamberth, Royce C., **322**
Landmark Legal Foundation, **258, 516**
Landow, Nathan, **172, 441**
Lane, Cliff, **40**
Lane Processing, Inc., **41**
Langston, Robert E., **184**
Lantos, Tom, **328, 370**
Larry King Live, **237-238, 287**
Lasater, Dan, **41**
   background, **62**
   charges of drug money laundering, **64, 233**
   Clinton administration ties to Lasater and Co., **63**
   Clinton's pardon of, **46, 519**
   drug parties, **63**
   employment of Roger Clinton, **63**
   Lasater's deal (cocaine), **59**
   pardon of, **46, 64**
   savings and loan controversy, **64, 233**
   sentencing of, **46**
Lasater and Company, **63**
Latham, John, **213**
Lauramoore, John, **210**
Lauramoore, Marilyn, **210**
Lawhorn, Johnny, Jr., **277**
Lawrence Livermore, **397**
Le Bistro nightclub (Little Rock, Ark.), **64**
Le Brun, Charles, **430**
Le Quang Uyen, **296**
Leach, Jim:
   Whitewater and, **226-227**
Lear, Norman, **48**
Leaves of Grass (Whitman), **339**
LeBleu, Conway, **280**
Lee, Peter, **385**
Lee, Wen Ho, **390-392**
Legacy (Lowry), **136**
Legal Times, **117**
Legal Services Corporation, **38, 53**
Lehman Brothers, **499**

Lehrer, Jim, **155, 475-476**
Levin, Carl and, **394**
Lewinsky, Bernie, **470**
Lewinsky, Michael, **451**
Lewinsky, Monica Samille:
   blue dress of, Introduction ix, **456, 474, 479-480**
   "break up day,"
   Clinton denial of affair, Introduction ix, **451, 477**
   at Clinton Radio City party, **455**
   Clinton's abuse of power and, **508-509**
   Clinton's DNA test, **480**
   Clinton's reported phone sex and, **453, 455, 481**
   Clinton's relationship with, **452-468**
   Clinton's testimony regarding, **480-481**
   cover stories of, **456, 467**
   Drudge Report, **471**
   "dump day," **456**
   false affidavit of, **271, 467-469**
   gifts exchanged between Clinton and, **455-456, 462-463, 465-466, 474**
   grand jury testimony, **480, 482**
   Hay-Adams Hotel (Washington, D.C.), **470**
   House vote and, **513**
   immunity agreement, **479**
   interviews of, **458-461, 467**
   job situation of, **454, 456-457**
   Jones case and, **467-468**
   Jones witness list and, **463-464**
   Leaves of Grass (Whitman), **456, 474**
   "Mission Accomplished," **467**
   obstruction of justice and, **466, 469**
   Ritz Carlton Hotel (Pentagon City, Va.), **468-469**
   "talking points," **468**
   taped conversations between, **460-461**
   Tripp and, **455-458, 460-461, 464-466, 468-470**
   UN, **432**

wagging his finger, Introduction ix, **451**, **477**
Watergate Hotel (Washington, D.C.), **451**, **460**, **474**
Willey and, **468**
Wilshire Courtyard Marriott (Los Angeles, Ca.), **462**
Lewis and Clark college, **451**
Lewis, Jean, **221**, **223**, **225**, **228-230**
Lewis, John, **369**
Libonati, John, **329**
Libya and, **379**, **385**
Liddy, G. Gordon, **283**
Filegate, **327**
Lieberman, Evelyn:
election of **1996**, **344**
Foster and, **185-186**
Lewinsky and, **453-455**
Lieberman, Joseph I., **483**
Limbaugh, David, **364-365**
Limbaugh, Rush, **164**, **283**, **285**, **346**
Lindsey, Bruce, **40**
Brown and, **300**
election of **1996**, **343**
Foster and, **176**
Lewinsky and, **269**, **463**, **473** **475**, **478**
Marriott Hotel (Washington, D.C.), **336**
nuclear codes lost, **338**
Travelgate, **132**
Tripp and, **457**
Troopergate, **205-207**
Waco and, **103**
Whitewater, **208**, **223**, **225-226**, **228**
Lindsey, Clayton, **192**
Lippo America, **496**
Lippo Group, **251**, **301**, **494**
Liu Chaoying, **383**, **500**, **502**, **503**
Liu Huaquing, **383-384**, **500**, **503**
Livingston, Bob, **510**, **512**
Livingstone, Craig,
Filegate, **324-326**, **328-331**
Foster and, **183**, **185-186**, **195**

fund-raising scandal, **499**
Travelgate and, **124**
Locke, George "Butch," **41**, **63**
Lockhart, Joe, **146**
Lockheed Martin and, **375**
Lodge, Edward, **115**
Loewe, Rudi, **17**
Logan, Hillman, **210**
Long Beach Naval Station, **377**, **383-384**
Loral Corporation, **305**, **372**, **375**, **378**, **381**, **386-388**, **400**
Lord, Winston, **25**
Los Alamos Lavatory, **377-378**, **385**, **389**, **391**, **397**, **402**
Los Angeles Times, **123**, **147**, **205-206**, **303**, **451**, **488**, **500-501**, **503-505**
Lowe, Lynn, **31-32**
Lowry, Rich, **136**
Lucas, Shawn, **280**
Ludwig, Eugene, **227-228**
Lum, Gene, **292-293**, **301**, **304**, **306-307**, **318**, **323**
Lum, Nora, **292-293**, **301**, **304**, **306-307**, **318**, **323**
Luntz, Frank, **287**, **345**, **483**
Luzzatto, Anne, **316**
Ly Tranh Binh, **294-298**
Lynch, Larry, **98-100**
Lynch, Loretta,
election **1992**, **235**
Whitewater and, **235**
Lyons, James,
election of **1992**, **76**
Foster and, **171**, **176**
Whitewater and, **223**

M
M-16s, **58**
Ma, Robert, **499**
MacAndrews & Forbes, **467**
Mackay, Donald, **222**, **225**
Macy's (department store), **520**

Madsen, Lillian, **294-295**
Madison Guaranty Savings and Loan Association, **212**, **214-215**, **217**, **220**, **222-224**, **226**, **228**, **233**, **235**, **238**
Madison Square Garden (NY), **37**
Magisono, Gus (a.k.a. Kenneth Fadley), **113**
Magladry, Bruce, **430-431**
Magraw, Sergeant Major Michael
Magraw, **545**
Magruder, Dan (a.k.a. Donald Gregg), **56**
Mahoney, Mary Caitrin, **276-277**, **483**
Magaziner, Ira, **158-159**, **163**, **165**
Mahathir, Mohammed, **261**
Malcolm X, **527**
Manila (**1995**):
  Abdul Hakim Murad, **408**
  Aida Farsical, **408**
  Dona Josefa apartment building, **408**
  Mohammed Jamal Khalifa, **408**
  Nap Taas, **408**
  "Project Bojinka," **409**
  Ramzi Yousef, **409**
Manzanares, Robert, **332**
Maraniss, David, **26**
Marceca, Anthony B., **326**, **328-329**, **331**, **333**
Marcus, Jerome, **258**
Margolis, David, **188**
Mariano, E. Connie, **480**
Maritime Administration, **503**
Marriott Hotel (Washington, D.C.), **336**
Martens, Darnell, **123-125**, **129**
Martha's Vineyard, **12**, **482**
Martin, Florence, **273**
Martin, Joseph W., Jr., **287**
Martin, Mark, **336**
Martin, Wayne, **98**, **100**, **102**
Massey, Richard, **214**
Master Marketing, **216**, **222**
Matesa, Zlatko, **308**, **310**
Matos, Adolfo, **521**

Matsch, Richard, **360**
Matsui, Robert, **495**
Matthews, Charles, **236**
Matthews, Chris, **445**
Matthews, Sylvia, **475**
Maughan, Robert, **132**, **134**
Maulden, Jerry, **299**
May 19th Communist Organization, **526**
Mayer, Jane, **479**
Mayer, Peter, **440-441**
McAlare, Robert, **281**
McAuliffe, Terry, **364**, **493**
McCarthy, Eugene, **8**, **12**, **341**
McCaughy, Elizabeth, **161**
McClellan, John L., **29**
McClendon, Sarah, **54**
McCloud, David J., **278**
McColl, Hugh, **282**
McCuen, William J., **442**
McCurdy, Dave, **356-357**
McCurry, Mike:
  Brown and, **321**
  China and, **387**
  fund-raising scandal, **485**
  Jones and, **264**, **448**
  Lewinsky and, **479**
McDonald, Neil, **26**
McDougal, James B.:
  Bank of Kingston, **209**
  death of, **238**, **277**
  FDIC investigation of, **218**
  Foster and, **172**
  guilty verdict, **238**
  HRC hired by, **212-213**
  indictment of, **218**
  Madison Guaranty and, **213-214**, **217**, **220**, **222-224**
  trial of, **218-219**
  Whitewater and, **171**, **208**, **212-220**, **230**, **232**, **235**, **237-238**
McDougal, Susan,
  guilty verdict, **238**

pardon of, **528**
Whitewater and, **171**, **208**, **216-218**, **235**, **237**
McDowell, Jerry, **127**
McGann, Eileen, **38**
McGovern, George, **20**, **136**
McGrath, Judy, **283**
McKeehan, Todd, **280**
McLarty, Thomas F. "Mack," III, **4**, **52**, **120**, **498**
    Brown and, **306**
    Foster and, **185**, **187**
    Travelgate and, **124-125**, **128-130**, **133**
    Troopergate and, **205**
    Whitewater and, **221**, **224**
McMahon, Henry, **94**
McMaskle, Keith, **273**
McMillan, William N., III, **264**
McNamara, Robert, **252**
McRae, Tom, **51**
McSorley, Richard, **13**
McSweeney, John, **131-132**, **134**
McTague, Jim, **537**
McVeigh, Timothy, **349**, **351-352**, **357**, **359-362**
    Daryl Bridges alias, **358**
    execution, **361**
    indictment, **359**
    sentencing of, **360**
McWethy, John, **353**
Medellin Cartel, **57**, **60**
Meet the Press NBC, **363**, **394**
Meissner, Charles F., **276**, **312**
Mena Intermountain Regional Airport (Ark.), **58**
    Clinton's denial of Mena operations, **54**
    cocaine traffic, **54-55**, **57-59**
    gun-running, **57-59**
Mendez, Olga A., **523**
Medlar Jones, Linda, **527**
Merletti, Lewis, **462**
Meyer, Maj. Fritz, **430**

Mfume, Kweisi, **137**
Miami Herald, **48**, **297**
Michelson, Lisa, **436**
Middleton, Mark, **498**
Mikva, Abner J., **486**
Milan, James, **273**
Milhollin, Gary, **372**
Miller, Charles Wilbourne, **278**
Miller, Dean, **116**
Miller, Marie B., **518**
Miller, Ron, **277**
Mills, Cheryl,
    Lewinsky and, **473-474**, **477**
Mills, Wilbur, **63**
Milosevic, Slobodan, **145-146**
Milton, Joyce, **28**, **37**
Miniter, Richard, **406**, **412**
Miss Emma, **201**
Miss Lang, **495**
Miss Marie's School for Little Folks, **4**
Missile defense system, **392**
Mission Energy, **301**
Mitchell, Andrea, **90**
Mitchell, George, **164-165**
Mitchell, Joni, **34**
Mixner, David, **12**, **89**
Mobile One Building (NY), **520**
Moler, Elizabeth, **389**, **393-394**
Molinari, Susan, **329**
Mondale, Eleanor, **463**
Monkey Business (boat), **48**
Monroe, Larry, **196**
Montano, Joe, **279**
Montgomery, Lt. Gen. Thomas, **142**
Moore, Rudy, **32**
Moose, Richard, **241**
Morgan, Charles Wilfred III, **529**
Morris, Dick, **454**
    Brown and, **306**
    Clinton gubernatorial campaigns, **30**, **35**, **38**, **41-42**, **50**, **52**
    election of **1994** and, **289-291**

election of **1996** and, **342-344**, **366**, **375**
fund-raising scandal and, **490**
Hamas, **546**
infidelity issue and, **346**
polls, **539-540**
terrorism and, **546-547**
Morris, Roger, **31**, **444**
Morris, Stephen J., **248**
Moscow, (Clinton's trip to), **16**, **80**
Moses, Stephen, **303**
Moss, Melissa, **323**
Motel Capri, **5**
Mother Theresa, **335**
Mountain View Maximum Security Prison (TX), **5**
Moussaoui, Zacarias, **361**
Moynihan, Daniel Patrick:
    fund-raising scandal and, **505**
    health care reform and, **162**
    impeachment, **507**
    Lewinsky, **483**
    Whitewater and, **228**
MSNBC, **436**, **445**, **447**
MTV, **282-283**, **458**
Muma, Dede, **437**
Munich, West Germany (Clinton trip to), **17**
Myers, Dee Dee:
    anchorwoman does Clinton's makeup and, **167**
    DUI, **334-335**
    election of **1992**, **70**
    election of **1994**, **288**
    Foster and, **191**
    health care reform and, **159**
    Jones and, **257**
    Travelgate, **123**, **130-131**
    Troopergate, **206**
    Whitewater and, **224-225**
Myers, Lisa, **444-447**
Myers, Rodney, **44**

N

Nannygate, **86-88**
NASCAR, **336**
Nash, Robert, **47**
National Association of Securities Dealers, **236**
National Building Museum, **462**
National Drug Control policy, **89**
National Enquirer, **76**
National Gallery (London, England), **10**
National Governors' Association, **70**, **163**
National Guard, **11**
National Hotel (Moscow), **16**
National Organization of Women (NOW), **263**
National Press Club, **402**
National Review, **421**
National Review Online, **539**
National Park Service (NPS), **534**
National Public Radio (NPR), **495**
National Security Agency (NSA), **368**, **371**, **379**, **411**, **544**
National Security Council (NSC), **7**, **388**, **425**, **457**, **502**
National Transportation Safety Board (NTSB), **425-426**, **431**, **433-437**, **439**
National War College (Ft. McNair), **91**, **527**
National Women's Educational Fund, **39**
NationsBank, **281**
Navarro, Joaquin, **283**
NBC News, **90**, **345**, **353**, **444-445**
Nella airfield (Ark.), **61**
Nelson, Sheffield, **444**
    campaign for governorship in **1990**, **51**
Netherlands Hotel (Kansas City, Mo.), **2**
Neuwirth, Stephen, **189**
New Hampshire primary (**1992**), **72-73**
New Mobilization Committee to End the War in Vietnam, **13**
New Statesman, **146**
New York *Daily News*, **538**

New York magazine, **40**
New York Observer, **535**
New York Post, **75**, **191-192**, **267**, **329**, **346**, **447**
New York Times, **56**, **85**, **108**, **116-117**, **150**, **164**, **190**, **198**, **212**, **219**, **223**, **227**, **231**, **249**, **272**, **297**, **370**, **376**, **378**, **380-381**, **388-389**, **391**, **417-418**, **431-434**, **437**, **444**, **521**, **523**, **525-526**, **530**, **533**, **535**, **539**
New Yorker magazine, **479**
Newbern, David, **23**
NewsHour,, **475-476**
Newsmax, **445**
Newsweek, **111**, **198**, **266**, **315**, **469**, **471**, **495**
Nguyen, Van Hao, **294-298**
Nichols, James, **357**
Nichols, Larry, **73**
Nichols, Terry, **349**, **357**, **359-360**, **362**
Nightline, **73**, **106**, **198**, **263**
Nightly News NBC, **446**
Nixon, Richard M., **20-21**, **492**, **518-519**
    Vietnam and, **14**, **246**
Nixon, Vic, **27**
Nixon, Walter, **507**
Ng Lap Seng, **497**
Noble County jail (Oklahoma), **357**
Noble, Ron, **99-100**
Norman, Greg, **426**, **456**
North, Oliver, **62**
North Korea, **385**
    The Agreed Framework, **151-152**
    Choma, **155**
    Hwang Jang-yop, **151-152**
    Kim Il-Sung, **148**
    Kim Jong-Il, **148**, **155**
    Kim Yong Nam, **150**
    Kim Yong Sam, **150**
    Kumchangni, **152-153**
    No-dong missile, **151**
    Taepo Dong-1 missile, **154**
    Taepo Dong-2 missile, **154**
    Yongbyon, **148**
Nuclear Nonproliferation Treaty (NPT), **148**
Nunn, Sam, **139**
Nussbaum, Bernard W.:
    attorney general search and, **87**
    Filegate and, **327-329**, **331**, **333**
    Foster and, **176**, **182**, **185-190**
    fund-raising scandal and, **486**
    resignation, **234**
    Travelgate, and, **131**, **133**
    Waco and, **103**
    Whitewater and, **221**, **223**, **225-226**, **229**

O

O'Connor, Jennifer, **129**
O'Connor, John Cardinal, **522**
O'Grady, Edward, **527**
O'Hare Airport (Chicago, IL), **356**
O'Leary, Hazel, **369**
O'Neill, Henry P., **186**
O'Reilly, Bill, **532**
Oak Ridge, **397**
Oakley, Meredith, **5**, **35**, **52**, **66**
Oakley, Robert, **407**
Oehler, Gordon, **385**, **388**
Oklahoma City bombing:
    Abraham Ahmad, **356**
    alerts to and rumors of bombing, **349**, **359**, **361**
    Bureau of Alcohol, Tobacco and Firearms (ATF), **361**
    Cactus Motel, **351-352**, **361**
    Clinton political revival and, **348**
    Congressional Task Force on Terrorism, **349**
    crime scene, **351-352**
    Dallas/Fort Worth International Airport, **353**
    Elohim City, **361-362**

evidence tampering, **360**
Hussain Al-Hussaini, **350**, **362**
investigation and trial, **352-362**
Marwan Al-Shehhi, **361**
Mid Kansas Co-op, **357**
Mohammed, **351**
Mohammed Atta, **361**
Noble County courthouse, **359**
Noble County jail (Oklahoma), **354**
Oklahoma Highway Patrol, **352**
Ryder truck and, **351**
Waco and, **348**, **359**
Will Rogers World Airport, **356**
Zacarias Moussaoui, **361**
Oklahoma *Gazette*, **357**
Old Executive Building (OEOB), **336**, **536**
Olson, Jeff, **18**
Olson, Kris, **18**
One Police Plaza (NY), **521**
On the Make, **35**, **66**
Operation Pursestrings, **17**, **19**
Operation Restore Hope, **139-140**
Oregon Hog Farm commune, **18**
Orenstein, Julian, **183**
Oslo, Norway (Clinton trip), **13**
Oslo Peace Institute, **13**
Ott, Capt. Ray, **438**
Ouachita National Forest (Ark.), **61**
Outlaw, Dailan, **497**
Oxford University:
    Clinton's first year at, **9**, **10**
    Clinton's overseas voyage to, **9**
    Clinton's second year at, **17**
    Tutorial system at, **9**

P

Padilla, Lana, **357**
Paige, Peter, **527**
PaineWebber, **295**
Pakis, Jack, **519-520**
Pakistan, **151**, **371**, **380**, **383**, **385**, **387-388**
Palladino, Jack, **76**, **235**
Palmer, Robert, **234**, **236**, **528**
Pan, Antonio, **497**
Panetta, Leon:
    Brown and, **306**, **323**
    election of **1996**, **343**
    fund-raising scandal, **488**, **493**
    Lewinsky and, **451**
    Travelgate, **124**, **133**
    Waco and, **109**
Parade magazine, **545**
Pardongate:
    Christmas pardons and, **524**
    criticism of, **524**, **531-532**
    explanation of, **530**
    FALN terrorists, **520-524**
    January 20 pardons, **524-529**
    New Square Four (Kalmen Stern, David Goldstein, Benjamin Berger and Jacob Elbaum) and, **526**
    pardon process and, **519**
Park Hyatt (Washington, D.C.), **466**
Parks, Gary, **174**
Parks, Jane, **66-67**, **173-174**
    Vantage Point, **66-67**
Parks, Jerry Luther:
    American Contract Services (Little Rock, Ark.), **174**
    Foster and, **173-174**
    Guardsmark (Little Rock, Ark.), **67**
    murder, **67**, **174**, **275**
Parsons, Maj. Thomas, **319**
Pascarella, Rocco, **521**
Pastorella, Richard, **521**
Patrick, Deval:
    Ruby Ridge and, **115-117**
Patrolmen's Benevolent Association (NY), **527**
Patterson, Larry:
    Mena airport and, **55**, **68**
    Jones and, **256**

INDEX 655

Troopergate, **202-205**
Patterson, Lt. Col. Robert "Buzz," **145, 337, 409-410, 544, 546**
Patton Boggs, **295-296**
Payne, Julia, **537**
Pearson, Daniel, **305-306**
Pelosi, Nancy, **379, 525**
Penn & Shoen, **344**
Pentagon bombing (**2001**), **547**
Perdue, Sally Miller:
    Clinton's affair with, **64**
Perelman, Ronald, **467**
Perot, H. Ross, **77, 80, 82, 287, 345-346**
Perroy, Deborah, **332**
Perry, Roger, **201, 203, 205**
Perry, William:
    China and, **368-369, 371**
    North Korea, **149, 154**
Peters, F. Whitten, **319**
Peterson, Chuck, **116**
Peterson, Michele, **332**
Philippines:
    al Qaeda, **408-409**
    bin Laden's operations in, **409**
Pilger, John, **146**
Pilon, Roger, **326-327**
Pine Bluff Commercial, **37**
Pittsburgh Tribune-Review, **182, 197, 316, 318 319, 321**
Pockrus, Theresa, **211**
Podesta, Anthony, **17, 19**
Podesta, John:
    Brown and, **323**
    Lewinsky and, **459, 474-475**
    nuclear codes, **338**
    Travelgate and, **133**
Pollock, Ellen, **192**
Pond, Betsy, **182, 187**
Porter, Richard, **258**
Posse Comitatus Act of **1878**, **96**
Potts, Larry:
    Ruby Ridge and, **116, 118**

Poulard, John, **50**
Powell, Gen. Colin:
    gays in military, **90**
    Haiti, **139**
    Somalia, **141, 143**
Prague, Czechoslovakia (Clinton trip), **17**
Presidential Legal Defense Trust (PLET), **497**
Price, Linda, **304**
Price, Stuart, **304**
Privacy Act, **479**
Proctor, William Jr., **518**
Prodi, Romano, **327**
Project Bojinka, **409-410**
Project Pursestrings, **17, 19**
Prosperi, Arnold Paul, **529**
Pryor, David, **22, 29-31, 46**
Purcell, Joe, **42**
Purdie, Jeff, **463**
Purkins, Marie A., **4**
Putting People First, **228**
Pyke, David, **462-463**
Pynoos, Rita, **534**

Q
Qian Qichen, **385**
Queen Noor, **289**
Quinn, Jack:
    Filegate, **324**
    Foster and, **185**
    fund-raising scandal, **495**
    pardon and, **525**

R
Rabinowitz, Dorothy, **445**
Rader, Robert E., **265**
Radio Factor (Bill O'Reilly), **532**
Raguz, Damir, **311**
Rainbow Coalition, **78**
Rainwater, Gene, **25**
Raiser, C. Victor, **274**
Raiser, Montgomery, **274**

Rand Corporation, **246**, **379**
Rasco, Carol, **165**
Rather, Dan, **515**
Ray, Robert:
    Filegate and, **332-333**
    Whitewater and, **238**
Raytheon (Garland, TX), **423**
Reagan, Michael, **283**
Reagan, Ronald, **39**, **83**, **136**, **168**, **287**, **288**, **334**, **542**
Red Guerilla Resistance, **527**
Redden, Yoly, **172**
Reed, Terry:
    Air Contra, **61**
    background, **61**
    Brown's assassination plan, **60-61**
    Clinton liability, **61-62**
    Compromised, **61-62**
    Contra pilot training, **61-62**
    North and, **62**
    Seal and, **61-62**
Rehnquist, William H., **514**
Reich, Robert, **9**
Reid, Morris, **308**, **310**
Reno, Janet:
    attorney general selected, **88**
    Brown and, **298**, **303**, **321**
    China and, **384**, **391**
    Filegate and, **328**
    Foster and, **173**, **195**
    fund-raising scandal and, **488**, **505**
    Hill and, **303**
    Jones and, **266**
    Lewinsky and, **469**
    Oklahoma City bombing and, **355**
    Ruby Ridge and, **119**
    State Department file search, **241**
    Travelgate, **126**
    TWA Flight **800**, **426**
    Waco and, **103-108**, **111-112**
    Whitewater and, **228-229**
Reno, John, **281**
Reno, Miriam Fisher, **281**
Republic of New Afrika, **527**
Republican party:
    in Arkansas, **11**
Reserve Officers Training Corps Program (ROTC), **11-13**, **31**
Resolution Trust Corporation (RTC), **219**, **221**, **223-224**, **229-230**, **232-233**, **236**
Reuters, **251**
Revlon Corp., **476**
Reynolds, Melvin, **528**
Reynolds, Scott J., **280**
Rhodes, Jeff, **273**
Rhodes, Gary, **280**
Rhodes Scholarship, **7**, **10**
Riady, James, **301**, **306**, **343**, **496**
Riady, Mochtar (Lippo Group):
    China and, **368**
    Vietnam and, **251**
Riady, Stephen, **301**, **306**
Rice, Donna, **48**
Rich, Denise, **525**, **529-530**, **537**
Rich, Marc, **524-525**, **531**
Rich Mountain Aviation, **57**
Rich, Seth, **279**
Richards, Ann, **94**
Richardson, Bill:
    China and, **402**
    Lewinsky and, **459-461**
Richenback, Paul, **394**
Richland, Dan, **123**
Ricks, Bob, **102**
The Right Mind, **272**
Riley, Richard, Jr., **528**
Ritz Carlton Hotel (Pentagon City, Va.), **468-469**
Rivera, Geraldo, **530**
Rivers, Dorothy, **529**
Rivlin, Alice:
    Drug Czar, **529**
    election of **1994**, **288-289**

health care reform and, **163**
Robb, Charles, **228**
Robert Trent Jones Golf Club, **294, 307, 458**
Robespierre, Maximilien, **161**
Robertson, William, **280**
Robinson, Tommy F., **51**
Robyn, Dorothy, **384**
Rockefeller, Winthrop, **7**
Roderick, Arthur, **114**
Roderiguez, Paul, **317**
Rodham, Dorothy Emma Howell, **27, 534**
Rodham, Hugh Ellsworth, **24**
Rodham, Hugh Ellsworth, Jr., **526, 529**
Rodham, Tony, **24**
Rodriguez, Felix (a.k.a. Max Gomez), **60-62**
Rodriguez, Miguel:
    Fort Marcy Park crime scene map, **196**
    Foster case probe, **196**
    grand jury and, **196-197**
    investigation, **196-197**
    Starr and, **196, 198**
Rodriguez, Robert, **95, 97**
Roelle, William, **221, 223**
Rogers, Jeff, **18**
Rogers, Richard, **115**
Rolla, John, **179, 184**
Rometsch, Ellen, **478**
Rood, Armistead, **19**
Roosevelt, Eleanor, **72**
Roosevelt, Franklin Delano, **72, 541**
Roper poll, **75**
Rossavik, Claudia, **352**
Rose, Nash, Williamson, Carroll, Clay & Giroir (Rose Law Firm), **28, 40, 47, 51, 126, 199, 204, 214, 216-217, 219, 232**
    Hillary's association with, **28, 47, 71**
    Hillary's income from, **28, 41**
    representation of Madison Guaranty, **214**
Rosen, Marvin, **343-344**

Rosenberg, Susan, **526-527**
Rosman, Adam, **134**
Ross, Thomas, **382**
Rostenkowski, Dan, **524**
Rowlands, Sherry, **346**
RU-486 (abortion pill), **89**
Rubin, James P., **388**
Rubin, Robert E.:
    health care reform and, **165**
    Waco and, **109**
Ruby Ridge:
    assault, **113-114**
    Bureau of Alcohol, Tobacco and Firearms (ATF), **113, 118-119**
    Legal Times, **117**
    "rules of engagement," **114**
    Spokane Spokesman-Review, **116**
    Striker (dog), **114**
    U.S. Constitution and, **117-118**
Ruddy, Christopher, **182, 191, 195, 197, 316, 318, 320-321**
Ruff, Charles, **278, 387, 473-474, 482**
Rule, Herbert, II, **28**
Rush Limbaugh Show, **284-285**
Russert, Tim, **394-395, 445**
Russia, **155**
Rutherford, Skip, **51-52**
Rutherford Institute, **265**
Rwanda:
    Arusha Agreement, **155-156**
    Clinton in, **156-157**
    Government of the Republic of Rwanda (Hutus), **155-157**
    Juvenal Habyarimana, **156**
    Kofi Annan, **156**
    Romeo Dallaire, **156-157**
    Rwandese Patriotic Front (Tutsis), **155-157**
    UN and, **156-157**
Ryan, Evan, **501**
Ryan, Jack, **229**

60 Minutes, 73, 95-96, 108, 442, 444
60 Minutes II, 515

S

Sabel, Tim, **280**
Sage, Byron, **100**, **103**
Salinger, Pierre, **434**
Salter, Scott, **189**
Sample, Penny, **123**, **132**
San Francisco Examiner, **76**
Sandia, **497**
Sanders, Elizabeth, **434**
Sanders, James, **431-434**
Santer, Jacques, **327**
Sarabyn, Charles, **97**, **100**, **108**
Schaffer, Archie, III, **213**, **524**
Schenck, Rev. Rob, **335**
Schippers, David P., **505**, **510**
Schwarzlose, Monroe, **36**
Shalala, Donna, **163**
Skadden, Arps, Slate, Meagher and From, **258**, **265**
Scaife, Richard Mellon, **199**
Scheibel, John, **370**
Schmitt, Eric, **388**
Schneider, Billie, **25**
Schneider, Steve, **100-102**
Schroeder, Michael, **100**
Schulhof, Mark, **240-241**
Schumer, Charles, **109**
Schwartz, Bernard, **305-306**, **371**, **374-376**, **378**, **381**, **387**
Schwartz, Dan, **76**
Scott, Marsha:
    affair with Clinton, **175**
    Foster and, **175**
    Lewinsky and, **456**
Scripps Howard News Service, **196-197**
Sculimbrene, Dennis, **328**, **330**
Seal, Berriman Adler:
    Air Contra supply operation, **57-59**
    Ben-Veniste and, **57**
    contact with Colombian cocaine cartels, **57**
    December 24, 1984 trip from Mena, **59**
    drug smuggling, **56**
    "Fat Lady" and, **58**
    Medellin Cartel, **57**
    murder of, **60**, **273**
    October 23, 1984 trip from Mena, **58-59**
    "Operation Screamer," **57**
    Rich Mountain Aviation, **57**
    relationship with CIA, **56**, **58-60**
    Salvation Army Center (Baton Rouge, La.), **60**
    Southern Air Transport, **58**
    snitch for the DEA, **57-58**
Secret Service:
    Clinton's whereabouts, **336**
    delay in Foster death notification, **184**
    Filegate and, **329-330**
    Foster death, **184**
    fund-raising scandal, **503-504**
    on Inauguration Day, **84**
    Jones and, **441**
    Lewinsky and, **463**, **466**, **476**
    MIG Group, **182**, **185**
    Parks murder, **174**
    visitor logs, Denise Rich and Beth Dozoretz, **525**
Security Bank, **235**
Sehic, Amir, **308-309**
Seidman, Ricki L., **272**
Seligman, Nicole, **476-477**
Senate Armed Services Committee, **392**
Senate Finance Committee, **152**
Senate Foreign Relations Committee:
    Clinton's staff work for, **7**
Senate Governmental Affairs Committee, **501**
Senate Intelligence Committee, **393**, **402**
Senate Whitewater Committee, **186**, **235**
Senate, U.S. (Clinton participation):
    Duffy's **1970** campaign, **19**

Fulbright's **1968** reelection campaign for, **8**
Senegal, **448**
Senft, Anthony, **521**
Sentelle, David, **195**
Sequoia Restaurant (Georgetown), **185**
Serbia, **145-148**, **379**
Serrano, Jose E., **523**
Sessions, William:
    firing and, **175**
    Foster and, **173**, **193**
    Travelgate and, **127-129**
    Waco and, **104**
Seventh Day Adventist Church (SDA), **93**
Shafer, Capt. Tim, **309-310**
Shaffer, Maj./Lt. Col. Tony, **422-424**
Shalala, Donna:
    health care reform and, **163**
Shapiro, Howard, **328**
Sheehy, Gail, **3**
Shelby, Richard C., **291**, **402**, **542**
Sherburne, Jane:
    Filegate and, **328**
Shelton, Bill, **275**
Shelton, Gen. Hugh, **321**, **338-339**, **418**, **421-422**
Shen Jueren, **495**
Sherrill, Martha, **335**
Shinn, David, **412**
Shock, Maurice, **17**
Shullaw, Richard, **16**
Simmons, Bill, **39**
Simpson, O.J., **370**
Simon & Schuster, **533**
Sister Souljah, **77**, **78**
Sklencar, Marge, **12**
"Slick Willie" nickname, **37**
Slater, Rodney, **47**
Sloan, Clifford, **189-190**, **223-224**
Small Business Administration (SBA), **220-221**, **223**, **312**
Smerick, Peter, **109**
Smermova, Marie, **17**
Smiley, Tavis (*BET Tonight*), **320**
Smith, Edye, **359**
Smith, Stephen, **220**, **234**, **236**
Smith, Steven A, **528**
Smith, Walter, **108**
Snead, Joseph, **195**
Snell, Wayne, **361-362**
Soesterberg Air Base, Netherlands, **166**
Solomon, Jerry, **505**
Somalia:
    Abu Hafs al Masry, **406**
    Al Itihaad al Islamiya, **406**
    bin Laden's operations in, **406-408**
    Black Hawk down, **145**, **156**
    civil war in, **142**
    Clinton and, **139-141**
    Delta Force, **144**
    Hassan Awali, **143**
    Islamist Habar Gidir, **142**
    Mohammed Atef, **406**
    Mohammed Farah Aideed, **141-144**, **406-407**
    Mohammed Ibrahim Makawi, **406**
    Operation Restore Hope, **139-140**
    Osman Hassan Ali (Ato), **143**
    Osman Salah, **143**
    Radio Tehran, **144**
    Somali Islamic Union Party (SIUP), **142**
    Task Force Ranger and, **141**
    UH-**60** Black Hawk helicopter, **143-144**
    UN in, **140-141**
    U.S. Military presence in, **139-145**
    warlords in, **141**
Sosnik, Douglas, **344**
South African Consulate (NY), **527**
Southeastern Legal Foundation, **516**
Spafford, Michael, **190**
Specter, Arlen, **118**
Speer, Jim, **435**
Speights, Nathaniel, **471**, **474**

Speilberg, Steven, **502**
Spence, Gerry:
    Jones and, **258**
    Ruby Ridge, **115**, **117**
Sperling Breakfast, **73**
Sperling, Godfrey, Jr., **73**
Spotila, John, **11**
Spotlight magazine, **358**
Squier, Robert, **344**
St. John's Peak (Sveti Ivan), **310-311**, **314**
Stacey, Terry, **433-434**
Stamps, J.C., **317**
Stanley, Mitchell, **220**
Stanton, Edwin, **491**
Star magazine, **73-75**, **346**
Starbucks (Washington, D.C.), **483**
Starr, John Robert, **41**
Starr, Kenneth, **76**, **306**
    Filegate and, **328**, **331**, **333**
    Foster and, **195-196**
    Foster suicide ruling, **198-199**
    Jones and, **266**, **271**, **448**
    Lewinsky and, **468-469**, **475**, **478-479**, **482**
    Whitewater and, **223**, **238**
Starr Report and, **453**, **462-463**, **475**
State Department,
    bin Laden and, **417-418**
    China and, **381-382**, **388**
    Kenya embassy bombing and, **417-419**
    Somalia and, **141**
    Tanzania embassy bombing and, **417-419**
State Department file search, **239-241**
Stearns, Rick, **17**
Stein, Jacob A., **479**
Steiner, Joshua, **231**
Stennis Airfield (Gulfport, Miss.), **58**
Stephanopoulos, George:
    American Banker, **282**
    arrested for, **335**
    attorney general nomination and, **87-88**
    Casey and, **231**
    commercial loan and, **280-282**
    election of **1992** and, **70**, **72-73**, **77**
    election of **1996** and, **342**, **344**
    Filegate and, **329**
    Jones and, **257**
    Lewinsky and, **477-478**
    Small Business Administration (SBA), **220-221**
    Steiner and, **231**
    Stephens and, **231-232**
    terrorism and, **546-547**
    Travelgate and, **131-132**
    Troopergate, **205**
    Waco and, **107**
    Whitewater and, **231-232**
    World Trade Center bombing (**1993**), **406**
Stephens, Inc., **28**, **120**
Stephens, Jackson T. "Jack," **28**, **41**
Stephens, Jay, **231-232**
Stephens, Wilton R. "Witt," **28**, **41**
Stern, Carl, **355**
Stern, Kalmen, **526**
Stewart, James, **207**
Stockdale, James:
    1992 V.P. Debate, **80-81**
    Hoa Lo prison (Hanoi Hilton), **81**
    view on Vietnam war protesters, **81**
Strauss, David, **488-489**
Strobel, Warren, **490**
Sudan:
    al Qaeda and, **412-415**
    Al-Quds al-Arabi, **415**
    Al-Shifa pharmaceutical plant, **418**
    Ali Osman Mohammed Taha, **412**
    bin Laden and, **412-415**
    bombing and,
    Carlos the Jackal, **413**
    CIA in, **412-414**
    Elfatih Erwa, **412-413**
    Ghazzi Selehedin Attaboni, **412**
    Hassan al-Turabi, **412-413**

Internal Security, **413**
Military Intelligence, **413**
Mukhabarat (external intelligence), **413**
as terrorism sponsor, **413**
Suettinger, Robert, **502**
Sullivan, Andrew, **405**
Sullivan, Richard, **500-502**
Sunday Telegraph, **54**
Svermova, Marie, **17**
Swann, Francis, **178**
Sweitzer, Donald, **341**
Swidler & Berlin, **184**
Sykes, Curtis, **345**
Syria and, **372**

T

Tabor, James, **101**
Taiwan and, **389-390**, **402**
Talbott, Nelson Strobridge, III (Strobe):
    China and, **378**
    Ron Brown and, **312**
    Oxford University and, **9**
Tamposi, Elizabeth, **239**
Tamraz, Roger, **299**
Tanner, John, **452**
Tanzania embassy bombing, **417**
Tarnoff, Peter, **310**
Tarver, Joseph, **240-241**
Tatom, Sam, **43**
Tegucigalpa, Honduras, **58-59**
Tenet, George:
    embassy bombings and, **418-419**
    TWA Flight **800** and, **434-435**
Thalheimer, Lee, **213**
Third Congressional District race (Ark.), **23-26**
The Third Terrorist (Davis), **348**, **357**
This Week, ABC-TV's, **232**, **387**, **478**, **507**
Thomases, Susan, **17**
    Foster and, **172**, **187**, **190**
    Travelgate and, **124-125**

Thomason, Harry, **50**, **84**, **123-126**, **129-130**, **132-133**, **482**
Thomason, Linda Bloodworth, **50**, **84**, **123**, **132**, **482**
Thomason, Richland & Martens (TRM), **123**
Thomasson, Patsy,
    evening of Foster's death, **182**, **185-187**
    Foster's desk search, **186**
    Lasater and, **63-64**
    Travelgate, **122**, **127**, **129**
Thorn, Victor, **279**
Thornburgh, Dick, **70**
Tidewater Inn (Easton, Md.), **172**
Time magazine, **84**, **125**, **198**, **315**, **346**, **370**, **500**
Timmerman, Kenneth, **369-371**
Timperlake, Edward, **365**, **375-376**, **380**, **505**
Tobe, Amy Weiss, **487**
Tomback, Andrew, **233**
The Tonight Show, **49-50**
Trafalgar Square (London, England), **10**
Traficant, James, **392**, **435**
Travel Office:
    Air Advantage (Ark.), **123**, **132**
    American Express Travel Services, **132**
    Arkansas Business, **121**
    beginnings, Andrew Jackson, **120**
    cronyism charges in, **125-127**, **132**
    firings in, **131**
    Nashville IRS District Office, **133**
    Peat Marwick audit in, **128-130**, **132**
    Secret Service, **131**
    Travel Weekly, **121**
    UltrAir, **124**, **133**
    Waco and, **108**, **110**
    White House Review, **127-130**, **132-133**
Traylor, Daniel, **257**
Trie, Yah Lin "Charlie," **301**, **379-380**, **497-500**
Triplett, William C., II, **365**, **375-376**,

380, 505
Tripp, Linda:
　Foster and, **176**
　Lewinsky and, **455-458, 460-461, 464-466, 468-470, 479**
　Parks murder, **174**
Tri-State Hospital, **2**
Troopergate:
　Booker Elementary, **203**
　Camelot Hotel (Little Rock, Ark.), **203**
　Harrison County Chamber of Commerce, **203**
　"Living with the Clintons" (Brock), **205**
　McDonald's, **202**
　telephone logs, **206**
Trucking industry, **31-32**
Trulock, Notra, **377, 389, 392-395**
Truman, Harry, **83, 334**
Truth About Hillary (Klein), **33-34, 40**
Tseng, Hank, **495**
Tsongas, Paul, **90**
Tucker, Jim Guy:
　campaign for governorship in **1978, 30-31**
　campaign for governorship in **1982, 42**
　campaign for governorship in **1990, 51**
　campaign for lieutenant governorship in **1990, 51**
　as congressman, **29**
　as governor, **201**
　guilty verdict, **238**
　indictments, **225**
　Troopergate and, **201**
　Whitewater and, **215, 220, 222, 224, 235, 237**
Tudjman, Franco, **308**
Tulley, Paul, **274**
Tuohey, Mark H. III, **190, 196**
TWA Flight **800**:
　Air Transport Association, **437**
　Airline Pilots Association (ALPA), **430**
　casualties, **425**
　Cooperative Engagement Capability missile test (CEC), **438**
　Docker's restaurant and, **437**
　evidence tampering, **435**
　Executive Order **13039, 431**
　Gabreski Airport, **428**
　International Association of Machinists and Aerospace Workers (IAMAW), **439**
　Mastic Beach High School, **428**
　MSNBC, **436**
　P-3 Orion, **438**
　Pan Am, **103, 427**
　Paris Match magazine, **431**
　PETN, traces on TWA **800** debris, **430**
　Press-Enterprise of Riverside, CA, **431-432**
　RDX traces on TWA **800** debris, **430**
　Teledyn Ryan aeronautical, **437**
　Teledyne Ryan BQM-34 Firebee I, **437**
　TWA and, **430**
　USS *Albuquerque,* **438**
　USS *Carr,* **438**
　USS *Normandy,* **438**
　USS *Trepang,* **438**
　USS *Wyoming,* **438**
　Westhampton High School, **429**
　White House Commission on Aviation Safety and Security, **436**
"Twenty-year project," **19**
Twersky, David, **526**
Tyrrell, R. Emmett, Jr., **3, 6, 39, 59-60, 66-67, 483**
Tyson, Don, **25, 31-32,**
Tyson Foods, **25, 28**
Tyson, Randall, **25**

U

Udolf, Bruce, **470**
Undercoffer, Jeffrey, **329**
University of Arkansas, **11, 24**
University of Arkansas Law School, **12**
　Bill Clinton as professor, **23**
　Bill Clinton's draft avoidance, **12-15**

University of Arkansas Medical Center, 67
University of Maryland, College Park, MD, 6
U.S. Capitol, 527
U.S. Chamber of Commerce, 163
U.S. Code, Title 18, Section 607, 486-487
U.S. Constitution, 334, 491
U.S. Consulate workers (Pakistan), 410
    Clinton reaction, 410
U.S. Military Training Center (Saudi Arabia), 410-411
    Clinton reaction, 411
U.S. News & World Report, 297
U.S. Park Police,
    briefcase, 177
    Foster crime scene, 178-180
    White House search, 188
U.S. Special Operations Command (SOCOM), 421-423
U.S.-Thai Business Council, 504
USA Today, 99, 285, 402
USS *Cole* attack (2000):
    Abd -al Muhsin al-Taifi, 420
    al Qaeda and, 420-421
    bin Laden and, 420-421
    Clinton response to, 421
    damage done by, 420
    warnings of, 422-423
USS *The Sullivans*, 419-420
USS *Theodore Roosevelt*, 91
USS *United States*, 9
Unlimited Access (Aldrich), 336
Urbina, Ricardo, 119

V
Van Eimeren, Robert, 132, 134
Van Natta, Don, 71, 432-433
Vandross, Luther, 84
Vanity Fair, 75
VE-Day, 334

Veasey, Bob, 314
Velazquez, Nydia M., 523
Vessey, Gen. John, 248
Viacom, 533
Vietnam:
    Dang Tan, 249-250
    Defense Intelligence Agency, 247-249
    Dien Bien Phu, 246
    Khoang Anya, 250
    Le Dinh, 250
    Le Duc Tho, 245-246
    National Alliance of Families, 252
    Nguyen, Manh Cam, 253
    Operation Homecoming, 246-247, 249
    Paris Peace Accords, 245
    Pham Van Dong, 246
    POW-MIA groups, 252
    Rand Corporation, 246
    Tran Van Quang, 247-248, 250
Vietnam Moratorium Committee, 12-13
Vietnam Veterans Memorial Wall, 167-168
Vietnam War, 7-10
    antiwar activities, 12, 13, 17, 25
    Clinton's opposition to, 10, 31
    Clinton's studies on, 7
    Clinton's views during Oxford years, 10, 17
    Clinton's work on the Fulbright committee, 7
Vignali, Carlos, 526
Vignali, Horatio, 526
Vita, Andrew, 435
Vo Van Kiet, 294
Voles, Lorraine, 485
Vlasto, Chris, 271

W
Waco, Texas compound:
    assault, 98-99, 103-105
    Bradley Fighting vehicles, 104
    Bureau of Alcohol, Tobacco, and Firearms

(ATF), **93-100**
Chemical and Biological Arms Control Institute, **106**
Chemical Weapons Convention, **105**
Dallas Morning News, **109-110**
Delta Force commandoes, **109-110**
Fort Hood, **96**
Hillcrest Baptist Medical Center, **104**
Infrared Technologies Corp., **111**
M-**60** tanks, **104**
McLennan County Sheriff's Dept., **93-94, 98**
methamphetamine lab, **93, 96**
National Firearms Act, **94**
O-chlorobenzalmalononnitrile (CS) gas, **104-105, 111**
"Operation Trojan Horse" ("Showtime"), **96-97**
Seventh-Day Adventist Church (SDA), **93**
"The Sinful Messiah," **97**
Texas Air National Guard, **94**
Texas Department of Public Safety, **109-110**
Texas Rangers, **100**
Waco: A New Revelation (McNulty), **110**
Waco Tribune Herald, **95, 97**
Wade, Chris, **215, 234-235, 528**
Wade, Richard, **127-128**
Wag the Dog, **419, 512**
Wagner, Carl, **17**
Wainwright, Duncan, **328**
Wal-Mart, **28**
Wald, Patricia, **86**
Walker, Bobby, **55**
Walker, Jon Parnell, **274-275**
Walker, Martin, **10**
Wall Street Journal, **72-73, 192, 445-446, 498, 531**
Wallerstein, Mitchell, **369**
Walsh, Lawrence, Iran-Contra investigation, **81**
Walters, Gary J., **535**

Wang Jun, **306, 379-380, 383, 498-499**
Ward, Seth, **222**
Washak, Petty Officer John, **420**
Washington County Democratic Central Committee (Ark.), **23**
Washington Post, **26, 48, 70, 76, 78, 87, 89, 111, 117, 135, 220, 226-227, 239-240, 249, 257-258, 293, 372, 379, 421, 451, 474-475, 479, 487, 493, 497, 510, 534-535**
Washington Times, **82, 85, 109, 121, 153, 186, 192, 230, 262-263, 266, 289, 305, 320, 329, 336, 341, 345, 371-372, 414, 442, 444, 448, 490, 494, 524, 531**
Watergate Hotel, **451, 460-461, 497**
Watergate report, **492**
Watkins, David, **120**
    Foster and, **171, 184, 187**
    Travelgate and, **121-122, 124, 125-127, 129-131, 133-134**
Watkins, Isabelle, **459**
Watkins, Larry S., **175**
Watson, William, **181**
Waters, Maxine, **138**
Watling, Belle *Gone With the Wind*, **288**
Wayne, John, **9**
Weather Underground, **526-527**
Weaver, Elisheba, **114**
Weaver, Randy, **113-119**
Weaver, Sammy, **113-115**
Weaver, Vicki, **114-118, 541**
Webb, E. Russell, **236**
Wecht, Cyril, **319**
Wei Jingsheng, **374**
Weicker, Lowell, **19**
Weigel, George, **89**
Weinberger, Casper, **81-82**
Weingarten, Reid, **298**
Weinig, Harvey, **529**
Weldon, Curt, **423**
Wellstone, Eileen, **10**
Western Building (NY), **520**

Wexner, Fran, **241**
Wheeler, Sharon, **96**
White, Frank, **37-38**, **41-43**, **47**
White, Ken, **322**
White, John, **381**
White, Mary Jo, **530-531**
White, Randy, **36**
Whitewater:
    101 River Development Inc., **208**
    Arkansas Public Service Division, **236**
    Arkansas Securities Commission, **213**
    Bank of Cherry Valley, **213**
    Bank of Kingston (soon becomes Madison Bank and Trust), **209**
    Black-Eyed Pea Restaurant (Little Rock, Ark.), **208**
    Capital Management Services Company, **220**
    Castle Grande Development, **215**
    Castle Sewer and Water Corporation, **222**
    Citizen's Bank of Flippin, **209**, **211**, **213**
    Citizens Bank of Jonesboro, **211**
    Federal Deposit Insurance Corporation (FDIC), **218**, **232**, **236**
    Federal Home Loan Bank Board, **212**, **216-217**
    First Bank of Arkansas, **235**
    Frost & Co., **218**
    land deal, **208-209**
    Lot 13, **209-211**, **227**
    Madison Bank and Trust, **209**, **212**
    National Association of Security Dealers, **236**
    Putting People First, **228**
    Resolution Trust Corp. (RTC), **223-226**, **229-233**, **236**
    Resolution Trust Corp. (RTC) (Kansas City), **219-221**, **229-230**
    Security Bank of Paragould, **212**, **215**, **235**
    Senate Whitewater Committee, **235**
    Small Business Administration, **220-221**, **223**
    Small Business Investment Company (SBIC), **216**
    Southloop Construction, **222**
    TCBY Yogurt, **218**
    Union National Bank, **209**
Whitewater Development Corporation, **208**, **211**, **226**, **228**, **235**
Wickam, DeWayne, **78**
Wilcher, Paul, **274**
Wilhelm, David, **70**
Wilhite, Jim, **274**
Willey, Ed, **275**
Willey, Kathleen:
    alleged groping of, **441**
    intimidation of, **441**
    Jones case and, **263-264**, **441**
    letters to Clinton from Willey, **443**
    Lewinsky and, **457**
    Tripp and, **465**
Williams and Connolly, **225-226**
Williams, Gareth, **279**
Williams, Jack L., **528**
Williams, Keith, **463**
Williams, Lee, **12**
Williams, Maggie:
    Foster and, **182**, **185-189**
    fund-raising scandal and, **490**, **501**
    Whitewater, **226**, **229**
Williams, Robert, **280**
Williamson, Tom, **13**
Willis, Carroll, **47**
Willis, Steve, **280**
Wilshire Courtyard Marriott (Los Angeles, Ca.), **462**
Wilson, James, **274**
Wilson, Sharlene:
    Clinton's "distinguishing characteristic," **65**
    Coachman's Inn (Little Rock, Ark.), **65**
    Cowboys Stadium, **65**
    Le Bistro (Little Rock, Ark.), **64**
    partying with Clinton, **65**

Wilson, Rear Adm. Thomas, **418-419**
Wilson, William R., **45**
Wilt, James L., **259**
Winters, Richard, **274**
Winthrop Rockefeller Foundation, **51**
Wire, Mike, **427**
Wiriadinata, Arief, **496**
Wiriadinata, Sonya, **496**
Wise, Barbara, **276**, **317**
Wisenberg, Sol, **468**, **480**
Wisner, Frank, **143**
WMUR-TV (N.H.), **167**
Wofford, Harris, **70**
Women, Infants, and Children (WIC) food aid program, **545**
Wood, Kimba, **87-88**
Wood, Mitchell Couey, **528**
Woodward, Bob, **364**, **487**
World News Tonight (ABC), **191**, **207**, **353**
World Trade Center, **521**
World Trade Center bombing (**1993**), **547**
    casualties, **405**
    Clinton's response to, **405-406**
    damage done by, **404-405**
    Khalid Shaikh Mohammad, **405**
    Mahmud Abouhalima, **404**
    Mohammed Salameh, **404**
    Ramzi Yousef, **404**
World Trade Center bombing (**2001**), **547**
World Wide Travel (Little Rock, Ark.):
    election of **1992** **77**, **121**, **129**
    Travelgate and, **120-122**, **130**, **132**
Worthern Bank, **28**, **77**, **120**, **496**
Worthen Tower, **230**
Wright, Gary, **131**, **134**
Wright, Onie Elizabeth "Betsey," **28**, **41**, **45**, **47**, **50-51**
    as architect of Clinton's comeback after **1980** defeat, **39-40**
    "bimbo eruptions," **76**, **78**
    "box room," **75-76**
    on Clinton's decision not to seek presidency in **1988**, **49**
    departure from Clinton administration, **50**
    drafting of state trooper's retraction of bribery statement, **45**
    election of **1992**, **75-76**, **78**
    McGovern campaign, **20**
    Troopergate and, **207**
    Whitewater and, **217**
Wright, Lindsey, and Jennings Law Firm, **40**
Wright, Susan Weber:
    disbarment and, **516-517**
    Jones and, **261**, **264**, **267**, **441**, **448**, **464**, **471**
Wynette, Tammy, **74**

X

Xiong Guangkai, **402**

Y

Yale Child Study Center, **20**
Yale Law School, **11**, **14**, **17-19**
    Barristers Union, **20**
    Bill Clinton's application to, **14**
    Bill Clinton's first year at, **18**
    Hillary's graduation from, **20**
Yale Review of Law and Social Action, **18**
Year of the Rat (Timperlake and Triplett), **365-366**
Yeltsin, Boris, **248**, **335**
Yemen, **403-404**
York, Byron, **421**
Young, Raymond "Buddy," **201**, **207**
Yousef, Ramzi:
    bin Laden's Philippines operations and, **408-409**
    bomb making and, **404**, **408-409**
    Manila (**1995**) and, **409**

Philippine airlines (PAL), **409**
Project Bojinka and, **409**
TWA Flight **800** and, **425**
U.S. Consulate (Pakistan), **410**
World Trade Center bombing (**1993**) and, **404**

Yugoslavia newspaper, **148**

Z

Zahn, Paula, **538**
Zwenig, Frances, **249**

www.ingramcontent.com/pod-product-compliance
Lightning Source LLC
Chambersburg PA
CBHW051751100526
44591CB00017B/2656